Oracle Database 12*c* DBA Handbook

About the Author

Bob Bryla is an Oracle 9*i*, 10*g*, 11*g*, and 12*c* Certified Professional with more than 20 years of experience in database design, database application development, training, and Oracle database administration. He is the primary Oracle DBA and database systems engineer at Epic in Verona, Wisconsin. He is a technical editor for a number of Oracle Press books, including several certification study guides for Oracle Database 10*g*, 11*g*, and 12*c*. He has also been known to watch science fiction movies and tinker with Android devices in his spare time.

About the Technical Editor

Scott Gossett is a technical director in the Oracle Advanced Technologies Solutions organization with more than 23 years of experience specializing in Oracle RAC, performance tuning, and high-availability databases. Prior to becoming a technical director, Scott was a senior principal instructor for Oracle Education for over 12 years, primarily teaching Oracle internals, performance tuning, RAC, and database administration. In addition, Scott is one of the architects and primary authors of the Oracle Certified Master exam. Scott has been a technical editor for twelve Oracle Press books.

Oracle Press™

Oracle Database 12*c* DBA Handbook

Bob Bryla

New York Chicago San Francisco
Athens London Madrid Mexico City
Milan New Delhi Singapore Sydney Toronto

Cataloging-in-Publication Data is on file with the Library of Congress

McGraw-Hill Education books are available at special quantity discounts to use as premiums and sales promotions, or for use in corporate training programs. To contact a representative, please visit the Contact Us pages at www.mhprofessional.com.

Oracle Database 12*c* DBA Handbook

1 2 3 4 5 6 7 8 9 0 DOC DOC 1 0 9 8 7 6 5

ISBN 978-0-07-179878-5
MHID 0-07-179878-1

Sponsoring Editor
Paul Carlstroem

Editorial Supervisor
Janet Walden

Project Manager
Shruti Awasthi,
Cenveo® Publisher Services

Acquisitions Coordinator
Amanda Russell

Technical Editor
Scott Gossett

Copy Editor
William McManus

Proofreader
Claire Splan

Indexer
Claire Splan

Production Supervisor
James Kussow

Composition
Cenveo Publisher Services

Illustration
Cenveo Publisher Services

Art Director, Cover
Jeff Weeks

To the gang at home: I couldn't have done it without you! And the pizzas. And the heavy metal. And several shows on the BBC.

—BB

Contents at a Glance

PART IV
Networked Oracle

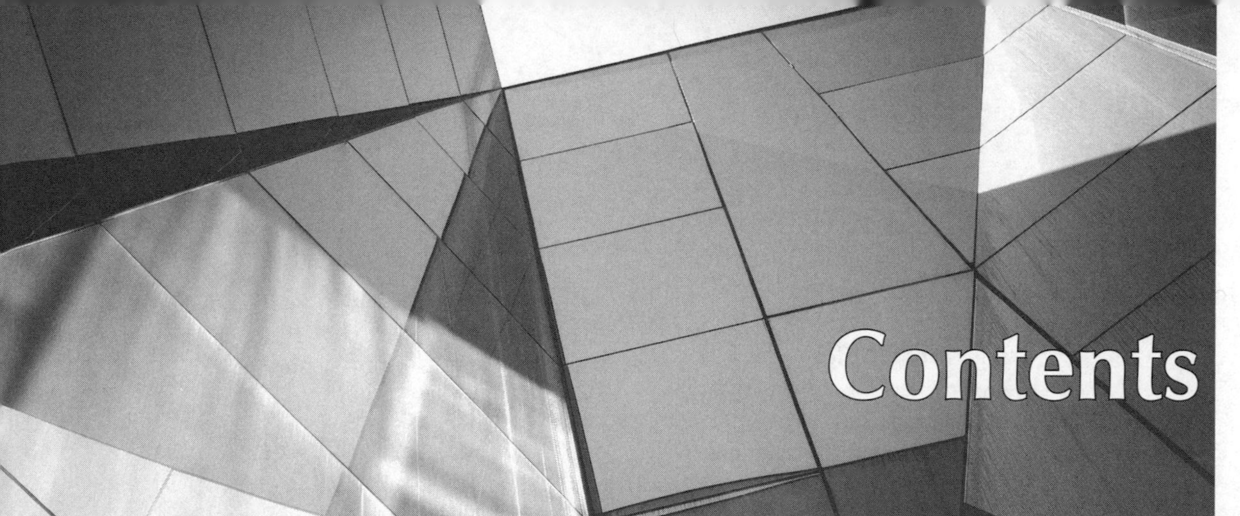

Contents

PART III
High Availability

Acknowledgments

Many technical books need the expertise of more than one person, and this one is no exception. The people I collaborated with for this book at Oracle Open World, Oracle Support, and in the Oracle Partner Network are too numerous to mention but all played an important role in this book.

Thanks also go out to all the people at McGraw-Hill Education who kept this book on a reasonable schedule and learned to be even more patient with me than ever before, including Paul Carlstroem and Amanda Russell. Thanks also to Scott Gossett, who gave me good advice when the theoretical met the practical.

Many of my professional colleagues at Epic were a source of both inspiration and guidance: James Slager, Scott Hinman, Joe Obbish, and Lonny Niederstadt. In this case, the whole is truly greater than the sum of its parts.

If you have any questions or comments about any part of this book, please do not hesitate to contact me at rjbdba@gmail.com.

—Bob Bryla

Introduction

Whether you're an experienced DBA, a new DBA, or an application developer, you need to understand how Oracle Database 12*c*'s features can help you best meet your customers' needs. In this book, you will find coverage of the newest features (including the In-Memory option) as well as ways of merging those features into the management of an Oracle database. The emphasis throughout is on managing the database's capabilities in an effective, efficient manner to deliver a quality product. The end result will be a database that is dependable, robust, secure, and extensible.

Several components are critical to this goal, and you'll see all of them covered here in depth after you are introduced to the Oracle Architecture, Oracle 12*c* upgrade issues, and tablespace planning in Part I; a well-designed logical and physical database architecture will improve performance and ease administration by properly distributing database objects.

You'll see appropriate monitoring, security, and tuning strategies for standalone and networked databases in Part II of this book. Backup and recovery strategies are provided to help ensure the database's recoverability. Each section focuses on both the features and the proper planning and management techniques for each area. Scalability and manageability are undeniably the biggest enhancements in Oracle Database 12*c*. Using pluggable databases (also known as multitenant or container databases) utilizes your server resources more effectively than single-instance pre-Oracle Database 12*c* databases, which means you can run many more database instances on a given server with the same performance as if you were running them on different servers. Because it's easy and fast to "unplug" a pluggable database from a container database and plug it back into another container database, you can migrate one or more pluggable databases to other servers when the need arises.

High availability is covered in all of its flavors in Part III: an introduction to Real Application Clusters (RAC), an extensive exposition on Recovery Manager (RMAN), and an overview of how to administer an Oracle Data Guard environment are a few of the topics covered in Part III.

Networking issues and the management of distributed and client/server databases are thoroughly covered. Oracle Net, networking configurations, materialized views, location transparency, and everything else you need to successfully implement a distributed or client/server database are described in detail in Part IV of this book. You'll also find real-world examples for every major configuration.

In addition to the commands needed to perform DBA activities, you will also see the Oracle Enterprise Manager Cloud Control 12*c* web pages from which you can perform similar functions. By following the techniques in this book, your systems can be designed and implemented so well that tuning efforts will be minimal. Administering the database will become easier as the users get a better product, while the database works—and works well.

Last but not least, no book with code samples would be complete without providing you the source code for the examples. Please visit www.OraclePressBooks.com to get the code sample file **12c DBA Handbook Code Listings.zip.**

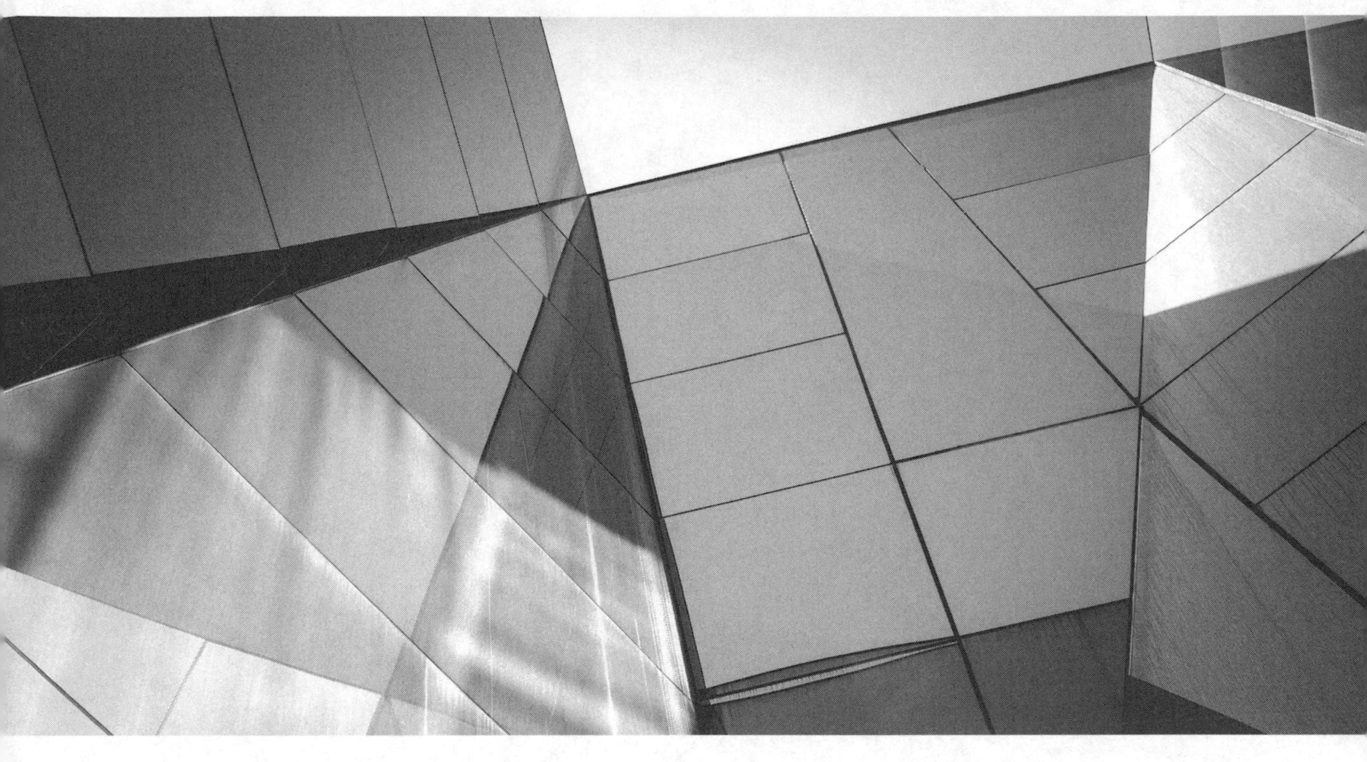

PART I

Database Architecture

CHAPTER 1

Getting Started with the Oracle Architecture

Oracle Database 12*c* is an evolutionary step from the previous release, Oracle Database 11*g*, which, in turn, was a truly revolutionary step from Oracle Database 10*g* in terms of its "set it and forget it" features. Oracle 12*c* continues the tradition of feature enhancement by making execution plan management more automated, adding new virtualization features, and significantly improving availability and failover capabilities. Part I of this book covers the basics of the Oracle architecture and lays the foundation for deploying a successful Oracle infrastructure by giving practical advice for a new installation or upgrading from a previous release of Oracle. To provide a good foundation for the Oracle 12*c* software, I cover server hardware and operating system configuration issues in the relevant sections.

In Part II of this book, I will cover several areas relevant to the day-to-day maintenance and operation of an Oracle 12*c* database. The first chapter in Part II discusses the requirements that a DBA needs to gather long before you mount the Oracle ISO image on your server. Successive chapters deal with ways the DBA can manage disk space, CPU usage, and adjust Oracle parameters to optimize the server's resources, using a variety of tools at the DBA's disposal for monitoring database performance. Query optimization in Oracle 12*c* is more automated than ever with the option to change a query plan on the fly if the optimizer sees that its original estimates for cardinality were off by a significant factor.

Part III of this book focuses on the high-availability aspects of Oracle 12*c*. This includes using Oracle's Recovery Manager (RMAN) to perform and automate database backups and recovery, along with other features, such as Oracle Data Guard, to provide a reliable and easy way to recover from a database failure. Features new to Oracle 12*c* such as container databases (multitenant databases) with their corresponding pluggable databases extend the concept of transportable tablespaces to the entire database in addition to more efficiently using the resources of a server hosting one or more container databases. Last, but certainly not least, we will explore how Oracle 12*c* Real Application Clusters (RAC) can at the same time provide extreme scalability and transparent failover capabilities to a database environment. Even if you don't use Oracle 12*c*'s RAC features, the standby features make Oracle 12*c* almost as available as a clustered solution; being able to easily switch between standby and primary databases as well as query a physical standby database provides a robust high-availability solution until you are ready to implement a RAC database.

In Part IV of this book, we will cover a variety of issues revolving around Networked Oracle. We cover not only how Oracle Net can be configured in an N-tier environment, but also how we manage large and distributed databases that may reside in neighboring cities or around the world.

In this chapter, we cover the basics of Oracle Database 12*c*, highlighting many of the features we will cover in the rest of the book as well as the basics of installing Oracle 12*c* using Oracle Universal Installer (OUI) and the Database Configuration Assistant (DBCA). We will take a tour of the elements that compose an instance of Oracle 12*c*, ranging from memory structures and disk structures to initialization parameters, tables, indexes, and PL/SQL. Each of these elements plays a large role in making Oracle 12*c* a highly scalable, available, and secure environment.

An Overview of Databases and Instances

Although the terms "database" and "instance" are often used interchangeably, they are quite different. They are very distinct entities in an Oracle datacenter, as you shall see in the following sections.

Databases

A *database* is a collection of data on disk in one or more files on a database server that collects and maintains related information. The database consists of various physical and logical structures, the table being the most important logical structure in the database. A table consists of rows and columns containing related data. At a minimum, a database must have at least tables to store useful information. Figure 1-1 shows a sample table containing four rows and three columns. The data in each row of the table is related: Each row contains information about a particular employee in the company.

In addition, a database provides a level of security to prevent unauthorized access to the data. Oracle Database 12*c* provides many mechanisms to facilitate the security necessary to keep confidential data confidential. Oracle Security and access control are covered in more detail in Chapter 9.

Files composing a database fall into two broad categories: database files and non-database files. The distinction lies in what kind of data is stored in each. Database files contain data and metadata; non-database files contain initialization parameters, logging information, and so forth. Database files are critical to the ongoing operation of the database on a moment-by-moment basis. Each of these physical storage structures is discussed later, in the section titled "Oracle Physical Storage Structures."

Instances

The main components of a typical enterprise server are one or more CPUs (each with multiple cores), disk space, and memory. Whereas the Oracle database is stored on a server's disk, an Oracle instance exists in the server's memory. An Oracle *instance* is composed of a large block of memory allocated in an area called the *System Global Area (SGA),* along with a number of background processes that interact between the SGA and the database files on disk.

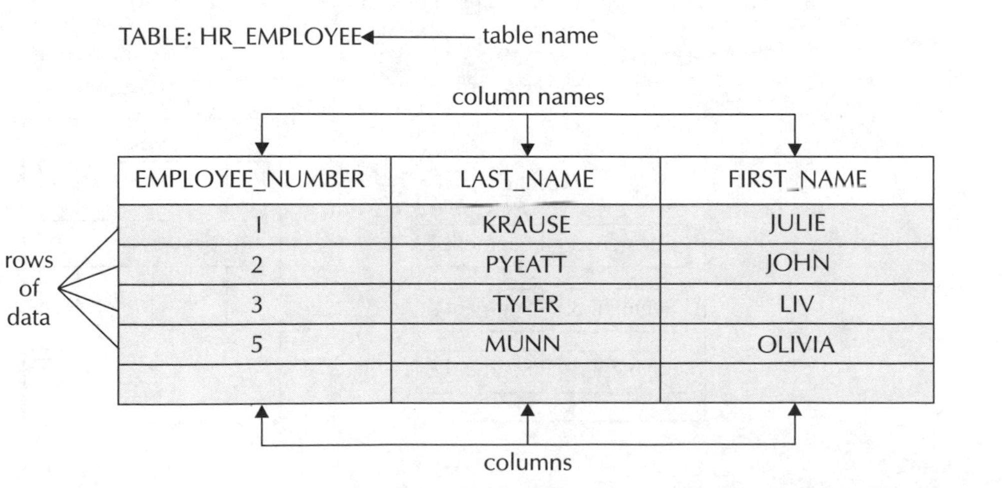

FIGURE 1-1. *Sample database table*

In an Oracle RAC, more than one instance will use the same database. Although the instances that share the database can be on the same server, most likely the instances will be on separate servers that are connected by a high-speed interconnect and access a database that resides on a specialized RAID-enabled disk subsystem. An Oracle Exadata database appliance is an example of database servers, I/O servers, and disk storage combined into one or more cabinets and is optimized for a RAC environment including dual InfiniBand interfaces to connect all of these devices at speeds up to 40 Gbps per interface. More details on how a RAC installation is configured are provided in Chapter 11.

Oracle Logical Storage Structures

The datafiles in an Oracle database are grouped together into one or more tablespaces. Within each tablespace, the logical database structures, such as tables and indexes, are segments that are further subdivided into extents and blocks. This logical subdivision of storage allows Oracle to have more efficient control over disk space usage. Figure 1-2 shows the relationship between the logical storage structures in a database.

Tablespaces

An Oracle *tablespace* consists of one or more datafiles; a datafile can be a part of one and only one tablespace. For an installation of Oracle 12*c*, a minimum of two tablespaces are created: the SYSTEM tablespace and the SYSAUX tablespace; a default installation of Oracle 12*c* creates six tablespaces.

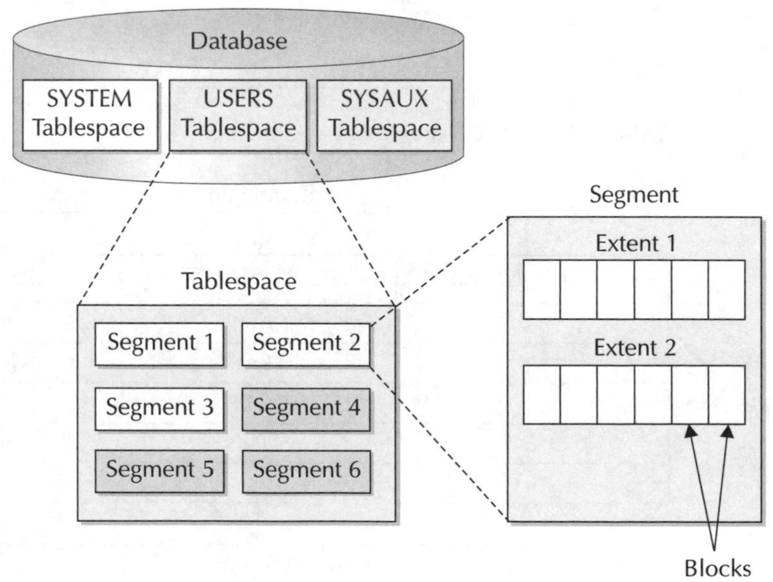

FIGURE 1-2. *Logical storage structures*

Oracle Database 10*g* and later allow you to create a special kind of tablespace called a *bigfile tablespace,* which can be as large as 128TB (terabytes). Using bigfiles makes tablespace management completely transparent to the DBA; in other words, the DBA can manage the tablespace as a unit without worrying about the size and structure of the underlying datafiles.

Using Oracle Managed Files (OMF) can make tablespace datafile management even easier. With OMF, the DBA specifies one or more locations in the file system where datafiles, control files, and redo log files will reside, and Oracle automatically handles the naming and management of these files. I discuss OMF in more detail in Chapter 4.

If a tablespace is *temporary,* the tablespace itself is permanent; only the segments saved in the tablespace are temporary. A temporary tablespace can be used for sorting operations and for tables that exist only for the duration of the user's session. Dedicating a tablespace for these kinds of operations helps to reduce the I/O contention between temporary segments and permanent segments stored in another tablespace, such as tables.

Tablespaces can be either *dictionary managed* or *locally managed.* In a dictionary-managed tablespace, extent management is recorded in data dictionary tables. Therefore, even if all application tables are in the USERS tablespace, the SYSTEM tablespace will still be accessed for managing Data Manipulation Language (DML) on application tables. Because all users and applications must use the SYSTEM tablespace for extent management, this creates a potential bottleneck for write-intensive applications. In a locally managed tablespace, Oracle maintains a bitmap in each datafile of the tablespace to track space availability. Only quotas are managed in the data dictionary, dramatically reducing the contention for data dictionary tables. There is really no good reason for creating dictionary-managed tablespaces. When you install Oracle 12*c*, the SYSTEM and SYSAUX tablespaces must be locally managed. For importing transportable tablespaces, a tablespace can be dictionary managed but it will be read-only.

Blocks

A database *block* is the smallest unit of storage in the Oracle database. The size of a block is a specific number of bytes of storage within a given tablespace within the database.

A block is usually a multiple of the operating system block size to facilitate efficient disk I/O. The default block size is specified by the Oracle initialization parameter DB_BLOCK_SIZE. As many as four other block sizes may be defined for other tablespaces in the database, although the blocks in the SYSTEM, SYSAUX, and any temporary tablespaces must be of the size DB_BLOCK_SIZE.

The default block size is 8K and all Oracle testing is performed using 8K blocks. Oracle best practices suggest using an 8K block size for all tablespaces unless there is a compelling reason to use a different size. One reason could be that the average row length for a table is 20K. Therefore, you might choose to use 32K blocks, but you should fully test to see if there is a performance gain.

Extents

The *extent* is the next level of logical grouping in the database. An extent consists of one or more database blocks. When you enlarge a database object, the space added to the object is allocated as an extent.

Segments

The next level of logical grouping in a database is the *segment.* A segment is a group of extents that form a database object that Oracle treats as a unit, such as a table or index. As a result, this is typically the smallest unit of storage that an end user of the database will deal with. Four types of segments are found in an Oracle database: table segments (non-partitioned tables and each partition of a partitioned table), index segments, temporary segments, and rollback segments.

Data Segment

Every table in the database resides in a single *data segment,* consisting of one or more extents; Oracle allocates more than one segment for a table if it is a partitioned table or a clustered table. Partitioned and clustered tables are discussed later in this chapter. Data segments include LOB (large object) segments that store LOB data referenced by a LOB locator column in a table segment (if the LOB is not stored inline in the table).

Index Segment

Each index is stored in its own *index segment.* As with partitioned tables, each partition of a partitioned index is stored in its own segment. Included in this category are LOB index segments; a table's non-LOB columns, a table's LOB columns, and the LOBs' associated indexes can all reside in their own tablespace to improve performance.

Temporary Segment

When a user's SQL statement needs disk space to complete an operation, such as a sorting operation that cannot fit in memory, Oracle allocates a *temporary segment*. Temporary segments exist only for the duration of the SQL statement.

Rollback Segment

As of Oracle 10*g,* legacy rollback segments only exist in the SYSTEM tablespace, and typically the DBA does not need to maintain the SYSTEM rollback segment. In previous Oracle releases, a rollback segment was created to save the previous values of a database DML operation in case the transaction was rolled back, and to maintain the "before" image data to provide read-consistent views of table data for other users accessing the table. Rollback segments were also used during database recovery for rolling back uncommitted transactions that were active when the database instance crashed or terminated unexpectedly.

Automatic Undo Management (AUM) handles the automatic allocation and management of rollback segments within an *undo tablespace*. Within an undo tablespace, the undo segments are structured similarly to rollback segments, except that the details of how these segments are managed is under control of Oracle, instead of being managed (often inefficiently) by the DBA. Automatic undo segments were available starting with Oracle9*i,* but manually managed rollback segments are still available in Oracle 12*c*. However, this functionality is deprecated as of Oracle 10*g,* and will no longer be available in future releases. In Oracle 12*c,* AUM is enabled by default; in addition, a PL/SQL procedure is provided to help you size the undo tablespace. Automatic Undo Management is discussed in detail in Chapter 7.

Oracle Logical Database Structures

In this section, we will cover the highlights of all major logical database structures, starting with tables and indexes. Next, I discuss the variety of datatypes we can use to define the columns of a table. When we create a table with columns, we can place restrictions, or *constraints,* on the columns of the table.

One of the many reasons we use a relational database management system (RDBMS) to manage our data is to leverage the security and auditing features of the Oracle database. We will review the ways we can segregate access to the database by user or by the object being accessed.

We'll also touch upon many other logical structures that can be defined by either the DBA or the user, including synonyms, links to external files, and links to other databases.

Tables

A *table* is the basic unit of storage in an Oracle database. Without any tables, a database has no value to an enterprise. Regardless of the type of table, data in a table is stored in *rows* and *columns,* similar to how data is stored in a spreadsheet. But that is where the similarity ends. The robustness of a database table due to the surrounding reliability, integrity, and scalability of the Oracle database makes a spreadsheet a poor second choice when deciding on a place to store critical information.

In this section, we will review the many different types of tables in the Oracle database and how they can satisfy most every data-storage need for an organization. You can find more details on how to choose between these types of tables for a particular application, and how to manage them, in Chapter 5 and Chapter 8.

Relational Tables

A *relational* table is the most common type of table in a database. A relational table is heap-organized; in other words, the rows in the table are stored in no particular order. In the CREATE TABLE command, you can specify the clause ORGANIZATION HEAP to define a heap-organized table, but because this is the default, the clause can be omitted.

Each row of a table contains one or more columns; each column has a datatype and a length. As of Oracle version 8, a column may also contain a user-defined object type, a nested table, or a VARRAY. In addition, a table can be defined as an object table. We will review object tables and objects later in this section.

The built-in Oracle datatypes are presented in Table 1-1. Oracle also supports ANSI-compatible datatypes; the mapping between the ANSI datatypes and Oracle datatypes is provided in Table 1-2.

Oracle Built-in Datatype	Description
VARCHAR2 (*size*) [BYTE | CHAR]	A variable-length character string with a maximum length of 32,767 bytes and a minimum length of 1 byte. CHAR indicates that character semantics are used to size the string; BYTE indicates that byte semantics are used. You can use 32767 as the maximum length of a VARCHAR2 column in Oracle Database 12*c* if you set the MAX_STRING_SIZE initialization parameter to EXTENDED.
NVARCHAR2(*size*)	A variable-length character string with a maximum length of 32,767 bytes.
NUMBER(*p*,*s*)	A number with a precision (*p*) and scale (*s*). The precision ranges from 1 to 38, and the scale can be from –84 to 127. A NUMBER column may require as little as 1 byte or as many as 22 bytes to store a given value.
LONG	A variable-length character data with a length up to 2GB ($2^{31} - 1$).
DATE	Date values from January 1st, 4712 B.C. to December 31st, 9999 A.D.
BINARY_FLOAT	A 32-bit floating point number.

TABLE 1-1. *Oracle Built-in Datatypes*

Oracle Built-in Datatype	Description
BINARY_DOUBLE	A 64-bit floating point number.
TIMESTAMP (*fractional_seconds*)	Year, month, day, hour, minute, second, and fractional seconds. Value of *fractional_seconds* can range from 0 to 9; in other words, up to one billionth of a second precision. The default is 6 (one millionth).
TIMESTAMP (*fractional_seconds*) WITH TIME ZONE	Contains a TIMESTAMP value in addition to a time zone displacement value. Time zone displacement can be an offset from UTC (such as –06:00) or a region name (e.g., US/Central).
TIMESTAMP (*fractional_seconds*) WITH LOCAL TIME ZONE	Similar to TIMESTAMP WITH TIMEZONE, except that (1) data is normalized to the database time zone when it is stored and (2) when retrieving columns with this datatype, the user sees the data in the session's time zone.
INTERVAL YEAR (*year_precision*) TO MONTH	Stores a time period in years and months. The value of *year_precision* is the number of digits in the YEAR field.
INTERVAL DAY (*day_precision*) TO SECOND (*fractional_seconds_precision*)	Stores a period of time as days, hours, minutes, seconds, and fractional seconds. The value for *day_precision* is from 0 to 9, with a default of 2. The value of *fractional_seconds_precision* is similar to the fractional seconds in a TIMESTAMP value; the range is from 0 to 9, with a default of 6.
RAW(*size*)	Raw binary data, with a maximum size of 2000 bytes.
LONG RAW	Raw binary data, variable length, up to 2GB in size.
ROWID	A base-64 string representing the unique address of a row in its corresponding table. This address is unique throughout the database.
UROWID [(*size*)]	A base-64 string representing the logical address of a row in an index-organized table. The maximum for *size* is 4000 bytes.
CHAR(*size*) [BYTE | CHAR]	A fixed-length character string of length *size*. The minimum size is 1, and the maximum is 2000 bytes. The BYTE and CHAR parameters are BYTE and CHAR semantics, as in VARCHAR2.
NCHAR(*size*)	A fixed-length character string up to 2000 bytes; the maximum *size* depends on the national character set definition for the database. The default *size* is 1.
CLOB	A character large object containing single-byte or multibyte characters; supports both fixed-width and variable-width character sets. The maximum size is (4GB – 1) * DB_BLOCK_SIZE.
NCLOB	Similar to CLOB, except that Unicode characters are stored from either fixed-width or variable-width character sets. The maximum size is (4GB – 1) * DB_BLOCK_SIZE.
BLOB	A binary large object; the maximum size is (4GB – 1) * DB_BLOCK_SIZE.
BFILE	A pointer to a large binary file stored outside the database. Binary files must be accessible from the server running the Oracle instance. The maximum size is 4GB.

TABLE 1-1. *Oracle Built-in Datatypes* (Continued)

ANSI SQL Datatype	Oracle Datatype
CHARACTER(n) CHAR(n)	CHAR(n)
CHARACTER VARYING(n) CHAR VARYING(n)	VARCHAR(n)
NATIONAL CHARACTER(n) NATIONAL CHAR(n) NCHAR(n)	NCHAR(n)
NATIONAL CHARACTER VARYING(n) NATIONAL CHAR VARYING(n) NCHAR VARYING(n)	NVARCHAR2(n)
NUMERIC(p,s) DECIMAL(p,s)	NUMBER(p,s)
INTEGER INT SMALLINT	NUMBER(38)
FLOAT(b) DOUBLE PRECISION REAL	NUMBER

TABLE 1-2. *ANSI-Equivalent Oracle Datatypes*

Temporary Tables

Temporary tables have been available since Oracle8*i*. They are temporary in the sense of the data that is stored in the table, not in the definition of the table itself. The command CREATE GLOBAL TEMPORARY TABLE creates a temporary table.

As long as other users have permissions to the table itself, they may perform SELECT statements or DML commands, such as INSERT, UPDATE, or DELETE, on a temporary table. However, each user sees their own and only their own data in the table. When a user truncates a temporary table, only the data that they inserted is removed from the table.

There are two different flavors of temporary data in a temporary table: temporary for the duration of the transaction, and temporary for the duration of the session. The longevity of the temporary data is controlled by the ON COMMIT clause; ON COMMIT DELETE ROWS removes all rows from the temporary table when a COMMIT or ROLLBACK is issued, and ON COMMIT PRESERVE ROWS keeps the rows in the table beyond the transaction boundary. However, when the user's session is terminated, all of the user's rows in the temporary table are removed.

There are a few other things to keep in mind when using temporary tables. Although you can create an index on a temporary table, the entries in the index are dropped along with the data rows, as with a regular table. Also, due to the temporary nature of the data in a temporary table, no redo information is generated for DML on temporary tables; however, undo information is created in the undo tablespace.

Index-Organized Tables

As you will find out later in the subsection on indexes, creating an index makes finding a particular row in a table more efficient. However, this adds a bit of overhead, because the database must maintain the data rows and the index entries for the table. What if your table does not have many columns, and access to the table occurs primarily on a single column? In this case, an *index-organized table (IOT)* might be the right solution. An IOT stores rows of a table in a B-tree index, where each node of the B-tree index contains the keyed (indexed) column along with one or more non-indexed columns.

The most obvious advantage of an IOT is that only one storage structure needs to be maintained instead of two; similarly, the values for the primary key of the table are stored only once in an IOT, versus twice in a regular table.

There are, however, a few disadvantages to using an IOT. Some tables, such as tables for logging events, may not need a primary key, or any keys for that matter; an IOT must have a primary key. Also, IOTs cannot be a member of a cluster. Finally, an IOT might not be the best solution for a table if it has a large number of columns and many of the columns are frequently accessed when table rows are retrieved.

Object Tables

Since Oracle 8, Oracle Database has supported many object-oriented features in the database. User-defined types, along with any defined methods for these object types, can make an implementation of an object-oriented (OO) development project in Oracle seamless.

Object tables have rows that are themselves objects, or instantiations of type definitions. Rows in an object table can be referenced by object ID (OID), in contrast to a primary key in a relational, or regular, table; however, object tables can still have both primary and unique keys, just as relational tables do.

Let's say, for example, that you are creating a Human Resources (HR) system from scratch, so you have the flexibility to design the database from an entirely OO point of view. The first step is to define an employee object, or type, by creating the type:

```
create type PERS_TYP as object
    (Last_Name          varchar2(45),
     First_Name         varchar2(30),
     Middle_Initial     char(1),
     Surname            varchar2(10),
     SSN                varchar2(15));
```

In this particular case, you're not creating any methods with the PERS_TYP object, but by default Oracle creates a constructor method for the type that has the same name as the type itself (in this case, PERS_TYP). To create an object table as a collection of PERS_TYP objects, you can use the familiar CREATE TABLE syntax, as follows:

```
create table pers of pers_typ;
```

To add an instance of an object to the object table, you can specify the constructor method in the INSERT command:

```
insert into pers
      values(pers_typ('Nickels','Randy','E','Ms.','123-45-6789'));
```

As of Oracle Database 10*g*, you do not need the constructor if the table consists of instances of a single object; here is the simplified syntax:

```
insert into pers values('Confused','Dazed','E','Ms.','123-45-6789');
```

References to instances of the PERS_TYP object can be stored in other tables as REF objects, and you can retrieve data from the PERS table without a direct reference to the PERS table itself.

More examples of how you can use objects to implement an object-oriented design project can be found in Chapter 5.

External Tables

External tables were introduced in Oracle9*i*. In a nutshell, *external tables* allow a user to access a data source, such as a text file, as if it were a table in the database. The metadata for the table is stored within the Oracle data dictionary, but the contents of the table are stored externally.

The definition for an external table contains two parts. The first and most familiar part is the definition of the table from the database user's point of view. This definition looks like any typical definition that you'd see in a CREATE TABLE statement.

The second part, however, is what differentiates an external table from a regular table. This is where the mapping between the database columns and the external data source occurs—what column(s) the data element starts in, how wide the column is, and whether the format of the external column is character or binary. The syntax for the default type of external table, ORACLE_LOADER, is virtually identical to that of a control file in SQL*Loader. This is one of the advantages of external tables; the user only needs to know how to access a standard database table to get to the external file.

There are a few drawbacks, however, to using external tables. You cannot create indexes on an external table, and no inserts, updates, or deletes can be performed on external tables. These drawbacks are minor when considering the advantages of using external tables for loading native database tables, for example, in a data warehouse environment.

Clustered Tables

If two or more tables are frequently accessed together (for example, an order table and a line-item detail table), then creating a *clustered table* might be a good way to boost the performance of queries that reference those tables. In the case of an order table with an associated line-item detail table, the order header information could be stored in the same block as the line-item detail records, thus reducing the amount of I/O needed to retrieve the order and line-item information.

Clustered tables also reduce the amount of space needed to store the columns the two tables have in common, also known as a *cluster key value*. The cluster key value is also stored in a *cluster* index. The cluster index operates much like a traditional index in that it will improve queries against the clustered tables when accessed by the cluster key value. In our example with orders and line items, the order number is only stored once, instead of repeating for each line-item detail row.

The advantages to clustering a table are reduced if frequent INSERT, UPDATE, and DELETE operations occur on the table relative to the number of SELECT statements against the table. In addition, frequent queries against individual tables in the cluster may also reduce the benefits of clustering the tables in the first place.

Hash Clusters

A special type of clustered table, a *hash cluster,* operates much like a regular clustered table, except that instead of using a cluster index, a hash cluster uses a hashing function to store and retrieve rows in a table. The total estimated amount of space needed for the table is allocated when the table is created, given the number of hash keys specified during the creation of the cluster. In our order-entry example, let's assume that our Oracle database needs to mirror the legacy data-entry system, which reuses order numbers on a periodic basis. Also, the order number is always a six-digit number. We might create the cluster for orders as in the following example:

```
create cluster order_cluster (order_number number(6))
     size 50
     hash is order_number hashkeys 1000000;

create table cust_order (
     order_number       number(6) primary key,
     order_date         date,
     customer_number    number)
cluster order_cluster(order_number);
```

Hash clusters have performance benefits when you select rows from a table using an equality comparison, as in this example:

```
select order_number, order_date from cust_order
     where order_number = 196811;
```

Typically, this kind of query will retrieve the row with only one I/O if the number of HASHKEYS is high enough and the HASH IS clause, containing the hashing function, produces an evenly distributed hash key.

Sorted Hash Clusters

Sorted hash clusters are new as of Oracle 10g. They are similar to regular hash clusters in that a hashing function is used to locate a row in a table. However, in addition, sorted hash clusters allow rows in the table to be stored by one or more columns of the table in ascending order. This allows the data to be processed more quickly for applications that lend themselves to first in, first out (FIFO) processing.

You create sorted hash clusters by first creating the cluster itself. Then you create the sorted hash cluster using the same syntax as regular clustered tables, with the addition of the SORT positional parameter after the column definitions within the cluster. Here is an example of creating a table in a sorted hash cluster:

```
create cluster order_detail_cluster (
     order_number number(6), order_timestamp timestamp)
     size 50 hash is order_number hashkeys 100;
create table order_detail (
     order_number       number,
     order_timestamp    timestamp sort,
     customer_number    number)
cluster order_detail_cluster (
     order_number,
     order_timestamp);
```

Due to the FIFO nature of a sorted hash cluster, when orders are accessed by ORDER_NUMBER the oldest orders are retrieved first based on the value of ORDER_TIMESTAMP.

Partitioned Tables

Partitioning a table (or index, as you will see in the next section) helps make a large table more manageable. A table may be partitioned, or even subpartitioned, into smaller pieces. From an application point of view, partitioning is transparent (that is, no explicit references to a particular partition are necessary in any end-user SQL). The only effect that a user may notice is that queries against the partitioned table using criteria in the WHERE clause that matches the partitioning scheme run a lot faster!

There are many advantages to partitioning from a DBA point of view. If one partition of a table is on a corrupted disk volume, the other partitions in the table are still available for user queries while the damaged volume is being repaired. Similarly, backups of partitions can occur over a period of days, one partition at a time, rather than requiring a single backup of the entire table.

Partitions are generally one of three types: range partitioned, hash partitioned, or list partitioned; as of Oracle 11*g*, you can also partition by parent/child relationships, application-controlled partitioning, and many combinations of basic partition types, including list-hash, list-list, list-range, and range-range. Each row in a partitioned table can exist in one, and only one, partition. The *partition key* directs the row to the proper partition; the partition key can be a composite key of up to 16 columns in the table. There are a few minor restrictions on the types of tables that can be partitioned; for example, a table containing a LONG or LONG RAW column cannot be partitioned. The LONG restriction should rarely be a problem; LOBs (CLOBs and BLOBs, character large objects and binary large objects) are much more flexible and encompass all the features of LONG and LONG RAW datatypes.

TIP
Oracle Corporation recommends that any table greater than 2GB in size be seriously considered for partitioning.

No matter what type of partitioning scheme is in use, each member of a partitioned table must have the same logical attributes, such as column names, datatypes, constraints, and so forth. The physical attributes for each partition, however, can be different depending on its size and location on disk. The key is that the partitioned table must be logically consistent from an application or user point of view.

Range Partitions A range partition is a partition whose partition key falls within a certain range. For example, visits to the corporate e-commerce website can be assigned to a partition based on the date of the visit, with one partition per quarter. A website visit on May 25, 2012, will be recorded in the partition with the name FY2012Q2, whereas a website visit on December 2, 2012, will be recorded in the partition with the name FY2012Q4.

List Partitions A list partition is a partition whose partition key falls within groups of distinct values. For example, sales by region of the country may create a partition for NY, CT, MA, and VT, and another partition for IL, WI, IA, and MN. Any sales from elsewhere in the world may be assigned to its own partition when the state code is missing.

Hash Partitions A hash partition assigns a row to a partition based on a hashing function, specifying the column or columns used in the hashing function, but not explicitly assigning the partition, only specifying how many partitions are available. Oracle will assign the row to a partition and ensure a balanced distribution of rows in each partition.

Hash partitions are useful when there is no clear list- or range-partitioning scheme given the types of columns in the table, or when the relative sizes of the partitions change frequently, requiring repeated manual adjustments to the partitioning scheme.

Composite Partitions Even further refinement of the partitioning process is available with composite partitions. For example, a table may be partitioned by range, and within each range, subpartitioned by list or by hash. New combinations in Oracle 11*g* include list-hash, list-list, list-range, and range-range partitioning.

Partitioned Indexes

You can also partition indexes on a table, either matching the partition scheme of the table being indexed (*local indexes*) or partitioned independently from the partition scheme of the table (*global indexes*). Local partitioned indexes have the advantage of increased availability of the index when partition operations occur; for example, archiving and dropping the partition FY2008Q4 and its local index will not affect index availability for the other partitions in the table.

Constraints

An Oracle *constraint* is a rule or rules that you can define on one or more columns in a table to help enforce a business rule. For example, a constraint can enforce the business rule that an employee's starting salary must be at least $25,000.00. Another example of a constraint enforcing a business rule is to require that if a new employee is assigned a department (although they need not be assigned to a particular department right away), the department number must be valid and exist in the DEPT table.

Six types of data integrity rules can be applied to table columns: null rule, unique column values, primary key values, referential integrity values, complex in-line integrity, and trigger-based integrity. We will touch upon each of these briefly in the following sections.

All the constraints on a table are defined either when the table is created or when the table is altered at the column level, except for triggers, which are defined according to which DML operation you are performing on the table. Constraints may be enabled or disabled at creation or at any point of time in the future; when a constraint is either enabled or disabled (using the keyword ENABLE or DISABLE), existing data in the table may or may not have to be validated (using the keyword VALIDATE or NOVALIDATE) against the constraint, depending on the business rules in effect.

For example, a table in an automaker's database named CAR_INFO containing new automobile data needs a new constraint on the AIRBAG_QTY column, where the value of this column must not be NULL and must have a value that is at least 1 for all new vehicles. However, this table contains data for model years before air bags were required, and as a result, this column is either 0 or NULL. One solution, in this case, would be to create a constraint on the AIRBAG_QTY table to enforce the new rule for new rows added to the table, but not to validate the constraint for existing rows.

Here is a table created with all constraint types. Each type of constraint is reviewed in turn in the following subsections.

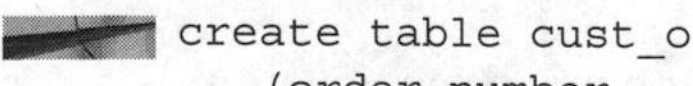

```
create table cust_order
    (order_number          number(6)       primary key,
     order_date            date            not null,
```

```
delivery_date           date,
warehouse_number        number          default 12,
customer_number         number          not null,
order_line_item_qty     number          check (order_line_item_qty < 100),
ups_tracking_number     varchar2(50)    unique,
foreign key (customer_number) references customer(customer_number));
```

NULL Rule

The NOT NULL constraint prevents NULL values from being entered into the ORDER_DATE or CUSTOMER_NUMBER column. This makes a lot of sense from a business rule point of view: Every order must have an order date, and an order doesn't make any sense unless a customer places it.

Note that a NULL value in a column doesn't mean that the value is blank or zero; rather, the value does not exist. A NULL value is not equal to anything, not even another NULL value. This concept is important when using SQL queries against columns that may have NULL values.

Unique Column Values

The UNIQUE integrity constraint ensures that a column or group of columns (in a composite constraint) is unique throughout the table. In the preceding example, the UPS_TRACKING_NUMBER column will not contain duplicate values.

To enforce the constraint, Oracle will create a unique index on the UPS_TRACKING_NUMBER column. If there is already a valid unique index on the column, Oracle will use that index to enforce the constraint.

A column with a UNIQUE constraint may also be declared as NOT NULL. If the column is not declared with the NOT NULL constraint, then any number of rows may contain NULL values, as long as the remaining rows have unique values in this column.

In a composite unique constraint that allows NULLs in one or more columns, the columns that are not NULL determine whether the constraint is being satisfied. The NULL column always satisfies the constraint, because a NULL value is not equal to anything.

Primary Key Values

The PRIMARY KEY integrity constraint is the most common type of constraint found in a database table. At most, only one primary key constraint can exist on a table. The column or columns that comprise the primary key cannot have NULL values.

In the preceding example, the ORDER_NUMBER column is the primary key. A unique index is created to enforce the constraint; if a usable unique index already exists for the column, the primary key constraint uses that index.

Referential Integrity Values

The referential integrity or FOREIGN KEY constraint is more complicated than the others we have covered so far because it relies on another table to restrict what values can be entered into the column with the referential integrity constraint.

In the preceding example, a FOREIGN KEY is declared on the CUSTOMER_NUMBER column; any values entered into this column must also exist in the CUSTOMER_NUMBER column of another table (in this case, the CUSTOMER table).

As with other constraints that allow NULL values, a column with a referential integrity constraint can be NULL without requiring that the referenced column contain a NULL value.

Furthermore, a FOREIGN KEY constraint can be self-referential. In an EMPLOYEE table whose primary key is EMPLOYEE_NUMBER, the MANAGER_NUMBER column can have a FOREIGN KEY declared against the EMPLOYEE_NUMBER column in the same table. This allows for the creation of a reporting hierarchy within the EMPLOYEE table itself.

Indexes should almost always be declared on a FOREIGN KEY column to improve performance; the only exception to this rule is when the referenced primary or unique key in the parent table is never updated or deleted.

Complex In-Line Integrity

More complex business rules may be enforced at the column level by using a CHECK constraint. In the preceding example, the ORDER_LINE_ITEM_QTY column must never exceed 99.

A CHECK constraint can use other columns in the row being inserted or updated to evaluate the constraint. For example, a constraint on the STATE_CD column would allow NULL values only if the COUNTRY_CD column is not USA. In addition, the constraint can use literal values and built-in functions such as TO_CHAR or TO_DATE, as long as these functions operate on literals or columns in the table.

Multiple CHECK constraints are allowed on a column. All the CHECK constraints must evaluate to TRUE to allow a value to be entered in the column. For example, we could modify the preceding CHECK constraint to ensure that ORDER_LINE_ITEM_QTY is greater than 0 in addition to being less than 100.

Trigger-Based Integrity

If the business rules are too complex to implement using unique constraints, a database *trigger* can be created on a table using the CREATE TRIGGER command along with a block of PL/SQL code to enforce the business rule.

Triggers are required to enforce referential integrity constraints when the referenced table exists in a different database. Triggers are also useful for many things outside the realm of constraint checking (auditing access to a table, for example). We cover database triggers in depth in Chapter 17.

Indexes

An Oracle *index* allows faster access to rows in a table when a small subset of the rows will be retrieved from the table. An index stores the value of the column or columns being indexed, along with the physical ROWID of the row containing the indexed value, except for index-organized tables (IOTs), which use the primary key as a logical ROWID. Once a match is found in the index, the ROWID in the index points to the exact location of the table row: which file, which block within the file, and which row within the block.

Indexes are created on a single column or multiple columns. Index entries are stored in a B-tree structure so that traversing the index to find the key value of the row uses very few I/O operations. An index may serve a dual purpose in the case of a unique index: Not only will it speed the search for the row, but it enforces a unique or primary key constraint on the indexed column. Entries within an index are automatically updated whenever the contents of a table row are inserted, updated, or deleted. When a table is dropped, all indexes created on the table are also automatically dropped.

Several types of indexes are available in Oracle, each suitable for a particular type of table, access method, or application environment. I will present the highlights and features of the most common index types in the following subsections.

Unique Indexes

A *unique index* is the most common form of B-tree index. It is often used to enforce the primary key constraint of a table. Unique indexes ensure that duplicate values will not exist in the column or columns being indexed. A unique index may be created on a column in the EMPLOYEE table for the Social Security Number because there should not be any duplicates in this column. However, some employees may not have a Social Security Number, so this column would contain a NULL value.

Non-Unique Indexes

A *non-unique* index helps speed access to a table without enforcing uniqueness. For example, we can create a non-unique index on the LAST_NAME column of the EMPLOYEE table to speed up our searches by last name, but we would certainly have many duplicates for any given last name.

A non-unique B-tree index is created on a column by default if no other keywords are specified in a CREATE INDEX statement.

Reverse Key Indexes

A *reverse key* index is a special kind of index used typically in an OLTP (online transaction processing) environment. In a reverse key index, all the bytes in each column's key value of the index are reversed. The REVERSE keyword specifies a reverse key index in the CREATE INDEX command. Here is an example of creating a reverse key index:

```
create index ie_line_item_order_number
        on line_item(order_number) reverse;
```

If an order number of 123459 is placed, the reverse key index stores the order number as 954321. Inserts into the table are distributed across all leaf keys in the index, reducing the contention among several writers all doing inserts of new rows. A reverse key index also reduces the potential for these "hot spots" in an OLTP environment if orders are queried or modified soon after they are placed. On the other hand, although a reverse key index reduces hot spots, it dramatically increases the number of blocks that have to be read from disks and increases the number of index block splits.

Function-Based Indexes

A *function-based index* is similar to a standard B-tree index, except that a transformation of a column or columns, declared as an expression, is stored in the index instead of the columns themselves.

Function-based indexes are useful in cases where names and addresses might be stored in the database as mixed case. A regular index on a column containing the value "SmiTh" would not return any values if the search criterion was "Smith". On the other hand, if the index stored the last names in all uppercase, all searches on last names could use uppercase. Here is an example of creating a function-based index on the LAST_NAME column of the EMPLOYEE table:

```
create index up_name on employee(upper(last_name));
```

As a result, searches using queries such as the following will use the index we just created instead of doing a full table scan:

```
select employee_number, last_name, first_name, from employee
     where upper(last_name) = 'SMITH';
```

Bitmap Indexes

A *bitmap index* has a significantly different structure from a B-tree index in the leaf node of the index. It stores one string of bits for each possible value (the cardinality) of the column being indexed. The length of the string of bits is the same as the number of rows in the table being indexed.

In addition to saving a tremendous amount of space compared to traditional indexes, a bitmap index can provide dramatic improvements in response time because Oracle can quickly remove potential rows from a query containing multiple WHERE clauses long before the table itself needs to be accessed. Multiple bitmaps can use logical AND and OR operations to determine which rows to access from the table.

Although you can use a bitmap index on any column in a table, it is most efficient when the column being indexed has a low *cardinality,* or number of distinct values. For example, the GENDER column in the PERS table will be either NULL, M, or F. The bitmap index on the GENDER column will have only three bitmaps stored in the index. On the other hand, a bitmap index on the LAST_NAME column will have close to the same number of bitmap strings as rows in the table itself! The queries looking for a particular last name will most likely take less time if a full table scan is performed instead of using an index. In this case, a traditional B-tree non-unique index makes more sense.

A variation of bitmap indexes called *bitmap join indexes* creates a bitmap index on a table column that is frequently joined with one or more other tables on the same column. This provides tremendous benefits in a data warehouse environment where a bitmap join index is created on a fact table and one or more dimension tables, essentially pre-joining those tables and saving CPU and I/O resources when an actual join is performed.

NOTE

Bitmap indexes are only available in the Enterprise Edition of Oracle 11g and 12c. Because bitmap indexes include extra overhead of locking and block splits when performing DML on the table, they are intended only for columns that are rarely updated.

Views

Views allow users to see a customized presentation of the data in a single table or even a join between many tables. A view is also known as a *stored query*—the query details underlying the view are hidden from the user of the view. A regular view does not store any data, only the definition, and the underlying query is run every time the view is accessed. An enhanced type of view, called a *materialized view,* allows the results of the query to be stored along with the definition of the query to speed processing, among other benefits. Object views, like traditional views, hide the details of the underlying table joins and allow object-oriented development and processing to occur in the database while the underlying tables are still in a relational format.

In the following subsections, we'll review the basics of the types of views a typical database user, developer, or DBA will create and use on a regular basis.

Regular Views

A *regular view,* or more commonly referred to as a *view,* is not allocated any storage; only its definition, a query, is stored in the data dictionary. The tables in the query underlying the view are called *base tables;* each base table in a view can be further defined as a view.

The advantages of a view are many. Views hide data complexity—a senior analyst can define a view containing the EMPLOYEE, DEPARTMENT, and SALARY tables to make it easier for upper management to retrieve information about employee salaries by using a SELECT statement against what appears to be a table but is actually a view containing a query that joins the EMPLOYEE, DEPARTMENT, and SALARY tables.

Views can also be used to enforce security. A view on the EMPLOYEE table called EMP_INFO may contain all columns except for SALARY, and the view can be defined as READ ONLY to prevent updates to the table:

```
create view emp_info as
    select employee_number, last_name,
           first_name, middle_initial, surname
from employee
with read only;
```

Without the READ ONLY clause, it is possible to update or add rows to a view, even to a view containing multiple tables. There are some constructs in a view that prevent it from being updatable, such as having a DISTINCT operator, an aggregate function, or a GROUP BY clause.

When Oracle processes a query containing a view, it substitutes the underlying query definition in the user's SELECT statement and processes the resulting query as if the view did not exist. As a result, the benefits of any existing indexes on the base tables are not lost when a view is used.

Materialized Views

In some ways, a *materialized view* is very similar to a regular view: The definition of the view is stored in the data dictionary, and the view hides the details of the underlying base query from the user. That is where the similarities end. A materialized view also allocates space in a database segment to hold the result set from the execution of the base query.

You can use a materialized view to replicate a read-only copy of a table to another database, with the same column definitions and data as the base table. This is the simplest implementation of a materialized view. To enhance the response time when a materialized view needs to be refreshed, a *materialized view log* can be created to refresh the materialized view. Otherwise, a full refresh is required when a refresh is required—the results of the base query must be run in their entirety to refresh the materialized view. The materialized view log facilitates incremental updates of the materialized views.

In a data warehouse environment, materialized views can store aggregated data from a GROUP BY ROLLUP or a GROUP BY CUBE query. If the appropriate initialization parameter values are set, such as QUERY_REWRITE_ENABLED, and the query itself allows for query rewrites (with the QUERY REWRITE clause), then any query that appears to do the same kind of aggregation as the materialized view will automatically use the materialized view instead of running the original query.

Regardless of the type of materialized view, it can be refreshed automatically when a committed transaction occurs in the base table, or it can be refreshed on demand.

Materialized views have many similarities to indexes: they are directly tied to a table and take up space, they must be refreshed when the base tables are updated, their existence is virtually transparent to the user, and they can aid in optimizing queries by using an alternate access path to return the results of a query.

More details on how to use materialized views in a distributed environment can be found in Chapter 17.

Object Views

Object-oriented (OO) application development environments are becoming increasingly prevalent, and the Oracle 12*c* database fully supports the implementation of objects and methods natively in the database. However, a migration from a purely relational database environment to a purely OO database environment is not an easy transition to make; few organizations have the time and resources to build a new system from the ground up. Oracle 12*c* makes the transition easier with object views. Object views allow the object-oriented applications to see the data as a collection of objects that have attributes and methods, while the legacy systems can still run batch jobs against the INVENTORY table. Object views can simulate abstract datatypes, OIDs, and references that a purely OO database environment would provide.

As with regular views, you can use INSTEAD OF triggers in the view definition to allow DML against the view by running a block of PL/SQL code instead of the actual DML statement supplied by the user or application.

Users and Schemas

Access to the database is granted to a database account known as a *user*. A user may exist in the database without owning any objects. However, if the user creates and owns objects in the database, those objects are part of a *schema* that has the same name as the database user. A schema can own any type of object in the database: tables, indexes, sequences, views, and so forth. The schema owner or DBA can grant access to these objects to other database users. The user always has full privileges and control over the objects in the user's schema.

When a user is created by the DBA (or by any other user with the CREATE USER system privilege), a number of other characteristics can be assigned to the user, such as which tablespaces are available to the user for creating objects, and whether the password is pre-expired.

You can authenticate users in the database with three methods: database authentication, operating system authentication, and network authentication. With database authentication, the encrypted password for the user is stored in the database. In contrast, operating system authentication makes an assumption that a user who is already authenticated by an operating system connection has the same privileges as a user with the same or similar name (depending on the value of the OS_AUTHENT_PREFIX initialization parameter). Network authentication uses solutions based on Public Key Infrastructure (PKI). These network authentication methods require Oracle 11*g* or 12*c* Enterprise Edition with the Oracle Advanced Security option.

Profiles

Database resources are not unlimited; therefore, a DBA must manage and allocate resources among all database users. Some examples of database resources are CPU time, concurrent sessions, logical reads, and connect time.

A database *profile* is a named set of resource limits that you can assign to a user. After Oracle is installed, the DEFAULT profile exists and is assigned to any user not explicitly assigned a profile. The DBA can add new profiles or change the DEFAULT profile to suit the needs of the enterprise. The initial values for the DEFAULT profile allow for unlimited use of all database resources.

Sequences

An Oracle *sequence* assigns sequential numbers, guaranteed to be unique unless the sequence is re-created or reset. It produces a series of unique numbers in a multi-user environment without the overhead of disk locking or any special I/O calls, other than what is involved in loading the sequence into the shared pool.

Sequences can generate numbers up to 38 digits in length; the series of numbers can be ascending or descending, the interval can be any user-specified value, and Oracle can cache blocks of numbers from a sequence in memory for even faster performance.

The numbers from sequences are guaranteed to be unique, but not necessarily sequential. If a block of numbers is cached, and the instance is restarted or a transaction that uses a number from a sequence is rolled back, the next call to retrieve a number from the sequence will not return the number that was not used in the original reference to the sequence.

Synonyms

An Oracle *synonym* is simply an alias to a database object, to simplify references to database objects and to hide the details of the source of the database objects. Synonyms can be assigned to tables, views, materialized views, sequences, procedures, functions, and packages. Like views, a synonym allocates no space in the database, other than its definition in the data dictionary.

Synonyms can be either public or private. A private synonym is defined in the schema of a user and is available only to the user. A public synonym is usually created by a DBA and is automatically available for use by any database user.

TIP

After creating a public synonym, make sure the users of the synonym have the correct privileges to the object referenced by the synonym.

When referencing a database object, Oracle first checks whether the object exists in the user's schema. If no such object exists, Oracle checks for a private synonym. If there is no private synonym, Oracle checks for a public synonym. If there is no public synonym, Oracle returns an error.

PL/SQL

Oracle PL/SQL is Oracle's procedural language extension to SQL. PL/SQL is useful when the standard DML and SELECT statements cannot produce the desired results in an easy fashion because of the lack of the procedural elements found in a traditional third-generation language such as C++ and Ada. Since Oracle Database 9*i*, the SQL processing engine is shared between SQL and PL/SQL, which means that all new features added to SQL are automatically available to PL/SQL.

In the next few sections, we'll take a whirlwind tour of the benefits of using Oracle PL/SQL.

Procedures/Functions

PL/SQL procedures and functions are examples of PL/SQL *named blocks*. A PL/SQL block is a sequence of PL/SQL statements treated as a unit for the purposes of execution, and it contains up to three sections: a variable declaration section, an executable section, and an exception section.

The difference between a procedure and function is that a function will return a single value to a calling program such as a SQL SELECT statement. A procedure, on the other hand, does not return a value, only a status code. However, procedures may have one or many variables that can be set and returned as part of the argument list to the procedure.

Procedures and functions have many advantages in a database environment. Procedures are compiled and stored in the data dictionary once; when more than one user needs to call the procedure, it is already compiled, and only one copy of the stored procedure exists in the shared pool. In addition, network traffic is reduced, even if the procedural features of PL/SQL are not used. One PL/SQL call uses up much less network bandwidth than several SQL SELECT and INSERT statements sent separately over the network, not to mention the reparsing that occurs for each statement sent over the network.

Packages

PL/SQL *packages* group together related functions and procedures, along with common variables and cursors. Packages consist of two parts: a package specification and a package body. In the package specification, the methods and attributes of the package are exposed; the implementation of the methods along with any private methods and attributes are hidden in the package body. Using a package instead of a standalone procedure or function allows the embedded procedure or function to be changed without invalidating any objects that refer to elements of the package specification, thus avoiding recompilation of the objects that reference the package.

Triggers

Triggers are a specialized type of a PL/SQL or Java block of code that is executed, or *triggered,* when a specified event occurs. The types of events can be DML statements on a table or view, DDL statements, and even database events such as startup or shutdown. The specified trigger can be refined to execute on a particular event for a particular user as part of an auditing strategy.

Triggers are extremely useful in a distributed environment to simulate a foreign key relationship between tables that do not exist in the same database. They are also very useful in implementing complex integrity rules that cannot be defined using the built-in Oracle constraint types.

More information on how triggers can be used in a robust distributed environment can be found in Chapter 17.

External File Access

In addition to external tables, there are a number of other ways Oracle can access external files:

- From SQL*Plus, either by accessing an external script containing other SQL commands to be run or by sending the output from a SQL*Plus SPOOL command to a file in the operating system's file system.
- Text information can be read or written from a PL/SQL procedure using the UTL_FILE built-in package; similarly, DBMS_OUTPUT calls within a PL/SQL procedure can generate text messages and diagnostics that can be captured by another application and saved to a text file.

- External data can be referenced by the BFILE datatype. A BFILE datatype is a pointer to an external binary file. Before BFILEs can be used in a database, a *directory alias* needs to be created with the CREATE DIRECTORY command that specifies a prefix containing the full directory path where the BFILE target is stored.
- DBMS_PIPE can communicate with any 3GL language that Oracle supports, such as C++, Ada, Java, or COBOL, and exchange information.
- UTL_MAIL, a package added in Oracle 10*g*, allows a PL/SQL application to send e-mails without knowing how to use the underlying SMTP protocol stack.

When using an external file as a data source, for either input or output, a number of cautions are in order. Carefully consider the following before you use an external data source:

- The database data and the external data may be frequently out of synch when one of the data sources changes without synchronizing with the other.
- It is important to make sure that the backups of the two data sources occur at nearly the same time to ensure that the recovery of one data source will keep the two data sources in synch.
- Script files may contain passwords; many organizations forbid the plain-text representation of any user account in a script file. In this situation, operating system validation may be a good alternative for user authentication.
- You should review the security of files located in a directory that is referenced by each DIRECTORY object. Extreme security measures on database objects are mitigated by lax security on referenced operating system files.

Database Links and Remote Databases

Database links allow an Oracle database to reference objects stored outside of the local database. The command CREATE DATABASE LINK creates the path to a remote database, which in turn allows access to objects in the remote database. A database link wraps together the name of the remote database, a method for connecting to the remote database, and a username/password combination to authenticate the connection to the remote database. In some ways, a database link is similar to a database synonym: A database link can be public or private, and it provides a convenient shorthand way to access another set of resources. The main difference is that the resource is outside of the database instead of in the same database, and therefore requires more information to resolve the reference. The other difference is that a synonym is a reference to a specific object, whereas a database link is a defined path used to access any number of objects in a remote database.

For links to work between databases in a distributed environment, the global database name of each database in the domain must be different. Therefore, it is important to assign the initialization parameters DB_NAME and DB_DOMAIN correctly.

To make using database links even easier, you can assign a synonym to a database link to make the table access even more transparent; the user does not know if the synonym accesses an object locally or on a distributed database. The object can move to a different remote database, or to the local database, and the synonym name can remain the same, making access to the object transparent to users.

How database links to remote databases are leveraged in a distributed environment is covered further in Chapter 17.

Oracle Physical Storage Structures

The Oracle database uses a number of physical storage structures on disk to hold and manage the data from user transactions. Some of these storage structures, such as the datafiles, redo log files, and archived redo log files, hold actual user data; other structures, such as control files, maintain the state of the database objects, and text-based alert and trace files contain logging information for both routine events and error conditions in the database. Figure 1-3 shows the relationship between these physical structures and the logical storage structures we reviewed in the earlier section "Oracle Logical Database Structures."

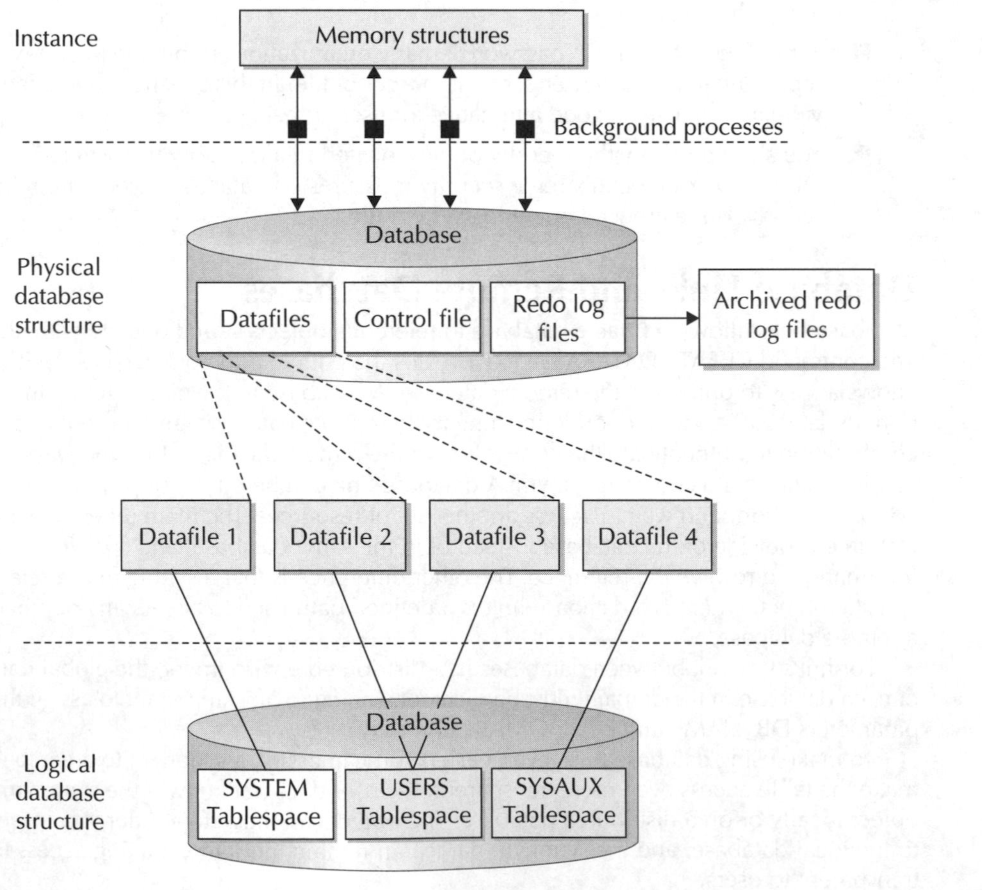

FIGURE 1-3. *Oracle physical storage structures*

Datafiles

Every Oracle database must contain at least one *datafile*. One Oracle datafile corresponds to one physical operating system file on disk. Each datafile in an Oracle database is a member of one and only one tablespace; a tablespace, however, can consist of many datafiles. (A bigfile tablespace consists of exactly one datafile.)

An Oracle datafile may automatically expand when it runs out of space, if the DBA created the datafile with the AUTOEXTEND parameter. The DBA can also limit the amount of expansion for a given datafile by using the MAXSIZE parameter. In any case, the size of the datafile is ultimately limited by the disk volume on which it resides.

TIP
The DBA often has to decide whether to allocate one datafile that can AUTOEXTEND indefinitely or to allocate many smaller datafiles with a limit to how much each can extend. In earlier releases of Oracle, you had no choice but to have multiple datafiles and manage the tablespace at the datafile level. Now that you can have bigfile tablespaces, you can manage most aspects at the tablespace level. Now that RMAN can back up a bigfile tablespace in parallel as well (since Oracle Database 11g), it makes sense to create one datafile and let it AUTOEXTEND when necessary.

The datafile is the ultimate resting place for all data in the database. Frequently accessed blocks in a datafile are cached in memory; similarly, new data blocks are not immediately written out to the datafile but rather are written to the datafile depending on when the database writer process is active. Before a user's transaction is considered complete, however, the transaction's changes are written to the redo log files.

Redo Log Files

Whenever data is added, removed, or changed in a table, index, or other Oracle object, an entry is written to the current *redo log file*. Every Oracle database must have at least two redo log files, because Oracle reuses redo log files in a circular fashion. When one redo log file is filled with *redo* log entries, the current log file is marked as ACTIVE, if it is still needed for instance recovery, or INACTIVE, if it is not needed for instance recovery; the next log file in the sequence is reused from the beginning of the file and is marked as CURRENT.

Ideally, the information in a redo log file is never used. However, when a power failure occurs, or some other server failure causes the Oracle instance to fail, the new or updated data blocks in the database buffer cache may not yet have been written to the datafiles. When the Oracle instance is restarted, the entries in the redo log file are applied to the database datafiles in a *roll forward* operation, to restore the state of the database up to the point where the failure occurred.

To be able to recover from the loss of one redo log file within a redo log group, multiple copies of a redo log file can exist on different physical disks. Later in this chapter, you will see how redo log files, archived log files, and control files can be *multiplexed* to ensure the availability and data integrity of the Oracle database.

Control Files

Every Oracle database has at least one *control file* that maintains the metadata of the database (in other words, data about the physical structure of the database itself). Among other things, the control file contains the name of the database, when the database was created, and the names and locations of all datafiles and redo log files. In addition, the control file maintains information used by RMAN, such as the persistent RMAN settings and the types of backups that have been performed on the database. RMAN is covered in depth in Chapter 12. Whenever any changes are made to the structure of the database, the information about the changes is immediately reflected in the control file.

Because the control file is so critical to the operation of the database, it can also be multiplexed. However, no matter how many copies of the control file are associated with an instance, only one of the control files is designated as primary for purposes of retrieving database metadata.

The ALTER DATABASE BACKUP CONTROLFILE TO TRACE command is another way to back up the control file. It produces a SQL script that you can use to re-create the database control file in case all multiplexed binary versions of the control file are lost due to a catastrophic failure.

This trace file can also be used, for example, to re-create a control file if the database needs to be renamed, or to change various database limits that could not otherwise be changed without re-creating the entire database. As of Oracle 10*g*, you can use the **nid** utility to rename the database without having to re-create the control file.

Archived Log Files

An Oracle database can operate in one of two modes: ARCHIVELOG or NOARCHIVELOG mode. When the database is in NOARCHIVELOG mode, the circular reuse of the redo log files (also known as the *online* redo log files) means that redo entries (the contents of previous transactions) are no longer available in case of a failure to a disk drive or another media-related failure. Operating in NOARCHIVELOG mode does protect the integrity of the database in the event of an instance failure or system crash, because all transactions that are committed but not yet written to the datafiles are available in the online redo log files.

In contrast, ARCHIVELOG mode sends a filled redo log file to one or more specified destinations and can be available to reconstruct the database at any given point in time in the event that a database media failure occurs. For example, if the disk drive containing the datafiles crashes, the contents of the database can be recovered to a point in time before the crash, given a recent backup of the datafiles and the redo log files that were generated since the backup occurred.

The use of multiple archived log destinations for filled redo log files is critical for one of Oracle's high-availability features known as Oracle Data Guard, formerly known as Oracle Standby Database. Oracle Data Guard is covered in detail in Chapter 13.

Initialization Parameter Files

When a database instance starts, the memory for the Oracle instance is allocated, and one of two types of *initialization parameter files* is opened: either a text-based file called **init<SID>.ora** (known generically as init.ora or a PFILE) or a server parameter file (otherwise known as an SPFILE). The instance first looks for an SPFILE in the default location for the operating system (**$ORACLE_HOME/dbs** on Unix, for example) as either **spfile<SID>.ora** or **spfile.ora**. If neither of these files exists, the instance looks for a PFILE with the name **init<SID>.ora**. Alternatively, the STARTUP command can explicitly specify a PFILE to use for startup.

Initialization parameter files, regardless of the format, specify file locations for trace files, control files, filled redo log files, and so forth. They also set limits on the sizes of the various structures in the SGA as well as how many users can connect to the database simultaneously.

Until Oracle9*i*, using the init.ora file was the only way to specify initialization parameters for the instance. Although init.ora is easy to edit with a text editor, it has some drawbacks. If a dynamic system parameter is changed at the command line with the ALTER SYSTEM command, the DBA must remember to change the init.ora file so that the new parameter value will be in effect the next time the instance is restarted.

An SPFILE makes parameter management easier and more effective for the DBA. If an SPFILE is in use for the running instance, any ALTER SYSTEM command that changes an initialization parameter can change the initialization parameter automatically in the SPFILE, change it only for the running instance, or both. No editing of the SPFILE is necessary, or even possible without corrupting the SPFILE itself.

Although you cannot mirror a parameter file or SPFILE per se, you can back up an SPFILE to an init.ora file, and both the init.ora and the SPFILE for the Oracle instance should be backed up using conventional operating system commands or using RMAN in the case of an SPFILE.

When the DBCA is used to create a database, an SPFILE is created by default.

Alert and Trace Log Files

When things go wrong, Oracle can and often does write messages to the *alert log* and, in the case of background processes or user sessions, *trace log* files.

The alert log file, located in the directory specified by the initialization parameter BACKGROUND_DUMP_DEST, contains both routine status messages and error conditions. When the database is started up or shut down, a message is recorded in the alert log, along with a list of initialization parameters that are different from their default values. In addition, any ALTFR DATABASE or ALTER SYSTEM commands issued by the DBA are recorded. Operations involving tablespaces and their datafiles are recorded here, too, such as adding a tablespace, dropping a tablespace, and adding a datafile to a tablespace. Error conditions, such as tablespaces running out of space, corrupted redo logs, and so forth, are also recorded here.

The trace files for the Oracle instance background processes are also located in BACKGROUND_DUMP_DEST. For example, the trace files for the Process Monitor (PMON) and System Monitor (SMON) contain an entry when an error occurs or when SMON needs to perform instance recovery; the trace files for the Queue Monitor (QMON) contain informational messages when it spawns a new process.

Trace files are also created for individual user sessions or connections to the database. These trace files are located in the directory specified by the initialization parameter USER_DUMP_DEST. Trace files for user processes are created in two situations: The first is when some type of error occurs in a user session because of a privilege problem, running out of space, and so forth. In the second situation, a trace file can be created explicitly with the command ALTER SESSION SET SQL_TRACE=TRUE. Trace information is generated for each SQL statement that the user executes, which can be helpful when tuning a user's SQL statement.

The alert log file can be deleted or renamed at any time; it is re-created the next time an alert log message is generated. The DBA will often set up a daily batch job (either through an operating system mechanism or using Oracle Enterprise Manager's scheduler) to rename and archive the alert log on a daily basis.

Backup Files

Backup files can originate from a number of sources, such as operating system copy commands or Oracle RMAN. If the DBA performs a "cold" backup (see the section titled "Backup/Recovery Overview" for more details on backup types), the backup files are simply operating system copies of the datafiles, redo log files, control files, archived redo log files, and so forth.

In addition to bit-for-bit image copies of datafiles (the default in RMAN), RMAN can generate full and incremental backups of datafiles, control files, archived redo log files, and SPFILEs that are in a special format, called *backupsets,* only readable by RMAN. RMAN backupset backups are generally smaller than the original datafiles because RMAN does not back up unused blocks.

Oracle Managed Files

Oracle Managed Files (OMF), introduced in Oracle version 9*i,* makes the DBA's job easier by automating the creation and removal of the datafiles that make up the logical structures in the database.

Without OMF, a DBA might drop a tablespace and forget to remove the underlying operating system files. This makes inefficient use of disk resources, and it unnecessarily increases backup time for datafiles that are no longer needed by the database.

OMF is well suited for small databases with a low number of users and a part-time DBA, where optimal configuration of a production database is not necessary. Even if the database is small, Oracle best practices recommend using Automatic Storage Management (ASM) for all of the datafiles that make up a database, and also recommend making only two disk groups—one for table and index segments (e.g., +DATA) and one for RMAN backups, a second copy of the control file, and copies of the archived redo logs (e.g., +RECOV). The initialization parameter DB_FILE_CREATE_DEST points to the +DATA disk group and DB_CREATE_ONLINE_DEST_1 points to the +DATA disk group and DB_CREATE_ONLINE_DEST_2 points to +RECOV. The same is true for the online log file destinations LOG_ARCHIVE_DEST_*n*.

Password Files

An Oracle *password file* is a file within the Oracle administrative or software directory structure on disk used to authenticate Oracle system administrators for tasks such as creating a database or starting up and shutting down the database. The privileges granted through this file are the SYSDBA and SYSOPER privileges. Authenticating any other type of user is done within the database itself; because the database may be shut down or not mounted, another form of administrator authentication is necessary in these cases.

The Oracle command-line utility **orapwd** creates a password file if one does not exist or is damaged. Because of the extremely high privileges granted via this file, it should be stored in a secure directory location that is not available to anyone except for DBAs and operating system administrators. Once this file is created, the initialization parameter REMOTE_LOGIN_PASSWORDFILE should be set to EXCLUSIVE to allow users other than SYS to use the password file. Also, the password file must be in the **$ORACLE_HOME/dbs** directory.

TIP
Create at least one user other than SYS or SYSTEM who has DBA privileges for daily administrative tasks. If there is more than one DBA administering a database, each DBA should have their own account with DBA privileges.

Alternatively, authentication for the SYSDBA and SYSOPER privileges can be done with OS authentication; in this case, a password file does not have to be created, and the initialization parameter REMOTE_LOGIN_PASSWORDFILE is set to NONE.

Multiplexing Database Files

To minimize the possibility of losing a control file or a redo log file, multiplexing of database files reduces or eliminates data-loss problems caused by media failures. Multiplexing can be somewhat automated by using an ASM instance, available starting in Oracle 10*g*. For a more budget-conscious enterprise, control files and redo log files can be multiplexed manually.

Automatic Storage Management

Using ASM is a multiplexing solution that automates the layout of datafiles, control files, and redo log files by distributing them across all available disks. When new disks are added to the ASM cluster, the database files are automatically redistributed across all disk volumes for optimal performance. The multiplexing features of an ASM cluster minimize the possibility of data loss and are generally more effective than a manual scheme that places critical files and backups on different physical drives.

Manual Multiplexing

Without a RAID or ASM solution, you can still provide some safeguards for your critical database files by setting some initialization parameters and providing an additional location for control files, redo log files, and archived redo log files.

Control Files

Control files can be multiplexed immediately when the database is created, or they can be multiplexed later with a few extra steps to manually copy them to multiple destinations. You can multiplex up to eight copies of a control file.

Whether you multiplex the control files when the database is created or you multiplex them later, the initialization parameter value for CONTROL_FILES is the same.

If you want to add another multiplexed location, you need to edit the initialization parameter file and add another location to the CONTROL_FILES parameter. If you are using an SPFILE instead of an init.ora file, then use a command similar to the following to change the CONTROL_FILES parameter:

```
alter system
     set control_files = '/u01/oracle/whse2/ctrlwhse1.ctl,
       /u02/oracle/whse2/ctrlwhse2.ctl,
       /u03/oracle/whse2/ctrlwhse3.ctl'
scope=spfile;
```

The other possible values for SCOPE in the ALTER SYSTEM command are MEMORY and BOTH. Specifying either one of these for SCOPE returns an error, because the CONTROL_FILES parameter cannot be changed for the running instance, only for the next restart of the instance. Therefore, only the SPFILE is changed.

In either case, the next step is to shut down the database. Copy the control file to the new destinations, as specified in CONTROL_FILES, and restart the database. You can always verify the names and locations of the control files by looking in one of the data dictionary views:

```
select value from v$spparameter where name='control_files';
```

This query will return one row for each multiplexed copy of the control file. In addition, the view V$CONTROLFILE contains one row for each copy of the control file along with its status.

Redo Log Files

Redo log files are multiplexed by changing a set of redo log files into a *redo log file group*. In a default Oracle installation, a set of three redo log files is created. As you learned in the previous section on redo log files, after each log file is filled, it starts filling the next in sequence. After the third is filled, the first one is reused. To change the set of three redo log files to a group, we can add one or more identical files as a companion to each of the existing redo log files. After the groups are created, the redo log entries are concurrently written to the group of redo log files. When the group of redo log files is filled, it begins to write redo entries to the next group. Figure 1-4 shows how a set of four redo log files can be multiplexed with four groups, each group containing three members.

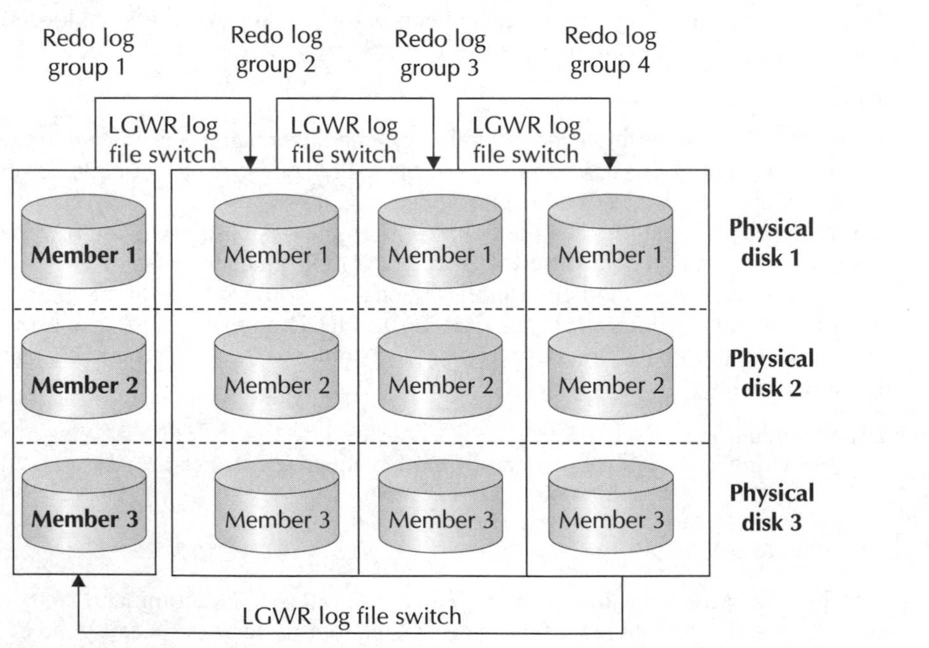

FIGURE 1-4. *Multiplexing redo log files*

Adding a member to a redo log group is very straightforward. In the ALTER DATABASE command, we specify the name of the new file and the group to add it to. The new file is created with the same size as the other members in the group:

```
alter database
    add logfile member '/u05/oracle/dc2/log_3d.dbf'
    to group 3;
```

If the redo log files are filling up faster than they can be archived, one possible solution is to add another redo log group. Here is an example of how to add a fifth redo log group to the set of redo log groups in Figure 1-4:

```
alter database
    add logfile group 5
    ('/u02/oracle/dc2/log_3a.dbf',
     '/u03/oracle/dc2/log_3b.dbf',
     '/u04/oracle/dc2/log_3c.dbf') size 250m;
```

All members of a redo log group must be the same size. However, the log file sizes between groups may be different. In addition, redo log groups may have a different number of members. In the preceding example, we started with four redo log groups, added an extra member to redo log group 3 (for a total of four members), and added a fifth redo log group with three members.

As of Oracle 10*g*, you can use the Redo Logfile Size Advisor to assist in determining the optimal size for redo log files to avoid excessive I/O activity or bottlenecks. See Chapter 8 for more information on how to use the Redo Logfile Size Advisor.

Archived Redo Log Files

If the database is in ARCHIVELOG mode, Oracle copies redo log files to a specified location before they can be reused in the redo log switch cycle.

Oracle Memory Structures

Oracle uses the server's physical memory to hold many things for an Oracle instance: the Oracle executable code itself, session information, individual processes associated with the database, and information shared between processes (such as locks on database objects). In addition, the memory structures contain user and data dictionary SQL statements, along with cached information that is eventually permanently stored on disk, such as data blocks from database segments and information about completed transactions in the database. The data area allocated for an Oracle instance is called the *System Global Area (SGA)*. The Oracle executables reside in the software code area. In addition, an area called the *Program Global Area (PGA)* is private to each server and background process; one PGA is allocated for each process. Figure 1-5 shows the relationships between these Oracle memory structures.

System Global Area

The *System Global Area* is a group of shared memory structures for an Oracle instance, shared by the users of the database instance. When an Oracle instance is started, memory is allocated for the SGA based on the values specified in the initialization parameter file or hard-coded in the Oracle software. Many of the parameters that control the size of the various parts of the SGA are dynamic; however, if the parameter SGA_MAX_SIZE is specified, the total size of all SGA areas

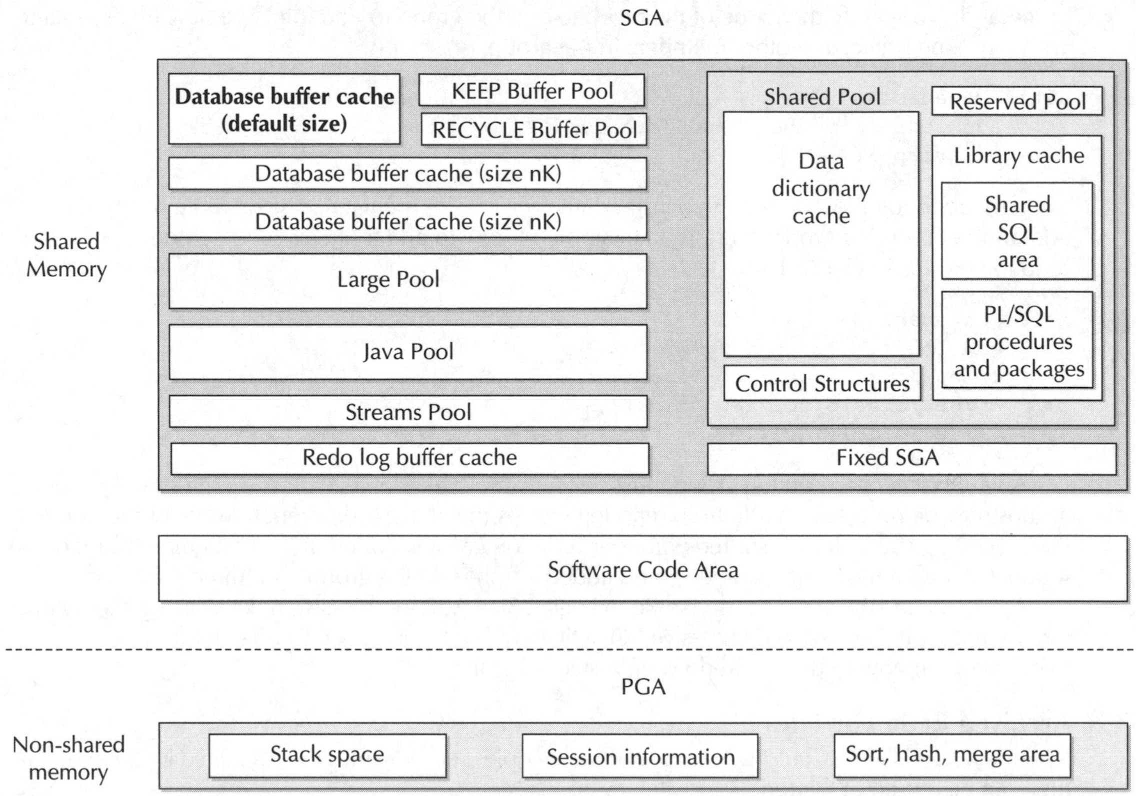

FIGURE 1-5. *Oracle logical memory structures*

must not exceed the value of SGA_MAX_SIZE. If SGA_MAX_SIZE is not specified, but the parameter SGA_TARGET is specified, Oracle automatically adjusts the sizes of the SGA components so that the total amount of memory allocated is equal to SGA_TARGET. SGA_TARGET is a dynamic parameter; it can be changed while the instance is running. The parameter MEMORY_TARGET, new to Oracle 11*g,* balances all memory available to Oracle between the SGA and the Program Global Area (discussed later in this chapter) to optimize performance.

Memory in the SGA is allocated in units of *granules.* A granule can be either 4MB or 16MB, depending on the total size of the SGA. If the SGA is less than or equal to 128MB, a granule is 4MB; otherwise, it is 16MB.

In the next few subsections, we will cover the highlights of how Oracle uses each section in the SGA. You can find more information on how to adjust the initialization parameters associated with these areas in Chapter 8.

Buffer Caches

The database *buffer cache* holds blocks of data from disk that have been recently read to satisfy a SELECT statement or that contain modified blocks that have been changed or added from a DML statement. As of Oracle9*i,* the memory area in the SGA that holds these data blocks is dynamic.

This is a good thing, considering that there may be tablespaces in the database with block sizes other than the default block size; tablespaces with up to five different block sizes (one block size for the default, and up to four others) require their own buffer cache. As the processing and transactional needs change during the day or during the week, the values of DB_CACHE_SIZE and DB_*n*K_CACHE_SIZE can be dynamically changed without restarting the instance to enhance performance for a tablespace with a given block size.

Oracle can use two additional caches with the same block size as the default (DB_CACHE_SIZE) block size: the KEEP buffer pool and the RECYCLE buffer pool. As of Oracle9*i*, both of these pools allocate memory independently of other caches in the SGA.

When a table is created, you can specify the pool where the table's data blocks will reside by using the BUFFER_POOL KEEP or BUFFER_POOL_RECYCLE clause in the STORAGE clause. For tables that you use frequently throughout the day, it would be advantageous to place this table into the KEEP buffer pool to minimize the I/O needed to retrieve blocks in the table.

Shared Pool

The *shared pool* contains two major subcaches: the library cache and the data dictionary cache. The shared pool is sized by the SHARED_POOL_SIZE initialization parameter. This is another dynamic parameter that can be resized as long as the total SGA size is less than SGA_MAX_SIZE or SGA_TARGET.

Library Cache The library cache holds information about SQL and PL/SQL statements that are run against the database. In the library cache, because it is shared by all users, many different database users can potentially share the same SQL statement.

Along with the SQL statement itself, the execution plan and parse tree of the SQL statement are stored in the library cache. The second time an identical SQL statement is run, by the same user or a different user, the execution plan and parse tree are already computed, improving the execution time of the query or DML statement.

If the library cache is sized too small, the execution plans and parse trees are flushed out of the cache, requiring frequent reloads of SQL statements into the library cache. See Chapter 8 for ways to monitor the efficiency of the library cache.

Data Dictionary Cache The data dictionary is a collection of database tables, owned by the SYS and SYSTEM schemas, that contain the metadata about the database, its structures, and the privileges and roles of database users. The data dictionary cache holds a subset of the columns from data dictionary tables after first being read into the buffer cache. Data blocks from tables in the data dictionary are used continually to assist in processing user queries and other DML commands.

If the data dictionary cache is too small, requests for information from the data dictionary will cause extra I/O to occur; these I/O-bound data dictionary requests are called *recursive calls* and should be avoided by sizing the data dictionary cache correctly.

Redo Log Buffer

The *redo log buffer* holds the most recent changes to the data blocks in the datafiles. When the redo log buffer is one-third full, or every three seconds, Oracle writes redo log records to the redo log files. As of Oracle 10*g*, the LGWR process will write the redo log records to the redo log files when 1MB of redo is stored in the redo log buffer. The entries in the redo log buffer, once written to the redo log files, are critical to database recovery if the instance crashes before the changed data blocks are written from the buffer cache to the datafiles. A user's committed transaction is not considered complete until the redo log entries have been successfully written to the redo log files.

Large Pool

The *large pool* is an optional area of the SGA. It is used for transactions that interact with more than one database, message buffers for processes performing parallel queries, and RMAN parallel backup and restore operations. As the name implies, the large pool makes available large blocks of memory for operations that need to allocate large blocks of memory at a time.

The initialization parameter LARGE_POOL_SIZE controls the size of the large pool and is a dynamic parameter as of Oracle9*i* release 2.

Java Pool

The *Java pool* is used by the Oracle JVM (Java Virtual Machine) for all Java code and data within a user session. Storing Java code and data in the Java pool is analogous to caching SQL and PL/SQL code in the shared pool.

Streams Pool

New as of Oracle 10*g*, the *streams pool* is sized by using the initialization parameter STREAMS_POOL_SIZE. The streams pool holds data and control structures to support the Oracle Streams feature of Oracle Enterprise Edition. Oracle Streams manages the sharing of data and events in a distributed environment. If the initialization parameter STREAMS_POOL_SIZE is uninitialized or set to zero, the memory used for Streams operations is allocated from the shared pool and may use up to 10 percent of the shared pool. For more information on Oracle Streams, see Chapter 17.

Program Global Area

The *Program Global Area* is an area of memory allocated and private for one process. The configuration of the PGA depends on the connection configuration of the Oracle database: either *shared server* or *dedicated.*

In a shared server configuration, multiple users share a connection to the database, minimizing memory usage on the server, but potentially affecting response time for user requests. In a shared server environment, the SGA holds the session information for a user instead of the PGA. Shared server environments are ideal for a large number of simultaneous connections to the database with infrequent or short-lived requests.

In a dedicated server environment, each user process gets its own connection to the database; the PGA contains the session memory for this configuration.

The PGA also includes a sort area. The sort area is used whenever a user request requires a sort, bitmap merge, or hash join operation.

As of Oracle9*i*, the PGA_AGGREGATE_TARGET parameter, in conjunction with the WORKAREA_SIZE_POLICY initialization parameter, can ease system administration by allowing the DBA to choose a total size for all work areas and let Oracle manage and allocate the memory between all user processes. As mentioned earlier in this chapter, the parameter MEMORY_TARGET manages the PGA and SGA memory as a whole to optimize performance.

Software Code Area

Software code areas store the Oracle executable files that are running as part of an Oracle instance. These code areas are static in nature and only change when a new release of the software is installed. Typically, the Oracle software code areas are located in a privileged memory area separate from other user programs.

Oracle software code is strictly read-only and can be installed either shared or non-shared. Installing Oracle software code as sharable saves memory when multiple Oracle instances are running on the same server at the same software release level.

Background Processes

When an Oracle instance starts, multiple background processes start. A *background process* is a block of executable code designed to perform a specific task. Figure 1-6 shows the relationship between the background processes, the database, and the Oracle SGA. In contrast to a foreground process, such as a SQL*Plus session or a web browser, a background process works behind the scenes. Together, the SGA and the background processes compose an Oracle instance.

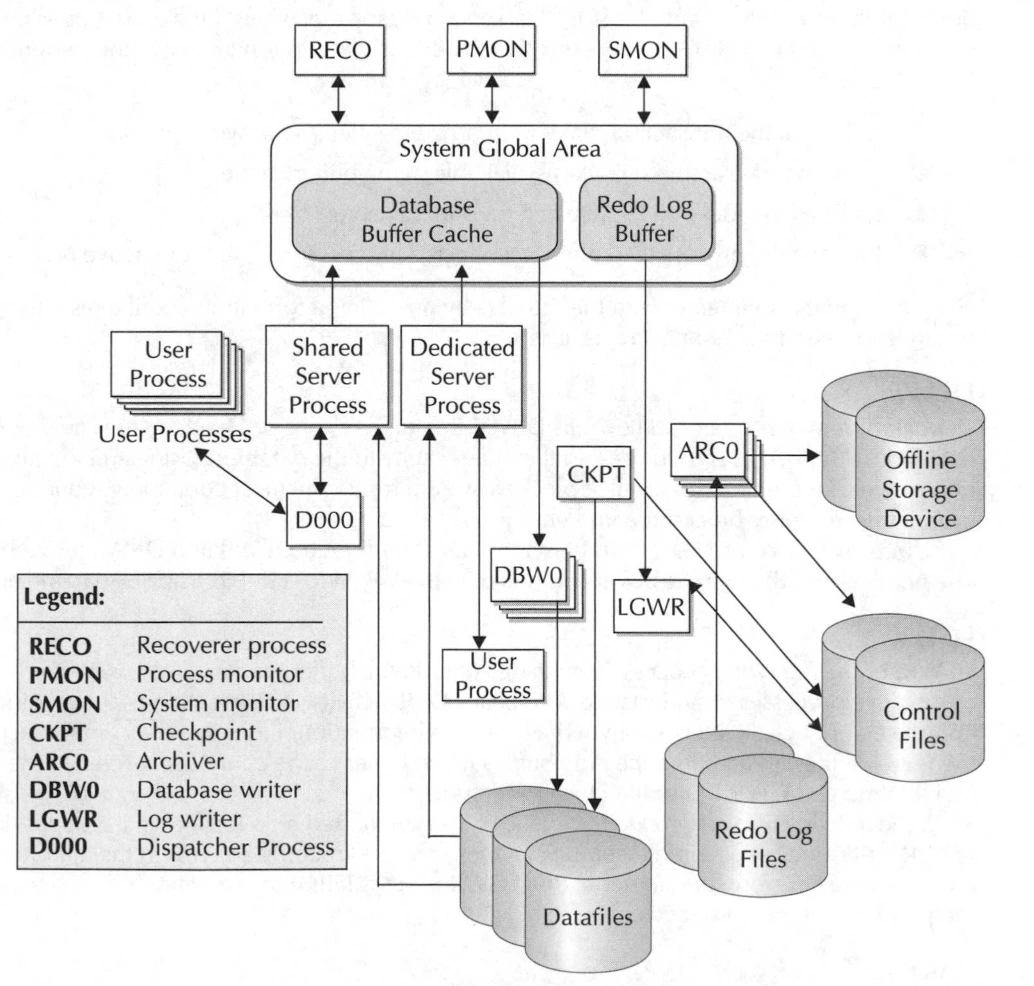

FIGURE 1-6. *Oracle background processes*

SMON

SMON is the *System Monitor* process. In the case of a system crash or instance failure, due to a power outage or CPU failure, the SMON process performs crash recovery by applying the entries in the online redo log files to the datafiles. In addition, temporary segments in all tablespaces are purged during system restart.

One of SMON's routine tasks is to coalesce the free space in tablespaces on a regular basis if the tablespace is dictionary managed.

PMON

If a user connection is dropped, or a user process otherwise fails, PMON, also known as the *Process Monitor,* does the cleanup work. It cleans up the database buffer cache along with any other resources that the user connection was using. For example, a user session may be updating some rows in a table, placing a lock on one or more of the rows. A thunderstorm knocks out the power at the user's desk, and the SQL*Plus session disappears when the workstation is powered off. Within moments, PMON will detect that the connection no longer exists and perform the following tasks:

- Roll back the transaction that was in progress when the power went out.
- Mark the transaction's blocks as available in the buffer cache.
- Remove the locks on the affected rows in the table.
- Remove the process ID of the disconnected process from the list of active processes.

PMON will also interact with the listeners by providing information about the status of the instance for incoming connection requests.

DBW*n*

The *database writer* process, known as DBWR in older versions of Oracle, writes new or changed data blocks (known as *dirty blocks*) in the buffer cache to the datafiles. Using an LRU algorithm, DBW*n* writes the oldest, least active blocks first. As a result, the most commonly requested blocks, even if they are dirty blocks, are in memory.

Up to 20 DBW*n* processes can be started, DBW0 through DBW9 and DBWa through DBWj. The number of DBW*n* processes is controlled by the DB_WRITER_PROCESSES parameter.

LGWR

LGWR, or the *log writer* process, is in charge of redo log buffer management. LGWR is one of the most active processes in an instance with heavy DML activity. A transaction is not considered complete until LGWR successfully writes the redo information, including the commit record, to the redo log files. In addition, the dirty buffers in the buffer cache cannot be written to the datafiles by DBW*n* until LGWR has written the redo information.

If the redo log files are grouped, and one of the multiplexed redo log files in a group is damaged, LGWR writes to the remaining members of the group and records an error in the alert log file. If all members of a group are unusable, the LGWR process fails and the entire instance hangs until the problem can be corrected.

ARC*n*

If the database is in ARCHIVELOG mode, then the *archiver process,* or ARC*n,* copies redo logs to one or more destination directories, devices, or network locations whenever a redo log fills up and redo information starts to fill the next redo log in sequence. Optimally, the archiver process finishes before the filled redo log is needed again; otherwise, serious performance problems occur—users cannot complete their transactions until the entries are written to the redo log files, and the redo log file is not ready to accept new entries because it is still being written to the archive location. There are at least three potential solutions to this problem: make the redo log files larger, increase the number of redo log groups, and increase the number of ARC*n* processes. Up to 30 ARC*n* processes can be started for each instance by increasing the value of the LOG_ARCHIVE_MAX_PROCESSES initialization parameter.

CKPT

The *checkpoint process,* or CKPT, helps to reduce the amount of time required for instance recovery. During a checkpoint, CKPT updates the header of the control file and the datafiles to reflect the last successful *System Change Number (SCN)*. A checkpoint occurs automatically every time a redo log file switch occurs. The DBW*n* processes routinely write dirty buffers to advance the checkpoint from where instance recovery can begin, thus reducing the *Mean Time to Recovery (MTTR)*.

RECO

The RECO, or *recoverer process,* handles failures of distributed transactions (that is, transactions that include changes to tables in more than one database). If a table in the CCTR database is changed along with a table in the WHSE database, and the network connection between the databases fails before the table in the WHSE database can be updated, RECO will roll back the failed transaction.

Backup/Recovery Overview

Oracle supports many different forms of backup and recovery. Some of them can be managed at the user level, such as export and import; most of them are strictly DBA-centric, such as online or offline backups and using operating system commands or the RMAN utility.

Details for configuring and using these backup and recovery methods can be found in Chapter 11 and also in Chapter 12.

Export/Import

You can use Oracle's logical data Export and Import utilities to back up and restore database objects. Export is considered a *logical* backup, because the underlying storage characteristics of the tables are not recorded, only the table metadata, user privileges, and table data. Depending on the task at hand, and whether you have DBA privileges or not, you can export either all tables in the database, all the tables of one or more users, or a specific set of tables. The corresponding import utility can selectively restore the previously exported objects.

One advantage to using Export and Import is that a database power user may be able to manage their own backups and recoveries, especially in a development environment. Also, a binary file generated by Export is typically readable across Oracle versions, making a transfer of a small set of tables from an older version to a newer version of Oracle fairly straightforward.

Export and Import are inherently "point in time" backups and therefore are not the most robust backup and recovery solutions if the data is volatile.

Previous releases of Oracle Database included the **exp** and **imp** commands, but these are not available in Oracle Database 12*c*. As of Oracle 10*g*, Oracle Data Pump replaces the legacy export and import commands and takes those operations to a new performance level. Exports to an external data source can be up to two times faster, and an import operation can be up to 45 times faster because Data Pump Import uses direct path loading, unlike traditional import. In addition, an export from the source database can be simultaneously imported into the target database without an intermediate dump file, saving time and administrative effort. Oracle Data Pump is implemented using the DBMS_DATAPUMP package with the **expdb** and **impdb** commands and includes numerous other manageability features, such as fine-grained object selection. Data Pump also keeps up with all new features of Oracle 12*c*, such as moving entire pluggable databases (PDBs) from one container database (CDB) to another. More information on Oracle Data Pump is provided in Chapter 17.

Offline Backups

One of the ways to make a physical backup of the database is to perform an *offline* backup. To perform an offline backup, the database is shut down and all database-related files, including datafiles, control files, SPFILEs, password files, and so forth, are copied to a second location. Once the copy operation is complete, the database instance can be started.

Offline backups are similar to export backups because they are point-in-time backups and therefore of less value if up-to-the-minute recovery of the database is required and the database is not in ARCHIVELOG mode. Another downside to offline backups is the amount of downtime necessary to perform the backup; any multinational company that needs 24/7 database access will most likely not do offline backups very often.

Online Backups

If a database is in ARCHIVELOG mode, it is possible to do *online* backups of the database. The database can be open and available to users even while the backup is in process. The procedure for doing online backups is as easy as placing a tablespace into a backup state by using the ALTER TABLESPACE USERS BEGIN BACKUP command, backing up the datafiles in the tablespace with operating system commands, and then taking the tablespace out of the backup state with the ALTER TABLESPACE USERS END BACKUP command.

RMAN

The backup tool Recovery Manager, known more commonly as *RMAN,* has been around since Oracle8. RMAN provides many advantages over other forms of backup. It can perform incremental backups of only changed data blocks in between full database backups while the database remains online throughout the backup.

RMAN keeps track of the backups via one of two methods: through the control file of the database being backed up, or through a recovery catalog stored in another database. Using the target database's control file for RMAN is easy, but it's not the best solution for a robust enterprise backup methodology. Although a recovery catalog requires another database to store the metadata for the target database along with a record of all backups, it is well worth it when all the control files in the target database are lost due to a catastrophic failure. In addition, a recovery catalog retains historical backup information that may be overwritten in the target database's control file if the value of CONTROL_FILE_RECORD_KEEP_TIME is set too low.

RMAN is discussed in detail in Chapter 12.

Security Capabilities

This section provides a brief overview of the different ways that Oracle 12*c* controls and enforces security in a database. An in-depth look at these and other security capabilities within Oracle is covered in Chapter 9.

Privileges and Roles

In an Oracle database, *privileges* control access to both the actions a user can perform and the objects in the database. Privileges that control access to actions in the database are called *system privileges,* whereas privileges that control access to data and other objects are called *object privileges*.

To make assignment and management of privileges easier for the DBA, a database *role* groups privileges together. To put it another way, a role is a named group of privileges. In addition, a role can itself have roles assigned to it.

Privileges and roles are granted and revoked with the GRANT and REVOKE commands. The user group PUBLIC is neither a user nor a role, nor can it be dropped; however, when privileges are granted to PUBLIC, they are granted to every user of the database, both present and future.

System Privileges

System privileges grant the right to perform a specific type of action in the database, such as creating users, altering tablespaces, or dropping any view. Here is an example of granting a system privilege:

```
grant drop any table to scott with admin option;
```

The user SCOTT can drop anyone's table in any schema. The WITH GRANT OPTION clause allows SCOTT to grant his newly granted privilege to other users.

Object Privileges

Object privileges are granted on a specific object in the database. The most common object privileges are SELECT, UPDATE, DELETE, and INSERT for tables, EXECUTE for a PL/SQL stored object, and INDEX for granting index-creation privileges on a table. In the following example, the user RJB can perform any DML on the JOBS table owned by the HR schema:

```
grant select, update, insert, delete on hr.jobs to rjb;
```

Auditing

To audit access to objects in the database by users, you can set up an audit trail on a specified object or action by using the AUDIT command. Both SQL statements and access to a particular database object can be audited; the success or failure of the action (or both) can be recorded in the audit trail table, SYS.AUD$, or in an OS file if specified by the AUDIT_TRAIL initialization parameter with a value of OS.

For each audited operation, Oracle creates an audit record with the username, the type of operation that was performed, the object involved, and a timestamp. Various data dictionary views, such as DBA_AUDIT_TRAIL and DBA_FGA_AUDIT_TRAIL, make interpreting the results from the raw audit trail table SYS.AUD$ easier.

CAUTION
Excessive auditing on database objects can have an adverse effect on performance. Start out with basic auditing on key privileges and objects, and expand the auditing when the basic auditing has revealed a potential problem.

Fine-Grained Auditing

The fine-grained auditing capability that was introduced in Oracle9*i* and enhanced in Oracle 10*g*, 11*g*, and Oracle 12*c* takes auditing one step further: Standard auditing can detect when a SELECT statement was executed on an EMPLOYEE table; fine-grained auditing will record an audit record containing specific columns accessed in the EMPLOYEE table, such as the SALARY column.

Fine-grained auditing is implemented using the DBMS_FGA package along with the data dictionary view DBA_FGA_AUDIT_TRAIL. The data dictionary view DBA_COMMON_AUDIT_TRAIL combines standard audit records in DBA_AUDIT_TRAIL with fine-grained audit records.

Virtual Private Database

The Virtual Private Database feature of Oracle, first introduced in Oracle8*i*, couples fine-grained access control with a secure application context. The security policies are attached to the data, and not to the application; this ensures that security rules are enforced regardless of how the data is accessed.

For example, a medical application context may return a predicate based on the patient identification number accessing the data; the returned predicate will be used in a WHERE clause to ensure that the data retrieved from the table is only the data associated with the patient.

Label Security

Oracle Label Security provides an out-of-the-box virtual private database (VPD) solution to restrict access to rows in any table based on the label of the user requesting the access and the label on the row of the table itself. Oracle Label Security administrators do not need any special programming skills to assign security policy labels to users and rows in the table.

This highly granular approach to data security can, for example, allow a DBA at an Application Service Provider (ASP) to create only one instance of an accounts receivable application and to use Label Security to restrict rows in each table to an individual company's accounts receivable information.

Real Application Clusters

Oracle's Real Application Clusters (RAC) feature allows more than one instance, on separate servers, to access the same database files.

A RAC installation can provide extreme high availability for both planned and unplanned outages. One instance can be restarted with new initialization parameters while the other instance is still servicing requests against the database. If one of the hardware servers crashes due to a fault of some type, the Oracle instance on the other server will continue to process transactions, even from users who were connected to the crashed server, transparently and with minimal downtime.

RAC, however, is not a software-only solution: The hardware that implements RAC has special requirements. The shared database should be on a RAID-enabled disk subsystem to ensure that

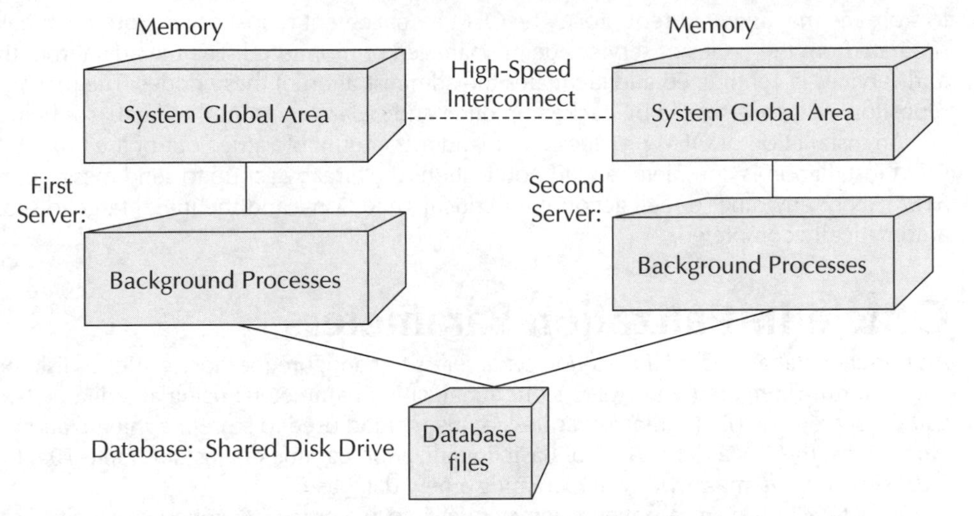

FIGURE 1-7. *A two-node Real Application Clusters (RAC) configuration*

each component of the storage system is fault tolerant. In addition, RAC requires a high-speed interconnect, or a private network, between the nodes in the cluster to support messaging and transfer of blocks from one instance to another using the Cache Fusion mechanism.

The diagram in Figure 1-7 shows a two-node RAC installation. How to set up and configure Real Application Clusters is discussed in depth in Chapter 10.

Oracle Streams

As a component of Oracle Enterprise Edition, *Oracle Streams* is the higher-level component of the Oracle infrastructure that complements Real Application Clusters. Oracle Streams allows the smooth flow and sharing of both data and events within the same database or from one database to another. It is another key piece in Oracle's long list of high-availability solutions, tying together and enhancing Oracle's message queuing, data replication, and event management functions. More information on how to implement Oracle Streams can be found in Chapter 17.

Oracle Enterprise Manager

Oracle Enterprise Manager (OEM) is a valuable set of tools that facilitates the comprehensive management of all components of an Oracle infrastructure, including Oracle database instances, Oracle application servers, and web servers. If a management agent exists for a third-party application, then OEM can manage the third-party application in the same framework as any Oracle-supplied target.

OEM is fully web-enabled via Internet Explorer, Firefox, or Chrome, and as a result any operating system platform that supports IE, Firefox, or Chrome can be used to launch the OEM console.

One of the key decisions to make when using OEM with Oracle Grid Control is the location to store the *management repository.* The OEM management repository is stored in a database separate from the nodes or services being managed or monitored. The metadata from the nodes and services is centralized and facilitates the administration of these nodes. The management repository database should be backed up often and separately from the databases being managed.

An installation of OEM provides a tremendous amount of value "out of the box." When the OEM installation is complete, e-mail notifications are already set up to send messages to the SYSMAN or any other e-mail account for critical conditions, and the initial target discovery is automatically completed.

Oracle Initialization Parameters

An Oracle database uses *initialization parameters* to configure memory settings, disk locations, and so forth. There are two ways to store initialization parameters: using an editable text file and using a server-side binary file. Regardless of the method used to store the initialization parameters, there is a defined set of basic initialization parameters (as of Oracle 10*g*) that every DBA should be familiar with when creating a new database.

As of Oracle 10*g*, initialization parameters fall into two broad categories: basic initialization parameters and advanced initialization parameters. As Oracle becomes more and more self-managing, the number of parameters that a DBA must be familiar with and adjust on a daily basis is reduced.

Basic Initialization Parameters

The list of Oracle 12*c* basic initialization parameters appears in Table 1-3 along with a brief description of each. In the sections that follow, I will give some further explanation and advice regarding how some of these parameters should be set, depending on the hardware and software environment, the types of applications, and the number of users in the database.

Some of these parameters will be revisited throughout this book, where we will present optimal values for SGA, PGA, and other parameters. Here are a few that you will set for every new database.

COMPATIBLE

The COMPATIBLE parameter allows a newer version of Oracle to be installed while restricting the feature set of the new version as if an older version of Oracle was installed. This is a good way to move forward with a database upgrade while remaining compatible with an application that may fail when it runs with the new version of the software. The COMPATIBLE parameter can then be bumped up as the applications are reworked or rewritten to work with the new version of the database.

The downside of using this parameter is that none of the new applications for the database can take advantage of new features until the COMPATIBLE parameter is set to the same value as the current release.

DB_NAME

DB_NAME specifies the local portion of the database name. It can be up to eight characters and must begin with an alphanumeric character. Once set, it can only be changed with the Oracle DBNEWID utility (**nid**); the DB_NAME is recorded in each datafile, redo log file, and control file in the database. At database startup, the value of this parameter must match the value of DB_NAME recorded in the control file.

Initialization Parameter	Description
CLUSTER_DATABASE	Enables this node to be a member of a cluster.
COMPATIBLE	Allows a new database version to be installed while ensuring compatibility with the release specified by this parameter.
CONTROL_FILES	Specifies the location of the control files for this instance.
DB_BLOCK_SIZE	Specifies the size of Oracle blocks. This block size is used for the SYSTEM, SYSAUX, and temporary tablespaces at database creation.
DB_CREATE_FILE_DEST	The default location for OMF datafiles. Also specifies the location of control files and redo log files if DB_CREATE_ONLINE_LOG_DEST_*n* is not set.
DB_CREATE_ONLINE_LOG_DEST_*n*	The default location for OMF control files and online redo log files.
DB_DOMAIN	The logical domain name where the database resides in a distributed database system (for example, us.oracle.com).
DB_NAME	A database identifier of up to eight characters. Prepended to the DB_DOMAIN value for a fully qualified name (for example, marketing.us.oracle.com).
DB_RECOVERY_FILE_DEST	The default location for the recovery area. Must be set along with DB_RECOVERY_FILE_DEST_SIZE.
DB_RECOVERY_FILE_DEST_SIZE	The maximum size, in bytes, for the files used for recovery in the recovery area location.
DB_UNIQUE_NAME	A globally unique name for the database. This distinguishes databases that have the same DB_NAME within the same DB_DOMAIN.
INSTANCE_NUMBER	In a RAC installation, the instance number of this node in the cluster.
JOB_QUEUE_PROCESSES	The maximum number of processes allowed for executing jobs, ranging from 0 to 1000.
LDAP_DIRECTORY_SYSAUTH	Enables or disables directory-based authorization for users with the SYSDBA and SYSOPER roles.
LOG_ARCHIVE_DEST_*n*	For ARCHIVELOG mode, up to 31 locations for sending archived log files.
LOG_ARCHIVE_DEST_STATE_*n*	Sets the availability of the corresponding LOG_ARCHIVE_DEST_*n* sites.
NLS_LANGUAGE	Specifies the default language of the database, including messages, day and month names, and sorting rules (for example, "AMERICAN").

TABLE 1-3. *Basic Initialization Parameters*

Initialization Parameter	Description
NLS_LENGTH_SEMANTICS	Specifies the default length semantics for VARCHAR2 or CHAR table columns. Its value is either 'BYTE' or 'CHAR'.
NLS_TERRITORY	The territory name used for day and week numbering (for example, 'SWEDEN', 'TURKEY', or 'AMERICA').
OPEN_CURSORS	The maximum number of open cursors per session.
PGA_AGGREGATE_TARGET	The total memory to allocate for all server processes in this instance.
PROCESSES	The maximum number of operating system processes that can connect to Oracle simultaneously. SESSIONS and TRANSACTIONS are derived from this value.
REMOTE_LISTENER	A network name resolving to an Oracle Net remote listener.
REMOTE_LOGIN_PASSWORDFILE	Specifies how Oracle uses password files. Required for RAC.
ROLLBACK_SEGMENTS	Names of private rollback segments to bring online, if undo management is not used for transaction rollback. There is rarely a need to change this parameter since Automatic Undo Management was introduced in Oracle Database 10*g*.
SESSIONS	The maximum number of sessions, and therefore simultaneous users, in the instance. Defaults to 1.1 * PROCESSES + 5. Oracle best practices dictates you let this parameter default except in rare circumstances.
SGA_TARGET	Specifies the total size of all SGA components; this parameter automatically determines DB_CACHE_SIZE, SHARED_POOL_SIZE, LARGE_POOL_SIZE, STREAMS_POOL_SIZE, and JAVA_POOL_SIZE.
SHARED_SERVERS	The number of shared server processes to allocate when an instance is started.
STAR_TRANSFORMATION_ENABLED	Controls query optimization when star queries are executed.
UNDO_MANAGEMENT	Specifies whether undo management is automatic (AUTO) or manual (MANUAL). If MANUAL is specified, rollback segments are used for undo management.
UNDO_TABLESPACE	The tablespace to use when UNDO_MANAGEMENT is set to AUTO.

TABLE 1-3. *Basic Initialization Parameters* (Continued)

DB_DOMAIN

DB_DOMAIN specifies the name of the network domain where the database will reside. The combination of DB_NAME and DB_DOMAIN must be unique within a distributed database system.

DB_RECOVERY_FILE_DEST and DB_RECOVERY_FILE_DEST_SIZE

When database recovery operations occur, either due to an instance failure or a media failure, it is convenient to have a *flash recovery area* to store and manage files related to a recovery or backup operation. Starting with Oracle 10*g*, the parameter DB_RECOVERY_FILE_DEST can be a directory location on the local server, a network directory location, or an ASM disk area. The parameter DB_RECOVERY_FILE_DEST_SIZE places a limit on how much space is allowed for the recovery or backup files.

These parameters are optional, but if they are specified, RMAN can automatically manage the files needed for backup and recovery operations. The size of this recovery area should be large enough to hold two copies of all datafiles, incremental RMAN backups, online redo logs, archived log files not yet backed up to tape, the SPFILE, and the control file.

CONTROL_FILES

The CONTROL_FILES parameter is not required when you create a database. If it is not specified, Oracle creates one control file in a default location, or if OMF is configured, in the location specified by either DB_CREATE_FILE_DEST or DB_CREATE_ONLINE_LOG_DEST_*n* and a secondary location specified by DB_RECOVERY_FILE DEST. Once the database is created, the CONTROL_FILES parameter reflects the names of the control file locations if you are using an SPFILE; if you are using a text initialization parameter file, you must add the location to this file manually.

However, it is strongly recommended that multiple copies of the control file be created on separate physical volumes. Control files are so critical to the database integrity and are so small that at least three multiplexed copies of the control file should be created on separate physical disks. In addition, the command ALTER DATABASE BACKUP CONTROLFILE TO TRACE should be executed to create a text-format copy of the control file in the event of a major disaster.

The following example specifies three locations for copies of the control file:

```
control_files = (/u01/oracle10g/test/control01.ctl,
                 /u03/oracle10g/test/control02.ctl,
                 /u07/oracle10g/test/control03.ctl)
```

DB_BLOCK_SIZE

The parameter DB_BLOCK_SIZE specifies the size of the default Oracle block in the database. At database creation, the SYSTEM, TEMP, and SYSAUX tablespaces are created with this block size. Ideally, this parameter is the same as or a multiple of the operating system block size for I/O efficiency.

Before Oracle9*i*, you might specify a smaller block size (4KB or 8KB) for OLTP systems and a larger block size (up to 32KB) for DSS (decision support system) databases. However, now that tablespaces with up to five block sizes can coexist in the same database, a smaller value for DB_BLOCK_SIZE is fine. However, 8KB is probably preferable as a minimum for any database, unless it has been rigorously proven in the target environment that a 4KB block size will not cause performance issues. Unless there are specific reasons (such as many tables with rows wider than 8KB), Oracle recommends that an 8KB block size is ideal for every database in Oracle Database 12*c*.

SGA_TARGET

Another way that Oracle 12*c* can facilitate a "set it and forget it" database is by the ability to specify a total amount of memory for all SGA components. If SGA_TARGET is specified, the parameters DB_CACHE_SIZE, SHARED_POOL_SIZE, LARGE_POOL_SIZE, STREAMS_POOL_SIZE, and JAVA_POOL_SIZE are automatically sized by Automatic Shared Memory Management (ASMM). If any of these four parameters are manually sized when SGA_TARGET is also set, ASMM uses the manually sized parameters as minimums.

Once the instance starts, the automatically sized parameters can be dynamically increased or decreased, as long as the parameter SGA_MAX_SIZE is not exceeded. The parameter SGA_MAX_SIZE specifies a hard upper limit for the entire SGA, and it cannot be exceeded or changed until the instance is restarted.

Regardless of how the SGA is sized, be sure that enough free physical memory is available in the server to hold the components of the SGA and all background processes; otherwise, excessive paging will occur and performance will suffer.

MEMORY_TARGET

Even though MEMORY_TARGET is not a "basic" parameter according to the Oracle documentation, it can greatly simplify instance memory management. This parameter specifies the Oracle system-wide usable memory; Oracle in turn reallocates memory between, for example, the SGA and PGA to optimize performances. This parameter is not available on some hardware and OS combinations. For example, MEMORY_TARGET is not available if your OS is Linux and huge pages are defined.

DB_CACHE_SIZE and DB_*n*K_CACHE_SIZE

The parameter DB_CACHE_SIZE specifies the size of the area in the SGA to hold blocks of the default size, including those from the SYSTEM, TEMP, and SYSAUX tablespaces. Up to four other caches can be defined if there are tablespaces with block sizes other than the SYSTEM and SYSAUX tablespaces. The value of *n* can be 2, 4, 8, 16, or 32; if the value of *n* is the same as the default block size, the corresponding DB_*n*K_CACHE_SIZE parameter is illegal. Although this parameter is not one of the basic initialization parameters, it becomes very basic when you transport a tablespace from another database with a block size other than DB_BLOCK_SIZE!

There are few advantages to a database containing multiple block sizes, however. Even though the tablespace handling OLTP applications can have a smaller block size and the tablespace with the data warehouse table can have a larger block size, an 8KB block is almost always the optimal block size unless you have very large row sizes and you therefore use a larger block size to prevent single rows from crossing a block boundary. However, be careful when allocating memory for multiple cache sizes so as not to allocate too much memory for one at the expense of another. If you must use multiple block sizes, then use Oracle's Buffer Cache Advisory feature to monitor the cache usage for each cache size in the view V$DB_CACHE_ADVICE to assist you in sizing these memory areas. More information on how to use the Buffer Cache Advisory feature can be found in Chapter 8.

SHARED_POOL_SIZE, LARGE_POOL_SIZE, STREAMS_POOL_SIZE, and JAVA_POOL_SIZE

The parameters SHARED_POOL_SIZE, LARGE_POOL_SIZE, STREAMS_POOL_SIZE, and JAVA_POOL_SIZE, which size the shared pool, large pool, streams pool, and Java pool, respectively, are automatically sized by Oracle if the SGA_TARGET initialization parameter is specified. More information on manually tuning these areas can be found in Chapter 8.

PROCESSES

The value for the PROCESSES initialization parameter represents the total number of processes that can simultaneously connect to the database. This includes both the background processes and the user processes; a good starting point for the PROCESSES parameter would be 50 for the background processes plus the number of expected maximum concurrent users; for a smaller database, 150 is a good starting point, because there is little or no overhead associated with making PROCESSES too big. A small departmental database would likely have a value of 256.

UNDO_MANAGEMENT and UNDO_TABLESPACE

Automatic Undo Management (AUM), introduced in Oracle9*i*, eliminates or at least greatly reduces the headaches in trying to allocate the right number and size of rollback segments to handle the undo information for transactions. Instead, a single undo tablespace is specified for all undo operations (except for a SYSTEM rollback segment), and all undo management is handled automatically when the UNDO_MANAGEMENT parameter is set to AUTO.

The remaining task for the DBA is sizing the undo tablespace. Data dictionary views such as V$UNDOSTAT and the Undo Advisor can help you adjust the size of the undo tablespace. Multiple undo tablespaces may be created; for example, a smaller undo tablespace is online during the day to handle relatively small transaction volumes, and a larger undo tablespace is brought online overnight to handle batch jobs and long-running queries that load the data warehouse and need transactional consistency. Only one undo tablespace may be active at any given time. In a RAC environment, each instance of the database has its own undo tablespace.

As of Oracle 11*g*, AUM is enabled by default. In addition, new PL/SQL procedures are available to supplement the information you get from the Undo Advisor and V$UNDOSTAT.

Advanced Initialization Parameters

The advanced initialization parameters include the balance of the initialization parameters not listed here, for a total of 368 of them in Release 1 of Oracle Database 12*c*. Most of these can be automatically set and tuned by the Oracle instance when the basic initialization parameters are set. We will review many of these throughout this book.

Summary

The Oracle database is the most advanced database technology available but its complexity can be understood when it's broken down into its core components. The database itself is the set of files where the tables and index reside; the instance, in contrast, consists of the memory structures on one or more servers that access the database files.

In this chapter I also reviewed the key database objects which for the most part are the variations on an Oracle table. Each type of table has a purpose that makes it suitable for OLTP, batch processing, or business intelligence.

Once your database objects exist, they must be backed up. They must also be secured from unauthorized access. Oracle Database does this with a combination of system and object privileges. Various types of auditing and security features ensure that only the right people can access the most sensitive information in your databases.

Finally, I gave a brief overview of some initialization parameters that you will likely configure in your environment and likely change later as your database grows. These parameters both the locations of key database files but also control how much memory is allocated for each Oracle feature. The variety of memory-related parameters give you the option to set only a couple of parameters and let Oracle manage the rest. If you need to fine-tune Oracle memory usage you can do that as well if your database environment is used for more than one type of application or the use of the database changes on an hourly basis.

CHAPTER 2

Upgrading to Oracle Database 12*c*

If you have previously installed an earlier version of the Oracle database server, you can upgrade your database to Oracle Database 12*c*. Multiple upgrade paths are supported; the right choice for you will depend on factors such as your current Oracle software version and your database size. In this chapter, you will see descriptions of these methods along with guidelines for their use.

If you have not used a version of Oracle prior to Oracle Database 12*c*, you can skip this chapter for now. However, you will likely need to refer to it when you upgrade from Oracle Database 12*c* to a later version or when you migrate data from a different database into your database.

Prior to beginning the upgrade, you should read the Oracle Database 12*c* Installation Guide for your operating system. A successful installation is dependent on a properly configured environment, including operating system patch levels and system parameter settings. Plan to get the installation and upgrade right the first time rather than attempting to restart a partially successful installation. Configure the system to support both the installation of the Oracle software and the creation of a usable starter database.

This chapter assumes that your installation of the Oracle Database 12*c* software completed successfully and that you have an Oracle database that uses an earlier version of the Oracle software on the same server. Note that whether you are installing from scratch or upgrading a previous version of Oracle Database, there are distinct advantages to installing the Oracle Database 12*c* software and creating the database in separate steps. When installing from scratch, you have greater control over initialization parameters, database file locations, memory allocation, and so forth when you create the database in a separate step; when upgrading from a previous release, installing the software first provides you with the Oracle Pre-Upgrade Information Tool that you use against the existing database to alert you to any potential compatibility problems when you upgrade to Oracle Database 12*c*. To upgrade that database, you have four options:

- *Use the Database Upgrade Assistant (DBUA) to guide and perform the upgrade in place.* The old database will become an Oracle 12*c* database during this process. DBUA supports both Oracle Real Application Clusters (RAC) and Automatic Storage Management (ASM); you can launch DBUA as part of the installation process or as a standalone tool after installation. Oracle strongly recommends using DBUA for Oracle Database major releases or patch release upgrades.
- *Perform a manual upgrade of the database.* The old database will become an Oracle 12*c* database during this process. While you have very precise control over every step of the process, this method is more susceptible to error if you miss a step or forget a prerequisite step.
- *Use Oracle Data Pump to move data from an earlier version of Oracle to the Oracle 12c database.* Two separate databases will be used: the old database as the source for the export and the new database as the target for the import. If you are upgrading from Oracle Database 11*g*, you will use Oracle Data Pump to move your data from the old database to the new database. Although Oracle Data Pump is the recommended migration method if available, the original import/export (**imp** and **exp**) are available to export from Oracle Database 10*g* and earlier and to import from an older release into Oracle Database 12*c*.
- *Copy data from an earlier version of Oracle to an Oracle 12c database.* Two separate databases will be used: the old database as the source for the copy and the new database

as the target for the copy. This method is the most straightforward because your migration consists primarily of CREATE TABLE AS SELECT SQL statements referencing the old and new databases. However, unless your database has very few tables and you aren't concerned with using existing SQL tuning sets, statistics, and so forth, Oracle does not recommend this method for production databases. One exception is if you're migrating to Oracle Exadata, in which case this method enables you to leverage Exadata features such as Hybrid Columnar Compression (HCC) and partitioning, outweighing any disadvantages of using this method.

Upgrading a database in place via either the Database Upgrade Assistant or the manual upgrade path is called a *direct upgrade*. Because a direct upgrade does not involve creating a second database for the one being upgraded, it may complete faster and require less disk space than an indirect upgrade.

NOTE
Direct upgrade of the database to version 12c is only supported if your present database is using one of these releases of Oracle: 10.2.0.5, 11.1.0.7, or 11.2.0.2 or later. If you are using any other release, you will first have to upgrade the database to one of those releases or you will need to use a different upgrade option.

Choosing an Upgrade Method

As described in the introduction, both direct upgrade and indirect upgrade paths are available. In this section, you will see a more detailed description of the options, followed by usage descriptions.

In general, the direct upgrade paths will perform the upgrade the fastest because they upgrade the database in place. The other methods involve copying data, either across a database link or via a Data Pump Export. For very large databases, the time required to completely re-create the database via the indirect methods may exclude them as viable options. One drawback to upgrading in place, however, is that none of the datafiles, tablespaces, or segments get reorganized and old objects that are now obsolete in Oracle Database 12*c* are still in the database.

The first direct method relies on the *Database Upgrade Assistant (DBUA)*. DBUA is an interactive tool that guides you through the upgrade process. DBUA evaluates your present database configuration and recommends modifications that can be implemented during the upgrade process. After you accept the recommendations, DBUA performs the upgrade in the background while a progress panel is displayed. DBUA is very similar in approach to the Database Configuration Assistant (DBCA). As discussed in Chapter 1, DBCA is a graphical interface to the steps and parameters required to make the upgrade a success.

The second direct method is called a *manual upgrade*. Whereas DBUA runs scripts in the background, the manual upgrade path involves database administrators running the scripts themselves. The manual upgrade approach gives you a great deal of control, but it also adds to the level of risk in the upgrade because you must perform the steps in the proper order.

You can use Oracle Data Pump Export/Import (first available with Oracle Database 10*g*) as an indirect method for upgrading a database. In this method, you export the data from the old version of the database and then import it into a database that uses the new version of the Oracle software. This process may require disk space for multiple copies of the data in the source database, in the Export dump file, and in the target database. In exchange for these costs, this method gives you great flexibility in choosing which data will be migrated. You can select specific tablespaces, schemas, tables, and rows to be exported.

In the Data Pump method, the original database is not upgraded; its data is extracted and moved, and the database can then either be deleted or be run in parallel with the new database until testing of the new database has been completed. In the process of performing the export/import, you are selecting and reinserting each row of the database. If the database is very large, the import process may take a long time, impacting your ability to provide the upgraded database to your users in a timely fashion. This is mainly because of your network's bandwidth limitations: if you have a 10-Gbps or faster network connection, then Data Pump can be run across the network in parallel for multiple schemas and even individual tables. See Chapter 12 for details on the Data Pump utilities.

In the data-copying method, you issue a series of CREATE TABLE AS SELECT . . . or INSERT INTO . . . SELECT commands that cross database links (see Chapter 16) to retrieve the source data. The tables are created in the Oracle 12*c* database based on queries of data from a separate source database. This method allows you to bring over data incrementally and to limit the rows and columns migrated. However, you will need to be careful that the copied data maintains all the necessary relationships among tables as well as any indexes or constraints. As with the Data Pump method, this method may require a significant amount of time for large databases.

NOTE

If you are changing the operating platform at the same time, you can use transportable tablespaces to move the data from the old database to the new database. For very large databases, this method may be faster than the other data-copying methods. See Chapter 17 for the details on transportable tablespaces.

Selecting the proper upgrade method requires you to evaluate the technical expertise of your team, the data that is to be migrated, and the allowable downtime for the database during the migration. In general, using DBUA will be the method of choice for very large databases, whereas using an indirect method may be more appropriate for smaller databases.

Before Upgrading

Prior to beginning the migration, you should back up the existing database and database software. If the migration fails for some reason and you are unable to revert the database or software to its earlier version, you will be able to restore your backup and re-create your database.

You should develop and test scripts that will allow you to evaluate the performance and functionality of the database following the upgrade. This evaluation may include the performance of specific database operations or the overall performance of the database under a significant user load.

Prior to executing the upgrade process on a production database, you should attempt the upgrade on a test database so that you can identify any missing components (such as operating system patches) and measure the time required for the upgrade.

Oracle Database 12*c* includes the Pre-Upgrade Information Tool called **preupgrd.sql**. This tool is included in the installation files in the directory **$ORACLE_HOME/rdbms/admin**. Copy this script to a location accessible by the old database, connect to the old database with SYSDBA privileges, and run this tool from a SQL*Plus session similar to the following:

```
SQL> @preupgrd.sql
```

This script produces a file called **preupgrade.log** containing the output from the script. Two other scripts are created by the pre-upgrade script: **preupgrade_fixups.sql** and **postupgrade_fixups.sql**. As the script names imply, they contain the commands to fix any issues with the existing database before the upgrade starts or to fix other issues that can only be fixed after the upgrade is completed. Any issues that cannot be fixed via the script are marked in the log file as *** USER ACTION REQUIRED ***.

The Pre-Upgrade Information Tool identifies invalid objects in the database. The list of invalid SYS or SYSTEM objects is stored in REGISTRY$SYS_INV_OBJS, and the list of non-SYS and non-SYSTEM objects is stored in REGISTRY$NONSYS_INV_OBJS. Typical invalid objects include corrupted indexes and triggers or other PL/SQL functions and procedures that will not compile due to missing objects or syntax problems.

Using the Database Upgrade Assistant

You can start the DBUA via the **dbua** command (in Unix environments) or by selecting Database Upgrade Assistant from the Oracle Configuration and Migration Tools menu option (in Windows environments). If you are using a Unix environment, you will need to enable an X Window display prior to starting DBUA.

When started, DBUA will display a Welcome screen. At the next screen, select the database you want to upgrade from the list of available databases. You can upgrade only one database at a time.

After you make your selection, the upgrade process begins. DBUA will perform pre-upgrade checks (such as for obsolete initialization parameters or files that are too small) using the **preupgrd.sql** script described earlier in this chapter. DBUA also includes the option to recompile invalid PL/SQL objects following the upgrade. To speed up the recompilation process, you can specify a degree of parallelism to run the recompiles in parallel. If you do not recompile these objects after the upgrade, the first user of these objects will be forced to wait while Oracle performs a run-time recompilation.

DBUA will then prompt you to back up the database as part of the upgrade process. If you have already backed up the database prior to starting DBUA, you may elect to skip this step. If you choose to have DBUA back up the database, it will use RMAN to create a backup in the location you specify. DBUA will also create a batch file in that directory to automate the restoration of those files to their earlier locations.

The next step is to choose whether to enable Oracle Enterprise Manager (OEM) to manage the database. If you enable the Oracle Management Agent, the upgraded database will automatically be available via OEM. If you are already using a centralized database and resource manager tool such as Oracle Enterprise Manager Cloud Control 12*c*, you can register the new database with Cloud Control at this time.

You will then be asked to finalize the security configuration for the upgraded database. As with the database-creation process, you can specify passwords for each privileged account or you can set a single password to apply to all the OEM user accounts.

Finally, you will be prompted for details on the flash recovery area location (see Chapter 14), the archive log setting, and the network configuration. A final summary screen displays your choices for the upgrade, and the upgrade starts when you accept them. After the upgrade has completed, DBUA will display the Checking Upgrade Results screen, showing the steps performed, the related log files, and the status. The section of the screen titled Password Management allows you to manage the passwords and the locked/unlocked status of accounts in the upgraded database.

If you are not satisfied with the upgrade results, you can choose the Restore option. If you used DBUA to perform the backup, the restoration will be performed automatically; otherwise, you will need to perform the restoration manually.

When you exit DBUA after successfully upgrading the database, DBUA removes the old database's entry in the network listener configuration file, inserts an entry for the upgraded database, and reloads the file.

Performing a Manual Direct Upgrade

In a manual upgrade, you must perform the steps that DBUA performs. The result will be a direct upgrade of the database in which you are responsible for (and control) each step in the upgrade process.

You should use the Pre-Upgrade Information Tool to analyze the database prior to its upgrade. As mentioned earlier in this chapter, this tool is provided in a SQL script that is installed with the Oracle Database 12*c* software; you will need to run it against the database to be upgraded. You should run that file *in the database to be upgraded* as a SYSDBA-privileged user. The results will show potential problems that should be addressed prior to the upgrade.

If there are no issues to resolve prior to the upgrade, you should shut down the database and perform an offline backup before continuing with the upgrade process. This ensures that if you have any serious problems with the database upgrade, you can always get back to the state of your old database as of when you started the upgrade process. The automated version of the database upgrade process includes an option to back up the current database using RMAN.

Once you have a backup that you can restore if needed, you are ready to proceed with the upgrade process. The process is detailed and script-based, so you should consult with the Oracle installation and upgrade documentation for your environment and version. The steps are as follows:

1. Copy configuration files (init.ora, spfile.ora, password file) from their old location to the new Oracle software home directory. By default, the configuration files are found in the **/dbs** subdirectory on Unix platforms and the **\database** directory on Windows platforms.
2. Remove obsolete and deprecated initialization parameter from the configuration files identified in the Pre-Upgrade Information Tool. Update any initialization parameters to at least the minimum values specified in the Pre-Upgrade Information Tool report. Use full pathnames in the parameter files.
3. If you are upgrading a cluster database, set the CLUSTER_DATABASE initialization parameter to FALSE. After the upgrade, you must set this initialization parameter back to TRUE.
4. Shut down the instance.
5. If you are using Windows, stop the service associated with the instance and delete the Oracle service at the command prompt using this command:

```
NET STOP OracleService<service_name>
ORADIM -DELETE -SID <instance_name>
```

Next, create the new Oracle Database 12*c* service using the ORADIM command, as shown here. The variables for this command are shown in the following table.

```
C:\> ORADIM -NEW -SID <SID> -INTPWD <PASSWORD> -MAXUSERS <USERS>
     -STARTMODE AUTO -PFILE <ORACLE_HOME>\<DATABASE>\INIT<SID>.ORA
```

Variable	**Description**
SID	The name of the SID (instance identifier) of the database you are upgrading.
PASSWORD	The password for the new release 12.1 database instance. This is the password for the user connected with SYSDBA privileges. If you do not specify INTPWD, operating system authentication is used and no password is required.
USERS	The maximum number of users who can be granted SYSDBA and SYSOPER privileges.
ORACLE_HOME	The release 12.1 Oracle home directory. Ensure that you specify the full pathname with the -PFILE option, including the drive letter of the Oracle home directory.
DATABASE	The database name.

6. If your operating system is Unix or Linux, make sure the environment variables ORACLE_HOME and PATH point to the new release 12.1 directories, ORACLE_SID is set to the existing database's SID, and the file **/etc/oratab** points to the new Oracle Database 12*c* home directory. In addition, any server or client-side scripts that set ORACLE_HOME must be changed to point to the new Oracle software home directory.
7. Log into the system as the owner of the Oracle Database 12*c* software.
8. Change your directory to the **$ORACLE_HOME/rdbms/admin** subdirectory under the Oracle software home directory.
9. Connect to SQL*Plus as a user with SYSDBA privileges.
10. Issue the STARTUP UPGRADE command.
11. Use the SPOOL command to log the results of the following steps.
12. Run the Perl script **catctl.pl** in the 12*c* environment, specifying the SQL script **catupgrd.sql** as one of the arguments. The **catctl.pl** script also allows for a parallel upgrade process, to reduce upgrade time. This script automatically determines which upgrade scripts must be run, runs them, and then shuts down the database.

    ```
    SQL> $ORACLE_HOME/perl/bin/perl catctl.pl catupgrd.sql
    ```

13. The database is shut down after running the Perl script. Next, restart the database as follows. The upgrade is complete.

    ```
    SQL> startup
    ```

    Run the post-upgrade tool, **utlu121s.sql**, to see if there are any upgrade issues. After fixing the issues, run this script again to make sure they are fixed.
14. Gather fixed object statistics to minimize object recompilation time:

    ```
    SQL> exec dbms_stats.gather_fixed_objects_stats;
    ```

15. Run **utlrp.sql** to compile any PL/SQL or Java procedures that still need recompilation:

```
SQL> @utlrp.sql
```

16. Verify that all objects and classes are valid:

```
SQL> @utluiobj.sql
```

NOTE
After the upgrade, you should never start your Oracle 12c database with the software from an earlier release.

Using Data Pump Export and Import

Export and Import provide you with an indirect method for the upgrade. You can create an Oracle 11*g* database alongside your existing database and use Data Pump Export and Import to move data from the old database to the new database. When the movement of the data is complete, you will need to point your applications to connect to the new database instead of the old database. You will also need to update any configuration files, version-specific scripts, and the networking configuration files (**tnsnames.ora** and **listener.ora**) to point to the new database.

The advantage to using the Export/Import method is that the existing database is unaffected throughout the upgrade process; however, to ensure that relational integrity remains intact and no new transactions are left behind in the old database, you can run the old database in restricted mode for the duration of the export and upgrade.

Export and Import Versions to Use

When you create an Export dump file via the Export utility, that file can be imported into all later releases of Oracle. When you create a Data Pump Export dump file, you can only import it into the same or later versions of Data Pump Export. Export dump files are not backward compatible, so if you ever need to revert to an earlier version of Oracle, you will need to carefully select the version of Export and Import used.

Note that when you are exporting in order to downgrade your database release, you should use the older version of the Export utility to minimize compatibility problems. You may still encounter compatibility problems if the newer version of the database uses new features (such as new datatypes) that the old version will not support.

Performing the Upgrade

Export the data from the source database using Data Pump Export (recommended) or Export/Import (Oracle Database 10*g*). Since a direct upgrade to Oracle Database 12*c* must be from a database running Oracle Database 10*g* or later, Data Pump Export will be available in that release and all interim releases. Perform a consistent export or perform the export when the database is not available for updates during and after the export.

Install the Oracle Database 12*c* software and create the target database. In the target database, pre-create the users and tablespaces needed to store the source data. If the source and target databases will coexist on the server, you need to be careful not to overwrite datafiles from one database with datafiles from the other. The Data Pump Import utility will attempt to execute the CREATE TABLESPACE commands found in the Data Pump Export dump file, and those commands will include the datafile names from the source database. By default, those commands will fail if the files already exist (although this can be overridden via Import's REUSE_DATAFILES=Y parameter). Pre-create the tablespaces with the proper datafile names to avoid this problem.

NOTE
You can export specific tablespaces, users, tables, and rows.

Once the database has been prepared, use Data Pump Import to load the data from the Export dump file into the target database. Review the log file for information about objects that did not import successfully. See Chapter 11 for detailed instructions on how to use Data Pump Export and Import.

Using the Data-Copying Method

The data-copying method requires that the source database and target database coexist. This method is most appropriate when the tables to be migrated are fairly small and few in number. As with the Data Pump Export/Import method, you must guard against transactions occurring in the source database during and after the extraction of the data. In this method, the data is extracted via queries across database links.

Create the target database using the Oracle Database 12*c* software-only installation and then pre-create the tablespaces, users, and tables to be populated with data from the source database. Create database links (see Chapter 16) in the target database that access accounts in the source database. Use commands such as INSERT INTO . . . SELECT to move data from the source database to the target.

The data-copying method allows you to bring over just the rows and columns you need; your queries limit the data migrated. You will need to be careful with the relationships between the tables in the source database so that you can re-create them properly in the target database. If you have a long application outage available for performing the upgrade and you need to modify the data structures during the migration, the data-copying method may be appropriate for your needs. Note that this method requires that the data be stored in multiple places at once, thus impacting your storage needs.

To improve the performance of this method, you may consider the following options:

- Disable all indexes and constraints until all the data has been loaded.
- Run multiple data-copying jobs in parallel.
- Use parallel query and DML to enhance the performance of individual queries and inserts.
- Use the APPEND hint to enhance the performance of inserts (direct-path insert).
- Collect statistics on the tables before re-creating the indexes. Oracle will automatically collect statistics on the indexes as they are being rebuilt.

As of Oracle 10*g*, you can use cross-platform transportable tablespaces. When transporting tablespaces, you export and import only the metadata for the tablespace, while the datafiles are physically moved to the new platform. For very large databases, the time required to move the datafiles may be significantly shorter than the time required to reinsert the rows. See Chapter 17 for details on the use of transportable tablespaces; see Chapter 8 for additional advice on performance tuning.

After Upgrading

Following the upgrade, you should double-check the configuration and parameter files related to the database, particularly if the instance name changed in the migration process. These files include

- The **tnsnames.ora** file
- The **listener.ora** file
- Programs that may have hard-coded instance names in them

NOTE
*You will need to manually reload the modified **listener.ora** file if you are not using DBUA to perform the upgrade.*

You should review your database initialization parameters to make sure deprecated and obsolete parameters have been removed; these should have been identified during the migration process when you ran the Pre-Upgrade Information Tool **preupgrd.sql**. Be sure to recompile any programs you have written that rely on the database software libraries.

Once the upgrade has completed, perform the functional and performance tests identified before the upgrade began. If there are issues with the database functionality, attempt to identify any parameter settings or missing objects that may be impacting the test results. If the problem cannot be resolved, you may need to revert to the prior release. If you performed a full backup before starting the upgrade, you should be able to easily revert to the old release with minimal downtime.

Summary

Upgrading a database from Oracle Database 11*g* to 12*c* is easy and you can accomplish the upgrade with one of several methods depending on your storage available and database size. If your options are few, the Database Upgrade Assistant (DBUA) will use a GUI interface to step you through all of the options that would otherwise require several complex OS commands.

Using Data Pump Export and Import has the advantage of being a logical migration: it gives you the option to change your physical database layout that may have been sub-optimal in the original database.

The data-copying method is the simplest method but is only appropriate if your database is small and there are few database objects. Both the old and new databases must be up and running at the same time; in addition, you must create INSERT statements to copy table data from the old database to the new database. After all table data is copied you create the appropriate indexes, create users, and grant permissions on the new tables.

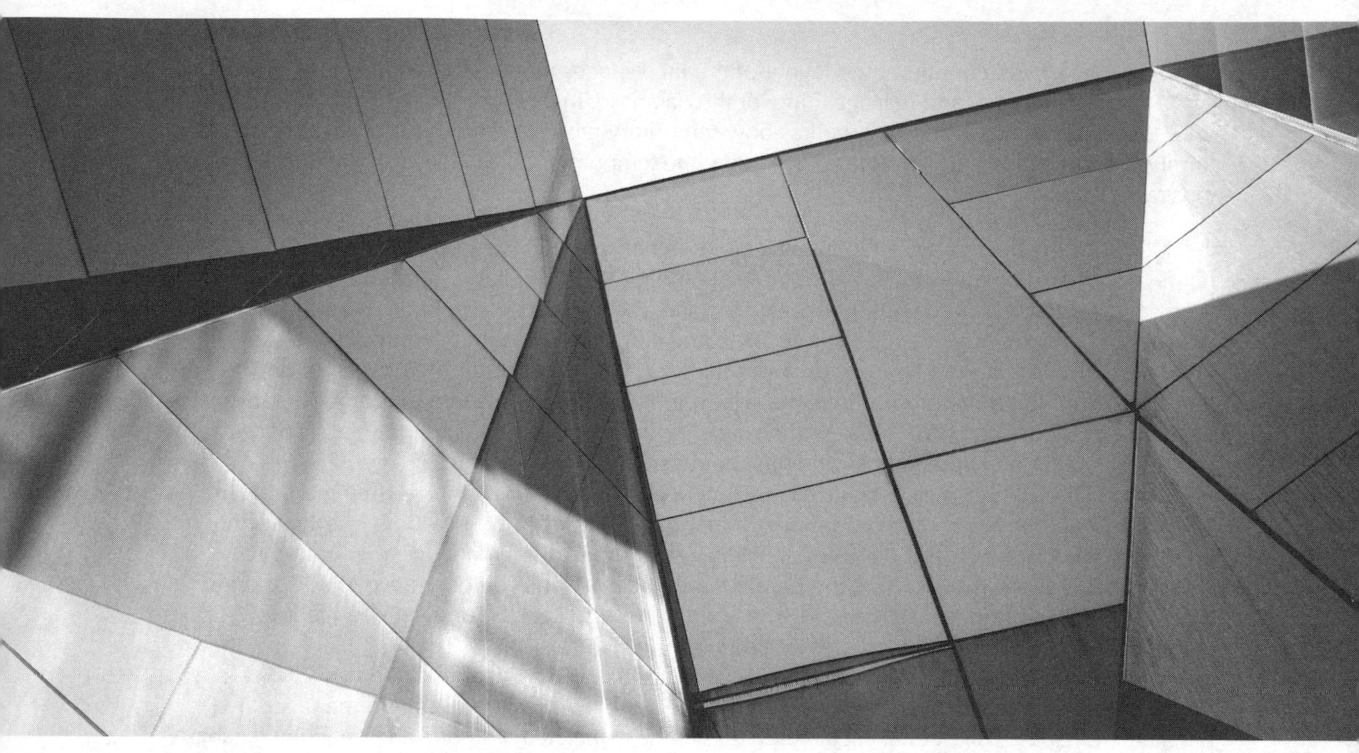

CHAPTER 3

Planning and Managing Tablespaces

How a DBA configures the layout of the tablespaces in a database directly affects the performance and manageability of the database. In this chapter, we'll review the different types of tablespaces as well as how temporary tablespace usage can drive the size and number of tablespaces in a database leveraging the temporary tablespace group feature introduced in Oracle 10*g*.

I'll also show how Oracle's Optimal Flexible Architecture (OFA), supported since Oracle 7, helps to standardize the directory structure for both Oracle executables and the database files themselves; Oracle Database 12*c* further enhances OFA to complement its original role of improving performance to enhancing security and simplifying cloning and upgrade tasks.

A default installation of Oracle provides the DBA with a good starting point, not only creating an OFA-compliant directory structure but also segregating segments into a number of tablespaces based on their function. We'll review the space requirements for each of these tablespaces and provide some tips on how to fine-tune the characteristics of these tablespaces.

Using Oracle Automatic Storage Management (ASM) as your logical volume manager makes tablespace maintenance easier and more efficient by automatically spreading out the segments within a tablespace across all disks of an ASM disk group. Adding datafiles to a tablespace is almost trivial when using ASM; using bigfile tablespaces means you only have to allocate a single datafile for the tablespace. In both cases, you don't need to specify, or even need to know, the name of the datafile itself within the ASM directory structure.

In Oracle Database 12*c*, container databases (CDBs) and pluggable databases (PDBs) in a multitenant database architecture change how some tablespaces are used and managed in a pluggable database. All permanent tablespaces can be associated with one and only one database—either the CDB or one PDB. In contrast, temporary tablespaces or temporary tablespace groups are managed at the CDB level and are used by all PDBs within the CDB. See Chapter 10 for an in-depth discussion of the Oracle Database 12*c* multitenant architecture.

At the end of the chapter, I'll provide some guidelines to help you place segments into different tablespaces based on their type, size, and frequency of access, as well as ways to identify hotspots in one or more tablespaces.

Tablespace Architecture

A prerequisite to competently setting up the tablespaces in your database is understanding the different types of tablespaces and how they are used in an Oracle database. In this section, we'll review the different types of tablespaces and give some examples of how they are managed. In addition, I'll review the types of tablespaces by category—permanent tablespaces (SYSTEM, SYSAUX, and so on), temporary tablespaces, undo tablespaces, and bigfile tablespaces—and describe their function. Finally, I'll also discuss Oracle's Optimal Flexible Architecture (OFA) and how it can ease maintenance tasks.

Tablespace Types

The primary types of tablespaces in an Oracle database are permanent, undo, and temporary. *Permanent* tablespaces contain segments that persist beyond the duration of a session or a transaction.

Although the undo tablespace may have segments that are retained beyond the end of a session or a transaction, it provides read consistency for SELECT statements that access tables being modified as well as provides undo data for a number of the Oracle Flashback features of the database. Primarily, however, undo segments store the previous values of columns being updated or deleted. This ensures that if a user's session fails before the user issues a COMMIT or a ROLLBACK, the UPDATEs, INSERTs, and DELETEs will be removed and will never be accessible by other sessions. Undo segments are never directly accessible by a user session, and undo tablespaces may only have undo segments.

As the name implies, temporary tablespaces contain transient data that exists only for the duration of the session, such as space to complete a sort operation that will not fit in memory.

Bigfile tablespaces can be used for any of these three types of tablespaces, and they simplify tablespace management by moving the maintenance point from the datafile to the tablespace. Bigfile tablespaces consist of one and only one datafile. There are a couple of downsides to bigfile tablespaces, however, and they will be presented later in this chapter.

Permanent

The SYSTEM and SYSAUX tablespaces are two examples of permanent tablespaces. In addition, any segments that need to be retained by a user or an application beyond the boundaries of a session or transaction should be stored in a permanent tablespace.

SYSTEM Tablespace User segments should never reside in the SYSTEM or SYSAUX tablespace, period. If you do not specify a default permanent or temporary tablespace when creating users, the database-level default permanent and temporary tablespaces are used.

If you use the Oracle Universal Installer (OUI) to create a database for you, a separate tablespace other than SYSTEM is created for both permanent and temporary segments. If you create a database manually, be sure to specify both a default permanent tablespace and a default temporary tablespace, as in the sample CREATE DATABASE command that follows.

```
CREATE DATABASE rjbdb
   USER SYS IDENTIFIED BY melsm25
   USER SYSTEM IDENTIFIED BY welisa45
   LOGFILE GROUP 1 ('/u02/oracle11g/oradata/rjbdb/redo01.log') SIZE 100M,
           GROUP 2 ('/u04/oracle11g/oradata/rjbdb/redo02.log') SIZE 100M,
           GROUP 3 ('/u06/oracle11g/oradata/rjbdb/redo03.log') SIZE 100M
   MAXLOGFILES 5
   MAXLOGMEMBERS 5
   MAXLOGHISTORY 1
   MAXDATAFILES 100
   MAXINSTANCES 1
   CHARACTER SET US7ASCII
   NATIONAL CHARACTER SET AL16UTF16
   DATAFILE '/u01/oracle11g/oradata/rjbdb/system01.dbf' SIZE 2G REUSE
   EXTENT MANAGEMENT LOCAL
   SYSAUX DATAFILE '/u01/oracle11g/oradata/rjbdb/sysaux01.dbf'
      SIZE 800M REUSE
   DEFAULT TABLESPACE USERS
      DATAFILE '/u03/oracle11g/oradata/rjbdb/users01.dbf'
      SIZE 4G REUSE
   DEFAULT TEMPORARY TABLESPACE TEMPTS1
      TEMPFILE '/u01/oracle11g/oradata/rjbdb/temp01.dbf'
      SIZE 500M REUSE
   UNDO TABLESPACE undotbs
      DATAFILE '/u02/oracle11g/oradata/rjbdb/undotbs01.dbf'
      SIZE 400M REUSE AUTOEXTEND ON MAXSIZE 2G;
```

As of Oracle 10*g*, the SYSTEM tablespace is locally managed by default; in other words, all space usage is managed by a bitmap segment in the first part of the first datafile for the tablespace. In a database where the SYSTEM tablespace is locally managed, the other tablespaces in the database must also be locally managed or they must be read-only. Using locally managed tablespaces takes some of the contention off the SYSTEM tablespace because space allocation and deallocation operations for a tablespace do not need to use data dictionary tables. More details on locally managed tablespaces can be found in Chapter 6. Other than to support the import of a transportable tablespace that is dictionary managed from a legacy database, there are no advantages to having a dictionary-managed tablespace in your database.

SYSAUX Tablespace Like the SYSTEM tablespace, the SYSAUX tablespace should not have any user segments. The contents of the SYSAUX tablespace, broken down by application, can be reviewed using Oracle Enterprise Manager Database Express (EM Express) or Cloud Control 12*c*. You can edit the SYSAUX tablespace in Cloud Control 12*c* by choosing Administration | Storage | Tablespaces and clicking the SYSAUX link in the tablespace list. Figure 3-1 shows a graphical representation of the space usage within SYSAUX.

If the space usage for a particular application that resides in the SYSAUX tablespace becomes too high or creates an I/O bottleneck through high contention with other applications that use the SYSAUX tablespace, you can move one or more of these applications to a different tablespace. Any SYSAUX occupant listed in Figure 3-1 that has a Change Tablespace link available can be moved by clicking the link and then choosing a destination tablespace in the field shown in Figure 3-2. The XDB objects will be moved to the SYSAUX2 tablespace. An example of moving a SYSAUX occupant to a different tablespace using the command line interface can be found in Chapter 6.

The SYSAUX tablespace can be monitored just like any other tablespace; later in this chapter, I'll show how EM Cloud Control can help us to identify hotspots in a tablespace.

Undo

Multiple undo tablespaces can exist in a database, but only one undo tablespace can be active at any given time for a single database instance. Undo tablespaces are used for rolling back transactions, for providing read consistency for SELECT statements that run concurrently with DML statements on the same table or set of tables, and for supporting a number of Oracle Flashback features, such as Flashback Query.

The undo tablespace needs to be sized correctly to prevent ORA-01555 "Snapshot too old" errors and to provide enough space to support initialization parameters such as UNDO_RETENTION. More information on how to monitor, size, and create undo tablespaces can be found in Chapter 7.

Temporary

More than one temporary tablespace can be online and active in the database, but until Oracle 10*g*, multiple sessions by the same user would use the same temporary tablespace because only one default temporary tablespace could be assigned to a user. To solve this potential performance bottleneck, Oracle supports *temporary tablespace groups*. A temporary tablespace group is a synonym for a list of temporary tablespaces.

A temporary tablespace group must consist of at least one temporary tablespace; it cannot be empty. Once a temporary tablespace group has no members, it no longer exists.

One of the big advantages of using temporary tablespace groups is to provide a single user with multiple sessions with the ability to use a different actual temporary tablespace for each session. In the diagram shown in Figure 3-3, the user OE has two active sessions that need temporary space for performing sort operations.

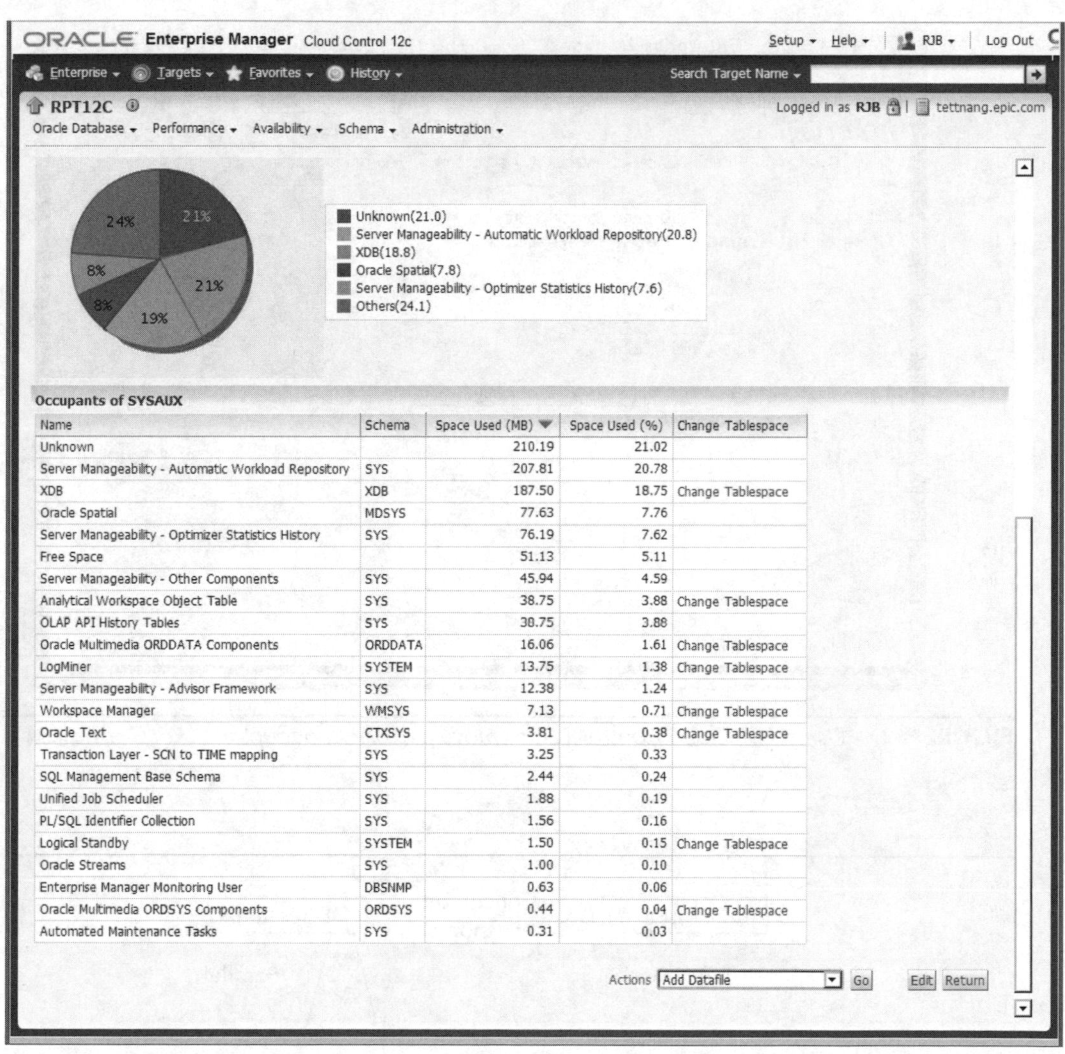

FIGURE 3-1. *EM Cloud Control 12*c *SYSAUX tablespace contents*

Instead of a single temporary tablespace being assigned to a user, the temporary tablespace group is assigned; in this example, the temporary tablespace group TEMPGRP has been assigned to OE. However, because there are three actual temporary tablespaces within the TEMPGRP temporary tablespace group, the first OE session may use temporary tablespace TEMP1, and the SELECT statement executed by the second OE session may use the other two temporary tablespaces, TEMP2 and TEMP3, in parallel. Before Oracle 10*g*, both sessions would use the same temporary tablespace, potentially causing a performance issue.

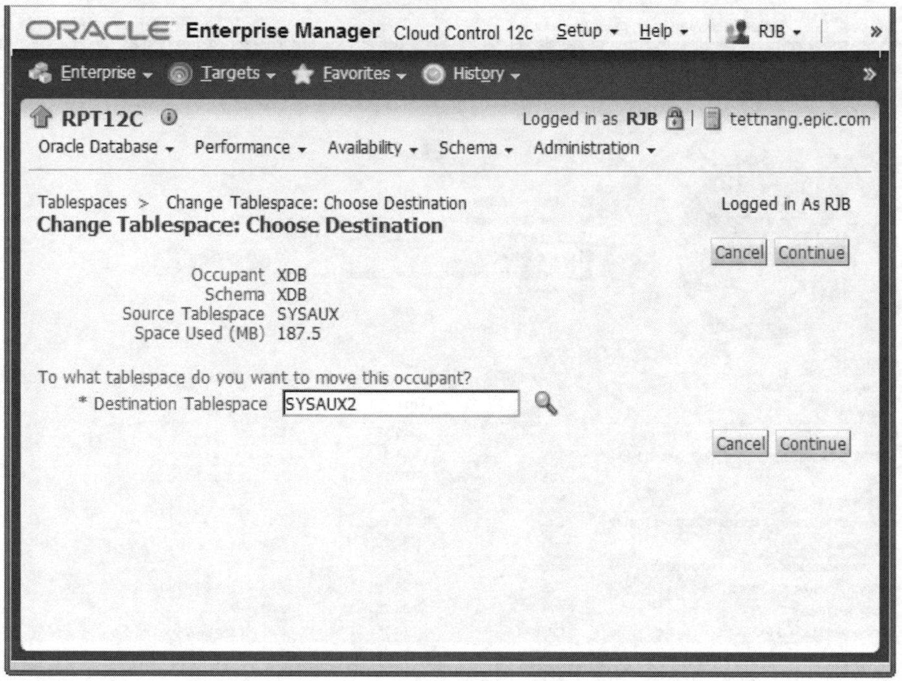

FIGURE 3-2. *Using EM Cloud Control 12c to move a SYSAUX occupant*

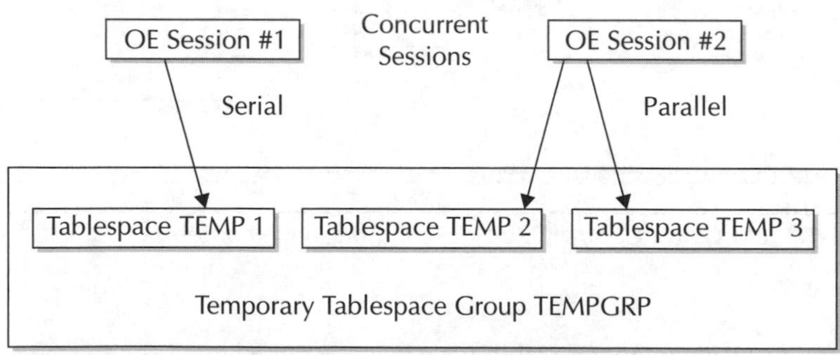

FIGURE 3-3. *Temporary tablespace group TEMPGRP*

Creating a temporary tablespace group is very straightforward. After creating the individual tablespaces TEMP1, TEMP2, and TEMP3, we can create a temporary tablespace group named TEMPGRP as follows:

```
SQL> alter tablespace temp1 tablespace group tempgrp;
Tablespace altered.
SQL> alter tablespace temp2 tablespace group tempgrp;
Tablespace altered.
SQL> alter tablespace temp3 tablespace group tempgrp;
Tablespace altered.
```

Changing the database's default temporary tablespace to TEMPGRP uses the same command as assigning an actual temporary tablespace as the default; temporary tablespace groups are treated logically the same as a temporary tablespace:

```
SQL> alter database default temporary tablespace tempgrp;
Database altered.
```

To drop a tablespace group, we must first drop all its members. Dropping a member of a tablespace group is accomplished by assigning the temporary tablespace to a group with an empty string (in other words, removing the tablespace from the group):

```
SQL> alter tablespace temp3 tablespace group '';
Tablespace altered.
```

As you might expect, assigning a temporary tablespace group to a user is identical to assigning a temporary tablespace to a user; this assignment can happen either when the user is created or at some point in the future. In the following example, the new user JENWEB is assigned the temporary tablespace TEMPGRP:

```
SQL> create user jenweb identified by pi4001
  2       default tablespace users
  3       temporary tablespace tempgrp;
User created.
```

Note that if we did not assign the tablespace during user creation, the user JENWEB would still be assigned TEMPGRP as the temporary tablespace because it is the database default from our previous CREATE DATABASE example.

A couple of changes were made to the data dictionary views in Oracle Database 10*g* and Oracle Database 11*g* to support temporary tablespace groups. The data dictionary view DBA_USERS still has the column TEMPORARY_TABLESPACE, as in previous versions of Oracle, but this column may now contain either the name of the temporary tablespace assigned to the user or the name of a temporary tablespace group:

```
SQL> select username, default_tablespace, temporary_tablespace
  2    from dba_users where username = 'JENWEB';

USERNAME                  DEFAULT_TABLESPACE TEMPORARY_TABLESPACE
-------------------- ------------------ --------------------
JENWEB                    USERS              TEMPGRP

1 row selected.
```

The new data dictionary view DBA_TABLESPACE_GROUPS shows the members of each temporary tablespace group:

```
SQL> select group_name, tablespace_name from dba_tablespace_groups;

GROUP_NAME                     TABLESPACE_NAME
------------------------------ ------------------------------
TEMPGRP                        TEMP1
TEMPGRP                        TEMP2
TEMPGRP                        TEMP3

3 rows selected.
```

As with most every other feature of Oracle that can be accomplished with the command line, assigning members to temporary tablespace groups or removing members from temporary tablespace groups can be performed using EM Cloud Control 12*c*. In Figure 3-4, we can add or remove members from a temporary tablespace group.

Bigfile

A bigfile tablespace eases database administration because it consists of only one datafile. The single datafile can be up to 128TB (terabytes) in size if the tablespace block size is 32KB; if you use the more common 8KB block size, 32TB is the maximum size of a bigfile tablespace. Many of the commands previously available only for maintaining datafiles can now be used at the tablespace level if the tablespace is a bigfile tablespace. Chapter 6 reviews how BIGFILE tablespaces are created and maintained.

The maintenance convenience of bigfile tablespaces can be offset by some potential disadvantages. Because a bigfile tablespace is a single datafile, a full backup of a single large datafile will take significantly longer than a full backup of several smaller datafiles (with the same total size as the single bigfile tablespace) even when Oracle uses multiple slave processes per datafile. If your bigfile tablespaces are read-only or if only changed blocks are backed up on a regular basis, the backup issue may not be critical in your environment. If you use the SECTION SIZE option in RMAN, available as of Oracle Database 11*g*, then an entire bigfile tablespace (and therefore the entire datafile) can be backed up in parallel.

Optimal Flexible Architecture

Oracle's Optimal Flexible Architecture (OFA) provides guidelines to ease the maintenance of the Oracle software and database files as well as improve the performance of the database by placing the database files such that I/O bottlenecks are minimized.

Although using OFA is not strictly enforced when you're installing or maintaining an Oracle environment, using OFA makes it easy for someone to understand how your database is organized on disk, preventing that phone call in the middle of the night during the week you're on vacation!

OFA is slightly different depending on the type of storage options you use: either an ASM environment or a standard operating system file system that may or may not be using a third-party logical volume manager or RAID-enabled disk subsystem. In either case, the Database Configuration Assistant can create an OFA-compliant datafile directory structure for you.

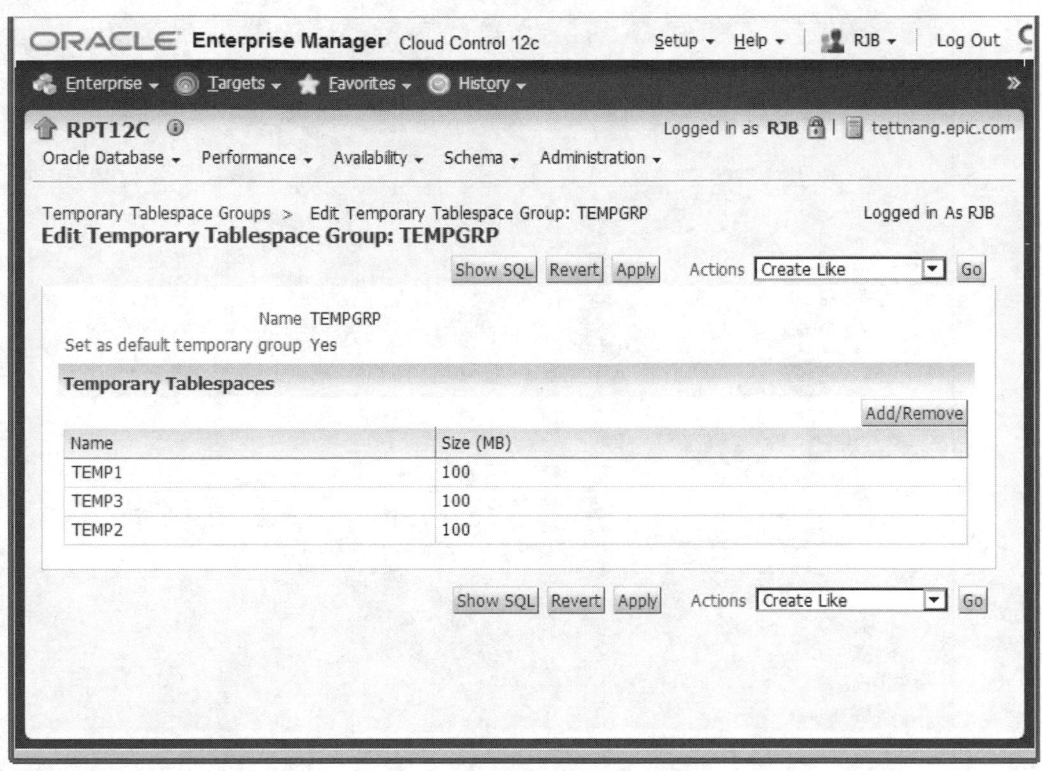

FIGURE 3-4. *Using EM Cloud Control 12c to edit temporary tablespace groups*

Non-ASM Environment

In a non-ASM environment on a Unix server, at least three file systems on separate physical devices are required to implement OFA recommendations. Starting at the top, the recommended format for a mount point is */<string const><numeric key>*, where *<string const>* can be one or several letters and *<numeric key>* is either two or three digits. For example, on one system we may have mount points **/u01**, **/u02**, **/u03**, and **/u04**, with room to expand to an additional 96 mount points without changing the file-naming convention. Figure 3-5 shows a typical Unix file system layout with an OFA-compliant Oracle directory structure.

There are two instances on this server: an ASM instance to manage disk groups and a standard RDBMS instance (**dw**).

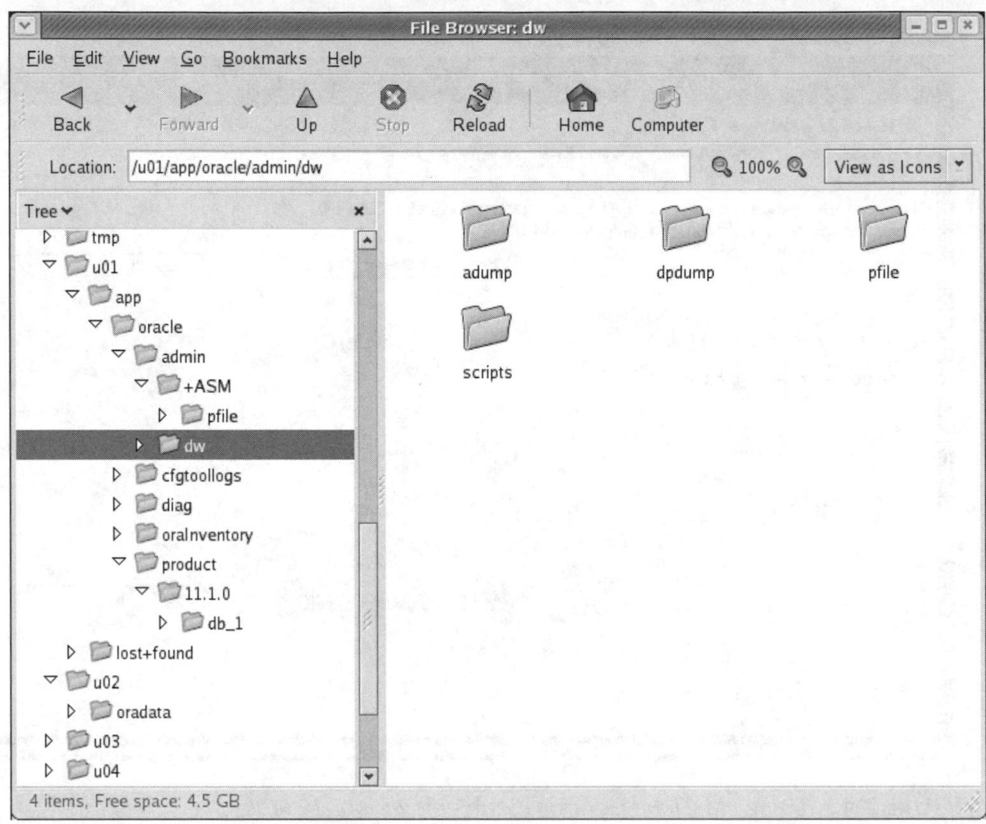

FIGURE 3-5. *OFA-compliant Unix directory structure*

Software Executables The software executables for each distinct product name reside in the directory /*<string const><numeric key>*/*<directory type>*/*<product owner>*, where *<string const>* and *<numeric key>* are defined previously, *<directory type>* implies the type of files installed in this directory, and *<product owner>* is the name of the user that owns and installs the files in this directory. For example, **/u01/app/oracle** would contain application-related files (executables) installed by the user **oracle** on the server. The directory **/u01/app/apache** would contain the executables for the middleware web server installed from a previous version of Oracle.

As of Oracle 10*g*, the OFA standard makes it easy for the DBA to install multiple versions of the database and client software within the same high-level directory. The OFA-compliant Oracle home path, corresponding to the environment variable ORACLE_HOME, contains a suffix that corresponds to the type and incarnation of the installation. For example, one installation of

Oracle 12*c*, one installation of Oracle 11*g*, two different installations of Oracle 10*g*, and one installation of Oracle9*i* may reside in the following three directories:

```
/u01/app/oracle/product/9.2.0.1
/u01/app/oracle/product/10.1.0/db_1
/u01/app/oracle/product/10.1.0/db_2
/u01/app/oracle/product/11.1.0/db_1
/u01/app/oracle/product/12.1.0/dbhome_1
```

At the same time, the Oracle client executables and configuration may be stored in the same parent directory as the database executables:

```
/u01/app/oracle/product/12.1.0/client_1
```

Some installation directories will never have more than one instance for a given product; for example, Oracle Grid Infrastructure (one installation per server) will be installed in the following directory given the previous installations:

```
/u01/app/oracle/product/12.1.0/grid
```

Because Grid Infrastructure can be installed only once on a system, it does not have an incrementing numeric suffix.

Database Files Any non-ASM Oracle datafiles reside in /<*mount point*>/oradata/<*database name*>, where <*mount point*> is one of the mount points we discussed earlier, and <*database name*> is the value of the initialization parameter DB_NAME. For example, **/u02/oradata/rac0** and **/u03/oradata/rac0** would contain the non-ASM control files, redo log files, and datafiles for the instance **rac0**, whereas **/u05/oradata/dev1** would contain the same files for the **dev1** instance on the same server. The naming convention for the different file types under the **oradata** directory are detailed in Table 3-1.

Although Oracle tablespace names can be as long as 30 characters, it is advisable to keep the tablespace names eight characters or less in a Unix environment. Because portable Unix filenames are restricted to 14 characters, and the suffix of an OFA datafile name is <*n*>.dbf, where *n* is two digits, a total of six characters are needed for the suffix in the file system. This leaves eight characters for the tablespace name itself.

File Type	Filename Format	Variables
Control files	control.ctl	None.
Redo log files	redo<*n*>.log	*n* is a two-digit number.
Datafiles	<*tn*>.dbf	*t* is an Oracle tablespace name, and *n* is a two-digit number.

TABLE 3-1. *OFA-Compliant Control File, Redo Log File, and Datafile Naming Conventions*

Only control files, redo log files, and datafiles associated with the database *<database name>* should be stored in the directory /*<mount point>*/oradata/*<database name>*. For the database **ord** managed without ASM, the datafile names are as follows:

```
SQL> select file#, name from v$datafile;

     FILE# NAME
---------- ------------------------------------
         1 /u05/oradata/ord/system01.dbf
         2 /u05/oradata/ord/undotbs01.dbf
         3 /u05/oradata/ord/sysaux01.dbf
         4 /u05/oradata/ord/users01.dbf
         5 /u09/oradata/ord/example01.dbf
         6 /u09/oradata/ord/oe_trans01.dbf
         7 /u05/oradata/ord/users02.dbf
         8 /u06/oradata/ord/logmnr_rep01.dbf
         9 /u09/oradata/ord/big_users.dbf
        10 /u08/oradata/ord/idx01.dbf
        11 /u08/oradata/ord/idx02.dbf
        12 /u08/oradata/ord/idx03.dbf
        13 /u08/oradata/ord/idx04.dbf
        14 /u08/oradata/ord/idx05.dbf
        15 /u08/oradata/ord/idx06.dbf
        16 /u08/oradata/ord/idx07.dbf
        17 /u08/oradata/ord/idx08.dbf
17 rows selected.
```

Other than file numbers 8 and 9, all the datafiles in the **ord** database are OFA compliant and are spread out over four different mount points. The tablespace name in file number 8 is too long, and file number 9 does not have a numeric two-digit counter to represent new datafiles for the same tablespace.

ASM Environment

In an ASM environment, the executables are stored in the directory structure presented previously; however, if you browsed the directory **/u02/oradata** in Figure 3-5, you would see no files. All the control files, redo log files, and datafiles for the instance **dw** are managed by the ASM instance +ASM on this server.

The actual datafile names are not needed for most administrative functions because ASM files are all Oracle Managed Files (OMF). This eases the overall administrative effort required for the database. Within the ASM storage structure, an OFA-like syntax is used to subdivide the file types even further:

```
SQL> select file#, name from v$datafile;

     FILE# NAME
---------- ----------------------------------------
         1 +DATA/dw/datafile/system.256.622426913
         2 +DATA/dw/datafile/sysaux.257.622426915
         3 +DATA/dw/datafile/undotbs1.258.622426919
```

```
         4 +DATA/dw/datafile/users.259.622426921
         5 +DATA/dw/datafile/example.265.622427181
5 rows selected.

SQL> select name from v$controlfile;

NAME
----------------------------------------
+DATA/dw/controlfile/current.260.622427059
+RECOV/dw/controlfile/current.256.622427123
2 rows selected.

SQL> select member from v$logfile;

MEMBER
----------------------------------------
+DATA/dw/onlinelog/group_3.263.622427143
+RECOV/dw/onlinelog/group_3.259.622427145
+DATA/dw/onlinelog/group_2.262.622427135
+RECOV/dw/onlinelog/group_2.258.622427137
+DATA/dw/onlinelog/group_1.261.622427127
+RECOV/dw/onlinelog/group_1.257.622427131
6 rows selected.
```

Within the disk groups +DATA and +RECOV, we see that each of the database file types, such as datafiles, control files, and online log files, has its own directory. Fully qualified ASM filenames have the format

```
+<group>/<dbname>/<file type>/<tag>.<file>.<incarnation>
```

where *<group>* is the disk group name, *<dbname>* is the database to which the file belongs, *<file type>* is the Oracle file type, *<tag>* is information specific to the file type, and the pair *<file>.<incarnation>* ensures uniqueness within the disk group.

Automatic Storage Management is covered in Chapter 6.

Oracle Installation Tablespaces

Table 3-2 lists the tablespaces created with a standard Oracle 12*c* installation using the Oracle Universal Installer (OUI); the EXAMPLE tablespace is optional; it is installed if you specify that you want the sample schemas created during the installation.

Tablespace	Type	Segment Space Management	Approx. Initial Allocated Size (MB)
SYSTEM	Permanent	Manual	790
SYSAUX	Permanent	Auto	1000
TEMP	Temporary	Manual	160
UNDOTBS1	Permanent	Manual	180
USERS	Permanent	Auto	255
EXAMPLE	Permanent	Auto	358

TABLE 3-2. *Standard Oracle Installation Tablespaces*

SYSTEM

As mentioned previously in this chapter, no user segments should ever be stored in the SYSTEM tablespace. The clause DEFAULT TABLESPACE in the CREATE DATABASE command helps to prevent this occurrence by automatically assigning a permanent tablespace for all users that have not explicitly been assigned a permanent tablespace. An Oracle installation performed using the OUI will automatically assign the USERS tablespace as the default permanent tablespace.

The SYSTEM tablespace will grow more quickly the more you use procedural objects such as functions, procedures, triggers, and so forth, because these objects must reside in the data dictionary. This also applies to abstract datatypes and Oracle's other object-oriented features.

SYSAUX

As with the SYSTEM tablespace, user segments should never be stored in the SYSAUX tablespace. If one particular occupant of the SYSAUX tablespace takes up too much of the available space or significantly affects the performance of other applications that use the SYSAUX tablespace, you should consider moving the occupant to another tablespace.

TEMP

Instead of one very large temporary tablespace, consider using several smaller temporary tablespaces and creating a temporary tablespace group to hold them. As you found out earlier in this chapter, this can improve the response time for applications that create many sessions with the same username. For Oracle container databases and pluggable databases (in Oracle's multitenant architecture, new to Oracle Database 12*c*), the container database owns the temporary tablespace used by all plugged-in databases.

UNDOTBS1

Even though a database may have more than one undo tablespace, only one undo tablespace can be active at any given time for a given instance. If more space is needed for an undo tablespace, and AUTOEXTEND is not enabled, another datafile can be added. One undo tablespace must be available for each node in a Real Application Clusters (RAC) environment because each instance manages its own undo.

USERS

The USERS tablespace is intended for miscellaneous segments created by each database user, and it's not appropriate for any production applications. A separate tablespace should be created for each application and segment type; later in this chapter I'll present some additional criteria you can use to decide when to segregate segments into their own tablespace.

EXAMPLE

In a production environment, the EXAMPLE tablespace should be dropped; it takes up hundreds of megabytes of disk space and has examples of all types of Oracle segments and data structures. A separate database should be created for training purposes with these sample schemas; for an existing training database, the sample schemas can be installed into the tablespace of your choice by using the scripts in **$ORACLE_HOME/demo/schema**.

Segment Segregation

As a general rule of thumb, you want to divide segments into different tablespaces based on their type, size, and frequency of access. Furthermore, each of these tablespaces would benefit from being on its own disk group or disk device; in practice, however, most shops will not have the luxury of storing each tablespace on its own device. The following list identifies some of the conditions you might use to determine how segments should be segregated among tablespaces. The list is not prioritized because the priority depends on your particular environment. Using ASM eliminates many of the contention issues listed with no additional effort by the DBA. ASM is discussed in detail in Chapter 4. In most of these scenarios the recommendations primarily enhance manageability over performance to enhance availability.

- Big segments and small segments should be in separate tablespaces, especially for manageability and reclaiming empty space from a large table.
- Table segments and their corresponding index segments should be in separate tablespaces (if you are not using ASM and each tablespace is stored in its own set of disks).
- A separate tablespace should be used for each application.
- Segments with low usage and segments with high usage should be in different tablespaces.
- Static segments should be separated from high DML segments.
- Read-only tables should be in their own tablespace.
- Staging tables for a data warehouse should be in their own tablespace.
- Tablespaces should be created with the appropriate block size, depending on whether segments are accessed row by row or in full table scans.
- Tablespaces should be allocated for different types of activity, such as primarily UPDATEs, primarily read-only, or temporary segment usage.
- Materialized views should be in a separate tablespace from the base table.
- For partitioned tables and indexes, each partition should be in its own tablespace.

Using EM Cloud Control 12*c*, you can identify overall contention on any tablespace by identifying hotspots, either at the file level or at the object level. We'll cover performance tuning, including resolving I/O contention issues, in Chapter 8.

Summary

The basic logical building block of a database is the tablespace. It consists of one or more physical datafiles, only one datafile if you create a bigfile tablespace. Whether you're creating a permanent, undo, or temporary tablespace you can create those tablespaces as bigfile tablespaces for ease of management.

When you create tablespaces or other objects, you can use Optimal Flexible Architecture (OFA) to automatically create an appropriate OS file name and directory location. This is even more useful in an ASM environment where you only need to specify the disk group name; Oracle puts it in the right directory location automatically and you may never need to know where in the ASM file structure Oracle places the object.

In a default Oracle database installation, Oracle creates five required tablespaces: SYSTEM, SYSAUX, TEMP, UNDOTBS1, and USERS; if you choose to install the sample schemas they will exist in the EXAMPLE tablespace. You will most likely create many more tablespaces in your environment to segregate applications to their own tablespace or to restrict how much disk space a tablespace may use for that application.

CHAPTER 4

Physical Database Layouts and Storage Management

Chapter 3 discussed the logical components of the database, tablespaces, and how to not only create the right number and types of tablespaces but also place table and index segments in the appropriate tablespace, based on their usage patterns and function. In this chapter, I'll focus more on the physical aspects of a database, the datafiles, and where to store them to maximize I/O throughput and overall database performance.

The assumption throughout this chapter is that you are using locally managed tablespaces with automatic segment space management. In addition to reducing the load on the SYSTEM tablespace by using bitmaps stored in the tablespace itself instead of freelists stored in the table or index header blocks, automatic segment space management (by specifying AUTOALLOCATE or UNIFORM) makes more efficient use of the space in the tablespace. As of Oracle 10*g*, the SYSTEM tablespace is created as locally managed. As a result, this requires all read-write tablespaces to also be locally managed.

In the first part of this chapter, I'll review some of the common problems and solutions when using traditional disk space management using a file system on a database server. In the second half of the chapter, I'll present an overview of Automatic Storage Management (ASM), a built-in logical volume manager that eases administration, enhances performance, and improves availability.

Traditional Disk Space Storage

In lieu of using a third-party logical volume or Oracle's Automatic Storage Management (discussed later in this chapter), you must be able to manage the physical datafiles in your database to ensure a high level of performance, availability, and recoverability. In general, this means spreading out your datafiles to different physical disks. In addition to ensuring availability by keeping mirrored copies of redo log files and control files on different disks, I/O performance is improved when users access tables that reside in tablespaces on multiple physical disks instead of one physical disk. Identifying an I/O bottleneck or a storage deficiency on a particular disk volume is only half the battle; once the bottleneck is identified, you need to have the tools and knowledge to move datafiles to different disks. If a datafile has too much space or not enough space, resizing an existing datafile is a common task.

In this section, I'll discuss a number of different ways to resize tablespaces, whether they are smallfile or bigfile tablespaces. In addition, I'll cover the most common ways to move datafiles, online redo log files, and control files to different disks.

Resizing Tablespaces and Datafiles

In an ideal database, all tablespaces and the objects within them are created at their optimal sizes. Resizing a tablespace proactively or setting up a tablespace to automatically extend can potentially avoid a performance hit when the tablespace expands or an application failure occurs if the datafile(s) within the tablespace cannot extend. More details on how to monitor space usage can be found in Chapter 6.

The procedures and methods available for resizing a tablespace are slightly different, depending on whether the tablespace is a *smallfile* or a *bigfile* tablespace. A smallfile tablespace, the only type of tablespace available before Oracle 10*g*, can consist of multiple datafiles. A bigfile tablespace, in contrast, consists of only one datafile, but the datafile can be much larger than a datafile in a smallfile tablespace: A bigfile tablespace with 32K blocks can have a datafile as large as 128TB. In addition, bigfile tablespaces must be locally managed.

Resizing a Smallfile Tablespace Using ALTER DATABASE

In the following examples, we attempt to resize the USERS tablespace, which contains one datafile, starting out at 5GB. First, we make it 15GB, then realize it's too big, and shrink it down to 10GB. Then, we attempt to shrink it too much. Finally, we try to increase its size too much.

```
SQL> alter database
  2      datafile '/u01/app/oracle/oradata/rmanrep/users01.dbf' resize 15g;
 Database altered.
SQL> alter database
  2      datafile '/u01/app/oracle/oradata/rmanrep/users01.dbf' resize 10g;
 Database altered.
SQL> alter database
  2      datafile '/u01/app/oracle/oradata/rmanrep/users01.dbf' resize 1g;
alter database
*
ERROR at line 1:
ORA-03297: file contains used data beyond requested RESIZE value
SQL> alter database
  2      datafile '/u01/app/oracle/oradata/rmanrep/users01.dbf' resize 100t;
alter database
*
ERROR at line 1:
ORA-00740: datafile size of (13421772800) blocks exceeds maximum file size
SQL> alter database
  2      datafile '/u01/app/oracle/oradata/rmanrep/users01.dbf' resize 50g;
alter database
*
ERROR at line 1:
ORA-01144: File size (6553600 blocks) exceeds maximum of 4194303 blocks
```

If the resize request cannot be supported by the free space available, or there is data beyond the requested decreased size, or an Oracle file size limit is exceeded, Oracle returns an error.

To avoid manual resizing of tablespaces reactively, we can instead be proactive and use the AUTOEXTEND, NEXT, and MAXSIZE clauses when modifying or creating a datafile. Table 4-1 lists the space-related clauses for modifying or creating datafiles in the ALTER DATAFILE and ALTER TABLESPACE commands.

In the following example, we set AUTOEXTEND to ON for the datafile **/u01/app/oracle/oradata/rmanrep/users01.dbf**, specify that each extension of the datafile is 500MB, and specify that the total size of the datafile cannot exceed 10GB:

```
SQL> alter database
  2      datafile '/u01/app/oracle/oradata/rmanrep/users01.dbf'
  3      autoextend on
  4      next 500MB
  5      maxsize 10g;
Database altered.
```

If the disk volume containing the datafile does not have the disk space available for the expansion of the datafile, we must either move the datafile to another disk volume or create a second datafile for the tablespace on another disk volume. In this example, we're going to add

Clause	Description
AUTOEXTEND	When this clause is set to ON, the datafile will be allowed to expand. When it's set to OFF, no expansion is allowed, and the other clauses are set to zero.
NEXT *<size>*	The size, in bytes, of the next amount of disk space to allocate for the datafile when expansion is required; the *<size>* value can be qualified with K, M, G, or T to specify the size in kilobytes, megabytes, gigabytes, or terabytes, respectively.
MAXSIZE *<size>*	When this clause is set to UNLIMITED, the size of the datafile is unlimited within Oracle, up to 128TB for a bigfile tablespace, and 128GB for a smallfile tablespace with 32K blocks (otherwise limited by the file system containing the datafile). Otherwise, MAXSIZE is set to the maximum number of bytes in the datafile, using the same qualifiers used in the NEXT clause: K, M, G, or T. Using the Oracle-recommended block size of 8K, the maximum size of a smallfile tablespace is therefore 32GB.

TABLE 4-1. *Datafile Extension Clauses*

a second datafile to the USERS tablespace on a different disk volume with an initial size of 500MB, allowing for the automatic extension of the datafile, with each extension 100MB and a maximum datafile size of 2000MB (2GB):

```
SQL> alter tablespace users
       add datafile '/u03/oradata/users02.dbf'
       size 500m
       autoextend on
       next 100m
       maxsize 2000m;
Tablespace altered.
```

Notice that when we modify an existing datafile in a tablespace, we use the ALTER DATABASE command, whereas when we add a datafile to a tablespace, we use the ALTER TABLESPACE command. As you will see shortly, using a bigfile tablespace simplifies these types of operations.

Resizing a Smallfile Tablespace Using EM Database Express

Using EM Database Express, we can use either of the methods described in the preceding section: increase the size and turn on AUTOEXTEND for the tablespace's single datafile, or add a second datafile.

Resizing a Datafile in a Smallfile Tablespace To resize a datafile in EM Database Express, from the database instance home page, choose Storage | Tablespaces. In Figure 4-1, the XPORT

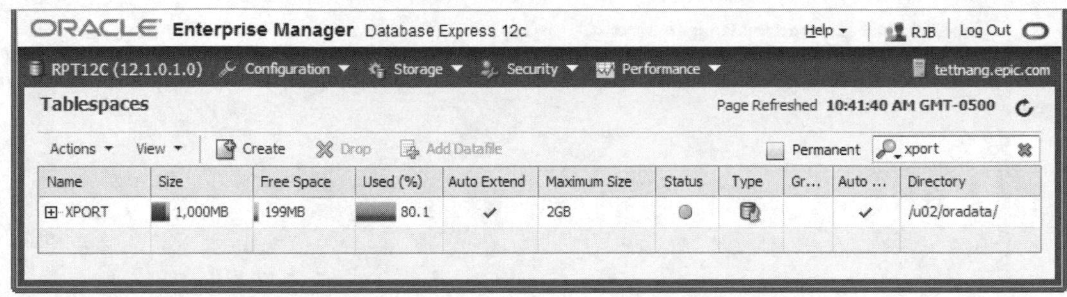

FIGURE 4-1. *Using EM Database Express to edit tablespace characteristics*

tablespace has been selected; it is over 80 percent full, so we will expand its size by extending the size of the existing datafile. This tablespace was originally created using this command:

```
create tablespace xport datafile '/u02/oradata/xport.dbf' size 1000m
   autoextend on next 500m maxsize 2000m;
```

Rather than let the tablespace's datafile autoextend, we will change the current size of the datafile to 2000MB from 1000MB.

By clicking the "+" icon to the left of XPORT, you can see the additional characteristics of the XPORT tablespace, as shown in Figure 4-2. The single datafile is **/u02/oradata/xport.dbf**.

With the single XPORT datafile selected, choose Actions | Resize, and you will see the Resize Datafile dialog box, shown in Figure 4-3, where you can change the size of the datafile. Change the file size to 2G (2000MB) and click OK.

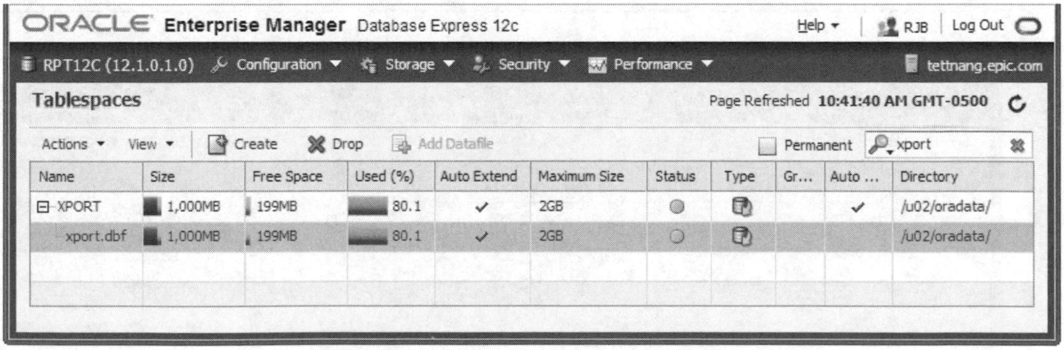

FIGURE 4-2. *Tablespace characteristics*

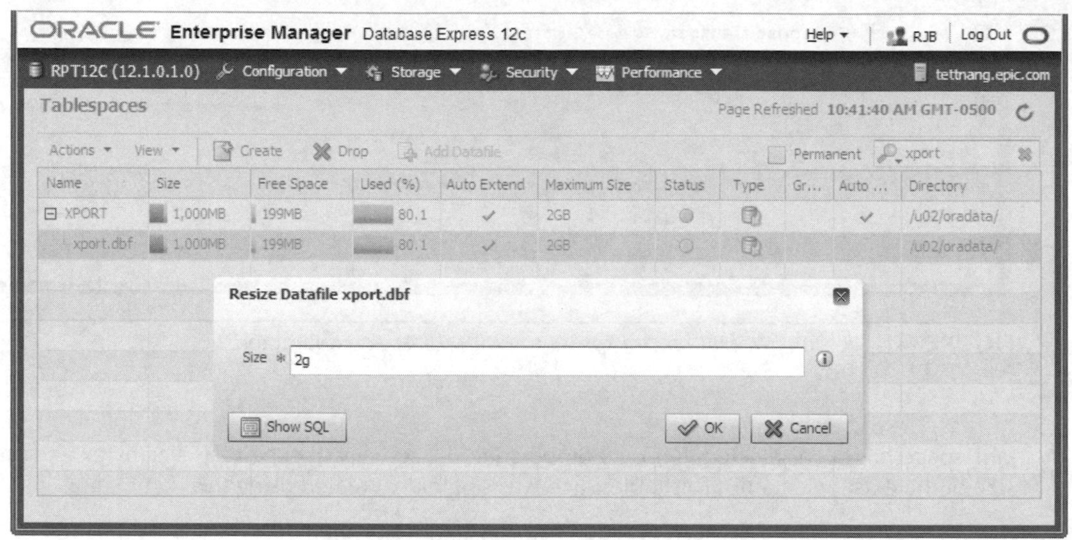

FIGURE 4-3. *Editing a tablespace's datafile*

Before committing the changes, it is often beneficial to review the SQL commands about to be executed by clicking the Show SQL button on almost any page where a DDL operation is going to be executed. It is a good way to brush up on your SQL command syntax! Here is the command that was executed when you clicked OK:

```
ALTER DATABASE DATAFILE '/u02/oradata/xport.dbf' RESIZE 2G
```

When you click OK, Oracle changes the size of the datafile. The Tablespaces reflects the successful operation and the new size of the datafile, as you can see in Figure 4-4.

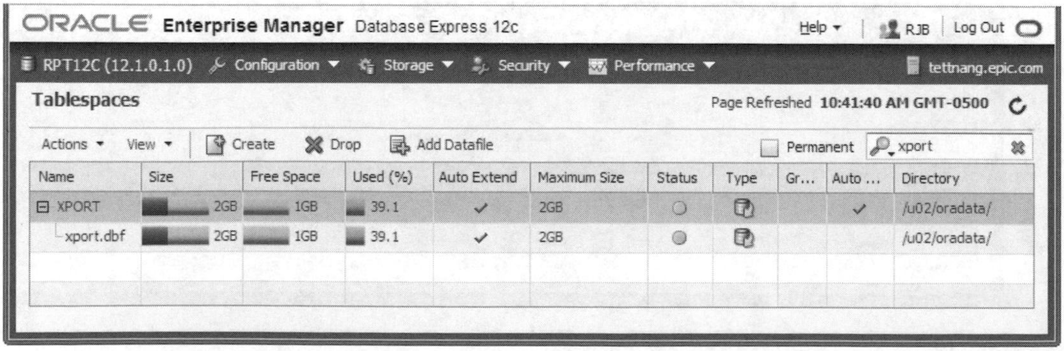

FIGURE 4-4. *Datafile resizing results*

Adding a Datafile to a Smallfile Tablespace Adding a datafile to a smallfile tablespace is just as easy as resizing a datafile using EM Database Express. In our preceding example, we expanded the datafile for the XPORT tablespace to 2000MB. Because the file system (**/u02**) containing the datafile for the XPORT tablespace is now at capacity, you will have to turn off AUTOEXTEND on the existing datafile and then create a new datafile on a different file system. To turn off AUTOEXTEND for the existing datafile from the Tablespaces page, choose Actions | Edit Auto Extend. In the dialog box that opens, uncheck the Auto Extend check box, as shown in Figure 4-5, and click OK. Here is the SQL command that is executed for this operation when you click OK:

```
ALTER DATABASE
     DATAFILE '/u02/oradata/xport.dbf'
     AUTOEXTEND OFF;
```

To add the second datafile on **/u04**, select the XPORT tablespace and click Add Datafile. You will see the dialog box shown in Figure 4-6. Specify the filename and directory location for the new datafile. Because you know that the **/u04** file system has at least 500MB free, specify **/u04/oradata** as the directory and **xport2.dbf** as the filename, although the filename itself need not contain the tablespace name. In addition, set the file size to 500MB. Do not check the Auto Extend check box.

After clicking OK, you see the new size of the XPORT tablespace's datafiles on the Tablespaces page, as shown in Figure 4-7.

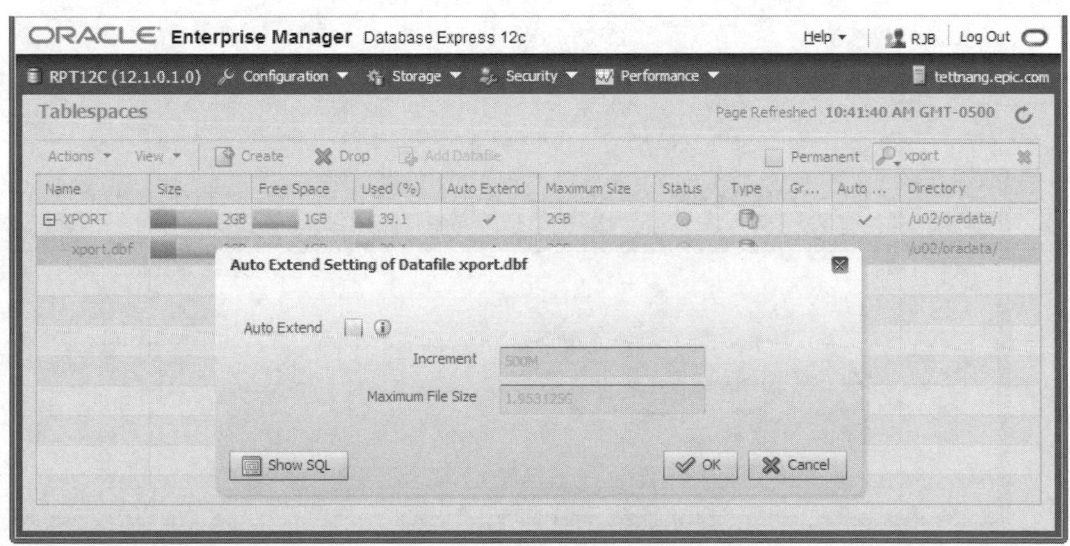

FIGURE 4-5. *Editing a tablespace's datafile characteristics*

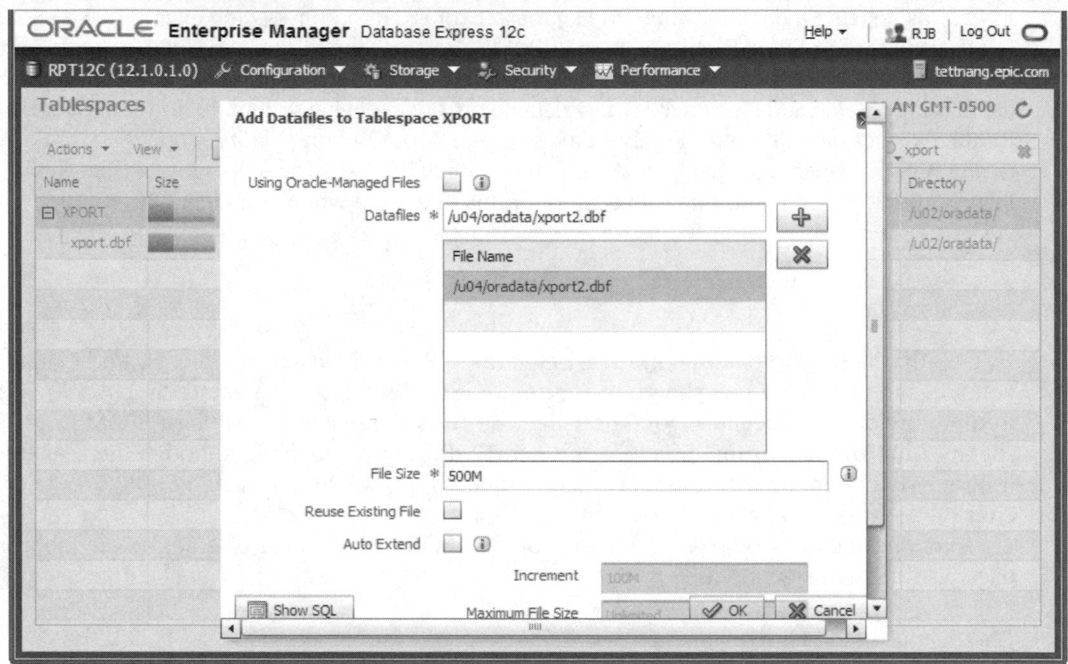

FIGURE 4-6. *Adding a datafile to the XPORT tablespace*

ORACLE Enterprise Manager Database Express 12c — Help | RJB | Log Out

RPT12C (12.1.0.1.0) Configuration Storage Security Performance — tettnang.epic.com

Tablespaces — Page Refreshed 10:41:40 AM GMT-0500

Actions View Create Drop Add Datafile — Permanent xport

Name	Size	Free Space	Used (%)	Auto Extend	Maximum Size	Status	Type	Gr...	Auto ...	Directory
XPORT	2GB	2GB	39.3		2GB				✓	...
xport.dbf	2GB	1GB	39.1		2GB					/u02/oradata/
xport2.dbf	500MB	499MB	.2		500MB					/u04/oradata/

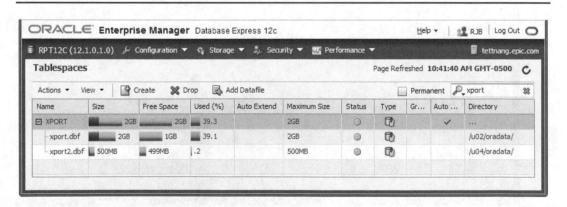

FIGURE 4-7. *Results of adding a datafile*

Dropping a Datafile from a Tablespace

In versions of Oracle Database prior to 11*g*, dropping a datafile from a tablespace was problematic; there was not a single command you could issue to drop a datafile unless you dropped the entire tablespace. You only had three alternatives:

- Live with it.
- Shrink it and turn off AUTOEXTEND.
- Create a new tablespace, move all the objects to the new tablespace, and drop the original tablespace.

Although creating a new tablespace was the most ideal approach from a maintenance and metadata point of view, performing the steps involved was error-prone and involved some amount of downtime for the tablespace, impacting availability.

Using Cloud Control 12*c* or EM Database Express, you can drop a datafile and minimize downtime, and let Cloud Control 12*c* or EM Database Express generate the scripts for you if you want to run it manually. Following our previous example in which we expanded the XPORT tablespace by adding a datafile, I'll step through an example of how you can remove the datafile by reorganizing the tablespace. On the Tablespaces page shown in Figure 4-7, select the datafile to be dropped (**xport2.dbf** in this case), and choose Actions | Drop, as shown in Figure 4-8.

If there are objects occupying the specified datafile to be dropped, you will have to reorganize the tablespace to move all of the objects to the first datafile or create a new tablespace and migrate the objects to the new tablespace.

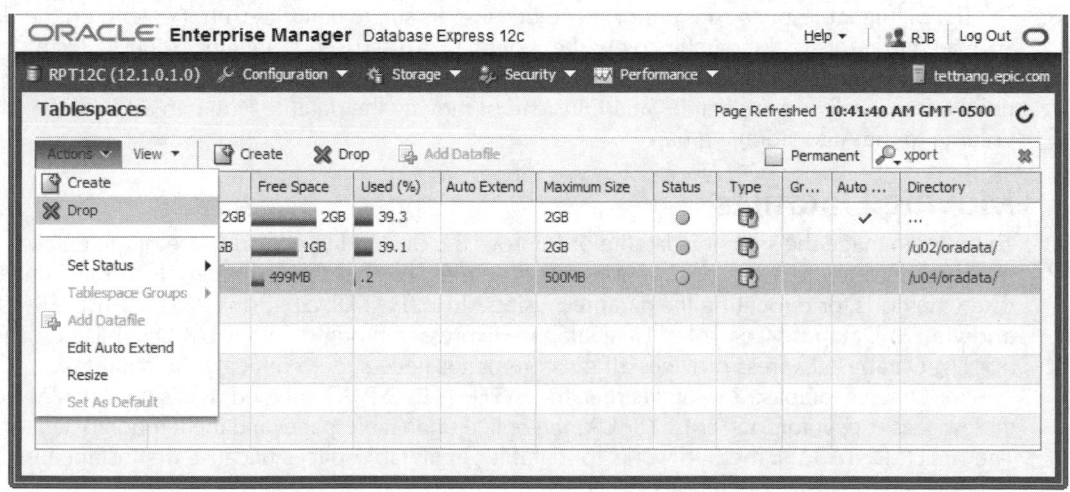

FIGURE 4-8. *Dropping a datafile*

Resizing a Bigfile Tablespace Using ALTER TABLESPACE

A bigfile tablespace consists of one and only one datafile. Although you will learn more about bigfile tablespaces in Chapter 6, this section presents a few details about how a bigfile tablespace can be resized. Most of the parameters available for changing the characteristics of a tablespace's datafile, such as the maximum size, whether it can extend at all, and the size of the extents, are now modifiable at the tablespace level. Let's start with a bigfile tablespace created as follows:

```
create bigfile tablespace dmarts
   datafile '/u05/oradata/dmarts.dbf' size 750m
   autoextend on next 100m maxsize 50g;
```

Operations that are valid only at the datafile level with smallfile tablespaces can be used with bigfile tablespaces at the tablespace level:

```
SQL> alter tablespace dmarts resize 1g;
Tablespace altered.
```

Although using ALTER DATABASE with the datafile specification for the DMARTS tablespace will work, the advantage of the ALTER TABLESPACE syntax is obvious: You don't have to or need to know where the datafile is stored. As you might suspect, trying to change datafile parameters at the tablespace level with smallfile tablespaces is not allowed:

```
SQL> alter tablespace users resize 500m;
alter tablespace users resize 500m
*
ERROR at line 1:
ORA-32773: operation not supported for smallfile tablespace USERS
```

If a bigfile tablespace runs out of space because its single datafile cannot extend on the disk, you need to relocate the datafile to another volume, as discussed in the next section. Using Automatic Storage Management, presented later in this chapter, can potentially eliminate the need to manually move datafiles at all: Instead of moving the datafile, you can add another disk volume to the ASM storage group.

Moving Datafiles

To better manage the size of a datafile or improve the overall I/O performance of the database, it may be necessary to move one or more datafiles in a tablespace to a different location. There are three methods for relocating the datafiles: using ALTER DATABASE, using ALTER TABLESPACE, and via EM Database Control or EM Database Express, although neither EM Database Control nor EM Database Express provides all the commands necessary to relocate the datafile.

For Oracle Database 11*g* and earlier, the ALTER TABLESPACE method works for datafiles in all tablespaces except for SYSTEM, SYSAUX, the online undo tablespace, and the temporary tablespace. The ALTER DATABASE method works for datafiles in all tablespaces because the instance is shut down when the move operation occurs.

If you are using Oracle Database 12*c*, you can move any datafile while the entire database is online, even from a traditional file system to ASM or vice versa. However, there is some slight overhead using this method, so you should be cognizant of your service-level agreement (SLA) and ensure that the move operation will not adversely affect response time.

Moving Datafiles with ALTER DATABASE

The steps for moving one or more datafiles (non-ASM) with ALTER DATABASE are as follows:

1. Connect to the database as SYSDBA and shut down the instance.
2. Use operating system commands to move the datafile(s).
3. Open the database in MOUNT mode.
4. Use ALTER DATABASE to change the references to the datafile in the database.
5. Open the database in OPEN mode.
6. Perform an incremental or full backup of the database that includes the control file.

In the following example, I will show you how to move the datafile of the XPORT tablespace from the file system **/u02** to the file system **/u06**. First, you connect to the database with SYSDBA privileges using the following command:

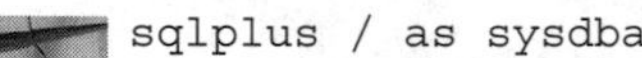

```
sqlplus / as sysdba
```

Next, you use a query against the dynamic performance views V$DATAFILE and V$TABLESPACE to confirm the names of the datafiles in the XPORT tablespace:

```
SQL> select d.name from
  2    v$datafile d join v$tablespace t using(ts#)
  3    where t.name = 'XPORT';

NAME
------------------------------------------------------------
/u02/oradata/xport.dbf

1 row selected.

SQL>
```

To complete step 1, shut down the database:

```
SQL> shutdown immediate;
Database closed.
Database dismounted.
ORACLE instance shut down.
SQL>
```

For step 2, you stay in SQL*Plus and use the "!" escape character to execute the operating system command to move the datafile:

```
SQL> ! mv /u02/oradata/xport.dbf /u06/oradata
```

In step 3, you start up the database in MOUNT mode so that the control file is available without opening the datafiles:

```
SQL> startup mount
ORACLE instance started.

Total System Global Area  422670336 bytes
Fixed Size                  1299112 bytes
Variable Size             230690136 bytes
Database Buffers          184549376 bytes
Redo Buffers                6131712 bytes
Database mounted.
```

For step 4, you change the pathname reference in the control file to point to the new location of the datafile:

```
SQL> alter database rename file
  2    '/u02/oradata/xport.dbf' to
  3    '/u06/oradata/xport.dbf';
Database altered.
```

In step 5, you open the database to make it available to users:

```
SQL> alter database open;
Database altered.
```

Finally, in step 6, you can make a backup copy of the updated control file:

```
SQL> alter database backup controlfile to trace;
Database altered.
SQL>
```

Alternatively, you can use RMAN to perform an incremental backup that includes a backup of the control file.

Moving Datafiles with ALTER TABLESPACE in Offline Mode (11*g* or earlier)

If the datafile you want to move is part of a tablespace other than SYSTEM, SYSAUX, the active undo tablespace, or the temporary tablespace, then it is preferable to use the ALTER TABLESPACE method to move a tablespace for one primary reason: The rest of the database, except for the tablespace whose datafile will be moved, remains available to all users during the entire operation.

The steps for moving one or more datafiles with ALTER TABLESPACE are as follows:

1. Using an account with the ALTER TABLESPACE privilege, take the tablespace offline.
2. Use operating system commands to move the datafile(s).
3. Use ALTER TABLESPACE to change the references to the datafile in the database.
4. Bring the tablespace back online.

In the ALTER DATABASE example, assume that you moved the datafile for the XPORT tablespace to the wrong file system. In this example, you'll move it from **/u06/oradata** to **/u05/oradata**:

```
alter tablespace xport offline;
Tablespace altered.

! mv /u06/oradata/xport.dbf /u05/oradata/xport.dbf

alter tablespace xport rename datafile
   '/u06/oradata/xport.dbf' to '/u05/oradata/xport.dbf';
Tablespace altered.

alter tablespace xport online;
Tablespace altered.
```

Note how this method is much more straightforward and much less disruptive than the ALTER DATABASE method. The only downtime for the XPORT tablespace is the amount of time it takes to move the datafile from one disk volume to another.

Moving Datafiles Online (Oracle Database 12*c*)

In Oracle Database 12*c*, you can move any datafile to or from an ASM disk group while the tablespace containing the datafile remains online. This enhances Oracle's ease of manageability for the DBA and the availability for the user.

In this example, the DMARTS tablespace resides on the **/u02** file system, and it needs to be moved to the +DATA disk group:

```
SQL> select ts#,ts.name,df.name
  2  from v$tablespace ts
  3     join v$datafile df
  4        using(ts#);

   TS# NAME                         NAME
------ ---------------------------- -------------------------
     0 SYSTEM                       +DATA/DWCDB/E7B2AFD1B8211
                                    382E043E3A0080A0732/DATAF
                                    ILE/system.375.827672253
. . .
     3 USERS                        +DATA/DWCDB/E7B2AFD1B8211
                                    382E043E3A0080A0732/DATAF
                                    ILE/users.377.827672261
    10 DMARTS                       /u02/oradata/dmartsbf.dbf

25 rows selected.
```

Moving the single datafile within the DMARTS tablespace to the +DATA disk group is accomplished with one command while the tablespace remains online:

```
SQL> alter database
  2     move datafile '/u02/oradata/dmartsbf.dbf'
  3     to '+DATA';

Database altered.
```

Moving Online Redo Log Files

Although it is possible to indirectly move online redo log files by dropping entire redo log groups and re-adding the groups in a different location, this solution will not work if there are only two redo log file groups, because a database will not open with only one redo log file group. Temporarily adding a third group and dropping the first or second group is an option if the database must be kept open; alternatively, the method shown here will move the redo log file(s) while the database is shut down.

In the following example, we have three redo log file groups with two members each. One member of each group is on the same volume as the Oracle software and should be moved to a different volume to eliminate any contention between log file filling and accessing Oracle software components. The method you will use here is very similar to the method used to move datafiles with the ALTER DATABASE method.

```
SQL> select group#, member from v$logfile
  2       order by group#, member;

    GROUP# MEMBER
---------- ---------------------------------------------
         1 /u01/app/oracle/oradata/redo01.log
         1 /u05/oradata/redo01.log
         2 /u01/app/oracle/oradata/redo02.log
         2 /u05/oradata/redo02.log
         3 /u01/app/oracle/oradata/redo03.log
         3 /u05/oradata/redo03.log
6 rows selected.

SQL> shutdown immediate;
Database closed.
Database dismounted.
ORACLE instance shut down.
SQL> ! mv /u01/app/oracle/oradata/redo0[1-3].log /u04/oradata

SQL> startup mount
ORACLE instance started.

Total System Global Area  422670336 bytes
Fixed Size                  1299112 bytes
Variable Size             230690136 bytes
Database Buffers          184549376 bytes
Redo Buffers                6131712 bytes
Database mounted.

SQL> alter database rename file '/u01/app/oracle/oradata/redo01.log'
  2      to '/u04/oradata/redo01.log';
Database altered.

SQL> alter database rename file '/u01/app/oracle/oradata/redo02.log'
  2      to '/u04/oradata/redo02.log';
Database altered.
```

```
SQL> alter database rename file '/u01/app/oracle/oradata/redo03.log'
  2      to '/u04/oradata/redo03.log';
Database altered.

SQL> alter database open;
Database altered.

SQL> select group#, member from v$logfile
  2      order by group#, member;

    GROUP# MEMBER
---------- ------------------------------------------
         1 /u04/oradata/redo01.log
         1 /u05/oradata/redo01.log
         2 /u04/oradata/redo02.log
         2 /u05/oradata/redo02.log
         3 /u04/oradata/redo03.log
         3 /u05/oradata/redo03.log

6 rows selected.

SQL>
```

The I/O for the redo log files no longer contends with the Oracle software; in addition, the redo log files are multiplexed between two different mount points, **/u04** and **/u05**.

Moving Control Files

Moving a control file when you use an initialization parameter file follows a procedure similar to the one you used for datafiles and redo log files: Shut down the instance, move the file with operating system commands, and restart the instance.

When you use a server parameter file (SPFILE), however, the procedure is a bit different. The initialization file parameter CONTROL_FILES is changed using ALTER SYSTEM . . . SCOPE=SPFILE when either the instance is running or it's shut down and opened in NOMOUNT mode. Because the CONTROL_FILES parameter is not dynamic, the instance must be shut down and restarted in either case.

In this example, you discover that you have three copies of the control file in your database, but they are not multiplexed on different disks. You will edit the SPFILE with the new locations, shut down the instance so that you can move the control files to different disks, and then restart the instance.

```
SQL> select name, value from v$spparameter
  2      where name = 'control_files';

NAME            VALUE
--------------- ---------------------------------------------------
control_files   /u01/app/oracle/oradata/control01.ctl
control_files   /u01/app/oracle/oradata/control02.ctl
control_files   /u01/app/oracle/oradata/control03.ctl

SQL> show parameter control_files
```

```
NAME             TYPE        VALUE
---------------- ----------- ------------------------------
control_files    string      /u01/app/oracle/oradata/contro
                             l01.ctl, /u01/app/oracle/orada
                             ta/control02.ctl, /u01/app/ora
                             cle/oradata/control03.ctl

SQL> alter system set control_files =
  2    '/u02/oradata/control01.ctl',
  3    '/u03/oradata/control02.ctl',
  4    '/u04/oradata/control03.ctl'
  5  scope = spfile;

System altered.

SQL> shutdown immediate
Database closed.
Database dismounted.
ORACLE instance shut down.
SQL> ! mv /u01/app/oracle/oradata/control01.ctl /u02/oradata
SQL> ! mv /u01/app/oracle/oradata/control02.ctl /u03/oradata
SQL> ! mv /u01/app/oracle/oradata/control03.ctl /u04/oradata

SQL> startup
ORACLE instance started.

Total System Global Area  422670336 bytes
Fixed Size                  1299112 bytes
Variable Size             230690136 bytes
Database Buffers          184549376 bytes
Redo Buffers                6131712 bytes
Database mounted.
Database opened.
SQL> select name, value from v$spparameter
  2  where name = 'control_files';

NAME            VALUE
--------------- ----------------------------------------------------
control_files   /u02/oradata/control01.ctl
control_files   /u03/oradata/control02.ctl
control_files   /u04/oradata/control03.ctl

SQL> show parameter control_files

NAME             TYPE        VALUE
---------------- ----------- ------------------------------
control_files    string      /u02/oradata/control01.ctl, /u
                             03/oradata/control02.ctl, /u04
                             /oradata/control03.ctl
SQL>
```

The three control files have been moved to separate file systems, no longer on the volume with the Oracle software and in a higher-availability configuration (if the volume containing one of the control files fails, two other volumes contain up-to-date control files).

NOTE
*In a default installation of Oracle Database 11*g *or 12*c *using ASM disks for tablespace storage and the flash recovery area, one copy of the control file is created in the default tablespace ASM disk and another in the flash recovery area.*

Making one or more copies of the control file to an ASM volume is just as easy: using the RMAN utility (described in detail in Chapter 12), restore a control file backup to an ASM disk location, as in this example:

```
RMAN> restore controlfile to
        '+DATA/dw/controlfile/control_bak.ctl';
```

The next step is identical to adding file system–based control files as I presented earlier in this section: change the CONTROL_FILES parameter to add the location **+DATA/dw/controlfile/control_bak.ctl** in addition to the existing control file locations, and then shut down and restart the database.

```
SQL> show parameter control_files

NAME                 TYPE        VALUE
-------------------- ----------- ------------------------------
control_files        string      /u02/oradata/control01.ctl, /u
                                 03/oradata/control02.ctl, /u04
                                 /oradata/control03.ctl, +DATA/
                                 dw/controlfile/control_bak.ctl
SQL>
```

Similarly, you can use the Linux utility **asmcmd** to make copies of the control file from one disk group to another, and change the CONTROL_FILES parameter to reflect the new control file location. I present an overview of the **asmcmd** command later in this chapter.

Automatic Storage Management

In Chapter 3, I presented some of the file naming conventions used for ASM objects. In this section, I'll delve more deeply into how we can create tablespaces—and ultimately datafiles behind the scenes—in an ASM environment with one or more disk groups.

When creating a new tablespace or other database structure, such as a control file or redo log file, you can specify a disk group as the storage area for the database structure instead of an operating system file. ASM takes the ease of use of Oracle Managed Files (OMF) and combines it with mirroring and striping features to provide a robust file system and logical volume manager that can even support multiple nodes in an Oracle Real Application Cluster (RAC). ASM eliminates the need to purchase a third-party logical volume manager.

ASM not only enhances performance by automatically spreading out database objects over multiple devices, but also increases availability by allowing new disk devices to be added to the database without shutting down the database; ASM automatically rebalances the distribution of files with minimal intervention.

We'll also review the ASM architecture. In addition, I'll show how you create a special type of Oracle instance to support ASM as well as how to start up and shut down an ASM instance. We'll review the new initialization parameters related to ASM and the existing initialization parameters that have new values to support an ASM instance. Also, I'll introduce the **asmcmd** command-line utility, new as of Oracle 10*g* Release 2, that gives you an alternate way to browse and maintain objects in your ASM disk groups. Finally, I'll use some raw disk devices on a Linux server to demonstrate how disk groups are created and maintained.

ASM Architecture

ASM divides the datafiles and other database structures into extents, and it divides the extents among all the disks in the disk group to enhance both performance and reliability. Instead of mirroring entire disk volumes, ASM mirrors the database objects to provide the flexibility to mirror or stripe the database objects differently depending on their type. Optionally, the objects do not have to be striped at all if the underlying disk hardware is already RAID enabled, part of a storage area network (SAN), or part of a network-attached storage (NAS) device.

Automatic rebalancing is another key feature of ASM. When an increase in disk space is needed, additional disk devices can be added to a disk group, and ASM moves a proportional number of files from one or more existing disks to the new disks to maintain the overall I/O balance across all disks. This happens in the background while the database objects contained in the disk files are still online and available to users. If the impact to the I/O subsystem is high during a rebalance operation, the speed at which the rebalance occurs can be reduced using an initialization parameter.

ASM requires a special type of Oracle instance to provide the interface between a traditional Oracle instance and the file system; the ASM software components are shipped with the Oracle database software and are always available as a selection when you're selecting the storage type for the SYSTEM, SYSAUX, and other tablespaces when the database is created.

Using ASM does not, however, prevent you from mixing ASM disk groups with manual Oracle datafile management techniques such as those I presented in Chapter 3 and earlier in this chapter. However, the ease of use and performance of ASM makes a strong case for eventually using ASM disk groups for all your storage needs.

Two Oracle background processes introduced in Oracle Database 10*g* support ASM instances: RBAL and ARB*n*. RBAL coordinates the disk activity for disk groups, whereas ORB*n*, where *n* can be a number from 0 to 9 or the letter A (Oracle Database 12*c*), performs the actual extent movement between disks in the disk groups.

For databases that use ASM disks, there are also two new background processes as of Oracle Database 10*g*: ASMB and RBAL. ASMB performs the communication between the database and the ASM instance, whereas RBAL performs the opening and closing of the disks in the disk group on behalf of the database.

Creating an ASM Instance

ASM requires a dedicated Oracle instance to manage the disk groups. An ASM instance generally has a smaller memory footprint, in the range of 100MB to 150MB, and is automatically configured when ASM (as part of the Grid Infrastructure) is specified as the database's file storage option when the Oracle software is installed and an existing ASM instance does not already exist, as you can see in the Oracle Universal Installer screen in Figure 4-9.

Oracle best practices for servers with over 128GB of memory recommend having the ASM instance's initialization parameters set to something close to this:

- SGA_TARGET=1250M (ASMM)
- PGA_AGGREGATE_TARGET=400M
- MEMORY_TARGET=0 or not set (No AMM)

As an example of disk devices used to create ASM disk groups, suppose our Linux server has two unused disks with the capacities listed in Table 4-2.

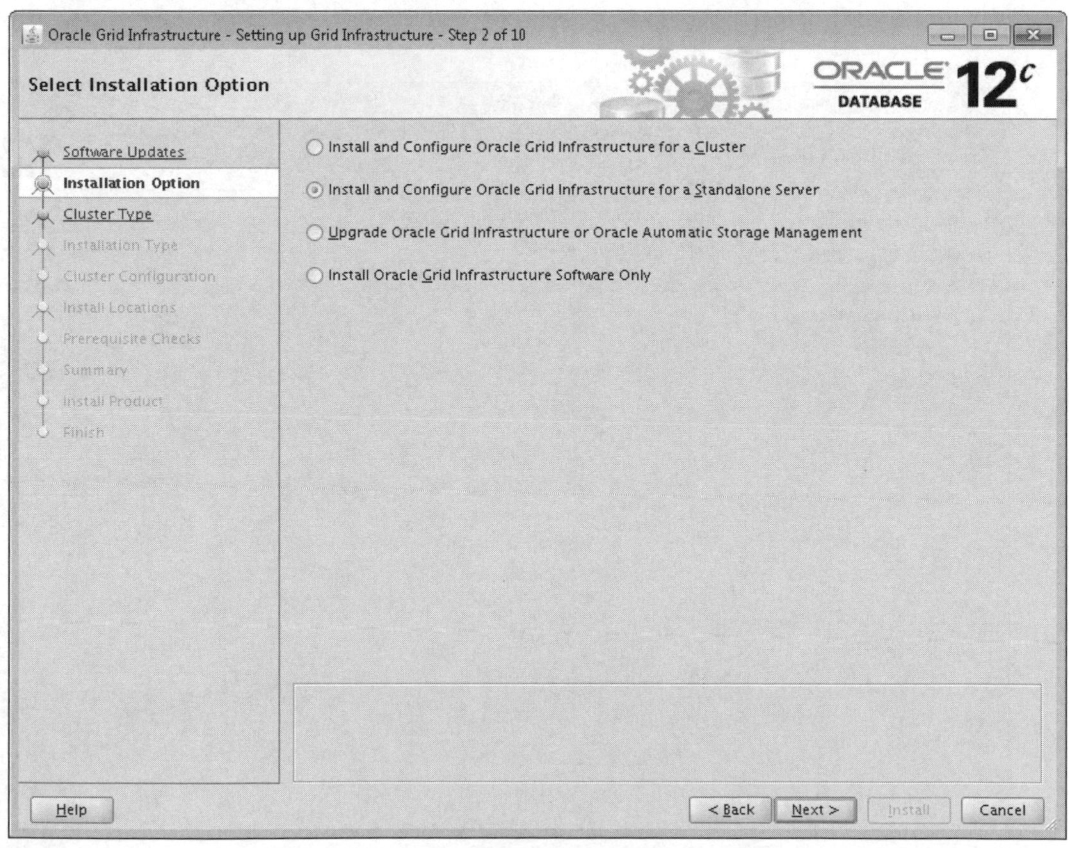

FIGURE 4-9. *Specifying Grid Infrastructure (ASM) as the database file storage method*

Device Name	Capacity
/dev/sdb1	32GB
/dev/sdc1	32GB

TABLE 4-2. *Raw Disks for ASM Disk Groups*

You configure the first disk group within the Oracle Universal Installer, as shown in Figure 4-10.

The name of the first disk group is DATA, and you will be using **/dev/sdb1** and **/dev/sdc1** to create the normal redundancy disk group. If an insufficient number of raw disks are selected for the desired redundancy level, OUI generates an error message. After the database is created, both the regular instance and the ASM instance are started.

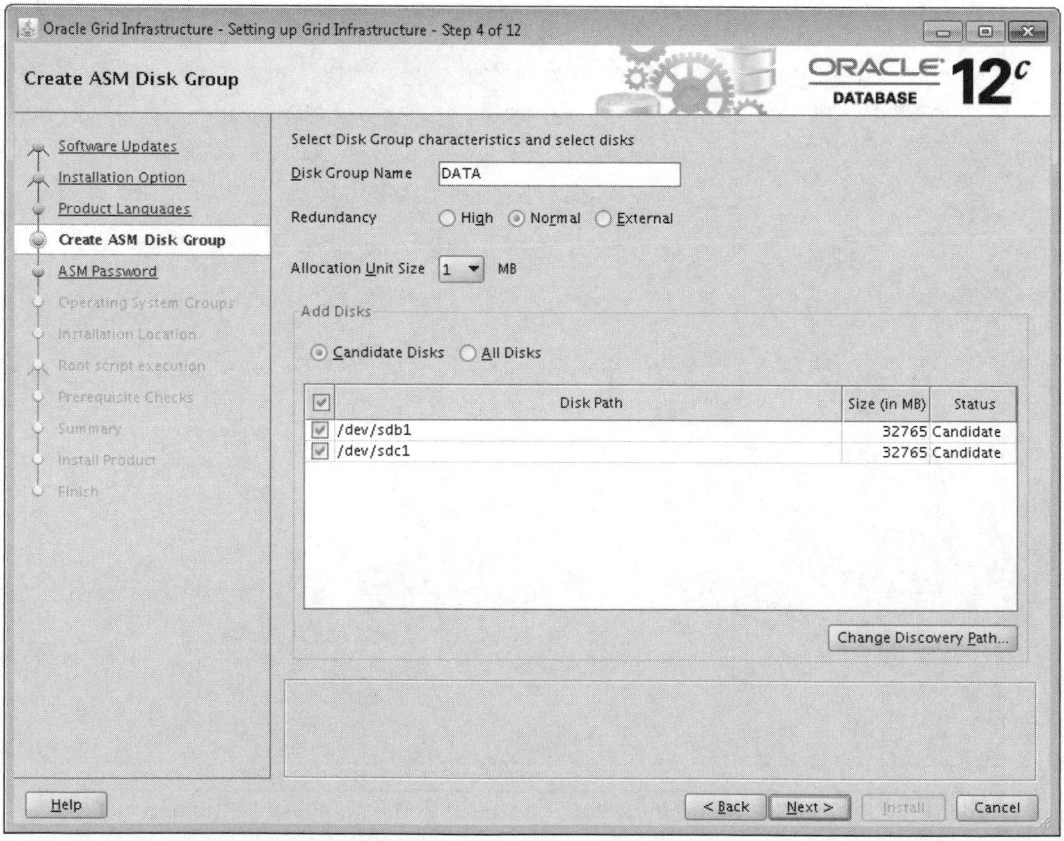

FIGURE 4-10. *Configuring the initial ASM disk group with OUI*

An ASM instance has a few other unique characteristics. Although it does have an initialization parameter file and a password file, it has no data dictionary, and therefore all connections to an ASM instance are via SYS and SYSTEM using operating system authentication only. If you are using Oracle Database 12*c*, however, you can create a password file and even put it in an ASM disk group, much like you can do with an RDBMS password file, as in this example:

```
[oracle@tettnang ~]$ . oraenv
ORACLE_SID = [RPT12C] ? +ASM
The Oracle base remains unchanged with value /u00/app/oracle
[oracle@tettnang ~]$ orapwd file=+DATA asm=y
Enter password for SYS: xxxxxxxxxxx
[oracle@tettnang ~]$ srvctl config asm -detail
ASM home: /u00/app/oracle/product/12.1.0/grid
Password file: +DATA/ASM/PASSWORD/pwdasm.406.834577299
ASM listener: LISTENER
Spfile: +DATA/ASM/ASMPARAMETERFILE/registry.253.826648367
ASM diskgroup discovery string: /dev/oracleasm/disks
ASM is enabled.
[oracle@tettnang ~]$
```

Disk group commands such as CREATE DISKGROUP, ALTER DISKGROUP, and DROP DISKGROUP are only valid in an ASM instance. Finally, an ASM instance is either in a NOMOUNT or MOUNT state; it is never in an OPEN state.

ASM Instance Components

ASM instances cannot be accessed using the variety of methods available with a traditional database. In this section, I'll talk about the privileges available to you that connect with SYSASM privilege. I'll also distinguish an ASM instance by the new and expanded initialization parameters (introduced in Oracle Database 10*g* and enhanced in Oracle Database 11*g* and 12*c*) available only for an ASM instance. At the end of this section, I'll present the procedures for starting and stopping an ASM instance along with the dependencies between ASM instances and the database instances they serve.

Accessing an ASM Instance

As mentioned earlier in the chapter, an ASM instance does not have a data dictionary, so access to the instance is restricted to users who can authenticate with the operating system—in other words, connecting as SYSASM by an operating system user in the **dba** group.

Users who connect to an ASM instance as SYSASM can perform all ASM operations, such as creating and deleting disk groups as well as adding and removing disks from disk groups. In Oracle Database 11*g* and 12*c*, a user with the SYSDBA privilege can still perform the same tasks as a user with SYSASM privileges, but that role is deprecated and will not have the same privileges as SYSASM in future releases.

The SYSOPER users have a much more limited set of commands available in an ASM instance. In general, the commands available to SYSOPER users give only enough privileges to perform routine operations for an already configured and stable ASM instance. The following list contains the operations available as SYSOPER:

- Starting up and shutting down an ASM instance
- Mounting or dismounting a disk group

- Altering a disk group's disk status from ONLINE to OFFLINE, or vice versa
- Rebalancing a disk group
- Performing an integrity check of a disk group
- Accessing the V$ASM_* dynamic performance views

In Oracle Database 12*c*, the following three new privileges for ASM instances have been added. These roles are task-oriented and help to enforce enterprise separation of duties requirements.

- **SYSBACKUP** Perform backup and recovery from RMAN or the SQL*Plus command line
- **SYSDG** Perform Data Guard operations with Data Guard Broker or at the **dgmgrl** command line
- **SYSKM** Manage encryption keys for Transparent Data Encryption (TDE)

ASM Initialization Parameters

A number of initialization parameters are either specific to ASM instances or have new values within an ASM instance. An SPFILE is highly recommended instead of an initialization parameter file for an ASM instance. For example, parameters such as ASM_DISKGROUPS will automatically be maintained when a disk group is added or dropped, potentially freeing you from ever having to manually change this value.

The ASM-related initialization parameters are presented next.

INSTANCE_TYPE For an ASM instance, the INSTANCE_TYPE parameter has a value of ASM. The default, for a traditional Oracle instance, is RDBMS.

DB_UNIQUE_NAME The default value for the DB_UNIQUE_NAME parameter is +ASM and is the unique name for a group of ASM instances within a cluster or on a single node.

ASM_POWER_LIMIT To ensure that rebalancing operations do not interfere with ongoing user I/O, the ASM_POWER_LIMIT parameter controls how fast rebalance operations occur. For Oracle Database 12*c*, the values range from 0 to 1024 (1 to 11 in Oracle Database 11*g* unless you are using version 11.2.0.2 and the COMPATIBLE.ASM disk group attribute is set to 11.2.0.2 or higher), with 1024 being the highest possible value; the default value is 1 (low I/O overhead). Because this is a dynamic parameter, you may set this to a low value during the day and set it higher overnight whenever a disk-rebalancing operation must occur.

ASM_DISKSTRING The ASM_DISKSTRING parameter specifies one or more strings, operating system dependent, to limit the disk devices that can be used to create disk groups. If this value is NULL, all disks visible to the ASM instance are potential candidates for creating disk groups. For the examples in this chapter for our test server, the value of the ASM_DISKSTRING parameter is **/dev/raw/***:

```
SQL> select name, type, value from v$parameter
  2      where name = 'asm_diskstring';

NAME                  TYPE VALUE
-------------- ---------- -------------------------
asm_diskstring           2 /dev/sd*
```

ASM_DISKGROUPS The ASM_DISKGROUPS parameter specifies a list containing the names of the disk groups to be automatically mounted by the ASM instance at startup or by the ALTER DISKGROUP ALL MOUNT command. Even if this list is empty at instance startup, any existing disk group can be manually mounted.

LARGE_POOL_SIZE The LARGE_POOL_SIZE parameter is useful for both regular and ASM instances; however, this pool is used differently for an ASM instance. All internal ASM packages are executed from this pool. The default value for this parameter is usually sufficient, which is 12MB for a single instance and 16GB in a RAC environment.

ASM_PREFERRED_READ_FAILURE_GROUPS The ASM_PREFERRED_READ_FAILURE_GROUPS parameter, new to Oracle Database 11*g*, contains a list of the preferred failure groups for a given database instance when using clustered ASM instances. This parameter is instance specific: each instance can specify a failure group that is closest to the instance's node (for example, a failure group on the server's local disk) to improve performance.

ASM Instance Startup and Shutdown

An ASM instance is started much like a database instance, except that the STARTUP command defaults to STARTUP MOUNT. Because there is no control file, database, or data dictionary to mount, the ASM disk groups are mounted instead of a database. The command STARTUP NOMOUNT starts up the instance but does not mount any ASM disks. In addition, you can specify STARTUP RESTRICT to temporarily prevent database instances from connecting to the ASM instance to mount disk groups.

NOTE
Even though the ASM instance is in a MOUNT state, the STATUS column is set to STARTED instead of MOUNTED, as in an RDBMS instance.

Performing a SHUTDOWN command on an ASM instance performs the same SHUTDOWN command on any database instances using the ASM instance; before the ASM instance finishes a shutdown, it waits for all dependent databases to shut down. The only exception to this is if you use the SHUTDOWN ABORT command on the ASM instance, which eventually forces all dependent databases to perform a SHUTDOWN ABORT.

For multiple ASM instances sharing disk groups, such as in a Real Application Clusters (RAC) environment, the failure of an ASM instance does not cause the database instances to fail. Instead, another ASM instance performs a recovery operation for the failed instance.

ASM Dynamic Performance Views

A few new dynamic performance views are associated with ASM instances. Table 4-3 contains the common ASM-related dynamic performance views. I'll provide further explanation, where appropriate, later in this chapter for some of these views.

ASM Filename Formats

All ASM files are Oracle Managed Files (OMF), so the details of the actual filename within the disk group is not needed for most administrative functions. When an object in an ASM disk group

View Name	Used in Standard Database?	Description
V$ASM_DISK	Yes	One row for each disk discovered by an ASM instance, whether used by a disk group or not. For a database instance, one row for each disk group in use by the instance.
V$ASM_DISKGROUP	Yes	For an ASM instance, one row for each disk group containing general characteristics of the disk group. For a database instance, one row for each disk group in use whether mounted or not.
V$ASM_FILE	No	One row for each file in every mounted disk group.
V$ASM_OPERATION	No	One row for each executing long-running operation in the ASM instance.
V$ASM_TEMPLATE	Yes	One row for each template in each mounted disk group in the ASM instance. For a database instance, one row for each template for each mounted disk group.
V$ASM_CLIENT	Yes	One row for each database using disk groups managed by the ASM instance. For a database instance, one row for the ASM instance if any ASM files are open.
V$ASM_ALIAS	No	One row for every alias in every mounted disk group.

TABLE 4-3. *ASM-Related Dynamic Performance Views*

is dropped, the file is automatically deleted. Certain commands will expose the actual filenames, such as ALTER DATABASE BACKUP CONTROLFILE TO TRACE, as well as some data dictionary and dynamic performance views. For example, the dynamic performance view V$DATAFILE shows the actual filenames within each disk group. Here is an example:

```
SQL> select file#, name, blocks from v$datafile;

     FILE# NAME                                          BLOCKS
---------- ---------------------------------------- ----------
         1 +DATA/dw/datafile/system.256.627432971         89600
         2 +DATA/dw/datafile/sysaux.257.627432973         77640
         3 +DATA/dw/datafile/undotbs1.258.627432975       12800
         4 +DATA/dw/datafile/users.259.627432977            640
         5 +DATA/dw/datafile/example.265.627433157        12800
         6 /u05/oradata/dmarts.dbf                        32000
         8 /u05/oradata/xport.dbf                         38400

7 rows selected.
```

ASM filenames can be one of six different formats. In the sections that follow, I'll give an overview of the different formats and the context where they can be used—either as a reference to an existing file, during a single-file creation operation, or during a multiple-file creation operation.

Fully Qualified Names

Fully qualified ASM filenames are used only when referencing an existing file. A fully qualified ASM filename has the format

```
+<group>/<dbname>/<file type>/<tag>.<file>.<incarnation>
```

where *group* is the disk group name, *dbname* is the database to which the file belongs, *file type* is the Oracle file type, *tag* is information specific to the file type, and the *file.incarnation* pair ensures uniqueness. Here is an example of an ASM file for the USERS tablespace:

```
+DATA/dw/datafile/users.259.627432977
```

The disk group name is +DATA, the database name is dw, it's a datafile for the USERS tablespace, and the file number/incarnation pair 259.627432977 ensures uniqueness if you decide to create another ASM datafile for the USERS tablespace.

Numeric Names

Numeric names are used only when referencing an existing ASM file. This allows you to refer to an existing ASM file by only the disk group name and the file number/incarnation pair. The numeric name for the ASM file in the preceding section is

```
+DATA.259.627432977
```

Alias Names

An alias can be used when either referencing an existing object or creating a single ASM file. Using the ALTER DISKGROUP ADD ALIAS command, a more readable name can be created for an existing or a new ASM file, and it's distinguishable from a regular ASM filename because it does not end in a dotted pair of numbers (the file number/incarnation pair), as shown here:

```
SQL> alter diskgroup data
  2      add directory '+data/purch';
Diskgroup altered.

SQL> alter diskgroup data
  2      add alias '+data/purch/users.dbf'
  3      for '+data/dw/datafile/users.259.627432977';
Diskgroup altered.

SQL>
```

Alias with Template Names

An alias with a template can only be used when creating a new ASM file. Templates provide a shorthand for specifying a file type and a tag when creating a new ASM file. Here's an example of an alias using a template for a new tablespace in the +DATA disk group:

```
SQL> create tablespace users2 datafile '+data(datafile)';
Tablespace created.
```

The template DATAFILE specifies COARSE striping, MIRROR for a normal-redundancy group, and HIGH for a high-redundancy group; it is the default for a datafile. Because we did not fully qualify the name, the ASM name for this diskgroup is as follows:

```
+DATA/dw/datafile/users2.267.627782171
```

I'll talk more about ASM templates in the upcoming section "ASM File Types and Templates."

Incomplete Names

An incomplete filename format can be used either for single-file or multiple-file creation operations. Only the disk group name is specified, and a default template is used depending on the type of file, as shown here:

```
SQL> create tablespace users5 datafile '+data1';
Tablespace created.
```

Incomplete Names with Template

As with incomplete ASM filenames, an incomplete filename with a template can be used either for single-file or multiple-file creation operations. Regardless of the actual file type, the template name determines the characteristics of the file.

Even though we are creating a tablespace in the following example, the striping and mirroring characteristics of an online log file (fine striping) are used for the new tablespace instead as the attributes for the datafile (coarse striping):

```
SQL> create tablespace users6 datafile '+data1(onlinelog)';
Tablespace created.
```

ASM File Types and Templates

ASM supports all types of files used by the database except for operating system executables. Table 4-4 contains the complete list of ASM file types; the ASM File Type and Tag columns are those presented previously for ASM file naming conventions.

The default ASM file templates referenced in the last column of Table 4-4 are presented in Table 4-5.

When a new disk group is created, a set of ASM file templates copied from the default templates in Table 4-5 is saved with the disk group; as a result, individual template characteristics can be changed and apply only to the disk group where they reside. In other words, the DATAFILE system template in disk group +DATA1 may have the default coarse striping, but the DATAFILE template in disk group +DATA2 may have fine striping. You can create your own templates in each disk group as needed.

When an ASM datafile is created with the DATAFILE template, by default the datafile is 100MB and autoextensible, and the maximum size is 32,767MB (32GB).

Administering ASM Disk Groups

Using ASM disk groups benefits you in a number of ways: I/O performance is improved, availability is increased, and the ease with which you can add a disk to a disk group or add an entirely new disk group enables you to manage many more databases in the same amount of time. Understanding the

Oracle File Type	ASM File Type	Tag	Default Template
Control files	controlfile	cf (control file) or bcf (backup control file)	CONTROLFILE
Data files	datafile	tablespace name.file#	DATAFILE
Online logs	online_log	log_thread#	ONLINELOG
Archive logs	archive_log	parameter	ARCHIVELOG
Temp files	temp	tablespace name.file#	TEMPFILE
RMAN datafile backup piece	backupset	Client specified	BACKUPSET
RMAN incremental backup piece	backupset	Client specified	BACKUPSET
RMAN archive log backup piece	backupset	Client specified	BACKUPSET
RMAN datafile copy	datafile	tablespace name.file#	DATAFILE
Initialization parameters	init	spfile	PARAMETERFILE
Broker config	drc	drc	DATAGUARDCONFIG
Flashback logs	rlog	thread#_log#	FLASHBACK
Change tracking bitmap	ctb	bitmap	CHANGETRACKING
Auto backup	autobackup	Client specified	AUTOBACKUP
Data Pump dumpset	dumpset	dump	DUMPSET
Cross-platform data files			XTRANSPORT

TABLE 4-4. *ASM File Types*

components of a disk group as well as correctly configuring a disk group are important goals for a successful DBA.

In this section, I'll delve more deeply into the details of the structure of a disk group. Also, I'll review the different types of administrative tasks related to disk groups and show how disks are assigned to failure groups; how disk groups are mirrored; and how disk groups are created, dropped, and altered. At the command line, I'll give you an introduction to the **asmcmd** command-line utility that you can use to browse, copy, and manage ASM objects.

Disk Group Architecture

As defined earlier in this chapter, a disk group is a collection of physical disks managed as a unit. Every ASM disk, as part of a disk group, has an ASM disk name that is either assigned by the DBA or automatically assigned when it is assigned to the disk group.

Files in a disk group are striped on the disks using either coarse striping or fine striping. *Coarse striping* spreads files in units of 1MB each across all disks. Coarse striping is appropriate for a system with a high degree of concurrent small I/O requests, such as an OLTP environment. Alternatively, *fine striping* spreads files in units of 128KB, is appropriate for traditional data warehouse environments or OLTP systems with low concurrency, and maximizes response time for individual I/O requests.

System Template	External Redundancy	Normal Redundancy	High Redundancy	Striping
CONTROLFILE	Unprotected	Two-way mirroring	Three-way mirroring	Fine
DATAFILE	Unprotected	Two-way mirroring	Three-way mirroring	Coarse
ONLINELOG	Unprotected	Two-way mirroring	Three-way mirroring	Fine
ARCHIVELOG	Unprotected	Two-way mirroring	Three-way mirroring	Coarse
TEMPFILE	Unprotected	Two-way mirroring	Three-way mirroring	Coarse
BACKUPSET	Unprotected	Two-way mirroring	Three-way mirroring	Coarse
XTRANSPORT	Unprotected	Two-way mirroring	Three-way mirroring	Coarse
PARAMETERFILE	Unprotected	Two-way mirroring	Three-way mirroring	Coarse
DATAGUARDCONFIG	Unprotected	Two-way mirroring	Three-way mirroring	Coarse
FLASHBACK	Unprotected	Two-way mirroring	Three-way mirroring	Fine
CHANGETRACKING	Unprotected	Two-way mirroring	Three-way mirroring	Coarse
AUTOBACKUP	Unprotected	Two-way mirroring	Three-way mirroring	Coarse
DUMPSET	Unprotected	Two-way mirroring	Three-way mirroring	Coarse

TABLE 4-5. *ASM File Template Defaults*

Disk Group Mirroring and Failure Groups

Before defining the type of mirroring within a disk group, you must group disks into failure groups. A *failure group* is one or more disks within a disk group that share a common resource, such as a disk controller, whose failure would cause the entire set of disks to be unavailable to the group. In most cases, an ASM instance does not know the hardware and software dependencies for a given disk. Therefore, unless you specifically assign a disk to a failure group, each disk in a disk group is assigned to its own failure group.

Once the failure groups have been defined, you can define the mirroring for the disk group; the number of failure groups available within a disk group can restrict the type of mirroring available for the disk group. There are three types of mirroring available: external redundancy, normal redundancy, and high redundancy.

External Redundancy External redundancy requires only one disk location and assumes that the disk is not critical to the ongoing operation of the database or that the disk is managed externally with high-availability hardware such as a RAID controller.

Normal Redundancy Normal redundancy provides two-way mirroring and requires at least two failure groups within a disk group. Failure of one of the disks in a failure group does not cause any downtime for the disk group or any data loss other than a slight performance hit for queries against objects in the disk group; when all disks in the failure group are online, read performance is typically improved because the requested data is available on more than one disk.

High Redundancy High redundancy provides three-way mirroring and requires at least three failure groups within a disk group. The failure of disks in two out of the three failure groups is for the most part transparent to the database users, as in normal redundancy mirroring.

Mirroring is managed at a very low level. Extents, not disks, are mirrored. In addition, each disk will have a mixture of both primary and mirrored (secondary and tertiary) extents on each disk. Although a slight amount of overhead is incurred for managing mirroring at the extent level, it provides the advantage of spreading out the load from the failed disk to all other disks instead of a single disk.

Disk Group Dynamic Rebalancing

Whenever you change the configuration of a disk group—whether you are adding or removing a failure group or a disk within a failure group—dynamic rebalancing occurs automatically to proportionally reallocate data from other members of the disk group to the new member of the disk group. This rebalance occurs while the database is online and available to users; any impact to ongoing database I/O can be controlled by adjusting the value of the initialization parameter ASM_POWER_LIMIT to a lower value.

Not only does dynamic rebalancing free you from the tedious and often error-prone task of identifying hot spots in a disk group, it also provides an automatic way to migrate an entire database from a set of slower disks to a set of faster disks while the entire database remains online. Faster disks are added as a new failure group in the existing disk group with the slower disks and the automatic rebalance occurs. After the rebalance operations complete, the failure groups containing the slower disks are dropped, leaving a disk group with only fast disks. To make this operation even faster, both the ADD and DROP operations can be initiated within the same ALTER DISKGROUP command.

As an example, suppose you want to create a new disk group with high redundancy to hold tablespaces for a new credit card authorization. Using the view V$ASM_DISK, you can view all disks discovered using the initialization parameter ASM_DISKSTRING, along with the status of the disk (in other words, whether it is assigned to an existing disk group or is unassigned). Here is the command:

```
SQL> select group_number, disk_number, name,
  2       failgroup, create_date, path from v$asm_disk;

GROUP_NUMBER DISK_NUMBER NAME       FAILGROUP  CREATE_DA PATH
------------ ----------- ---------- ---------- --------- ---------------
           0           0                                 /dev/sdj1
           0           1                                 /dev/sdk1
           0           2                                 /dev/sdl1
```

```
         0          3                                    /dev/sdm1
         2          1 RECOV_0001 RECOV_0001 08-JUL-13 /dev/sdg1
         2          0 RECOV_0000 RECOV_0000 08-JUL-13 /dev/sdh1
         1          1 DATA_0001  DATA_0001  08-JUL-13 /dev/sdd1
         1          0 DATA_0000  DATA_0000  08-JUL-13 /dev/sde1

8 rows selected.

SQL>
```

Out of the eight disks available for ASM, only four of them are assigned to two disk groups, DATA and RECOV, each in its own failure group. The disk group name can be obtained from the view V$ASM_DISKGROUP:

```
SQL> select group_number, name, type, total_mb, free_mb
  2       from v$asm_diskgroup;

GROUP_NUMBER NAME       TYPE     TOTAL_MB    FREE_MB
------------ ---------- ------ ---------- ----------
           1 DATA       NORMAL      24568      20798
           2 RECOV      NORMAL      24568      24090

SQL>
```

Note that if you had a number of ASM disks and disk groups, you could have joined the two views on the GROUP_NUMBER column and filtered the query result by GROUP_NUMBER. Also, you see from V$ASM_DISKGROUP that both of the disk groups are NORMAL REDUNDANCY groups consisting of two disks each.

Your first step is to create the disk group:

```
SQL> create diskgroup data2 high redundancy
  2         failgroup fg1 disk '/dev/sdj1' name d2a
  3         failgroup fg2 disk '/dev/sdk1' name d2b
  4         failgroup fg3 disk '/dev/sdl1' name d2c
  5         failgroup fg4 disk '/dev/sdm1' name d2d;

Diskgroup created.

SQL>
```

Looking at the dynamic performance views, you see the new disk group available in V$ASM_DISKGROUP and the failure groups in V$ASM_DISK:

```
SQL> select group_number, name, type, total_mb, free_mb
  2     from v$asm_diskgroup;

GROUP_NUMBER NAME       TYPE     TOTAL_MB    FREE_MB
------------ ---------- ------ ---------- ----------
           1 DATA       NORMAL      24568      20798
           2 RECOV      NORMAL      24568      24090
           3 DATA2      HIGH        16376      16221
```

```
SQL> select group_number, disk_number, name,
  2       failgroup, create_date, path from v$asm_disk;

GROUP_NUMBER DISK_NUMBER NAME       FAILGROUP  CREATE_DA PATH
------------ ----------- ---------- ---------- --------- ---------------
           3           3 D2D        FG4        13-JUL-13 /dev/sdj1
           3           2 D2C        FG3        13-JUL-13 /dev/sdk1
           3           1 D2B        FG2        13-JUL-13 /dev/sdl1
           3           0 D2A        FG1        13-JUL-13 /dev/sdm1
           2           1 RECOV_0001 RECOV_0001 08-JUL-13 /dev/sdg1
           2           0 RECOV_0000 RECOV_0000 08-JUL-13 /dev/sdh1
           1           1 DATA_0001  DATA_0001  08-JUL-13 /dev/sdd1
           1           0 DATA_0000  DATA_0000  08-JUL-13 /dev/sde1

8 rows selected.

SQL>
```

However, if disk space is tight, you don't need four members; for a high-redundancy disk group, only three failure groups are necessary, so you drop the disk group and re-create it with only three members:

```
SQL> drop diskgroup data2;

Diskgroup dropped.
```

If the disk group has any database objects other than disk group metadata, you have to specify the INCLUDING CONTENTS clause in the DROP DISKGROUP command. This is an extra safeguard to make sure that disk groups with database objects are not accidentally dropped. Here is the command:

```
SQL> create diskgroup data2 high redundancy
  2     failgroup fg1 disk '/dev/raw/raw5' name d2a
  3     failgroup fg2 disk '/dev/raw/raw6' name d2b
  4     failgroup fg3 disk '/dev/raw/raw7' name d2c;

Diskgroup created.

SQL> select group_number, disk_number, name,
  2        failgroup, create_date, path from v$asm_disk;

GROUP_NUMBER DISK_NUMBER NAME       FAILGROUP  CREATE_DA PATH
------------ ----------- ---------- ---------- --------- ---------------
           0           3                       13-JUL-13 /dev/sdj1
           3           2 D2C        FG3        13-JUL-13 /dev/sdk1
           3           1 D2B        FG2        13-JUL-13 /dev/sdl1
           3           0 D2A        FG1        13-JUL-13 /dev/sdm1
           2           1 RECOV_0001 RECOV_0001 08-JUL-13 /dev/sdg1
           2           0 RECOV_0000 RECOV_0000 08-JUL-13 /dev/sdh1
```

```
         1            1 DATA_0001  DATA_0001  08-JUL-13 /dev/sdd1
         1            0 DATA_0000  DATA_0000  08-JUL-13 /dev/sde1

8 rows selected.
SQL>
```

Now that the configuration of the new disk group has been completed, you can create a tablespace in the new disk group from the database instance:

```
SQL> create tablespace users3 datafile '+DATA2';
Tablespace created.
```

Because ASM files are OMF, you don't need to specify any other characteristics when you create the tablespace.

Disk Group Fast Mirror Resync

Mirroring the files in your disk groups improves performance and availability; when a failed disk in a disk group is repaired and brought back online, however, the re-mirroring of the entire new disk can be time consuming. There are occasions when a disk in a disk group needs to be brought offline because of a disk controller failure; the entire disk does not need remirroring, and only the data changed during the failed disk's downtime needs to be resynced. As a result, you can use the ASM fast mirror resync feature introduced in Oracle Database 11*g*.

To implement fast mirror resync, you set the time window within which ASM will not automatically drop the disk in the disk group when a transient planned or unplanned failure occurs. During the transient failure, ASM keeps track of all changed data blocks so that when the unavailable disk is brought back online, only the changed blocks need to be remirrored instead of the entire disk.

To set a time window for the DATA disk group, you must first set the compatibility level of the disk group to 11.1 or higher for both the RDBMS instance and the ASM instance (this only needs to be done once for the disk group):

```
SQL> alter diskgroup data set attribute
  2     'compatible.asm' = '12.1.0.0.0';

Diskgroup altered.

SQL> alter diskgroup data set attribute
  2     'compatible.rdbms' = '12.1.0.0.0';

Diskgroup altered.

SQL>
```

The only side effect to using a higher compatibility level for the RDBMS and ASM instance is that only other instances with a version number 12.1.0.0.0 or higher can access this disk group. Next, set the disk group attribute DISK_REPAIR_TIME as in this example:

```
SQL> alter diskgroup data set attribute
  2     'disk_repair_time' = '2.5h';

Diskgroup altered.

SQL>
```

The default disk repair time is 3.6 hours, which should be more than adequate for most planned and unplanned (transient) outages. Once the disk is back online, run this command to notify the ASM instance that the disk DATA_0001 is back online:

```
SQL> alter diskgroup data online disk data_0001;

Diskgroup altered.

SQL>
```

This command starts the background procedure to copy all changed extents on the remaining disks in the disk group to the disk DATA_0001 that is now back online.

Altering Disk Groups

Disks can be added and dropped from a disk group; also, most characteristics of a disk group can be altered without re-creating the disk group or impacting user transactions on objects in the disk group.

When a disk is added to a disk group, a rebalance operation is performed in the background after the new disk is formatted for use in the disk group. As mentioned earlier in this chapter, the speed of the rebalance is controlled by the initialization parameter ASM_POWER_LIMIT.

Continuing with our example in the preceding section, suppose you decide to improve the I/O characteristics of the disk group DATA by adding the last available disk to the disk group, as follows:

```
SQL> alter diskgroup data
  2      add failgroup d1fg3 disk '/dev/sdj1' name d1c;

Diskgroup altered.
```

The command returns immediately and the formatting and rebalancing continue in the background. You then check the status of the rebalance operation by checking the view V$ASM_OPERATION:

```
SQL> select group_number, operation, state, power, actual,
  2      sofar, est_work, est_rate, est_minutes from v$asm_operation;

GROUP_NUMBER OPERA STAT POWER ACTUA SOFAR EST_WORK EST_RATE EST_MINUTES
------------ ----- ---- ----- ----- ----- -------- -------- -----------
           1 REBAL RUN      1     1     3      964       60          16
```

Because the estimate for completing the rebalance operation is 16 minutes, you decide to allocate more resources to the rebalance operation and change the power limit for this particular rebalance operation:

```
SQL> alter diskgroup data rebalance power 700;
Diskgroup altered.
```

Checking the status of the rebalance operation confirms that the estimated time to completion has been reduced to 2 minutes instead of 16:

```
SQL> select group_number, operation, state, power, actual,
  2      sofar, est_work, est_rate, est_minutes from v$asm_operation;

GROUP_NUMBER OPERA STAT POWER ACTUA SOFAR EST_WORK EST_RATE EST_MINUTES
------------ ----- ---- ----- ----- ----- -------- -------- -----------
           1 REBAL RUN    700     8    16      605      118           2
```

About four minutes later, you check the status once more:

```
SQL> /
no rows selected
```

Finally, you can confirm the new disk configuration from the V$ASM_DISK and V$ASM_DISKGROUP views:

```
SQL> select group_number, disk_number, name,
  2  failgroup, create_date, path from v$asm_disk;

GROUP_NUMBER DISK_NUMBER NAME       FAILGROUP  CREATE_DA PATH
------------ ----------- ---------- ---------- --------- ---------------
           1           2 D1C        D1FG3      13-JUL-13 /dev/sdj1
           3           2 D2C        FG3        13-JUL-13 /dev/sdk1
           3           1 D2B        FG2        13-JUL-13 /dev/sdl1
           3           0 D2A        FG1        13-JUL-13 /dev/sdm1
           2           1 RECOV_0001 RECOV_0001 08-JUL-13 /dev/sdg1
           2           0 RECOV_0000 RECOV_0000 08-JUL-13 /dev/sdh1
           1           1 DATA_0001  DATA_0001  08-JUL-13 /dev/sdd1
           1           0 DATA_0000  DATA_0000  08-JUL-13 /dev/sde1

8 rows selected.

SQL> select group_number, name, type, total_mb, free_mb
  2      from v$asm_diskgroup;

GROUP_NUMBER NAME       TYPE     TOTAL_MB    FREE_MB
------------ ---------- ------ ---------- ----------
           1 DATA       NORMAL      28662      24814
           2 RECOV      NORMAL      24568      24090
           3 DATA2      HIGH        12282      11820

SQL>
```

Note that the disk group DATA is still normal redundancy, even though it has three failure groups. The I/O performance of SELECT statements against objects in the DATA disk group will not necessarily be improved due to additional copies of extents available in the disk group, but

ALTER DISKGROUP Command	Description
alter diskgroup ... drop disk	Removes a disk from a failure group within a disk group and performs an automatic rebalance
alter diskgroup ... drop ... add	Drops a disk from a failure group and adds another disk, all in the same command
alter diskgroup ... mount	Makes a disk group available to all instances
alter diskgroup ... dismount	Makes a disk group unavailable to all instances
alter diskgroup ... check all	Verifies the internal consistency of the disk group

TABLE 4-6. *Disk Group ALTER Commands*

the availability of the disk group will be higher since it can tolerate the loss of one disk and still maintain normal redundancy.

Other disk group ALTER commands are listed in Table 4-6.

Using the asmcmd Command

The **asmcmd** utility, added in Oracle 10*g* Release 2, is a command-line utility that provides you an easy way to browse and maintain objects within ASM disk groups by using a command set similar to Linux shell commands such as **ls** and **mkdir**. The hierarchical nature of objects maintained by the ASM instance lends itself to a command set similar to what you would use to browse and maintain files in a Linux file system.

Before you can use **asmcmd**, you must ensure that the environment variables ORACLE_BASE, ORACLE_HOME, and ORACLE_SID are set to point to the ASM instance; for the ASM instance used in this chapter, these variables are set as follows:

```
ORACLE_BASE=/u01/app/oracle
ORACLE_HOME=/u01/app/oracle/product/12.1.0/grid
ORACLE_SID=+ASM
```

In addition, you must be logged into the operating system as a user in the dba group, since the **asmcmd** utility connects to the database with SYSDBA privileges. The operating system user is usually **oracle** but can be any other user in the dba group.

You can use **asmcmd** one command at a time by using the format **asmcmd *command***, or you can start **asmcmd** interactively by typing just **asmcmd** at the Linux shell prompt. To get a list of available commands, use **help** from the ASMCMD> for more details. Table 4-7 lists the **asmcmd** commands and a brief description of their purpose; the **asmcmd** commands available only in Oracle Database 11*g* and 12*c* are noted in the middle column.

When you start **asmcmd**, you start out at the root node of the ASM instance's file system; unlike in a Linux file system, the root node is designated by a plus sign (+) instead of a leading forward slash (/), although subsequent directory levels use a forward slash. In this example, you

asmcmd Command	11g, 12c Only	Description
cd		Change the directory to the specified directory.
cp	Y	Copy files between ASM disk groups, both in the same instance and in remote instances.
du		Recursively displays total disk space usage for the current directory and all subdirectories.
exit		Terminate **asmcmd** and return to the operating system shell prompt.
find		Find all occurrences of the name (using wildcards as well), starting with the specified directory.
help		List the **asmcmd** commands.
ls		List the contents of the current directory.
lsct		List information about current ASM client databases.
lsdg		List all disk groups and their attributes.
lsdsk	Y	List all disks visible to this ASM instance.
md_backup	Y	Create metadata backup script for specified disk groups.
md_restore	Y	Restore disk groups from a backup.
mkalias		Create an alias for system-generated ASM filenames.
mkdir		Create an ASM directory.
pwd		Display the current ASM directory.
remap	Y	Repair a range of corrupted or damaged physical blocks on a disk.
rm		Remove ASM files or directories.
rmalias		Remove an ASM alias, but not the target of the alias.

TABLE 4-7. *asmcmd Command Summary*

start **asmcmd** and query the existing disk groups, along with the total disk space used within all disk groups:

```
[oracle@dw ~]$ asmcmd
ASMCMD> ls -l
State    Type    Rebal  Unbal  Name
MOUNTED  NORMAL  N      N      DATA/
MOUNTED  HIGH    N      N      DATA2/
MOUNTED  NORMAL  N      N      RECOV/
ASMCMD> du
Used_MB      Mirror_used_MB
   2143                4399
ASMCMD> pwd
+
ASMCMD>
```

As with the Linux shell **ls** command, you can append **–l** to get a more detailed listing of the objects retrieved by the command. The **ls** command shows the three disk groups in the ASM instance used throughout this chapter, +DATA, +DATA2, and +RECOV.

Note also that the **du** command only shows the used disk space and total disk space used across mirrored disk groups; to get the amount of free space in each disk group, use the **lsdg** command instead.

In this example, you want to find all files that have the string **user** in the filename:

```
ASMCMD> pwd
+
ASMCMD> find . user*
+DATA/DW/DATAFILE/USERS.259.627432977
+DATA/DW/DATAFILE/USERS2.267.627782171
+DATA/purch/users.dbf
+DATA2/DW/DATAFILE/USERS3.256.627786775
ASMCMD> ls -l +DATA/purch/users.dbf
Type      Redund  Striped  Time      Sys  Name
                                     N    users.dbf =>
                                          +DATA/DW/DATAFILE/USERS.259.627432977
ASMCMD>
```

Note the line with **+DATA/purch/users.dbf**: the **find** command finds all ASM objects; in this case, it finds an alias as well as datafiles that match the pattern.

Finally, you can perform file backups to external file systems or even other ASM instances. This example uses the **cp** command to back up the database's SPFILE to the **/tmp** directory on the host's file system:

```
ASMCMD> pwd
+data/DW
ASMCMD> ls
CONTROLFILE/
DATAFILE/
ONLINELOG/
PARAMETERFILE/
TEMPFILE/
spfiledw.ora
ASMCMD> cp spfiledw.ora /tmp/BACKUPspfiledw.ora
source +data/DW/spfiledw.ora
target /tmp/BACKUPspfiledw.ora
copying file(s)...
file, /tmp/BACKUPspfiledw.ora, copy committed.
ASMCMD> exit
[oracle@dw ~]$ ls -l /tmp/BACKUP*
-rw-r-----  1 oracle oinstall 2560 Jul 13 09:47 /tmp/BACKUPspfiledw.ora
[oracle@dw ~]$
```

This example also shows how all database files for the database **dw** are stored within the ASM file system. It looks like they are stored on a traditional host file system, but instead are managed by ASM, providing built-in performance and redundancy features (optimized for use with Oracle Database 12*c*), making the DBA's life a bit easier when it comes to datafile management.

Summary

Oracle Database provides you with a wealth of tools to easily manage your tablespaces and datafiles. If you are creating smallfile tablespaces, you can manage tablespace size at the datafile level; if you create your tablespaces as bigfile tablespaces you can manage disk space and other attributes at the tablespace level. There are very few reasons why you wouldn't want to create all new tablespaces as bigfile tablespaces.

Using ASM for your disk storage provides both ease of use and performance benefits. The setup of an ASM instance only takes a few steps and once it's set up you may never have to change any parameters of the ASM instance. When you have to add or drop disks from an ASM disk group, Oracle automatically relocates database objects across all disks to maintain performance; no manual rebalancing operation is required. It's automatic! If you must really dig deep into the internal ASM disk structure, Oracle provides an OS command called **asmcmd** which gives you Linux-like access to the directory structure within the ASM disk groups.

PART II

Database Management

CHAPTER 5

Developing and Implementing Applications

Managing application development can be a difficult process. From a DBA's perspective, the best way to manage the development process is to become an integral part of teams involved in the process. In this chapter, you will learn the guidelines for migrating applications into databases and the technical details needed for implementation, including the sizing of database objects.

This chapter focuses on the design and creation of applications that use the database. These activities should be integrated with the database-planning activities described in Chapter 3 and Chapter 4. The following chapters in this part of the book address the monitoring and tuning activities that follow the database creation.

Implementing an application in a database by merely running a series of CREATE TABLE commands fails to integrate the creation process with the other major areas (planning, monitoring, and tuning). The DBA must be involved in the application development process in order to correctly design the database that will support the end product. The methods described in this chapter will also provide important information for structuring the database monitoring and tuning efforts.

The first section of this chapter addresses overall design and implementation considerations that directly impact performance. The following sections focus on implementation details such as resource management, sizing tables and indexes, quiescing the database for maintenance activities, and managing packaged applications.

Tuning by Design: Best Practices

At least 50 percent of the time—conservatively—performance problems are designed into an application. During the design of the application and the related database structures, the application architects may not know all the ways in which the business will use the application data over time. As a result, there may be some components whose performance is poor during the initial release, whereas other problems will appear later as the business usage of the application changes and increases.

In some cases, the fix will be relatively straightforward: changing an initialization parameter, adding an index, or rescheduling large operations to off-hours. In other cases, the problem cannot be fixed without altering the application's architecture. For example, an application may be designed to heavily reuse functions for all data access so that functions call other functions, which call additional functions, even to perform the simplest database actions. As a result, a single database call may result in tens of thousands of function calls and database accesses. Such an application will usually not scale well; as more users are added to the system, the CPU burden of the number of executions per user will slow the performance for the individual users. Tuning the individual SQL statements executed as part of that application may yield little performance benefit; the statements themselves may be well-tuned already. Rather, it is the sheer number of executions that leads to the performance problem.

The following best practices may seem overly simplistic, but they are violated over and over in database applications, and those violations directly result in performance problems. There are always exceptions to the rules. The next change to your software or environment may allow you to violate the rules without affecting your performance. In general, though, following these rules will allow you to meet performance requirements as the application usage increases.

Do As Little As Possible

End users do not care, in general, if the underlying database structures are fully normalized to Fifth Normal Form or if they are laid out in compliance with object-oriented standards. Users want to perform a business process, and the database application should be a tool that helps that business process complete as quickly as possible. The focus of your design should not be the achievement of theoretical design perfection; it should always be on the end user's ability to do his or her job. Therefore, you should simplify the processes involved at every step in the application.

This can be a difficult point to negotiate with application development teams. If application development teams or enterprise architects insist on perfectly normalized data models, DBAs should point out the number of database steps involved in even the simplest transaction. For example, INSERTs for a complex transaction (such as a line item for an invoice) may involve many code table lookups as well as multiple INSERTs. For a single user this may not present a problem, but with many concurrent users this design may lead to performance issues or locking issues. From a performance-planning perspective, INSERTs should involve as few tables as possible, and queries should retrieve data that is already stored in a format that is as close as possible to the final format requested by the users. Fully normalized databases and object-oriented designs tend to require a high number of joins during complex queries. Although you should strive to maintain a manageable data model, the first emphasis should be on the functionality of the application and its ability to meet the business's performance needs.

In Your Application Design, Strive to Eliminate Logical Reads

In the past, there was a heavy focus on eliminating physical reads. Although this is still a good idea, no physical reads occur unless logical reads require them.

Let's take a simple example. Select the current time from DUAL using the SYSDATE function. If you need the time to an accuracy of one second, the value will change 86,400 times per day. Yet there are application designers who repeatedly perform this query, executing it millions of times per day. Such a query likely performs few physical reads throughout the day. Therefore, if you are focused solely on tuning the physical I/O, you would likely disregard it. However, it can significantly impact the performance of the application. How? By using the CPU resources available. Each execution of the query will force Oracle to perform work, using processing power to find and return the correct data. As more and more users execute the command repeatedly, you may find that the number of logical reads used by the query exceeds all other queries. In some cases, multiple processors on the server are dedicated to servicing repeated small queries of this sort. If multiple users need to read the same data, you should store it in a table or in a package variable.

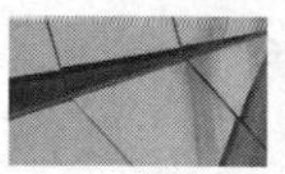

NOTE

*Even though the DUAL table has been an internal (memory-based) table since Oracle Database 10g, accessing it will not generate consistent gets as long as you don't use * as the column list in a query referencing DUAL.*

Consider the following real-world example. A programmer wanted to implement a pause in a program, forcing it to wait 30 seconds between two steps. Because the performance of the environment would not be consistent over time, the programmer coded the routine in the following format (shown in pseudo-code):

```
perform Step 1
select SysDate from DUAL into a StartTime variable
begin loop
   select SysDate from DUAL in a CurrentTime variable;
   Compare CurrentTime with the StartTime variable value.
   If 30 seconds have passed, exit the loop;
      Otherwise repeat the loop, calculating SysDate again.
end loop
Perform Step 2.
```

Is this a reasonable approach? Absolutely not! It will do what the developer wanted, but at a significant cost to the application. What's more, there is nothing a DBA can do to improve its performance. In this case, the cost will not be due to I/O activity, as the DUAL table will stay in the instance's memory area, but rather due to CPU activity. Every time this program is run, by every user, the database will spend 30 seconds consuming as many CPU resources as the system can support. In this particular case the SELECT SYSDATE FROM DUAL query accounts for over 40 percent of all the CPU time used by the application. All of that CPU time is wasted. Tuning the database initialization parameters will not solve the problem. Tuning the individual SQL statement will not help; the application design must be revised to eliminate the needless execution of commands. For instance, in this case the developer could have used a SLEEP command at the operating system level or within a PL/SQL program using the DBMS_LOCK.SLEEP procedure to enforce the same behavior without the database accesses.

For those who still favor tuning based on the buffer cache hit ratio (wait-based tuning is preferable in 11*g* and 12*c*), this database has a hit ratio of almost 100 percent due to the high number of completely unnecessary logical reads without related physical reads. The buffer cache hit ratio compares the number of logical reads to the number of physical reads; if 10 percent of the logical reads require physical reads, the buffer cache hit ratio is 90 percent. Low hit ratios identify databases that perform a high number of physical reads; extremely high hit ratios such as found in this example may identify databases that perform an excessive number of logical reads. You must look beyond the buffer cache hit ratio to the commands that are generating the logical reads and the physical reads.

In Your Application Design, Strive to Avoid Trips to the Database

Remember that you are tuning an application, not a query. When tuning database operations, you may need to combine multiple queries into a single procedure so that the database can be visited once rather than multiple times for each screen. This bundled-query approach is particularly relevant for "thin-client" applications that rely on multiple application tiers. Look for queries that are interrelated based on the values they return, and see if there are opportunities to transform them into single blocks of code. The goal is not to make a monolithic query that will never complete; the goal is to avoid doing work that does not need to be done. In this case, the constant back-and-forth communication between the database server, the application server, and the end user's computer is targeted for tuning.

This problem is commonly seen on complex data-entry forms in which each field displayed on the screen is populated via a separate query. Each of those queries is a separate trip to the database. As with the example in the previous section, the database is forced to execute large numbers of related queries. Even if each of those queries is tuned, the burden from the number of commands multiplied by the number of users will consume a large percentage of the CPU resources available on the server. Such a design may also impact the network usage, but the network is seldom the problem: the issue is the number of times the instance is accessed.

Within your packages and procedures, you should strive to eliminate unnecessary database accesses. Store commonly needed values in local variables instead of repeatedly querying the database. If you don't need to make a trip to the database for information, don't make it. That sounds simple, but you would be amazed at how often application developers fail to consider this advice.

There is no initialization parameter that can make this change take effect. It is a design issue and requires the active involvement of developers, designers, DBAs, and application users in the application performance planning and tuning process.

For Reporting Systems, Store the Data the Way the Users Will Query It

If you know which queries will be executed, such as via parameterized reports, you should strive to store the data so that Oracle will do as little work as possible to transform the format of the data in your tables into the format presented to the user. This may require the creation and maintenance of materialized views or reporting tables. That maintenance is, of course, extra work for the database and DBA to perform—but it is performed in batch mode and does not directly affect the end user. The end user, on the other hand, benefits from the ability to perform the query faster. The database as a whole will perform fewer logical and physical reads because the accesses to the base tables to populate and refresh the materialized views are performed infrequently when compared to the end-user queries against the views.

Avoid Repeated Connections to the Database

Opening a database connection may take more time than the commands you execute within that connection. If you need to connect to the database, keep the connection open and reuse the connection. See Chapter 17 for more information on Oracle Net and optimizing database connections.

One application designer took normalization to the extreme, moving all code tables into their own database. As a result, most operations in the order-processing system repeatedly opened database links to access the code tables, thus severely hampering the performance of the application. Again, tuning the database initialization parameters is not going to lead to the greatest performance benefit; the application is slow by design.

Use the Right Indexes

In an effort to eliminate physical reads, some application developers create numerous indexes on every table. Aside from their impact on data load times, many of the indexes may never be needed to support queries. In OLTP applications, you should not use bitmap indexes; if a column has few distinct values, you should consider leaving it unindexed. The optimizer supports "skip-scan" index accesses, so it may choose an index on a set of columns even if the leading column of the index is not a limiting condition for the query. For platforms such as Oracle Exadata, you may need very few if any indexes at all to run a query as fast as possible with the added bonus of not needing to maintain those indexes during DML operations.

Do It As Simply As Possible

Once you have eliminated the performance costs of unnecessary logical reads, unneeded database trips, unmanaged connections, and inappropriate indexes, take a look at the commands that remain.

Go Atomic

You can use SQL to combine many steps into one large query. In some cases, this may benefit your application: you can create stored procedures and reuse the code and thus reduce the number of database trips performed. However, you can take this too far, creating large queries that fail to complete quickly enough. These queries commonly include multiple sets of grouping operations, inline views, and complex multi-row calculations against millions of rows.

If you are performing batch operations, you may be able to break such a query into its atomic components, creating temporary tables to store the data from each step. If you have an operation that takes hours to complete, you almost always can find a way to break it into smaller component parts. Divide and conquer the performance problem.

For example, a batch operation may combine data from multiple tables, perform joins and sorts, and then insert the result into a table. On a small scale, this may perform satisfactorily. On a large scale, you may have to divide this operation into multiple steps:

1. Create a work table (possibly as an Oracle global temporary table). Insert rows into it from one of the source tables for the query, selecting only those rows and columns that you care about later in the process.
2. Create a second work table for the columns and rows from the second table.
3. Create any needed indexes on the work tables. Note that all the steps to this point can be parallelized: the inserts, the queries of the source tables, and the creation of the indexes.
4. Perform the join, again parallelized. The join output may go into another work table.
5. Perform any sorts needed. Sort as little data as possible.
6. Insert the data into the target table.

Why go through all these steps? Because you can tune them individually, you may be able to tune them to complete much faster individually than Oracle can complete them as a single command. For batch operations, you should consider making the steps as simple as possible. You will need to manage the space allocated for the work tables, but this approach can generate significant benefits to your batch-processing performance.

Eliminate Unnecessary Sorts

As part of the example in the preceding section, the sort operation was performed last. In general, sort operations are inappropriate for OLTP applications. Sort operations do not return any rows to the user until the entire set of rows is sorted. Row operations, on the other hand, return rows to the user as soon as those rows are available.

Consider the following simple test: Perform a full table scan of a large table. As soon as the query starts to execute, the first rows are displayed. Now, perform the same full table scan but add an ORDER BY clause on an unindexed column. No rows will be displayed until all the rows have been sorted. Why does this happen? Because for the second query Oracle performs a SORT ORDER BY operation on the results of the full table scan. Because it is a set operation, the set must be completed before the next operation is performed.

Now, imagine an application in which there are many queries executed within a procedure. Each of the queries has an ORDER BY clause. This turns into a series of nested sorts: no operation can start until the one before it completes.

Note that UNION operations perform sorts. If it is appropriate for the business logic, use a UNION ALL operation in place of a UNION, because a UNION ALL does not perform a sort.

NOTE
A UNION ALL operation does not eliminate duplicate rows from the result set, so it may generate more rows and therefore different results than a UNION.

Eliminate the Need to Use Undo

When performing a query, Oracle will need to maintain a read-consistent image of the rows queried. If a row is modified by another user, the database will need to query the undo segment to see the row as it existed at the time your query began. Application designs that call for queries to frequently access data that others may be changing at the same time force the database to do more work: it has to look in multiple locations for one piece of data. Again, this is a design issue. DBAs may be able to configure the undo segment areas to reduce the possibility of queries encountering "Snapshot too old" errors, but correcting the fundamental problem requires a change to the application design.

Tell the Database What It Needs to Know

Oracle's optimizer relies on statistics when it evaluates the thousands of possible paths to take during the execution of a query. How you manage those statistics can significantly impact the performance of your queries.

Keep Your Statistics Updated

How often should you gather statistics? With each major change to the data in your tables, you should collect statistics on those tables. If you have partitioned the tables, you can analyze them on a partition-by-partition basis. As of Oracle Database 10*g*, you can use the Automatic Statistics Gathering feature to automate the collection of statistics. By default, that process gathers statistics during a maintenance window from 10 P.M. to 6 A.M. each night and all day on weekends. Of course, manual statistics gathering is still available when you have volatile tables that are being dropped or deleted during the day, or when bulk-loaded tables increase in size by more than 10 percent. For partitioned tables on Oracle Database 11*g* or 12*c*, incremental statistics keep global statistics up to date when partition-level statistics are created or updated. Oracle Database 12*c* takes statistics gathering to a new level by allowing concurrent statistics collection on tables in a schema or partitions within a table. In addition, a new hybrid histogram type in Oracle Database 12*c* combines a height-based histogram with a frequency histogram.

Because the analysis job is usually a batch operation performed after hours, you can tune it by improving sort and full table scan performance at the session level. If you are performing the analysis manually, increase the settings for the DB_FILE_MULTIBLOCK_READ_COUNT parameter at the session level or the PGA_AGGREGATE_TARGET parameter at the system level to gathering the statistics. If you are not using PGA_AGGREGATE_TARGET or do not want to modify a system-wide setting, increase SORT_AREA_SIZE (which is modifiable at the session level) instead. The result will be enhanced performance for the sorts and full table scans the analysis performs.

CAUTION
Increasing the DB_FILE_MULTIBLOCK_READ_COUNT parameter in a RAC database environment can cause performance problems when too many blocks are shipped across the interconnect. This value is platform-dependent but is 1MB on most platforms.

Hint Where Needed

In most cases, the cost-based optimizer (CBO) selects the most efficient execution path for queries. However, you may have information about a better path. You may give Oracle a hint to influence the join operations, the overall query goal, the specific indexes used, or the parallelism of the query.

Maximize the Throughput in the Environment

In an ideal environment, there is never a need to query information outside the buffer cache; all of the data stays in memory all of the time. Unless you are working with a very small database, however, this is not a realistic approach. In this section, you will see guidelines for maximizing the throughput of the environment.

Use the Appropriate Database Block Size

You should use an 8KB block size for all tablespaces unless otherwise recommended by Oracle support or if you have rows with a very large average row length greater than 8KB. All Oracle development and testing, especially for database appliances such as Exadata, uses 8KB block sizes.

Design to Throughput, Not Disk Space

If you take an application that is running on eight 256GB disks and move it to a single 2TB disk, will the application run faster or slower? In general, it will run slower because the throughput of the single disk is unlikely to be equal to the combined throughput of the eight separate disks. Rather than designing your disk layout based on the space available (a common method), design it based on the throughput of the disks available. You may decide to use only part of each disk. The remaining space on the disk will not be used by the production application unless the throughput available for that disk improves.

Avoid the Use of the Temporary Segments

Whenever possible, perform all sorts in memory. Any operation that writes to the temporary segments is potentially wasting resources. Oracle uses temporary segments when the SORT_AREA_SIZE parameter (or PGA_AGGREGATE_TARGET, if it is used) does not allocate enough memory to support the sorting requirements of operations. Sorting operations include index creations, ORDER BY clauses, statistics gathering, GROUP BY operations, and some joins. As noted earlier in this chapter, you should strive to sort as few rows as possible. When performing the sorts that remain, perform them in memory.

Divide and Conquer Your Data

If you cannot avoid performing expensive operations on your database, you can attempt to split the work into more manageable chunks. Often you can severely limit the number of rows acted on by your operations, substantially improving performance.

Use Partitions

Partitions can benefit end users, DBAs, and application support personnel. For end users, there are two potential benefits: improved query performance and improved availability for the database. Query performance may improve because of *partition elimination*. The optimizer knows which partitions may contain the data requested by a query. As a result, the partitions that will not participate are eliminated from the query process. Because fewer logical and physical reads are needed, the query should complete faster.

NOTE
The Partitioning Option is an extra-cost option for the Enterprise Edition of the database software.

The availability improves because of the benefits partitions generate for DBAs and application support personnel. Many administrative functions can be performed on single partitions, allowing the rest of the table to be unaffected. For example, you can truncate a single partition of a table. You can split a partition, move it to a different tablespace, or switch it with an existing table (so that the previously independent table is then considered a partition). You can gather statistics on one partition at a time. All these capabilities narrow the scope of administrative functions, reducing their impact on the availability of the database as a whole.

Use Materialized Views

You can use materialized views to divide the types of operations users perform against your tables. When you create a materialized view, you can direct users to query the materialized view directly or you can rely on Oracle's query rewrite capability to redirect queries to the materialized view. As a result, you will have two copies of the data—one that services the input of new transactional data, and a second (the materialized view) that services queries. As a result, you can take one of them offline for maintenance without affecting the availability of the other. Also, the materialized view can pre-join tables and pre-generate aggregations so that user queries perform as little work as possible.

Use Parallelism

Almost every major operation can be parallelized, including queries, inserts, object creations, and data loads. The parallelism options allow you to involve multiple processors and I/O channels in the execution of a single command, effectively dividing the command into multiple smaller coordinated commands. As a result, the command may perform better. You can specify a degree of parallelism at the object level and can override it via hints in your queries.

Test Correctly

In most development methodologies, application testing has multiple phases, including module testing, full system testing, and performance stress testing. Many times, the full system test and performance stress test are not performed adequately due to time constraints as the application nears its delivery deadline. The result is that applications are released into production without any way to guarantee that the functionality and performance of the application as a whole will meet the needs of the users. This is a serious and significant flaw and should not be tolerated by any user of the application. Users do not need just one component of the application to function properly; they need the entire application to work properly in support of a business process. If they cannot do a day's worth of business in a day, the application fails.

This is a key tenet regarding identifying the need for tuning: *If the application slows the speed of the business process, it should be tuned.* The tests you perform must be able to determine if the application will hinder the speed of the business process under the expected production load.

Test with Large Volumes of Data

As described earlier in this chapter, objects within the database function differently after they have been used for some time. For example, a table's PCTUSED setting may make it likely that blocks will be only half-used or rows will be chained. Each of these scenarios causes performance problems that will only be seen after the application has been used for some time.

A further problem with data volume concerns indexes. As a B-tree index grows in size, it may split internally—in other words, an additional level is added to the index. As a result, you can picture the new level as being an index within the index. The additional level in the index increases the negative effect of the index on data load rates. You will not see this impact until *after* the index is split. Applications that work acceptably for the first week or two in production only to suddenly falter after the data volume reaches critical levels do not support the business needs. In testing, there is no substitute for production data loaded at production rates while the tables already contain a substantial amount of data. When leaf blocks are split and index maintenance occurs, Oracle has to lock all branch blocks above the leaf, including the root block. During this maintenance operation, contention will occur from other sessions that need to access the index.

Test with Many Concurrent Users

Testing with a single user does not reflect the expected production usage of most database applications. You must be able to determine if concurrent users will encounter deadlocks, data consistency issues, or performance problems. For example, suppose an application module uses a work table during its processing. Rows are inserted into the table, manipulated, and then queried. A separate application module does similar processing and uses the same table. When executed at the same time, the two processes attempt to use each other's data. Unless you are testing with multiple users executing multiple application functions simultaneously, you may not discover this problem and the business data errors it will generate.

Testing with many concurrent users will also help to identify areas in the application where users frequently use undo segments to complete their queries, thus impacting performance.

Test the Impact of Indexes on Your Load Times

Every INSERT, UPDATE, or DELETE of an indexed column may be slower than the same transaction against an unindexed table. There are some exceptions—sorted data has much less of an impact, for example—but the rule is generally true. The impact is dependent on your operating environment, the data structures involved, and the degree to which the data is sorted.

How many rows per second can you insert in your environment? Perform a series of simple tests. Create a table with no indexes and insert a large number of rows into it. Repeat the tests to reduce the impact of physical reads on the timing results. Calculate the number of rows inserted per second. In most environments you can insert tens of thousands of rows per second into the database. Perform the same test in your other database environments so you can identify any that are significantly different from the others.

Now consider your application. Are you able to insert rows into your tables via your application at anywhere near the rate you just calculated? Many applications run at less than 5 percent of the rate the environment will support. They are bogged down by unneeded indexes or the type of code design issues described earlier in this chapter. If your application's load rate decreases, say, from 40 rows per second to 20 rows per second, your tuning focus should not be solely on how that decrease occurred but also on how the application managed to get only 40 rows per second inserted in an environment that supports thousands of rows inserted per second. Adding another index is easy to do but will add three times the amount of overhead during DML operations (INSERT, DELETE, UPDATE, MERGE).

Make All Tests Repeatable

Most regulated industries have standards for tests. Their standards are so reasonable that *all* testing efforts should follow them. Among the standards is that all tests must be repeatable. To be compliant with the standards, you must be able to re-create the data set used, the exact action performed, the exact result expected, and the exact result seen and recorded. Pre-production tests for validation of the application must be performed on the production hardware. Moving the application to different hardware requires retesting the application. The tester and the business users must sign off on all tests.

Most people, on hearing those restrictions, would agree that they are good steps to take in any testing process. Indeed, your business users may be expecting that the people developing the application are following such standards, even if they are not required by the industry. But are they followed? And if not, then why not? The two commonly cited reasons for not following such standards are time and cost. Such tests require planning, personnel resources, business user involvement, and time for execution and documentation. Testing on production-caliber hardware may require the purchase of additional servers. Those are the most evident costs, but what is the business cost of failing to perform such tests? The testing requirements for validated systems in some healthcare industries were implemented because those systems directly impact the integrity of critical products such as the safety of the blood supply. If your business has critical components served by your application (and if it does not, then why are you building the application?), you must consider the costs of insufficient, rushed testing and communicate those potential costs to the business users. The evaluation of the risks of incorrect data or unacceptably slow performance must involve the business users. In turn, that may lead to an extended deadline to support proper testing.

In many cases, the rushed testing cycle occurs because a testing standard was not in place at the start of the project. If there is a consistent, thorough, and well-documented testing standard in place at the enterprise level when the project starts, the testing cycle will be shorter when it is finally executed. Testers will have known long in advance that repeatable data sets will be needed. Templates for tests will be available. If there is an issue with any test result, or if the application needs to be retested following a change, the test can be repeated. Also, the application users will know that the testing is robust enough to simulate the production usage of the application. In addition, the testing environment must support automation of tasks that will be automated in production, especially if the developers used many manual processes in the development environment. If the system fails the tests for performance reasons, the problem may be a design issue (as described in the previous sections) or a problem with an individual query.

Standard Deliverables

How do you know if an application is ready to be migrated to a production environment? The application development methodology must clearly define, both in format and in level of detail, the required deliverables for each stage of the life cycle. These should include specifications for each of the following items:

- Entity relationship diagram
- Physical database diagram

- Space requirements
- Tuning goals for queries and transaction processing
- Security requirements
- Data requirements
- Query execution plans
- Acceptance test procedures

In the following sections, you will see descriptions of each of these items.

Entity Relationship Diagram

The *entity relationship (E-R) diagram* illustrates the relationships that have been identified among the entities that make up the application. E-R diagrams are critical for providing an understanding of the goals of the system. They also help to identify interface points with other applications and to ensure consistency in definitions across the enterprise.

Physical Database Diagram

A *physical database diagram* shows the physical tables generated from the entities and the columns generated from the defined attributes in the logical model; most, if not all, data modeling tools support the automatic translation of a logical database diagram to the physical database design. A physical database diagramming tool is usually capable of generating the DDL necessary to create the application's objects.

You can use the physical database diagram to identify tables that are most likely to be involved in transactions. You should also be able to identify which tables are commonly used together during a data entry or query operation. You can use this information to effectively plan the distribution of these tables (and their indexes) across the available physical devices (or among ASM disk groups) to reduce the amount of I/O contention encountered.

In data warehousing applications, the physical database diagram should show the aggregations and materialized views accessed by user queries. Although they contain derived data, they are critical components of the data access path and must be documented.

Space Requirements

The space requirements deliverable should show the initial space requirements for each database table and index. The recommendations for the proper size of tables, clusters, and indexes are shown in the "Sizing Database Objects" section later in this chapter.

Tuning Goals for Queries and Transaction Processing

Changes to the application design may have significant impact on the application's performance. Application design choices may also directly affect your ability to tune the application. Because application design has such a great effect on the DBA's ability to tune its performance, the DBA must be involved in the design process.

You must identify the performance goals of a system *before* it goes into production. The role of expectation in perception cannot be overemphasized. If the users have an expectation that the system will be at least as fast as an existing system, anything less will be unacceptable. The estimated response time for each of the most-used components of the application must be defined and approved.

It is important during this process to establish two sets of goals: reasonable goals and "stretch" goals. *Stretch goals* represent the results of concentrated efforts to go beyond the hardware and software constraints that limit the system's performance. Maintaining two sets of performance goals helps to focus efforts on those goals that are truly mission-critical versus those that are beyond the scope of the core system deliverables. In terms of the goals, you should establish control boundaries for query and transaction performance; the application performance will be judged to be "out of control" if the control boundaries are crossed.

Security Requirements

The development team must specify the account structure the application will use, including the ownership of all objects in the application and the manner in which privileges will be granted. All roles and privileges must be clearly defined. The deliverables from this section will be used to generate the account and privilege structure of the production application (see Chapter 10 for a full review of Oracle's security capabilities).

Depending on the application, you may need to specify the account usage for batch accounts separately from that of online accounts. For example, the batch accounts may use the database's automatic login features, whereas the online users have to manually sign in. Your security plans for the application must support both types of users.

Like the space requirements deliverable, security planning is an area in which the DBA's involvement is critical. The DBA should be able to design an implementation that meets the application's needs while fitting in with the enterprise database security plan.

Data Requirements

The methods for data entry and retrieval must be clearly defined. Data-entry methods must be tested and verified while the application is in the test environment. Any special data-archiving requirements of the application must also be documented because they will be application specific.

You must also describe the backup and recovery requirements for the application. These requirements can then be compared to the enterprise database backup plans (see Chapter 13 for guidelines). Any database recovery requirements that go beyond the site's standard will require modifying the site's backup standard or adding a module to accommodate the application's needs.

Query Execution Plans

Execution plans are the steps that the database will go through while executing queries. They are generated via the EXPLAIN PLAN or SET AUTOTRACE commands or the SQL Monitoring tool, as described in Chapter 8. Recording the execution plans for the most important queries against the database will aid in planning the index usage and tuning goals for the application. Generating them prior to production implementation will simplify tuning efforts and identify potential performance problems before the application is released. Generating the explain plans for your most important queries will also facilitate the process of performing code reviews of the application.

If you are implementing a third-party application, you may not have visibility to all the SQL commands the application is generating. As described in Chapter 8, you can use Oracle's automated tuning and monitoring utilities to identify the most resource-intensive queries performed between two points in time; many of the new automated tuning features introduced in Oracle Database 12*c*, such as improved accuracy of automatic degree of parallelism (DOP) and adaptive SQL plan management, can help you fix issues with queries that are not easily visible or accessible.

Acceptance Test Procedures

Developers and users should very clearly define what functionality and performance goals must be achieved before the application can be migrated to production. These goals will form the foundation of the test procedures that will be executed against the application while it is in the test environment.

The procedures should also describe how to deal with unmet goals. The procedures should very clearly list the functional goals that must be met before the system can move forward. A second list of noncritical functional goals should also be provided. This separation of functional capabilities will aid in both resolving scheduling conflicts and structuring appropriate tests.

NOTE
As part of acceptance testing, all interfaces to the application should be tested and their input and output verified.

Resource Management

You can use the Database Resource Manager to control the allocation of system resources among database users. The Database Resource Manager gives DBAs more control over the allocation of system resources than is possible with operating system controls alone.

Implementing the Database Resource Manager

You can use the Database Resource Manager to allocate percentages of system resources to classes of users and jobs. For example, you could allocate 75 percent of the available CPU resources to your online users, leaving 25 percent to your batch users. To use the Database Resource Manager, you will need to create resource plans, resource consumer groups, and resource plan directives.

Prior to using the Database Resource Manager commands, you must create a "pending area" for your work. To create a pending area, use the CREATE_PENDING_AREA procedure of the DBMS_RESOURCE_MANAGER package. When you have completed your changes, use the VALIDATE_PENDING_AREA procedure to check the validity of the new set of plans, subplans, and directives. You can then either submit the changes (via SUBMIT_PENDING_AREA) or clear the changes (via CLEAR_PENDING_AREA). The procedures that manage the pending area do not have any input variables, so a sample creation of a pending area uses the following syntax:

```
execute dbms_resource_manager.create_pending_area();
```

If the pending area is not created, you will receive an error message when you try to create a resource plan.

To create a resource plan, use the CREATE_PLAN procedure of the DBMS_RESOURCE_MANAGER package. The syntax for the CREATE_PLAN procedure is shown in the following listing:

```
CREATE_PLAN
   (plan                        IN VARCHAR2,
    comment                     IN VARCHAR2,
    cpu_mth                     IN VARCHAR2 DEFAULT 'EMPHASIS',
    active_sess_pool_mth        IN VARCHAR2 DEFAULT
'ACTIVE_SESS_POOL_ABSOLUTE',
    parallel_degree_limit_mth   IN VARCHAR2 DEFAULT
          'PARALLEL_DEGREE_LIMIT_ABSOLUTE',
    queueing_mth                IN VARCHAR2 DEFAULT 'FIFO_TIMEOUT')
```

When you create a plan, give the plan a name (in the *plan* variable) and a comment. By default, the CPU allocation method will use the "emphasis" method, allocating CPU resources based on percentage. The following example shows the creation of a plan called DEVELOPERS:

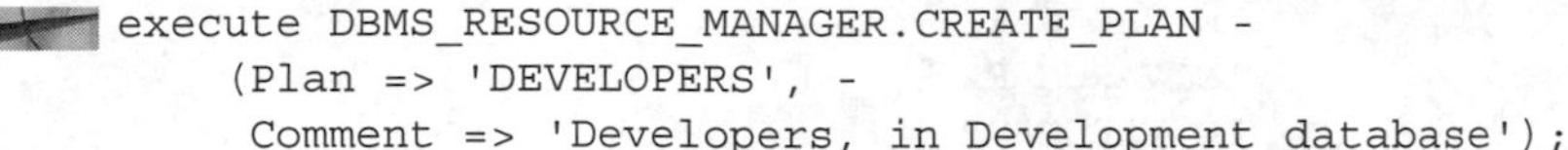

```
execute DBMS_RESOURCE_MANAGER.CREATE_PLAN -
    (Plan => 'DEVELOPERS', -
     Comment => 'Developers, in Development database');
```

NOTE
*The hyphen (-) character is a continuation character in SQL*Plus, allowing a single command to span multiple lines.*

In order to create and manage resource plans and resource consumer groups, you must have the ADMINISTER_RESOURCE_MANAGER system privilege enabled for your session. DBAs have this privilege with the WITH ADMIN OPTION. To grant this privilege to non-DBAs, you must execute the GRANT_SYSTEM_PRIVILEGE procedure of the DBMS_RESOURCE_MANAGER_PRIVS package. The following example grants the user LYNDAG the ability to manage the Database Resource Manager:

```
execute DBMS_RESOURCE_MANAGER_PRIVS.GRANT_SYSTEM_PRIVILEGE -
   (grantee_name => 'LYNDAG',  -
    privilege_name => 'ADMINISTER_RESOURCE_MANAGER', -
    admin_option => TRUE);
```

You can revoke LYNDAG's privileges via the REVOKE_SYSTEM_PRIVILEGE procedure of the DBMS_RESOURCE_MANAGER package.

With the ADMINISTER_RESOURCE_MANAGER privilege enabled, you can create a resource consumer group using the CREATE_CONSUMER_GROUP procedure within DBMS_RESOURCE_MANAGER. The syntax for the CREATE_CONSUMER_GROUP procedure is shown in the following listing:

```
CREATE_CONSUMER_GROUP
    (consumer_group IN VARCHAR2,
     comment        IN VARCHAR2,
     cpu_mth        IN VARCHAR2 DEFAULT 'ROUND-ROBIN')
```

You will be assigning users to resource consumer groups, so give the groups names that are based on the logical divisions of your users. The following example creates two groups—one for online developers and a second for batch developers:

```
execute DBMS_RESOURCE_MANAGER.CREATE_CONSUMER_GROUP -
 (Consumer_Group => 'Online_developers', -
  Comment => 'Online developers');

execute DBMS_RESOURCE_MANAGER.CREATE_CONSUMER_GROUP -
 (Consumer_Group => 'Batch_developers', -
  Comment => 'Batch developers');
```

Once the plan and resource consumer groups are established, you need to create resource plan directives and assign users to the resource consumer groups. To assign directives to a plan, use the CREATE_PLAN_DIRECTIVE procedure of the DBMS_RESOURCE_MANAGER package. The syntax for the CREATE_PLAN_DIRECTIVE procedure is shown in the following listing:

```
CREATE_PLAN_DIRECTIVE
    (plan                      IN VARCHAR2,
     group_or_subplan          IN VARCHAR2,
     comment                   IN VARCHAR2,
     cpu_p1                    IN NUMBER   DEFAULT NULL,
     cpu_p2                    IN NUMBER   DEFAULT NULL,
     cpu_p3                    IN NUMBER   DEFAULT NULL,
     cpu_p4                    IN NUMBER   DEFAULT NULL,
     cpu_p5                    IN NUMBER   DEFAULT NULL,
     cpu_p6                    IN NUMBER   DEFAULT NULL,
     cpu_p7                    IN NUMBER   DEFAULT NULL,
     cpu_p8                    IN NUMBER   DEFAULT NULL,
     active_sess_pool_p1       IN NUMBER   DEFAULT UNLIMITED,
     queueing_p1               IN NUMBER   DEFAULT UNLIMITED,
     parallel_degree_limit_p1  IN NUMBER   DEFAULT NULL,
     switch_group              IN VARCHAR2 DEFAULT NULL,
     switch_time               IN NUMBER   DEFAULT UNLIMITED,
     switch_estimate           IN BOOLEAN  DEFAULT FALSE,
     max_est_exec_time         IN NUMBER   DEFAULT UNLIMITED,
     undo_pool                 IN NUMBER   DEFAULT UNLIMITED,
     max_idle_time             IN NUMBER   DEFAULT NULL,
     max_idle_time_blocker     IN NUMBER   DEFAULT NULL,
     switch_time_in_call       IN NUMBER   DEFAULT NULL);
```

The multiple CPU variables in the CREATE_PLAN_DIRECTIVE procedure support the creation of multiple levels of CPU allocation. For example, you could allocate 75 percent of all your CPU resources (level 1) to your online users. Of the remaining CPU resources (level 2), you could allocate 50 percent to a second set of users. You could split the remaining 50 percent of resources available at level 2 to multiple groups at a third level. The CREATE_PLAN_DIRECTIVE procedure supports up to eight levels of CPU allocations.

The following example shows the creation of the plan directives for the ONLINE_DEVELOPERS and BATCH_DEVELOPERS resource consumer groups within the DEVELOPERS resource plan:

```
execute DBMS_RESOURCE_MANAGER.CREATE_PLAN_DIRECTIVE -
 (Plan => 'DEVELOPERS', -
  Group_or_subplan => 'ONLINE_DEVELOPERS', -
  Comment => 'online developers', -
  Cpu_p1 => 75, -
  Cpu_p2=> 0, -
  Parallel_degree_limit_p1 => 12);

execute DBMS_RESOURCE_MANAGER.CREATE_PLAN_DIRECTIVE -
 (Plan => 'DEVELOPERS', -
  Group_or_subplan => 'BATCH_DEVELOPERS', -
  Comment => 'Batch developers', -
  Cpu_p1 => 25, -
  Cpu_p2 => 0, -
  Parallel_degree_limit_p1 => 6);
```

In addition to allocating CPU resources, the plan directives restrict the parallelism of operations performed by members of the resource consumer group. In the preceding example, batch developers are limited to a degree of parallelism of 6, reducing their ability to consume system resources. Online developers are limited to a degree of parallelism of 12.

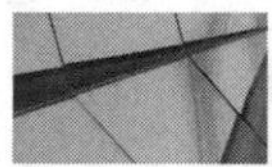

NOTE
*Oracle Database 12*c *includes runaway query management to proactively prevent queries that have hit their limit in one consumer group to affect other consumer groups where that same query may appear.*

To assign a user to a resource consumer group, use the SET_INITIAL_CONSUMER_GROUP procedure of the DBMS_RESOURCE_MANAGER package. The syntax for the SET_INITIAL_CONSUMER_GROUP procedure is shown in the following listing:

```
SET_INITIAL_CONSUMER_GROUP
   (user           IN VARCHAR2,
    consumer_group IN VARCHAR2)
```

If a user has never had an initial consumer group set via the SET_INITIAL_CONSUMER_GROUP procedure, the user is automatically enrolled in the resource consumer group named DEFAULT_CONSUMER_GROUP.

To enable the Resource Manager within your database, set the RESOURCE_MANAGER_PLAN database initialization parameter to the name of the resource plan for the instance. Resource plans can have subplans, so you can create tiers of resource allocations within the instance. If you do not set a value for the RESOURCE_MANAGER_PLAN parameter, resource management is not performed in the instance.

You can dynamically alter the instance to use a different resource allocation plan using the RESOURCE_MANAGER_PLAN initialization parameter; for example, you could create a resource plan for your daytime users (DAYTIME_USERS) and a second for your batch users (BATCH_USERS). You could create a job that each day executes this command at 6:00 A.M.:

```
alter system set resource_manager_plan = 'DAYTIME_USERS';
```

Then at a set time in the evening, you could change consumer groups to benefit the batch users:

```
alter system set resource_manager_plan = 'BATCH_USERS';
```

The resource allocation plan for the instance will thus be altered without needing to shut down and restart the instance.

When using multiple resource allocation plans in this fashion, you need to make sure you don't accidentally use the wrong plan at the wrong time. For example, if the database is down during a scheduled plan change, your job that changes the plan allocation may not execute. How will that affect your users? If you use multiple resource allocation plans, you need to consider the impact of using the wrong plan at the wrong time. To avoid such problems, you should try to minimize the number of resource allocation plans in use.

In addition to the examples and commands shown in this section, you can update existing resource plans (via the UPDATE_PLAN procedure), delete resource plans (via DELETE_PLAN), and cascade the deletion of a resource plan plus all its subplans and related resource consumer groups (DELETE_PLAN_CASCADE). You can update and delete resource consumer groups via the UPDATE_CONSUMER_GROUP and DELETE_CONSUMER_GROUP procedures, respectively. Resource plan directives may be updated via UPDATE_PLAN_DIRECTIVE and deleted via DELETE_PLAN_DIRECTIVE.

When you are modifying resource plans, resource consumer groups, and resource plan directives, you should test the changes prior to implementing them. To test your changes, create a pending area for your work. To create a pending area, use the CREATE_PENDING_AREA procedure of the DBMS_RESOURCE_MANAGER package. When you have completed your changes, use the VALIDATE_PENDING_AREA procedure to check the validity of the new set of plans, subplans, and directives. You can then either submit the changes (via SUBMIT_PENDING_AREA) or clear the changes (via CLEAR_PENDING_AREA). The procedures that manage the pending area do not have any input variables, so a sample validation and submission of a pending area uses the following syntax:

```
execute DBMS_RESOURCE_MANAGER.CREATE_PLAN_DIRECTIVE(
   plan => 'DEVELOPERS', -
   GROUP_OR_SUBPLAN => 'SYS_GROUP', -
   COMMENT => 'System USER SESSIONS AT LEVEL 1', -
   MGMT_P1 => 90, -
   PARALLEL_DEGREE_LIMIT_P1 => 16);
execute DBMS_RESOURCE_MANAGER.VALIDATE_PENDING_AREA();
execute DBMS_RESOURCE_MANAGER.SUBMIT_PENDING_AREA();
```

Switching Consumer Groups

Three of the parameters in the CREATE_PLAN_DIRECTIVE procedure allow sessions to switch consumer groups when resource limits are met. As shown in the previous section, the parameters for CREATE_PLAN_DIRECTIVE include SWITCH_GROUP, SWITCH_TIME, and SWITCH_ESTIMATE.

The SWITCH_TIME value is the length of time, in seconds, a job can run before it is switched to another consumer group. The default SWITCH_TIME value is NULL (unlimited). You should set the SWITCH_GROUP parameter value to the group the session will be switched to once the SWITCH_TIME limit is reached. By default, SWITCH_GROUP is NULL. If you set SWITCH_GROUP to the value CANCEL_SQL, the current call will be canceled when the switch criteria is met. If the SWITCH_GROUP value is KILL_SESSION, the session will be killed when the switch criteria is met.

You can use the third parameter, SWITCH_ESTIMATE, to tell the database to switch the consumer group for a database call before the operation even begins to execute. If you set SWITCH_ESTIMATE to TRUE, Oracle will use its execution time estimate to automatically switch the consumer group for the operation instead of waiting for it to reach the SWITCH_TIME value.

You can use the group-switching features to minimize the impact of long-running jobs within the database. You can configure consumer groups with different levels of access to the system resources and customize them to support fast jobs as well as long-running jobs. The ones that reach the SWITCH_TIME limit will be redirected to the appropriate groups before they even execute.

Using SQL Profiles

As of Oracle 10*g*, you can use SQL profiles to further refine the SQL execution plans chosen by the optimizer. SQL profiles are particularly useful when you are attempting to tune code that you do not have direct access to (for example, within a packaged application). The SQL profile consists of statistics that are specific to the statement, allowing the optimizer to know more about the exact selectivity and cost of the steps in the execution plan.

SQL profiling is part of the automatic tuning capability presented in Chapter 8. Once you accept a SQL profile recommendation, it is stored in the data dictionary. To control a SQL profile's usage you can use a category attribute. See Chapter 8 for further details on the use of the automatic tools for detection and diagnosis of SQL performance issues.

Sizing Database Objects

Choosing the proper space allocation for database objects is critical. Developers should begin estimating space requirements before the first database objects are created. Afterward, the space requirements can be refined based on the actual usage statistics. In the following sections, you will see the space estimation methods for tables, indexes, and clusters. You'll also see methods for determining the proper settings for PCTFREE and PCTUSED.

NOTE

You can enable Automatic Segment Space Management (ASSM) when you create a tablespace; you cannot enable this feature for existing tablespaces. If you are using ASSM, Oracle ignores the PCTUSED, FREELISTS, and FREELIST GROUPS parameters. All new tablespaces should use ASSM and be locally managed.

Why Size Objects?

You should size your database objects for three reasons:

- To preallocate space in the database, thereby minimizing the amount of future work required to manage objects' space requirements
- To reduce the amount of space wasted due to overallocation of space
- To improve the likelihood of a dropped free extent being reused by another segment

You can accomplish all these goals by following the sizing methodology shown in the following sections. This methodology is based on Oracle's internal methods for allocating space to database objects. Rather than rely on detailed calculations, the methodology relies on approximations that will dramatically simplify the sizing process while simplifying the long-term maintainability of the database.

The Golden Rule for Space Calculations

Keep your space calculations simple, generic, and consistent across databases. There are far more productive ways to spend your work time than performing extremely detailed space calculations that Oracle may ignore anyway. Even if you follow the most rigorous sizing calculations, you cannot be sure how Oracle will load the data into the table or index.

In the following section, you'll see how to simplify the space-estimation process, freeing you to perform much more useful DBA functions. These processes should be followed whether you are generating the DEFAULT STORAGE values for a dictionary managed tablespace or the extent sizes for locally managed tablespaces.

The Ground Rules for Space Calculations

Oracle follows a set of internal rules when allocating space:

- Oracle only allocates whole blocks, not parts of blocks.
- Oracle allocates sets of blocks rather than individual blocks.
- Oracle may allocate larger or smaller sets of blocks, depending on the available free space in the tablespace.

Your goal should be to work with Oracle's space-allocation methods instead of against them. If you use consistent extent sizes, you can largely delegate the space allocation to Oracle.

The Impact of Extent Size on Performance

There is no direct performance benefit gained by reducing the number of extents in a table. In some situations (such as for parallel queries), having multiple extents in a table can significantly reduce I/O contention and enhance your performance. Regardless of the number of extents in your tables, they need to be properly sized; as of Oracle Database 10*g*, you should rely on automatic (system-managed) extent allocation if the objects in the tablespace are of varying sizes. Unless you know the precise amount of space you need for each object and the number and size of extents, use AUTOALLOCATE when you create a tablespace, as in this example:

```
create tablespace users12
   datafile '+DATA' size 100m
   extent management local autoallocate;
```

The EXTENT MANAGEMENT LOCAL clause is the default for CREATE TABLESPACE; AUTOALLOCATE is the default for tablespaces with local extent management.

Oracle reads data from tables in two ways: by ROWID (usually immediately following an index access) and via full table scans. If the data is read via ROWID, the number of extents in the table is not a factor in the read performance. Oracle will read each row from its physical location (as specified in the ROWID) and retrieve the data.

If the data is read via a full table scan, the size of your extents can impact performance to a very small degree. When reading data via a full table scan, Oracle will read multiple blocks at a time. The number of blocks read at a time is set via the DB_FILE_MULTIBLOCK_READ_COUNT database initialization parameter and is limited by the operating system's I/O buffer size. For example, if your database block size is 8KB and your operating system's I/O buffer size is 128KB, you can read up to 16 blocks per read during a full table scan. In that case, setting DB_FILE_MULTIBLOCK_READ_COUNT to a value higher than 16 will not affect the performance of the full table scans. Ideally, the product of DB_FILE_MULTIBLOCK_READ_COUNT * BLOCK_SIZE should therefore be 1MB.

Estimating Space Requirements for Tables

You use the CREATE_TABLE_COST procedure of the DBMS_SPACE package to estimate the space required by a table. The procedure determines the space required for a table based on attributes such as the tablespace storage parameters, the tablespace block size, the number of rows, and the average row length. The procedure is valid for both dictionary-managed and locally managed tablespaces.

TIP
When you create a new table using Oracle Cloud Control 12c (or Oracle Enterprise Manager DB Control in previous versions), you can click the Estimate Table Size button to estimate table size for a given estimated row count.

There are two versions of the CREATE_TABLE_COST procedure (it is overloaded so you can use the same procedure both ways). The first version has four input variables: TABLESPACE_NAME, AVG_ROW_SIZE, ROW_COUNT, and PCT_FREE. Its output variables are USED_BYTES and ALLOC_BYTES. The second version's input variables are TABLESPACE_NAME, COLINFOS, ROW_COUNT, and PCT_FREE; its output variables are USED_BYTES and ALLOC_BYTES. Descriptions of the variables are provided in the following table:

Parameter	Description
TABLESPACE_NAME	The tablespace in which the object will be created.
AVG_ROW_SIZE	The average length of a row in the table.
COLINFOS	The description of the columns.
ROW_COUNT	The anticipated number of rows in the table.
PCT_FREE	The pctfree setting for the table.
USED_BYTES	The space used by the table's data. This value includes the overhead due to the pctfree setting and other block features.
ALLOC_BYTES	The space allocated to the table's data, based on the tablespace characteristics. This value takes the tablespace extent size settings into account.

For example, if you have an existing tablespace named USERS, you can estimate the space required for a new table in that tablespace. In the following example, the CREATE_TABLE_COST procedure is executed with values passed for the average row size, the row count, and the PCTFREE setting. The USED_BYTES and ALLOC_BYTES variables are defined and are displayed via the DBMS_OUTPUT.PUT_LINE procedure:

```
declare
   calc_used_bytes NUMBER;
   calc_alloc_bytes NUMBER;
begin
   DBMS_SPACE.CREATE_TABLE_COST (
       tablespace_name => 'USERS',
       avg_row_size => 100,
       row_count => 5000,
       pct_free => 10,
       used_bytes => calc_used_bytes,
       alloc_bytes => calc_alloc_bytes
   );
   DBMS_OUTPUT.PUT_LINE('Used bytes: '||calc_used_bytes);
   DBMS_OUTPUT.PUT_LINE('Allocated bytes: '||calc_alloc_bytes);
end;
/
```

The output of this PL/SQL block will display the used and allocated bytes calculated for these variable settings. You can easily calculate the expected space usage for multiple combinations of space settings prior to creating the table. Here is the output from the preceding example:

```
Used bytes: 66589824
Allocated bytes: 66589824

PL/SQL procedure successfully completed.
```

NOTE
*You must use the SET SERVEROUTPUT ON command to enable the script's output to be displayed within a SQL*Plus session.*

Estimating Space Requirements for Indexes

Similarly, you can use the CREATE_INDEX_COST procedure of the DBMS_SPACE package to estimate the space required by an index. The procedure determines the space required for a table based on attributes such as the tablespace storage parameters, the tablespace block size, the number of rows, and the average row length. The procedure is valid for both dictionary-managed and locally managed tablespaces.

For index space estimations, the input variables include the DDL commands executed to create the index and the name of the local plan table (if one exists). The index space estimates rely on the statistics for the related table. You should be sure those statistics are correct before starting the space-estimation process; otherwise, the results will be skewed.

The variables for the CREATE_INDEX_COST procedure are described in the following table:

Parameter	Description
DDL	The CREATE INDEX command
USED_BYTES	The number of bytes used by the index's data
ALLOC_BYTES	The number of bytes allocated for the index's extents
PLAN_TABLE	The plan table to use (the default is NULL)

Because the CREATE_INDEX_COST procedure bases its results on the table's statistics, you cannot use this procedure until the table has been created, loaded, and analyzed. The following example estimates the space required for a new index on the BOOKSHELF table. The tablespace designation is part of the CREATE INDEX command passed to the CREATE_INDEX_COST procedure as part of the DDL variable value.

```
declare
   calc_used_bytes NUMBER;
   calc_alloc_bytes NUMBER;
begin
   DBMS_SPACE.CREATE_INDEX_COST (
      ddl => 'create index EMP_FN on EMPLOYEES '||
        '(FIRST_NAME) tablespace USERS',
       used_bytes => calc_used_bytes,
      alloc_bytes => calc_alloc_bytes
   );
```

```
    DBMS_OUTPUT.PUT_LINE('Used bytes = '||calc_used_bytes);
    DBMS_OUTPUT.PUT_LINE('Allocated bytes = '||calc_alloc_bytes);
end;
/
```

The output of the script will show the used and allocated bytes values for the proposed index for the employee's first name:

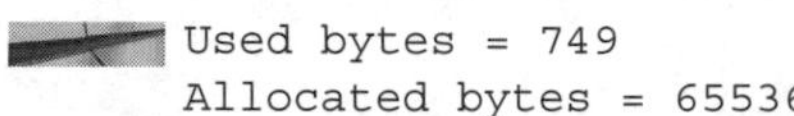

```
Used bytes = 749
Allocated bytes = 65536

PL/SQL procedure successfully completed.
```

Estimating the Proper Value for PCTFREE

The PCTFREE value represents the percentage of *each* data block that is reserved as free space. This space is used when a row that has already been stored in that data block grows in length, either by updates of previously NULL fields or by updates of existing values to longer values. The size of a row can increase (and therefore move the row within a block) during an update when a NUMBER column increases its precision or a VARCHAR2 column increases in length.

There is no single value for PCTFREE that will be adequate for all tables in all databases. To simplify space management, choose a consistent set of PCTFREE values:

- For indexes whose key values are rarely changed: 2
- For tables whose rows seldom change: 2
- For tables whose rows frequently change: 10 to 30

Why maintain free space in a table or index even if the rows seldom change? Oracle needs space within blocks to perform block maintenance functions. If there is not enough free space available (for example, to support a large number of transaction headers during concurrent inserts), Oracle will allocate part of the block's PCTFREE area. You should choose a PCTFREE value that supports this allocation of space. To reserve space for transaction headers in INSERT-intensive tables, set the INITRANS parameter to a non-default value (the minimum is 2). In general, your PCTFREE area should be large enough to hold several rows of data.

NOTE

Oracle automatically allows up to 255 concurrent update transactions for any data block, depending on the available space in the block; the space occupied by the transaction entries will take up no more than half of the block.

Because PCTFREE is tied to the way in which updates occur in an application, determining the adequacy of its setting is a straightforward process. The PCTFREE setting controls the number of rows that are stored in a block in a table. To see if PCTFREE has been set correctly, first determine the number of rows in a block. You can use the DBMS_STATS package to gather statistics. If the PCTFREE setting is too low, the number of migrated rows will steadily increase due to total row length increase. You can monitor the database's V$SYSSTAT view (or the Automatic Workload Repository) for increasing values of the "table fetch continued row" action; these indicate the need for the database to access multiple blocks for a single row.

Chained rows occur when the entire row will not fit in an empty block or the number of columns in a row is greater than 255. As a result, part of the row is stored in the first block and the rest of the row in one or more successive blocks.

NOTE
When rows are moved due to inadequate space in the PCTFREE area, the move is called a row migration. *Row migration will impact the performance of your transactions.*

The DBMS_STATS procedure, while powerful, does not collect statistics on chained rows. You can still use the ANALYZE command, which is otherwise deprecated in favor of DBMS_STATS, to reveal chained rows, as in this example:

```
analyze table employees list chained rows;
```

NOTE
For indexes that will support a large number of INSERTs, PCTFREE may need to be as high as 50 percent if the INSERTs are always in the middle of the index, but otherwise 10 percent is usually adequate for indexes on increasing values of a numeric column.

Reverse Key Indexes

In a reverse key index, the values are stored backwards (in reverse order). For example, a value of 2201 is stored as 1022. If you use a standard index, consecutive values are stored near each other. In a reverse key index, consecutive values are not stored near each other. If your queries do not commonly perform range scans and you are concerned about I/O contention (in a RAC database environment) or concurrency contention (**buffer busy waits** statistic in Automatic Database Diagnostic Monitor) in your indexes, reverse key indexes may be a tuning solution to consider. When sizing a reverse key index, follow the same method used to size a standard index, as shown in the prior sections of this chapter.

There is a downside to reverse key indexes, however: they need a high value for PCTFREE to allow for frequent INSERTs, and must be rebuilt often, more often than a standard B-tree index.

Sizing Bitmap Indexes

If you create a bitmap index, Oracle will dynamically compress the bitmaps generated. The compression of the bitmap may result in substantial storage savings. To estimate the size of a bitmap index, estimate the size of a standard (B-tree) index on the same columns using the methods provided in the preceding sections of this chapter. After calculating the space requirements for the B-tree index, divide that size by 10 to determine the most likely maximum size of a bitmap index for those columns. In general, bitmap indexes will be between 2 and 10 percent of the size of a comparable B-tree index for a bitmap index with low cardinality. The size of the bitmap index will depend on the variability and number of distinct values in the indexed columns; if a bitmap index is created on a high-cardinality column, the space occupied by a bitmap index may exceed the size of a B-tree index on the same column!

NOTE
Bitmap indexes are only available in Oracle Enterprise Edition and Standard Edition One.

Sizing Index-Organized Tables

An index-organized table is stored sorted by its primary key. The space requirements of an index-organized table closely mirror those of an index on all of the table's columns. The difference in space estimation comes in calculating the space used per row, because an index-organized table does not have RowIDs.

The following listing gives the calculation for the space requirement per row for an index-organized table (note that this storage estimate is for the entire row, including its out-of-line storage):

```
Row length for sizing = Average row length
                        + number of columns
                        + number of LOB columns
                        + 2 header bytes
```

Enter this value as the row length when using the CREATE_TABLE_COST procedure for the index-organized table.

Sizing Tables That Contain Large Objects (LOBs)

LOB data (in BLOB or CLOB datatypes) is usually stored apart from the main table. You can use the LOB clause of the CREATE TABLE command to specify the storage attributes for the LOB data, such as a different tablespace. In the main table, Oracle stores a LOB locator value that points to the LOB data. When the LOB data is stored out of line, between 36 and 86 bytes of control data (the LOB locator) remain inline in the row piece.

Oracle does not always store the LOB data apart from the main table. In general, the LOB data is not stored apart from the main table until the LOB data and the LOB locator value total more than 4000 bytes. Therefore, if you will be storing short LOB values, you need to consider their impact on the storage of your main table. If your LOB values are less than 32,768 characters, you may be able to use VARCHAR2 datatypes instead of LOB datatypes in Oracle Database 12c for the data storage, but those VARCHAR2 columns will still be stored out of line as a SecureFile LOB.

NOTE
You can define VARCHAR2 columns up to 32,767 characters in length in Oracle Database 12c if you set the initialization parameter MAX_STRING_SIZE=EXTENDED.

To explicitly specify where the LOB will reside if its size is 4000 bytes or less, use the DISABLE STORAGE IN ROW or ENABLE STORAGE IN ROW clause in the LOB storage clause of the CREATE TABLE statement. If a LOB is stored inline, and its value starts out with a size less than 4000 bytes, it will migrate to out of line. If an out-of-line LOB's size becomes less than 4000 bytes, it stays out of line.

Sizing Partitions

You can create multiple *partitions* of a table. In a partitioned table, multiple separate physical partitions constitute the table. For example, a SALES table may have four partitions: SALES_NORTH,

SALES_SOUTH, SALES_EAST, and SALES_WEST. You should size each of those partitions using the table-sizing methods described earlier in this chapter. You should size the partition indexes using the index-sizing methods shown earlier in this chapter.

Using Global Temporary Tables

You can create global temporary tables (GTTs) to hold temporary data during your application processing. The table's data can be specific to a transaction or maintained throughout a user's session. When the transaction or session completes, the data is truncated from the table.

To create a GTT, use the CREATE GLOBAL TEMPORARY TABLE command. To automatically delete the rows at the end of the transaction, specify ON COMMIT DELETE ROWS, as shown here:

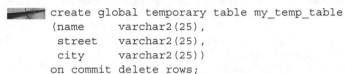

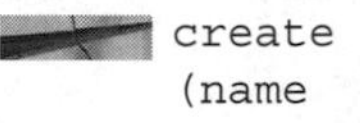

```
create global temporary table my_temp_table
(name      varchar2(25),
 street    varchar2(25),
 city      varchar2(25))
on commit delete rows;
```

You can then insert rows into MY_TEMP_TABLE during your application processing. When you commit, Oracle will truncate MY_TEMP_TABLE. To keep the rows for the duration of your session, specify ON COMMIT PRESERVE ROWS instead.

From the DBA perspective, you need to know if your application developers are using this feature. If they are, you need to account for the space required by their temporary tables during their processing. Temporary tables are commonly used to improve processing speeds of complex transactions, so you may need to balance the performance benefit against the space costs. You can create indexes on temporary tables to further improve processing performance, again at the cost of increased space usage.

NOTE
GTTs and their indexes do not allocate any space until the first INSERT into them occurs. When they are no longer in use, their space is deallocated. In addition, if you are using PGA_AGGREGATE TARGET, Oracle will try to create the tables in memory and will only write them to a temporary tablespace if necessary.

Supporting Tables Based on Abstract Datatypes

User-defined datatypes, also known as abstract datatypes, are a critical part of object-relational database applications. Every abstract datatype has related constructor methods used by developers to manipulate data in tables. Abstract datatypes define the structure of data: for example, an ADDRESS_TY datatype may contain attributes for address data, along with methods for manipulating that data. When you create the ADDRESS_TY datatype, Oracle will automatically create a constructor method called ADDRESS_TY. The ADDRESS_TY constructor method contains parameters that match the datatype's attributes, facilitating inserts of new values into the datatype's format. In the following sections, you will see how to create tables that use abstract datatypes, along with information on the sizing and security issues associated with that implementation.

You can create tables that use abstract datatypes for their column definitions. For example, you could create an abstract datatype for addresses, as shown here:

```
create type address_ty as object
(street    varchar2(50),
city       varchar2(25),
state      char(2),
zip        number);
```

Once the ADDRESS_TY datatype has been created, you can use it as a datatype when creating your tables, as shown in the following listing:

```
create table customer
(name      varchar2(25),
 address    address_ty);
```

When you create an abstract datatype, Oracle creates a constructor method for use during inserts. The constructor method has the same name as the datatype, and its parameters are the attributes of the datatype. When you insert records into the CUSTOMER table, you need to use the ADDRESS_TY datatype's constructor method to insert address values, as shown here:

```
insert into customer values
  ('Joe',address_ty('My Street', 'Some City', 'NY', 10001));
```

In this example, the INSERT command calls the ADDRESS_TY constructor method in order to insert values into the attributes of the ADDRESS_TY datatype.

The use of abstract datatypes increases the space requirements of your tables by 8 bytes for each datatype used. If a datatype contains another datatype, you should add 8 bytes for each of the datatypes.

Using Object Views

The use of abstract datatypes may increase the complexity of your development environment. When you query the attributes of an abstract datatype, you must use a syntax different from the syntax you use against tables that do not contain abstract datatypes. If you do not implement abstract datatypes in all your tables, you will need to use one syntax for some of your tables and a separate syntax for other tables and you will need to know ahead of time which queries use abstract datatypes.

For example, the CUSTOMER table uses the ADDRESS_TY datatype described in the previous section:

```
create table customer
(name      varchar2(25),
 address    address_ty);
```

The ADDRESS_TY datatype, in turn, has four attributes: STREET, CITY, STATE, and ZIP. If you want to select the STREET attribute value from the ADDRESS column of the CUSTOMER table, you may write the following query:

```
select address.street from customer;
```

However, this query will *not* work. When you query the attributes of abstract datatypes, you must use correlation variables for the table names. Otherwise, there may be an ambiguity regarding the object being selected. To query the STREET attribute, use a correlation variable (in this case, "C") for the CUSTOMER table, as shown in the following example:

```
select c.address.street from customer c;
```

As shown in this example, you need to use correlation variables for queries of abstract datatype attributes *even if the query only accesses one table*. There are therefore two features of queries against abstract datatype attributes: the notation used to access the attributes and the correlation variables requirement. In order to implement abstract datatypes consistently, you may need to alter your SQL standards to support 100-percent usage of correlation variables. Even if you use correlation variables consistently, the notation required to access attribute values may cause problems as well, because you cannot use a similar notation on tables that do not use abstract datatypes.

Object views provide an effective compromise solution to this inconsistency. The CUSTOMER table created in the previous examples assumes that an ADDRESS_TY datatype already exists. But what if your tables already exist? What if you had previously created a relational database application and are trying to implement object-relational concepts in your application without rebuilding and re-creating the entire application? What you would need is the ability to overlay object-oriented (OO) structures such as abstract datatypes on existing relational tables. Oracle provides *object views* as a means for defining objects used by existing relational tables.

If the CUSTOMER table already exists, you could create the ADDRESS_TY datatype and use object views to relate it to the CUSTOMER table. In the following listing, the CUSTOMER table is created as a relational table, using only the normally provided datatypes:

```
create table customer
(name         varchar2(25) primary key,
 street       varchar2(50),
 city         varchar2(25),
 state        char(2),
 zip          varchar2(10));
```

If you want to create another table or application that stores information about people and addresses, you may choose to create the ADDRESS_TY datatype. However, for consistency, that datatype should be applied to the CUSTOMER table as well. The following examples will use the ADDRESS_TY datatype created in the preceding section.

To create an object view, use the CREATE VIEW command. Within the CREATE VIEW command, specify the query that will form the basis of the view. The code for creating the CUSTOMER_OV object view on the CUSTOMER table is shown in the following listing:

```
create view customer_ov (name, address) as
select name, address_ty(street, city, state, zip)
from customer;
```

The CUSTOMER_OV view will have two columns: NAME and ADDRESS (the latter is defined by the ADDRESS_TY datatype). Note that you cannot specify OBJECT as an option within the CREATE VIEW command.

Several important syntax issues are presented in this example. When a table is built on existing abstract datatypes, you select column values from the table by referring to the names of the columns (such as NAME) instead of their constructor methods. When creating the object view, however, you refer to the names of the constructor methods (such as ADDRESS_TY) instead. Also, you can use WHERE clauses in the query that forms the basis of the object view. You can therefore limit the rows that are accessible via the object view.

If you use object views, you as the DBA will administer relational tables the same way as you did before. You will still need to manage the privileges for the datatypes (see the following section of this chapter for information on security management of abstract datatypes), but the table and index structures will be the same as they were before the creation of the abstract datatypes. Using the relational structures will simplify your administration tasks while allowing developers to access objects via the object views of the tables.

You can also use object views to simulate the references used by row objects. Row objects are rows within an object table. To create an object view that supports row objects, you need to first create a datatype that has the same structure as the table, as shown here:

```
create or replace type customer_ty as object
(name          varchar2(25),
 street        varchar2(50),
 city          varchar2(25),
 state         char(2),
 zip           varchar2(10));
```

Next, create an object view based on the CUSTOMER_TY type while assigning *object identifier,* or OID, values to the rows in CUSTOMER:

```
create view customer_ov of customer_ty
with object identifier (name) as
select name, street, city, state, zip
from customer;
```

The first part of this CREATE VIEW command gives the view its name (CUSTOMER_OV) and tells Oracle that the view's structure is based on the CUSTOMER_TY datatype. An OID identifies the row object. In this object view, the NAME column will be used as the OID.

If you have a second table that references CUSTOMER via a foreign key or primary key relationship, you can set up an object view that contains references to CUSTOMER_OV. For example, the CUSTOMER_CALL table contains a foreign key to the CUSTOMER table, as shown here:

```
create table customer_call
(name            varchar2(25),
 call_number     number,
 call_date       date,
 constraint customer_call_pk
     primary key (name, call_number),
 constraint customer_call_fk foreign key (name)
    references customer(name));
```

The NAME column of CUSTOMER_CALL references the same column in the CUSTOMER table. Because you have simulated OIDs (called *pkOIDs*) based on the primary key of CUSTOMER, you need to create references to those OIDs. Oracle provides an operator called MAKE_REF that creates the references (called *pkREFs*). In the following listing, the MAKE_REF operator is used to create references from the object view of CUSTOMER_CALL to the object view of CUSTOMER:

```
create view customer_call_ov as
select make_ref(customer_ov, name) name,
       call_number,
       call_date
from customer_call;
```

Within the CUSTOMER_CALL_OV view, you tell Oracle the name of the view to reference and the columns that constitute the pkREF. You could now query CUSTOMER_OV data from within CUSTOMER_CALL_OV by using the DEREF operator on the CUSTOMER_ID column:

```
select deref(ccov.name)
from customer_call_ov ccov
where call_date = trunc(sysdate);
```

You can thus return CUSTOMER data from your query without directly querying the CUSTOMER table. In this example, the CALL_DATE column is used as a limiting condition for the rows returned by the query.

Whether you use row objects or column objects, you can use object views to shield your tables from the object relationships. The tables are not modified; you administer them the way you always did. The difference is that the users can now access the rows of CUSTOMER as if they are row objects.

From a DBA perspective, object views allow you to continue creating and supporting standard tables and indexes while the application developers implement the advanced object-relational features as a layer above those tables.

Security for Abstract Datatypes

The examples in the previous sections assumed that the same user owned the ADDRESS_TY datatype and the CUSTOMER table. What if the owner of the datatype is not the table owner? What if another user wants to create a datatype based on a datatype you have created? In the development environment, you should establish guidelines for the ownership and use of abstract datatypes just as you would for tables and indexes.

For example, what if the account named ORANGE_GROVE owns the ADDRESS_TY datatype, and the user of the account named CON_K tries to create a PERSON_TY datatype? I'll show you the problem with type ownership, and then show you an easy solution later in this section. For example, CON_K executes the following command:

```
create type person_ty as object
(name      varchar2(25),
 address   address_ty);
```

If CON_K does not own the ADDRESS_TY abstract datatype, Oracle will respond to this CREATE TYPE command with the following message:

```
Warning: Type created with compilation errors.
```

The compilation errors are caused by problems creating the constructor method when the datatype is created. Oracle cannot resolve the reference to the ADDRESS_TY datatype because CON_K does not own a datatype with that name.

CON_K will not be able to create the PERSON_TY datatype (which includes the ADDRESS_TY datatype) unless ORANGE_GROVE first grants her EXECUTE privilege on the type. The following listing shows this GRANT command in action:

```
grant execute on address_ty to con_k;
```

NOTE
You must also grant EXECUTE privilege on the type to any user who will perform DML operations on the table.

Now that the proper GRANTs are in place, CON_K can create a datatype that is based on ORANGE_GROVE's ADDRESS_TY datatype:

```
create or replace type person_ty as object
(name      varchar2(25),
 address  orange_grove.address_ty);
```

CON_K's PERSON_TY datatype will now be successfully created. However, using datatypes based on another user's datatypes is not trivial. For example, during INSERT operations, you must fully specify the name of the owner of each type. CON_K can create a table based on her PERSON_TY datatype (which includes ORANGE_GROVE's ADDRESS_TY datatype), as shown in the following listing:

```
create table con_k_customers
(customer_id  number,
 person       person_ty);
```

If CON_K owned the PERSON_TY and ADDRESS_TY datatypes, an INSERT into the CUSTOMER table would use the following format:

```
insert into con_k_customers values
(1,person_ty('John Smith',
   address_ty('522 Main Street','Half Moon Bay','CA','94019-1922')));
```

This command will not work. During the INSERT, the ADDRESS_TY constructor method is used, and ORANGE_GROVE owns it. Therefore, the INSERT command must be modified to specify ORANGE_GROVE as the owner of ADDRESS_TY. The following example shows the corrected INSERT statement, with the reference to ORANGE_GROVE shown in bold:

```
insert into con_k_customers values
(1,person_ty('John Smith',
 orange_grove.address_ty('522 Main Street','Half Moon Bay','CA','94019-1922')));
```

Solving this problem is easy: you can create and use a public synonym for a datatype. Continuing with the previous examples, ORANGE_GROVE can create a public synonym like so and grant EXECUTE privileges on the type:

```
create public synonym pub_address_ty for address_ty;
grant execute on address_ty to public;
```

As a result, any user, including CON_K, can now reference the type using the synonym for creating new tables or types:

```
create or replace type person_ty as object
     (name      varchar2(25),
      address   pub_address_ty);
```

In a relational-only implementation of Oracle, you grant the EXECUTE privilege on procedural objects, such as procedures and packages. Within the object-relational implementation of Oracle, the EXECUTE privilege is extended to cover abstract datatypes as well, as you can see in the example earlier in this section. The EXECUTE privilege is used because abstract datatypes can include methods—in other words, PL/SQL functions and procedures that operate on the datatypes. If you grant someone the privilege to use your datatype, you are granting the user the privilege to execute the methods you have defined on the datatype. Although ORANGE_GROVE did not yet define any methods on the ADDRESS_TY datatype, Oracle automatically creates constructor methods that are used to access the data. Any object (such as PERSON_TY) that uses the ADDRESS_TY datatype uses the constructor method associated with ADDRESS_TY.

You cannot create public types, but as you saw earlier in this section, you can create public synonyms for your types to ease datatype management; one solution would be to create all types using a single schema name and create the appropriate synonyms. The users who reference the type do not have to know the owner of the types to use them effectively.

Indexing Abstract Datatype Attributes

In the preceding example, the CON_K_CUSTOMERS table was created based on a PERSON_TY datatype and an ADDRESS_TY datatype. As shown in the following listing, the CON_K_CUSTOMERS table contains a scalar (non-object-oriented) column CUSTOMER_ID and a PERSON column that is defined by the PERSON_TY abstract datatype:

```
create table george_customers
(customer_id     number,
 person          person_ty);
```

From the datatype definitions shown in the previous section of this chapter, you can see that PERSON_TY has one column, NAME, followed by an ADDRESS column defined by the ADDRESS_TY datatype.

When referencing columns within the abstract datatypes during queries, updates, and deletes, specify the full path to the datatype attributes. For example, the following query returns the CUSTOMER_ID column along with the NAME column. The NAME column is an attribute of the datatype that defines the PERSON column, so you refer to the attribute as PERSON.NAME, as shown here:

```
select c.customer_id, c.person.name
  from con_k_customers c;
```

You can refer to attributes within the ADDRESS_TY datatype by specifying the full path through the related columns. For example, the STREET column is referred to as PERSON.ADDRESS.STREET, which fully describes its location within the structure of the table. In the following example, the CITY column is referenced twice, once in the list of columns to select and once within the WHERE clause:

```
select c.person.name,
       c.person.address.city
  from con_k_customers c
 where c.person.address.city like 'C%';
```

Because the CITY column is used with a range search in the WHERE clause, the optimizer may be able to use an index when resolving the query. If an index is available on the CITY column, Oracle can quickly find all the rows that have CITY values starting with the letter *C,* specified in the predicate.

To create an index on a column that is part of an abstract datatype, you need to specify the full path to the column as part of the CREATE INDEX command. To create an index on the CITY column (which is part of the ADDRESS column), you can execute the following command:

```
create index i_con_k_customers_city
on con_k_customers(person.address.city);
```

This command will create an index named I_CON_K_CUSTOMER_CITY on the PERSON .ADDRESS.CITY column. Whenever the CITY column is accessed, the optimizer will evaluate the SQL used to access the data and determine if the new index can be useful to improve the performance of the access.

When creating tables based on abstract datatypes, you should consider how the columns within the abstract datatypes will be accessed. If, like the CITY column in the previous example, certain columns will commonly be used as part of limiting conditions in queries, they should be indexed. In this regard, the representation of multiple columns in a single abstract datatype may hinder your application performance, because it may obscure the need to index specific columns within the datatype.

When you use abstract datatypes, you become accustomed to treating a group of columns as a single entity, such as the ADDRESS columns or the PERSON columns. It is important to remember that the optimizer, when evaluating query access paths, will consider the columns individually. You therefore need to address the indexing requirements for the columns even when you are using abstract datatypes. In addition, remember that indexing the CITY column in one table that uses the ADDRESS_TY datatype does not affect the CITY column in a second table that uses the ADDRESS_TY datatype. If there is a second table named BRANCH that uses the ADDRESS_TY datatype, then *its* CITY column will not be indexed unless you explicitly create an index for it. Also keep in mind that extra indexes on abstract datatypes adds three times the overhead for each additional index, much like an index on non-abstract datatypes.

Quiescing and Suspending the Database

You can temporarily quiesce or suspend the database during your maintenance operations. Using these options allows you to keep the database open during application maintenance, avoiding the time or availability impact associated with database shutdowns.

While the database is quiesced, no new transactions will be permitted by any accounts other than SYS and SYSTEM. New queries or attempted logins will appear to hang until you unquiesce the database. The quiesce feature is useful when performing table maintenance or complicated data maintenance. To use the quiesce feature, you must first enable the Database Resource Manager, as described earlier in this chapter. In addition, the RESOURCE_MANAGER_PLAN initialization parameter must have been set to a valid plan when the database was started, and it must not have been disabled following database startup.

While logged in as SYS or SYSTEM (other SYSDBA privileged accounts cannot execute these commands), quiesce the database as follows:

```
alter system quiesce restricted;
```

Any non-DBA sessions logged into the database will continue until their current command completes, at which point they will become inactive. Currently inactive sessions will stay quiesced. In Real Application Clusters configurations, all running instances will be quiesced.

To see if the database is in quiesced state, log in as SYS or SYSTEM and execute the following query:

```
select active_state from v$instance;
```

The ACTIVE_STATE column value will be either NORMAL (unquiesced), QUIESCING (active non-DBA sessions are still running), or QUIESCED.

To unquiesce the database, use the following command:

```
alter system unquiesce;
```

Instead of quiescing the database, you can suspend it. A suspended database performs no I/O to its datafiles and control files, allowing the database to be backed up without I/O interference. To suspend the database, use the following command:

```
alter system suspend;
```

NOTE
Do not use the ALTER SYSTEM SUSPEND command unless you have put the database in hot backup mode.

Although the ALTER SYSTEM SUSPEND command can be executed from any SYSDBA privileged account, you can only resume normal database operations from the SYS and SYSTEM accounts. Use SYS and SYSTEM to avoid potential errors while resuming the database operations. In Real Application Clusters configurations, all instances will be suspended. To see the current status of the instance, use the following command:

```
select database_status from v$instance;
```

The database will be either SUSPENDED or ACTIVE. To resume the database, log in as SYS or SYSTEM and execute the following command:

```
alter system resume;
```

Supporting Iterative Development

Iterative development methodologies typically consist of a series of rapidly developed prototypes. These prototypes are used to define the system requirements as the system is being developed. These methodologies are attractive because of their ability to show the customers something tangible as development is taking place. However, there are a few common pitfalls that occur during iterative development that undermine its effectiveness.

First, effective *versioning* is not always used. Creating multiple versions of an application allows certain features to be "frozen" while others are changed. It also allows different sections of the application to be in development while others are in test. Too often, one version of the application is used for every iteration of every feature, resulting in an end product that is not adequately flexible to handle changing needs (which was the alleged purpose of the iterative development).

Second, the prototypes are not always thrown away. Prototypes are developed to give the customer an idea of what the final product will look like; they should not be intended as the foundation of a finished product. Using them as a foundation will not yield the most stable and flexible system possible. When performing iterative development, treat the prototypes as temporary legacy systems.

Third, the divisions between development, test, and production environments are clouded. The methodology for iterative development must very clearly define the conditions that have to be met before an application version can be moved to the next stage. It may be best to keep the prototype development completely separate from the development of the full application.

Finally, unrealistic timelines are often set. The same deliverables that applied to the structured methodology apply to the iterative methodology. The fact that the application is being developed at an accelerated pace does not imply that the deliverables will be any quicker to generate.

Iterative Column Definitions

During the development process, your column definitions may change frequently. You can drop columns from existing tables. You can drop a column immediately, or you can mark it as UNUSED to be dropped at a later time. If the column is dropped immediately, the action may impact performance. If the column is marked as UNUSED, there will be no impact on performance. The column can actually be dropped at a later time when the database is less heavily used.

To drop a column, use either the SET UNUSED clause or the DROP clause of the ALTER TABLE command. You cannot drop a pseudo-column, a column of a nested table, or a partition key column.

In the following example, column COL2 is dropped from a table named TABLE1:

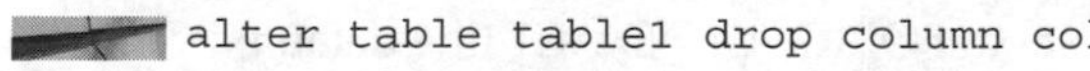

```
alter table table1 drop column col2;
```

You can mark a column as UNUSED, as shown here:

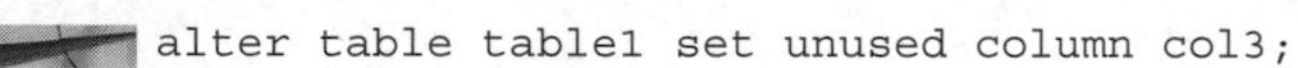

```
alter table table1 set unused column col3;
```

NOTE

As of Oracle Database 12c, you can use SET UNUSED COLUMN . . . ONLINE to prevent blocking locks on the table and therefore enhance availability.

Marking a column as UNUSED does not release the space previously used by the column. You can also drop any unused columns:

```
alter table table1 drop unused columns;
```

You can query USER_UNUSED_COL_TABS, DBA_UNUSED_COL, and ALL_UNUSED_COL_TABS to see all tables with columns marked as UNUSED.

NOTE
Once you have marked a column as UNUSED, you cannot access that column. If you export the table after designating a column as UNUSED, the column will not be exported.

You can drop multiple columns in a single command, as shown in the following example:

```
alter table table1 drop (col4, col5);
```

NOTE
When dropping multiple columns, you should not use the COLUMN keyword of the ALTER TABLE command. The multiple column names must be enclosed in parentheses, as shown in the preceding example.

If the dropped columns are part of primary keys or unique constraints, you will also need to use the CASCADE CONSTRAINTS clause as part of your ALTER TABLE command. If you drop a column that belongs to a primary key, Oracle will drop both the column and the primary key index.

If you cannot immediately arrange for a maintenance period during which you can drop the columns, mark them as UNUSED. During a later maintenance period, you can complete the maintenance from the SYS or SYSTEM account.

Forcing Cursor Sharing

Ideally, application developers should use bind variables in their programs to maximize the reuse of their previously parsed commands in the shared SQL area. If bind variables are not in use, you may see many very similar statements in the library cache: queries that differ only in the literal value in the WHERE clause.

Statements that are identical except for their literal value components are called *similar* statements. Similar statements can reuse previously parsed commands in the shared SQL area if the CURSOR_SHARING initialization parameter is set to FORCE. Use EXACT (the default) if the SQL statements must match exactly including all literals.

NOTE
As of Oracle Database 12c, a value of SIMILAR for CURSOR_SHARING has been deprecated and FORCE should be used instead.

Managing Package Development

Imagine a development environment with the following characteristics:

- None of your standards are enforced.
- Objects are created under the SYS or SYSTEM account.
- Proper distribution and sizing of tables and indexes is only lightly considered.
- Every application is designed as if it were the only application you intend to run in your database.

As undesirable as these conditions are, they are occasionally encountered during the implementation of purchased packaged applications. Properly managing the implementation of packages involves many of the same issues that were described for the application development processes in the previous sections. This section will provide an overview of how packages should be treated so they will best fit with your development environment.

Generating Diagrams

Most CASE tools have the ability to *reverse-engineer* packages into a physical database diagram. Reverse engineering consists of analyzing the table structures and generating a physical database diagram that is consistent with those structures, usually by analyzing column names, constraints, and indexes to identify key columns. However, normally there is no one-to-one correlation between the physical database diagram and the entity relationship diagram. Entity relationship diagrams for packages can usually be obtained from the package vendor; they are helpful in planning interfaces to the package database.

Space Requirements

Most Oracle-based packages provide fairly accurate estimates of their database resource usage during production usage. However, they usually fail to take into account their usage requirements during data loads and software upgrades. You should carefully monitor the package's undo requirements during large data loads. A spare DATA tablespace may be needed as well if the package creates copies of all its tables during upgrade operations.

Tuning Goals

Just as custom applications have tuning goals, packages must be held to tuning goals as well. Establishing and tracking these control values will help to identify areas of the package in need of tuning (see Chapter 8).

Security Requirements

Unfortunately, many packages that use Oracle databases fall into one of two categories: either they were migrated to Oracle from another database system, or they assume they will have full DBA privileges for their object owner accounts.

If the packages were first created on a different database system, their Oracle port very likely does not take full advantage of Oracle's functional capabilities, such as sequences, triggers, and methods. Tuning such a package to meet your needs may require modifying the source code.

If the package assumes that it has full DBA authority, it must not be stored in the same database as any other critical database application. Most packages that require DBA authority do so in order to add new users to the database. You should determine exactly which system-level privileges the package administrator account actually requires (such as CREATE SESSION and CREATE USER, for example). You can create a specialized system-level role to provide this limited set of system privileges to the package administrator.

Packages that were first developed on non-Oracle databases may require the use of the same account as another Oracle-ported package. For example, ownership of a database account called SYSADM may be required by multiple applications. The only way to resolve this conflict with full confidence is to create the two packages in separate databases.

Data Requirements

Any processing requirements that the packages have, particularly on the data-entry side, must be clearly defined. These requirements are usually well documented in package documentation.

Version Requirements

Applications you support may have dependencies on specific versions and features of Oracle. If you use packaged applications, you will need to base your kernel version upgrade plans on the vendor's support for the different Oracle versions. Furthermore, the vendor may switch the optimizer features it supports. For example, it may require that your COMPATIBLE parameter be set to a specific value. Your database environment will need to be as flexible as possible in order to support these changes.

Because of these restrictions outside of your control, you should attempt to isolate the packaged application to its own instance. If you frequently query data across applications, the isolation of the application to its own instance will increase your reliance on database links. You need to evaluate the maintenance costs of supporting multiple instances against the maintenance costs of supporting multiple applications in a single instance.

Execution Plans

Generating execution plans requires accessing the SQL statements that are run against the database. The shared SQL area in the SGA maintains the SQL statements that are executed against the database (accessible via the V$SQL_PLAN view). Matching the SQL statements against specific parts of the application is a time-consuming process. You should attempt to identify specific areas whose functionality and performance are critical to the application's success and work with the package's support team to resolve performance issues. You can use the Automated Workload Repository (see Chapter 8) to gather all the commands generated during testing periods and then determine the explain plans for the most resource-intensive queries in that set. If the commands are still in the shared SQL area, you can see the statistics via V$SQL and the explain plan via V$SQL_PLAN and see both of them using Cloud Control 12*c*.

Acceptance Test Procedures

Purchased packages should be held to the same functional requirements that custom applications must meet. The acceptance test procedures should be developed before the package has been selected; they can be generated from the package-selection criteria. By testing in this manner, you will be testing for the functionality you need rather than what the package developers thought you wanted.

Be sure to specify what your options are in the event the package fails its acceptance test for functional or performance reasons. Critical success factors for the application should not be overlooked just because it is a purchased application.

The Testing Environment

When establishing a testing environment, follow these guidelines:

- It should be larger than your production environment. You need to be able to forecast future performance and test scalability.
- It must contain known data sets, explain plans, performance results, and data result sets.
- It must be used for each release of the database and tools, as well as for new features.
- It must support the generation of multiple test conditions to enable the evaluation of the features' business costs. You do not want to have to rely on point analysis of results; ideally, you can determine the cost/benefit curves of a feature as the database grows in size.
- It must be flexible enough to allow you to evaluate different licensing cost options.
- It must be actively used as a part of your technology implementation methodology.

When testing transaction performance, be sure to track the incremental load rate over time. In general, the indexes on a table will slow the performance of loads when they reach a second internal level. See Chapter 8 for details on indexes and load performance.

When testing, your sample queries should represent each of the following groups:

- Queries that perform joins, including merge joins, nested loops, outer joins, and hash joins
- Queries that use database links
- DML statements that use database links
- Each type of DML statement (INSERT, UPDATE, and DELETE statements)
- Each major type of DDL statement, including table creations, index rebuilds, and grants
- Queries that use parallelism (if that option is in use in your environment)

The sample set should not be fabricated; it should represent your operations, and it must be repeatable. Generating the sample set should involve reviewing your major groups of operations as well as the OLTP operations executed by your users. The result will not reflect every action within the database, but will allow you to be aware of the implications of upgrades and thus allow you to mitigate your risk and make better decisions about implementing new options.

Summary

Creating an effective Oracle database is much more than the CREATE DATABASE command. There are many prerequisites to consider such as the overall architecture of the application: what are the service level agreements with the eventual users of the system? Has the data model been completed and verified to contain the data elements that end users require?

From a development point of view you must decide which Oracle features are best suited for the application and its growth pattern. Using Oracle features such as partitioning, materialized views, and parallelism will ensure adequate response times and efficient use of the database server itself.

Once the database is up and running, your job as a DBA is not over—you must monitor the database to ensure that the SLAs are being met and predict when a hardware upgrade is necessary along with the required disk space needed to ensure that the system will be available when users need it.

CHAPTER 6

Monitoring Space Usage

A good DBA has a toolset in place to monitor the database, both proactively monitoring various aspects of the database, such as transaction load, security enforcement, space management, and performance monitoring, and effectively reacting to any potentially disastrous system problems. Transaction management, performance tuning, memory management, and database security and auditing are covered in Chapters 7 through 10. In this chapter, we'll address how a DBA can effectively and efficiently manage the disk space used by database objects in the different types of tablespaces: the SYSTEM tablespace, the SYSAUX tablespace, temporary tablespaces, undo tablespaces, and tablespaces of different sizes.

To reduce the amount of time it takes to manage disk space, it is important for the DBA not only to understand how the applications will be using the database, but also to provide guidance during the design of the database application. Designing and implementing the database application, including tablespace layouts and expected growth of the database, have been covered in Chapters 3, 4, and 5.

In this chapter, I'll also provide some scripts that need not much more than SQL*Plus and the knowledge to interpret the results. These scripts are good for a quick look at the database's health at a given point in time—for example, to see if there is enough disk space to handle a big SQL*Loader job that evening or to diagnose some response-time issues for queries that normally run quickly.

Oracle provides a number of built-in packages to help the busy DBA manage space and diagnose problems. For example, Oracle Segment Advisor, introduced in Oracle Database 10*g*, helps to determine if a database object has space available for reuse, given how much fragmentation exists in the object. Other features of Oracle, such as Resumable Space Allocation, allow a long-running operation that runs out of disk space to be suspended until the DBA can intervene and allocate enough additional disk space to complete the operation. As a result, the long-running job will not have to be restarted from the beginning.

We'll also cover some of the key data dictionary and dynamic performance views that give us a close look at the structure of the database and a way to optimize space usage. Many of the scripts provided in this chapter use these views.

At the end of this chapter, we'll cover two different methods for automating some of the scripts and Oracle tools: using the DBMS_SCHEDULER built-in package as well as using the Oracle Enterprise Manager (OEM) infrastructure.

Space usage for tablespaces will be the primary focus in this chapter, along with the objects contained within the tablespaces. Other database files, such as control files and redo log files, take up disk space, but as a percentage of the total space used by a database they are small. We will, however, briefly consider how archived log files are managed, because the number of archived log files will increase indefinitely at a pace proportional to how much DML activity occurs in the database. Therefore, a good plan for managing archived log files will help keep disk space usage under control.

Common Space Management Problems

Space management problems generally fall into one of three categories: running out of space in a regular tablespace, not having enough undo space for long-running queries that need a consistent "before" image of the tables, and insufficient space for temporary segments. Although we may still have some fragmentation issues within a database object such as a table or index, locally managed tablespaces solve the problem of tablespace fragmentation.

Each of these three problem areas are addressed by using the techniques described in the following sections.

Running Out of Free Space in a Tablespace

If a tablespace is not defined with the AUTOEXTEND attribute, then the total amount of space in all the datafiles that compose the tablespace limits the amount of data that can be stored in the tablespace. If the AUTOEXTEND attribute is defined, then one or more of the datafiles that compose the tablespace will grow to accommodate the requests for new segments or the growth of existing segments. Even with the AUTOEXTEND attribute, the amount of space in the tablespace is ultimately limited by the amount of disk space on the physical disk drive or storage group. If you have created a bigfile tablespace, you have only one datafile, but that single datafile has the same constraints as a datafile in a smallfile tablespace.

The AUTOEXTEND attribute is the default if you don't specify the SIZE parameter in the CREATE TABLESPACE command and you are using Oracle Managed Files (OMF), so you'll actually have to go out of your way to prevent a datafile from autoextending. In Oracle Database 11*g* or 12*c*, with the initialization parameter DB_CREATE_FILE_DEST set to an ASM or file system location, you can run a CREATE TABLESPACE command like this:

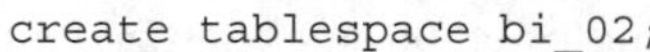

```
create tablespace bi_02;
```

In this case, the tablespace BI_02 is created with the default initial extent size of 100MB in a single datafile, AUTOEXTEND is on, and the next extent is 100MB when the first datafile fills up. In addition, extent management is set to LOCAL, space allocation is AUTOALLOCATE, and segment space management is set to AUTO.

The conclusion to be reached here is that we want to monitor the free and used space within a tablespace to detect trends in space usage over time, and as a result be proactive in making sure that enough space is available for future space requests. You can use the DBMS_SERVER_ALERT package (with a PL/SQL call or via Cloud Control 12*c*) to automatically notify you when a tablespace reaches a warning or critical space threshold level, either at a percent used, space remaining, or both.

Insufficient Space for Temporary Segments

A *temporary segment* stores intermediate results for database operations such as sorts, index builds, DISTINCT queries, UNION queries, or any other operation that necessitates a sort/merge operation that cannot be performed in memory. Temporary segments should be allocated in a temporary tablespace, which was introduced in Chapter 1. Under no circumstances should the SYSTEM tablespace be used for temporary segments; when the database is created, a non-SYSTEM tablespace should be specified as a default temporary tablespace for users who are not otherwise assigned a temporary tablespace. If the SYSTEM tablespace is locally managed (which is preferred and the default since Oracle Database 10*g*), a default temporary tablespace must be defined when the database is created.

When there is not enough space available in the user's default temporary tablespace, and either the tablespace cannot be autoextended or the tablespace's AUTOEXTEND attribute is disabled, the user's query or DML statement fails.

Too Much or Too Little Undo Space Allocated

Undo tablespaces have simplified the management of rollback information by managing undo information automatically within the tablespace. The DBA does not have to define the number and size of the rollback segments for the kinds of activity occurring in the database; as of Oracle 10*g*, manual rollback management has been deprecated.

Not only does an undo segment allow a rollback of an uncommitted transaction, it provides for read consistency of long-running queries that begin before INSERTs, UPDATEs, and DELETEs occur on a table. The amount of undo space available for providing read consistency is under the control of the DBA and is specified as the number of seconds that Oracle will attempt to guarantee that "before" image data is available for long-running queries.

As with temporary tablespaces, we want to make sure we have enough space allocated in an undo tablespace for peak demands without allocating more than is needed. As with any tablespace, we can use the AUTOEXTEND option when creating the tablespace to allow for unexpected growth of the tablespace without reserving too much disk space up front.

Undo segment management is discussed in detail in Chapter 7, whereas the tools to help size the undo tablespaces are discussed later in this chapter.

Fragmented Tablespaces and Segments

A tablespace that is locally managed uses bitmaps to keep track of free space, which, in addition to eliminating the contention on the data dictionary, eliminates wasted space because all extents are either the same size (with uniform extent allocation) or are multiples of the smallest size (with autoallocation). For migrating from a dictionary-managed tablespace, we will review an example that converts a dictionary-managed tablespace to a locally managed tablespace. In a default installation of Oracle Database 10*g* or later using the Database Configuration Assistant (DBCA), all tablespaces, including the SYSTEM and SYSAUX tablespaces, are created as locally managed tablespaces.

By default, starting with Oracle Database 11*g*, you don't need to specify many options in the CREATE TABLESPACE statement to get a locally managed tablespace with Automatic Segment Space Management (ASSM):

```
create tablespace users4
   datafile '+DATA'
   size 250m autoextend on next 250m maxsize 2g
   uniform size 8m;
tablespace USERS4 created.

select tablespace_name, initial_extent, next_extent,
   extent_management, allocation_type, segment_space_management
from dba_tablespaces
where tablespace_name='USERS4';

TABLESPACE_NAME INITIAL_EXTENT NEXT_EXTENT EXTENT_MAN ALLOCATIO SEGMEN
--------------- -------------- ----------- ---------- --------- ------
USERS4                 8388608     8388608 LOCAL      UNIFORM   AUTO
```

Only the UNIFORM clause is required if you want fixed extent sizes; otherwise, the default is AUTOALLOCATE and therefore Oracle manages the extent sizes.

This tablespace will be created with an initial size of 250MB, and it can grow as large as 2000MB (2GB); extents will be locally managed with a bitmap, and every extent in this tablespace will be exactly 8MB in size. Space within each segment (table or index) will be managed automatically with a bitmap instead of freelists.

Even with efficient extent allocation, table and index segments may eventually contain a lot of free space due to UPDATE and DELETE statements. As a result, a lot of unused space can be reclaimed by using some of the scripts provided later in this chapter, as well as by using Oracle Segment Advisor.

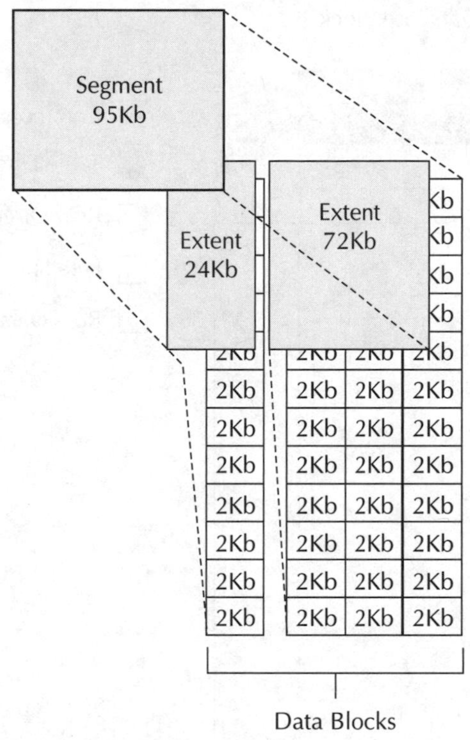

FIGURE 6-1. *Oracle segments, extents, and blocks*

Oracle Segments, Extents, and Blocks

Chapter 1 provided an overview of tablespaces and the logical structures contained within them. Also briefly presented were datafiles, allocated at the operating system level, as the building blocks for tablespaces. Being able to effectively manage disk space in the database requires an in-depth knowledge of tablespaces and datafiles, as well as the components of the segments stored within the tablespaces, such as tables and indexes. At the lowest level, a tablespace segment consists of one or more extents, each extent comprising one or more data blocks. Figure 6-1 shows the relationship between segments, extents, and blocks in an Oracle database.

In the following sections are the details of data blocks, extents, and segments with the focus on space management.

Data Blocks

A *data block* is the smallest unit of storage in the database. Ideally, an Oracle block is a multiple of the operating system block to ensure efficient I/O operations. The default block size for the database is specified with the DB_BLOCK_SIZE initialization parameter; this block size is used for the SYSTEM, TEMP, and SYSAUX tablespaces at database creation and cannot be changed without re-creating the database.

The format for a data block is presented in Figure 6-2.

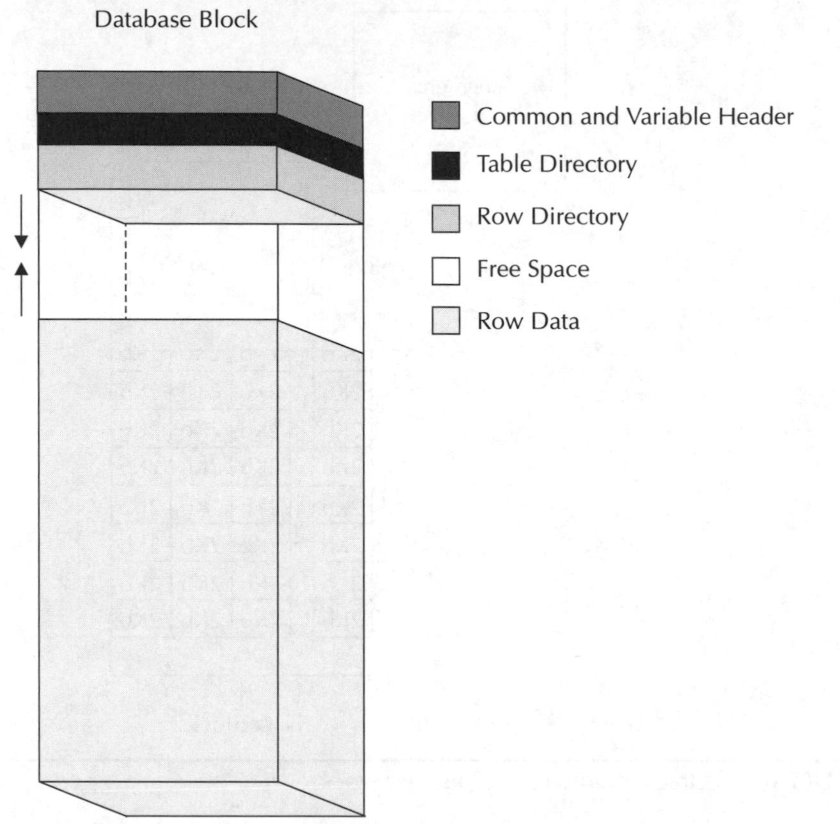

FIGURE 6-2. *Contents of an Oracle data block*

Every data block contains a *header* that specifies what kind of data is in the block: table rows or index entries. The *table directory* section has information about the table with rows in the block; a block can have rows from only one table or entries from only one index, unless the table is a clustered table, in which case the table directory identifies all the tables with rows in this block. The *row directory* provides details of the specific rows of the table or index entries in the block.

The space for the header, table directory, and row directory is a very small percentage of the space allocated for a block; our focus, then, is on the *free space* and *row data* within the block.

Within a newly allocated block, free space is available for new rows and updates to existing rows; the updates may increase or decrease the space allocated for the row if there are varying-length columns in the row or a non-NULL value is changed to a NULL value, or vice versa. Space is available within a block for new inserts until there is less than a certain percentage of space available in the block defined by the PCTFREE parameter, specified when the segment is created. Once there is less than PCTFREE space in the block, no inserts are allowed. If freelists are used to manage space within the blocks of a segment, then new inserts are allowed on the table when used space within the block falls below PCTUSED.

A row may span more than one block if the row size is greater than the block size or an updated row no longer fits into the original block. In the first case, a row that is too big for a block is stored in a *chain* of blocks; this may be unavoidable if a row contains columns that exceed even the largest block size allowed, which in Oracle 11*g* is 32KB.

In the second case, an update to a row in a block may no longer fit in the original block, and as a result Oracle will *migrate* the data for the entire row to a new block and leave a pointer in the first block to point to the location in the second block where the updated row is stored. As you may infer, a segment with many migrated rows may cause I/O performance problems because the number of blocks required to satisfy a query can double. In some cases, adjusting the value of PCTFREE or rebuilding the table may result in better space utilization and I/O performance. More tips on how to improve I/O performance can be found in Chapter 8.

Starting with Oracle9*i* Release 2, you can use Automatic Segment Space Management (ASSM) to manage free space within blocks; you enable ASSM in locally managed tablespaces by using the SEGMENT SPACE MANAGEMENT AUTO keywords in the CREATE TABLESPACE command (although this is the default for locally managed tablespaces).

Using ASSM reduces segment header contention and improves simultaneous insert concurrency; this is because the free space map in a segment is spread out into a bitmap block within each extent of the segment. As a result, you dramatically reduce waits because each process performing INSERT, UPDATE, or DELETE operations will likely be accessing different blocks instead of one freelist or one of a few freelist groups. In addition, each extent's bitmap block lists each block within the extent along with a four-bit "fullness" indicator defined as follows (with room for future expansion from values 6–15):

- **0000** Unformatted block
- **0001** Block full
- **0010** Less than 25 percent free space available
- **0011** 25 percent to 50 percent free space
- **0100** 50 percent to 75 percent free space
- **0101** Greater than 75 percent free space

In a RAC database environment, using ASSM segments means you no longer need to create multiple freelist groups. In addition, you no longer need to specify PCTUSED, FREELISTS, or FREELIST GROUPS parameters when you create a table; if you specify any of these parameters, they are ignored.

Extents

An *extent* is the next level of logical space allocation in a database; it is a specific number of blocks allocated for a specific type of object, such as a table or index. An extent is the minimum number of blocks allocated at one time; when the space in an extent is full, another extent is allocated.

When a table is created, an *initial* extent is allocated. Once the space is used in the initial extent, *incremental* extents are allocated. In a locally managed tablespace, these subsequent extents can either be the same size (using the UNIFORM keyword when the tablespace is created) or optimally sized by Oracle (AUTOALLOCATE). For extents that are optimally sized, Oracle starts with a minimum extent size of 64KB and increases the size of subsequent extents as multiples of the initial extent as the segment grows. In this way, fragmentation of the tablespace is virtually eliminated.

When the extents are sized automatically by Oracle, the storage parameters INITIAL, NEXT, and MINEXTENTS are used as a guideline, along with Oracle's internal algorithm, to determine the best extent sizes. In the following example, a table created in the USERS tablespace (during installation of a new database, the USERS tablespace is created with AUTOALLOCATE enabled) does not use the storage parameters specified in the CREATE TABLE statement:

```
SQL> create table t_autoalloc (c1 char(2000))
  2  storage (initial 1m next 2m)
  3  tablespace users;

Table created.

SQL> begin
  2     for i in 1..3000 loop
  3        insert into t_autoalloc values ('a');
  4     end loop;
  5  end;
  6  /

PL/SQL procedure successfully completed.

SQL>  select segment_name, extent_id, bytes, blocks
  2     from user_extents where segment_name = 'T_AUTOALLOC';

SEGMENT_NAME  EXTENT_ID      BYTES     BLOCKS
------------ ---------- ---------- ----------
T_AUTOALLOC           0      65536          8
T_AUTOALLOC           1      65536          8
. . .
T_AUTOALLOC          15      65536          8
T_AUTOALLOC          16    1048576        128
. . .
T_AUTOALLOC          22    1048576        128

23 rows selected.
```

Unless a table is truncated or the table is dropped, any blocks allocated to an extent remain allocated for the table, even if all rows have been deleted from the table. The maximum number of blocks ever allocated for a table is known as the *high-water mark (HWM).*

Segments

Groups of extents are allocated for a single *segment*. A segment must be wholly contained within one and only one tablespace. Every segment represents one and only one type of database object, such as a table, a partition of a partitioned table, an index, or a temporary segment. For partitioned tables, every partition resides in its own segment; however, a cluster (with two or more tables) resides within a single segment. Similarly, a partitioned index consists of one segment for each index partition.

Temporary segments are allocated in a number of scenarios. When a sort operation cannot fit in memory, such as a SELECT statement that needs to sort the data to perform a DISTINCT, GROUP BY, or UNION operation, a temporary segment is allocated to hold the intermediate results of the sort. Index creation also typically requires the creation of a temporary segment. Because allocation and deallocation of temporary segments occur often, it is highly desirable to create a tablespace specifically to hold temporary segments. This helps to distribute the I/O required for a given operation, and it reduces the possibility that fragmentation may occur in other tablespaces due to the allocation and deallocation of temporary segments. When the database is created, a *default temporary tablespace* can be created for any new users who do not have a specific temporary tablespace assigned; if the SYSTEM tablespace is locally managed (which it should be for any new database), a separate temporary tablespace must be created to hold temporary segments.

How space is managed within a segment depends on how the tablespace containing the block is created. If the tablespace is locally managed (the default and recommended), space in segments can be managed with either freelists or bitmaps. Oracle strongly recommends that all new tablespaces be created as locally managed and that free space within segments be managed automatically with bitmaps. Automatic Segment Space Management allows more concurrent access to the bitmap lists in a segment compared to freelists; in addition, tables that have widely varying row sizes make more efficient use of space in segments that are automatically managed.

As mentioned earlier, in the section titled "Data Blocks," if a segment is created with Automatic Segment Space Management, bitmaps are used to manage the space within the segment. As a result, the PCTUSED, FREELIST, and FREELIST GROUPS keywords within a CREATE TABLE or CREATE INDEX statement are ignored. The three-level bitmap structure within the segment indicates whether blocks below the HWM are full (less than PCTFREE), 0 to 25 percent free, 25 to 50 percent free, 50 to 75 percent free, 75 to 100 percent free, or unformatted.

Data Dictionary Views and Dynamic Performance Views

A number of data dictionary views and dynamic performance views are critical in understanding how disk space is being used in your database. The data dictionary views that begin with DBA_ are of a more static nature, whereas the V$ views, as expected, are of a more dynamic nature and give you up-to-date statistics on how space is being used in the database.

In the next few sections, I'll highlight the space management views and provide some quick examples; later in this chapter, you'll see how these views form the basis of Oracle's space management tools.

DBA_TABLESPACES

The view DBA_TABLESPACES contains one row for each tablespace, whether native or currently plugged in from another database. It contains default extent parameters for objects created in the tablespace that don't specify INITIAL and NEXT values. The EXTENT_MANAGEMENT column indicates whether the tablespace is locally managed or dictionary managed. As of Oracle 10*g*, the column BIGFILE indicates whether the tablespace is a smallfile or a bigfile tablespace. Bigfile tablespaces are discussed later in this chapter.

In the following query we retrieve the tablespace type and the extent management type for all tablespaces within the database:

```
SQL> select tablespace_name, block_size,
  2           contents, extent_management from dba_tablespaces;
```

```
TABLESPACE_NAME                  BLOCK_SIZE CONTENTS  EXTENT_MAN
-------------------------------- ---------- --------- ----------
SYSTEM                                 8192 PERMANENT LOCAL
SYSAUX                                 8192 PERMANENT LOCAL
UNDOTBS1                               8192 UNDO      LOCAL
TEMP                                   8192 TEMPORARY LOCAL
USERS                                  8192 PERMANENT LOCAL
EXAMPLE                                8192 PERMANENT LOCAL
DMARTS                                16384 PERMANENT LOCAL
XPORT                                  8192 PERMANENT LOCAL
USERS2                                 8192 PERMANENT LOCAL
USERS3                                 8192 PERMANENT LOCAL
USERS4                                 8192 PERMANENT LOCAL

11 rows selected.
```

In this example, all the tablespaces are locally managed; in addition, the DMARTS tablespace has a larger block size to improve response time for data mart tables that are typically accessed hundreds or thousands of rows at a time.

DBA_SEGMENTS

The data dictionary view DBA_SEGMENTS has one row for each segment in the database. This view is not only good for retrieving the size of the segment, in blocks or bytes, but also for identifying the owner of the object and the tablespace where an object resides:

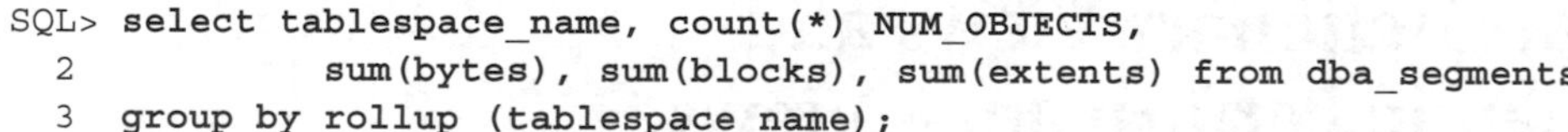

```
SQL> select tablespace_name, count(*) NUM_OBJECTS,
  2           sum(bytes), sum(blocks), sum(extents) from dba_segments
  3  group by rollup (tablespace_name);

TABLESPACE_NAME  NUM_OBJECTS SUM(BYTES) SUM(BLOCKS) SUM(EXTENTS)
---------------- ----------- ---------- ----------- ------------
DMARTS                     2   67108864        4096           92
EXAMPLE                  418   81068032        9896          877
SYSAUX                  5657  759103488       92664         8189
SYSTEM                  1423  732233728       89384         2799
UNDOTBS1                  10   29622272        3616           47
USERS                     44   11665408        1424           73
XPORT                      1  134217728       16384           87
                        7555 1815019520      217464        12164
```

DBA_EXTENTS

The DBA_EXTENTS view is similar to DBA_SEGMENTS, except that DBA_EXTENTS drills down further into each database object. There is one row in DBA_EXTENTS for each extent of each segment in the database, along with the FILE_ID and BLOCK_ID of the datafile containing the extent:

```
SQL> select owner, segment_name, tablespace_name,
  2         extent_id, file_id, block_id, bytes from dba_extents
  3  where segment_name = 'AUD$';
```

```
OWNER    SEGMENT_NAM TABLESPACE  EXTENT_ID    FILE_ID  BLOCK_ID      BYTES
----- ------------ ---------- ---------- ---------- ---------- ----------
SYS      AUD$        SYSTEM              3          1     32407     196608
SYS      AUD$        SYSTEM              4          1     42169     262144
SYS      AUD$        SYSTEM              5          2       289     393216
SYS      AUD$        SYSTEM              2          1     31455     131072
SYS      AUD$        SYSTEM              1          1     30303      65536
SYS      AUD$        SYSTEM              0          1       261      16384
```

In this example, the table AUD$ owned by SYS has extents in two different datafiles that compose the SYSTEM tablespace.

DBA_FREE_SPACE

The view DBA_FREE_SPACE is broken down by datafile number within the tablespace. You can easily compute the amount of free space in each tablespace by using the following query:

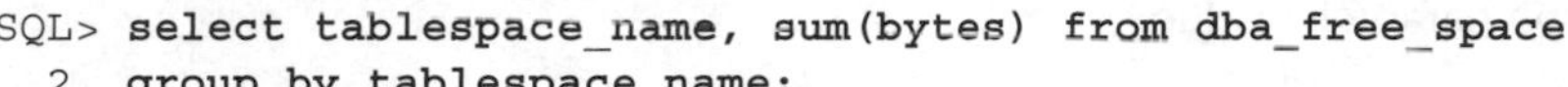

```
SQL> select tablespace_name, sum(bytes) from dba_free_space
  2  group by tablespace_name;

TABLESPACE_NAME  SUM(BYTES)
---------------- ----------
DMARTS            194969600
XPORT             180289536
SYSAUX             44105728
UNDOTBS1           75169792
USERS3            104792064
USERS4            260046848
USERS               1376256
USERS2            104792064
SYSTEM             75104256
EXAMPLE            23724032

10 rows selected.
```

Note that the free space does not take into account the space that would be available if and when the datafiles in a tablespace are autoextended. Also, any space allocated to a table for rows that are later deleted will be available for future inserts into the table, but it is not counted in the preceding query results as space available for other database objects. When a table is truncated, however, the space is made available for other database objects.

DBA_LMT_FREE_SPACE

The view DBA_LMT_FREE_SPACE provides the amount of free space, in blocks, for all tablespaces that are locally managed, and it must be joined with DBA_DATA_FILES to get the tablespace names.

DBA_THRESHOLDS

Introduced in Oracle Database 10*g*, DBA_THRESHOLDS contains the currently active list of the different metrics that gauge the database's health and specify a condition under which an alert will be issued if the metric threshold reaches or exceeds a specified value.

The values in this view are typically maintained via the OEM interface; in addition, the DBMS_SERVER_ALERT built-in PL/SQL package can set and get the threshold values with the SET_THRESHOLD and GET_THRESHOLD procedures, respectively. To read alert messages in the alert queue, you can use the DBMS_AQ and DBMS_AQADM packages, or OEM can be configured to send a pager or e-mail message when the thresholds have been exceeded.

For a default installation of Oracle Database 12*c*, a number of thresholds are configured, including the following:

- At least one user session is blocked every minute for three consecutive minutes.
- Any segments are not able to extend for any reason.
- The total number of concurrent processes comes within 80 percent of the PROCESSES initialization parameter value.
- More than two invalid objects exist for any individual database user.
- The total number of concurrent user sessions comes within 80 percent of the SESSIONS initialization parameter value.
- There are more than 1200 concurrent open cursors.
- There are more than 100 logons per second.
- A tablespace is more than 85 percent full (warning) or more than 97 percent full (critical).
- User logon time is greater than 1000 milliseconds (1 second).

DBA_OUTSTANDING_ALERTS

The data dictionary view DBA_OUTSTANDING_ALERTS contains one row for each active alert in the database, until the alert is cleared or reset. One of the fields in this view, SUGGESTED_ACTION, contains a recommendation for addressing the alert condition.

DBA_OBJECT_USAGE

If an index is not being used, it not only takes up space that could be used by other objects, but the overhead of maintaining the index whenever an INSERT, UPDATE, or DELETE occurs is wasted. By using the ALTER INDEX . . . MONITORING USAGE command, the data dictionary view DBA_OBJECT_USAGE will be updated when the index has been accessed indirectly because of a SELECT statement.

NOTE
V$OBJECT_USAGE is deprecated as of Oracle Database 12c and is retained for backward compatibility; use DBA_OBJECT_USAGE or USER_OBJECT_USAGE instead.

DBA_ALERT_HISTORY

After an alert in DBA_OUTSTANDING_ALERTS has been addressed and cleared, a record of the cleared alert is available in the view DBA_ALERT_HISTORY.

V$ALERT_TYPES

The dynamic performance view V$ALERT_TYPES contains the 175 alert conditions (as of Oracle 12*c*, Release 1) that can be monitored. The GROUP_NAME column categorizes the alert conditions by type. For example, for space management issues, we would use alerts with a GROUP_NAME of "Space":

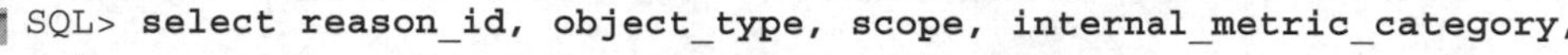

```
SQL> select reason_id, object_type, scope, internal_metric_category,
  2        internal_metric_name from v$alert_types
  3        where group_name = 'Space';

 REASON_ID OBJECT_TYPE          SCOPE    INTERNAL_METRIC_CATE INTERNAL_METRIC_NA
---------- -------------------- -------- -------------------- ------------------
       123 RECOVERY AREA        Database Recovery_Area        Free_Space
         1 SYSTEM               Instance
         0 SYSTEM               Instance
       133 TABLESPACE           Database problemTbsp          bytesFree
         9 TABLESPACE           Database problemTbsp          pctUsed
        12 TABLESPACE           Database Suspended_Session    Tablespace
        10 TABLESPACE           Database Snap_Shot_Too_Old    Tablespace
        13 ROLLBACK SEGMENT     Database Suspended_Session    Rollback_Segment
        11 ROLLBACK SEGMENT     Database Snap_Shot_Too_Old    Rollback_Segment
        14 DATA OBJECT          Database Suspended_Session    Data_Object
        15 QUOTA                Database Suspended_Session    Quota

11 rows selected.
```

Using the alert with REASON_ID=123 as an example, an alert can be initiated when the free space in the database recovery area falls below a specified percentage.

V$UNDOSTAT

Having too much undo space and having not enough undo space are both problems. Although an alert can be set up to notify the DBA when the undo space is not sufficient to provide enough transaction history to satisfy Flashback queries or enough "before" image data to prevent "Snapshot Too Old" errors, a DBA can be proactive by monitoring the dynamic performance view V$UNDOSTAT during heavy database usage periods.

V$UNDOSTAT displays historical information about the consumption of undo space for ten-minute intervals. By analyzing the results from this table, a DBA can make informed decisions when adjusting the size of the undo tablespace or changing the value of the UNDO_RETENTION initialization parameter.

V$SORT_SEGMENT

The view V$SORT_SEGMENT can be used to view the allocation and deallocation of space in a temporary tablespace's sort segment. The column CURRENT_USERS indicates how many distinct users are actively using a given segment. V$SORT_SEGMENT is only populated for temporary tablespaces.

V$TEMPSEG_USAGE

From the perspective of users requesting temporary segments, the view V$TEMPSEG_USAGE identifies the locations, types, and sizes of the temporary segments currently being requested. Unlike V$SORT_SEGMENT, V$TEMPSEG_USAGE will contain information about temporary segments in both temporary and permanent tablespaces. Later in this chapter, I'll introduce the improved and simplified temporary tablespace management tools available since Oracle Database 11*g*.

Space Management Methodologies

In the following sections, we will consider various features of Oracle 12*c* to facilitate the efficient use of disk space in the database. Locally managed tablespaces offer a variety of advantages to the DBA, improving the performance of the objects within the tablespace, as well as easing administration of the tablespace. Fragmentation of a tablespace is a thing of the past. Another feature, Oracle Managed Files, eases datafile maintenance by automatically removing files at the operating system level when a tablespace or other database object is dropped. Bigfile tablespaces, introduced in Oracle 10*g*, simplify datafile management because one (and only one) datafile is associated with a bigfile tablespace. This moves the maintenance point up one level from the datafile to the tablespace. We'll also review a couple other features introduced in earlier releases: undo tablespaces and multiple block sizes.

Locally Managed Tablespaces

Prior to Oracle8*i*, there was only one way to manage free space within a tablespace: by using data dictionary tables in the SYSTEM tablespace. If a lot of INSERT, DELETE, and UPDATE activity occurred anywhere in the database, there was the potential for a "hot spot" to occur in the SYSTEM tablespace where the space management occurred. Oracle removed this potential bottleneck by introducing *locally managed tablespaces (LMTs)*. A locally managed tablespace tracks free space in the tablespace with bitmaps, as discussed in Chapter 1. These bitmaps can be managed very efficiently because they are very compact compared to a freelist of available blocks. Because they are stored within the tablespace itself, instead of in the data dictionary tables, contention in the SYSTEM tablespace is reduced.

Since Oracle Database 10*g*, by default, all tablespaces are created as locally managed tablespaces, including the SYSTEM and SYSAUX tablespaces. When the SYSTEM tablespace is locally managed, you can no longer create any dictionary-managed tablespaces in the database that are read/write. A dictionary-managed tablespace may still be plugged into the database from an earlier version of Oracle, but it is read-only.

An LMT can have objects with one of two types of extents: automatically sized or all of a uniform size. If extent allocation is set to UNIFORM when the LMT is created, all extents, as expected, are the same size. Because all extents are the same size, there can be no fragmentation. Gone is the classic example of a 51MB segment that can't be allocated in a tablespace with two free 50MB extents because the two 50MB extents are not adjacent.

On the other hand, automatic segment extent management within a locally managed tablespace allocates space based on the size of the object. Initial extents are small, and if the object stays small, very little space is wasted. If the table grows past the initial extent allocated for the segment, subsequent extents to the segment are larger. Extents in an autoallocated LMT have sizes of 64KB, 1MB, 8MB, and 64MB, and the extent size increases as the size of the segment increases, up to a maximum of 64MB. In other words, Oracle is specifying what the values of INITIAL, NEXT, and

PCTINCREASE are automatically, depending on how the object grows. Although it seems like fragmentation can occur in a tablespace with autoallocation, in practice the fragmentation is minimal because a new object with a 64KB initial segment size will fit nicely in a 1MB, 4MB, 8MB, or 64MB block preallocated for all other objects with an initial 64KB extent size.

Given an LMT with either automatically managed extents or uniform extents, the free space within the segment itself can be AUTO or MANUAL. With AUTO segment space management, a bitmap is used to indicate how much space is used in each block. As mentioned earlier in the chapter, the parameters PCTUSED, FREELISTS, and FREELIST GROUPS no longer need to be specified when the segment is created. In addition, the performance of concurrent DML operations is improved because the segment's bitmap allows concurrent access. In a freelist-managed segment, the data block in the segment header that contains the freelist is locked out to all other writers of the block when a single writer is looking for a free block in the segment. Although allocating multiple freelists for very active segments does somewhat solve the problem, it is another structure that the DBA has to manage.

Another advantage of LMTs is that rollback information is reduced or eliminated when any LMT space-related operation is performed. Because the update of a bitmap in a tablespace is not recorded in a data dictionary table, no rollback information is generated for this transaction.

Other than third-party applications, such as older versions of SAP that require dictionary-managed tablespaces, there are no other reasons for creating new dictionary-managed tablespaces in Oracle 12*c*. As mentioned earlier, compatibility is provided in part to allow dictionary-managed tablespaces from previous versions of Oracle to be "plugged into" an Oracle 12*c* database (as a transportable tablespace). An Oracle 11*g* database as a whole can be "plugged into" a container database (CDB) in a multitenant architecture. But if the SYSTEM tablespace is locally managed, any dictionary-managed tablespaces must be opened read-only. Later in this chapter, you'll see some examples where we can optimize space and performance by moving a tablespace from one database to another and allocating additional data buffers for tablespaces with different sizes.

Migrating a dictionary-managed tablespace to a locally managed tablespace is very straightforward using the DBMS_SPACE_ADMIN built-in package:

```
execute sys.dbms_space_admin.tablespace_migrate_to_local('USERS');
```

If you're upgrading your database from Oracle 11*g* to 12*c*, you must also convert the SYSTEM tablespace to an LMT; if so, a number of prerequisites are in order:

- Before starting the migration, shut down the database and perform a cold backup of the database.
- Any non-SYSTEM tablespaces that are to remain read/write should be converted to LMTs.
- The default temporary tablespace must not be SYSTEM.
- If automatic undo management is being used, the undo tablespace must be online.
- For the duration of the conversion, all tablespaces except for the undo tablespace must be set to read-only.
- The database must be started in RESTRICTED mode for the duration of the conversion.

If any of these conditions are not met, the TABLESPACE_MIGRATE_TO_LOCAL procedure will not perform the migration.

Using OMF to Manage Space

In a nutshell, *Oracle-Managed Files (OMF)* simplifies the administration of an Oracle database. At database creation time, or later by changing a couple parameters in the initialization parameter file, the DBA can specify a number of default locations for database objects such as datafiles, redo log files, and control files. Prior to Oracle9*i*, the DBA had to remember where the existing datafiles were stored by querying the DBA_DATA_FILES and DBA_TEMP_FILES views. On many occasions, a DBA would drop a tablespace but would forget to delete the underlying datafiles, thus wasting space and the time it took to back up files that were no longer used by the database.

Using OMF, Oracle not only automatically creates and deletes the files in the specified directory location but also ensures that each filename is unique. This avoids corruption and database downtime in a non-OMF environment due to existing files being overwritten by a DBA inadvertently creating a new datafile with the same name as an existing datafile, and using the REUSE clause. OMF fits in nicely with Automatic Storage Management (ASM) to make datafile creation as simple as specifying +DATA as the destination for the datafile to reside. ASM will automatically put the datafile into an ASM subdirectory divided by database name and object type:

```
[oracle@oel63 ~]$ asmcmd
ASMCMD> pwd
+
ASMCMD> cd data
ASMCMD> ls
ASM/
CDB01/
COMPLREF/
orapwasm
ASMCMD> cd complref
ASMCMD> ls
CONTROLFILE/
DATAFILE/
ONLINELOG/
PARAMETERFILE/
TEMPFILE/
spfilecomplref.ora
ASMCMD> ls -l datafile
Type      Redund  Striped  Time             Sys  Name
DATAFILE  UNPROT  COARSE   NOV 21 23:00:00  Y    EXAMPLE.270.821312609
DATAFILE  UNPROT  COARSE   NOV 21 23:00:00  Y    SYSAUX.257.821312437
DATAFILE  UNPROT  COARSE   NOV 21 23:00:00  Y    SYSTEM.258.821312493
DATAFILE  UNPROT  COARSE   NOV 21 23:00:00  Y    UNDOTBS1.260.821312561
DATAFILE  UNPROT  COARSE   NOV 21 23:00:00  Y    USERS.259.821312559
ASMCMD>
```

If you set the initialization parameter DB_FILE_CREATE_DEST to +DATA, you don't even have to specify the disk group +DATA in the CREATE TABLESPACE command.

In a test or development environment, OMF reduces the amount of time the DBA must spend on file management and lets him or her focus on the applications and other aspects of the test database. OMF has an added benefit for packaged Oracle applications that need to create tablespaces: The scripts that create the new tablespaces do not need any modification to include a datafile name, thus increasing the likelihood of a successful application deployment.

Migrating to OMF from a non-OMF environment is easy, and it can be accomplished over a longer time period. Non-OMF files and OMF files can coexist indefinitely in the same database. When the appropriate initialization parameters are set, all new datafiles, control files, and redo log files can be created as OMF files, while the previously existing files can continue to be managed manually until they are converted to OMF, if ever.

The OMF-related initialization parameters are detailed in Table 6-1. Note that the operating system path specified for any of these initialization parameters must already exist; Oracle will not create the directory. Also, these directories must be writable by the operating system account that owns the Oracle software (which on most platforms is **oracle**).

Bigfile Tablespaces

Bigfile tablespaces, introduced in Oracle 10*g,* take OMF files to the next level. In a bigfile tablespace, a single datafile is allocated, and it can be up to 8EB (exabytes, a million terabytes) in size.

Bigfile tablespaces can only be locally managed with Automatic Segment Space Management. If a bigfile tablespace is used for automatic undo or for temporary segments, then segment space management must be set to MANUAL.

Bigfile tablespaces can save space in the System Global Area (SGA) and the control file because fewer datafiles need to be tracked; similarly, all ALTER TABLESPACE commands on bigfile tablespaces need not refer to datafiles because one and only one datafile is associated with each bigfile tablespace. This moves the maintenance point from the physical (datafile) level to the logical (tablespace) level, simplifying administration. One downside to bigfile tablespaces is that a backup of a bigfile tablespace uses a single process; a number of smaller tablespaces, however, can be backed up using parallel processes and will most likely take less time to back up than a single bigfile tablespace.

Initialization Parameter	**Description**
DB_CREATE_FILE_DEST	The default operating system file directory where datafiles and tempfiles are created if no pathname is specified in the CREATE TABLESPACE command. This location is used for redo log files and control files if DB_CREATE_ONLINE_LOG_DEST_*n* is not specified.
DB_CREATE_ONLINE_LOG_DEST_*n*	Specifies the default location to store redo log files and control files when no pathname is specified for redo log files or control files at database-creation time. Up to five destinations can be specified with this parameter, allowing up to five multiplexed control files and five members of each redo log group.
DB_RECOVERY_FILE_DEST	Defines the default pathname in the server's file system where RMAN backups, archived redo logs, and flashback logs are located. Also used for redo log files and control files if neither DB_CREATE_FILE_DEST nor DB_CREATE_ONLINE_LOG_DEST_*n* is specified.

TABLE 6-1. *OMF-Related Initialization Parameters*

Bigfile tablespaces can be backed up using multiple processes by setting SECTION SIZE when using RMAN. For example, RMAN level 0 backups that are scripted to include the SECTION SIZE 64G parameter to allow parallel backups of big file tablespaces. Oracle will automatically use a single process for any file smaller than 64GB.

Creating a bigfile tablespace is as easy as adding the BIGFILE keyword to the CREATE TABLESPACE command:

```
SQL> create bigfile tablespace whs01
  2       datafile '/u06/oradata/whs01.dbf' size 10g;
Tablespace created.
```

If you are using OMF, then the DATAFILE clause can be omitted. To resize a bigfile tablespace, you can use the RESIZE clause:

```
SQL> alter tablespace whs01 resize 80g;
Tablespace altered.
```

In this scenario, even 80GB is not big enough for this tablespace, so we will let it autoextend 20GB at a time:

```
SQL> alter tablespace whs01 autoextend on next 20g;
Tablespace altered.
```

Notice in both cases that we do not need to refer to a datafile; there is only one datafile, and once the tablespace is created, we no longer need to worry about the details of the underlying datafile and how it is managed.

Bigfile tablespaces are intended for use with Automatic Storage Management, discussed in the next section.

Automatic Storage Management

Using *Automatic Storage Management (ASM)* can significantly reduce the administrative overhead of managing space in a database because a DBA need only specify an ASM *disk group* when allocating space for a tablespace or other database object. Database files are automatically distributed among all available disks in a disk group, and the distribution is automatically updated whenever the disk configuration changes. For example, when a new disk volume is added to an existing disk group in an ASM instance, all datafiles within the disk group are redistributed to use the new disk volume. ASM was introduced in Chapter 4. In this section, we'll revisit some other key ASM concepts from a storage management point of view and provide more examples.

Because ASM automatically places datafiles on multiple disks, performance of queries and DML statements is improved because the I/O is spread out among several disks. Optionally, the disks in an ASM group can be mirrored to provide additional redundancy and performance benefits.

Using ASM provides a number of other benefits. In many cases, an ASM instance with a number of physical disks can be used instead of a third-party volume manager or network-attached storage (NAS) subsystem. As an added benefit over volume managers, ASM maintenance operations do not require a shutdown of the database if a disk needs to be added or removed from a disk group.

In the next few sections, we'll delve further into how ASM works, with an example of how to create a database object using ASM.

Disk Group Redundancy

A *disk group* in ASM is a collection of one or more ASM disks managed as a single entity. Disks can be added or removed from a disk group without shutting down the database. Whenever a disk is added or removed, ASM automatically rebalances the datafiles on the disks to maximize redundancy and I/O performance.

In addition to the advantages of high redundancy, a disk group can be used by more than one database. This helps to maximize the investment in physical disk drives by easily reallocating disk space among several databases whose disk space needs may change over the course of a day or the course of a year.

As explained in Chapter 4, the three types of disk groups are normal redundancy, high redundancy, and external redundancy. The normal-redundancy and high-redundancy groups require that ASM provide the redundancy for files stored in the group. The difference between normal redundancy and high redundancy is in the number of *failure groups* required: A normal-redundancy disk group typically has two failure groups, and a high-redundancy disk group will have at least three failure groups. A failure group in ASM would roughly correspond to a redo log file group member using traditional Oracle datafile management. External redundancy requires that the redundancy be provided by a mechanism other than ASM (for example, with a hardware third-party RAID storage array). Alternatively, a disk group might contain a non-mirrored disk volume that is used for a read-only tablespace that can easily be re-created if the disk volume fails.

ASM Instance

ASM requires a dedicated Oracle instance, typically on the same node as the database that is using an ASM disk group. In an Oracle Real Application Clusters (RAC) environment, each node in a RAC database has an ASM instance. In Oracle Database 12*c*, an Oracle Flex ASM instance can reside on a physical server that does not host a database instance.

An ASM instance never mounts a database; it only coordinates the disk volumes for other database instances. In addition, all database I/O from an instance goes directly to the disks in a disk group. Disk group maintenance, however, is performed in the ASM instance; as a result, the memory footprint needed to support an ASM instance can be as low as 275MB but is typically at least 2GB in a production environment.

For more details on how to configure ASM or Oracle Flex ASM for use with RAC, see Chapter 12.

Background Processes

Several Oracle background processes exist in an ASM instance. The RBAL background process coordinates the automatic disk group rebalance activity for a disk group. Other ASM background processes, ARB0 through ARB9 and ARBA, perform the actual rebalance activity in parallel. When ASM transactions terminate abnormally, the ASM processes ARS*n* (where *n* is a number from 0 to 9) perform the recovery.

Creating Objects Using ASM

Before a database can use an ASM disk group, the group must be created by the ASM instance. In the following example, a new disk group, LYUP25, is created to manage the Unix disk volumes /dev/hda1, /dev/hda2, /dev/hda3, /dev/hdb1, /dev/hdc1, and /dev/hdd4:

```
SQL> create diskgroup LYUP25 normal redundancy
  2        failgroup mir1 disk  '/dev/hda1','/dev/hda2','/dev/hda3',
  3        failgroup mir2 disk  '/dev/hdb1','/dev/hdc1','/dev/hdd4';
```

When normal redundancy is specified, at least two failure groups must be specified to provide two-way mirroring for any datafiles created in the disk group.

In the database instance that is using the disk group, OMF is used in conjunction with ASM to create the datafiles for the logical database structures. In the following example, we set the initialization parameter DB_CREATE_FILE_DEST using a disk group so that any tablespaces created using OMF will automatically be named and placed in the disk group LYUP25:

```
db_create_file_dest = '+LYUP25'
```

Creating a tablespace in the disk group is straight to the point:

```
SQL> create tablespace lob_video;
```

Once an ASM file is created, the automatically generated filenames can be found in V$DATAFILE and V$LOGFILE, along with manually generated filenames. All typical database files can be created using ASM, except for administrative files, including trace files, alert logs, backup files, export files, and core dump files.

OMF is a handy option when you want to let Oracle manage the datafile naming for you, whether the datafile is on a conventional file system or in an ASM disk group. You can also mix and match: some of your datafiles can be OMF-named, and others explicitly named.

Undo Management Considerations

Creating an undo tablespace provides a number of benefits for both the DBA and a typical database user. For the DBA, the management of rollback segments is a thing of the past (the past century!): all undo segments are managed automatically by Oracle in the undo tablespace. In addition to providing a read-consistent view of database objects to database readers when a long transaction against an object is in progress, an undo tablespace can provide a mechanism for a user to recover rows from a table.

A big enough undo tablespace will minimize the possibility of getting the classic "Snapshot too old" error message, but how much undo space is enough? If it is undersized, then the availability window for flashback queries is short; if it is sized too big, disk space is wasted and backup operations may take longer than necessary.

A number of initialization parameter files control the allocation and use of undo tablespaces. The UNDO_MANAGEMENT parameter specifies whether AUTOMATIC undo management is used, and the UNDO_TABLESPACE parameter specifies the undo tablespace itself. To change undo management from rollback segments to automatic undo management (changing the value of UNDO_MANAGEMENT from MANUAL to AUTO), the instance must be shut down and restarted for the change to take effect; you can change the value of UNDO_TABLESPACE while the database is open. The UNDO_RETENTION parameter specifies, in seconds, the minimum amount of time that undo information should be retained for Flashback queries. However, with an undersized undo tablespace and heavy DML usage, some undo information may be overwritten before the time period specified in UNDO_RETENTION.

Introduced in Oracle Database 10*g* was the RETENTION GUARANTEE clause of the CREATE UNDO TABLESPACE command. In essence, an undo tablespace with a RETENTION GUARANTEE will not overwrite unexpired undo information at the expense of failed DML operations when there is not enough free undo space in the undo tablespace. More details on using this clause can be found in Chapter 7.

The following initialization parameters enable automatic undo management with the undo tablespace UNDO04 using a retention period of at least 24 hours:

```
undo_management = auto
undo_tablespace = undo04
undo_retention = 86400
```

The dynamic performance view V$UNDOSTAT can assist in sizing the undo tablespace correctly for the transaction load during peak processing periods. The rows in V$UNDOSTAT are inserted at ten-minute intervals and give a snapshot of the undo tablespace usage:

```
SQL> select to_char(end_time,'yyyy-mm-dd hh24:mi') end_time,
  2         undoblks, ssolderrcnt from v$undostat;

END_TIME           UNDOBLKS SSOLDERRCNT
------------------ -------- -----------
2013-07-23 10:28        522           0
2013-07-23 10:21       1770           0
2013-07-23 10:11        857           0
2013-07-23 10:01       1605           0
2013-07-23 09:51       2864           3
2013-07-23 09:41        783           0
2013-07-23 09:31       1543           0
2013-07-23 09:21       1789           0
2013-07-23 09:11        890           0
2013-07-23 09:01       1491           0
```

In this example, a peak in undo space usage occurred between 9:41 A.M. and 9:51 A.M., resulting in a "Snapshot too old" error for three queries. To prevent these errors, the undo tablespace should be either manually resized or allowed to autoextend.

SYSAUX Monitoring and Usage

The SYSAUX tablespace, introduced in Oracle 10*g*, is an auxiliary tablespace to the SYSTEM tablespace, and it houses data for several components of the Oracle database that either required their own tablespace or used the SYSTEM tablespace in previous releases of Oracle. These components include the Enterprise Manager Repository, formerly in the tablespace OEM_REPOSITORY, as well as LogMiner, Oracle Spatial, and Oracle Text, all of which formerly used the SYSTEM tablespace for storing configuration information. The current occupants of the SYSAUX tablespace can be identified by querying the V$SYSAUX_OCCUPANTS view:

```
SQL> select occupant_name, occupant_desc, space_usage_kbytes
  2         from v$sysaux_occupants;

OCCUPANT_NAME OCCUPANT_DESC                            SPACE_USAGE_KBYTES
------------- ---------------------------------------- ------------------
LOGMNR        LogMiner                                              14080
LOGSTDBY      Logical Standby                                        1536
SMON_SCN_TIME Transaction Layer - SCN to TIME map                    3328
              ping
```

```
PL/SCOPE       PL/SQL Identifier Collection                    1600
STREAMS        Oracle Streams                                  1024
AUDIT_TABLES   DB audit tables                                    0
XDB            XDB                                           192000
AO             Analytical Workspace Object Table              39680
XSOQHIST       OLAP API History Tables                        39680
XSAMD          OLAP Catalog                                       0
SM/AWR         Server Manageability - Automatic Wo           716800
               rkload Repository
SM/ADVISOR     Server Manageability - Advisor Fram            19264
               ework
SM/OPTSTAT     Server Manageability - Optimizer St           164928
               atistics History
SM/OTHER       Server Manageability - Other Compon            47040
               ents
STATSPACK      Statspack Repository                               0
SDO            Oracle Spatial                                 79488
WM             Workspace Manager                               7296
ORDIM          Oracle Multimedia ORDSYS Components              448
ORDIM/ORDDATA  Oracle Multimedia ORDDATA Component            16448
ORDIM/ORDPLUG  Oracle Multimedia ORDPLUGINS Compon                0
INS            ents
ORDIM/SI_INFO  Oracle Multimedia SI_INFORMTN_SCHEM                0
RMTN_SCHEMA    A Components
EM             Enterprise Manager Repository                      0
TEXT           Oracle Text                                     3776
ULTRASEARCH    Oracle Ultra Search                                0
ULTRASEARCH_D  Oracle Ultra Search Demo User                      0
EMO_USER
EXPRESSION_FI  Expression Filter System                           0
LTER
EM_MONITORING  Enterprise Manager Monitoring User               704
_USER
TSM            Oracle Transparent Session Migratio                0
               n User
SQL_MANAGEMEN  SQL Management Base Schema                      2496
T_BASE
AUTO_TASK      Automated Maintenance Tasks                      320
JOB_SCHEDULER  Unified Job Scheduler                           5184

31 rows selected.
```

If the SYSAUX tablespace is taken offline or otherwise becomes corrupted, only these components of the Oracle database will be unavailable; the core functionality of the database will be unaffected. In any case, the SYSAUX tablespace helps to take the load off of the SYSTEM tablespace during normal operation of the database.

To monitor the usage of the SYSAUX tablespace, you can query the column SPACE_USAGE_KBYTES on a routine basis, and it can alert the DBA when the space usage grows beyond a certain level. If the space usage for a particular component requires a dedicated tablespace to be allocated for the component, such as for the Oracle Text repository, the procedure identified in the MOVE_PROCEDURE column of the V$SYSAUX_OCCUPANTS view will move the application to another tablespace:

```
SQL> select occupant_name, move_procedure from v$sysaux_occupants
  2     where occupant_name = 'TEXT';

OCCUPANT_NAME    MOVE_PROCEDURE
---------------- ------------------------------------------------
EM               DRI_MOVE_CTXSYS
```

If a component is not being used in the database at all, such as for TSM or Ultra Search, a negligible amount of space is used in the SYSAUX tablespace.

Archived Redo Log File Management

It is important to consider space management for objects that exist outside of the database, such as archived redo log files. In ARCHIVELOG mode, an online redo log file is copied to the destination(s) specified by LOG_ARCHIVE_DEST_*n* (where *n* is a number from 1 to 10) or by DB_RECOVERY_FILE_DEST (the flash recovery area) if none of the LOG_ARCHIVE_DEST_*n* values are set.

The redo log being copied must be copied successfully to at least one of the destinations before it can be reused by the database. The LOG_ARCHIVE_MIN_SUCCEED_DEST parameter defaults to 1 and must be at least 1. If none of the copy operations are successful, the database will be suspended until at least one of the destinations receives the log file. Running out of disk space is one possible reason for this type of failure.

If the destination for the archived log files is on a local file system, an operating system shell script can monitor the space usage of the destination, or it can be scheduled with DBMS_SCHEDULER or with Oracle Cloud Control 12*c*.

Built-in Space Management Tools

Oracle 12*c* provides a number of built-in tools that a DBA can use on demand to determine if there are any problems with disk space in the database. Most, if not all, of these tools can be manually configured and run by calling the appropriate built-in package. In this section, we'll cover the packages and procedures used to query the database for space problems or advice on space management. In addition, I'll show you the new initialization parameter used by the Automatic Diagnostic Repository to identify the alert and trace file location. Later in this chapter, you'll see how some of these tools can be automated to notify the DBA via e-mail or pager when a problem is imminent; many, if not all, of these tools are available on demand via the Oracle Cloud Control 12*c* web interface.

Segment Advisor

Frequent inserts, updates, and deletes on a table may, over time, leave the space within a table fragmented. Oracle can perform *segment shrink* on a table or index. Shrinking the segment makes the free space in the segment available to other segments in the tablespace, with the potential to improve future DML operations on the segment because fewer blocks may need to be retrieved for the DML operation after the segment shrink. Segment shrink is very similar to online table redefinition in that space in a table is reclaimed. However, segment shrink can be performed in place without the additional space requirements of online table redefinition.

To determine which segments will benefit from segment shrink, you can invoke *Segment Advisor* to perform growth trend analysis on specified segments. In this section, we'll invoke Segment Advisor on some candidate segments that may be vulnerable to fragmentation.

In the example that follows, we'll set up Segment Advisor to monitor the HR.EMPLOYEES table. In recent months, there has been high activity on this table; in addition, a new column, WORK_RECORD, has been added to the table, which HR uses to maintain comments about the employees:

```
SQL> alter table hr.employees add (work_record varchar2(4000));
Table altered.
SQL> alter table hr.employees enable row movement;
Table altered.
```

We have enabled ROW MOVEMENT in the table so that shrink operations can be performed on the table if recommended by Segment Advisor.

After Segment Advisor has been invoked to give recommendations, the findings from Segment Advisor are available in the DBA_ADVISOR_FINDINGS data dictionary view. To show the potential benefits of shrinking segments when Segment Advisor recommends a shrink operation, the view DBA_ADVISOR_RECOMMENDATIONS provides the recommended shrink operation along with the potential savings, in bytes, for the operation.

To set up Segment Advisor to analyze the HR.EMPLOYEES table, we will use an anonymous PL/SQL block, as follows:

```
-- begin Segment Advisor analysis for HR.EMPLOYEES
--  rev. 1.1  RJB    07/30/2013
--
-- SQL*Plus variable to retrieve the task number from Segment Advisor
variable task_id number

-- PL/SQL block follows
declare
    name varchar2(100);
    descr varchar2(500);
    obj_id number;
begin
    name := ''; -- unique name generated from create_task
    descr := 'Check HR.EMPLOYEE table';
    dbms_advisor.create_task
         ('Segment Advisor', :task_id, name, descr, NULL);
    dbms_advisor.create_object
         (name, 'TABLE', 'HR', 'EMPLOYEES', NULL, NULL, obj_id);
    dbms_advisor.set_task_parameter(name, 'RECOMMEND_ALL', 'TRUE');
    dbms_advisor.execute_task(name);
end;

PL/SQL procedure successfully completed.

SQL> print task_id

   TASK_ID
----------
       384

SQL>
```

The procedure DBMS_ADVISOR.CREATE_TASK specifies the type of advisor; in this case, it is Segment Advisor. The procedure will return a unique task ID and an automatically generated name to the calling program; we will assign our own description to the task.

Within the task, identified by the uniquely generated name returned from the previous procedure, we identify the object to be analyzed with DBMS_ADVISOR.CREATE_OBJECT. Depending on the type of object, the second through the sixth arguments vary. For tables, we only need to specify the schema name and the table name.

Using DBMS_ADVISOR.SET_TASK_PARAMETER, we tell Segment Advisor to give all possible recommendations about the table. If we want to turn off recommendations for this task, we would specify FALSE instead of TRUE for the last parameter.

Finally, we initiate the Segment Advisor task with the DBMS_ADVISOR.EXECUTE_TASK procedure. Once it is done, we display the identifier for the task so we can query the results in the appropriate data dictionary views.

Now that we have a task number from invoking Segment Advisor, we can query DBA_ADVISOR_FINDINGS to see what we can do to improve the space utilization of the HR.EMPLOYEES table:

```
SQL> select owner, task_id, task_name, type,
  2         message, more_info from dba_advisor_findings
  3         where task_id = 384;

OWNER         TASK_ID TASK_NAME  TYPE
---------- ------- --------- ------
RJB                 6 TASK_00003 INFORMATION

MESSAGE
--------------------------------------------------
Perform shrink, estimated savings is 107602 bytes.

MORE_INFO
---------------------------------------------------------------------------
Allocated Space:262144: Used Space:153011: Reclaimable Space :107602:
```

The results are fairly self-explanatory. We can perform a segment shrink operation on the table to reclaim space from numerous INSERT, DELETE, and UPDATE operations on the HR.EMPLOYEES table. Because the WORK_RECORD column was added to the HR.EMPLOYEES table after the table was already populated, we may have created some chained rows in the table; in addition, since the WORK_RECORD column can be up to 4000 bytes long, updates or deletes of rows with big WORK_RECORD columns may create blocks in the table with free space that can be reclaimed. The view DBA_ADVISOR_RECOMMENDATIONS provides similar information:

```
SQL> select owner, task_id, task_name, benefit_type
  2  from dba_advisor_recommendations
  3  where task_id = 384;

OWNER         TASK_ID TASK_NAME
---------- ------- ----------
RJB               384 TASK_00003

BENEFIT_TYPE
--------------------------------------------------
Perform shrink, estimated savings is 107602 bytes.
```

In any case, we will shrink the segment HR.EMPLOYEES to reclaim the free space. As an added time-saving benefit to the DBA, the SQL needed to perform the shrink is provided in the view DBA_ADVISOR_ACTIONS:

```
SQL> select owner, task_id, task_name, command, attr1
  2       from dba_advisor_actions where task_id = 384;

OWNER      TASK_ID TASK_NAME  COMMAND
---------- ------- ---------- -----------------
RJB              6 TASK_00003 SHRINK SPACE

ATTR1
-----------------------------------------------------
alter table HR.EMPLOYEES shrink space

1 row selected.

SQL> alter table HR.EMPLOYEES shrink space;
Table altered.
```

As mentioned earlier, the shrink operation does not require extra disk space and does not prevent access to the table during the operation, except for a very short period of time at the end of the process to free the unused space. All indexes are maintained on the table during the operation.

In addition to freeing up disk space for other segments, there are other benefits to shrinking a segment. Cache utilization is improved because fewer blocks need to be in the cache to satisfy SELECT or other DML statements against the segment. Also, because the data in the segment is more compact, the performance of full table scans is improved.

There are a couple of caveats and minor restrictions in Oracle Database 12c. First, segment shrink will not work on SecureFile LOB segments, IOT mapping tables, tables with function-based indexes, and ROWID-based materialized views. If a table is compressed, only certain compression types are eligible for shrinking, such as advanced compression using ROW STORE COMPRESS ADVANCED. You could uncompress the table before shrinking it—but then you'd be better off using ALTER TABLE . . . MOVE ONLINE and specifying the same compression storage parameters for the move.

Undo Advisor and the Automatic Workload Repository

Starting with Oracle 10g, *Undo Advisor* provides tuning information for the undo tablespace, whether it's sized too large, it's too small, or the undo retention (via the initialization parameter UNDO_RETENTION) is not set optimally for the types of transactions that occur in the database.

Using Undo Advisor is similar to using Segment Advisor in that we will call the DBMS_ADVISOR procedures and query the DBA_ADVISOR_* data dictionary views to see the results of the analysis.

Undo Advisor, however, relies on another feature introduced in Oracle 10g—the *Automatic Workload Repository (AWR)*. The Automatic Workload Repository, built into every Oracle database, contains snapshots of all key statistics and workloads in the database at 60-minute intervals by default. The statistics in the AWR are kept for seven days, after which the oldest statistics are dropped. Both the snapshot intervals and the retention period can be adjusted to suit your environment, however. The AWR maintains the historical record of how the database is being used over time and helps to diagnose and predict problems long before they can cause a database outage.

To set up Undo Advisor to analyze undo space usage, we will use an anonymous PL/SQL block similar to what we used for Segment Advisor. Before we can use Segment Advisor, however, we need to determine the timeframe to analyze. The data dictionary view DBA_HIST_SNAPSHOT contains the snapshot numbers and date stamps; we will look for the snapshot numbers from 8:00 P.M. Saturday, July 21, 2013 through 9:30 P.M. Saturday, July 21, 2013:

```
SQL> select snap_id, begin_interval_time, end_interval_time
         from DBA_HIST_SNAPSHOT
     where begin_interval_time > '21-Jul-13 08.00.00 PM' and
             end_interval_time < '21-Jul-13 09.31.00 PM'
     order by end_interval_time desc;

   SNAP_ID BEGIN_INTERVAL_TIME           END_INTERVAL_TIME
---------- ----------------------------- ---------------------------
         8 21-JAN-07 09.00.30.828 PM   21-JAN-07 09.30.14.078 PM
         7 21-JAN-07 08.30.41.296 PM   21-JAN-07 09.00.30.828 PM
         6 21-JAN-07 08.00.56.093 PM   21-JAN-07 08.30.41.296 PM
```

Given these results, we will use a SNAP_ID range from 6 to 8 when we invoke Undo Advisor. The PL/SQL anonymous block is as follows:

```
-- begin Undo Advisor analysis
--  rev. 1.1  RJB    7/16/2013
--
-- SQL*Plus variable to retrieve the task number from Segment Advisor
variable task_id number

declare
    task_id     number;
    name        varchar2(100);
    descr       varchar2(500);
    obj_id      number;
begin
    name := ''; -- unique name generated from create_task
    descr := 'Check Undo Tablespace';
    dbms_advisor.create_task
         ('Undo Advisor', :task_id, name, descr);
    dbms_advisor.create_object
         (name, 'UNDO_TBS', NULL, NULL, NULL, 'null', obj_id);
    dbms_advisor.set_task_parameter(name, 'TARGET_OBJECTS', obj_id);
    dbms_advisor.set_task_parameter(name, 'START_SNAPSHOT', 6);
    dbms_advisor.set_task_parameter(name, 'END_SNAPSHOT', 8);
    dbms_advisor.set_task_parameter(name, 'INSTANCE', 1);
    dbms_advisor.execute_task(name);
end;

PL/SQL procedure successfully completed.

SQL> print task_id
```

```
TASK_ID
-------
    527
```

As with Segment Advisor, we can review the DBA_ADVISOR_FINDINGS view to see the problem and the recommendations.

```
SQL> select owner, task_id, task_name, type,
  2      message, more_info from dba_advisor_findings
  3      where task_id = 527;

OWNER        TASK_ID TASK_NAME  TYPE
---------- ------- ---------- -------------
RJB              527 TASK_00003 PROBLEM

MESSAGE
----------------------------------------------------
The undo tablespace is OK.

MORE_INFO
--------------------------------------------------------------------
```

In this particular scenario, Undo Advisor indicates that there is enough space allocated in the undo tablespace to handle the types and volumes of queries run against this database.

Index Usage

Although indexes provide a tremendous benefit by speeding up queries, they can have an impact on space usage in the database. If an index is not being used at all, the space occupied by an index can be better used elsewhere; if we don't need the index, we also can save processing time for INSERT, UPDATE, and DELETE operations that have an impact on the index. Index usage can be monitored with the dynamic performance view V$OBJECT_USAGE. In our HR schema, we suspect that the index on the JOB_ID column of the EMPLOYEES table is not being used. We turn on monitoring for this index as follows:

```
SQL> alter index hr.emp_job_ix monitoring usage;
Index altered.
```

We take a quick look at the V$OBJECT_USAGE view to make sure this index is being monitored:

```
SQL> select * from v$object_usage;
INDEX_NAME      TABLE_NAME      MON USED START_MONITORING
--------------- --------------- --- ---- -------------------
EMP_JOB_IX      EMPLOYEES       YES NO   07/24/2013 10:04:55
```

The column USED will tell us if this index is accessed to satisfy a query. After a full day of typical user activity, we check V$OBJECT_USAGE again and then turn off monitoring:

```
SQL> alter index hr.emp_job_ix nomonitoring usage;
Index altered.
SQL> select * from v$object_usage;
```

```
INDEX_NAME   TABLE_NAME     MON USED START_MONITORING    END_MONITORING
---------- --------------- --- ---- ------------------- -------------------
EMP_JOB_IX   EMPLOYEES      NO  YES  07/24/2013 10:04:55 07/25/2013 11:39:45
```

Sure enough, the index appears to be used at least once during a typical day.

On the other end of the spectrum, an index may be accessed too frequently. If key values are inserted, updated, and deleted frequently, an index can become less efficient in terms of space usage. The following commands can be used as a baseline for an index after it is created, and then run periodically to see if the space usage becomes inefficient:

```
SQL> analyze index hr.emp_job_ix validate structure;
Index analyzed.
SQL> select pct_used from index_stats where name = 'EMP_JOB_IX';
  PCT_USED
----------
        78
```

NOTE
Running ANALYZE INDEX . . . VALIDATE STRUCTURE will temporarily lock the index in exclusive mode and therefore no DML can occur on the table while the ANALYZE is running.

The PCT_USED column indicates the percentage of the allocated space for the index in use. Over time, the EMPLOYEES table is heavily used, due to the high turnover rate of employees at the company, and this index, among others, is not using its space efficiently, as indicated by the following ANALYZE command and SELECT query, so we decide that a rebuild is in order:

```
SQL> analyze index hr.emp_job_ix validate structure;
Index analyzed.
SQL> select pct_used from index_stats where name = 'EMP_JOB_IX';
  PCT_USED
----------
        26
SQL> alter index hr.emp_job_ix rebuild online;
Index altered.
```

Notice the inclusion of the ONLINE option in the ALTER INDEX . . . REBUILD statement. The indexed table can remain online with minimal overhead while the index is rebuilding. In rare circumstances, such as on longer key lengths, you may not be able to use the ONLINE option.

Space Usage Warning Levels

Earlier in this chapter, we reviewed the data dictionary view DBA_THRESHOLDS, which contains a list of the active metrics to measure a database's health. In a default installation of Oracle 12*c*, use the following SELECT statement to see some of the 22 built-in thresholds:

```
SQL> select metrics_name, warning_operator warn, warning_value wval,
  2     critical_operator crit, critical_value cval,
  3     consecutive_occurrences consec
  4     from dba_thresholds;
```

```
METRICS_NAME                     WARN WVAL          CRIT CVAL          CONSEC
-------------------------------- ---- ------------- ---- ------------- ------
Average Users Waiting Counts     GT   10            NONE               3
. . .
Blocked User Session Count       GT   0             NONE               15
Current Open Cursors Count       GT   1200          NONE               3
Database Time Spent Waiting (%)  GT   30            NONE               3
. . .
Logons Per Sec                   GE   100           NONE               2
Session Limit %                  GT   90            GT   97            3
Tablespace Bytes Space Usage     LE   0             LE   0             1
Tablespace Space Usage           GE   85            GE   97            1

22 rows selected.
```

In terms of space usage, we see that the warning level for a given tablespace is when the tablespace is 85 percent full, and the space is at a critical level when it reaches 97 percent full. In addition, this condition need only occur during one reporting period, which by default is one minute. For the other conditions in this list, the condition must be true anywhere between 2 and 15 consecutive reporting periods before an alert is issued.

To change the level at which an alert is generated, we can use the DBMS_SERVER_ALERT .SET_THRESHOLD procedure. In this example, we want to be notified sooner if a tablespace is running out of space, so we will update the warning threshold for alert notification from 85 percent down to 60 percent:

```
--
-- PL/SQL anonymous procedure to update the Tablespace Space Usage threshold
--

declare
     /* OUT */
     warning_operator   number;
     warning_value      varchar2(100);
     critical_operator  number;
     critical_value     varchar2(100);
     observation_period number;
     consecutive_occurrences number;
     /* IN */
     metrics_id         number;
     instance_name      varchar2(50);
     object_type        number;
     object_name        varchar2(50);

     new_warning_value varchar2(100) := '60';
begin
     metrics_id := DBMS_SERVER_ALERT.TABLESPACE_PCT_FULL;
     object_type := DBMS_SERVER_ALERT.OBJECT_TYPE_TABLESPACE;
     instance_name := 'dw';
     object_name := NULL;
```

```
-- retrieve the current values with get_threshold
     dbms_server_alert.get_threshold(
          metrics_id, warning_operator, warning_value,
          critical_operator, critical_value,
          observation_period, consecutive_occurrences,
          instance_name, object_type, object_name);

-- update the warning threshold value from 85 to 60
     dbms_server_alert.set_threshold(
          metrics_id, warning_operator, new_warning_value,
          critical_operator, critical_value,
          observation_period, consecutive_occurrences,
          instance_name, object_type, object_name);

end;

PL/SQL procedure successfully completed.
```

Checking DBA_THRESHOLDS again, we see the warning level has been changed to 60 percent:

```
SQL> select metrics_name, warning_operator warn, warning_value wval
  2      from dba_thresholds;

METRICS_NAME                       WARN WVAL
---------------------------------- ---- -------------
Average Users Waiting Counts       GT   10
. . .
Blocked User Session Count         GT   0
Current Open Cursors Count         GT   1200
Database Time Spent Waiting (%)    GT   30
. . .
Logons Per Sec                     GE   100
Session Limit %                    GT   90
Tablespace Bytes Space Usage       LE   0
Tablespace Space Usage             GE   60

22 rows selected.
```

A detailed example of how to use Oracle's Advanced Queuing to subscribe to queue alert messages is beyond the scope of this book. Later in this chapter, I will, however, show some examples of how to use Cloud Control 12*c* to set up asynchronous notification of alert conditions using e-mail, a pager, or a PL/SQL procedure.

Resumable Space Allocation

The Oracle database provides a way to suspend long-running operations in the event of space allocation failures. Once the DBA is notified and the space allocation problem has been corrected, the long-running operation can complete. The long-running operation does not have to be restarted from the beginning.

Three types of space management problems can be addressed with Resumable Space Allocation:

- Out of space in the tablespace
- Maximum extents reached in the segment
- Space quota exceeded for a user

The DBA can automatically make statements resumable by setting the initialization parameter RESUMABLE_TIMEOUT to a value other than 0. This value is specified in seconds. At the session level, a user can enable resumable operations by using the ALTER SESSION ENABLE RESUMABLE command:

```
SQL> alter session enable resumable timeout 3600;
```

In this case, any long-running operation that may run out of space will suspend for up to 3600 seconds (60 minutes) until the space condition is corrected. If it is not corrected within the time limit, the statement fails.

In the scenario that follows, the HR department is trying to add the employees from the branch office EMPLOYEES table to an EMPLOYEE_SEARCH table that contains employees throughout the company. Without Resumable Space Allocation, the HR user receives an error, as follows:

```
SQL> insert into employee_search
   2     select * from employees;
insert into employee_search
*
ERROR at line 1:
ORA-01653: unable to extend table HR.EMPLOYEE_SEARCH by 128
           in tablespace USERS9
```

After running into this problem many times, the HR user decides to use Resumable Space Allocation to prevent a lot of rework whenever there are space problems in the database, and tries the operation again:

```
SQL> alter session enable resumable timeout 3600;
Session altered.
SQL> insert into hr.employee_search
  2      select * from hr.employees;
```

The user does not receive a message, and it is not clear that the operation has been suspended. However, in the alert log (managed by the Automatic Diagnostic Repository as of Oracle Database 11*g*), the XML message reads as follows:

```
<msg time='2013-07-23T22:58:26.749-05:00'
    org_id='oracle' comp_id='rdbms'
   client_id='' type='UNKNOWN' level='16'
   host_id='dw' host_addr='192.168.2.95' module='SQL*Plus' pid='1843'>
<txt> ORA-01653: unable to extend table
         HR.EMPLOYEE_SEARCH by 128 in tablespace USERS9
</txt>
</msg>
```

The DBA receives a pager alert, set up in OEM, and checks the data dictionary view DBA_RESUMABLE:

```
SQL> select user_id, instance_id, status, name, error_msg
  2  from dba_resumable;

  USER_ID INSTANCE_ID STATUS    NAME                 ERROR_MSG
---------- ----------- --------- -------------------- --------------------
       80           1 SUSPENDED User HR(80), Session ORA-01653: unable to
                                  113, Instance 1      extend table HR.EMP
                                                     LOYEE_SEARCH by 128
                                                     in tablespace USERS9
```

The DBA notices that the tablespace USERS9 does not allow autoextend, and modifies the tablespace to allow growth:

```
SQL> alter tablespace users9
  2       add datafile '+DATA'
  3       size 100m autoextend on;
Tablespace altered.
```

The user session's INSERT completes successfully, and the status of the resumable operation is reflected in the DBA_RESUMABLE view:

```
  USER_ID INSTANCE_ID STATUS    NAME                 ERROR_MSG
--------- ---------- -------- -------------------- -------------------
       80           1 NORMAL    User HR(80), Session
                                  113, Instance 1
```

The alert log file also indicates a successful resumption of this operation:

```
<msg time='2013-07-23T23:06:31.178-05:00'
    org_id='oracle' comp_id='rdbms'
    client_id='' type='UNKNOWN' level='16'
    host_id='dw' host_addr='192.168.2.95' module='SQL*Plus'
    pid='1843'>
<txt>statement in resumable session &apos;User HR(80),
   Session 113, Instance 1&apos; was resumed </txt>
</msg>
```

In Figure 6-3, you can see the tablespace USERS9 space alert appear on the instance's home page in the Incidents and Problems section, in addition to the previous alert warning you that the USERS9 tablespace was nearly full about 15 minutes before the HR user temporarily ran out of space! In Figure 6-4, the Alert History page shows the most recent alerts, which include the tablespace full condition.

As far as the user is concerned, the operation took longer than expected but still completed successfully. Another way to provide more information to the user is to set up a special type of trigger introduced in Oracle9*i* called a *system trigger.* A system trigger is like any other trigger, except it is based on some type of system event rather than on a DML statement against a table. Here is a template for a system trigger that fires on an AFTER SUSPEND event:

```
create or replace trigger resumable_notify
   after suspend on database  -- fired when resumable space event occurs
```

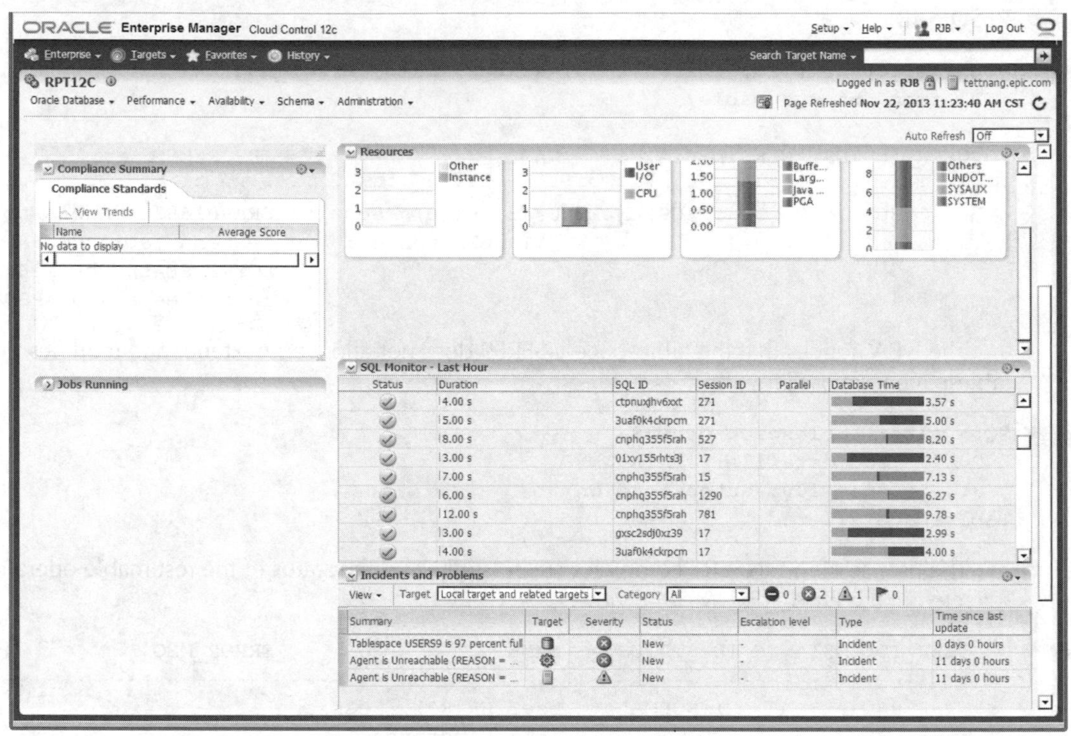

FIGURE 6-3. *Incidents and Problems section on the instance home page*

```
declare
     -- variables, if required
begin
     -- give DBA 2 hours to resolve
     dbms_resumable.set_timeout(7200);
     -- check DBA_RESUMABLE for user ID, then send e-mail
     utl_mail.send ('lyngrv@rjbdba.com', . . . );
end;
```

Managing Alert and Trace Files with ADR

New as of Oracle Database 11*g*, the Automatic Diagnostic Repository (ADR) is a system-managed repository for storing database alert logs, trace files, and any other diagnostic data previously controlled by several other initialization parameters.

The initialization parameter DIAGNOSTIC_DEST sets the base location for all diagnostic directories; in the examples that follow, the database **dw** has a value of **/u01/app/oracle** for the

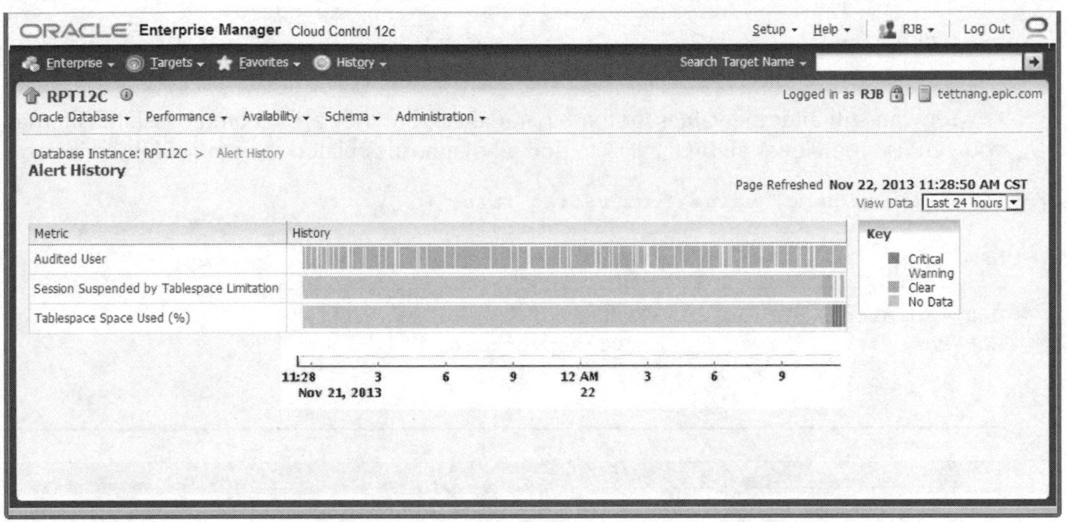

FIGURE 6-4. *Alert History page*

parameter DIAGNOSTIC_DEST. Figure 6-5 shows a typical directory structure starting with the subdirectory **/u01/app/oracle/diag**.

Notice that there are separate directories for the ASM databases and the database (RDBMS) instances; within the **rdbms** directory, you can see the **dw** directory twice: the first-level directory is the database **dw**, and the second **dw** is the *instance* **dw**. If this were a RAC database, you would see each instance of the **dw** database under the first-level **dw** directory. In fact, Oracle strongly recommends that all instances within a RAC database have the same value for DIAGNOSTIC_DEST.

Because the location of all logging and diagnostic information is controlled by the initialization parameter DIAGNOSTIC_DEST, the following initialization parameters are ignored:

- BACKGROUND_DUMP_DEST
- USER_DUMP_DEST
- CORE_DUMP_DEST

For backward compatibility, however, you can still use these as read-only parameters to determine the location of the alert log, trace files, and core dumps:

```
SQL> show parameter dump_dest

NAME                                 TYPE        VALUE
------------------------------------ ----------- ------------------------------
background_dump_dest                 string      /u01/app/oracle/diag/rdbms/dw/
                                                 dw/trace
```

```
core_dump_dest                     string     /u01/app/oracle/diag/rdbms/dw/
                                              dw/cdump
user_dump_dest                     string     /u01/app/oracle/diag/rdbms/dw/
                                              dw/trace
```

You can still alter the values for these parameters, but they are ignored by ADR. Alternatively, you can use the view V$DIAG_INFO to find all diagnostic-related directories for the instance:

```
SQL> select name, value from v$diag_info;

NAME                      VALUE
------------------------- ---------------------------------------------
Diag Enabled              TRUE
ADR Base                  /u01/app/oracle
```

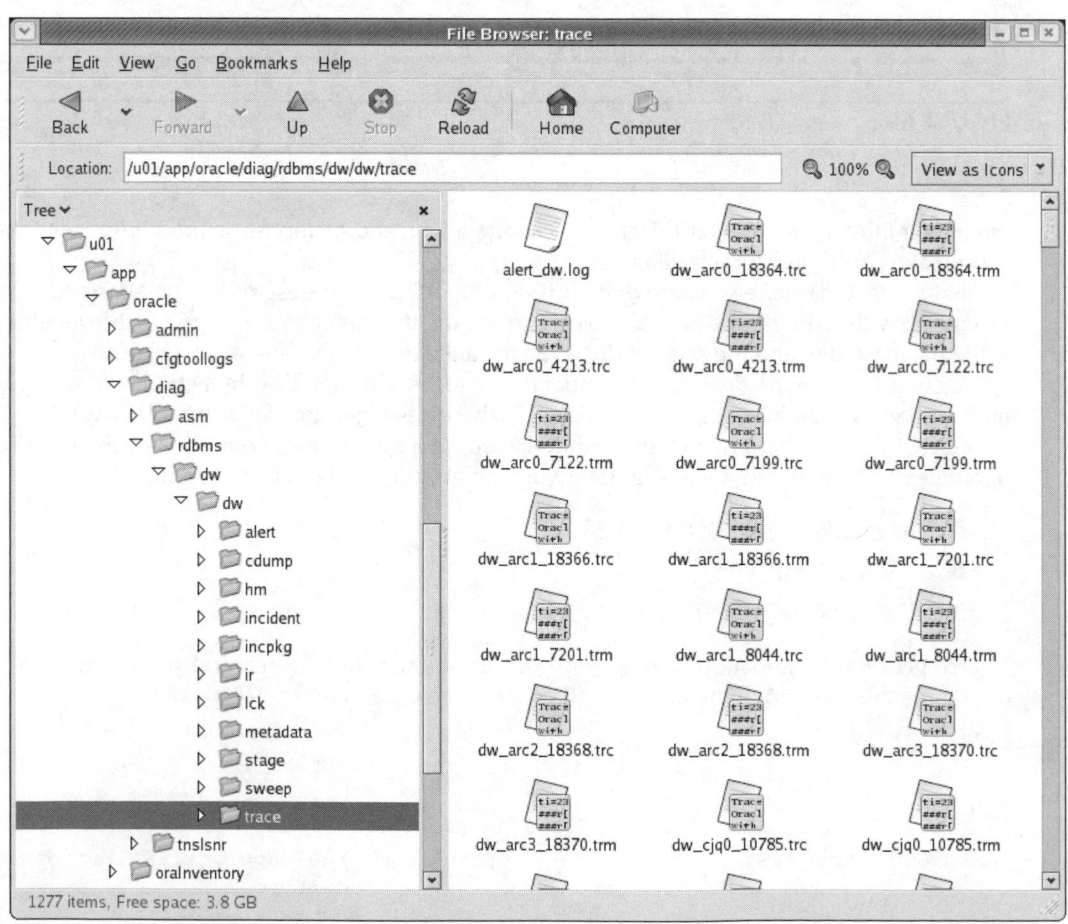

FIGURE 6-5. *ADR directory structure*

```
ADR Home                       /u01/app/oracle/diag/rdbms/dw/dw
Diag Trace                     /u01/app/oracle/diag/rdbms/dw/dw/trace
Diag Alert                     /u01/app/oracle/diag/rdbms/dw/dw/alert
Diag Incident                  /u01/app/oracle/diag/rdbms/dw/dw/incident
Diag Cdump                     /u01/app/oracle/diag/rdbms/dw/dw/cdump
Health Monitor                 /u01/app/oracle/diag/rdbms/dw/dw/hm
Default Trace File             /u01/app/oracle/diag/rdbms/dw/dw/trace/dw_ora
                               _28810.trc

Active Problem Count           0
Active Incident Count          0

11 rows selected.
```

OS Space Management

Outside of the Oracle environment, space should be monitored by the system administrator with a thorough understanding from the DBA as to the parameters in place for autoextending datafiles. Setting AUTOEXTEND ON with large NEXT values for a tablespace will allow a tablespace to grow and accommodate more inserts and updates, but this will fail if the server's disk volumes do not have the space available. Better yet is to use ASM: The storage administrator will allocate one or more large blocks of disk space or entire disks from a storage appliance, allowing the Oracle DBA to manage the space entirely from a database perspective.

Space Management Scripts

In this section, I provide a couple scripts you can run on an as-needed basis, or you can schedule them to run on a regular basis to proactively monitor the database.

These scripts take the dictionary views and give a more detailed look at a particular structure. The functionality of some of these scripts might overlap with the results provided by some of the tools I've mentioned earlier in the chapter, but they might be more focused and in some cases provide more detail about the possible space problems in the database.

Segments That Cannot Allocate Additional Extents

In the following script, we want to identify segments (most likely tables or indexes) that cannot allocate additional extents:

```
select s.tablespace_name, s.segment_name,
       s.segment_type, s.owner
from dba_segments s
where s.next_extent >=
      (select max(f.bytes)
       from dba_free_space f
       where f.tablespace_name = s.tablespace_name)
or s.extents = s.max_extents
order by tablespace_name, segment_name;

TABLESPACE_NAME    SEGMENT_NAME             SEGMENT_TYPE      OWNER
------------------ ------------------------ ----------------- ---------------
USERS9             EMPLOYEE_SEARCH          TABLE             HR
```

In this example, we're using a correlated subquery to compare the size of the next extent to the amount of free space left in the tablespace. The other condition we're checking is whether the next extent request will fail because the segment is already at the maximum number of extents.

The reason these objects might be having problems is most likely one of two possibilities: The tablespace does not have room for the next extent for this segment, or the segment has the maximum number of extents allocated. To solve this problem, the DBA can extend the tablespace by adding another datafile or by exporting the data in the segment and re-creating it with storage parameters that more closely match its growth pattern. Since Oracle9*i*, using locally managed tablespaces instead of dictionary-managed tablespaces solves this problem when disk space is not the issue, because the maximum number of extents in an LMT is unlimited.

Used and Free Space by Tablespace and Datafile

The following SQL*Plus script breaks down the space usage of each tablespace, which is further broken down by datafile within each tablespace. This is a good way to see how space is used and extended within each datafile of a tablespace, and it may be useful for load balancing when you're not using ASM or other high-availability storage.

```
--
-- Free space within non-temporary datafiles, by tablespace.
--
-- No arguments.
-- 1024*1024*1000 = 1048576000 = 1GB to match Cloud Control
--

column free_space_gb format 9999999.999
column allocated_gb  format 9999999.999
column used_gb       format 9999999.999
column tablespace    format a12
column filename      format a20

select ts.name tablespace, trim(substr(df.name,1,100)) filename,
    df.bytes/1048576000 allocated_gb,
    ((df.bytes/1048576000) - nvl(sum(dfs.bytes)/1048576000,0)) used_gb,
    nvl(sum(dfs.bytes)/1048576000,0) free_space_gb
from v$datafile df
      join dba_free_space dfs on df.file# = dfs.file_id
      join v$tablespace ts on df.ts# = ts.ts#
group by ts.name, dfs.file_id, df.name, df.file#, df.bytes
order by filename;

TABLESPACE   FILENAME             ALLOCATED_GB    USED_GB FREE_SPACE_GB
------------ -------------------- ------------ ---------- -------------
DMARTS       +DATA/dw/datafile/dm          .25  .0640625       .1859375
             arts.269.628621093
EM_REP       +DATA/dw/datafile/em          .25  .0000625       .2499375
             _rep.270.628640521
EXAMPLE      +DATA/dw/datafile/ex           .1   .077375        .022625
             ample.265.627433157
SYSAUX       +DATA/dw/datafile/sy     .7681875     .7145       .0536875
             saux.257.627432973
```

```
SYSTEM          +DATA/dw/datafile/sy          .77   .7000625       .0699375
                stem.256.627432971
UNDOTBS1        +DATA/dw/datafile/un         .265   .0155625       .2494375
                dotbs1.258.627432975
USERS           +DATA/dw/datafile/us        .0125   .0111875       .0013125
                ers.259.627432977
USERS2          +DATA/dw/datafile/us           .1   .0000625       .0999375
                ers2.267.627782171
USERS4          +DATA/dw/datafile/us          .25       .002           .248
                ers4.268.628561597
USERS9          +DATA/dw/datafile/us          .01   .0000625       .0099375
                ers9.271.628727991
USERS9          +DATA/dw/datafile/us          .01   .0000625       .0099375
                ers9.272.628729587
USERS9          +DATA/dw/datafile/us          .05   .0000625       .0499375
                ers9.273.628730561
USERS3          +DATA2/dw/datafile/u           .1   .0000625       .0999375
                sers3.256.627786775
XPORT           /u05/oradata/xport.d           .3   .1280625       .1719375
                bf

14 rows selected.
```

Only the USERS9 tablespace has more than one datafile in this database. To include temporary tablespaces on this report, you can use a UNION query to combine this query with a similar query based on V$TEMPFILE.

Automating and Streamlining the Notification Process

Although any of the scripts and packages presented earlier in this chapter can be executed on demand, some of them can and should be automated, not only to save time for the DBA but also to be proactive and catch problems long before they cause a system outage.

Two of the primary methods for automating the scripts and packages are DBMS_SCHEDULER and Oracle Cloud Control 12*c*. Each of these methods has its advantages and disadvantages. DBMS_SCHEDULER can provide more control over how the task is scheduled and can be set up using only a command-line interface. Oracle Cloud Control, on the other hand, uses a completely web-based environment that allows a DBA to oversee a database environment from wherever there is access to a web browser.

Using DBMS_SCHEDULER

The DBMS_SCHEDULER package has been available since Oracle Database 11*g*. It provides new features and functionality over the previous job scheduler package, DBMS_JOB. Although DBMS_JOB is still available in Oracle Database 12*c*, it is deprecated and no longer supported.

DBMS_SCHEDULER contains many of the procedures you'd expect from a scheduling package: CREATE_JOB, DROP_JOB, DISABLE, STOP_JOB, and COPY_JOB. In addition, DBMS_SCHEDULER makes it easy to automatically repeat job executions with CREATE_SCHEDULE and to partition jobs into categories based on resource usage with the CREATE_JOB_CLASS procedure.

Cloud Control and Monitoring

Not only can Oracle Enterprise Manager present most database administration tasks in a graphical, web-based environment, it can automate some of the routine tasks that a DBA might perform on a daily basis. In this section, we'll cover the OEM-equivalent functionality to Segment Advisor and Undo Advisor, covered previously in this chapter.

Segment Advisor

Figure 6-6 shows the home page for the RPT12C database in Cloud Control. Many of the space management functions, including Segment Advisor, are available directly from this home page, especially when there is a pending alert.

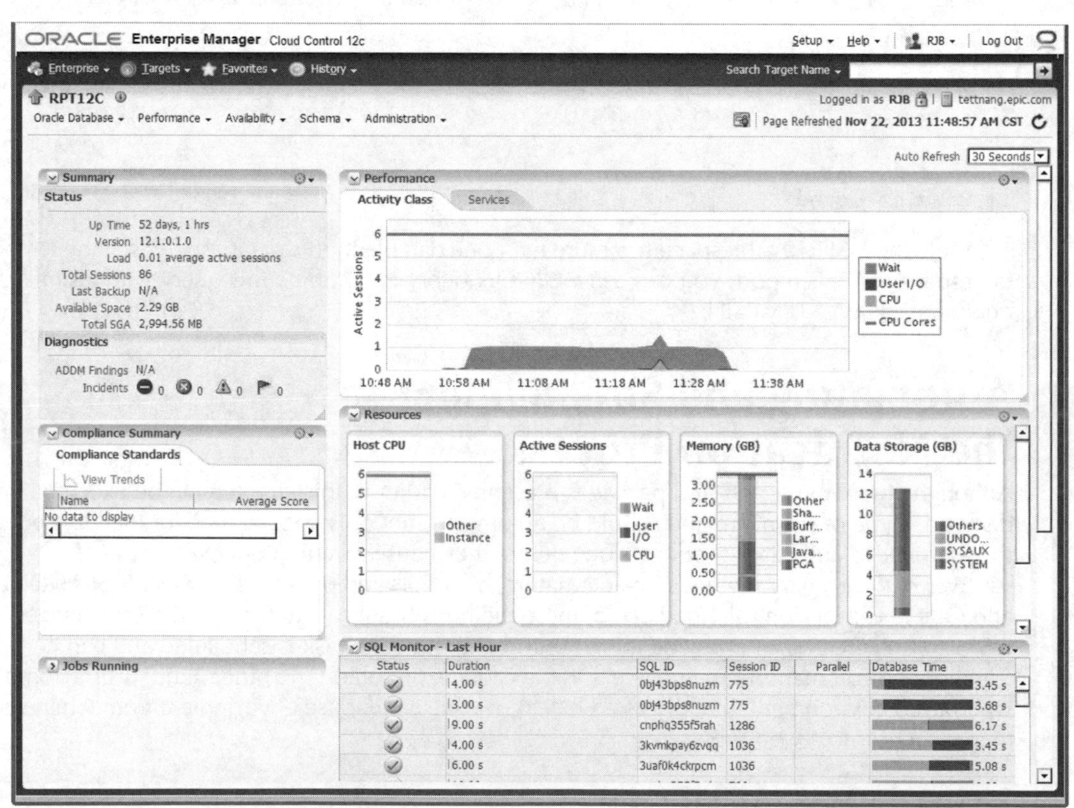

FIGURE 6-6. *OEM home page*

The home page lists general availability information of the instance, including the instance name, host name, CPU usage, and session information. Links to the advisors are in the drop-down lists in the upper-left corner.

If there is not an outstanding space-related alert, and you want to run Segment Advisor, go to the Advisor Central page by choosing Performance | Advisor Central; you will see the page shown in Figure 6-7. Click the Segment Advisor link, and you will see the page shown in Figure 6-8. Select the Schema Objects radio button and click Next.

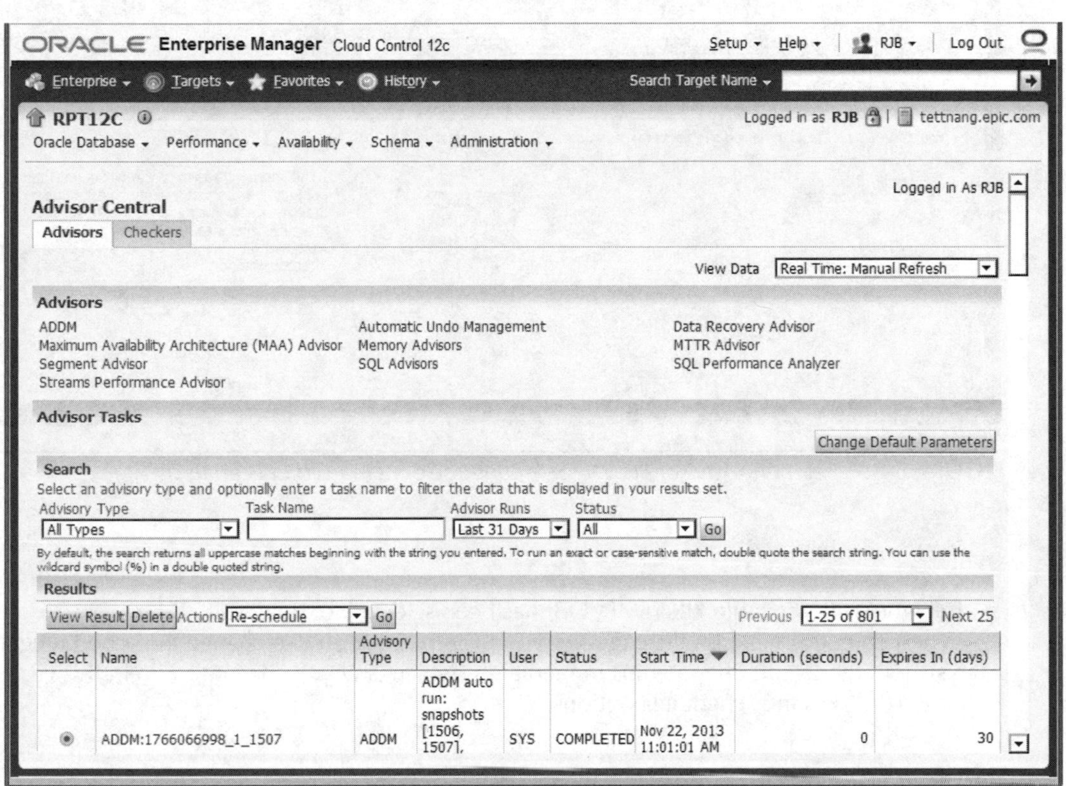

FIGURE 6-7. *Advisor Central page*

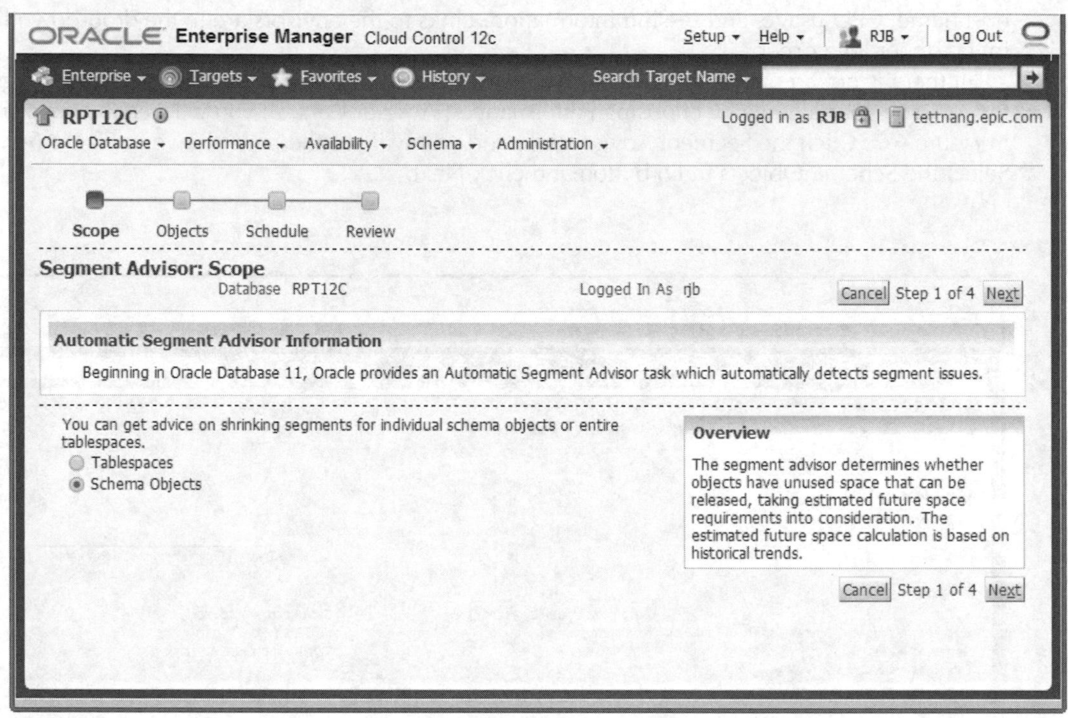

FIGURE 6-8. *Segment Advisor Step 1: Selecting the Schema Objects analysis type*

In Figure 6-9, the table HR.TEMP_OBJ has been selected for analysis.

When you click Next on the page shown in Figure 6-9, you can change the scheduling for the analysis job; by default, the job runs immediately, which is what you want to do in this case. Figure 6-10 shows the scheduling options.

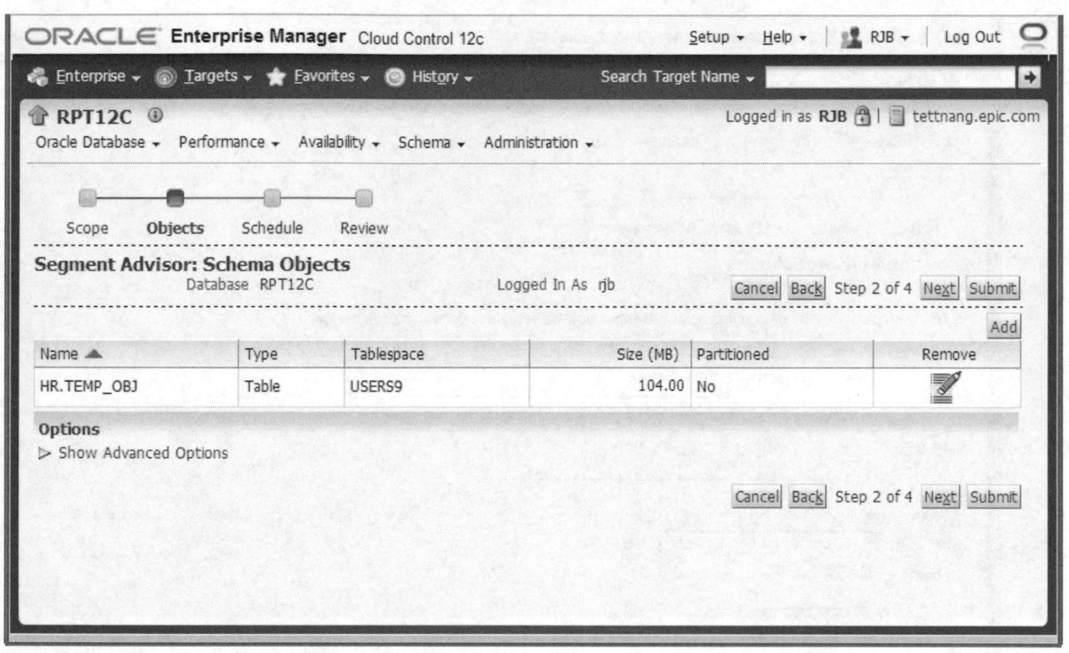

FIGURE 6-9. *Segment Advisor Step 2: Selected objects*

When you click Next in Figure 6-10, you see the review page shown in Figure 6-11. You can click Show SQL if you are curious or if you want to use the SQL statements in your own custom batch job.

As you might suspect, clicking Submit on the page shown in Figure 6-11 submits the job to be run either immediately or at the specified time. The next page you see is the Advisors tab, shown in Figure 6-12. When the job completes you will see the completion status on this page.

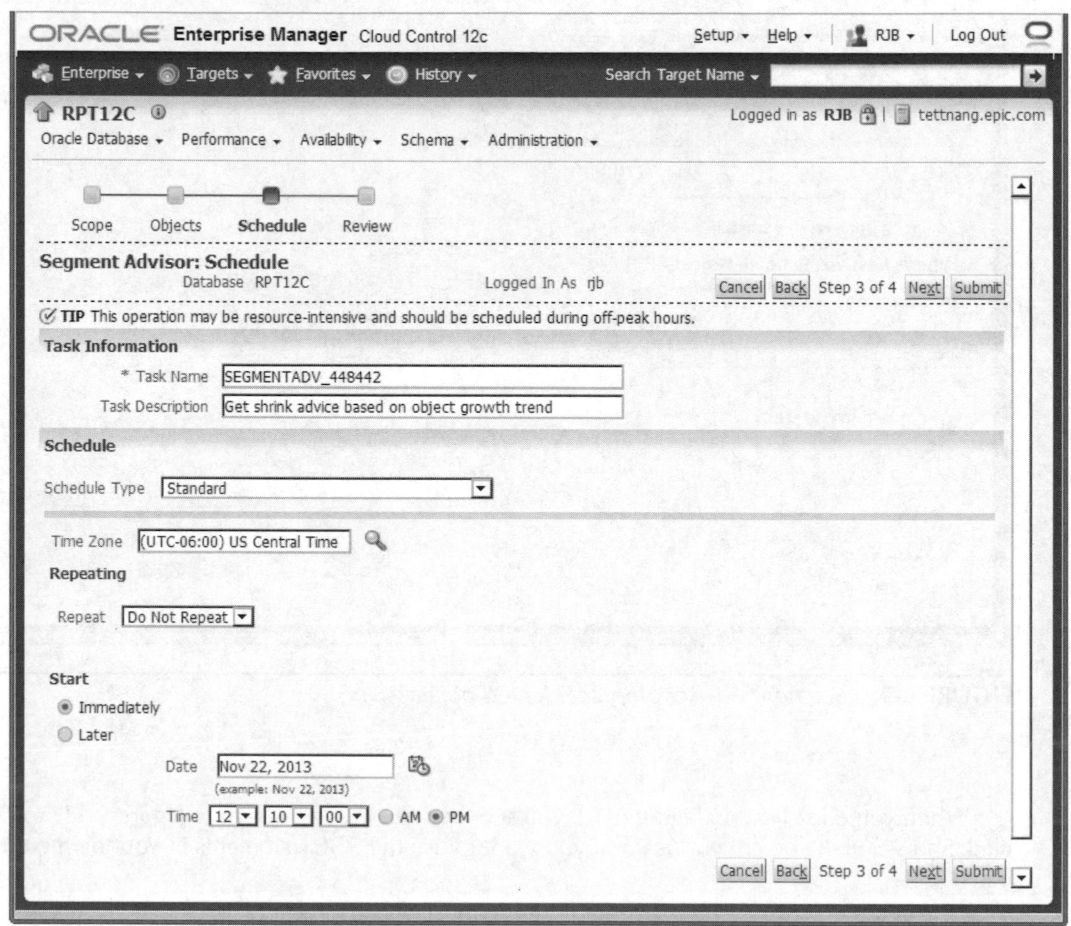

FIGURE 6-10. *Segment Advisor Step 3: Scheduling options*

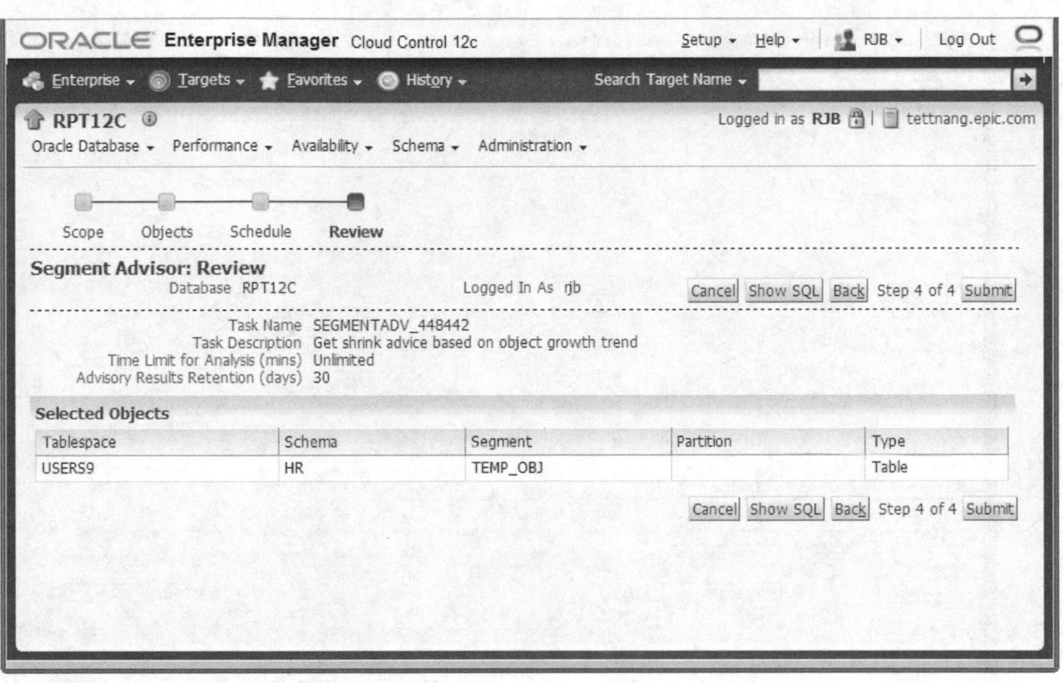

FIGURE 6-11. *Segment Advisor Step 4: Review*

Click the Segment Advisor link in the Results section shown in Figure 6-12, and you will see the Recommendations page shown in Figure 6-13.

The Segment Advisor results in Figure 6-13 indicate that the table TEMP_OBJ in the USERS9 tablespace would benefit from a shrink operation, potentially improving access to the table and freeing up space in the USERS9 tablespace. To implement the recommendation, click the

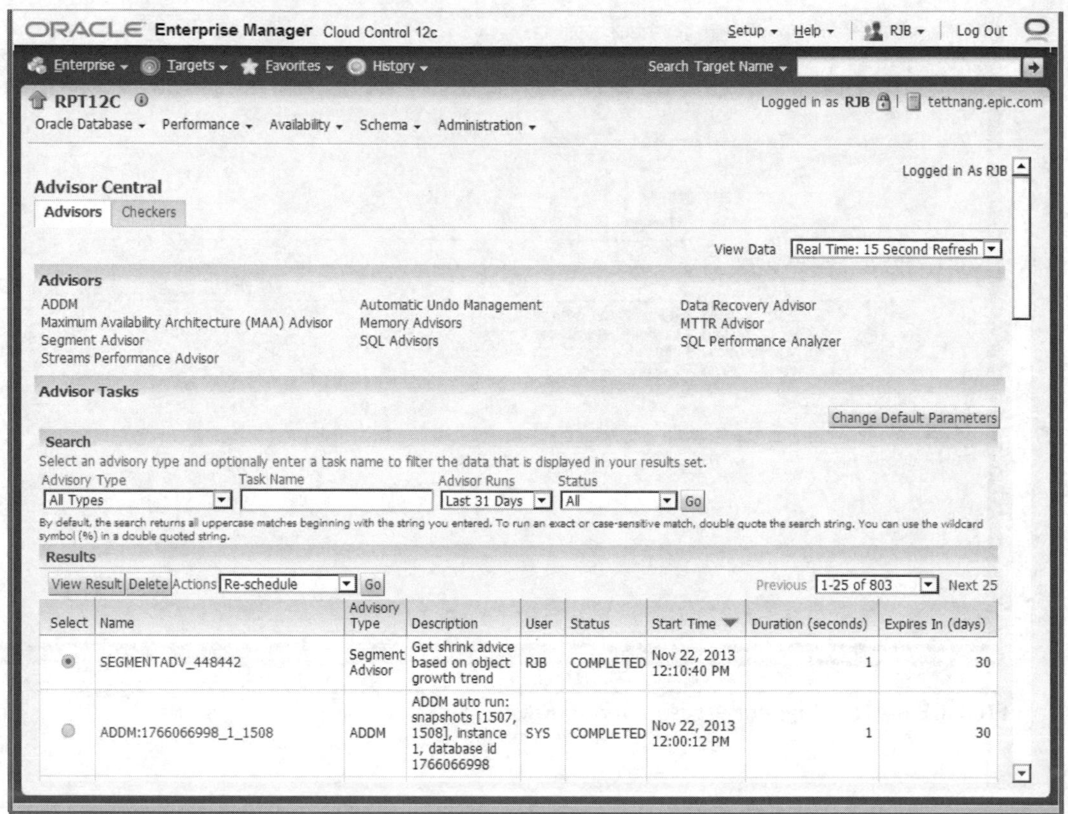

FIGURE 6-12. *Advisors and Advisor Tasks*

Recommendation Details link shown in Figure 6-13, and on the page shown in Figure 6-14, you can click the Shrink button in the Recommendation column to perform the shrink operation on the TEMP_OBJ table.

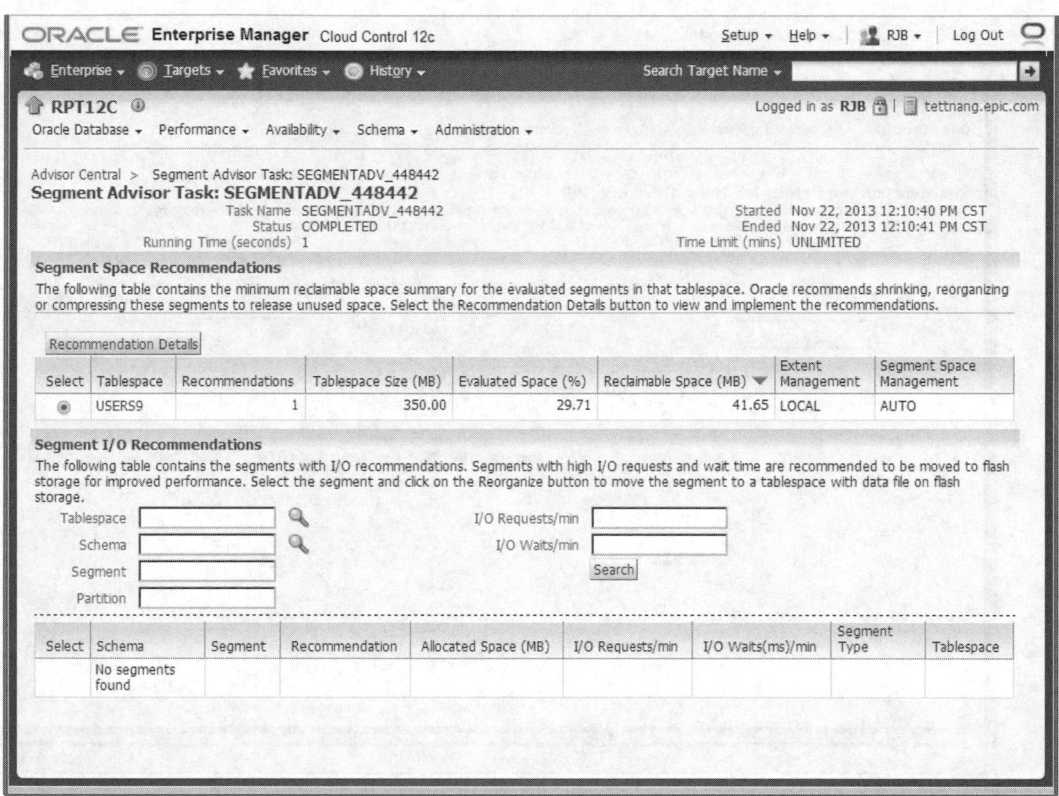

FIGURE 6-13. *Segment Advisor results*

Undo Advisor

To start Automatic Undo Management Advisor, start at the page shown previously in Figure 6-7, and click the Automatic Undo Management link at the top of the page. In Figure 6-15, you see the current settings for the undo tablespace UNDOTBS1.

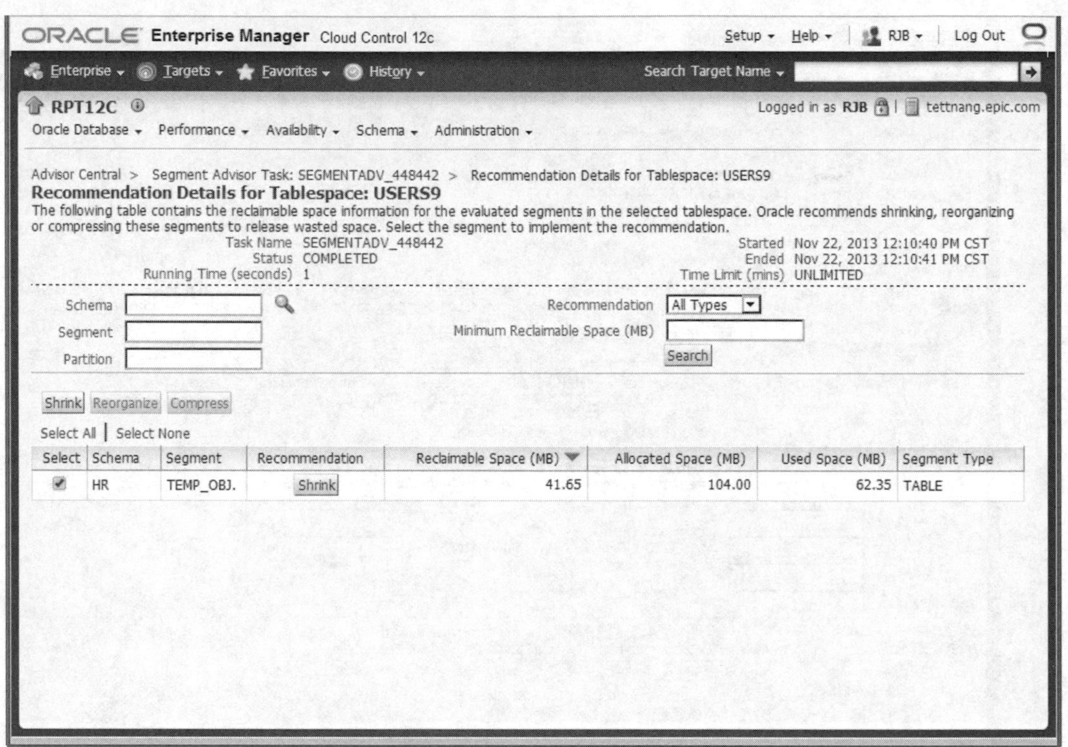

FIGURE 6-14. *Implementing Segment Advisor recommendations*

Given the recent SQL load in this database, the current size of the undo tablespace (265MB) is sufficient (with AUTOEXTEND set at 5MB increments) to satisfy the undo data needs for similar queries in the future. However, you're expecting to add some data warehouse tables and you may have long-running queries that may exceed the current 15-minute undo retention window, and you want to maintain overall system performance by avoiding frequent extensions to the existing

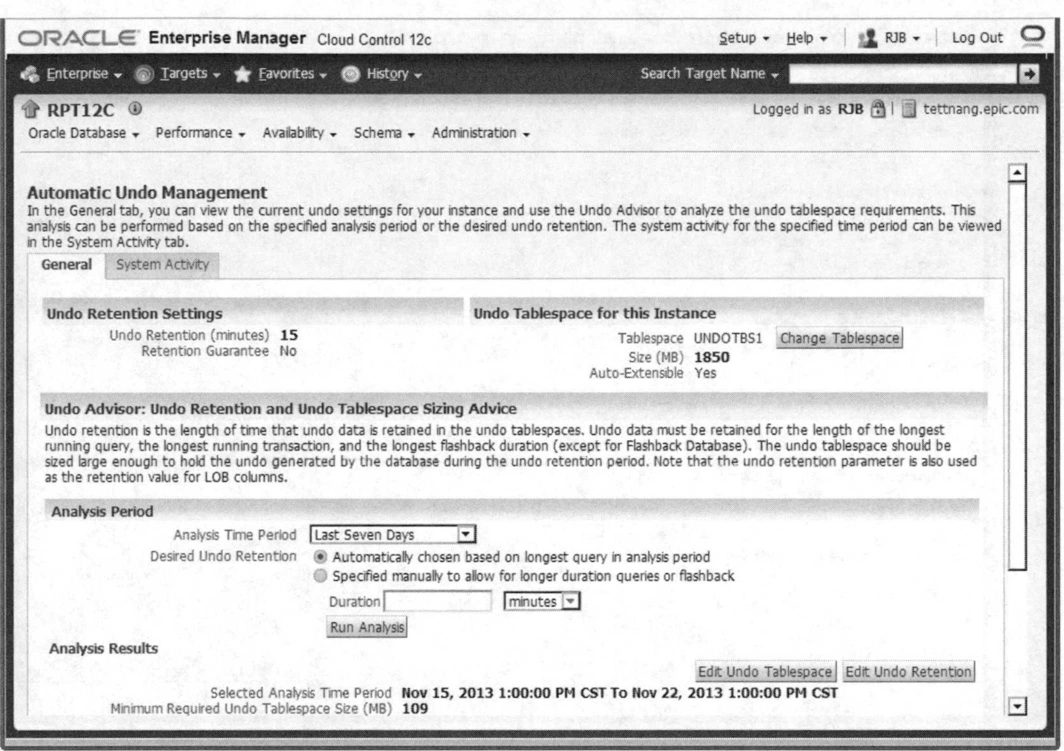

FIGURE 6-15. *Undo Advisor current settings and options*

undo tablespace. Therefore, you probably need to increase the size of the undo tablespace; in Figure 6-15, specify 90 minutes in the Duration text box and click the Run Analysis button. The analysis is performed immediately; at the bottom of Figure 6-16, you see that the minimum required undo tablespace size is 143MB.

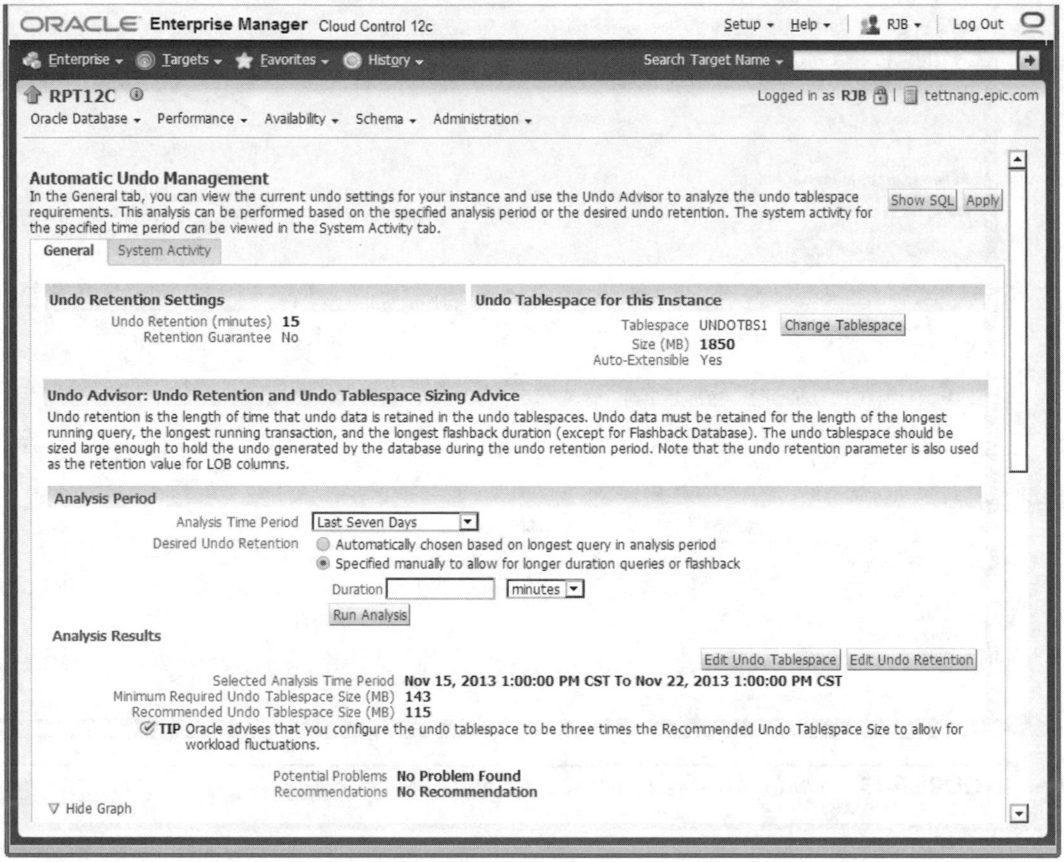

FIGURE 6-16. *Undo Advisor recommendations*

You don't need to change your undo tablespace size immediately; the beauty of Undo Advisor is that you can change the time period for analysis and retention to see what your disk requirements will be in a given scenario.

Summary

It seems you never have enough disk space to hold all of the objects and their data in the database. Even with the ever declining price per GB of storage and the advancements in solid state storage, each GB still has a price attached to it. Given a finite amount of disk space, you must understand how this storage is structured in the database and how to query the structures themselves. You must understand the hierarchy of storage components in the database and this chapter explained that hierarchy with blocks, extents, segments, datafiles, and tablespaces.

Once you know how the storage is structured, you must be able to query that storage metadata. Oracle provides a number of data dictionary and dynamic performance views to show you where and how your storage is allocated. Data dictionary views such as DBA_SEGMENTS shows you the tables, indexes, and materialized views; DBA_EXTENTS shows how those segments were allocated. Dynamic performance views such as V$UNDOSTAT have real-time information about the UNDO tablespace and its occupants.

Oracle not only provides you with these views but gives you an advisor framework to proactively alert you to impending space issues based on thresholds you provide. You can be alerted to space usage at several levels including the tablespace, disk group, and even OS level so that you can maintain an SLA that mandates little or no downtime.

CHAPTER 7

Managing Transactions with Undo Tablespaces

In Chapter 6, we touched briefly on how the space in an undo tablespace is managed, along with views such as V$UNDOSTAT that can help the DBA monitor and size the undo tablespace. In this chapter, we'll delve much more deeply into the configuration and management of the undo tablespace, and how we may resolve the sometimes conflicting requirements of providing enough undo for read consistency while also ensuring that DML statements will not fail.

To start off this chapter, we'll do a quick review of transactions from a database user's point of view so that you will better understand how to support the user's transactions with the appropriately sized undo tablespace. Next, we'll cover the basics of how to create an undo tablespace, either during database creation or later using the familiar CREATE TABLESPACE command. Undo segments fulfill a number of requirements for database users, and I will enumerate and explain each of those requirements in some detail.

Oracle provides a number of ways to monitor and, as a result, more precisely size undo tablespaces. The package DBMS_ADVISOR can be used to analyze the undo tablespace usage, as we did in Chapter 6; we will investigate this package in more detail and look at how Oracle Enterprise Manager Cloud Control can make it easy to perform the analysis. Oracle Database 12*c* further refines the resource requirements for undo by allowing the undo against temporary tables to be stored in a temporary tablespace.

I'll also review the different types of Oracle Flashback features that rely on an adequately sized undo tablespace to recover from a number of different user error scenarios. All the major Flashback features at the query, table, or transaction level are covered in this chapter; Flashback Database is covered in Chapter 16.

Rollback segments from previous Oracle releases were hard to manage and were usually sized too large or too small by most DBAs; Oracle strongly recommends that all new databases use Automatic Undo Management and that databases upgraded from a previous version of Oracle be converted to using Automatic Undo Management. We won't cover any aspects of manual undo management here except for how to migrate from rollback segments to automatic undo.

Transaction Basics

A *transaction* is a collection of SQL DML statements that is treated as a logical unit; the failure of any of the statements in the transaction implies that none of the other changes made to the database in the transaction should be permanently saved to the database. Once the DML statements in the transaction have successfully completed, the application or SQL*Plus user will issue a COMMIT to make the changes permanent. In the classic banking example, a transaction that transfers a dollar amount from one account to another is successful only if both the debit of one account (an UPDATE of the savings account balance) and the credit of another account (an UPDATE of the checking account balance) are successful. Failure of either or both statements invalidates the entire transaction. When the application or SQL*Plus user issues a COMMIT, if only one or the other of the UPDATE statements is successful, the bank will have some very unhappy customers!

A transaction is initiated implicitly. After a COMMIT of a previous transaction is completed, and at least one row of a table is inserted, updated, or deleted, a new transaction is implicitly created (an UPDATE with a predicate returning no rows does not create a transaction slot). Also, any DDL commands such as CREATE TABLE and ALTER INDEX will commit an active transaction and begin a new transaction. You can name a transaction by using the SET TRANSACTION . . . NAME '*transaction_name*' command. Although this provides no direct benefit to the application, the name assigned to the transaction is available in the dynamic performance view V$TRANSACTION and allows a DBA to monitor long-running transactions; in addition, the transaction name helps the DBA resolve in-doubt transactions in distributed database environments. The SET TRANSACTION command, if used, must be the first statement within the transaction.

Within a given transaction, you can define a *savepoint*. A savepoint allows the sequence of DML commands within a transaction to be partitioned so that it is possible to roll back one or more of the DML commands after the savepoint, and subsequently submit additional DML commands or commit the DML commands performed before the savepoint. Savepoints are created with the SAVEPOINT *savepoint_name* command. To undo the DML commands since the last savepoint, you use the command ROLLBACK TO SAVEPOINT *savepoint_name*.

A transaction is implicitly committed if a user disconnects from Oracle normally; if the user process terminates abnormally, the most recent transaction is rolled back.

Undo Basics

Undo tablespaces facilitate the rollback of logical transactions. In addition, undo tablespaces support a number of other features, including read consistency, various database-recovery operations, and Flashback functions.

Rollback

As described in the previous section, any DML command within a transaction—whether the transaction is one or one hundred DML commands—may need to be rolled back. When a DML command makes a change to a table, the old data values changed by the DML command are recorded in the undo tablespace within a system-managed undo segment or a rollback segment.

When an entire transaction is rolled back (that is, a transaction without any savepoints), Oracle undoes all the changes made by DML commands since the beginning of the transaction using the corresponding undo records, releases the locks on the affected rows, if any, and the transaction ends.

If part of a transaction is rolled back to a savepoint, Oracle undoes all changes made by DML commands after the savepoint. All subsequent savepoints are lost, all locks obtained after the savepoint are released, and the transaction remains active.

Read Consistency

Undo provides *read consistency* for users who are reading rows that are involved in a DML transaction by another user. In other words, all users who are reading the affected rows will see no changes in the rows until they issue a new query after the DML user commits the transaction. Undo segments are used to reconstruct the data blocks back to a read-consistent version and, as a result, provide the previous values of the rows to any user issuing a SELECT statement before the transaction commits.

For example, user CLOLSEN begins a transaction at 10:00 that is expected to commit at 10:15, with various updates and insertions to the EMPLOYEES table. As each INSERT, UPDATE, and DELETE occurs on the EMPLOYEES table, the old values of the table are saved in the undo tablespace. When the user SUSANP issues a SELECT statement against the EMPLOYEES table at

10:08, none of the changes made by CLOLSEN are visible to anyone except CLOLSEN; the undo tablespace provides the previous values of CLOLSEN's changes for SUSANP and all other users. Even if the query from SUSANP does not finish until 10:20, the table still appears to be unchanged until a new query is issued after the changes are committed. Until CLOLSEN performs a COMMIT at 10:15, the data in the table appears unchanged as of 10:00.

If there is not enough undo space available to hold the previous values of changed rows, the user issuing the SELECT statement may receive an "ORA-01555: Snapshot Too Old" error. Later in this chapter, we will discuss ways in which we can address this issue.

Database Recovery

Undo tablespaces are also a key component of instance recovery. The online redo logs bring both committed and uncommitted transactions forward to the point in time of the instance crash; the undo data is used to roll back any transactions that were not committed at the time of the crash or instance failure.

Flashback Operations

The data in the undo tablespace is used to support the various types of Flashback options: Flashback Table, Flashback Query, and the package DBMS_FLASHBACK. Flashback Table will restore a table as of a point of time in the past, Flashback Query lets you view a table as of an SCN or time in the past, and DBMS_FLASHBACK provides a programmatic interface for Flashback operations. Flashback Data Archive, new as of Oracle Database 11*g*, stores and tracks all transactions on a specified table for a specified time period; in a nutshell, Flashback Data Archive stores undo data for a specific table in a specific tablespace outside of the global undo tablespace. Also new as of Oracle Database 11*g* is Flashback Transaction Backout that can roll back an already committed transaction and its dependent transactions while the database is online. All these Flashback options are covered in more detail at the end of this chapter.

Managing Undo Tablespaces

Creating and maintaining undo tablespaces is a "set it and forget it" operation once the undo requirements of the database are understood. Within the undo tablespace, Oracle automatically creates, sizes, and manages the undo segments, unlike previous versions of Oracle in which the DBA would have to manually size and constantly monitor rollback segments.

In the next couple sections, we'll review the processes used to create and manage undo tablespaces, including the relevant initialization parameters. In addition, we'll review some scenarios where we may create more than one undo tablespace and how to switch between undo tablespaces.

Creating Undo Tablespaces

Undo tablespaces can be created in two ways: at database creation or with the CREATE TABLESPACE command after the database is created. As with any other tablespace in Oracle 12*c*, the undo tablespace can be a bigfile tablespace, further easing the maintenance of undo tablespaces.

Creating an Undo Tablespace with CREATE DATABASE

A database may have more than one undo tablespace, although only one can be active at a time. Here's what creating an undo tablespace at database creation looks like:

```
create database ord
     user sys identified by ds88dkw2
     user system identified by md78s233
     sysaux datafile '/u02/oradata/ord/sysaux001.dbf' size 1g
     default temporary tablespace temp01
        tempfile '/u03/oradata/ord/temp001.dbf' size 150m
     undo tablespace undotbs01
        datafile '/u01/oradata/ord/undo001.dbf' size 500m;
```

If the undo tablespace cannot be successfully created in the CREATE DATABASE command, the entire operation fails. The error must be corrected, any files remaining from the operation must be deleted, and the command must be reissued.

Although the UNDO TABLESPACE clause in the CREATE DATABASE command is optional, if it is omitted and Automatic Undo Management is enabled (the default), an undo tablespace is still created with an autoextensible datafile with an initial size of 10MB and the default name SYS_UNDOTBS.

Creating an Undo Tablespace with CREATE TABLESPACE

Any time after the database is created, a new undo tablespace can be created. An undo tablespace is created just as any other tablespace with the addition of the UNDO keyword:

```
create undo tablespace undotbs02
   datafile '/u01/oracle/rbdb1/undo0201.dbf'
   size 500m reuse autoextend on;
```

Most DML won't need more than 500MB of UNDO space, so we start out this tablespace at only 500MB and allow it to grow for the occasional larger or one-time DML statements that might need more.

Extents in an undo tablespace must be system managed; in other words, you can only specify EXTENT MANAGEMENT as LOCAL AUTOALLOCATE.

Creating an Undo Tablespace Using EM Cloud Control

Creating an undo tablespace is straightforward using Enterprise Manager Cloud Control. From the instance's home page, navigate to Administration | Storage | Tablespaces . You will be presented with a list of existing tablespaces; click the Create button. In Figure 7-1, we're creating a new undo tablespace named UNDO_BATCH. This undo tablespace will be used for all transactions running during the overnight batch window even if SELECT statements are running. Specify Undo Retention Guarantee as well. I'll explain how that works later in this chapter.

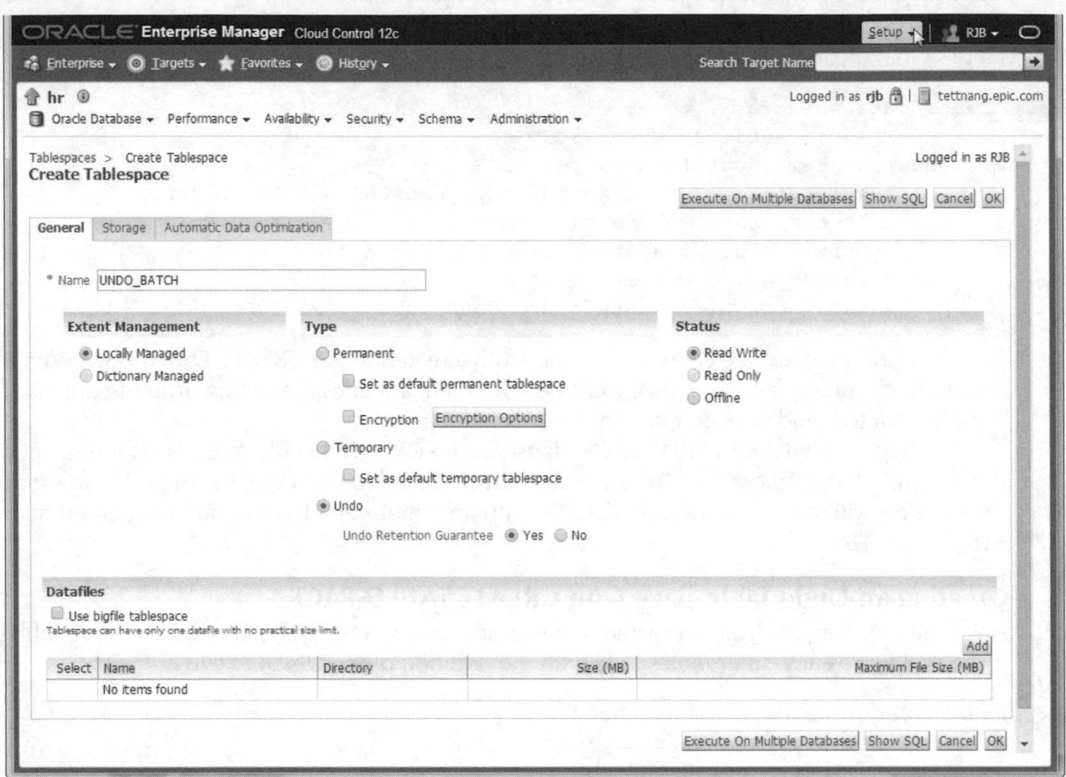

FIGURE 7-1. *Using EM Database Cloud Control to create an undo tablespace*

At the bottom of the screen, click Add and specify the name of the datafile to use for the undo tablespace, as indicated in Figure 7-2. In this example, you use the ASM disk group DATA for the datafile with a size of 500MB and 100MB more each time it extends. Click Continue to return to the page shown in Figure 7-1.

Clicking the Storage tab allows us to specify extent allocation, although for an undo tablespace it must be automatic. If we are supporting multiple block sizes, we can specify the block size for the undo tablespace. Figure 7-3 shows that we are specifying automatic extent allocation and a block size of 8192, the default and only block size defined for the database.

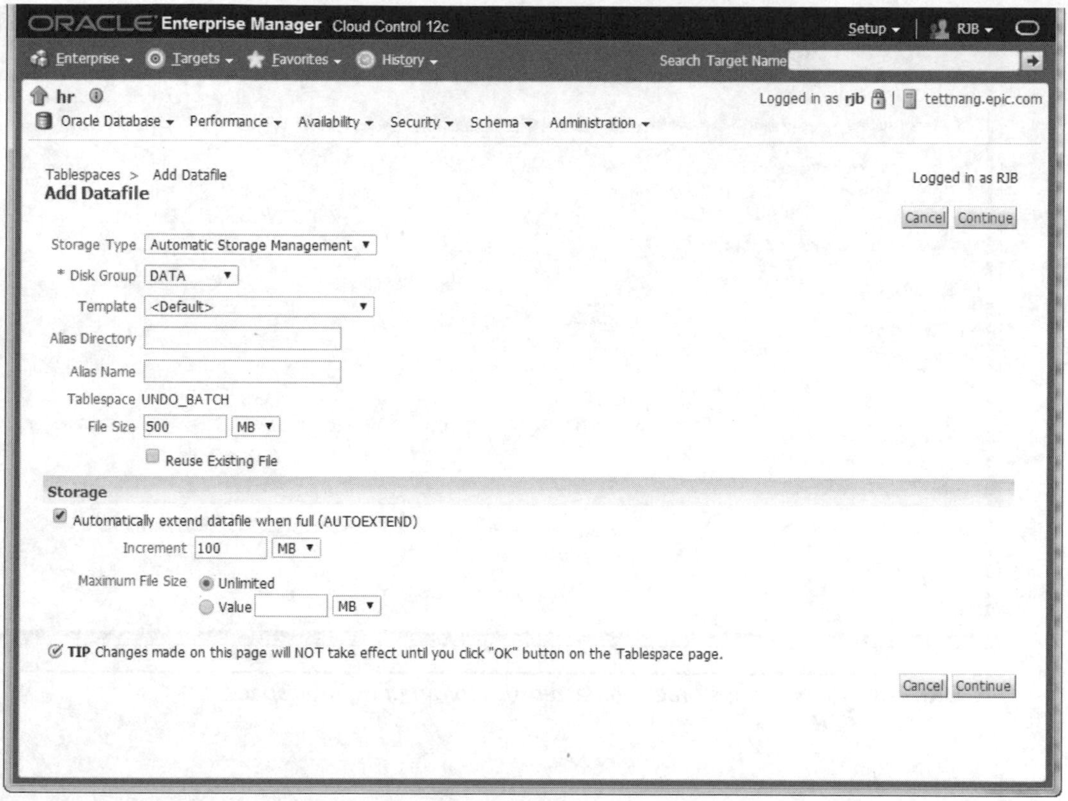

FIGURE 7-2. *Specifying a datafile for a new undo tablespace*

As with most every EM Cloud Control maintenance screen, we can view the actual SQL commands that will be executed when we are ready to create the tablespace. In Figure 7-4, we clicked the Show SQL button to preview the SQL commands used to create the tablespace.

After we click OK on the screen shown in Figure 7-3, the new undo tablespace is created successfully, as shown in Figure 7-5.

Note that EM Cloud Control, although a big timesaver for the DBA, does not cover every possible scenario, nor does it prevent the DBA from trying to create an undo tablespace with the wrong parameters. On the Storage tab in Figure 7-3, we could have specified Uniform under Extent Allocation, but when we then tried to create the undo tablespace, it would have failed with an error message. As mentioned earlier in this chapter, undo tablespaces must have automatically allocated extents.

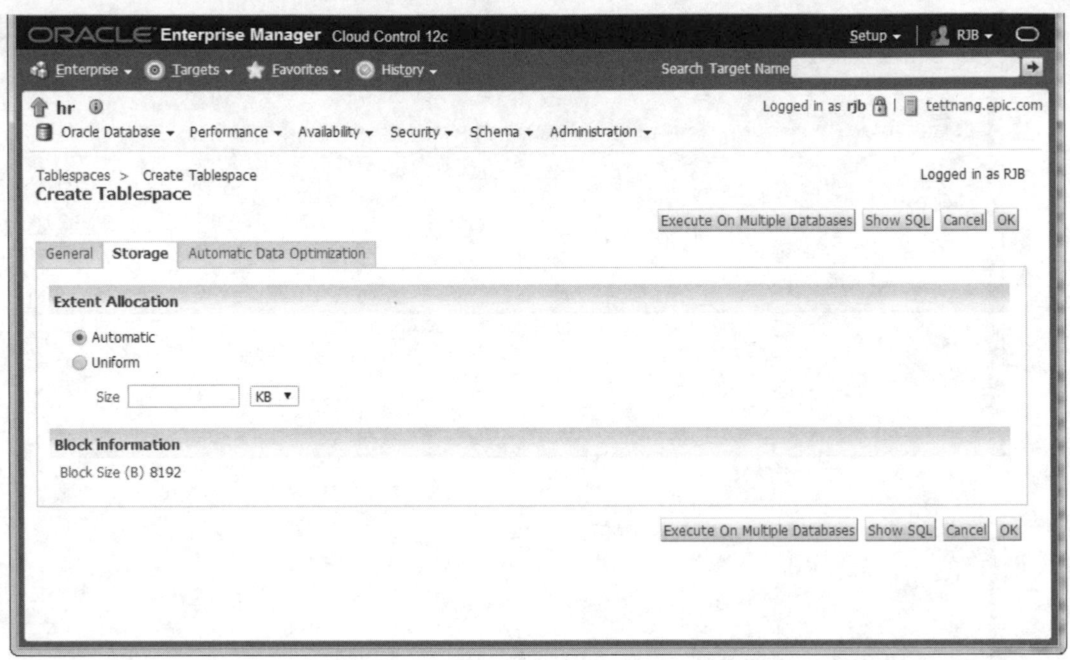

FIGURE 7-3. *Specifying storage characteristics for an undo tablespace*

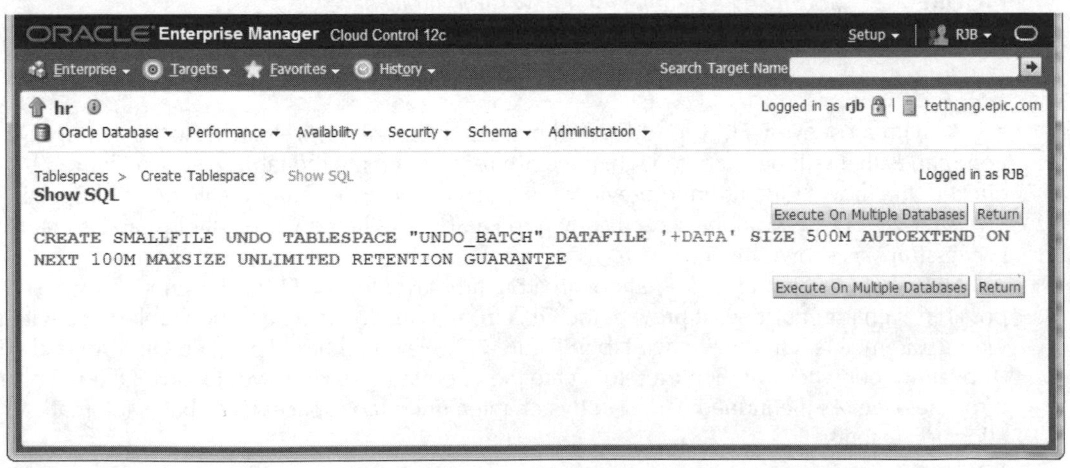

FIGURE 7-4. *Previewing SQL commands to create an undo tablespace*

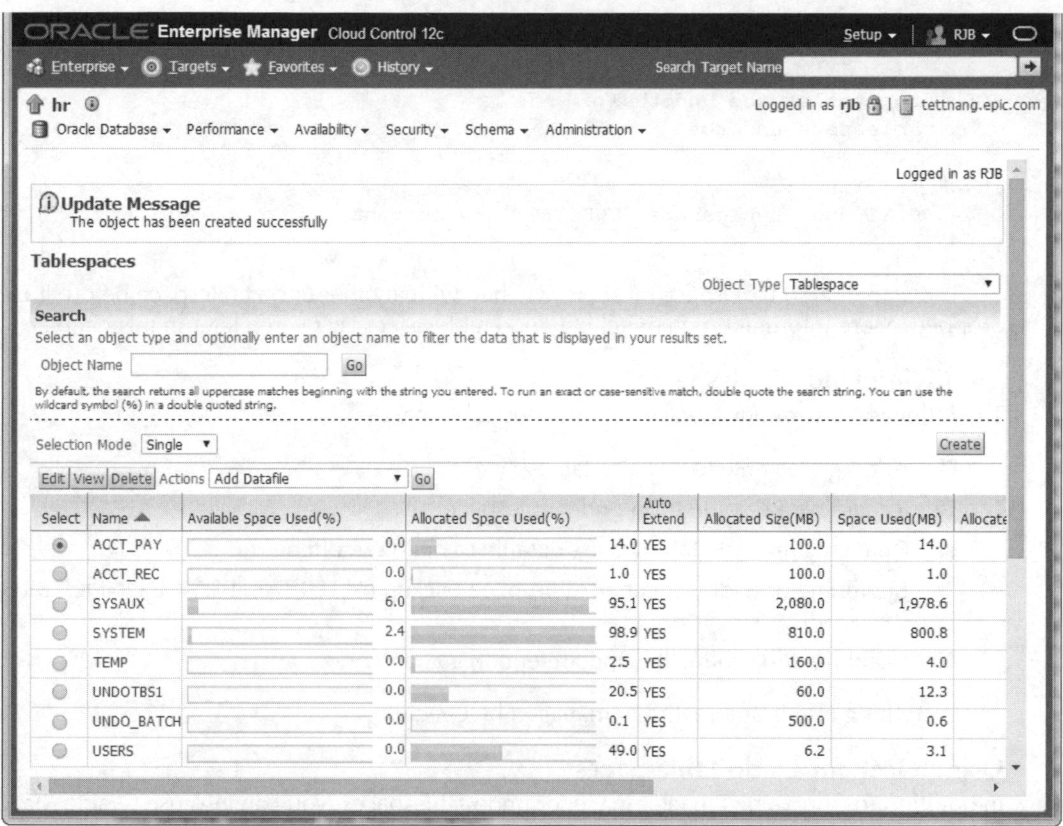

FIGURE 7-5. *Create undo tablespace confirmation*

Dropping Undo Tablespaces

Dropping an undo tablespace is similar to dropping any other tablespace; the only restriction is that the undo tablespace being dropped must not be the active undo tablespace or still have undo data for an uncommitted transaction. You may, however, drop an undo tablespace that has unexpired undo information, which may cause a long-running query to fail. To drop the tablespace we created in the previous section, we use the DROP TABLESPACE command:

```
SQL> drop tablespace undo_batch;
Tablespace dropped.
SQL>
```

The clause INCLUDING CONTENTS is implied when dropping an undo tablespace. However, to remove the operating system data files when the tablespace is dropped, you must specify INCLUDING CONTENTS AND DATAFILES. Trying to drop the active undo tablespace is not allowed:

```
SQL> drop tablespace undotbs1;
drop tablespace undotbs1
*
ERROR at line 1:
ORA-30013: undo tablespace 'UNDOTBS1' is currently in use
SQL>
```

The active undo tablespace must be switched with another undo tablespace before it can be dropped. More information on switching undo tablespaces is covered later in this chapter.

Modifying Undo Tablespaces

The following operations are allowed on undo tablespaces:

- Adding a datafile to an undo tablespace
- Renaming a datafile in an undo tablespace
- Changing an undo tablespace's datafile to online or offline
- Beginning or ending an open tablespace backup (ALTER TABLESPACE UNDOTBS BEGIN BACKUP)
- Enabling or disabling the undo retention guarantee

Everything else is automatically managed by Oracle.

Using OMF for Undo Tablespaces

In addition to using a bigfile tablespace for undo tablespaces, you can also use Oracle Managed Files (OMF) to automatically name (and locate, if you're not using ASM) an undo tablespace; the initialization parameter DB_CREATE_FILE_DEST contains the location where an undo tablespace will be created if the DATAFILE clause is not specified in the CREATE UNDO TABLESPACE command. In the following example, we create an undo tablespace using OMF in an ASM disk group:

```
SQL> show parameter db_create_file_dest
NAME                                 TYPE        VALUE
------------------------------------ ----------- ------------------------------
db_create_file_dest                  string      +DATA

SQL> create undo tablespace undo_bi;
Tablespace created.

SQL> select ts.name ts_name, df.name df_name, bytes
  2  from v$tablespace ts join v$datafile df using(ts#)
  3  where ts.name = 'UNDO_BI';

TS_NAME      DF_NAME                                             BYTES
------------ ------------------------------------------- ----------
UNDO_BI      +DATA/dw/datafile/undo_bi.275.629807457      104857600

SQL>
```

Because we did not specify a datafile size either, the tablespace defaults to a size of 100MB; in addition, the datafile is autoextensible with an unlimited maximum size, limited only by the file system.

Undo Tablespace Dynamic Performance Views

A number of dynamic performance views and data dictionary views contain information about undo tablespaces, user transactions, and undo segments. Table 7-1 contains the view names and their descriptions.

The views in Table 7-1 are described in more detail later in this chapter.

Undo Tablespace Initialization Parameters

The following sections describe the initialization parameters needed to specify the undo tablespace for the database as well as control how long Oracle will retain undo information in the database.

UNDO_MANAGEMENT

The parameter UNDO_MANAGEMENT defaults to MANUAL in Oracle Database 10*g*, and AUTO in Oracle Database 11*g* and 12*c*. Setting the parameter UNDO_MANAGEMENT to AUTO places the database in Automatic Undo Management mode. At least one undo tablespace must exist in the database for this parameter to be valid, whether UNDO_TABLESPACE is specified or not. UNDO_MANAGEMENT is not a dynamic parameter; therefore, the instance must be restarted whenever UNDO_MANAGEMENT is changed from AUTO to MANUAL, or vice versa.

UNDO_TABLESPACE

The UNDO_TABLESPACE parameter specifies which undo tablespace will be used for Automatic Undo Management. If UNDO_MANAGEMENT is not specified or is set to MANUAL, and UNDO_TABLESPACE is specified, the instance will not start.

View	Description
DBA_TABLESPACES	Tablespace names and characteristics, including the CONTENTS column, which can be PERMANENT, TEMPORARY, or UNDO; the undo RETENTION column is NOT APPLY, GUARANTEE, or NOGUARANTEE.
DBA_UNDO_EXTENTS	All undo segments in the database, including their size, their extents, the tablespace where they reside, and current status (EXPIRED or UNEXPIRED).
V$UNDOSTAT	The amount of undo usage for the database at ten-minute intervals; contains at most 1008 rows (7 days).
V$ROLLSTAT	Rollback segment statistics, including size and status.
V$TRANSACTION	Contains one row for each active transaction for the instance.

TABLE 7-1. *Undo Tablespace Views*

NOTE
UNDO_TABLESPACE is used in a Real Application Clusters (RAC) environment to assign a particular undo tablespace to an instance, where the total number of undo tablespaces in the database is the same or more than the number of instances in the cluster.

Conversely, if UNDO_MANAGEMENT is set to AUTO and there is no undo tablespace in the database, the instance will start, but then the SYSTEM rollback segment will be used for all undo operations, and a message is written to the alert log. Any user DML that attempts to make changes in non-SYSTEM tablespaces will, in addition, receive the error message "ORA-01552: cannot use system rollback segment for non-system tablespace 'USERS,'" and the statement fails.

UNDO_RETENTION

UNDO_RETENTION specifies a minimum amount of time that undo information is retained for queries. In automatic undo mode, UNDO_RETENTION defaults to 900 seconds. This value is valid only if there is enough space in the undo tablespace to support read-consistent queries; if active transactions require additional undo space, an unexpired undo may be used to satisfy the active transactions and may cause "ORA-01555: Snapshot Too Old" errors.

The column TUNED_UNDORETENTION of the dynamic performance view V$UNDOSTAT gives the tuned undo retention time for each time period; the status of the undo tablespace usage is updated in V$UNDOSTAT every ten minutes:

```
SQL> show parameter undo_retention

NAME                                 TYPE        VALUE
------------------------------------ ----------- ---------------
undo_retention                       integer     900

SQL> select to_char(begin_time,'yyyy-mm-dd hh24:mi'),
  2  undoblks, txncount, tuned_undoretention
  3  from v$undostat where rownum = 1;

TO_CHAR(BEGIN_TI   UNDOBLKS   TXNCOUNT TUNED_UNDORETENTION
---------------- ---------- ---------- -------------------
2014-08-05 16:07          9         89                 900
1 row selected.
SQL>
```

Because the transaction load is very light during the most recent time period, and the instance has just recently started up, the value in the TUNED_UNDORETENTION column is the same as the minimum specified in the UNDO_RETENTION initialization parameter: 900 seconds (15 minutes). You may even set UNDO_RETENTION to 24 hours or more to facilitate AS OF queries for users without needing DBA intervention.

TIP
You don't need to specify UNDO_RETENTION unless you have Flashback or LOB retention requirements; the UNDO_RETENTION parameter is not used for managing transaction rollback.

Multiple Undo Tablespaces

As mentioned earlier in this chapter, a database can have multiple undo tablespaces, but only one of them can be active for a given instance at any one time. In this section, I'll show an example of switching to a different undo tablespace while the database is open.

NOTE
In a RAC environment, one undo tablespace is required for each instance in the cluster.

In our **dw** database, we have three undo tablespaces:

```
SQL> select tablespace_name, status from dba_tablespaces
  2       where contents = 'UNDO';

TABLESPACE_NAME                STATUS
------------------------------ ---------
UNDOTBS1                          ONLINE
UNDO_BATCH                        ONLINE
UNDO_BI                           ONLINE

3 rows selected.
```

But only one of the undo tablespaces is active:

```
SQL> show parameter undo_tablespace

NAME                           TYPE        VALUE
------------------------------ ----------- ----------------------
undo_tablespace                string      UNDOTBS1
```

For overnight processing, we change the undo tablespace from UNDOTBS1 to the tablespace UNDO_BATCH, which is much larger to support higher DML activity. The disk containing the daytime undo tablespace is much faster but has a limited amount of space; the disk containing the overnight undo tablespace is much larger, but slower. As a result, we use the smaller undo tablespace to support OLTP during the day, and the larger undo tablespace for our data mart and data warehouse loads, as well as other aggregation activities, at night when response time is not as big of an issue.

NOTE
Other than special circumstances described in this section, it is unlikely that you will be switching undo tablespaces for a given instance. Oracle's best practices suggest that you create a single undo tablespace per instance that is large enough to handle all transaction loads; in other words, "set it and forget it."

About the time the undo tablespace is going to be switched, the user HR is performing some maintenance operations on the HR.EMPLOYEES table, and she has an active transaction in the current undo tablespace:

```
SQL> connect hr/hr@dw;
Connected.
SQL> set transaction name 'Employee Maintenance';
Transaction set.
SQL> update employees set commission_pct = commission_pct * 1.1;
107 rows updated.
SQL>
```

Checking V$TRANSACTION, you see HR's uncommitted transaction:

```
SQL> select t.status, t.start_time, t.name
  2    from v$transaction t join v$session s on t.ses_addr = s.saddr
  3    where s.username = 'HR';

STATUS         START_TIME           NAME
-------------- -------------------- -------------------------
ACTIVE         08/05/14 17:41:50    Employee Maintenance

1 row selected.
```

You change the undo tablespace as follows:

```
SQL> alter system set undo_tablespace=undo_batch;
System altered.
```

HR's transaction is still active, and therefore the old undo tablespace still contains the undo information for HR's transaction, leaving the undo segment still available with the following status until the transaction is committed or rolled back:

```
SQL> select r.status
  2     from v$rollstat r join v$transaction t on r.usn=t.xidusn
  3                       join v$session s on t.ses_addr = s.saddr
  4     where s.username = 'HR';

STATUS
---------------
PENDING OFFLINE

1 row selected.
```

Even though the current undo tablespace is UNDO_BATCH, the daytime tablespace UNDOTBS1 cannot be taken offline or dropped until HR's transaction is committed or rolled back:

```
SQL> show parameter undo_tablespace

NAME                         TYPE        VALUE
---------------------------- ----------- ----------------------
undo_tablespace              string      UNDO_BATCH
```

```
SQL> alter tablespace undotbs1 offline;
alter tablespace undotbs1 offline
*
ERROR at line 1:
ORA-30042: Cannot offline the undo tablespace
```

The error message ORA-30042 applies if you try to offline an undo tablespace that is in use—either it is the current undo tablespace or it still has pending transactions. Note that if we switch back to the daytime tablespace before HR commits or rolls back the original transaction, the status of HR's rollback segment reverts to ONLINE:

```
SQL> alter system set undo_tablespace=undotbs1;
System altered.
SQL> select r.status
  2     from v$rollstat r join v$transaction t on r.usn=t.xidusn
  3                        join v$session s on t.ses_addr = s.saddr
  4     where s.username = 'HR';

STATUS
---------------
ONLINE

1 row selected.
```

Sizing and Monitoring the Undo Tablespace

There are three types of undo data in the undo tablespace: *active* or *unexpired*, *expired*, and *unused*. Active or unexpired is undo data that is still needed for read consistency, even after a transaction has been committed. Once all queries needing the active undo data have completed and the undo retention period is reached, the active undo data becomes *expired*. Expired undo data may still be used to support other Oracle features, such as the Flashback features, but it is no longer needed to support read consistency for long-running transactions. Unused undo data is space in the undo tablespace that has never been used.

As a result, the minimum size for an undo tablespace is enough space to hold the before-image versions of all data from all active transactions that have not yet been committed or rolled back. If the space allocated to the undo tablespace cannot even support the changes to uncommitted transactions to support a rollback operation, the user will get the error message "ORA-30036: unable to extend segment by *space_qty* in undo tablespace *tablespace_name*." In this situation, the DBA must increase the size of the undo tablespace, or as a stopgap measure the user can split up a larger transaction into smaller ones while still maintaining any required business rules.

Manual Methods

The DBA can use a number of manual methods to correctly size the undo tablespace. As demonstrated in Chapter 6, we can review the contents of the dynamic performance view

V$UNDOSTAT to see the undo segment usage at ten-minute intervals. In addition, the column SSOLDERRCNT indicates how many queries failed with a "Snapshot too old" error:

```
SQL> select to_char(end_time,'yyyy-mm-dd hh24:mi') end_time,
  2>       undoblks, ssolderrcnt from v$undostat;

END_TIME           UNDOBLKS SSOLDERRCNT
---------------- ---------- -----------
2014-08-02 20:17         45           0
2014-08-02 20:07        116           0
2014-08-02 19:57       2763           0
2014-08-02 19:47         23           0
2014-08-02 19:37      45120           2
2014-08-02 19:27        119           0
2014-08-02 19:17        866           0
```

Between 19:27 and 19:37 we have a spike in undo usage, resulting in some failed queries. As a rule of thumb, you can use the following calculations:

```
undo_tablespace_size = UR * UPS + overhead
```

In this formula, UR equals undo retention in seconds (from the initialization parameter UNDO_RETENTION), UPS equals undo blocks used per second (maximum), and overhead equals undo metadata, usually a very small number relative to the overall size. For example, if a database has an 8KB block size, UNDO_RETENTION equals 43200 (12 hours), and we generate 500 undo blocks every second, all of which must be retained for at least 12 hours, our total undo space must be

```
undo_tablespace_size = 43200 * 500 * 8192 = 176947200000 = 177GB
```

Add about 10 to 20 percent to this calculation to allow for unexpected situations. Alternatively, you can enable autoextend for the datafiles in the undo tablespace. Although this calculation is useful as a starting point, Oracle 10*g*'s and Oracle 11*g*'s built-in advisors, using trending analysis, can give a better overall picture of undo space usage and recommendations.

Undo Advisor

Oracle 12*c*'s Undo Advisor automates a lot of the tasks necessary to fine-tune the amount of space required for an undo tablespace. In Chapter 6, we reviewed two examples of using Undo Advisor: via the EM Cloud Control interface and using the PL/SQL DBMS_ADVISOR packages within the Automatic Workload Repository (AWR) to programmatically choose a time period to analyze and perform the analysis.

The Automatic Undo Management GUI screen is shown in Figure 7-6.

UNDO_RETENTION is currently set to 15 minutes and the size of the active undo tablespace (UNDOTBS1) is 60MB. In this example, if we want a read-consistent view of table data for 720 minutes, clicking the Run Analysis button tells us that we only need an undo tablespace size of only 36MB (and ideally three times this amount) to support workload fluctuations. Therefore, our undo tablespace would be sized adequately for future growth at 108MB.

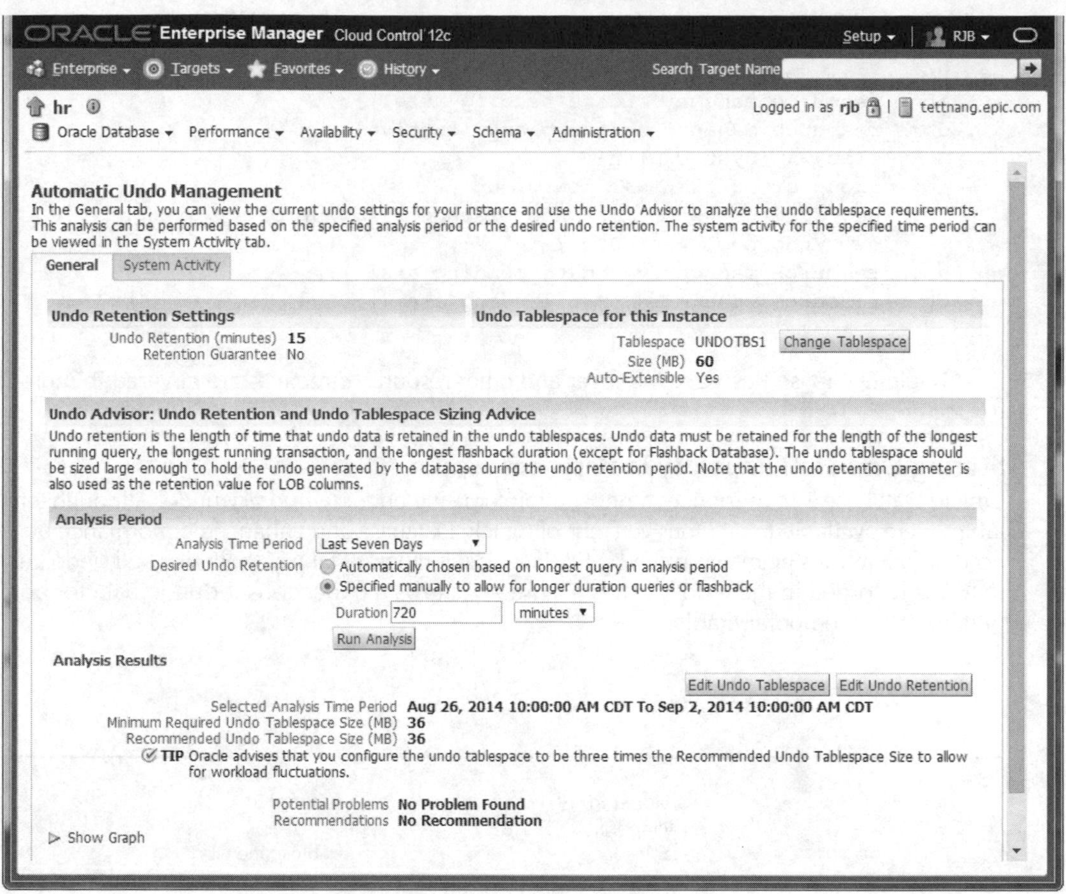

FIGURE 7-6. *Tablespace characteristics*

Controlling Undo Usage

Since Oracle9*i*, Oracle's Database Resource Manager can help to control undo space usage by user or by group of users within a resource consumer group via the UNDO_POOL directive. Each consumer group can have its own undo pool; when the total undo generated by a group exceeds the assigned limit, the current transaction generating the undo is terminated and generates the error message "ORA-30027: Undo quota violation—failed to get *number* (bytes)." The session will have to wait until the DBA increases the size of the undo pool or until other transactions from users in the same consumer group complete.

In the following example, we change the default value of UNDO_POOL from NULL (unlimited) to 50000KB (50MB) for users in the resource consumer group LOW_GROUP:

```
begin
    dbms_resource_manager.create_pending_area();
    dbms_resource_manager.update_plan_directive(
         plan => 'system_plan',
         group_or_subplan => 'low_group',
         new_comment => 'Limit undo space for low priority groups',
         new_undo_pool => 50000);
    dbms_resource_manager.validate_pending_area();
    dbms_resource_manager.submit_pending_area();
end;
```

Oracle Database Resource Manager and other resource directives are covered in more detail in Chapter 5.

Storing Undo in Temporary Tablespaces

Oracle Database 12*c* introduces a new option for using undo: *temporary* undo. Although temporary tables were available in previous versions of Oracle Database and enhanced performance because no redo operations were generated by DML against temporary tables, there was still undo generated that was recorded in the redo log files. Figure 7-7 shows the locations for undo data for both persistent and temporary tables.

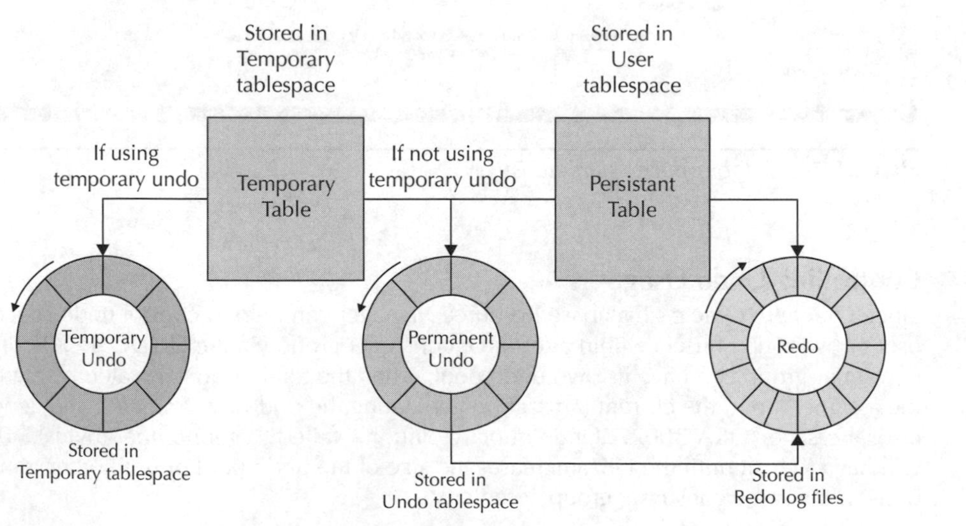

FIGURE 7-7. *Temporary undo architecture*

Undo is still required for a temporary table to ensure consistent reads and transaction rollback to a savepoint for the temporary table used in a single session, but the undo does not have to reside in the database's default undo tablespace. Instead, the undo for temporary tables can reside in the temporary tablespace itself and therefore not generate additional vectors in the online redo log files.

To enable temporary undo at the database level, change the initialization parameter TEMP_UNDO_ENABLED:

```
SQL> alter system set temp_udno_enabled=true;
```

Temporary undo can also be enabled at the session level. To use temporary undo, the COMPATIBLE initialization parameter must be set to at least 12.1.0.0.0.

Read Consistency vs. Successful DML

For OLTP databases, generally we want DML commands to succeed at the expense of read-consistent queries. For a DSS environment, however, we may want long-running queries to complete without getting a "Snapshot too old" error. Although increasing the UNDO_RETENTION parameter or increasing the size of the undo tablespace helps to ensure that undo blocks are available for read-consistent queries, undo tablespaces have another characteristic to help ensure that queries will run to completion: the RETENTION GUARANTEE setting.

Undo retention guarantee is set at the tablespace level, and it can be altered at any time. Setting a retention guarantee for an undo tablespace ensures that any unexpired undo within the tablespace should be retained even if it means that DML transactions might not have enough undo space to complete successfully. By default, a tablespace is created with NOGUARANTEE, unless you specify the GUARANTEE keyword, either when the tablespace is created or later with ALTER TABLESPACE:

```
SQL> alter tablespace undotbs1 retention guarantee;
Tablespace altered.

SQL> select tablespace_name, retention
  2     from dba_tablespaces
  3     where tablespace_name = 'UNDOTBS1';

TABLESPACE_NAME                RETENTION
------------------------------ -----------
UNDOTBS1                       GUARANTEE

1 row selected.
```

For non-undo tablespaces, the value of RETENTION is always NOT APPLY.

Flashback Features

In this section we'll discuss the Flashback features supported by undo tablespaces or Flashback Data Archive: Flashback Query, Flashback Table, Flashback Version Query, and Flashback Transaction Query. In addition, we'll cover the highlights of using the DBMS_FLASHBACK package. As of Oracle Database 11*g*, these features are collectively known as the Oracle Total Recall Option.

Flashback Database and Flashback Drop are covered in Chapter 16. Flashback Database uses Flashback logs in the Flash Recovery Area instead of undo in an undo tablespace to provide the Flashback functionality. Flashback Drop places dropped tables into a virtual recycle bin within the tablespace and they remain there until the user retrieves them with FLASHBACK TABLE . . . TO BEFORE DROP command or empties the recycle bin, or else until the space is needed by new permanent objects in the tablespace.

To further extend the self-service capabilities of Oracle Database 12*c*, the DBA can grant system and object privileges to users to allow them to fix their own problems, usually without any DBA intervention. In the following example, we're enabling the user SCOTT to perform Flashback operations on specific tables and to access transaction metadata across the database:

```
SQL> grant insert, update, delete, select on hr.employees to scott;
Grant succeeded.
SQL> grant insert, update, delete, select on hr.departments to scott;
Grant succeeded.
SQL> grant flashback on hr.employees to scott;
Grant succeeded.
SQL> grant flashback on hr.departments to scott;
Grant succeeded.
SQL> grant select any transaction to scott;
Grant succeeded.
```

Flashback Query

The AS OF clause is available in a SELECT query to retrieve the state of a table as of a given timestamp or SCN. You might use this to find out which rows in a table were deleted since midnight, or you might want to just do a comparison of the rows in a table today versus what was in the table yesterday.

In the following example, HR is cleaning up the EMPLOYEES table and deletes two employees who no longer work for the company:

```
SQL> delete from employees
  2  where employee_id in (195,196);
2 rows deleted.

SQL> commit;
Commit complete.

SQL>
```

Normally, HR will copy these rows to the EMPLOYEES_ARCHIVE table first, but she forgot to do that this time; HR doesn't need to put those rows back into the EMPLOYEES table, but she needs to get the two deleted rows and put them into the archive table. Because HR knows she deleted the rows less than an hour ago, we can use a relative timestamp value with Flashback Query to retrieve the rows:

```
SQL>  insert into hr.employees_archive
  2      select * from hr.employees
  3         as of timestamp systimestamp - interval '60' minute
```

```
  4          where hr.employees.employee_id not in
  5               (select employee_id from hr.employees);

2 rows created.

SQL> commit;
Commit complete.
```

Because we know that EMPLOYEE_ID is the primary key of the table, we can use it to retrieve the employee records that existed an hour ago but do not exist now. Note also that we didn't have to know which records were deleted; we essentially compared the table as it exists now versus an hour ago and inserted the records that no longer exist into the archive table.

TIP
It is preferable to use the SCN for Flashback over a timestamp; SCNs are exact, whereas the timestamp values are only stored every three seconds to support Flashback operations. As a result, enabling Flashback using timestamps may be off by as much as 1.5 seconds.

Although we could use Flashback Table to get the entire table back, and then archive and delete the affected rows, in this case it is much simpler to merely retrieve the deleted rows and insert them directly into the archive table.

Another variation of Flashback Table is to use Create Table As Select (CTAS) with the subquery being a Flashback Query:

```
SQL> delete from employees where employee_id in (195,196);
2 rows deleted.

SQL> commit;
Commit complete.

SQL> create table employees_deleted as
  2         select * from employees
  3            as of timestamp systimestamp - interval '60' minute
  4            where employees.employee_id not in
  5                  (select employee_id from employees);
Table created.

SQL> select employee_id, last_name from employees_deleted;

EMPLOYEE_ID LAST_NAME
----------- -------------------------
        195 Jones
        196 Walsh

2 rows selected.
```

This is known as an *out-of-place restore* (in other words, restoring the table or a subset of the table to a different location than the original). This has the advantage of being able to further manipulate the missing rows, if necessary, before placing them back in the table; for example, after reviewing the out-of-place restore, an existing referential integrity constraint may require that you insert a row into a parent table before the restored row can be placed back in the child table.

One of the disadvantages of an out-of-place restore using CTAS is that neither constraints nor indexes are rebuilt automatically.

DBMS_FLASHBACK

An alternative to Flashback Query is the package DBMS_FLASHBACK. One of the key differences between the DBMS_FLASHBACK package and Flashback Query is that DBMS_FLASHBACK operates at the session level, whereas Flashback Query operates at the object level.

Within a PL/SQL procedure or a user session, DBMS_FLASHBACK can be enabled and all subsequent operations, including existing applications, can be carried out without the AS OF clause being added to SELECT statements. After DBMS_FLASHBACK is enabled as of a particular timestamp or SCN, the database appears as if the clock was turned back to the timestamp or SCN until DBMS_FLASHBACK is disabled. Although DML is not allowed when DBMS_FLASHBACK is enabled, a cursor can be opened in a PL/SQL procedure before DBMS_FLASHBACK is enabled to allow data from a previous point in time to be inserted or updated in the database as of the current point in time.

Table 7-2 lists the procedures available within DBMS_FLASHBACK.

The procedures that enable and disable Flashback mode are relatively simple to use. The complexity usually lies within a PL/SQL procedure, for example, that creates cursors to support DML commands.

In the following example, we'll revisit HR's deletion of the EMPLOYEES rows and how HR can restore those to the table using the DBMS_FLASHBACK package. In this scenario, HR will put the

Procedure	Description
DISABLE	Disables Flashback mode for the session
ENABLE_AT_SYSTEM_CHANGE_NUMBER	Enables Flashback mode for the session, specifying an SCN
ENABLE_AT_TIME	Enables Flashback mode for the session, using the SCN closest to the TIMESTAMP specified
GET_SYSTEM_CHANGE_NUMBER	Returns the current SCN
TRANSACTION_BACKOUT	Backs out a transaction and all dependent transactions using transaction names or transaction identifiers (XIDs)

TABLE 7-2. *DBMS_FLASHBACK Procedures*

deleted employee rows back into the table and instead add a termination date column to the table to reflect the date at which the employees left the company:

```
SQL> delete from hr.employees where employee_id in (195,196);
2 rows deleted.

SQL> commit;
Commit complete.
```

About ten minutes later, HR decides to get those rows back using DBMS_FLASHBACK, and enables Flashback for her session:

```
SQL> execute dbms_flashback.enable_at_time(
  2              to_timestamp(sysdate - interval '45' minute));
PL/SQL procedure successfully completed.
```

Next, HR verifies that the two deleted rows existed as of 45 minutes ago:

```
SQL> select employee_id, last_name from hr.employees
  2     where employee_id in (195,196);

EMPLOYEE_ID LAST_NAME
----------- -------------------------
        195 Jones
        196 Walsh

SQL>
```

To put the rows back into the HR.EMPLOYEES table, HR writes an anonymous PL/SQL procedure to create a cursor to hold the deleted rows, disable Flashback Query, then reinsert the rows:

```
declare
     -- cursor to hold deleted rows before closing
     cursor del_emp is
         select * from employees where employee_id in (195,196);
     del_emp_rec del_emp%rowtype; -- all columns of the employee row
begin
     -- open the cursor while still in Flashback mode
     open del_emp;
     -- turn off Flashback so we can use DML to put the rows
     -- back into the EMPLOYEES table
     dbms_flashback.disable;
     loop
          fetch del_emp into del_emp_rec;
          exit when del_emp%notfound;
          insert into employees values del_emp_rec;
     end loop;
     commit;
     close del_emp;
end; -- anonymous PL/SQL procedure
```

Note that HR could have enabled Flashback within the procedure; in this case, HR enabled it outside of the procedure to run some ad hoc queries, and then used the procedure to create the cursor, turn off Flashback, and reinsert the rows.

Flashback Transaction Backout

A given transaction in a complex application may be consistent and atomic, but the validity of the transaction may not be validated until many other transactions have taken place; in other words, the ill effects of an earlier transaction may cause other transactions to further modify the same data as the original transaction. Trying to manually track the interdependent successive transactions is tedious and error-prone. Flashback Transaction makes it easy to identify and roll back the offending transaction and optionally all dependent transactions.

To enable Flashback Transaction Backout, enable archiving (if it is not already in ARCHIVELOG mode) while the database is mounted (but not open):

```
alter database archivelog;
```

Next, run these commands to create at least one archived redo log file and to add additional transaction information to the log files.

```
alter system archive log current;
alter database add supplemental log data;
```

Adding the supplemental log data will have a noticeable impact on performance in a heavy DML environment. Be sure to monitor system resources before and after you enable the additional logging to assess the cost of the logging operation. Finally, open the database:

```
alter database open;
```

You leverage Flashback Transaction Backout features via the DBMS_FLASHBACK procedure TRANSACTION_BACKOUT. After you run DBMS_FLASHBACK.TRANSACTION_BACKOUT, the DML against the related tables is performed but not committed; you must then review the tables DBA_FLASHBACK_TRANSACTION_STATE and DBA_FLASHBACK_TRANSACTION_REPORT to see if the correct transactions were rolled back. You must then manually perform either a COMMIT or a ROLLBACK.

Flashback Table

The Flashback Table feature not only restores the state of rows in a table as of a point of time in the past, but also restores the table's indexes, triggers, and constraints while the database is online, increasing the overall availability of the database. The table can be restored as of a timestamp or an SCN. Flashback Table is preferable to other Flashback methods if the scope of user errors is small and limited to one or very few tables. It's also the most straightforward method if you know that you want to restore the table to a point in the past unconditionally. For recovering the state of a larger number of tables, Flashback Database may be a better choice. Flashback Table cannot be used on a standby database and cannot reconstruct all DDL operations, such as adding and dropping columns. See Chapter 14 for a way to recover a single table from an RMAN backup.

To use Flashback Table on a table or tables, you must enable *row movement* on the table before performing the Flashback operation, although row movement need not be in effect when the user error occurs. Row movement is also required to support Oracle's segment shrink functionality; because row movement will change the ROWID of a table row, do not enable row movement if your applications depend on the ROWID being the same for a given row until the row is deleted. Because none of our applications reference our tables by ROWID, we can safely enable row movement for the HR tables:

```
SQL> alter table employees enable row movement;
Table altered.
SQL> alter table departments enable row movement;
Table altered.
SQL> alter table jobs enable row movement;
Table altered.
```

The next day, the HR user accidentally deletes all the rows in the EMPLOYEES table due to a cut-and-paste error from an existing script:

```
SQL> delete from hr.employees
  2  /
107 rows deleted.

SQL> commit
  2  ;
Commit complete.

SQL> where employee_id = 195
SP2-0734: unknown command beginning "where empl..." - rest of line ignored.
```

Because the undo tablespace is large enough and the HR user notices the problem within the retention period, the HR user can bring back the entire table quickly without calling the DBA:

```
SQL> flashback table employees
  2      to timestamp systimestamp - interval '15' minute;
Flashback complete.

SQL> select count(*) from employees;
  COUNT(*)
----------
       107
```

If two or more tables have a parent/child relationship with foreign key constraints, and rows were inadvertently deleted from both tables, they can be flashed back in the same FLASHBACK command:

```
SQL>  flashback table employees, departments
  2         to timestamp systimestamp - interval '15' minute;
Flashback complete.
```

The HR user can also use EM Cloud Control to flash back one or more tables by choosing Availability | Perform Recovery to open the Perform Recovery page, shown in Figure 7-8.

In simple scenarios, using the command line would take less time and is probably more straightforward; however, if you have unknown dependencies or if the command-line syntax is unfamiliar to you, then EM Cloud Control is a better option.

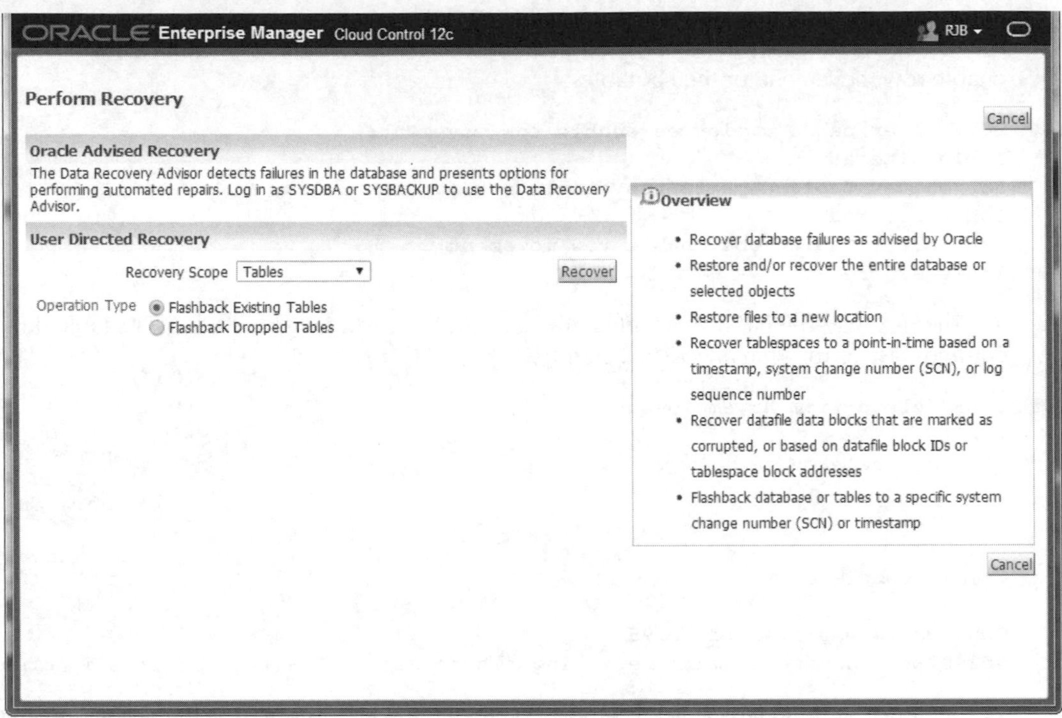

FIGURE 7-8. *EM Cloud Control Perform Recovery page*

Flashback Version Query

Flashback Version Query, another Flashback feature that relies on undo data, provides a finer level of detail than an AS OF query: Whereas the Flashback methods presented up to now bring back rows of a table or an entire table for a particular point in time, Flashback Version Query returns the entire history of a given row between two SCNs or timestamps.

For the examples in this and the next section, the user HR makes a number of changes to the HR.EMPLOYEES and HR.DEPARTMENTS tables:

```
SQL> select dbms_flashback.get_system_change_number from dual;
GET_SYSTEM_CHANGE_NUMBER
------------------------
                 4011365

SQL> update hr.employees set salary = salary*1.2 where employee_id=195;
1 row updated.

SQL> select dbms_flashback.get_system_change_number from dual;
GET_SYSTEM_CHANGE_NUMBER
------------------------
                 4011381
```

```
SQL> delete from hr.employees where employee_id = 196;
1 row deleted.

SQL> select dbms_flashback.get_system_change_number from dual;
GET_SYSTEM_CHANGE_NUMBER
------------------------
                 4011409

SQL> insert into hr.departments values (660,'Security', 100, 1700);
1 row created.

SQL> select dbms_flashback.get_system_change_number from dual;
GET_SYSTEM_CHANGE_NUMBER
------------------------
                 4011433

SQL> update hr.employees set manager_id = 100 where employee_id = 195;
1 row updated.

SQL> commit;
Commit complete.

SQL> select dbms_flashback.get_system_change_number from dual;
GET_SYSTEM_CHANGE_NUMBER
------------------------
                 4011464
SQL> update hr.employees set department_id = 660 where employee_id = 195;
1 row updated.

SQL> select dbms_flashback.get_system_change_number from dual;
GET_SYSTEM_CHANGE_NUMBER
------------------------
                 4011470

SQL> update hr.employees set salary = salary*1.2 where employee_id=195;
1 row updated.

SQL> commit;
Commit complete.

SQL> select dbms_flashback.get_system_change_number from dual;
GET_SYSTEM_CHANGE_NUMBER
------------------------
                 4011508
SQL>
```

The next day, the HR user is out of the office, and the other HR department employees (who use the HR user account) want to know what rows and tables were changed. Using Flashback Version Query, the user HR can see not only the values of a column at a particular time, but the entire history of changes between specified timestamps or SCNs.

A Flashback Version Query uses the VERSIONS BETWEEN clause to specify a range of SCNs or timestamps for analysis of a given table (in this case, the EMPLOYEES table). When VERSIONS BETWEEN is used in a Flashback Version Query, a number of pseudocolumns are available to help identify the SCN and timestamp of the modifications, as well as the transaction ID and the type of operation performed on the row. Table 7-3 shows the pseudocolumns available with Flashback Version Queries.

The HR user runs a Flashback Version Query to see the changes to any key columns in HR.EMPLOYEES for the two employees with IDs 195 and 196:

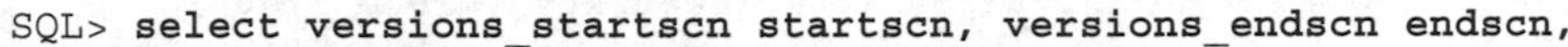

```
SQL> select versions_startscn startscn, versions_endscn endscn,
  2         versions_xid xid, versions_operation oper,
  3         employee_id empid, last_name name, manager_id mgrid, salary sal
  4  from hr.employees
  5  versions between scn 4011365 and 4011508
  6  where employee_id in (195,196);

 STARTSCN    ENDSCN XID              OPER EMPID NAME     MGRID        SAL
--------- --------- ---------------- ---- ----- -------- ----- ----------
  4011507           1100120025000000 U      195 Jones      100       4032
  4011463   4011507 0E001A0024000000 U      195 Jones      100       3360
            4011463                         195 Jones      123       2800
  4011463           0E001A0024000000 D      196 Walsh      124       3100
            4011463                         196 Walsh      124       3100
```

The rows are presented with the most recent changes first. Alternatively, HR could have filtered the query by TIMESTAMP or displayed the TIMESTAMP values, but either can be used in a Flashback Query or Flashback Table operation, if required later. From this output, we see that one employee was deleted and that another employee received two pay adjustments instead of one. It's also worth noting that some of the transactions contain only one DML command, and others have two. In the next section, we'll attempt to correct one or more of these problems.

Pseudocolumn	Description
VERSIONS_START{SCN|TIME}	The starting SCN or timestamp when the change was made to the row.
VERSION_END{SCN|TIME}	The ending SCN or timestamp when the change was no longer valid for the row. If this is NULL, either the row version is still current or the row was deleted.
VERSIONS_XID	The transaction ID of the transaction that created the row version.
VERSIONS_OPERATION	The operation performed on the row (I=Insert, D=Delete, U=Update).

TABLE 7-3. *Flashback Version Query Pseudocolumns*

Column Name	Description
XID	Transaction ID number
START_SCN	SCN for the first DML in the transaction
START_TIMESTAMP	Timestamp of the first DML in the transaction
COMMIT_SCN	SCN when the transaction was committed
COMMIT_TIMESTAMP	Timestamp when the transaction was committed
LOGON_USER	User who owned the transaction
UNDO_CHANGE#	Undo SCN
OPERATION	DML operation performed: DELETE, INSERT, UPDATE, BEGIN, or UNKNOWN
TABLE_NAME	Table changed by DML
TABLE_OWNER	Owner of the table changed by DML
ROW_ID	ROWID of the row modified by DML
UNDO_SQL	SQL statement to undo the DML operation

TABLE 7-4. *FLASHBACK_TRANSACTION_QUERY Columns*

Flashback Transaction Query

Once we have identified any erroneous or incorrect changes to a table, we can use Flashback Transaction Query to identify any other changes that were made by the transaction containing the inappropriate changes. Once identified, all changes within the transaction can be reversed as a group, typically to maintain referential integrity or the business rules used to process the transaction in the first place.

A Flashback Transaction Query, unlike a Flashback Version Query, does not reference the table involved in DML transactions; instead, you query the data dictionary view FLASHBACK_TRANSACTION_QUERY, the columns of which are summarized in Table 7-4.

To further investigate the changes that were made to the EMPLOYEES table, we will query the view FLASHBACK_TRANSACTION_QUERY with the oldest transaction from the query in the previous section:

```
SQL> select start_scn, commit_scn, logon_user,
  2       operation, table_name, undo_sql
  3  from flashback_transaction_query
  4  where xid = hextoraw('0E001A0024000000');

START_SCN COMMIT_SCN LOGON_USER  OPERATION    TABLE_NAME
--------- ---------- ---------- ------------ --------------
UNDO_SQL
----------------------------------------------------------------------
```

```
   4011380     4011463 HR          UPDATE       EMPLOYEES
update "HR"."EMPLOYEES" set "MANAGER_ID" = '123' where ROWID =
'AAARAxAAFAAAAHGABO';

   4011380     4011463 HR          INSERT       DEPARTMENTS
delete from "HR"."DEPARTMENTS" where ROWID = 'AAARAsAAFAAAAA3AAb';

   4011380     4011463 HR          DELETE       EMPLOYEES
insert into "HR"."EMPLOYEES"("EMPLOYEE_ID","FIRST_NAME",
"LAST_NAME","EMAIL","PHONE_NUMBER","HIRE_DATE","JOB_ID","SALARY",
"COMMISSION_PCT","MANAGER_ID","DEPARTMENT_ID","WORK_RECORD")
values ('196','Alana','Walsh','AWALSH','650.507.9811',
TO_DATE('24-APR-08', 'DD-MON-RR'),'SH_CLERK','3100',
NULL,'124','50',NULL);

   4011380     4011463 HR          UPDATE       EMPLOYEES
update "HR"."EMPLOYEES" set "SALARY" = '2800' where
ROWID = 'AAARAxAAFAAAAHGABO';

   4011380     4011463 HR          BEGIN
```

We confirm what we already expected—that another user in the HR department made the deletion and salary update (thus pointing out the usefulness of assigning separate user accounts for each member of the HR department). The UNDO_SQL column contains the actual SQL code that can be used to reverse the effect of the transaction. Note, however, that in this example, this is the first transaction to occur between the SCNs of interest. If other transactions made further updates to the same columns, we may want to review the other updates before running the SQL code in the UNDO_SQL column.

Flashback Data Archive

Regulations such as Sarbanes-Oxley and HIPAA require strict control and tracking requirements for customer and patient data; keeping a historical record of all changes to rows in critical tables is error prone and requires custom applications or database triggers to maintain repositories for the historical changes. Every time you create a new application or update a table in an application that requires historical tracking, you must make changes to your tracking application as well. As of Oracle Database 11*g*, you can use Flashback Data Archive to automatically save historical changes to all key tables for as long as regulatory agencies or your stakeholders require.

Flashback Data Archive is implemented natively in Oracle Database 11*g*; in a nutshell, you create one or more repository areas (one of which can be the default), assign a default retention period for objects in the repository, and then mark the appropriate tables for tracking.

A Flashback Data Archive acts much like an undo tablespace; however, a Flashback Data Archive only records UPDATE and DELETE statements, but not INSERT statements. In addition, undo data is typically retained for a period of hours or days for all objects; rows in Flashback Data Archives can span years or even decades. Flashback Data Archive has a much narrower focus as well, recording only historical changes to table rows; Oracle uses data in an undo tablespace for read-consistency in long-running transactions and to roll back uncommitted transactions.

You can access data in a Flashback Data Archive just as you do with Flashback Query: using the AS OF clause in a SELECT statement. In the next few sections, I'll show you how to create a Flashback Data Archive, assign permissions to users and objects, and query historical data in a Flashback Data Archive.

Creating an Archive

You can create one or several Flashback Data Archives in existing tablespaces using the CREATE FLASHBACK ARCHIVE command; however, Oracle best practice recommends that you use dedicated tablespaces. All archives must have a default retention period using the RETENTION clause and can optionally be identified as the default archive using the DEFAULT keyword. The disk quota in an archive is limited by the disk space within the tablespace unless you assign a maximum amount of disk space in the archive using the QUOTA keyword.

In this example, you first create a dedicated tablespace for your Flashback Data Archive:

```
SQL> create tablespace fbda1
  2  datafile '+data' size 10g;

Tablespace created.
SQL>
```

Next, you create three Flashback Data Archives: one for the ES department with no quota limit and a ten-year retention period, a second one for the finance department with a 500MB limit and a seven-year retention period, and a third for all other users in the USERS4 tablespace as the default with a 250MB limit and a two-year retention period:

```
SQL> create flashback archive fb_es
  2  tablespace fbda1 retention 10 year;

Flashback archive created.

SQL> create flashback archive fb_fi
  2  tablespace fbda1 quota 500m
  3  retention 7 year;

Flashback archive created.

SQL> create flashback archive default fb_dflt
  2  tablespace users4 quota 250m
  3  retention 2 year;

Flashback archive created.

SQL>
```

You cannot specify more than one tablespace in the CREATE FLASHBACK ARCHIVE command; you must use the ALTER FLASHBACK ARCHIVE command to add a tablespace, as you'll see a bit later in this chapter, in the section "Managing Flashback Data Archives."

Using Flashback Data Archive Data Dictionary Views

Two new data dictionary views support Flashback Data Archives: DBA_FLASHBACK_ARCHIVE and DBA_FLASHBACK_ARCHIVE_TS. DBA_FLASHBACK_ARCHIVE lists the archives, and DBA_FLASHBACK_ARCHIVE_TS displays the tablespace-to-archive mapping:

```
SQL> select flashback_archive_name, flashback_archive#,
  2      retention_in_days, status
  3  from dba_flashback_archive;

FLASHBACK_AR FLASHBACK_ARCHIVE# RETENTION_IN_DAYS STATUS
------------ ------------------ ----------------- -------
FB_ES                         1              3650
FB_FI                         2              2555
FB_DFLT                       3               730 DEFAULT

SQL> select * from dba_flashback_archive_ts;

FLASHBACK_AR FLASHBACK_ARCHIVE# TABLESPACE QUOTA_IN_M
------------ ------------------ ---------- ----------
FB_ES                         1 FBDA1
FB_FI                         2 FBDA1      500
FB_DFLT                       3 USERS4     250

SQL>
```

The view DBA_FLASHBACK_ARCHIVE_TABLES tracks the tables enabled for flashback archiving. I'll show you the contents of this view later in this chapter after enabling a table for flashback archiving.

Assigning Flashback Data Archive Permissions

A user must have the FLASHBACK ARCHIVE ADMINISTER system privilege to create or modify Flashback Data Archives, and the FLASHBACK ARCHIVE object privilege to enable tracking on a table. Once tracking is enabled, a user doesn't need any specific permissions to use the AS OF clause in a SELECT statement other than the SELECT permission on the table itself.

The FLASHBACK_ARCHIVE_ADMINSTER privilege also includes adding and removing tablespaces from an archive, dropping an archive, and performing an ad hoc purge of history data.

Managing Flashback Data Archives

You can easily add another tablespace to an existing archive; use the ALTER FLASHBACK ARCHIVE command like this to add the USERS3 tablespace to the FB_DFLT archive with a quota of 400MB:

```
SQL> alter flashback archive fb_dflt
  2  add tablespace users3 quota 400m;

Flashback archive altered.

SQL>
```

You can purge archive data with the PURGE clause; in this example, you want to purge all rows in the FB_DFLT archive before January 1, 2010:

```
SQL> alter flashback archive fb_dflt
  2  purge before timestamp
  3  to_timestamp('2010-01-01 00:00:00', 'YYYY-MM-DD HH24:MI:SS');
```

Assigning a Table to a Flashback Data Archive

You assign a table to an archive either at table creation using the standard CREATE TABLE syntax with the addition of the FLASHBACK ARCHIVE clause, or later with the ALTER TABLE command, as in this example:

```
SQL> alter table hr.employees flashback archive fb_es;

Table altered.
```

Note that the previous command specified a specific archive for the HR.EMPLOYEES table; if you did not specify an archive, Oracle would assign FB_DFLT. You can review the tables that use Flashback Data Archive by querying the data dictionary view DBA_FLASHBACK_ARCHIVE_TABLES:

```
SQL> select * from dba_flashback_archive_tables;

TABLE_NAME             OWNER_NAME FLASHBACK_AR ARCHIVE_TABLE_NAME
---------------------- ---------- ------------ --------------------
EMPLOYEES              HR         FB_ES        SYS_FBA_HIST_70313
```

Querying Flashback Data Archives

Querying the historical data for a table in a Flashback Data Archive is as easy as using the AS OF clause in a table when you are using DML activity stored in an undo tablespace. In fact, users will not know whether they are retrieving historical data from the undo tablespace or from a Flashback Data Archive.

In this scenario, much like in the scenarios earlier in this chapter, one of the employees in the HR department deletes an employee row in the EMPLOYEES table and forgets to archive it to the EMPLOYEE_HISTORY table first; with Flashback Data Archive enabled for the EMPLOYEES table, the HR employee can rely on the FB_ES archive to satisfy any queries on employees no longer in the EMPLOYEE table. This is the DELETE statement from three weeks ago:

```
SQL> delete from employees where employee_id = 169;

1 row deleted.

SQL>
```

The HR employee needs to find the hire date for employee 169, so she retrieves the historical information from the EMPLOYEES table with the AS OF clause specifying a time four weeks ago:

```
SQL> select employee_id, last_name, hire_date
  2  from employees
  3  as of timestamp (systimestamp - interval '28' day)
```

```
  4  where employee_id = 169;

EMPLOYEE_ID LAST_NAME                 HIRE_DATE
----------- ------------------------- ---------
        169 Bloom                     23-MAR-98

SQL>
```

Whether Oracle is using an undo tablespace or a Flashback Data Archive for a query containing AS OF is completely transparent to the user.

Flashback and LOBs

Undo data for LOB columns in a table can take up gigabytes of disk space even for a single row; therefore, to enable flashback operations for LOB columns, you must explicitly specify the RETENTION keyword in the storage clause for the LOB. This keyword is mutually exclusive with the PCTVERSION keyword, which specified a percentage of the table space for old versions of the LOBs. If you use the RETENTION keyword, old versions of a LOB are retained for the amount of time specified by the UNDO_RETENTION parameter, just as any other table rows in the undo tablespace.

Migrating to Automatic Undo Management

To migrate your environment from manually managed rollback segments to Automatic Undo Management, you need to know one thing: how large to size the undo tablespace based on the usage of the rollback segments in manual undo mode. With all manual rollback segments online, execute the procedure DBMS_UNDO_ADV.RBU_MIGRATION to return the size, in megabytes, of the current rollback segment utilization:

```
SQL> variable undo_size number
SQL> begin
  2        :undo_size := dbms_undo_adv.rbu_migration;
  3  end;
  4  /

PL/SQL procedure successfully completed.

SQL> print :undo_size

 UNDO_SIZE
----------
      2840

SQL>
```

In this example, an undo tablespace created to replace the rollback segments should be at least 2840MB, or 2.84GB, to support the undo requirements currently supported by rollback segments.

Summary

Rarely does an Oracle database environment support only OLTP with constant DML or only BI queries. Even though your e-commerce database primarily takes customer orders, you need to run real-time analytic queries during the day along with the hourly extracts to the data warehouse. As a result you have at least two conflicting priorities for space in your undo tablespace. You need to have enough space in the undo tablespace to roll back failed transactions in addition to providing read consistency for long-running queries initiated while hundreds or even thousands of transactions are running against the same database.

The last three versions of Oracle Database (including 12*c*) have new features that leverage undo data beyond transaction consistency and read consistency, in particular the Flashback Query features covered in this chapter. As a result, your undo tablespace seems to get bigger with every release and requires a longer retention period for the undo data. This is not a problem as long as you, the DBA, understand your workload and set parameters such as UNDO_RETENTION appropriately along with specifying the RETENTION GUARANTEE parameter for a given undo tablespace.

The key to successful undo management involves using not only the tools available for reactive management such as Oracle Enterprise Manager Cloud Control 12*c* but also the extensive procedures in the DBMS_ADVISOR PL/SQL package to analyze your database on a regular basis and size your undo tablespace for the constantly changing workload—both the type of workload and the inevitable size of your workload as the demand for database consolidation increases.

CHAPTER 8

Database Tuning

From a tuning perspective, every system has a performance bottleneck that may move from component to component over a time period of days or even weeks The goal of performance design is to make sure that the physical limitations of the applications and the associated hardware—I/O throughput rates, memory sizes, query performance, and so on—do not impact the business performance. If the application performance limits the business process it is supposed to be supporting, the application must be tuned. During the design process, the limits of the application environment must be evaluated, including the hardware and the design of the application's interactions with the database. No environment provides infinite computing capacity, so every environment is designed to fail at some performance point. In the process of designing the application, you should strive to have your performance needs amply served by the performance capabilities of the environment.

Performance tuning is a part of the life cycle of every database application, and the earlier performance is addressed (preferably before going into production), the more likely it will be successfully resolved. As noted in previous chapters, most performance problems are not isolated symptoms but rather are the result of the system design. Tuning efforts should therefore focus on identifying and fixing the underlying flaws that result in unacceptable performance.

Tuning is the final step in a four-step process: planning, implementing, and monitoring must precede it. If you tune only for the sake of tuning, you are failing to address the full cycle of activity and will likely never resolve the underlying flaws that caused the performance problem.

Most of the database objects that can be tuned are discussed elsewhere in this book—for example, undo segments are covered thoroughly in Chapter 7. This chapter only discusses the tuning-related activities for such objects, while their own chapters cover planning and monitoring activities.

As of Oracle Database 10*g*, and significantly enhanced in Oracle Database 11*g* and 12*c*, you can take advantage of new tuning tools and features, including the Automated Workload Repository (AWR). For ease of use, and to take advantage of numerous automated monitoring and diagnostic tools, Oracle Cloud Control 12*c* is the Oracle-recommended tool on a routine basis as a central dashboard for all monitoring and performance tools. Before jumping into the Cloud Control tools, however, I'll present some of the prerequisites and principles behind effective proactive and reactive tuning methods.

In the following sections, you will see tuning activities for the following areas:

- Application design
- SQL
- Memory usage
- Data access
- Data manipulation
- Network traffic
- Physical storage
- Logical storage
- Tuning using the Automatic Workload Repository
- Managing resources in a PDB
- Performing Database Replay

Tuning Application Design

Why should a DBA tuning guide include a section on application design? And why should this section come first? Because nothing you can do as a DBA will have as great an impact on the system performance as the design of the application. The requirements for making the DBA's involvement in application development a reality are described in Chapter 5. In designing an application, you can take several steps to make effective and proper use of the available technology, as described in the following sections.

Effective Table Design

No matter how well designed your database is, poor table design will lead to poor performance. Not only that, but overly rigid adherence to relational table designs will lead to poor performance. That is due to the fact that while fully relational table designs (said to be in the *third normal form* or even *fourth* or *fifth normal form*) are logically desirable, they are usually physically undesirable in anything but OLTP environments.

The problem with such designs is that although they accurately reflect the ways in which an application's data is related to other data, they do not reflect the normal access paths that users will employ to access that data. Once the user's access requirements are evaluated, the fully relational table design will become unworkable for many large queries. Typically, the first problems will occur with queries that return a large number of columns. These columns are usually scattered among several tables, forcing the tables to be joined together during the query. If one of the joined tables is large, the performance of the whole query may suffer unless a software/hardware platform such as Oracle Exadata or Oracle In-Memory Database filters the table columns themselves to only return the desired columns.

In designing the tables for an application, developers should first develop the model in third normal form (3NF) and then consider denormalizing data to meet specific requirements—for example, creating small derived tables (or materialized views) from large, static tables. Can that data be dynamically derived from the large, static tables on demand? Of course. But if the users frequently request it, and the data is largely unchanging, then it makes sense to periodically store that data *in the format in which the users will ask for it.*

For example, some applications store historical data and current data in the same table. Each row may have a timestamp column, so the current row in a set is the one with the most recent timestamp. Every time a user queries the table for a current row, the user will need to perform a subquery, such as the following:

```
where timestamp_col =
   (select max(timestamp_col)
    from table
    where emp_no=196811)
```

If two such tables are joined, there will be two subqueries. In a small database, this may not present a performance problem, but as the number of tables and rows increase, performance problems will follow. Partitioning the historical data away from the current data or storing the historical data in a separate table will involve more work for the DBAs and developers but should improve the long-term performance of the application.

User-centered table design, rather than theory-centered table design, will yield a system that better meets the users' requirements; this is not to say that you should not *design* the database using 3NF and 4NF methodologies: it's a good starting point for revealing business requirements and a prerequisite for the physical database design. Physical database design options include separating a single table into multiple tables, and the reverse—combining multiple tables into one. The emphasis should be on providing the users the most direct path possible to the data they want in the format they want.

Distribution of CPU Requirements

When effectively designed and given adequate hardware, an Oracle database application will process I/O requests without excessive waits, will use memory areas without swapping and paging memory to disk, and will use the CPU threads without generating high load averages. Data that is read into memory by one process will be stored in memory and reused by many processes before it is aged out of memory. SQL commands are reused via the shared SQL area (the *shared pool*), further reducing the burden on the system.

If the I/O burdens of the system are reduced, the CPU burden may increase. You have several options for managing the CPU resources:

- Schedule the CPU load. You should time long-running batch queries or update programs to run at off-peak hours. Rather than run them at lower operating system priority while online users are performing transactions, run them at normal operating system priority at an appropriate time. Maintaining their normal priority level while scheduling the jobs appropriately will minimize potential locking, undo, and CPU conflicts.
- Take advantage of the opportunity to physically shift CPU requirements from one server to another. Wherever possible, isolate the database server from the application's CPU requirements. The data distribution techniques described in the networking chapters of this book will result in data being stored in its most appropriate place, and the CPU requirements of the application may be separated from the I/O requirements against the database.
- Consider using Oracle's Real Application Clusters (RAC) technology on traditional hardware platforms or on the Exadata engineered system platform to spread the database access requirements for a single database across multiple instances. See Chapter 12 for a review of RAC features.
- Use the database resource management features. You can use the Database Resource Manager to establish resource allocation plans and resource consumer groups. You can use Oracle's capabilities to change the resource allocations available to the consumer groups. See Chapter 5 for details on creating and implementing resource consumer groups and resource plans via the Database Resource Manager.
- Use Parallel Query to distribute the processing requirements of SQL statements among multiple CPUs. Parallelism can be used by almost every SQL, DML, and DDL command, including SELECT, CREATE TABLE AS SELECT, CREATE INDEX, RECOVER, partition management, and the SQL*Loader Direct Path loading options.

The degree to which a transaction is parallelized depends on the defined degree of parallelism for the transaction. Each table has a defined degree of parallelism, and a query can override the default degree of parallelism by using the PARALLEL hint. Using Automatic Degree of Parallelism (Auto DOP), Oracle evaluates the number of CPUs available on the server and the number of disks on which the table's data is stored in order to determine the default degree of parallelism.

The maximum available parallelism level is set at the instance level. The PARALLEL_MAX_SERVERS initialization parameter sets the maximum number of parallel query server processes that can be used at any one time by all the processes in the database. For example, if you set PARALLEL_MAX_SERVERS to 32 for your instance, and you run a query that uses 30 parallel query server processes for its query and sorting operations, then only two parallel query server processes are available for all the rest of the users in the database. Therefore, you need to carefully manage the parallelism you allow for your queries and batch operations. The PARALLEL_ADAPTIVE_MULTI_USER parameter, when set to TRUE, enables an adaptive algorithm designed to improve performance in multi-user environments using parallel execution. The algorithm automatically reduces the requested degree of parallelism according to the system load at query startup time. The effective degree of parallelism is based on the default degree of parallelism, or the degree from the table, or hints, divided by a reduction factor.

For each table, you can set a default degree of parallelism via the PARALLEL clause of the CREATE TABLE and ALTER TABLE commands. The *degree of parallelism* tells Oracle how many parallel query server processes to attempt to use for each part of the operation. For example, if a query that performs both table scanning and data sorting operations has a degree of parallelism of 8, there could be 16 parallel query server processes used—eight for scanning and eight for sorting. You can also specify a degree of parallelism for an index when it is created, via the PARALLEL clause of the CREATE INDEX command.

The minimum number of parallel query server processes started is set via the PARALLEL_MIN_SERVERS initialization parameter. In general, you should set this parameter to a very low number (less than 12) unless the system is actively used at all hours of the day. Setting this parameter to a low value will force Oracle to repeatedly start new query server processes, but it will greatly decrease the amount of memory held by idle parallel query server processes during low-use periods. If you set a high value for PARALLEL_MIN_SERVERS, you may frequently have idle parallel query server processes on your server, holding onto the memory they had previously acquired but not performing any functions.

Parallelizing operations distributes their processing requirements across multiple CPUs; however, you should use these features carefully. If you use a degree of parallelism of 5 for a large query, you will have five separate processes accessing the data (and five more receiving the processed rows). If you have that many processes accessing the data, you may create contention for the disks on which the data is stored, thus hurting performance. When using Parallel Query, you should selectively apply it to those tables whose data is well distributed over many physical devices. Also, you should avoid using it for all tables; as noted earlier, a single query may use all the available parallel query server processes, eliminating the parallelism for all the rest of the transactions in your database.

Effective Application Design

In addition to the application design topics described later in this chapter are several general guidelines for Oracle applications.

First, applications should minimize the number of times they request data from the database. Options include the use of sequences, the use of PL/SQL blocks, and the denormalization of tables. You can use distributed database objects such as materialized views to help reduce the number of times a database is queried.

NOTE
Even mildly inefficient SQL can impact your database's performance if it is executed frequently enough. SQL that generates few or no physical I/O reads still consumes CPU resources.

Second, different users of the same application should query the database in a very similar fashion. Consistent access paths increase the likelihood that requests may be resolved by information that is already available in the System Global Area (SGA). The sharing of data includes not only the tables and rows retrieved but also the queries that are used. If the queries are identical, a parsed version of a query may already exist in the shared SQL pool, reducing the amount of time needed to process the query. Cursor-sharing enhancements in the optimizer increase the likelihood of statement reuse within the shared pool—but the application needs to be designed with statement reuse in mind.

Third, you should restrict the use of dynamic SQL. Dynamic SQL, by definition, is undefined until run time; an application's dynamic SQL may select a couple of rows the first time, perform several full table scans of the order table the second time, and inadvertently perform a Cartesian join the third time (or consciously perform a Cartesian join using the CROSS JOIN keyword in a SELECT statement!). In addition, there is no way to guarantee that a dynamically generated SQL statement is syntactically correct until run time. Dynamically generated SQL is a double-edged sword: you have the flexibility to create your SQL on the fly based on user input, but you open yourself up to SQL injection attacks for both your in-house applications and your external website applications.

Fourth, you should minimize the number of times you open and close sessions in the database. If the application repeatedly opens a session, executes a small number of commands, and then closes the session, the performance of the SQL may be a minor factor in the overall performance. The session management may cost more than any other step in the application.

When stored procedures are used, the same code may be executed multiple times, taking advantage of the shared pool. You can also manually compile procedures, functions, and packages to avoid run-time compilation. When you create a procedure, Oracle automatically compiles it. If the procedure later becomes invalid, the database must recompile it before executing it. To avoid incurring this compilation cost at run time, use the ALTER PROCEDURE command shown here:

```
alter procedure user_util.update_benefits compile;
```

You can view the SQL text for all procedures in a database via the TEXT column in the DBA_SOURCE view. The USER_SOURCE view will display the procedures owned by the user performing the query. Text for packages, functions, and package bodies is also accessible via the DBA_SOURCE and USER_SOURCE views, which in turn reference a table named SYS.SOURCE$.

The first two design guidelines discussed—limiting the number of user accesses and coordinating their requests—require the application developer to know as much as possible about how the data is to be used and the access paths involved. For this reason, it is critical that users be as involved in the application design as they are in the table design. If the users spend long hours drawing pictures of tables with the data modelers and little time with the application developers discussing the access paths, the application will most likely not meet the users' needs. The access paths should be discussed as part of the data modeling exercise.

Tuning SQL

As with application design, the tuning of SQL statements seems far removed from a DBA's duties. However, DBAs should be involved in reviewing the SQL that is written as part of the application. A well-designed application may still experience performance problems if the SQL it uses is poorly tuned. Application design and SQL problems cause most of the performance problems in properly designed databases.

The key to tuning SQL is to minimize the search path that the database uses to find the data. In most Oracle tables, each row has a ROWID associated with it. The ROWID contains information about the physical location of the row—its file, the block within that file, and the row within the database block.

When a query with no WHERE clause is executed, the database will usually perform a *full table scan,* reading every block from the table under the high-water mark (HWM). During a full table scan, the database locates the first block of the table and then reads sequentially through all the other blocks in the table. For large tables, full table scans can be very time-consuming.

When specific rows are queried, the database may use an index to help speed the retrieval of the desired rows. An index maps logical values in a table to their RowIDs—which in turn map them to specific physical locations. Indexes may either be unique—in which case there is no more than one occurrence for each value—or nonunique. Indexes only store RowIDs for NOT NULL values in the indexed columns.

You may index several columns together. This is called a *concatenated* or *composite* index, and it will be used if its leading column is used in the query's WHERE clause. The optimizer can also use a "skip-scan" approach in which a concatenated index is used even if its leading column is not in the query's WHERE clause.

Indexes must be tailored to the access path needed. Consider the case of a three-column, concatenated index. As shown in the following listing, this index is created on the CITY, STATE, and ZIP columns of the EMPLOYEE table:

```
create index city_st_zip_ndx
on employee(city, state, zip)
tablespace indexes;
```

If a query of the form

```
select *
from employee
where state='NJ';
```

is executed, then the leading column of the index (CITY) is not in the WHERE clause. Oracle can use two types of index-based accesses to retrieve the rows—a skip-scan of the index or a full scan of the index. The optimizer will select an execution path based on the index's statistics—its size, the size of the table, and the selectivity of the index. If users will frequently run this type of query, the index's columns may need to be reordered with STATE first in order to reflect the actual usage pattern.

An *index range scan* is another index-based optimization that Oracle can use to efficiently retrieve selective data. Oracle uses an index range scan when the variable in the WHERE clause is equal to, less than, or greater than the specified constant and the variable is the leading column if the index is a multi-part index. No ORDER BY clause is required if you want the rows returned in the index order, as in this example where you are looking for employees hired before August 1st, 2012:

```
select * from EMPLOYEE where hire_date < '1-AUG-2012';
```

However, if you are using Parallel Query to retrieve these rows using the index, then you will need the ORDER BY clause to return the rows in the index order.

It is critical that the table's data be as ordered as possible. If users are frequently executing *range* queries—selecting those values that are within a specified range—then having the data ordered may require fewer data blocks to be read while resolving the query, thus improving performance. The ordered entries in the index will point to a set of neighboring blocks in the table rather than blocks that are scattered throughout the datafile(s); this assumes that the data was ordered when loaded or the query has a GROUP BY clause using the indexed column(s).

For example, consider a range query of the following type:

```
select *
from employee
where empno between 1 and 100;
```

This range query will require fewer data blocks to be read if the physical rows in the EMPLOYEE table are ordered by the EMPNO column. To guarantee that the rows are properly ordered in the table, copy the rows to a temporary table with an ORDER BY clause, TRUNCATE the original table, and reload the rows from the newly sorted table. In addition, you should use online segment shrink to reclaim fragmented free space below the HWM for tables with frequent DML activity; this improves cache utilization and requires fewer blocks to be scanned in full table scans. You use the ALTER TABLE . . . SHRINK SPACE command to compact the free space in a table.

Impact of Order on Load Rates

Indexes impact the performance of both queries and data loads. During INSERT operations, the rows' order has a significant impact on load performance. Even in heavily indexed environments, properly ordering the rows prior to INSERT may improve load performance by 50 percent. This assumes you only have one index—you can't load rows in index order if you have more than one index! Keep in mind that each additional index adds three times the overhead for DML operations when maintaining the index.

As an index grows, Oracle allocates new blocks. If a new index entry is added beyond the previous entry, the new entry will be added to the last block in the index. If the new entry causes Oracle to exceed the space available in that block, the entry will be moved to a new block. There is very little performance impact from this block allocation.

If the inserted rows are not ordered, new index entries will be written to existing index node blocks. If there is no more room in the block where the new value is added, and the block is not the last block in the index, the block's entries will be split in two. Half the index entries will be left in the original block, and half will be moved to a new block. As a result, the performance suffers during loads (because of the additional space management activity) and during queries (because the index contains more unused space, requiring more blocks to be read for the same number of entries read).

NOTE
There is a significant drop in load performance when an index increases its number of internal levels. To see the number of levels, analyze an index and then select its BLEVEL column value from DBA_INDEXES.

Because of the way Oracle manages its indexes internally, load rates will be affected each time a new index is added (because it is unlikely that inserted rows will be sorted correctly for multiple columns). From a load rate perspective, favor fewer multicolumn indexes over multiple single-column indexes.

Additional Indexing Options

If the data is not very selective, you may consider using *bitmap indexes*. As described in Chapter 18, bitmap indexes are most effective for queries against large, static data sets with few distinct values. You can create both bitmap indexes and normal (B-tree) indexes on the same table, and Oracle will perform any necessary index conversions dynamically during query processing. See Chapter 18 for details on using bitmap indexes.

NOTE
Avoid creating bitmap indexes on tables modified by online transactions; data warehouse tables, however, are excellent candidates for bitmap indexes.

If two tables are frequently queried together, then *clusters* may be effective in improving performance. Clusters store rows from multiple tables in the same physical data blocks, based on their logical values (the cluster key).

Queries in which a column's value is compared to an exact value (rather than a range of values) are called *equivalence* queries. A *hash cluster* stores a row in a specific location based on its value in the cluster key column. Every time a row is inserted, its cluster key value is used to determine in which block it should be stored; this same logic can be used during queries to quickly find data blocks that are needed for retrieval. Hash clusters are designed to improve the performance of equivalence queries; they will not be as helpful in improving the performance of the range queries discussed earlier. Performance will be significantly worse with range queries, queries that force a full table scan, or for hash clusters that are frequently updated.

Reverse indexes provide another tuning solution for equivalence queries. In a reverse index, the bytes of the index are stored in reverse order. In a traditional index, two consecutive values are stored next to each other. In a reverse index, consecutive values are not stored next to each other. For example, the values 2004 and 2005 are stored as 4002 and 5002, respectively, in a reverse index. Although not appropriate for range scans, reverse indexes may reduce contention for index blocks if many equivalence queries are performed. Reverse key indexes may need to be rebuilt quite often to perform well. They should also include a large value for PCTFREE to allow for inserts.

NOTE
You cannot reverse a bitmap index.

You can create *function-based indexes* on expressions involving columns. This query could not use a B-tree index on the NAME column:

```
select * from employee
where upper(name) = 'JONES';
```

However, the query

```
select * from employee
where name = 'JONES';
```

could, because the second query does not perform a function on the NAME column. Instead of creating an index on the column NAME, you can create an index on the column expression UPPER(NAME), as shown in the following example:

```
create index emp_upper_name on
employee(upper(name));
```

Although function-based indexes can be useful, be sure to consider the following points when creating them:

- Can you restrict the functions that will be used on the column? If so, can you restrict all functions from being performed on the column?
- Do you have adequate storage space for the additional indexes?
- When you drop the table, you will be dropping more indexes (and therefore more extents) than before. How will that impact the time required to drop the table? (This is less of a consideration if you are using locally managed tablespaces, which you should be using if you're running Oracle Database 10*g* or later.)

Function-based indexes are useful, but you should implement them sparingly. The more indexes you create on a table, the longer all INSERT, UPDATE, and DELETE operations will take. Of course, this applies to creating any additional indexes on a table, regardless of type.

Text indexes use Oracle's text options (Oracle Text) to create and manage lists of words and their occurrences—similar to the way a book's index works. Text indexes are most often used to support applications that perform searches on portions of words with wildcards.

Partitioned tables can have indexes that span all partitions (global indexes) or indexes that are partitioned along with the table partitions (local indexes). From a query-tuning perspective, local indexes may be preferable because they contain fewer entries than global indexes.

Generating Explain Plans

How can you determine which access path the database will use to perform a query? This information can be viewed via the EXPLAIN PLAN command. This command will evaluate the execution path for a query and will place its output into a table (named PLAN_TABLE) in the database. A sample EXPLAIN PLAN command is shown in the following listing:

```
explain plan
 for
select *
 from BOOKSHELF
 where title like 'M%';
```

The first line of this command tells the database that it is to explain its execution plan for the query without actually executing the query. You can optionally include a SET STATEMENT_ID clause to label the explain plan in PLAN_TABLE. Following the keyword FOR, the query to be analyzed is listed.

The account that is running this command must have a plan table in its schema. Oracle provides the CREATE TABLE commands needed for this table. The file, named **utlxplan.sql**, is located in the **$ORACLE_HOME/rdbms/admin** directory. Oracle creates a single PLAN_TABLE available for all users.

NOTE
You should drop and re-create the plan table following each Oracle upgrade because new columns may be added by the upgrade scripts.

Query the plan table using the DBMS_XPLAN procedure:

```
select * from table(DBMS_XPLAN.DISPLAY);
```

You can also use the Oracle-supplied script in **$ORACLE_HOME/rdbms/admin/utlxpls.sql** to query the plan table for serial execution, or the **$ORACLE_HOME/rdbms/admin/utlxplp.sql** for parallel execution.

This query will report on the types of operations the database must perform to resolve the query. The output will show the steps of the query execution in a hierarchical fashion, illustrating the relationships between the steps. For example, you may see an index-based step that has a TABLE ACCESS BY INDEX ROWID step as its parent, indicating that the index step is processed first and the RowIDs returned from the index are used to retrieve specific rows from the table.

You can use the SET AUTOTRACE ON command in SQL*Plus to automatically generate the EXPLAIN PLAN output and trace information for every query you run. The autotrace-generated output will not be displayed until after the query has completed, whereas the EXPLAIN PLAN output is generated without running the command. To enable autotrace-generated output, a plan table must either be created in the schema in which the autotrace utility will be used or created in the SYSTEM schema with access granted to the schema that will use the autotrace utility. The script plustrce.sql, located in the **$ORACLE_HOME/sqlplus/admin** directory, must also be run as SYS before you can SET AUTOTRACE ON. Users must have the PLUSTRACE role enabled prior to executing SET AUTOTRACE ON. For an installation or upgrade to Oracle Database 10g or later, this script is run automatically.

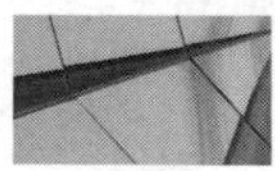

NOTE
To show the EXPLAIN PLAN output without running the query, use the SET AUTOTRACE TRACEONLY EXPLAIN command.

If you use the parallel query options or query remote databases, an additional section of the SET AUTOTRACE ON output will show the text of the queries executed by the parallel query server processes or the query executed within the remote database.

To disable the autotrace feature, use the SET AUTOTRACE OFF command.

The following listing shows how to turn on autotrace and generate an explain plan:

```
set autotrace traceonly explain

select *
 from BOOKSHELF
 where Title like 'M%';

Execution Plan
----------------------------------------------------------
   0      SELECT STATEMENT Optimizer=ALL_ROWS (Cost=3 Card=2 Bytes=80)
   1    0   TABLE ACCESS (BY INDEX ROWID) OF 'BOOKSHELF' (TABLE) (Cost
          =3 Card=2 Bytes=80)
   2    1     INDEX (RANGE SCAN) OF 'SYS_C004834' (INDEX (UNIQUE)) (Co
          st=1 Card=2)
```

To understand the explain plan, read the order of operations within the hierarchy from inside out, until you come to a set of operations at the same level of indentation; then read from top to bottom. In this example, there are no operations at the same level of indentation; therefore, you read the order of operations from inside out. The first operation is the index range scan, followed by the table access; the SELECT STATEMENT operation displays the output to the user. Each operation has an ID value (the first column) and a parent ID value (the second number; it is blank in the topmost operation). In more complex explain plans, you may need to use the parent ID values to determine the order of operations.

This plan shows that the data returned to the user comes via a TABLE ACCESS BY INDEX ROWID operation. The RowIDs are supplied by an index range scan of a unique index.

Each step is assigned a "cost." The cost is cumulative, reflecting the cost of that step plus the costs of all its child steps. You can use the cost values to identify steps that contribute the greatest amount to the overall cost of the query and then target them for specific tuning efforts.

When evaluating the output of the EXPLAIN PLAN command, you should make sure that the most selective indexes (that is, the most nearly unique indexes) are used by the query. If a nonselective index is used, you may be forcing the database to perform unnecessary reads to resolve the query. A full discussion of SQL tuning is beyond the scope of this book, but you should focus your tuning efforts on making sure that the most resource-intensive SQL statements are using the most selective indexes possible.

In general, transaction-oriented applications (such as multi-user systems used for data entry) judge performance by the time it takes to return the first row of a query. For transaction-oriented applications, you should focus your tuning efforts on using indexes to reduce the database's response time to the query.

If the application is batch oriented (with large transactions and reports), you should focus on improving the time it takes to complete the overall transaction instead of the time it takes to return the first row from the transaction. Improving the overall throughput of the transaction may require using full table scans in place of index accesses—and may improve the overall performance of the application.

If the application is distributed across multiple databases, focus on reducing the number of times database links are used in queries. If a remote database is frequently accessed during a query, the cost of accessing that remote database is paid each time the remote data is accessed. Even if the cost of accessing the remote data is low, accessing it thousands of times will eventually place a performance burden on your application. See the section "Reducing Network Traffic" later in this chapter for additional tuning suggestions for distributed databases.

Tuning Memory Usage

In Oracle Database 10*g*, you were able to use the Automatic Workload Repository (AWR) toolset to gather and manage statistical data (as described later in this chapter). As of Oracle Database 11*g*, new initialization parameters were introduced such as MEMORY_TARGET to further automate the overall memory used by Oracle—helping you tune the database automatically when you don't have time to read the AWR reports! With Oracle Database 12*c*, you can now tune your SQL statements with "zero effort." This seems like marketing hype at first glance, but in some cases it's true, because the Oracle optimizer can use an *adaptive execution plan* by stopping a plan after initial execution and making run-time adjustments to the plan after finding variations in the initial cardinality estimates.

The data block buffer cache and the shared pool are managed via a *least recently used (LRU)* algorithm. A preset area is set aside to hold values; when it fills, the least recently used data is eliminated from memory and written back to disk. An adequately sized memory area keeps the most frequently accessed data in memory; accessing less frequently used data requires physical reads.

Managing SGA Pools

You can see the queries performing the logical and physical reads in the database via the V$SQL view. V$SQL reports the cumulative number of logical and physical reads performed for each query currently in the shared pool, as well as the number of times each query was executed. The following script shows the SQL text for the queries in the shared pool, with the most I/O-intensive queries listed first. The query also displays the number of logical reads (buffer gets) per execution:

```
select buffer_gets,
       disk_reads,
       executions,
       buffer_gets/executions b_e,
       sql_text
from v$sql where executions != 0
order by disk_reads desc;
```

If the shared pool has been flushed, queries executed prior to the flush will no longer be accessible via V$SQL. However, the impact of those queries can still be seen, provided the users are still logged in. The V$SESS_IO view records the cumulative logical reads and physical reads performed for each user's session. You can query V$SESS_IO for each session's hit ratio, as shown in the following listing:

```
select sess.username,
       sess_io.block_gets,
       sess_io.consistent_gets,
       sess_io.physical_reads,
       round(100*(sess_io.consistent_gets
          +sess_io.block_gets-sess_io.physical_reads)/
         (decode(sess_io.consistent_gets,0,1,
```

```
              sess_io.consistent_gets+sess_io.block_gets)),2)
                session_hit_ratio
from v$sess_io sess_io, v$session sess
where sess.sid = sess_io.sid
  and sess.username is not null
order by username;
```

To see the objects whose blocks are currently in the data block buffer cache, query the X$BH table in SYS's schema, as shown in the following query (note that the SYS and SYSTEM objects are excluded from the output so the DBA can focus on the application tables and indexes present in the SGA):

```
select object_name,
       object_type ,
       count(*) num_buff
from x$bh a, sys.dba_objects b
where a.obj = b.object_id
  and owner not in ('sys','system')
group by object_name, object_type;
```

NOTE
You can query the NAME and KIND columns from V$CACHE to see similar data if you are not connected as the SYS user.

There are multiple cache areas within the data block buffer cache:

- **DEFAULT cache** This is the standard cache for objects that use the default database block size for the database.
- **KEEP cache** This is dedicated to objects you wish to keep in memory at all times. In general, this area is used for small tables with few transactions. This cache is good for lookup tables for such things as state codes, ZIP codes, and salesperson data.
- **RECYCLE cache** This is dedicated to objects you wish to flush from memory quickly. Like the KEEP cache, the RECYCLE cache isolates objects in memory so that they do not interfere with the normal functioning of the DEFAULT cache. The KEEP and RECYCLE cache sizes only apply to the default database block size.
- **Block size–specific caches (DB_*n*K_CACHE_SIZE)** Oracle supports multiple database block sizes within a single database; you must create a cache for each non-default database block size.

With all the areas of the SGA—the data block buffers, the dictionary cache, and the shared pool—the emphasis should be on sharing data among users. Each of these areas should be large enough to hold the most commonly requested data from the database. In the case of the shared pool, it should be large enough to hold the parsed versions of the most commonly used queries. When they are adequately sized, the memory areas in the SGA can dramatically improve the performance of individual queries and of the database as a whole.

The sizes of the KEEP and RECYCLE buffer pools do not reduce the available space in the data block buffer cache. For a table to use one of the new buffer pools, specify the name of the buffer pool via the BUFFER_POOL parameter within the table's STORAGE clause. For example, if you want a table to be quickly removed from memory, assign it to the RECYCLE pool. The default pool is named DEFAULT, so you can use the ALTER TABLE command to redirect a table to the DEFAULT pool at a later date. Here is an example of assigning a table to the KEEP buffer pool:

```
create table state_cd_lookup
 (state_cd   char(2),
  state_nm   varchar2(50)
 )
storage (buffer_pool keep);
```

If you do not set a size for the KEEP and RECYCLE pools, all of the data and index blocks assigned to those areas go to the default buffer cache.

You can use the LARGE_POOL_SIZE initialization parameter to specify the size of the large pool allocation heap in bytes. The large pool allocation heap is used in shared server systems for session memory, by parallel execution for message buffers, and by backup processes for I/O buffers. By default, the large pool is not created.

As of Oracle Database 10*g*, you can use Automatic Shared Memory Management (ASMM). To activate ASMM, set a nonzero value for the SGA_TARGET database initialization parameter. After you set SGA_TARGET to the size of the SGA you want (that is, all of the caches added together), you can then set the other cache-related parameters (DB_CACHE_SIZE, SHARED_POOL_SIZE, JAVA_POOL_SIZE, and LARGE_POOL_SIZE) each to 0; if you provide values for these parameters, those values will serve as the lower bound for the automatic tuning algorithm. Shut down and restart the database for the changes to take effect; the database will then begin actively managing the size of the different caches. You can monitor the size of the caches at any time via the V$SGASTAT dynamic performance view. Oracle Database 11*g* takes the automation a step farther: you can set MEMORY_TARGET to the total amount of memory available to Oracle. The amount of memory specified in MEMORY_TARGET is allocated between the SGA and PGA automatically; when MEMORY_TARGET is set, SGA_TARGET and PGA_AGGREGATE_TARGET are set to 0 and ignored.

As the workload in the database changes, the database will alter the cache sizes to reflect the needs of the application. For example, if there is a heavy batch-processing load at night and a more intensive online transaction load during the day, the database may alter the cache sizes as the load changes. These changes occur automatically, without DBA intervention. If you specify a value for a pool in your initialization parameter file, Oracle will use that as the minimum value for that pool.

NOTE
DBAs can create KEEP and RECYCLE pools in the buffer cache. KEEP and RECYCLE pools are not affected by the dynamic cache resizing and are not part of the DEFAULT buffer pool.

You may wish to selectively "pin" packages in the shared pool. Pinning packages in memory immediately after starting the database will increase the likelihood that a large enough section of contiguous free space is available in memory. As shown in the following listing, the KEEP procedure of the DBMS_SHARED_POOL package designates the packages to pin in the shared pool:

```
execute dbms_shared_pool.keep('APPOWNER.ADD_CLIENT','P');
```

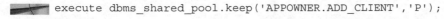

Pinning of packages is more closely related to application management than application tuning, but it can have a performance impact. If you can avoid dynamic management of fragmented memory areas, you minimize the work Oracle has to do when managing the shared pool.

Specifying the Size of the SGA

To enable the automatic management of the caches, set the SGA_TARGET initialization parameter to the size of the SGA.

If you choose to manage the caches manually, you can set the SGA_MAX_SIZE parameter to the size of the SGA. You can then specify the sizes for the individual caches; they can be dynamically altered while the database is running via the ALTER SYSTEM command.

You can also set SGA_TARGET to a size smaller than SGA_MAX_SIZE. Oracle will use the value of SGA_TARGET to initially set the individual caches and can grow them over time to occupy more memory up to SGA_MAX_SIZE. This is a good way to determine what the total memory requirements should be before deploying your database in a production environment.

Parameter	Description
SGA_MAX_SIZE	The maximum size to which the SGA can grow.
SHARED_POOL_SIZE	The size of the shared pool.
DB_BLOCK_SIZE	The default database block size for the database.
DB_CACHE_SIZE	The cache size specified in bytes.
DB_*n*K_CACHE_SIZE	If you will be using multiple database block sizes within a single database, you must specify a DB_CACHE_SIZE parameter value and at least one DB_*n*K_CACHE_SIZE parameter value. For example, if your standard database block size is 4KB, you can also specify a cache for the 8KB block size tablespaces via the DB_8K_CACHE_SIZE parameter.

For example, you may specify the following:

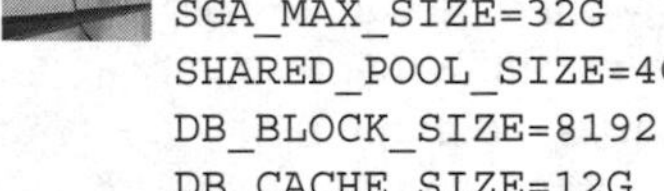

```
SGA_MAX_SIZE=32G
SHARED_POOL_SIZE=4G
DB_BLOCK_SIZE=8192
DB_CACHE_SIZE=12G
DB_4K_CACHE_SIZE=4G
```

With these parameters, 4MB will be available for data queried from objects in tablespaces with 4KB block sizes. Objects using the standard 8KB block size will use the 160MB cache. While the database is open, you can change the SHARED_POOL_SIZE and DB_CACHE_SIZE parameter values via the ALTER SYSTEM command.

NOTE

With few exceptions, Oracle recommends a single block size of 8KB. Even on Oracle engineered systems such as Exadata the recommended and only block size is 8KB.

SGA_TARGET is a dynamic parameter and can be changed through Cloud Control or with the ALTER SYSTEM command.

SGA_TARGET can be increased up to the value of SGA_MAX_SIZE. It can be reduced until any one of the auto-tuned components reaches its minimum size—either a user-specified minimum or an internally determined minimum. Both of these parameters can be used to tune the SGA.

Using the Cost-Based Optimizer

With each release of its software, Oracle has added new features to its optimizer and has enhanced existing features. Effective use of the cost-based optimizer requires that the tables and indexes in your application be analyzed regularly. The frequency with which you analyze the objects depends on the rate of change within the objects. For batch transaction applications, you should reanalyze the objects after each large set of batch transactions. For OLTP applications, you should reanalyze the objects on a time-based schedule (such as via a weekly or nightly process).

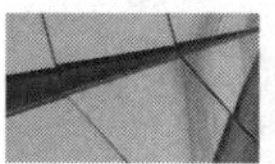

NOTE

As of Oracle Database 10g Release 1, the rule-based optimizer is deprecated. There is no reason to use it unless you are supporting a legacy application that only runs under previous versions of Oracle Database.

Statistics on objects are gathered via executions of the DBMS_STATS package's procedures. If you analyze a table, its associated indexes are automatically analyzed as well. You can analyze a schema (via the GATHER_SCHEMA_STATS procedure) or a specific table (via GATHER_TABLE_STATS). You can also analyze only the indexed columns, thus speeding the analysis process. In general, you should analyze a table's indexes each time you analyze the table. In the following listing, the PRACTICE schema is analyzed:

```
execute dbms_stats.gather_schema_stats('PRACTICE', 'COMPUTE');
```

You can view the statistics on tables and indexes via DBA_TABLES, DBA_TAB_COL_STATISTICS, and DBA_INDEXES. Some column-level statistics are still provided in DBA_TAB_COLUMNS, but they are provided there strictly for backward compatibility. The statistics for the columns of partitioned tables are found in DBA_PART_COL_STATISTICS.

NOTE

As of Oracle Database 10g, statistics are automatically gathered in a default installation using the automated maintenance tasks infrastructure (AutoTask) during maintenance windows.

When the command in the preceding listing is executed, all the objects belonging to the PRACTICE schema will be analyzed using the GATHER AUTO option of DBMS_STATS.GATHER_SCHEMA_STATS. You can also choose to estimate statistics based on a specified percentage of the table's rows, but using the GATHER AUTO option gathers additional statistics that can further improve execution plans.

Tuning Data Access

Even if your tables are properly configured and indexed, your performance may suffer if there are wait events caused by file accesses. In the following sections, I'll present some general recommendations related to file and tablespace configuration.

As the old saying goes, the best kind of I/O is the I/O you don't have to do. Given that you do have to perform some I/O, your best investment in database configuration is to use Automatic Storage Management (ASM). While you can get the same general level of performance from a well-tuned OS file system (with optimal queue depths, SAN configuration, and so forth), ASM makes management of Oracle storage easier while at the same time maintaining optimal performance.

Identifying Chained Rows

When a data segment is created, a PCTFREE value is specified. The PCTFREE parameter tells the database how much space should be kept free in each data block. The free space is used when rows that are already stored in the data block extend in length via UPDATE operations.

If an UPDATE to a row causes that row to no longer completely fit in a single data block, that row may be moved to another data block, or the row may be *chained* to another block. If you are storing rows whose length is greater than the Oracle block size, you will automatically have chaining.

Chaining affects performance because it requires Oracle to look in multiple physical locations for data from the same logical row. By eliminating unnecessary chaining, you reduce the number of physical reads needed to return data from a datafile.

You can avoid chaining by setting the proper value for PCTFREE during the creation of data segments. The default value, 10, should be increased if your application will frequently update NULL values to non-NULL values, or if long text values are frequently updated.

If you must perform mass updates of a table, it will be much faster and more efficient to re-create the table and perform the update as part of the process. No rows will be chained or migrated utilizing this method.

You should only use the ANALYZE command to collect information about chained rows and to collect information about freelist blocks. The ANALYZE command has an option that detects and records chained rows in tables. Its syntax is

```
analyze table table_name list chained rows into CHAINED_ROWS;
```

The ANALYZE command will put the output from this operation into a table called CHAINED_ROWS in your local schema. The SQL to create the CHAINED_ROWS table is in a file named **utlchain.sql**, in the **$ORACLE_HOME/rdbms/admin** directory. The following query will select the most significant columns from the CHAINED_ROWS table:

```
select
       owner_name,        /*owner of the data segment*/
       table_name,        /*name of the table with the chained rows*/
       cluster_name,      /*name of the cluster, if it is clustered*/
       head_rowid         /*rowid of the first part of the row*/
from chained_rows;
```

The output will show the RowIDs for all chained rows, allowing you to quickly see how many of the rows in the table are chained. If chaining is prevalent in a table, that table should be rebuilt with a higher value for PCTFREE.

You can see the impact of row chaining by querying V$SYSSTAT. The V$SYSSTAT entry for the "table fetch continued row" statistic will be incremented each time Oracle selects data from a chained row. This statistic will also be incremented when Oracle selects data from a *spanned row*—a row that is chained because it is greater than a block in length. Tables with LONG, BLOB, CLOB, and NCLOB datatypes are likely to have spanned rows. The "table fetch continued row" statistic is also available in the AWR reports (or Statspack reports in Oracle Database 10*g* and earlier).

In addition to chaining rows, Oracle will occasionally move rows. If a row exceeds the space available to its block, the row may be inserted into a different block. The process of moving a row from one block to another is called *row migration,* and the moved row is called a *migrated* row. During row migration, Oracle has to dynamically manage space in multiple blocks and access the freelist (the list of blocks available for INSERT operations). A migrated row does not appear as a chained row, but it does impact the performance of your transactions. See Chapter 6 for an example of using the DBMS_ADVISOR package to find and reorganize tables with chained rows.

TIP

Accessing a migrated row increments the count in the "table fetch continued row" statistic.

Using Index-Organized Tables

An *index-organized table (IOT)* is an index in which an entire row is stored, rather than just the key values for the row. Rather than storing a RowID for the row, the primary key for the row is treated as the row's logical identifier. Rows in IOTs do not have RowIDs.

Within the IOT, the rows are stored sorted by their primary key values. Thus, any range query that is based on the primary key may benefit because the rows are stored near each other (see the section "Tuning SQL" earlier in this chapter for the steps involved in ordering the data within normal tables). Additionally, any equivalence query based on the primary key may benefit because the table's data is all stored in the index. In the traditional table/index combination, an index-based access requires an index access followed by a table access. In an IOT, only the IOT is accessed; there is no companion index.

However, the performance gains from a single index access in place of a normal index/table combination access may be minimal—any index-based access should be fast. To help improve performance further, index-organized tables offer additional features:

- **An overflow area** By setting the PCTTHRESHOLD parameter when the IOT is created, you can store the primary key data apart from the row data. If the row's data exceeds the threshold of available space in the block, it will dynamically be moved to an overflow area. You can designate the overflow area to be in a separate tablespace, improving your ability to distribute the I/O associated with the table.
- **Secondary indexes** You can create secondary indexes on the IOT. Oracle will use the primary key values as the logical RowIDs for the rows.
- **Reduced storage requirements** In a traditional table/index combination, the same key values are stored in two places. In an IOT, they are stored once, reducing the storage requirements.

TIP

When specifying an overflow area, you can use the INCLUDING COLUMN clause to specify the column (and all successive columns in the table definition) that will be stored in the overflow area:

```
create table ord_iot
   (order_id number,
    order_date date,
    order_notes varchar2(1000), primary key(order_id,order_date))
     organization index including order_date
     overflow tablespace over_ord_tab
     PARTITION BY RANGE (order_date)
       (PARTITION p1 VALUES LESS THAN ('01-JAN-2009')
           TABLESPACE data01,
       PARTITION p2 VALUES LESS THAN ('01-JAN-2010')
           TABLESPACE data02,
       PARTITION p3 VALUES LESS THAN ('01-JAN-2011')
           TABLESPACE data03,
       PARTITION p4 VALUES LESS THAN ('01-JAN-2012')
           TABLESPACE data04,
       PARTITION p5 VALUES LESS THAN ('01-JAN-2013')
           TABLESPACE data05,
        PARTITION p6 VALUES LESS THAN (MAXVALUE)
           TABLESPACE data06);
```

Both ORDER_DATE and ORDER_NOTES will be stored in the overflow area.

To create an IOT, use the ORGANIZATION INDEX clause of the CREATE TABLE command. You must specify a primary key when creating an IOT. Within an IOT, you can drop columns or mark them as inactive via the SET UNUSED clause of the ALTER TABLE command.

Tuning Issues for Index-Organized Tables

Like indexes, IOTs may become internally fragmented over time, as values are inserted, updated, and deleted. To rebuild an IOT, use the MOVE clause of the ALTER TABLE command. In the following example, the EMPLOYEE_IOT table is rebuilt, along with its overflow area:

```
alter table EMPLOYEE_IOT
move tablespace DATA
overflow tablespace DATA_OVERFLOW;
```

You should avoid storing long rows of data in IOTs. In general, you should avoid using an IOT if the data is longer than 75 percent of the database block size. If the database block size is 4KB, and your rows will exceed 3KB in length, you should investigate the use of normal tables and indexes instead of IOTs. The longer the rows are, and the more transactions are performed against the IOT, the more frequently it will need to be rebuilt.

NOTE

You cannot use LONG datatypes in IOTs, but you can use LOBs. You shouldn't be using LONG datatypes any more anyway—their use will be deprecated in a future version of Oracle. CLOBs have all the functionality of LONG datatypes and more.

As noted earlier in this chapter, indexes impact data load rates. For best results, the primary key index of an IOT should be loaded with sequential values to minimize the costs of index management.

Tuning Data Manipulation

Several data manipulation tasks—usually concerning the manipulation of large quantities of data—may involve the DBA. You have several options when loading and deleting large volumes of data, as described in the following sections.

Bulk Inserts: Using the SQL*Loader Direct Path Option

When used in the Conventional Path mode, SQL*Loader reads records from a file, generates INSERT commands, and passes them to the Oracle kernel. Oracle then finds places for those rows in free blocks in the table and updates any associated indexes.

In Direct Path mode, SQL*Loader creates formatted data blocks and writes directly to the datafiles. This requires occasional checks with the database to get new locations for data blocks, but no other I/O with the database kernel is required. The result is a data load process that is dramatically faster than Conventional Path mode.

If the table is indexed, the indexes will be placed in DIRECT PATH state during the load. After the load is complete, the new keys (index column values) will be sorted and merged with the existing keys in the index. To maintain the temporary set of keys, the load will create a temporary index segment that is at least as large as the largest index on the table. The space requirements for this can be minimized by presorting the data and using the SORTED INDEXES clause in the SQL*Loader control file.

To minimize the amount of dynamic space allocation necessary during the load, the data segment that you are loading into should already be created, with all the space it will need already allocated. You should also presort the data on the columns of the largest index in the table. Sorting the data and leaving the indexes on the table during a Direct Path load will usually yield better performance than if you were to drop the indexes before the load and then re-create them after it completed.

However, keep in mind that direct path load operations always use new extents. Therefore, if you use parallel DELETEs and then follow it with parallel direct path loads, you will potentially have an ever-increasing amount of free space in every block, and the disk space allocated to the table will increase much faster than you expect.

To take advantage of the Direct Path option, the table cannot be clustered, and there can be no other active transactions against it. During the load, only NOT NULL, UNIQUE, and PRIMARY KEY constraints will be enforced; after the load has completed, the CHECK and FOREIGN KEY constraints can be automatically reenabled. To force this to occur, use the REENABLE DISABLED_CONSTRAINTS clause in the SQL*Loader control file.

The only exception to this reenabling process is that table insert triggers, when reenabled, are not executed for each of the new rows in the table. A separate process must manually perform whatever commands were to have been performed by this type of trigger.

The SQL*Loader Direct Path loading option provides significant performance improvements over the SQL*Loader Conventional Path loader in loading data into Oracle tables by bypassing SQL processing, buffer cache management, and unnecessary reads for the data blocks. The Parallel Data Loading option of SQL*Loader allows multiple processes to load data into the same table, utilizing spare resources on the system and thereby reducing the overall elapsed times for loading. Given enough CPU and I/O resources, this can significantly reduce the overall loading times.

To use Parallel Data Loading, start multiple SQL*Loader sessions using the PARALLEL keyword (otherwise, SQL*Loader puts an exclusive lock on the table). Each session is an independent session requiring its own control file. The following listing shows an example of a Direct Path load using the DIRECT=TRUE parameter on the command line:

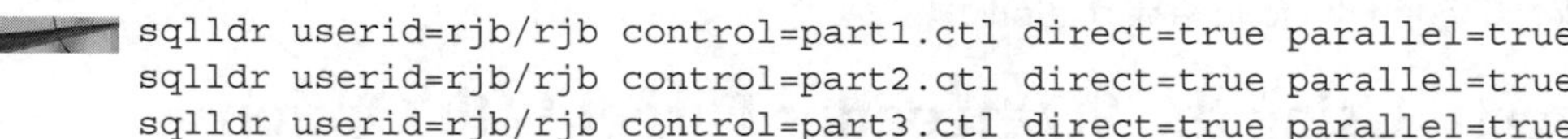

```
sqlldr userid=rjb/rjb control=part1.ctl direct=true parallel=true
sqlldr userid=rjb/rjb control=part2.ctl direct=true parallel=true
sqlldr userid=rjb/rjb control=part3.ctl direct=true parallel=true
```

Each session creates its own log, bad, and discard files (**part1.log**, **part2.log**, **part3.log**, **part1.bad**, **part2.bad**, and so on) by default. Because you have multiple sessions loading data into the same table, only the APPEND option is allowed for Parallel Data Loading. The SQL*Loader REPLACE, TRUNCATE, and INSERT options are not allowed for Parallel Data Loading. If you need to delete the table's data before starting the load, you must manually delete the data (via DELETE or TRUNCATE commands). You cannot use SQL*Loader to delete the rows automatically if you are using Parallel Data Loading.

NOTE

*If you use Parallel Data Loading, indexes are not maintained by the SQL*Loader session. Before starting the loading process, you must drop all indexes on the table and disable all its PRIMARY KEY and UNIQUE constraints. After the loads complete, you can re-create the table's indexes.*

In serial Direct Path loading (PARALLEL=FALSE), SQL*Loader loads data into extents in the table. If the load process fails before the load completes, some data could be committed to the table prior to the process failure. In Parallel Data Loading, each load process creates temporary segments for loading the data. The temporary segments are later merged with the table. If a Parallel Data Loading process fails before the load completes, the temporary segments will not have been merged with the table. If the temporary segments have not been merged with the table being loaded, no data from the load will have been committed to the table.

You can use the SQL*Loader FILE parameter to direct each data loading session to a different datafile. By directing each loading session to its own datafile, you can balance the I/O load of the loading processes. Data loading is very I/O intensive and must be distributed across multiple disks for parallel loading to achieve significant performance improvements over serial loading.

After a Parallel Data Load, each session may attempt to reenable the table's constraints. As long as at least one load session is still underway, attempting to reenable the constraints will fail. The final loading session to complete should attempt to reenable the constraints, and should succeed. You should check the status of your constraints after the load completes. If the table being loaded has PRIMARY KEY and UNIQUE constraints, you can create the associated indexes in parallel prior to enabling the constraints.

Bulk Data Moves: Using External Tables

You can query data from files outside the database via an object called an *external table*. An external table's structure is defined via the ORGANIZATION EXTERNAL clause of the CREATE TABLE command; its syntax closely resembles the SQL*Loader control file syntax.

You cannot manipulate rows in an external table, and you cannot index it—every access of the table results in a full table scan (that is, a full scan of the file at the operating system level). As a result, the performance of queries against external tables tends to be worse than that of queries against tables stored within the database. However, external tables offer a couple of potential benefits for systems that load large sets of data:

- Because the data is not stored within the database, the data is only stored once (outside the database, rather than both outside and inside the database), thus saving space.
- Because the data is never loaded into the database, the data-loading time is eliminated.

Given that you cannot index external tables, they are most useful for operations in which large volumes of data are accessed once serially by batch programs. For example, many data warehousing environments have a staging area in which data is loaded into temporary tables prior to rows being inserted into the tables users will query. Instead of loading the data into those temporary tables, you can access the operating system files directly via external tables, saving time and space.

From an architectural perspective, external tables allow you to focus your database contents on the objects users will most commonly use—small codes tables, aggregation tables, and transaction tables—while keeping very large data sets outside the database. You can replace the files accessed by the external tables at any time without incurring any transaction overhead within the database.

Bulk Inserts: Common Traps and Successful Tricks

If your data is not being inserted from a flat file, SQL*Loader will not be a useful solution. For example, if you need to move a large set of data from one table to another, you will likely want to avoid having to write the data to a flat file and then read it back into the database. The fastest way to move data in your database is to move it from one table to another without going out to the operating system.

When you're moving data from one table to another, there are several common methods for improving the performance of the data migration:

- Tuning the structures (removing indexes and triggers)
- Disabling constraints during the data migration
- Using hints and options to improve the transaction performance

The first of the tips, tuning the structures, involves disabling any triggers or indexes that are on the table into which data is being loaded. For example, if you have a row-level trigger on the target table, that trigger will be executed for every row inserted into the table. If possible, disable the triggers prior to the data load. If the trigger should be executed for every inserted row, you may be able to do a bulk operation once the rows have been inserted, rather than a repeated operation during each INSERT. If properly tuned, the bulk operation will complete faster than the repeated trigger executions. You will need to be sure that the bulk operations execute for all rows that have not already been processed by the triggers.

In addition to disabling triggers, you should disable the indexes on the target table prior to starting the data load. If the indexes are left on the table, Oracle will dynamically manage the indexes as each row is inserted. Rather than continuously manage the index, drop it prior to the start of the load and re-create it when the load has completed.

NOTE
Disabling indexes and triggers resolves most of the performance problems associated with large table-to-table data migration efforts.

In addition to disabling indexes, you should consider disabling constraints on the table. If the source data is already in a table in the database, you can check that data for its adherence to your constraints (such as foreign keys or CHECK constraints) prior to loading it into your target table. Once the data has been loaded, you can reenable the constraints.

If none of those options gives you adequate performance, you should investigate the options Oracle has introduced for data migration tuning. Those options include the following:

- **The APPEND hint for INSERT commands** Like the SQL*Loader Direct Path option, the APPEND hint loads blocks of data into a table, starting at the HWM for the table. Use of the APPEND hint will increase your space usage.
- **The NOLOGGING option** If you are performing a CREATE TABLE AS SELECT command, use the NOLOGGING option to avoid writing to the redo logs during the operation. If the database utilizes a standby (Data Guard) server, then FORCE LOGGING will be the default behavior so that the inserted data will be logged into the redo logs regardless of the use of the NOLOGGING option.
- **The PARALLEL option** Parallel Query uses multiple processes to accomplish a single task. For a CREATE TABLE AS SELECT operation, you can parallelize both the CREATE TABLE portion and the query. If you use the PARALLEL option, you should also use the NOLOGGING option; otherwise, the parallel operations will have to wait due to serialized writes to the online redo log files. However, Oracle best practices suggest logging all operations in a production database.

Before using any of these advanced options, you should first investigate the target table's structures to make sure you've avoided the common traps cited earlier in this section.

You can also use programming logic to force INSERTs to be processed in arrays rather than as an entire set. For example, PL/SQL, Java, and C support array INSERTs, thus reducing the size of the transactions required to process a large set of data.

Bulk Deletes: The TRUNCATE Command

Occasionally, users attempt to delete all the rows from a table at once. When they encounter errors during this process, they complain that the rollback segments are too small, when in fact their transaction is too large.

A second problem occurs once the rows have all been deleted. Even though the segment no longer has any rows in it, it still maintains all the space that was allocated to it. Therefore, deleting all those rows saved not a single byte of allocated space.

The TRUNCATE command resolves both of these problems. It is a DDL command, not a DML command, *so it cannot be rolled back*. Once you have used the TRUNCATE command on a table, its rows are gone, and none of its DELETE triggers are executed in the process. However, the table retains all its dependent objects—such as grants, indexes, and constraints.

The TRUNCATE command is the fastest way to delete large volumes of data. Because it will delete all the rows in a table, this may force you to alter your application design so that no protected rows are stored in the same table as the rows to be deleted. If you use partitions, you can truncate one partition of a table without affecting the rest of the table's partitions (see Chapter 18).

A sample TRUNCATE command for a table is shown here:

```
truncate table EMPLOYEE drop storage;
```

This example, in which the EMPLOYEE table's rows are deleted, shows a powerful feature of TRUNCATE. The DROP STORAGE clause is used to deallocate the non-INITIAL space from the table (this is the default option). Therefore, you can delete all of a table's rows and reclaim all but its initial extent's allocated space, without dropping the table.

The TRUNCATE command also works for clusters. In this example, the REUSE STORAGE option is used to leave all allocated space empty within the segment that acquired it:

```
truncate cluster EMP_DEPT reuse storage;
```

When this example command is executed, all the rows in the EMP_DEPT cluster will be instantly deleted.

To truncate a partition, you need to know its name. In the following example, the partition named PART3 of the EMPLOYEE table is truncated via the ALTER TABLE command:

```
alter table EMPLOYEE
truncate partition PART3
drop storage;
```

The rest of the partitions of the EMPLOYEE table will be unaffected by the truncation of the PART3 partition. See Chapter 18 for details on creating and managing partitions.

As an alternative, you can create a PL/SQL program that uses dynamic SQL to divide a large DELETE operation into multiple smaller transactions with a COMMIT after each group of rows.

Using Partitions

You can use partitions to isolate data physically. For example, you can store each month's transactions in a separate partition of an ORDERS table. If you perform a bulk data load or deletion on the table, you can customize the partitions to tune the data manipulation operation. For example:

- You can truncate a partition and its indexes without affecting the rest of the table.
- You can drop a partition, via the DROP PARTITION clause of the ALTER TABLE command.
- You can drop a partition's local index.
- You can set a partition to NOLOGGING, reducing the impact of large transactions.

From a performance perspective, the chief advantage of partitions lies in their ability to be managed apart from the rest of the table. For example, being able to truncate a partition enables you to delete a large amount of data from a table (but not all of the table's data) without generating any redo information. In the short term, the beneficiary of this performance improvement is the DBA; in the longer term, the entire enterprise benefits from the improved availability of the data. See Chapter 18 for details on implementing partitions and subpartitions.

You can use the EXCHANGE PARTITION option to greatly reduce the impact your data-loading processes have on system availability. Start by creating an empty table that has the same column structure as your partitioned table. Load your data into the new table and then analyze the new table. Create indexes on the new table to match the partitioned table's indexes; the indexes must be local, and not global, indexes. When these steps are complete, alter the partitioned table using the EXCHANGE PARTITION clause to exchange an empty partition with the new table you populated. All the loaded data will now be accessible via the partitioned table. There is little impact to the system availability during this step because it is a DDL operation.

Reducing Network Traffic

As databases and the applications that use them become more distributed, the network that supports the servers may become a bottleneck in the process of delivering data to the users. Because DBAs typically have little control over the network management, it is important to use the database's capabilities to reduce the number of network packets required for the data to be delivered. Reducing network traffic will reduce your reliance on the network and thus eliminate a potential cause of performance problems.

Replication of Data Using Materialized Views

You can manipulate and query data from remote databases. However, it is not desirable to have large volumes of data constantly sent from one database to another. To reduce the amount of data being sent across the network, you should consider different data replication options.

In a purely distributed environment, each data element exists in one database. When data is required, it is accessed from remote databases via database links. This purist approach is similar to implementing an application strictly in third normal form—an approach that will not easily support any major production application. Modifying the application's tables to improve data retrieval performance involves denormalizing data. The denormalization process deliberately stores redundant data in order to shorten users' access paths to the data.

In a distributed environment, replicating data accomplishes this goal. Rather than force queries to cross the network to resolve user requests, selected data from remote servers is replicated to the local server. This can be accomplished via a number of means, as described in the following sections.

Replicated data is out of date as soon as it is created. Replicating data for performance purposes is therefore most effective when the source data is very infrequently changed or when the business processes can support the use of old data.

Oracle's distributed capabilities offer a means of managing the data replication within a database. *Materialized views* replicate data from a master source to multiple targets. Oracle provides tools for refreshing the data and updating the targets at specified time intervals.

Materialized views may be read-only or updatable. The management issues for materialized views are covered in Chapter 19; in this section, you will see their performance-tuning aspects.

Before creating a materialized view for replication, you should first create a database link to the source database. The following example creates a private database link called HR_LINK, using the LOC service name:

```
create database link hr_link
connect to hr identified by in4quandry
using 'loc';
```

The CREATE DATABASE LINK command, as shown in this example, has several parameters:

- The name of the link (HR_LINK, in this case).
- The account to connect to.
- The service name of the remote database (as found in the **tnsnames.ora** file for the server). In this case, the service name is LOC.

Materialized views automate the data replication and refresh processes. When materialized views are created, a *refresh interval* is established to schedule refreshes of replicated data. Local updates can be prevented, and transaction-based refreshes can be used. Transaction-based refreshes, available for many types of materialized views, send from the master database only those rows that have changed for the materialized view. This capability, described later in this chapter, may significantly improve the performance of your refreshes.

The syntax used to create the materialized view on the local server is shown in the following example, where the materialized view is given a name (LOCAL_EMP) and its storage parameters are specified. Its base query is given as well as its refresh interval. In this case, the materialized view is told to immediately retrieve the master data and then to perform the refresh operation again in seven days (SYSDATE+7).

```
create materialized view local_emp
pctfree 5
tablespace data_2
storage (initial 100m next 100m pctincrease 0)
refresh fast
      start with sysdate
      next sysdate+7
as select * from employee@hr_link;
```

The REFRESH FAST clause tells the database to use a materialized view log to refresh the local materialized view. The ability to use materialized view logs during refreshes is only available if the materialized view's base query is simple enough that Oracle can determine which row in the materialized view will change when a row changes in the source tables.

When a materialized view log is used, only the changes to the master table are sent to the targets. If you use a complex materialized view, you must use the REFRESH COMPLETE clause in place of the REFRESH FAST clause. In a complete refresh, the refresh completely replaces the existing data in the materialized view's underlying table.

Materialized view logs must be created in the master database, via the CREATE MATERIALIZED VIEW LOG command. An example of the CREATE MATERIALIZED VIEW LOG command is shown here:

```
create materialized view log on EMPLOYEE
tablespace DATA
storage (initial 500k next 100k pctincrease 0);
```

The materialized view log is always created in the same schema as the master table.

You can use simple materialized views with materialized view logs to reduce the amount of network traffic involved in maintaining the replicated data. Because only the changes to the data will be sent via a materialized view log, the maintenance of simple materialized views should use fewer network resources than complex materialized views require, particularly if the master tables are large, fairly static tables. If the master tables are not static, the volume of transactions sent via the materialized view log may not be any less than would be sent to perform a complete refresh. For details on the refresh capabilities of materialized views, see Chapter 19.

Regardless of the refresh option chosen, you should index the materialized view's base table to optimize queries against the materialized view. From a performance perspective, your goal is to present the users with the data they want in the format they want as quickly as possible. By creating materialized views on remote data, you can avoid traversing database links during queries. By creating materialized views on local data, you can prevent users from repeatedly aggregating large volumes of data, presenting them instead with pre-aggregated data that answers their most common queries.

Using Remote Procedure Calls

When using procedures in a distributed database environment, you can use one of two options: to create a local procedure that references remote tables or to create a remote procedure that is called by a local application.

The proper location for the procedure depends on the distribution of the data and the way the data is to be used. The emphasis should be on minimizing the amount of data that must be sent through the network to resolve the data request. The procedure should reside within the database that contains most of the data used during the procedure's operations.

For example, consider this procedure:

```
create procedure my_raise (my_emp_no in number, raise in number)
as
begin
      update employee@hr_link
      set salary = salary+raise
      where empno = my_emp_no;
end;
/
```

In this case, the procedure only accesses a single table (EMPLOYEE) on a remote node (as indicated by the database link HR_LINK). To reduce the amount of data sent across the network, move this procedure to the remote database identified by the database link HR_LINK and remove the reference to that database link from the FROM clause in the procedure. Then, call the procedure from the local database by using the database link, as shown here:

```
execute my_raise@hr_link(1234,2000);
```

In this case, two parameters are passed to the procedure—MY_EMP_NO is set to 1234, and RAISE is set to 2000. The procedure is invoked using a database link to tell the database where to find the procedure.

The tuning benefit of performing a remote procedure call is that all of the procedure's processing is performed in the database where the data resides. The remote procedure call minimizes the amount of network traffic necessary to complete the procedure's processing.

To maintain location transparency, you may create a local synonym that points to the remote procedure. The database link name will be specified in the synonym so that user requests will automatically use the remote database:

```
create synonym my_raise for my_raise@hr_link;
```

A user could then enter the command

```
execute my_raise(1234,2000);
```

and it would execute the remote procedure defined by the synonym MY_RAISE.

Using the Automatic Workload Repository

In Oracle Database 10*g* and earlier, Statspack gathers and reports on database statistics, albeit in a strictly text-based format! As of Oracle 10*g*, the Automatic Workload Repository (AWR) provides enhancements to the Statspack concept, generating all statistics found in Statspack, and more. In addition, the AWR is highly integrated with OEM, making it easy to analyze and fix a performance problem.

NOTE
*Statspack is still available in Oracle Database 12*c *as a free option. To use AWR reports, you must be licensed for the Diagnostics pack.*

Like Statspack, the AWR collects and maintains performance statistics for problem detection and self-tuning purposes. You can generate reports on the AWR data, and you can access it via views and through Cloud Control 12*c*. You can report on recent session activity as well as the overall system statistics and SQL usage.

The AWR captures the system statistics on an hourly basis (taking "snapshots" of the database) and stores the data in its repository tables. As with Statspack, the space requirements of the AWR will increase as the historical retention period is increased or the interval between snapshots is decreased. By default, seven days' worth of data is maintained in the AWR. You can see the snapshots that are stored in the AWR via the DBA_HIST_SNAPSHOT view.

To enable the AWR, set the STATISTICS_LEVEL initialization parameter to TYPICAL or ALL. If you set STATISTICS_LEVEL to BASIC, you can take manual snapshots of the AWR data, but they will not be as comprehensive as those performed automatically by the AWR. Setting STATISTICS_LEVEL to ALL adds timed OS statistics and plan execution statistics to those gathered with the TYPICAL setting.

Managing Snapshots

To take a manual snapshot, use the CREATE_SNAPSHOT procedure of the DBMS_WORKLOAD_REPOSITORY package:

```
execute dbms_workload_repository.create_snapshot ();
```

To alter the snapshot settings, use the MODIFY_SNAPSHOT_SETTINGS procedure. You can modify the retention (in minutes) and the interval (in minutes) for snapshots. The following example changes the interval to 30 minutes for the current database:

```
execute  dbms_workload_repository.modify_snapshot_settings
( interval => 30);
```

To drop a range of snapshots, use the DROP_SNAPSHOT_RANGE procedure, specifying the start and end of the snapshot IDs to drop:

```
execute dbms_workload_repository.drop_snapshot_range
     (low_snap_id => 1, high_snap_id => 10);
```

Managing Baselines

You can designate a set of snapshots as a baseline for the performance of the system. The baseline data will be retained for later comparisons with snapshots. Use the CREATE_BASELINE procedure to specify the beginning and ending snapshots for the baseline:

```
execute dbms_workload_repository.create_baseline
   (start_snap_id => 1, end_snap_id => 10,
   baseline_name => 'Monday baseline');
```

When you create a baseline, Oracle will assign an ID to the baseline; you can view past baselines via the DBA_HIST_BASELINE view. The snapshots you specify for the beginning and ending of the baseline are maintained until you drop the baseline. To drop the baseline, use the DROP_BASELINE procedure:

```
execute dbms_workload_repository.drop_baseline
(baseline_name => 'Monday baseline', cascade => FALSE);
```

If you set the CASCADE parameter of the DROP_BASELINE procedure to TRUE, the related snapshots will be dropped when the baseline is dropped.

You can see the AWR data via Cloud Control 12*c* or via the data dictionary views listed earlier in this section. Additional views supporting the AWR include V$ACTIVE_SESSION_HISTORY (sampled every second), DBA_HIST_SQL_PLAN (execution plans), and DBA_HIST_WR_CONTROL (for the AWR settings).

Generating AWR Reports

You can generate reports from the AWR either via Cloud Control 12*c* or via the reporting scripts provided. The **awrrpt.sql** script generates a report based on the differences in statistics between the beginning and ending snapshots. A second report, **awrrpti.sql**, displays a report based on the beginning and ending snapshots for a specified database and instance.

Both **awrrpt.sql** and **awrrpti.sql** are located in the **$ORACLE_HOME/rdbms/admin** directory. When you execute a report (from any DBA account), you will be prompted for the type of report (HTML or text), the number of days for which snapshots will be listed, the beginning and ending snapshot IDs, and the name for the output file. For RAC environments, you can use **awrgrpt.sql** to report most of the statistics across all instances.

Running the Automatic Database Diagnostic Monitor Reports

Rather than relying on manual reporting against the AWR table (much as you did with Statspack in previous versions of Oracle), you can use the Automatic Database Diagnostic Monitor (ADDM). Because it is based on AWR data, ADDM requires that the STATISTICS_LEVEL parameter be set (either to TYPICAL or ALL, as recommended earlier). You can access ADDM via the Performance Analysis section of Cloud Control 12*c*, or you can run an ADDM report manually.

To run ADDM against a set of snapshots, use the **addmrpt.sql** script located in the **$ORACLE_HOME/rdbms/admin** directory.

NOTE
You must have the ADVISOR system privilege in order to execute ADDM reports.

Within SQL*Plus, execute the **addmrpt.sql** script. You will be prompted for the beginning and ending snapshot IDs for the analysis and a name for the output file.

To view the ADDM data, you can use Cloud Control 12*c* or the advisor data dictionary views. The advisor views include DBA_ADVISOR_TASKS (existing tasks), DBA_ADVISOR_LOG (status and progress on tasks), DBA_ADVISOR_RECOMMENDATIONS (completed diagnostic tasks plus recommendations), and DBA_ADVISOR_FINDINGS. You can implement the recommendations to address the findings identified via ADDM. Figure 8-1 shows a typical AWR report, generated from the default baseline; in this example, the snapshot began on 14-Sep-2013 and ended on 22-Sep-2013. This database seems to be lightly loaded with plenty of CPU and memory resources; for example, latch contention is nonexistent, and there is enough memory to perform all sorting without using disk.

Using Automatic SQL Tuning Advisor

New as of Oracle Database 11*g*, Automatic SQL Tuning Advisor runs during the default maintenance window (using AutoTask) and targets the highest-load SQL statements collected in the AWR. Once the automatic SQL tuning begins during a maintenance window, the following steps are performed by the Automatic SQL Tuning Advisor:

1. Identify repeated high-load SQL from AWR statistics. Recently tuned SQL and recursive SQL are ignored.
2. Tune high-load SQL using calls to the SQL Tuning Advisor.
3. Create SQL Profiles for the high-load SQL; performance is tested both with and without the profile.
4. If the performance is better by at least a factor of three, automatically keep the profile; otherwise, note the improvement in the tuning report.

Instance Efficiency Percentages (Target 100%)

Buffer Nowait %:	99.99	Redo NoWait %:	100.00
Buffer Hit %:	96.86	In-memory Sort %:	100.00
Library Hit %:	97.50	Soft Parse %:	92.77
Execute to Parse %:	88.03	Latch Hit %:	99.99
Parse CPU to Parse Elapsd %:	97.79	% Non-Parse CPU:	39.29

Shared Pool Statistics

	Begin	End
Memory Usage %:	60.22	58.20
% SQL with executions>1:	83.61	93.20
% Memory for SQL w/exec>1:	61.80	57.38

Top 5 Timed Foreground Events

Event	Waits	Time(s)	Avg wait (ms)	% DB time	Wait Class
db file sequential read	85,419	264	3	59.77	User I/O
DB CPU		139		31.42	
direct path read	10,288	35	3	7.84	User I/O
db file parallel read	272	4	16	0.98	User I/O
db file scattered read	505	2	5	0.54	User I/O

Host CPU (CPUs: 24 Cores: 12 Sockets: 2)

Load Average Begin	Load Average End	%User	%System	%WIO	%Idle
1.94	2.11	2.9	0.8	2.9	96.2

Instance CPU

%Total CPU	%Busy CPU	%DB time waiting for CPU (Resource Manager)
0.2	5.1	0.0

Memory Statistics

	Begin	End
Host Mem (MB):	96,867.3	96,867.3
SGA use (MB):	3,504.0	3,504.0
PGA use (MB):	373.7	409.5
% Host Mem used for SGA+PGA:	4.00	4.04

FIGURE 8-1. *Sample AWR report via Cloud Control 12c*

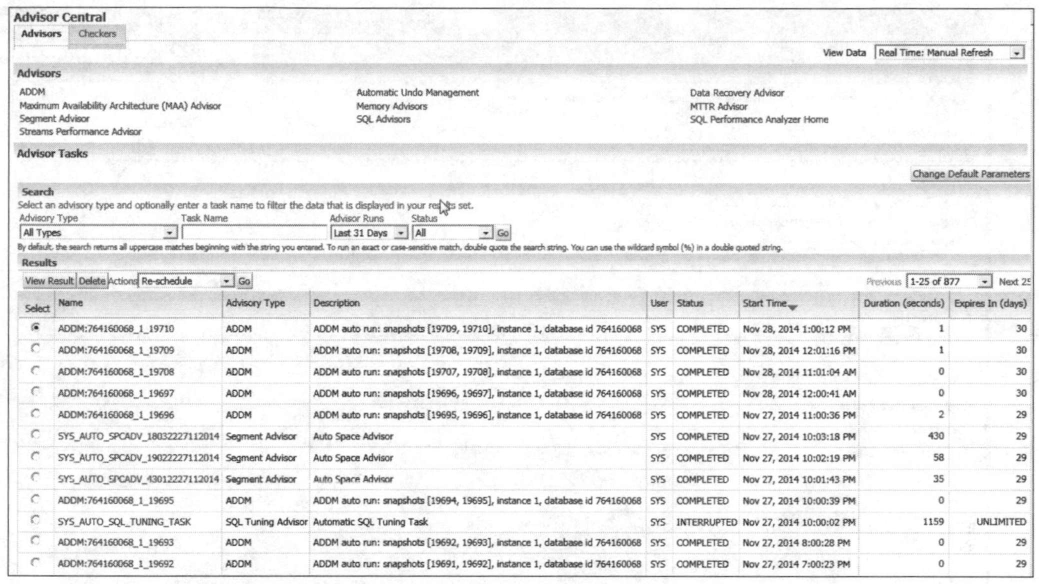

FIGURE 8-2. *Cloud Control 12*c *Advisor Central summary*

Figure 8-2 shows a summary of the Advisor tasks from Advisor Central; in this example, you can see a summary of the results for the Automatic Database Diagnostic Monitor (ADDM), Segment Advisor, and SQL Tuning Advisor.

Clicking the SQL Tuning Advisor result link, you can see the Automatic SQL Tuning Result Summary in Figure 8-3. On this database, the SQL Tuning Advisor found 124 potential SQL statements that could be improved by implementing a SQL Profile, adding one or more indexes, collecting statistics more often, or rewriting the SQL statement.

Performance Tuning in a Multitenant Environment

In Chapter 11 I cover the basics of Oracle's multitenant architecture. This includes the different types of containers available: the root container (container database, or CDB) that at a minimum comprises the root database, a seed database, and zero or more pluggable databases (PDBs). Oracle 12*c* databases can be standalone databases as well and converted to PDBs. I also distinguish between common and local users: common users have privileges across all PDBs within a container, whereas local users see the PDB as a standalone database (non-CDB). In a multitenant environment, the traditional USER_, ALL_, and DBA_ data dictionary views are supplemented with CDB_ views that are visible across the entire container to common users.

As you might expect, tuning a multitenant container database (the container itself or one of the PDBs) is much like tuning a non-CDB in that you're tuning a single instance with many different applications (PDBs) sharing and competing for the same server resources. This is in line with the multitenant database architecture in that there is minimal or no difference between a CDB and a non-CDB from a usage, compatibility, and tuning perspective.

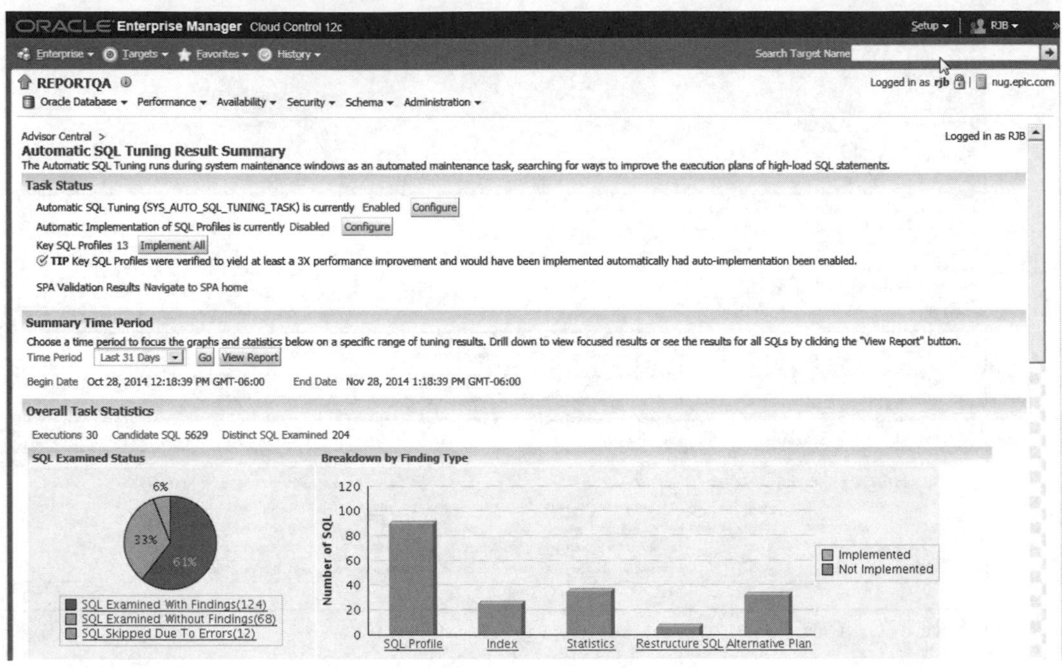

FIGURE 8-3. *Automatic SQL Tuning Advisor results*

The keys to performance tuning a PDB are monitoring and resource allocation. Not only must you tune individual SQL statements within a PDB, but you also must decide what percentage of the server's resources a PDB can have if all PDBs are active. Many of the same tools you use for a non-CDB database are also used for a CDB, such as the SQL Tuning Advisor and the familiar AWR and ADDM reports. The big difference in a CDB environment is that tuning SQL statements happens at the PDB level, whereas the AWR, ASH, and ADDM reports are at the instance (CDB) level.

As you will find out in Chapter 11, some initialization parameters can also be set at the PDB level if the default value at the CDB level is not appropriate. I'll show you how to change some of these parameters at the PDB level in a tuning scenario.

Even though there is database activity at the CDB level, the bulk of the activity should be occurring in each PDB from a logical perspective. Remember that from an instance perspective, it's still one database instance. Therefore, the standard Oracle tuning methodologies still apply to a CDB environment.

At the CDB level, you want to optimize the amount of memory you need to host one or more PDBs; that's the reason you're using a multitenant environment in the first place! In the following sections, I'll review the standard tuning methodologies as well as how you can change initialization parameters at the PDB level. Using performance reports such as the ASH, ADDM, and AWR reports helps you identify performance issues for the CDB, and using the SQL Tuning Advisor helps you optimize your SQL activity within each PDB.

Tuning Methodology

The standard Oracle tuning methodology developed and refined over the last several releases of Oracle Database still apply to multitenant environments. The overall steps are as follows:

1. Identify the tuning goal:
   a. Reduce elapsed time for individual queries?
   b. Increase the number of users without buying new hardware?
   c. Optimize memory usage?
   d. Reduce disk space usage (compression, normalization)?
2. Determine the cause of the bottleneck (OS, network, I/O); usually it's one cause.
3. Tune the application from the top down:
   a. Review the application design.
   b. Modify the database design (denormalization, materialized views, data warehouse).
   c. Tune the SQL code.
   d. Tune the instance.
4. Use database analysis tools once you finish step 3:
   a. Collect statistics at the instance and OS levels.
   b. Use the AWR report to identify wait events and poorly performing SQL.
   c. Use the SQL Tuning Advisor, memory advisors, and other advisors to tune and reduce elapsed time, CPU, and I/O.
5. After tuning one or more components, start again at step 2 if the tuning goal has not yet been met.

The biggest focus of any tuning effort is identifying when to stop tuning. In other words, you need to identify the goal for a tuning effort after several users complain that "the database is slow." Identifying the performance issue, reevaluating the service-level agreements (SLAs) in place, and monitoring database growth and the user base are important factors in deciding how much time you want to spend tuning a database (CDB or non-CDB) before you reach the decision that you need faster hardware, a faster network, or a new database design.

Sizing the CDB

Adjusting parameters at the CDB level is much like tuning a single instance in a non-CDB environment that has several applications with different resource and availability requirements. It's worth mentioning again that a CDB *is* a single database instance, but with the added features of the multitenant environment, you have much more control over resource consumption among the several applications (each in their own PDB) in addition to the strong isolation between the applications from a security perspective.

Tuning CDB Memory and CPU Resources

Tuning the memory in a CDB means you're changing the same memory areas as in a non-CDB:

- Buffer cache (SGA)
- Shared pool (SGA)
- Program Global Area (PGA)

When you calculate the memory requirements for a CDB, your first estimate should be the sum of all corresponding memory requirements for each non-CDB that will become a PDB. Of course, you will eventually want to reduce the total memory footprint for the CDB based on a number of factors. For example, not all PDBs will be active at the same time; therefore, you will likely not need as much total memory allocated to the CDB.

Using Enterprise Manager Cloud Control 12*c* is a good way to see resource usage across the CDB. In Figure 8-4, the container CDB01 has three PDBs active and two inactive.

The total memory allocated for the CDB is approximately 5GB. Three non-CDBs would likely use 5GB or more each; all five PDBs in CDB01 may perform just fine in a total of 5GB.

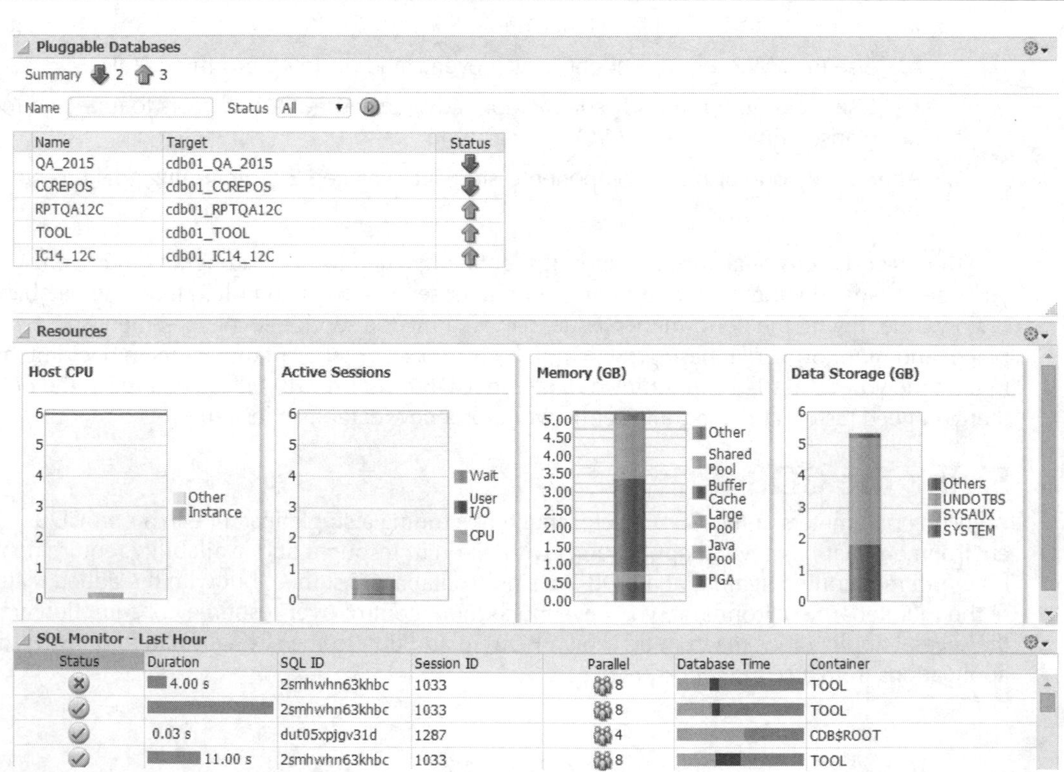

FIGURE 8-4. *Viewing PDB resource usage within a CDB using Cloud Control 12*c

There are a few different approaches to resource allocation among PDBs within a CDB:

- **None** Let each PDB use all resources of the CDB if no other PDB is active; when multiple PDBs need resources, they are divided equally.
- **Minimum** Each PDB gets a minimum guaranteed resource allocation.
- **Minimum/maximum** Each PDB gets both a minimum guaranteed resource allocation and a maximum.

Resource usage allocation in a CDB is measured in *shares*. By default, all PDBs can consume all resources allocated to the CDB. I cover more details on how shares are allocated and calculated later in the chapter.

Modifying Initialization Parameters

As you will find out in Chapter 11, there is only one SPFILE per CDB instance. All database parameters are stored in the CDB's SPFILE, but 171 of those parameters (out of a total of 367 for Oracle Database 12*c* 12.1.0.1) can be changed at the PDB level. The column ISPDB_MODIFIABLE is an easy way to see which parameters you can change at the PDB level:

```
SQL> select ispdb_modifiable,count(ispdb_modifiable)
  2  from v$parameter
  3  group by ispdb_modifiable;

ISPDB COUNT(ISPDB_MODIFIABLE)
----- -----------------------
TRUE                      171
FALSE                     196

SQL>
```

When you unplug a PDB, its customized parameters stay with the unplugged PDB and are set when that PDB is plugged back in regardless of which PDB it is plugged into. When a PDB is cloned, the custom parameters are cloned as well. At the container level, you can also look at the data dictionary view PDB_SPFILE$ to see which parameters are different across PDBs:

```
select pdb_uid,pdb_name,name,value$
from pdb_spfile$ ps
   join cdb_pdbs cp
      on ps.pdb_uid=cp.con_uid;

   PDB_UID PDB_NAME         NAME                           VALUE$
---------- ---------------- ------------------------------ ----------
1258510409 TOOL             sessions                       200
1288637549 RPTQA12C         cursor_sharing                 'FORCE'
1288637549 RPTQA12C         star_transformation_enabled    TRUE
1288637549 RPTQA12C         open_cursors                   300
```

In the TOOL PDB, the SESSIONS parameter is different from the default (at the CDB level); the RPTQA12C PDB has three non-default parameters set.

Using Memory Advisors

The buffer cache in a CDB, shared across all PDBs, behaves much like the buffer cache in a non-CDB: The same LRU algorithms are used to determine when and if a block should stay in the buffer cache. Because the buffer cache is shared, the PDB's container ID (CON_ID) is also stored in each block. The same container ID is stored in the other SGA and PGA memory areas, such as the shared pool in the SGA and the global PGA. The memory advisors from previous versions of Oracle Database work in much the same way in a multitenant environment; sizing recommendations are at the CDB (instance) level. Individual memory parameters that can be adjusted at the PDB level are limited to SORT_AREA_SIZE and SORT_AREA_RETAINED_SIZE, although in general Oracle best practices dictate that you only set PGA_AGGREGATE_TARGET and let Oracle manage the other memory areas.

Figure 8-5 shows the output from the SGA Memory Advisor launched from Cloud Control 12*c*.

Even with several PDBs in the CDB01 container, it appears that the total memory for the CDB can be reduced by at least 1GB and retain good performance for all PDBs.

To accommodate a potentially larger number of sessions in a CDB, the parameter PGA_AGGREGATE_LIMIT was added to place a hard limit on the amount of PGA memory used. The existing parameter PGA_AGGREGATE_TARGET was useful in previous releases as a soft limit but only for tunable memory. Several sessions using untunable memory (such as PL/SQL applications that allocate large memory arrays) could potentially use up all available PGA memory, causing swap activity at the OS level and affecting performance across all instances on the server. Thus, the parameter PGA_AGGREGATE_LIMIT was added to abort PGA memory requests by one or more non-SYSTEM connections to get under this limit.

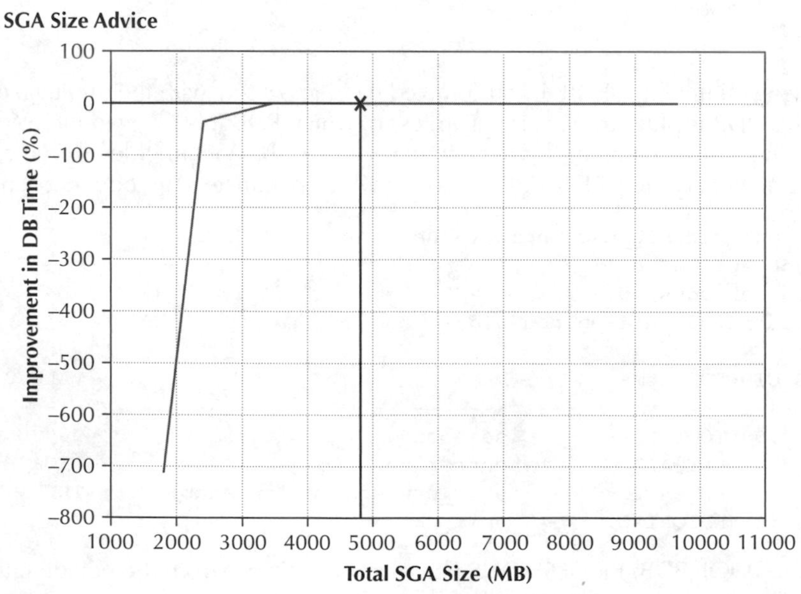

FIGURE 8-5. *CDB SGA Memory Advisor in Cloud Control 12c*

Leveraging AWR Reports

As with all previously described Oracle tuning tools, AWR snapshots include a container ID number, and that container ID is reflected in any AWR report. Figure 8-6 shows an excerpt of the SQL statements executed during the three-hour window specified for the AWR report.

The SQL statements run during this window were from two PDBs and the root container. As in a non-CDB environment, your tuning effort will focus first on the statements with the longest elapsed time along with statements whose total time across multiple executions is at the top of the list.

Using the SQL Tuning Advisor

When you run the SQL Tuning Advisor against one or more SQL statements, such as those in Figure 8-6, the advisor runs only in the context of a single PDB. In other words, the recommendations are based only on the performance and resource usage within the PDB. Even if the same SQL statement is run in multiple PDBs, the schema names, statistics, data volumes, and initialization parameters can and will likely be different between PDBs. Therefore, if any recommendations are implemented, they are applied in only a single PDB.

Other new and enhanced SQL Tuning features in Oracle Database 12*c* can be used for CDBs and non-CDBs:

- Adaptive SQL plan management
- Automatic SQL plan baseline evolution
- SQL management base
- SQL plan directives
- Improved statistics gathering performance

The usage of these tools is beyond the scope of this book.

SQL ordered by Elapsed Time

- Resources reported for PL/SQL code includes the resources used by all SQL statements called by the code.
- % Total DB Time is the Elapsed Time of the SQL statement divided into the Total Database Time multiplied by 100
- %Total - Elapsed Time as a percentage of Total DB time
- %CPU - CPU Time as a percentage of Elapsed Time
- %IO - User I/O Time as a percentage of Elapsed Time
- Captured SQL account for 118.9% of Total DB Time (s): 216
- Captured PL/SQL account for 11.0% of Total DB Time (s): 216

Elapsed Time (s)	Executions	Elapsed Time per Exec (s)	%Total	%CPU	%IO	SQL Id	SQL Module	PDB Name	SQL Text
46.45	3	15.48	21.54	27.70	9.92	2smhwhn63khbc	SQL*Plus	TOOL	insert /*+ parallel(8) */ int...
33.03	165	0.20	15.31	95.94	2.03	dt2babdaankpq	EM Realtime Connection		select dbms_report.get_report(...
22.73	165	0.14	10.54	96.82	2.65	6fwy90bgdvdfn	EM Realtime Connection		with base_metrics as (select...
19.88	2	9.94	9.22	95.55	2.82	gsbdfku007tup	Admin Connection		select output from table(dbms_...
15.23	240	0.06	7.06	98.61	0.00	5yv7yvjgjxugg			select TIME_WAITED_MICRO from ...
14.36	117	0.12	6.66	90.79	2.91	fhf8upax5cxsz	MMON_SLAVE		BEGIN sys.dbms_auto_report_int...
12.64	117	0.11	5.86	91.75	3.16	0w26sk6t6gg98	MMON_SLAVE		SELECT XMLTYPE(DBMS_REPORT.GET...
8.63	117	0.07	4.00	88.42	4.47	7r24h5ucyjggz	MMON_SLAVE		WITH MONITOR_DATA AS (SELECT I...
7.66	4	1.91	3.55	32.30	10.03	8fypn587m9tc5	SQL*Plus	TOOL	insert into temp_objects selec...
7.54	165	0.05	3.49	99.35	0.00	01w7zgb118hpb	EM Realtime Connection		select xmlelement("references...
6.19	1,437	0.00	2.87	96.95	0.28	fnq8p3fj3r5as			select /*+ no_monitor */ job, ...
5.07	78	0.07	2.35	98.94	0.00	5m2z5vch05wap	EM Realtime Connection		select end_time endTime, round...
4.44	49	0.09	2.06	98.51	0.14	g57kbmvd1gqfk	EM Realtime Connection		select dbms_sqltune.report_sql...
3.97	6	0.66	1.84	21.87	62.07	4t8wz8471kxf2	EM Realtime Connection	RPTQA12C	WITH F AS (select tablespace_n...
3.62	2	1.81	1.68	73.18	26.94	a3a61zmn8t5k4	SQL*Plus	TOOL	select owner, status, count(ob...
3.57	6	0.60	1.66	98.86	0.10	2vwhap18bjf9h	ClarityDataTransferService.exe	RPTQA12C	SELECT DISTINCT CC.COLUMN_NAME...

FIGURE 8-6. *AWR report in a multitenant environment*

Managing Resource Allocation Within a PDB

In the previous section, I introduced the concept of resource sharing within a CDB by using shares. I'll expand on that concept by showing how you can allocate shares among PDBs within a CDB. In addition, I'll talk about resource management within a PDB, which is much like how Resource Manager operates in a non-CDB environment and previous versions of Oracle Database.

Once a portion of resources is allocated to a PDB, Resource Manager will prioritize resource requests by users. In both cases you'll use the DBMS_RESOURCE_MANAGER package to create and deploy resource allocations.

Using Shares to Manage Inter-PDB Resources

Each PDB that's plugged into a CDB competes for the resources of the CDB—primarily CPU, parallel servers, and, in the case of Oracle Exadata, I/O. How much of each resource a PDB gets depends on how many *shares* that PDB was assigned when it was created.

NOTE
Neither consumer groups (using Resource Manager) nor shares can be defined for the root container.

By default, each PDB gets one share unless otherwise specified. When a new PDB is added or an existing PDB is unplugged, the number of shares each PDB has remains the same. Table 8-1 shows a CDB with four PDBs: HR, BI, REPOS, and TOOL. The BI PDB has three shares, and the rest have one each, the default.

The TOOL database, for example, is guaranteed 16.67 percent of the server's CPU resources if needed. If one or more of the other PDBs are not active, TOOL can use its default allocation if there is no activity in the other PDBs.

Suppose you create a PDB called NCAL and don't specify the number of shares; it defaults to 1, with the results shown in Table 8-2.

The minimum CPU guaranteed for each PDB is automatically recalculated based on the new total number of shares. Each PDB with one share now gets 14.29 percent of the CPU resources, and the amount of CPU resources available (at a minimum) for the BI PDB is now 42.86 percent.

Creating and Modifying Resource Manager Plans

To further refine the resource consumption, you can set limits within each PDB using Resource Manager. From the perspective of the PDB, all resources are controlled by directives created using DBMS_RESOURCE_MANAGER. The amount of CPU, Exadata I/O, and concurrent parallel servers

PDB Name	Shares	CPU Percent (Maximum)
HR	1	16.67 percent
BI	3	50 percent
REPOS	1	16.67 percent
TOOL	1	16.67 percent

TABLE 8-1. *PDBs and Share Allocation for Four PDBs*

PDB Name	Shares	CPU Percent (Maximum)
HR	1	14.29 percent
BI	3	42.86 percent
REPOS	1	14.29 percent
TOOL	1	14.29 percent
NCAL	1	14.29 percent

TABLE 8-2. *PDBs and Share Allocation for Five PDBs After Adding a New One*

used by the PDB default to 100 percent but can be adjusted down to 0 percent depending on the time of day or other circumstances.

The resource plan itself is created at the CDB level, and you create directives for each PDB within the CDB. You can also specify a set of default directives for those PDBs that do not have an explicit set of directives.

Identifying Parameters to Limit PDB Resource Usage

As part of the utilization plan for each PDB, there are two key limits you can control: the utilization limit for CPU, Exadata I/Os, and parallel servers and a parallel server limit. These plan directive limits are UTILIZATION_LIMIT and PARALLEL_SERVER_LIMIT, respectively.

The resource directive UTILIZATION_LIMIT defines the percentage of CPU, I/Os, and parallel servers available to a PDB. If UTILIZATION_LIMIT is set at 30, then the PDB can use no more than 30 percent of the resources available to the CDB.

To further refine the resource limits, you can use PARALLEL_SERVER_LIMIT to define the maximum percentage of the CDB's PARALLEL_SERVERS_TARGET value; this value overrides the UTILIZATION_LIMIT directive but only for parallel resources. The default is 100 percent.

Creating the CDB Resource Plan

The steps for creating a CDB resource plan are similar to those for creating a resource plan in a non-CDB, but with additional steps for each PDB. You create and manage the resource plan from the root container only. Table 8-3 lists the steps and corresponding DBMS_RESOURCE_MANAGER calls needed to create and configure the CDB resource plan.

Other key procedures in DBMS_RESOURCE_MANAGER include UPDATE_CDB_PLAN to change the characteristics of the CDB resource plan and DELETE_CDB_PLAN to delete the resource plan and all of its directives. To update and delete individual CDB plan directives, use UPDATE_CDB_PLAN_DIRECTIVE and DELETE_CDB_PLAN_DIRECTIVE.

Here is an example of creating a CDB resource plan for the CDB01 container and defining the plan directives for two of the PDBs in the CDB.

1. Create a pending area for the CDB plan:

```
SQL> connect / as sysdba
Connected.
SQL> exec dbms_resource_manager.create_pending_area();

PL/SQL procedure successfully completed.
```

Step	Description	DBMS_RESOURCE_MANAGER Procedure
1	Create a pending area.	CREATE_PENDING_AREA
2	Create a CDB resource plan.	CREATE_CDB_PLAN
3	Create PDB directives.	CREATE_CDB_PLAN_DIRECTIVE
4	Update default PDB directives.	UPDATE_CDB_DEFAULT_DIRECTIVE
5	Update default AutoTask directives.	UPDATE_CDB_AUTOTASK_DIRECTIVE
6	Validate the pending area.	VALIDATE_PENDING_AREA
7	Submit the pending area.	SUBMIT_PENDING_AREA

TABLE 8-3. *Steps to Create a Resource Plan with DBMS_RESOURCE_MANAGER Calls*

2. Create a resource plan that manages the TOOL and CCREPOS PDBs to minimize CPU and other resource usage:

```
SQL> begin
       dbms_resource_manager.create_cdb_plan(
          plan     => 'low_prio_apps',
          comment  => 'TOOL and repository database low priority');
     end;
     /

PL/SQL procedure successfully completed.
SQL>
```

3. Create a plan directive that gives both the TOOL and CCREPOS PDBs one share. The utilization limit for TOOL should be 50 percent, and for CCREPOS it will be 75 percent:

```
SQL> begin
       dbms_resource_manager.create_cdb_plan_directive(
          plan => 'low_prio_apps',
          pluggable_database => 'tool',
          shares => 1,
          utilization_limit => 50,
          parallel_server_limit => 50);
     end;
     /

PL/SQL procedure successfully completed.

SQL> begin
       dbms_resource_manager.create_cdb_plan_directive(
           plan => 'low_prio_apps',
          pluggable_database => 'ccrepos',
          shares => 1,
          utilization_limit => 75,
```

```
              parallel_server_limit => 75);
      end;
      /

PL/SQL procedure successfully completed.

SQL>
```

4. Validate and submit the pending area:

```
SQL> exec dbms_resource_manager.validate_pending_area();

PL/SQL procedure successfully completed.

SQL> exec dbms_resource_manager.submit_pending_area();

PL/SQL procedure successfully completed.

SQL>
```

5. Finally, make this resource manager plan the current plan:

```
SQL> alter system set resource_manager_plan='low_prio_apps';
System altered.
SQL>
```

Viewing Resource Plan Directives

In Oracle Database 12*c* you have a data dictionary view called DBA_CDB_RSRC_PLAN_DIRECTIVES to see all of the current resource plans. Querying that view, you can see the resource plans you just created for TOOL and CCREPOS:

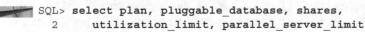

```
SQL> select plan, pluggable_database, shares,
       utilization_limit, parallel_server_limit
     from dba_cdb_rsrc_plan_directives
     order by plan,pluggable_database;

PLAN                       PLUGGABLE_DATABASE SHARES UTILIZA PARALLEL_
-------------------------- ------------------ ------ ------- ---------
DEFAULT_CDB_PLAN           ORA$AUTOTASK                   90       100
DEFAULT_CDB_PLAN           ORA$DEFAULT_PDB_DI      1     100       100
                           RECTIVE
DEFAULT_MAINTENANCE_PLAN   ORA$AUTOTASK                   90       100
DEFAULT_MAINTENANCE_PLAN   ORA$DEFAULT_PDB_DI      1     100       100
                           RECTIVE

LOW_PRIO_APPS              CCREPOS                 1      75        75
LOW_PRIO_APPS              ORA$AUTOTASK                   90       100
LOW_PRIO_APPS              ORA$DEFAULT_PDB_DI      1     100       100
                           RECTIVE
LOW_PRIO_APPS              TOOL                    1      50        50
ORA$INTERNAL_CDB_PLAN      ORA$AUTOTASK
```

```
ORA$INTERNAL_CDB_PLAN       ORA$DEFAULT_PDB_DI
                            RECTIVE
ORA$QOS_CDB_PLAN            ORA$AUTOTASK                    90        100
ORA$QOS_CDB_PLAN            ORA$DEFAULT_PDB_DI     1       100        100
                            RECTIVE
```

In previous releases of Oracle Database and for non-CDBs in Oracle Database 12*c*, the corresponding data dictionary view is DBA_RSRC_PLAN_DIRECTIVES.

Managing Resources Within a PDB

Resource plans can manage workloads within a PDB as well. These resource plans manage workloads just as they do in a non-CDB and, not surprisingly, are called PDB resource plans. There are a few restrictions and differences with PDB plans. Table 8-4 shows the parameter and feature differences between non-CDB and PDB resource plans.

Regardless of the container type, you still view resource plans using the V$RSRC_PLAN dynamic performance view. To find the active CDB resource plan, select the row in V$RSRC_PLAN with CON_ID=1.

Migrating Non-CDB Resource Plans

You will likely convert and plug in many non-CDBs as well as creating new PDBs. This process is straightforward, and all of your applications should work as expected. If the non-CDB has a resource plan, it will be converted as well, as long as it meets these conditions:

- There are no more than eight consumer groups.
- There are no subplans.
- All resource allocations are on level 1.

In other words, the migrated resource plan must be compatible with a new PDB resource plan that follows the rules in the previous section. If the plan violates any of these conditions, the plan is converted during the plug-in operation to a plan that is compatible with a PDB. This plan may be unsuitable; you can drop, modify, or create a new resource plan. The original plan is saved in DBA_RSRC_PLAN_DIRECTIVES with the STATUS column having a value of LEGACY.

Resource Plan Feature	Non-CDB	PDB
Multilevel plans	Yes	No
Consumer groups	Maximum: 32	Maximum: 8
Subplans	Yes	No
CREATE_PLAN_DIRECTIVE parameter	N/A	SHARE
CREATE_PLAN_DIRECTIVE parameter	MAX_UTILIZATION_LIMIT	UTILIZATION_LIMIT
CREATE_PLAN_DIRECTIVE parameter	PARALLEL_TARGET_ PERCENTAGE	PARALLEL_SERVER_LIMIT

TABLE 8-4. *Differences Between Non-CDB and PDB Resource Plans*

Performing Database Replay

The Database Replay functionality from previous Oracle Database releases has also been enhanced in Oracle Database 12*c* to include simultaneous workload replays as a planning tool for estimating how multiple non-CDBs will perform in a CDB environment. You can take production workloads from multiple servers in a non-CDB environment and play them back in various configurations on a single new server to simulate how well they would coexist in a multitenant environment.

Analyze the Source Database Workloads

When you capture workloads for potential multitenant deployment, the workloads are typically in different business units and locations; the peak load for each application is likely at different times of the day, which makes these applications ideal candidates for consolidation. Figure 8-7 shows a typical set of workloads from applications currently on different servers.

You can also analyze existing PDBs and capture workloads to see how they would perform as a PDB of another CDB on a different server. The general steps you'll follow as part of this analysis phase are as follows:

1. Capture the workload of an existing non-CDB or PDB.
2. Optionally export the AWR snapshots for the database.
3. Restore the candidate database onto the target system.
4. Make changes to the imported candidate database as needed, such as upgrading to Oracle Database 12*c*.
5. Copy the generated workload files to the target system.
6. Process the workload as a one-time prerequisite step.
7. Repeat steps 1–6 for all other candidate databases.
8. Configure the target system for replay (such as the workload replay client processes).
9. Replay the workloads for all PDBs within the single CDB on the target system.

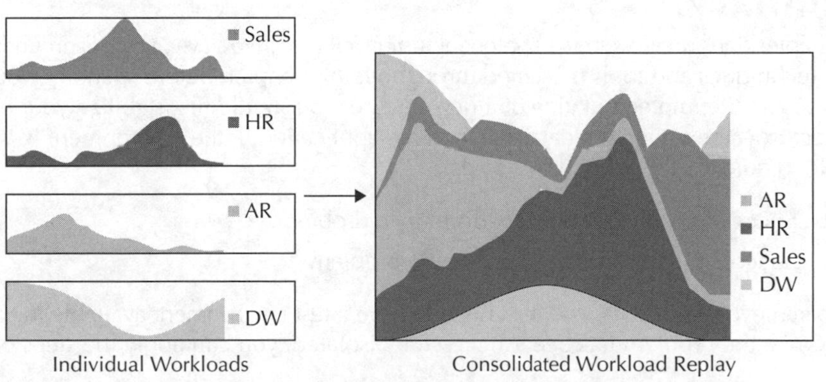

FIGURE 8-7. *Candidate workloads for multitenant consolidation*

Capture Source Database Workloads

On the source database server, you'll capture the workload for a typical 8-hour or 24-hour period. You'll want all captured workloads to cover the same time period. To optimize the performance of the replay test, you can optionally export AWR snapshots, SQL profiles, and SQL tuning sets.

Process Workloads on Target System

After you import the candidate database into a PDB of the new CDB, you import the workload generated on the source server. You preprocess the workload files in preparation for the replay, which needs to happen only once for each imported workload. It's recommended that you replay each imported workload individually to ensure that there are no extreme variations in performance compared to that database's performance on the original server.

Replay Workloads on Target CDB

After all PDBs have been created and preprocessed, remap any connections that might refer to objects that don't exist on the target system. Create a replay schedule that will replay each workload at the same time and rate that it does on the source system. You can create multiple schedules to see how workloads can be shifted to optimize the CDB's overall performance.

Verify Replay Results

After the replay session is complete, review the reports generated by Consolidated Database Replay to see, for example, if the response time and overall SLA of the databases on their original servers can be met by this consolidation platform. If there are severe regressions, then you can use the tuning methodologies discussed earlier in this chapter and run the replay again. Even after tuning, you may find that the server needs more CPUs or memory. Ideally, you'll find out that each database runs just as fast as or faster than it did on the original server!

Last, but not least, having accurate and easy-to-manage diagnostic information for your CDB and PDBs is more important than ever. The Automatic Diagnostic Repository (ADR) has the same structure as in previous releases, and the CDB and the PDBs within the CDB have their own subdirectories under the ADR Base directory.

Summary

This chapter does not cover every potential tuning solution. However, there is an underlying approach to the techniques and tools presented throughout this chapter. Before spending your time and resources on the implementation of a new feature, you should first stabilize your environment and architecture—the server, the database, and the application. If the environment is stable, you should be able to quickly accomplish two goals:

1. Successfully re-create the performance problem.
2. Successfully isolate the cause of the problem.

To achieve these goals, you may need to have a test environment available for your performance tests. Once the problem has been successfully isolated, you can apply the steps outlined in this chapter to the problem. In general, your tuning approach should mirror the order of the sections of this chapter:

1. Evaluate application design.
2. Tune SQL.
3. Tune memory usage.
4. Tune data access.
5. Tune data manipulation.
6. Tune network traffic.
7. Tune physical and logical storage.
8. Use the AWR to tune queries.
9. Manage PDB resources.
10. Leverage Database Replay for resource planning.

Depending on the nature of your application, you may choose a different order for the steps, or you may combine steps.

If the application design cannot be altered and the SQL cannot be altered, you can tune the memory and disk areas used by the application. As you alter the memory and disk area settings, you must be sure to revisit the application design and SQL implementation to be sure that your changes do not adversely impact the application. The need to revisit the application design process is particularly important if you choose to use a data replication method, because the timeliness of the replicated data may cause problems within the business process served by the application.

Finally, you'll need to expand your tuning expertise to include tuning pluggable databases in a multitenant environment. This tuning expertise is easy to come by: The container database can be tuned as a traditional single-instance database and individual statements within a pluggable database can be tuned with the tools you're already familiar with such as the SQL Tuning Advisor. Resource management in a multitenant environment adds the concept of a *share* to allocate resources among several pluggable tenants in a container database. Within each pluggable database you'll once again be able to use the Resource Manager tools you're familiar with from previous versions of Oracle Database.

CHAPTER 9

In-Memory Option

In Chapter 8, we talked about tuning methodologies and other ways to maximize throughput and minimize response time. One of the most useful and powerful new features of Oracle Database 12*c*, the In-Memory option (available starting with version 12.1.0.2), adds another tool you can use to make your queries run faster than ever before.

This chapter gives a high-level overview of the Oracle In-Memory option, what system requirements you need to use it effectively, and what it can and cannot do. I'll give a few real-world examples of how In-Memory works and review the dynamic performance views you need to use to identify how well In-Memory is working in your environment.

Overview of Oracle In-Memory Option

The considerations for using the In-Memory option are primarily licensing costs and how much memory you can allocate to the In-Memory column store. As of version 12.1.0.2, the licensing costs for In-Memory are comparable to that of RAC licensing; memory prices go down every year, but because the bottleneck moves from I/O to the memory, your server's memory bus and memory speed become critical to the performance of In-Memory as a whole.

The In-Memory (IM) column store is allocated as part of the SGA; therefore, your total SGA size (SGA_MAX_SIZE) includes the memory you want to allocate to the IM column store. As the name implies, the IM column store contains one or more columns from a table stored in the SGA alongside the table's row store in the buffer cache and on disk. Any changes to values in the IM column are kept in synch with the row store in the buffer cache and, of course, in the table's datafile.

You don't necessarily have to enable the IM column store for each table—you can enable it for a single column, or you can enable it for an entire tablespace by default. For a partitioned table, one partition can default to residing in the IM column store while the rest of the partitions are stored only in the row store.

Using the IM column store gives the most benefit in these scenarios:

- Query aggregates
- Scanning a very large number of rows using operators such as =, <, >, and IN
- Frequently retrieving a very small number of columns from a table with a large number of columns
- Joins between a small table and a large table (e.g., a data warehouse dimension table and fact table)

If you have the memory available, you can store most columns of your biggest tables in the IM column store continuously; once the column resides in the IM column store, it is maintained alongside the row store on disk and is removed from the IM column store only if pushed out by another, more frequently accessed column of another table or if the database instance is restarted. Using ALTER TABLE to disable the IM column store for that column immediately invalidates and flushes the contents of that column from the SGA.

System Requirements and Setup

The requirements to use the IM column store are not much more than what you likely already have—you probably need a bit more memory and maybe another CPU, but your I/O requirements will be somewhat less demanding since you will almost certainly be doing less I/O. You may not even need more CPU threads, because the processing required to manage the IM column store in memory is offset by reduced I/O, and therefore your elapsed time, especially in a batch or data warehouse environment, is going to be significantly reduced.

The most important hardware component for implementing the IM column store is the additional memory required to hold the tables or table columns in memory. The memory bandwidth, not just the amount of memory, becomes much more critical because the bottleneck in throughput has moved from the I/O subsystem to memory; you're using the existing buffer cache to hold table rows (the row cache) while maintaining some or all columns in the dedicated IM column store.

Do you need to have enough memory to hold all of your tables and all columns in memory? Not at all. Most likely only a small subset of columns in your biggest tables are accessed most often. In addition, any given table column will be stored in memory at one of four compression levels; which level of compression you choose depends on the type and distribution of the data in the column as well as the CPU resources available. A primary key column will not compress much at all regardless of the compression type, but a column such as SERVICE_DATE or LOCATION_ID will compress nicely.

You won't need an Exadata engineered system to effectively use the IM column store. A monolithic traditional server with lots of fast memory will actually give you some of the advantages of an Exadata system at a somewhat lower total cost of ownership (TCO).

If you already have an Exadata engineered system, you can certainly take advantage of the IM column store. While the Exadata storage subsystem leverages many of the algorithms used by the IM column store, having several tables' columns in memory across nodes in an Exadata RAC environment still reduces the amount of I/O required by the storage subsystem. The best performing I/O is still the I/O that you don't have to do!

In-Memory Case Study

Using the IM column store is easy, as long as you understand its limitations and requirements. Setting up the initialization parameters is easy, but you must also be cognizant of which initialization parameters cannot be changed while the instance is running and the dependencies on those parameters. In this section I'll present the main initialization parameters you need to set and show you how to mark entire tablespaces, tables, or columns to leverage the IM column store.

Initialization Parameters

The key parameters for using the IM column store are INMEMORY_SIZE, SGA_TARGET, and SGA_MAX_SIZE. On a server with 384GB of RAM, you start by defining the total size of the SGA, including the IM column store, leaving room for the OS and the PGA. You don't want to set the IM column store area too big since you still need space in the SGA for the shared pool and the standard buffer cache; you can still use SGA_TARGET in this scenario, but keep in mind that the target size must include the total size of the IM column store:

```
alter system set sga_max_size=240g scope=spfile;
alter system set inmemory_size=128g scope=spfile;
alter system set sga_target=200g scope=spfile;
```

Restart the instance after setting these parameters. If the value for SGA_TARGET is too low or, worse yet, less than the value of INMEMORY_SIZE, your instance will not start and you'll need to create a temporary text-based initialization file (PFILE) to get the instance started again!

Since the parameters SGA_MAX_SIZE and INMEMORY_SIZE are static, you might need to control use of the IM column store in other ways until you can restart the instance. For example, you can set INMEMORY_QUERY to DISABLE either at the system level to turn off all use of the IM column store or at the session level to easily test query performance with and without the IM column store, even if the table columns in the query might currently be in the IM column store for other sessions.

Marking Tablespaces, Tables, and Columns

Your other point of control for using the IM column store is, of course, marking tables and columns to use the IM column store. You can perform this operation while the instance is up and running. Keep in mind, though, that turning off and then turning on the IM column store attribute for a column will require a repopulation operation, which can temporarily affect performance of the instance due to higher CPU usage during the repopulation process.

If you want all of your IM-enabled tables to reside in a single tablespace, you can mark the entire tablespace that way and automatically enable the IM column store for any table created in or moved to that tablespace by using the ALTER TABLESPACE command:

```
alter tablespace users default inmemory;
```

The defaults that go along with the INMEMORY setting may be fine for you—but you also have the option to fine-tune how much compression should be used, whether the compression should favor SELECT statements or DML statements, and what priority this tablespace's objects will have in the IM column store when there is not enough room to hold all the selected columns simultaneously:

```
alter tablespace users default inmemory
   memcompress for query low priority high;
```

You can always override the settings at the table level or column level even if the table resides in a tablespace whose default setting is INMEMORY. Marking the ORDER_PROC table for residency in the IM column store is as easy as this:

```
alter table order_proc
   inmemory memcompress for query high;
```

Specifying QUERY HIGH means that all columns of ORDER_PROC are stored with relatively high compression but still suitable for frequent SELECT query activity. However, knowing that the ORDER_PROC table has 215 columns and that you will likely not need to use all of those columns in most reports, you want to be more selective. If most of your big reports only need the ORDER_PROC_ID, PROC_CODE, and PANEL_PROC_ID columns, you can instead mark just those columns:

```
alter table clarity.order_proc
   inmemory memcompress for query high
   (
       order_proc_id,proc_code,panel_proc_id
   );
```

If you need the flexibility, you can even mark some columns with a different compression level if desired.

Query Performance Before and After

As I mentioned earlier in this chapter, you may not have the memory to keep all desired columns in the IM column store. You also might need to keep memory contention in check by keeping

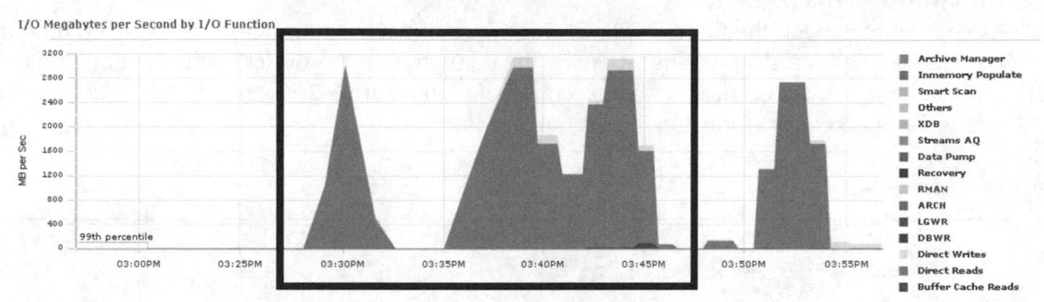

FIGURE 9-1. *Report batch with IM column store inactive*

some of the smaller tables' columns out of the IM column store and instead relying on the SGA buffer cache with traditional I/O. While some queries are using the IM column store, the others may not need as much CPU at any given moment because they are bound by I/O waits (even though the disk is fast—but usually not as fast as server memory). In this example, a daily report batch consisting of about 4000 reports consumes I/O at a rate of about 3 GBps, maxing out the throughput of the I/O subsystem. Figure 9-1 shows the I/O throughput and type for this report batch.

After some analysis, you determine that a small number of tables, though large, account for most of the long-running queries. In addition, only about 20 columns across those big tables account for all columns referenced in the reports. Therefore, you mark those tables for INMEMORY and QUERY HIGH as in the example in the previous section. After taking a few minutes to construct the ALTER TABLE statements, you rerun the report batch to see the results of your new IM column store configuration. In Figure 9-2 you see that even your minimal level of analysis has yielded significant results:

Not only is the elapsed time reduced from about 20 minutes to 12 minutes, the overall I/O consumption has been cut by about two-thirds. The queries in the latter portion of the report batch are referencing many of the same columns as queries in the beginning of the report batch (although probably with different predicates and aggregation). With some additional analysis you might be able to reduce the elapsed time even more, but in this case the I/O subsystem now has additional bandwidth for other database instances by offloading the I/O to the IM column store.

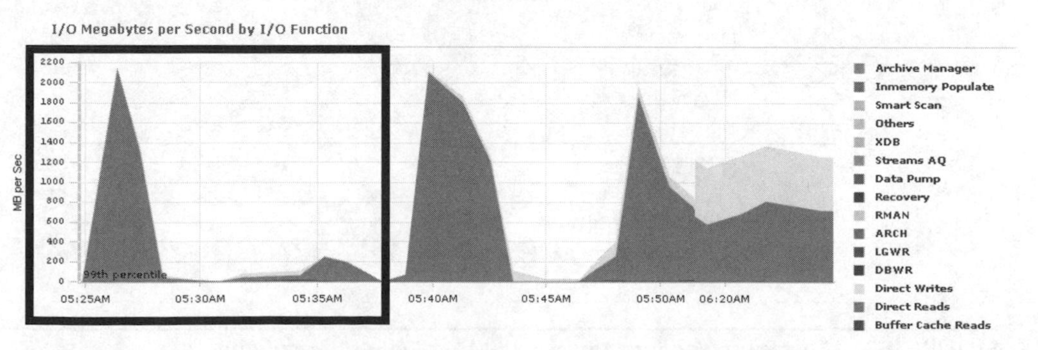

FIGURE 9-2. *Report batch with IM column store active*

Execution Plans

As you might expect, the Oracle optimizer is aware of the execution costs of using column data from the IM column store versus retrieving the column from the buffer cache via traditional I/O against the row store on disk. In the execution plan in Figure 9-3, every column referenced in the query was marked for storage in the IM column store.

Plan Statistics | Plan | Parallel | Activity

Plan Hash Value 1831788054 | Plan Note

Operation	Name	Line ID	Estimated Rows	Cost
SELECT STATEMENT		0		
PX COORDINATOR		1		
PX SEND QC (ORDER)	:TQ10006	2	781K	62K
SORT ORDER BY		3	781K	62K
PX RECEIVE		4	781K	62K
PX SEND RANGE	:TQ10005	5	781K	62K
HASH JOIN		6	781K	62K
JOIN FILTER CREATE	:BF0000	7	685K	55K
PX RECEIVE		8	685K	55K
PX SEND BROADCAST	:TQ10004	9	685K	55K
HASH JOIN RIGHT OUTER BUFFERED		10	685K	55K
PX RECEIVE		11	4,616	9
PX SEND BROADCAST	:TQ10000	12	4,616	9
PX SELECTOR		13		
TABLE ACCESS INMEMORY FULL	CLARITY_DEP	14	4,616	9
FILTER		15		
HASH JOIN RIGHT OUTER		16	685K	55K
PX RECEIVE		17	14K	2
PX SEND BROADCAST	:TQ10001	18	14K	2
PX SELECTOR		19		
TABLE ACCESS INMEMORY FULL	CLARITY_SER_DEPT	20	14K	2
HASH JOIN RIGHT OUTER		21	1,073K	55K
PX RECEIVE		22	88K	20
PX SEND HASH	:TQ10002	23	88K	20
PX SELECTOR		24		
TABLE ACCESS INMEMORY FULL	CLARITY_SER	25	88K	20
PX RECEIVE		26	1,073K	55K
PX SEND HASH	:TQ10003	27	1,073K	55K
PX BLOCK ITERATOR		28	1,073K	55K
TABLE ACCESS FULL	PAT_ENC	29	1,073K	55K
JOIN FILTER USE	:BF0000	30	16M	7,112

FIGURE 9-3. *Execution plan for a query with IM column store columns*

Most of the steps referencing tables confirm that the IM column store is being used:

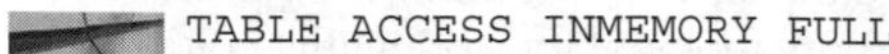

```
TABLE ACCESS INMEMORY FULL
```

However, it appears that the table PAT_ENC is being accessed in the buffer cache using traditional I/O. The optimizer cost for using a full table scan came out lower than using the copy in the IM column store. This could be the case for several reasons. For example, the columns in PAT_ENC could be marked for the IM column store as CAPACITY HIGH, meaning that the CPU cost for decompressing and scanning those columns in the IM column store was higher than retrieving the uncompressed columns that were already in the buffer cache.

You'll also see cases where every column of every table in a query is in the IM column store as QUERY LOW but the optimizer still chooses to use one of the table's indexes on disk. This costing decision makes sense if the number of rows retrieved is low—retrieving a couple of blocks of an index from disk will often take less time or resources than scanning an entire table's column values in memory.

Data Dictionary Views

There are only a few dynamic performance views you'll use to see the status of your IM column store: V$IM_SEGMENTS, V$INMEMORY_AREA, and, an old favorite, V$SGA.

V$IM_SEGMENTS

The V$IM_SEGMENTS view is clearly the most granular and important view you'll use to monitor the status of your IM column store.

```
SQL> select segment_name, inmemory_compression,
  2>      inmemory_size,bytes
  3> from v$im_segments;

SEGMENT_NAME            INMEMORY_COMPRESS    INMEMORY_SIZE            BYTES
----------------------- ------------------ ----------------- ---------------
PATIENT                 FOR QUERY HIGH         137,822,208      588,251,136
RES_DB_MAIN             FOR QUERY HIGH         963,248,128    1,342,177,280
IB_RECEIVER             FOR QUERY LOW          371,785,728    1,549,795,328
CLARITY_DEP             FOR QUERY HIGH           1,179,648          589,824
IB_MESSAGES             FOR QUERY LOW          440,991,744    2,469,396,480
HSP_WQ_HISTORY          FOR QUERY HIGH       1,953,628,160    5,161,091,072
HSP_WORKQUEUES          FOR QUERY HIGH           1,179,648          720,896
CLARITY_EMP             FOR QUERY HIGH           3,276,800       16,777,216
. . .
LPF_PREF_LISTS          FOR QUERY LOW           32,702,464       45,088,768
ORD_PRFLST_TRK          FOR QUERY LOW        1,361,969,152    2,697,986,048
PAT_ENC_HSP             FOR QUERY LOW          495,190,016    5,786,042,368

33 rows selected.

SQL>
```

Note that even for columns marked as FOR QUERY LOW, the compression ratios are quite high; in the case of PAT_ENC_HSP, the compression ratio is approximately 12:1. The column's compression (primarily due to repeating column values) reduces both the memory footprint for storing that column and the time it takes to scan all column values. This somewhat offsets the CPU cost of "uncompressing" the column values when using them in a query.

Other columns in V$IM_SEGMENTS show the status of the IM column store population process (POPULATE_STATUS), the type of segment in the IM column store (SEGMENT_TYPE: TABLE, TABLE PARTITION, or TABLE SUBPARTITION), and the column's priority for the population process and its retention in the IM column store (INMEMORY_PRIORITY).

V$INMEMORY_AREA

The view V$INMEMORY_AREA shows a high-level status of each pool in the IM column store. The two pools have a distinctly different purpose: the 1MB pool stores the actual column values in memory while the 64KB pool contains the metadata about the column values stored in the 1MB pool:

```
SQL> select pool,alloc_bytes,used_bytes,populate_status
  2> from v$inmemory_area;

POOL                  ALLOC_BYTES        USED_BYTES POPULATE_STATUS
--------------- ----------------- ----------------- --------------------
1MB POOL          109,511,180,288    16,715,350,016 DONE
64KB POOL          27,900,510,208       206,372,864 DONE

SQL>
```

As you might expect, the 64KB pool is going to be much smaller and take up less memory than the 1MB pool as long as you're storing columns from tables with millions of rows instead of only hundreds of rows.

V$SGA

The view V$SGA has the same rows as in previous releases of Oracle Database along with the new row for the In-Memory Area:

```
SQL> select name,value from v$sga;

NAME                            VALUE
-------------------- ----------------
Fixed Size                  6,875,568
Variable Size          32,212,256,336
Database Buffers       87,509,958,656
Redo Buffers              529,993,728
In-Memory Area        137,438,953,472

SQL>
```

Summary

The In-Memory option, new in Oracle Database 12*c* (12.1.0.2), is one of the most useful and powerful features second only to the multitenant architecture. You can speed up your queries by a magnitude or more by keeping some or all columns of a table in a special compressed format in a new area of the SGA known as the In-Memory column store. This column store works side by side with the traditional row store that maintains tables in row format on disk and whose data blocks reside in the SGA buffer cache or a session's private PGA area. All of your applications work as before and the IM column store stays in synch with any DML operations on the underlying table in the row store on disk.

The increased speed of queries using the IM column store and the significant reduction of I/O come at a price, however. You'll need more memory allocated in the SGA and potentially more CPU resources to perform the compress and decompress operations on the column store. However, the higher CPU and memory demands are typically offset by the reduction of I/O and the accompanying wait events, meaning not only that your elapsed time for any given query is much shorter, but also that you'll more easily meet your customer's SLA. Or, in another scenario, your shorter execution times mean that you'll be able to run more queries in the same amount of time.

CHAPTER 10

Database Security and Auditing

To protect one of the most vital assets to a company—its data—you as a DBA must be keenly aware of how Oracle can protect corporate data and the different tools you have at your disposal. The Oracle-provided tools and mechanisms fall into three broad categories: authentication, authorization, and auditing.

Authentication includes methods used to identify who is accessing the database, ensuring that you are who you say you are, regardless of what resources you are requesting of the database. Even if you are merely trying to access the daily lunch menu at the cafeteria, it is important that you identify yourself correctly to the database. If, for example, the web-based database application presents customized content based on the user account, you want to make sure you get the lunch menu for your branch office in Houston, Texas, and not the one for the home office in Buffalo, New York!

Authorization provides access to various objects in the database once you are authenticated by the database. Some users may be authorized to run a report against the daily sales table, some users may be developers and therefore need to create tables and reports, whereas others may only be allowed to see the daily lunch menu. Some users may never log in at all, but their schema may own a number of tables for a particular application, such as payroll or accounts receivable. Additional authorization methods are provided for database administrators, due to the extreme power that a database administrator has. Because a DBA can shut down and start up a database, an additional level of authorization is provided.

Authorization goes well beyond simple access to a table or a report; it also includes the rights to use system resources in the database as well as privileges to perform certain actions in the database. A given database user might be allowed to use only 15 seconds of CPU time per session, for example, or to be idle only for five minutes before being disconnected from the database. Another database user might be granted the privilege to create or drop tables in any other user's schema, but not be able to create synonyms or view data dictionary tables. Fine-grained access control gives the DBA more control over how database objects are accessed. For example, standard object privileges will either give a user access to an entire row of a table or give the user no access at all; using fine-grained access control, a DBA can create a policy implemented by a stored procedure that restricts access based on time of day, where the request originates, which column of the table is being accessed, or all three.

At the end of the section on database authorization, I will present a short example of a *Virtual Private Database (VPD)* to provide methods for defining, setting, and accessing application attributes along with the predicates (usually WHERE clauses) to control which data is accessible or returned to the user of the application.

Auditing in an Oracle database encompasses a number of different levels of monitoring in the database. At a high level, auditing can record both successful and unsuccessful attempts to log in, access an object, or perform an action. Fine-grained auditing (FGA) can record not only what objects are accessed, but what columns of a table are accessed when an insert, update, or delete is being performed on the data in the column. Fine-grained auditing is to auditing what fine-grained access control is to standard authorization: more precise control and information about the objects being accessed or actions being performed.

DBAs must use auditing judiciously so as not to be overwhelmed by audit records or create too much overhead by implementing continuous auditing. On the flip side, auditing can help to protect company assets by monitoring who is using what resource, at what time, and how often, as well as whether the access was successful or not. Therefore, auditing is another tool that the DBA should be using on a continuous basis to monitor the security health of the database.

Non-database Security

All the methodologies presented later in the chapter are useless if access to the operating system is not secure or the physical hardware is not in a secure location. In this section, I'll discuss a few of the elements outside of the database itself that need to be secure before the database can be considered secure.

The following are a few things that need to be considered outside of the database:

- **Operating system security** Unless the Oracle database is running on its own dedicated hardware with only the **root** and **oracle** user accounts enabled, operating system security must be reviewed and implemented. Ensure that the software is installed with the **oracle** account and not the **root** account. You may also consider using another account instead of **oracle** as the owner of the software and the database files, to eliminate an easy target for a hacker. Ensure that the software and the database files are readable only by the **oracle** account and the group that **oracle** belongs to. Other than the Oracle executables that require it, turn off the SUID (set UID, or running with root privileges) bit on files that don't require it. Don't send passwords (operating system or Oracle) to users via e-mail in plain text. Finally, remove any system services that are not required on the server to support the database, such as telnet and ftp.
- **Securing backup media** Ensure that the database backup media—whether tape, disk, or CD/DVD-ROM—is accessible by a limited number of people. A secure operating system and robust, encrypted passwords on the database are of little value if a hacker can obtain backup copies of the database and load them onto another server. The same applies to any server that contains data replicated from your database.
- **Background security checks** Screening of employees that deal with sensitive database data—whether it be a DBA, auditor, or operating system administrator—is a must.
- **Security education** Ensure that all database users understand the security and usage policies of the IT infrastructure. Requiring that users understand and follow the security policies emphasizes the critical nature and value of the data to the company, including the information in the database. A well-educated user will be more likely to resist attempts at system access from a hacker's social-engineering skills.
- **Controlled access to hardware** All computer hardware that houses the database should be located in a secure environment that is accessible only with badges or security access codes.

Database Authentication Methods

Before the database can allow a person or application access to objects or privileges in the database, the person or application must be authenticated; in other words, the identity of who is attempting access to the database needs to be validated.

In this section, I'll give an overview of the most basic method used to allow access to the database—the user account, otherwise known as *database authentication*. In addition, I'll show how to reduce the number of passwords a user needs to remember by allowing the operating system to authenticate the user and, as a result, automatically connect the user to the database. Using 3-tier authentication via an application server, network authentication, or Oracle's Identity Management can reduce the number of passwords even further. Finally, I'll talk about using a password file to authenticate DBAs when the database is down and cannot provide authentication services.

Database Authentication

In an environment where the network is protected from the outside environment with firewalls and the network traffic between the client and the database server uses some method of encryption, authentication by the database is the most common and easiest method to authenticate the user with the database. All information needed to authenticate the user is stored in a table within the SYSTEM tablespace.

Very special database operations, such as starting up or shutting down the database, require a different and more secure form of authentication, either by using operating system authentication or by using password files.

Network authentication relies on third-party authentication services such as the Distributed Computing Environment (DCE), Kerberos, Public Key Infrastructure (PKI), and Remote Authentication Dial-In User Service (RADIUS). Although at first glance 3-tier authentication appears to be a network authentication method, it is different in that a middle tier, such as Oracle Application Server, authenticates the user while maintaining the client's identity on the server. In addition, the middle tier provides connection pooling services and implements business logic for the client.

Later in this chapter, in the section titled "User Accounts," we'll go through all the options available to the DBA for setting up accounts in the database for authentication.

Database Administrator Authentication

The database is not always available to authenticate a DBA, such as when it is down because of an unplanned outage or for an offline database backup. To address this situation, Oracle uses a *password file* to maintain a list of database users who are allowed to perform functions such as starting up and shutting down the database, initiating backups, and so forth.

Alternatively, a DBA can use operating system authentication, which we discuss in the next section. The flowchart shown in Figure 10-1 identifies the options for a DBA when deciding what method will work the best in their environment.

For connecting locally to the server, the main consideration is the convenience of using the same account for both the operating system and the Oracle server versus maintaining a password file. For a remote administrator, the security of the connection is the driving factor when choosing an authentication method. Without a secure connection, a hacker could easily impersonate a user with the same account as that of an administrator on the server itself and gain full access to the database with OS authentication.

NOTE
When using a password file for authentication, ensure that the password file itself is in a directory location that is only accessible by the operating system administrators and the user or group that owns the Oracle software installation.

We will discuss system privileges in greater detail later in this chapter. For now, though, you need to know that three particular system privileges give administrators special authentication in the database:

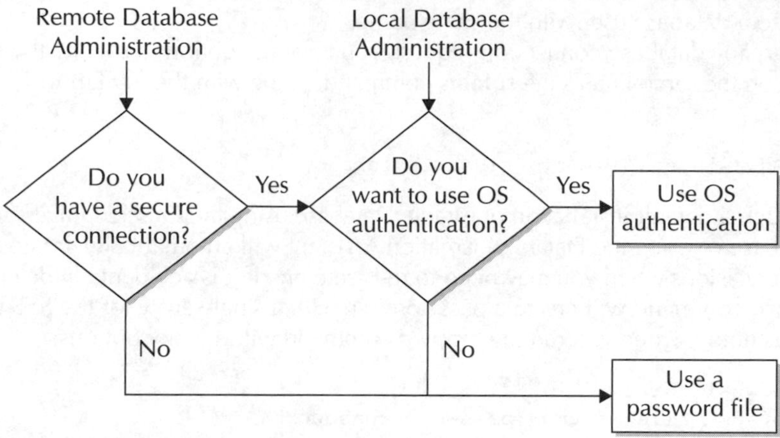

FIGURE 10-1. *Authentication method flowchart*

- **SYSOPER** An administrator with the SYSOPER privilege can start up and shut down the database, perform online or offline backups, archive the current redo log files, and connect to the database when it is in RESTRICTED SESSION mode.
- **SYSDBA** The SYSDBA privilege contains all the rights of SYSOPER, with the addition of being able to create a database and grant the SYSDBA or SYSOPER privilege to other database users.
- **SYSASM** As of Oracle Database 11*g*, the SYSASM privilege is specific to an ASM instance to manage database storage.

Oracle Database 12*c* has three additional privileges to further enhance Oracle's support for separation of duties: SYSBACKUP, SYSDG, and SYSKM.

To connect to the database from a SQL*Plus session, you append AS SYSDBA or AS SYSOPER to your CONNECT command. Here's an example:

```
[oracle@kthanid ~]$ sqlplus /nolog
SQL*Plus: Release 12.1.0.2.0 Production on Tue Oct 28 10:18:22 2014

Copyright (c) 1982, 2014, Oracle.  All rights reserved.

SQL> connect rjb/rjb as sysdba;
Connected.
SQL> show user
USER is "SYS"
SQL>
```

Other than the additional privileges available to the users who connect as SYSDBA or SYSOPER, the default schema is also different for these users when they connect to the database. Users who connect with the SYSDBA or SYSASM privilege connect as the SYS user; the SYSOPER privilege sets the user to PUBLIC. Each of the privileges SYSKM, SYSBACKUP, and SYSDG connects to a database user with the same name.

As with any database connection request, you have the option to specify the username and password on the same line as the **sqlplus** command, along with the SYSDBA or SYSOPER keyword:

```
[oracle@dw ~]$ sqlplus rjb/rjb as sysdba
```

Although a default installation of Oracle Database using the Oracle Universal Installer with a seed database or using the Database Creation Assistant will automatically create a password file, there are occasions when you may need to re-create one if it is accidentally deleted or damaged. The **orapwd** command will create a password file with a single entry for the SYS user and other options, as noted, when you run the **orapwd** command without any options:

```
[oracle@dw ~]$ orapwd
Usage: orapwd file=<fname> password=<password>
     entries=<users> force=<y/n> ignorecase=<y/n> nosysdba=<y/n>

  where
    file - name of password file (required),
    password - password for SYS (optional),
    entries - maximum number of distinct DBA (required),
    force - whether to overwrite existing file (optional),
    ignorecase - passwords are case-insensitive (optional),
    nosysdba - whether to shut out the SYSDBA logon
      (optional Database Vault only).

  There must be no spaces around the equal-to (=) character.
[oracle@dw ~]$
```

Once you re-create the password file, you will have to grant the SYSDBA and SYSOPER privileges to those database users who previously had those privileges. In addition, if the password you provided in the **orapwd** command is not the same password that the SYS account has in the database, this is not a problem: when you connect using CONNECT / AS SYSDBA, you're using operating system authentication. And just to reiterate, if the database is down or in MOUNT mode, you must use operating system authentication or the password file. Also worth noting is that operating system authentication takes precedence over password file authentication, so as long as you fulfill the requirements for operating system authentication, the password file will not be used for authentication if it exists.

CAUTION
As of Oracle Database 11g, database passwords are case sensitive. To disable case sensitivity, set the SEC_CASE_SENSITIVE_LOGON initialization parameter to FALSE.

The system initialization parameter REMOTE_LOGIN_PASSWORDFILE controls how the password file is used for the database instance. It has three possible values: NONE, SHARED, and EXCLUSIVE.

If the value is NONE, then Oracle ignores any password file that exists. Any privileged users must be authenticated by other means, such as by operating system authentication, which is discussed in the next section.

With a value of SHARED, multiple databases can share the same password file, but only the SYS user is authenticated with the password file, and the password for SYS cannot be changed. As a result, this method is not the most secure, but it does allow a DBA to maintain more than one database with a single SYS account.

TIP
If a shared password file must be used, ensure that the password for SYS is at least 12 characters long and includes a combination of upper- and lowercase alphabetic, numeric, and special characters to fend off a brute-force attack.

A value of EXCLUSIVE binds the password file to only one database, and other database user accounts can exist in the password file. As soon as the password file is created, use this value to maximize the security of SYSDBA or SYSOPER connections.

The dynamic performance view V$PWFILE_USERS lists all the database users who have one of the six available privileges, as shown here:

```
SQL> select * from v$pwfile_users;

USERNAME                       SYSDB SYSOP SYSAS SYSBA SYSDG SYSKM     CON_ID
------------------------------ ----- ----- ----- ----- ----- ----- ----------
SYS                            TRUE  TRUE  FALSE FALSE FALSE FALSE          0
SYSDG                          FALSE FALSE FALSE FALSE TRUE  FALSE          0
SYSBACKUP                      FALSE FALSE FALSE TRUE  FALSE FALSE          0
SYSKM                          FALSE FALSE FALSE FALSE FALSE TRUE           0
RJB                            TRUE  FALSE FALSE FALSE FALSE FALSE          0

5 rows selected.

SQL>
```

Operating System Authentication

If a DBA chooses to implement *operating system authentication,* a database user is automatically connected to the database when they use the following SQL*Plus syntax:

```
SQL> sqlplus /
```

This method is similar to how an administrator connects to the database, without the AS SYSDBA or AS SYSOPER clause. The main difference is that the operating system account authorization methods are used instead of an Oracle-generated and -maintained password file.

In fact, administrators can also use operating system authentication to connect using AS SYSDBA or AS SYSOPER. If the administrator's operating system login account is in the Unix group **dba** (or the Windows group ORA_DBA), the administrator can connect to the database using AS SYSDBA. Similarly, if the operating system login account is in the Unix group **oper** (or the Windows group ORA_OPER), the administrator can connect to the database using AS SYSOPER without the need for an Oracle password file.

The Oracle server makes the assumption that if the user is authenticated by an operating system account, then the user is also authenticated for the database. With operating system authentication, Oracle does not need to maintain passwords in the database, but it still maintains the usernames. The usernames are still needed to set the default schema and tablespaces in addition to providing information for auditing.

In a default Oracle 12*c* installation, as well as in previous releases of Oracle, operating system authentication is enabled for user accounts if you create database users with the identified externally clause. The prefix for the database username must match the value of the initialization parameter OS_AUTHENT_PREFIX; the default value is OPS$. Here's an example:

```
SQL> create user ops$corie identified externally;
```

When the user logs into the operating system with the account CORIE, she is automatically authenticated in the Oracle database as if the account OPS$CORIE was created with database authentication.

Setting the value of OS_AUTHENT_PREFIX to a null string allows the database administrator and the operating system account administrator to use identical usernames when using external authentication.

Using IDENTIFIED GLOBALLY is similar to using IDENTIFIED EXTERNALLY in that the authentication is done outside of the database. However, with a globally identified user, authentication is performed by an enterprise directory service such as Oracle Internet Directory (OID). OID facilitates ease of account maintenance for DBAs and the convenience of single sign-on for database users who need to access more than just a single database or service.

Network Authentication

Authentication by a network service is another option available to the DBA to authenticate users in the database. Although a complete treatment is beyond the scope of this book, I will give a brief summary of each method and its components. These components include Secure Sockets Layer (SSL), Distributed Computing Environment (DCE), Kerberos, PKI, RADIUS, and directory-based services.

Secure Sockets Layer Protocol

Secure Sockets Layer (SSL) is a protocol originally developed by Netscape Development Corporation for use in web browsers. Because it is a public standard and open source, it faces continuous scrutiny by the programming community to ensure that there are no holes or "back doors" that can compromise its robustness.

At a minimum, a server-side certificate is required for authentication. Client authentication is also doable with SSL to validate the client, but setting up certificates may become a large administrative effort.

Using SSL over TCP/IP requires only slight changes to the listener configuration by adding another protocol (TCPS) at a different port number in the **listener.ora** file. In the following excerpt, configured with Oracle Net Configuration Assistant (**netca**), the listener named LISTENER on the server **dw10g** will accept traffic via TCP on port 1521 and SSL TCP traffic on port 2484:

```
# listener.ora Network Configuration File:
   /u01/app/oracle/product/12.1.0/network/admin/listener.ora
```

```
# Generated by Oracle configuration tools.
SID_LIST_LISTENER =
  (SID_LIST =
    (SID_DESC =
      (SID_NAME = PLSExtProc)
      (ORACLE_HOME = /u01/app/oracle/product/12.1.0)
      (PROGRAM = extproc)
    )
    (SID_DESC =
      (GLOBAL_DBNAME = dw.world)
      (ORACLE_HOME = /u01/app/oracle/product/12.1.0)
      (SID_NAME = dw)
    )
  )

LISTENER =
  (DESCRIPTION_LIST =
    (DESCRIPTION =
      (ADDRESS_LIST =
        (ADDRESS = (PROTOCOL = TCP)(HOST = dw12c)(PORT = 1521))
      )
      (ADDRESS_LIST =
        (ADDRESS = (PROTOCOL = TCPS)(HOST = dw12c)(PORT = 2484))
      )
    )
  )
```

Distributed Computing Environment

The Distributed Computing Environment (DCE) provides a number of services, such as remote procedure calls, distributed file services, and distributed time service, in addition to a security service. DCE supports distributed applications in a heterogeneous environment on all major software and hardware platforms.

DCE is one of the protocols that support single sign-on (SSO); once a user authenticates with DCE, they can securely access any Oracle database configured with DCE without specifying a username or password.

Kerberos

Kerberos is another trusted third-party authentication system that, like DCE, provides SSO capabilities. Oracle fully supports Kerberos version 5 with Oracle Advanced Security under the Enterprise Edition of Oracle Database 12*c*.

As with other middleware authentication solutions, the basic premise is that passwords should never be sent across the network; all authentication is brokered by the Kerberos server. In Kerberos terminology, a password is a "shared secret."

Public Key Infrastructure

Public Key Infrastructure (PKI) comprises a number of components. It is implemented using the SSL protocol and is based on the concept of secret private keys and related public keys to facilitate secure communications between the client and server.

To provide identification and authentication services, PKI uses certificates and certificate authorities (CAs). In a nutshell, a certificate is an entity's public key validated by a trusted third party (a certificate authority), and it contains information such as the certificate user's name, an expiration date, the public key, and so forth.

RADIUS

Remote Authentication Dial-In User Service (RADIUS) is a lightweight protocol used for authentication as well as authorization and accounting services. In an Oracle environment, the Oracle server acts as the client to a RADIUS server when an authorization request is sent from an Oracle client.

Any authentication method that supports the RADIUS standard—whether it be token cards, smart cards, or SecurID ACE—can easily be added to the RADIUS server as a new authentication method without any changes being made on the client or server configuration files, such as **sqlnet.ora**.

3-Tier Authentication

In a 3-tier or multitier environment, an application server can provide authentication services for a client and provide a common interface to the database server, even if the clients use a variety of different browsers or "thick" client applications. The application server, in turn, is authenticated with the database and demonstrates that the client is allowed to connect to the database, thus preserving the identity of the client in all tiers.

In multitier environments, both users and middle tiers are given the fewest possible privileges necessary to do their jobs. The middle tier is granted permission to perform actions on behalf of a user with a command such as the following:

```
alter user kmourgos
    grant connect through oes_as
    with role all except ordmgmt;
```

In this example, the application server service OES_AS is granted permission to perform actions on behalf of the database user KMOURGOS. The user KMOURGOS has been assigned a number of roles, and they can all be enabled through the application server, except for the ORDMGMT role. As a result, when KMOURGOS connects through the application server, he is permitted to access, via the Web, all tables and privileges granted to him via roles, except for the order management functions. Because of the business rules in place at his company, all access to the order management applications must be done via a direct connection to the database. Roles are discussed in detail in the section titled "Creating, Assigning, and Maintaining Roles" later in this chapter.

Client-Side Authentication

Client-side authentication is one way to authenticate users in a multitier environment, but Oracle strongly discourages this method unless all clients are on a secure network, inside a firewall, with no connections allowed to the database from outside the firewall. In addition, users should not have any administrative rights on any workstation that can connect to the database.

If an Oracle user is created with the IDENTIFIED EXTERNALLY attribute, and the initialization parameter REMOTE_OS_AUTHENT is set to TRUE, then an attacker can easily authenticate himself on the workstation with a local user account that matches the **oracle** user account, and as a result gain access to the database.

As a result, it is strongly recommended that the REMOTE_OS_AUTHENT parameter be set to FALSE. The database will have to be stopped and restarted for this change to take effect.

NOTE
As of Oracle Database 11g, the parameter REMOTE_OS_AUTHENT is deprecated. There are several other, more secure ways to allow remote access to the database.

User Accounts

In order to gain access to the database, a user must provide a *username* to access the resources associated with that account. Each username must have a password and is associated with one and only one schema in the database; some accounts may have no objects in the schema, but instead would have the privileges granted to that account to access objects in other schemas.

In this section, I'll explain the syntax and give examples for creating, altering, and dropping users. In addition, I'll show you how to become another user without explicitly knowing the password for the user.

Creating Users

The CREATE USER command is fairly straightforward. It has a number of parameters, the most important of which are listed in Table 10-1 along with a brief description of each one.

In the following example, we are creating a user (KLYNNE) to correspond with the user Jeff K. Lynne, employee number 100 in the HR.EMPLOYEES table from the sample schemas installed with the database:

```
SQL> create user klynne identified by KLYNNE901
  2      account unlock
  3      default tablespace users
  4      temporary tablespace temp;
User created.
```

The user KLYNNE is authenticated by the database with an initial password of KLYNNE901. The second line is not required; all accounts are created unlocked by default. Both the default permanent tablespace and default temporary tablespace are defined at the database level, so the last two lines of the command aren't required unless you want a different default permanent tablespace or a different temporary tablespace for the user.

Even though the user KLYNNE has been either explicitly or implicitly assigned a default permanent tablespace, he cannot create any objects in the database until we provide both a quota and the rights to create objects in their own schema.

A *quota* is simply a space limit, by tablespace, for a given user. Unless a quota is explicitly assigned or the user is granted the UNLIMITED TABLESPACE privilege (privileges are discussed later in this chapter), the user cannot create objects in their own schema. In the following example, we're giving the KLYNNE account a quota of 250MB in the USERS tablespace:

```
SQL> alter user KLYNNE quota 250M on users;
User altered.
```

Parameter	Usage
username	The name of the schema, and therefore the user, to be created. The username can be up to 30 characters long and cannot be a reserved word unless it is quoted (which is not recommended).
IDENTIFIED { BY *password* | EXTERNALLY | GLOBALLY AS '*extname*' }	Specifies how the user will be authenticated: by the database with a password, by the operating system (local or remote), or by a service (such as Oracle Internet Directory).
DEFAULT TABLESPACE *tablespace*	The tablespace where permanent objects are created, unless a tablespace is explicitly specified during creation.
TEMPORARY TABLESPACE *tablespace*	The tablespace where temporary segments are created during sort operations, index creation, and so forth.
QUOTA { *size* | UNLIMITED } ON *tablespace*	The amount of space allowed for objects created on the specified tablespace. Size is in kilobytes (K) or megabytes (M).
PROFILE *profile*	The profile assigned to this user. Profiles are discussed later in this chapter. If a profile is not specified, the DEFAULT profile is used.
PASSWORD EXPIRE	At first logon, the user must change their password.
ACCOUNT {LOCK | UNLOCK}	Specifies whether the account is locked or unlocked. By default, the account is unlocked.
ENABLE EDITIONS	Allows this user to create one or more versions of editionable objects in their schema.
CONTAINER = {CURRENT | ALL}	Creates a single user account in the current container of a multitenant database or in all containers (a common user). If the account is a common user, it must begin with C## or c##; local users must not begin with C## or c##.

TABLE 10-1. *Options for the CREATE USER Command*

Note that we could have granted this quota at the time the account was created, along with almost every other option in the CREATE USER command. A default role, however, can only be assigned after the account is created. (Role management is discussed later in this chapter.)

Unless we grant some basic privileges to a new account, the account cannot even log in; therefore, we need to grant at least the CREATE SESSION privilege or the CONNECT role (roles are discussed in detail later in this chapter). For Oracle Database 10*g* Release 1 and earlier, the CONNECT role contains the CREATE SESSION privilege, along with other basic privileges, such as CREATE TABLE and ALTER SESSION; as of Oracle Database 10*g* Release 2, the CONNECT role only has the CREATE SESSION privilege and therefore is deprecated. In the following example, we grant KLYNNE the CREATE SESSION and CREATE TABLE privileges:

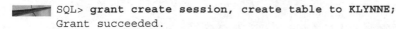

```
SQL> grant create session, create table to KLYNNE;
Grant succeeded.
```

Now the user KLYNNE has a quota on the USERS tablespace as well as the privileges to create objects in that tablespace.

All these options for CREATE USER are available in the web-based Oracle Cloud Control 12*c* interface, as demonstrated in Figure 10-2.

As with any Cloud Control operation, the Show SQL button shows the actual SQL commands, such as CREATE and GRANT, that will be run when the user is created. This is a great way to take advantage of the web interface's ease of use, while at the same time brushing up on your SQL command syntax!

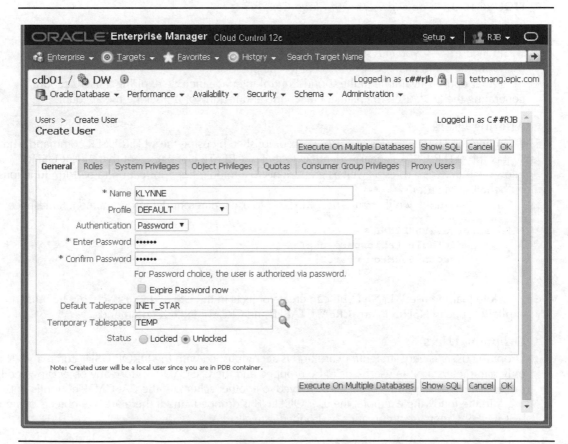

FIGURE 10-2. *Creating users with Cloud Control*

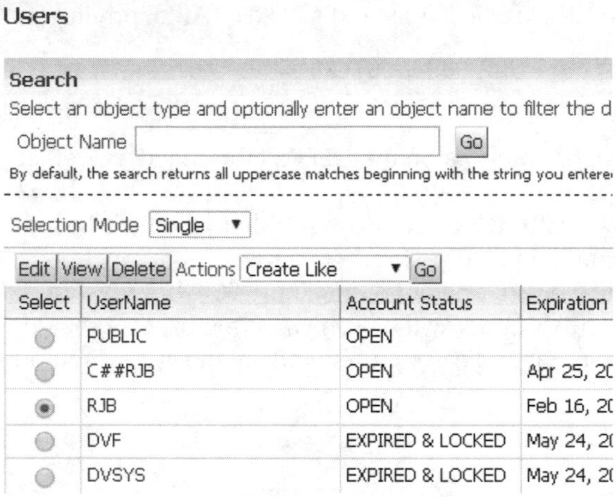

Users

Search

Select an object type and optionally enter an object name to filter the d

Object Name [ ] Go

By default, the search returns all uppercase matches beginning with the string you entere

Selection Mode Single

Edit View Delete Actions Create Like Go

Select	UserName	Account Status	Expiration
○	PUBLIC	OPEN	
○	C##RJB	OPEN	Apr 25, 2C
◉	RJB	OPEN	Feb 16, 2C
○	DVF	EXPIRED & LOCKED	May 24, 2(
○	DVSYS	EXPIRED & LOCKED	May 24, 2(

FIGURE 10-3. *Copying users with Cloud Control*

In Figure 10-3, you can see that it's also very easy to pick an existing user and create a new user with the same characteristics except for the password.

Other options available in the Cloud Control interface include expiring a user account, generating the DDL used to create the account, and locking or unlocking the account.

Altering Users

Changing the characteristics of a user is accomplished by using the ALTER USER command. The syntax for ALTER USER is nearly identical to that of CREATE USER, except that ALTER USER allows you to assign roles as well as grant rights to a middle-tier application to perform functions on behalf of the user.

In this example, we'll change user KLYNNE to use a different default permanent tablespace:

```
SQL> alter user KLYNNE
  2       default tablespace users2
  3       quota 500M on users2;
User altered.
```

Note that the user KLYNNE still can create objects in the USERS tablespace, but he must explicitly specify USERS in any CREATE TABLE and CREATE INDEX commands.

Dropping Users

Dropping users is very straightforward and is accomplished with the DROP USER command. The only parameters are the username to be dropped and the CASCADE option; any objects owned by the user must be explicitly dropped or moved to another schema if the CASCADE option is not used. In the following example, the user QUEENB is dropped, and if there are any objects owned by QUEENB, they are automatically dropped as well:

```
SQL> drop user queenb cascade;
User dropped.
```

If any other schema objects, such as views or packages, rely on objects dropped when the user is dropped, the other schema objects are marked INVALID and must be recoded to use other objects and then recompiled. In addition, any object privileges that were granted by the first user to a second user via the WITH GRANT OPTION clause are automatically revoked from the second user if the first user is dropped.

Becoming Another User

To debug an application, a DBA sometimes needs to connect as another user to simulate the problem. Without knowing the actual plain-text password of the user, the DBA can retrieve the encrypted password from the database, change the password for the user, connect with the changed password, and then change back the password using an undocumented clause of the ALTER USER command. It is assumed that the DBA has access to the DBA_USERS table, along with the ALTER USER privilege. If the DBA has the DBA role, then these two conditions are satisfied.

The first step is to retrieve the encrypted password for the user, which is stored in the table DBA_USERS:

```
SQL> select password from user$
  2       where username = 'KLYNNE';

PASSWORD
------------------------------
83C7CBD27A941428

1 row selected.
```

Save this password using cut and paste in a GUI environment, or save it in a text file to retrieve later. The next step is to temporarily change the user's password and then log in using the temporary password:

```
SQL> alter user KLYNNE identified by temp_pass;
User altered.
SQL> connect KLYNNE/temp_pass@tettnang:1521/dw;
Connected.
```

At this point, you can debug the application from KLYNNE's point of view. Once you are done debugging, change the password back using the undocumented BY VALUES clause of ALTER USER:

```
SQL> alter user KLYNNE identified by values '83C7CBD27A941428';
User altered.
```

Connecting with the KLYNNE user guarantees that you will see exactly what KLYNNE will see when running the application. In some scenarios, however, you can avoid having to change passwords by using the ALTER SESSION command with the CURRENT_SCHEMA option.

```
[oracle@yeb ~]$ sqlplus / as sysdba
SQL> alter session set current_schema=KLYNNE;
Session altered.
SQL> show user
USER is "SYS"
```

```
SQL> create table emp2
  2  (employee_id        number,
  3   salary             number);
Table created.
SQL> select owner,table_name from dba_tables where owner='KLYNNE';

OWNER                          TABLE_NAME
------------------------------ ------------------------------
KLYNNE                          EMP2

SQL>
```

All DML and SELECT commands will run in the context of the user specified by CURRENT_SCHEMA parameter.

User-Related Data Dictionary Views

A number of data dictionary views contain information related to users and characteristics of users. Table 10-2 lists the most common views and tables. The equivalent views in a multitenant environment begin with CDB_ instead of DBA_.

Database Authorization Methods

Once a user is authenticated with the database, the next step is to determine what types of objects, privileges, and resources the user is permitted to access or use. In this section, we'll review how profiles can control not only how passwords are managed but also how profiles can put limits on various types of system resources.

In addition, we'll review the two types of privileges in an Oracle database: system privileges and object privileges. Both of these privileges can be assigned directly to users, or indirectly through roles, another mechanism that can make a DBA's job easier when assigning privileges to users.

Data Dictionary View	Description
DBA_USERS	Contains usernames, encrypted passwords, account status, and default tablespaces.
DBA_TS_QUOTAS	Disk space usage and limits by user and tablespace, for users who have quotas that are not UNLIMITED.
DBA_PROFILES	Profiles that can be assigned to users with resource limits assigned to the profiles.
USER_HISTORY$	Password history with usernames, encrypted passwords, and datestamps. Used to enforce password reuse rules if you set the initialization parameter RESOURCE_LIMIT to TRUE and limit password reuse using the ALTER PROFILE parameters PASSWORD_REUSE_*.

TABLE 10-2. *User-Related Data Dictionary Views and Tables*

Managing profiles and privileges in a multitenant environment is similar to managing those in a non-CDB environment with a few exceptions; see Chapter 11 for more details.

At the end of this section, we'll cover the Virtual Private Database (VPD) features of Oracle and how it can be used to provide more precise control over what parts of a table can be seen by a user based on a set of DBA-defined credentials assigned to the user. To help make the concepts clearer, we'll step through an implementation of a VPD from beginning to end.

Profile Management

There never seems to be enough CPU power or disk space or I/O bandwidth to run a user's query. Because all these resources are inherently limited, Oracle provides a mechanism to control how much of these resources a user can use. An Oracle *profile* is a named set of resource limits providing this mechanism.

In addition, profiles can be used as an authorization mechanism to control how user passwords are created, reused, and validated. For example, we may wish to enforce a minimum password length, along with a requirement that at least one upper- and lowercase letter appear in the password. In this section, we'll look at how profiles manage passwords and resources.

The CREATE PROFILE Command

The CREATE PROFILE command does double duty; we can create a profile to limit the connect time for a user to 120 minutes:

```
create profile lim_connect limit
   connect_time 120;
```

Similarly, we can limit the number of consecutive times a login can fail before the account is locked:

```
create profile lim_fail_login limit
   failed_login_attempts 8;
```

Or, we can combine both types of limits in a single profile:

```
create profile lim_connectime_faillog limit
   connect_time 120
   failed_login_attempts 8;
```

How Oracle responds to one of the resource limits being exceeded depends on the type of limit. When one of the connect time or idle time limits is reached (such as CPU_PER_SESSION), the transaction in progress is rolled back, and the session is disconnected. For most other resource limits (such as PRIVATE_SGA), the current transaction is rolled back, an error is returned to the user, and the user has the option to commit or roll back the transaction. If an operation exceeds a limit for a single call (such as LOGICAL_READS_PER_CALL), the operation is aborted, the current statement is rolled back, and an error is returned to the user. The rest of the transaction remains intact; the user can then roll back, commit, or attempt to complete the transaction without exceeding statement limits.

Oracle provides the DEFAULT profile, which is applied to any new user if no other profile is specified. The following query against the data dictionary view DBA_PROFILES reveals the limits for the DEFAULT profile.

```
SQL> select *
  2  from dba_profiles
  3  where profile = 'DEFAULT';

PROFILE      RESOURCE_NAME                    RESOURCE LIMIT          COM
------------ -------------------------------- -------- -------------- ---
DEFAULT      COMPOSITE_LIMIT                  KERNEL   UNLIMITED      NO
DEFAULT      SESSIONS_PER_USER                KERNEL   UNLIMITED      NO
DEFAULT      CPU_PER_SESSION                  KERNEL   UNLIMITED      NO
DEFAULT      CPU_PER_CALL                     KERNEL   UNLIMITED      NO
DEFAULT      LOGICAL_READS_PER_SESSION        KERNEL   UNLIMITED      NO
DEFAULT      LOGICAL_READS_PER_CALL           KERNEL   UNLIMITED      NO
DEFAULT      IDLE_TIME                        KERNEL   UNLIMITED      NO
DEFAULT      CONNECT_TIME                     KERNEL   UNLIMITED      NO
DEFAULT      PRIVATE_SGA                      KERNEL   UNLIMITED      NO
DEFAULT      FAILED_LOGIN_ATTEMPTS            PASSWORD 10             NO
DEFAULT      PASSWORD_LIFE_TIME               PASSWORD 180            NO
DEFAULT      PASSWORD_REUSE_TIME              PASSWORD UNLIMITED      NO
DEFAULT      PASSWORD_REUSE_MAX               PASSWORD UNLIMITED      NO
DEFAULT      PASSWORD_VERIFY_FUNCTION         PASSWORD NULL           NO
DEFAULT      PASSWORD_LOCK_TIME               PASSWORD 1              NO
DEFAULT      PASSWORD_GRACE_TIME              PASSWORD 7              NO

16 rows selected.

SQL>
```

The only real restrictions in the DEFAULT profile limit the number of consecutive unsuccessful login attempts (FAILED_LOGIN_ATTEMPTS) to ten before the account is locked and the number of days before a password must be changed (PASSWORD_LIFE_TIME) to 180. In addition, no password verification function is enabled.

Profiles and Password Control

Table 10-3 lists and describes the password-related profile parameters. All units of time are specified in days (to specify any of these parameters in minutes, for example, divide by 1440):

```
SQL> create profile lim_lock limit password_lock_time 5/1440;
Profile created.
```

In this example, an account will only be locked for five minutes after the specified number of login failures.

A parameter value of UNLIMITED means that there is no bound on how much of the given resource can be used. DEFAULT means that this parameter takes its values from the DEFAULT profile.

The parameters PASSWORD_REUSE_TIME and PASSWORD_REUSE_MAX must be used together; setting one without the other has no useful effect. In the following example, we create a profile that sets PASSWORD_REUSE_TIME to 20 days and PASSWORD_REUSE_MAX to 5:

```
create profile lim_reuse_pass limit
    password_reuse_time 20
    password_reuse_max 5;
```

Password Parameter	Description
FAILED_LOGIN_ATTEMPTS	The number of failed login attempts before the account is locked.
PASSWORD_LIFE_TIME	The number of days the password can be used before it must be changed. If it is not changed within PASSWORD_GRACE_TIME, the password must be changed before logins are allowed.
PASSWORD_REUSE_TIME	The number of days a user must wait before reusing a password; this parameter is used in conjunction with PASSWORD_REUSE_MAX.
PASSWORD_REUSE_MAX	The number of password changes that have to occur before a password can be reused; this parameter is used in conjunction with PASSWORD_REUSE_TIME.
PASSWORD_LOCK_TIME	How many days the account is locked after FAILED_LOGIN_ATTEMPTS attempts. After this time period, the account is automatically unlocked.
PASSWORD_GRACE_TIME	The number of days after which an expired password must be changed. If it is not changed within this time period, the account is expired and the password must be changed before the user can log in successfully.
PASSWORD_VERIFY_FUNCTION	A PL/SQL script to provide an advanced password-verification routine. If NULL is specified (the default), no password verification is performed.

TABLE 10-3. *Password-Related Profile Parameters*

For users with this profile, their password can be reused after 20 days if the password has been changed at least five times. If you specify a value for either of these, and UNLIMITED for the other, a user can never reuse a password.

As with most other operations, profiles can easily be managed with Oracle Cloud Control. Figure 10-4 shows an example of changing the DEFAULT profile to disconnect the user after only 15 minutes of inactivity.

If we wanted to provide tighter control over how passwords are created and reused, such as a mixture of upper- and lowercase characters in every password, we need to enable the PASSWORD_VERIFY_FUNCTION limit in each applicable profile. Oracle provides a template for enforcing an organization's password policy. It's located in **$ORACLE_HOME/rdbms/admin/utlpwdmg.sql**. Some key sections of this script follow:

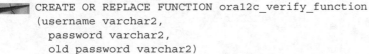

```
CREATE OR REPLACE FUNCTION ora12c_verify_function
(username varchar2,
  password varchar2,
  old_password varchar2)
  RETURN boolean IS
```

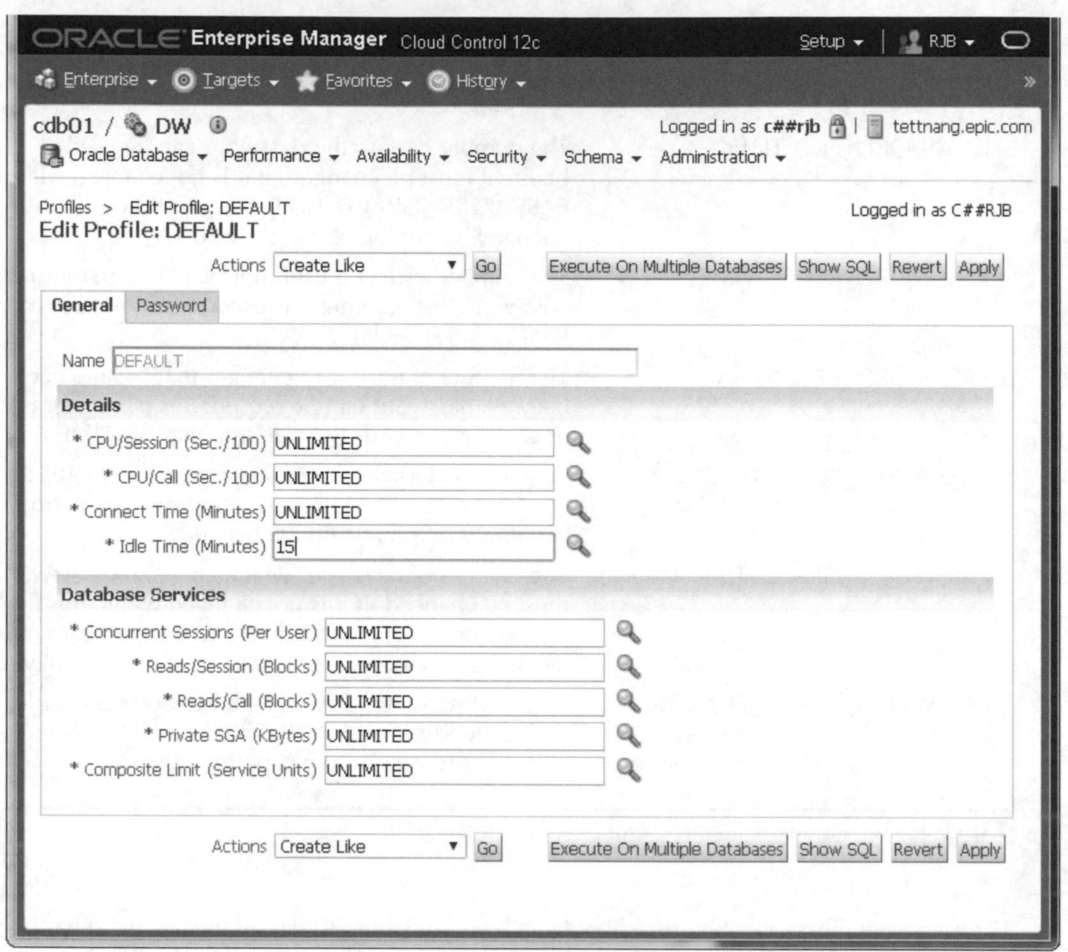

FIGURE 10-4. *Changing password limits with Oracle Cloud Control*

```
n boolean;
m integer;
differ integer;
isdigit boolean;
ischar  boolean;
ispunct boolean;
db_name varchar2(40);
digitarray varchar2(20);
```

```
   punctarray varchar2(25);
   chararray varchar2(52);
   i_char varchar2(10);
   simple_password varchar2(10);
   reverse_user varchar2(32);

BEGIN
   digitarray:= '0123456789';
   chararray:= 'abcdefghijklmnopqrstuvwxyzABCDEFGHIJKLMNOPQRSTUVWXYZ';
. . .
   -- Check if the password is same as the username reversed
   FOR i in REVERSE 1..length(username) LOOP
     reverse_user := reverse_user || substr(username, i, 1);
   END LOOP;
   IF NLS_LOWER(password) = NLS_LOWER(reverse_user) THEN
     raise_application_error(-20003, 'Password same as username reversed');
   END IF;
. . .
   -- Everything is fine; return TRUE ;
   RETURN(TRUE);
END;
/

-- This script alters the default parameters for Password Management
-- This means that all the users on the system have Password Management
-- enabled and set to the following values unless another profile is
-- created with parameter values set to different value or UNLIMITED
-- is created and assigned to the user.

ALTER PROFILE DEFAULT LIMIT
PASSWORD_LIFE_TIME 180
PASSWORD_GRACE_TIME 7
PASSWORD_REUSE_TIME UNLIMITED
PASSWORD_REUSE_MAX UNLIMITED
FAILED_LOGIN_ATTEMPTS 10
PASSWORD_LOCK_TIME 1 PASSWORD_VERIFY_FUNCTION ora12c_verify_function;
```

The script provides the following functionality for password complexity:

- Ensures that the password is not the same as the username
- Ensures that the password is at least four characters long
- Checks to make sure the password is not a simple, obvious word, such as ORACLE or DATABASE
- Requires that the password contains one letter, one digit, and one punctuation mark
- Ensures that the password is different from the previous password by at least three characters

To use this policy, the first step is to make your own custom changes to this script. For example, you may wish to have several different verify functions, one for each country or business unit, to match the database password complexity requirements to that of the operating systems in use in a particular country or business unit. Therefore, you can rename this function as VERIFY_FUNCTION_US_MIDWEST, for example. In addition, you might want to change the list of simple words to include names of departments or buildings at your company.

Once the function is successfully compiled, you can either alter an existing profile to use this function with the ALTER PROFILE command, or create a new profile that uses this function. In the following example, we're changing the DEFAULT profile to use the function VERIFY_FUNCTION_US_MIDWEST:

```
SQL> alter profile default limit
  2       password_verify_function verify_function_us_midwest;
Profile altered.
```

For all existing users who are using the DEFAULT profile, or for any new users who use the DEFAULT profile, their password will be checked by the function VERIFY_FUNCTION_US_MIDWEST. If the function returns a value other than TRUE, the password is not allowed, and the user must specify a different password. If a user has a current password that does not conform to the rules in this function, it is still valid until the password is changed, at which time the new password must be validated by the function.

Profiles and Resource Control

The list of resource-control profile options that can appear after CREATE PROFILE *profilename* LIMIT are explained in Table 10-4. Each of these parameters can either be an integer, UNLIMITED, or DEFAULT.

As with the password-related parameters, UNLIMITED means that there is no bound on how much of the given resource can be used. DEFAULT means that this parameter takes its values from the DEFAULT profile.

The COMPOSITE_LIMIT parameter allows you to control a group of resource limits when the types of resources typically used varies widely by type; it allows a user to use a lot of CPU time but not much disk I/O during one session, and vice versa during another session, without being disconnected by the policy.

By default, all resource costs are zero:

```
SQL> select * from resource_cost;

RESOURCE_NAME                     UNIT_COST
-------------------------------- ----------
CPU_PER_SESSION                           0
LOGICAL_READS_PER_SESSION                 0
CONNECT_TIME                              0
PRIVATE_SGA                               0

4 rows selected.
```

To adjust the resource cost weights, use the ALTER RESOURCE COST command. In this example, we change the weightings so that CPU_PER_SESSION favors CPU usage over connect time by a factor of 25 to 1; in other words, a user is more likely to be disconnected because of CPU usage than connect time:

Resource Parameter	Description
SESSIONS_PER_USER	The maximum number of sessions a user can simultaneously have
CPU_PER_SESSION	The maximum CPU time allowed per session, in hundredths of a second
CPU_PER_CALL	Maximum CPU time for a statement parse, execute, or fetch operation, in hundredths of a second
CONNECT_TIME	Maximum total elapsed time, in minutes
IDLE_TIME	Maximum continuous inactive time in a session, in minutes, while a query or other operation is not in progress
LOGICAL_READS_PER_SESSION	Total number of data blocks read per session, either from memory or disk
LOGICAL_READS_PER_CALL	Maximum number of data blocks read for a statement parse, execute, or fetch operation
COMPOSITE_LIMIT	Total resource cost, in *service units,* as a composite weighted sum of CPU_PER_SESSION, CONNECT_TIME, LOGICAL_READS_PER_SESSION, and PRIVATE_SGA
PRIVATE_SGA	Maximum amount of memory a session can allocate in the shared pool, in bytes, kilobytes, or megabytes

TABLE 10-4. *Resource-Related Profile Parameters*

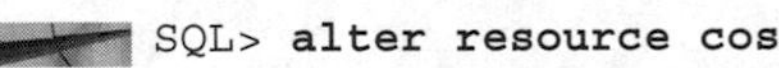

```
SQL> alter resource cost
  2       cpu_per_session 50
  3       connect_time 2;
Resource cost altered.

SQL> select * from resource_cost;

RESOURCE_NAME                     UNIT_COST
-------------------------------- ---------
CPU_PER_SESSION                         50
LOGICAL_READS_PER_SESSION                0
CONNECT_TIME                             2
PRIVATE_SGA                              0

4 rows selected.
```

CPU (Seconds)	Connect (Seconds)	Composite Cost	Exceeded?
0.05	100	(50*5) + (2*100) = 450	Yes
0.02	30	(50*2) + (2*30) = 160	No
0.01	150	(50*1) + (2*150) = 350	Yes
0.02	5	(50*2) + (2*5) = 110	No

TABLE 10-5. *Resource Usage Scenarios*

The next step is to create a new profile or modify an existing profile to use a composite limit:

```
SQL> create profile lim_comp_cpu_conn limit
  2       composite_limit 250;

Profile created.
```

As a result, users assigned to the profile LIM_COMP_CPU_CONN will have their session resources limited using the following formula to calculate cost:

```
composite_cost = (50 * CPU_PER_SESSION) + (2 * CONNECT_TIME);
```

Table 10-5 provides some examples of resource usage to see if the composite limit of 250 is exceeded.

The parameters PRIVATE_SGA and LOGICAL_READS_PER_SESSION are not used in this particular example, so unless they are specified otherwise in the profile definition, they default to whatever their value is in the DEFAULT profile. The goal of using composite limits is to give users some leeway in the types of queries or DML they run. On some days, they may run a lot of queries that perform numerous calculations but don't access a lot of table rows; on other days, they may do a lot of full table scans but not stay connected very long. In these situations, we don't want to limit a user by a single parameter, but instead by total resource usage weighted by the availability of each resource on the server.

System Privileges

A *system privilege* is a right to perform an action on any object in the database, as well as other privileges that do not involve objects at all, but rather things like running batch jobs, altering system parameters, creating roles, and even connecting to the database itself. There are 237 system privileges in Release 1 of Oracle 12*c* (12.1.0.2). All of them can be found in the data dictionary table SYSTEM_PRIVILEGE_MAP:

```
SQL> select * from system_privilege_map;

PRIVILEGE  NAME                                      PROPERTY
---------  ----------------------------------------  ----------
       -3  ALTER SYSTEM                                       0
       -4  AUDIT SYSTEM                                       0
       -5  CREATE SESSION                                     0
       -6  ALTER SESSION                                      0
       -7  RESTRICTED SESSION                                 0
```

```
      -10 CREATE TABLESPACE                                   0
      -11 ALTER TABLESPACE                                    0
      -12 MANAGE TABLESPACE                                   0
      -13 DROP TABLESPACE                                     0
      -15 UNLIMITED TABLESPACE                                0
      -20 CREATE USER                                         0
      -21 BECOME USER                                         0
      -22 ALTER USER                                          0
      -23 DROP USER                                           0
. . .
     -318 INSERT ANY MEASURE FOLDER                           0
     -319 CREATE CUBE BUILD PROCESS                           0
     -320 CREATE ANY CUBE BUILD PROCESS                       0
     -321 DROP ANY CUBE BUILD PROCESS                         0
     -322 UPDATE ANY CUBE BUILD PROCESS                       0
     -326 UPDATE ANY CUBE DIMENSION                           0
     -327 ADMINISTER SQL MANAGEMENT OBJECT                    0
     -350 FLASHBACK ARCHIVE ADMINISTER                        0

237 rows selected.
```

Table 10-6 lists some of the more common system privileges, along with a brief description of each.

Granting System Privileges

Privileges are granted to a user, role, or PUBLIC using the GRANT command; privileges are revoked using the REVOKE command. PUBLIC is a special group that includes all database users, and it's convenient shorthand for granting privileges to everyone in the database.

To grant the user SCOTT the ability to create stored procedures and synonyms, you can use a command like the following:

```
SQL> grant create procedure, create synonym to scott;
Grant succeeded.
```

Revoking privileges is just as easy:

```
SQL> revoke create synonym from scott;
Revoke succeeded.
```

If you wish to allow grantees the right to grant the same privilege to someone else, you include WITH ADMIN OPTION when you grant the privilege. In the preceding example, we want the user SCOTT to be able to grant the CREATE PROCEDURE privilege to other users. To accomplish this, we need to re-grant the CREATE PROCEDURE privilege:

```
SQL> grant create procedure to scott with admin option;
Grant succeeded.
```

Now the user SCOTT may issue the GRANT CREATE PROCEDURE command. Note that if SCOTT's permission to grant his privileges to others is revoked, the users he granted the privileges to retain the privileges.

System Privilege	Capability
ALTER DATABASE	Make changes to the database, such as changing the state of the database from MOUNT to OPEN, or recover a database.
ALTER SYSTEM	Issue ALTER SYSTEM statements: Switch to the next redo log group and change system-initialization parameters in the SPFILE.
AUDIT SYSTEM	Issue AUDIT statements.
CREATE DATABASE LINK	Create database links to remote databases.
CREATE ANY INDEX	Create an index in any schema; CREATE INDEX is granted along with CREATE TABLE for the user's schema.
CREATE PROFILE	Create a resource/password profile.
CREATE PROCEDURE	Create a function, procedure, or package in your own schema.
CREATE ANY PROCEDURE	Create a function, procedure, or package in any schema.
CREATE SESSION	Connect to the database.
CREATE SYNONYM	Create a private synonym in your own schema.
CREATE ANY SYNONYM	Create a private synonym in any schema.
CREATE PUBLIC SYNONYM	Create a public synonym.
DROP ANY SYNONYM	Drop a private synonym in any schema.
DROP PUBLIC SYNONYM	Drop a public synonym.
CREATE TABLE	Create a table in your own schema.
CREATE ANY TABLE	Create a table in any schema.
CREATE TABLESPACE	Create a new tablespace in the database.
CREATE USER	Create a user account/schema.
ALTER USER	Make changes to a user account/schema.
CREATE VIEW	Create a view in your own schema.
SYSDBA	Create an entry in the external password file, if enabled; also, perform startup/shutdown, alter a database, create a database, recover a database, create an SPFILE, and connect when the database is in RESTRICTED SESSION mode.
SYSOPER	Create an entry in the external password file, if enabled; also, perform startup/shutdown, alter a database, recover a database, create an SPFILE, and connect when the database is in RESTRICTED SESSION mode.

TABLE 10-6. *Common System Privileges*

Data Dictionary View	Description
DBA_SYS_PRIVS	System privileges assigned to roles and users
SESSION_PRIVS	All system privileges in effect for this user for the session, granted directly or via a role
ROLE_SYS_PRIVS	Current session privileges granted to a user via a role

TABLE 10-7. *System Privilege Data Dictionary Views*

System Privilege Data Dictionary Views

Table 10-7 contains the data dictionary views related to system privileges (see Chapter 11 for the equivalent views in a multitenant environment).

Object Privileges

In contrast to a system privilege, an *object privilege* is a right to perform a particular type of action on a specific object, such as a table or a sequence, that is not in the user's own schema. As with system privileges, you use the grant and revoke commands to grant and revoke privileges on objects.

As with system privileges, you can grant object privileges to PUBLIC or a specific user; a user with the object privilege may pass it on to others by granting the object privilege with the WITH GRANT OPTION clause.

CAUTION
Only grant object or system privileges to PUBLIC when the privilege is truly required by all current and future users of the database.

Some schema objects, such as clusters and indexes, rely on system privileges to control access. In these cases, the user can change these objects if they own the objects or have the ALTER ANY CLUSTER or ALTER ANY INDEX system privilege.

A user with objects in their own schema automatically has all object privileges on those objects and can grant any object privilege on these objects to any user or another role, with or without the GRANT OPTION clause.

In Table 10-8 are the object privileges available for different types of objects; some privileges are only applicable to certain types of objects. For example, the INSERT privilege only makes sense with tables, views, and materialized views; the EXECUTE privilege, on the other hand, is applicable to functions, procedures, and packages, but not tables.

It's worth noting that DELETE, UPDATE, and INSERT privileges cannot be granted to materialized views unless they are updatable. Some of these object privileges overlap with system privileges; for example, if you don't have the FLASHBACK object privilege on a table, you can still perform flashback queries if you have the FLASHBACK ANY TABLE system privilege.

Object Privilege	Capability
ALTER	Can alter a table or sequence definition.
DELETE	Can delete rows from a table, view, or materialized view.
EXECUTE	Can execute a function or procedure, with or without a package.
DEBUG	Allowed to view PL/SQL code in triggers defined on a table, or SQL statements that reference a table. For object types, this privilege allows access to all public and private variables, methods, and types defined on the object type.
FLASHBACK	Allows flashback queries on tables, views, and materialized views using retained undo information.
INDEX	Can create an index on a table.
INSERT	Can insert rows into a table, view, or materialized view.
ON COMMIT REFRESH	Can create a refresh-on-commit materialized view based on a table.
QUERY REWRITE	Can create a materialized view for query rewrite based on a table.
READ	Can read the contents of an operating system directory using an Oracle DIRECTORY definition.
REFERENCES	Can create a foreign key constraint that references another table's primary key or unique key.
SELECT	Can read rows from a table, view, or materialized view, in addition to reading current or next values from a sequence.
UNDER	Can create a view based on an existing view.
UPDATE	Can update rows in a table, view, or materialized view.
WRITE	Can write information to an operating system directory using an Oracle DIRECTORY definition.

TABLE 10-8. *Object Privileges*

In the following example, the DBA grants SCOTT full access to the table HR.EMPLOYEES, but only allows SCOTT to pass on the SELECT object privilege to other users:

```
SQL> grant insert, update, delete on hr.employees to scott;
Grant succeeded.
SQL> grant select on hr.employees to scott with grant option;
Grant succeeded.
```

Note that if the SELECT privilege on the table HR.EMPLOYEES is revoked from SCOTT, the SELECT privilege is also revoked from anyone he granted the privilege.

Table Privileges

The types of privileges that can be granted on a table fall into two broad categories: DML operations and DDL operations. DML operations include DELETE, INSERT, SELECT, and UPDATE, whereas DDL operations include adding, dropping, and changing columns in the table as well as creating indexes on the table.

When granting DML operations on a table, it is possible to restrict those operations only to certain columns. For example, we may want to allow SCOTT to see and update all the rows and columns in the HR.EMPLOYEES table except for the SALARY column. To do this, we first need to revoke the existing SELECT privilege on the table:

```
SQL> revoke update on hr.employees from scott;
Revoke succeeded.
```

Next, we will let SCOTT update all the columns except for the SALARY column:

```
SQL> grant update (employee_id, first_name, last_name, email,
  2               phone_number, hire_date, job_id, commission_pct,
  3               manager_id, department_id)
  4   on hr.employees to scott;

Grant succeeded.
```

SCOTT will be able to update all columns in the HR.EMPLOYEES table except for the SALARY column:

```
SQL> update hr.employees set first_name = 'Steve' where employee_id = 100;
1 row updated.
SQL> update hr.employees set salary = 50000 where employee_id = 203;
update hr.employees set salary = 50000 where employee_id = 203
          *
ERROR at line 1:
ORA-01031: insufficient privileges
```

This operation is also easy to perform with the web-based Cloud Control, as demonstrated in Figure 10-5.

View Privileges

Privileges on views are similar to those granted on tables. Rows in a view can be selected, updated, deleted, or inserted, assuming that the view is updatable. To create a view, first you need either the CREATE VIEW system privilege (to create a view in your own schema) or the CREATE ANY VIEW system privilege (to create a view in any schema). Even to create the view, you must also have at least SELECT object privileges on the underlying tables of the view, along with INSERT, UPDATE, and DELETE, if you wish to perform those operations on the view and the view is updatable. Alternatively, you can have the SELECT ANY TABLE, INSERT ANY TABLE, UPDATE ANY TABLE, or DELETE ANY TABLE privileges if the underlying objects are not in your schema.

To allow others to use your view, you must also have permissions on the view's base tables with the GRANT OPTION, or you must have the system privileges with the ADMIN OPTION. For example, if you are creating a view against the HR.EMPLOYEES table, you must have been granted the SELECT object privilege WITH GRANT OPTION on HR.EMPLOYEES, or you must have the SELECT ANY TABLE system privilege WITH ADMIN OPTION.

Procedure Privileges

For procedures, functions, and the packages that contain procedures and functions, the EXECUTE privilege is the only object privilege that can be applied. Since Oracle8*i,* procedures and functions can be run either from the perspective of the *definer,* the creator of the procedure or function, or from the *invoker,* the user who is running the procedure or function.

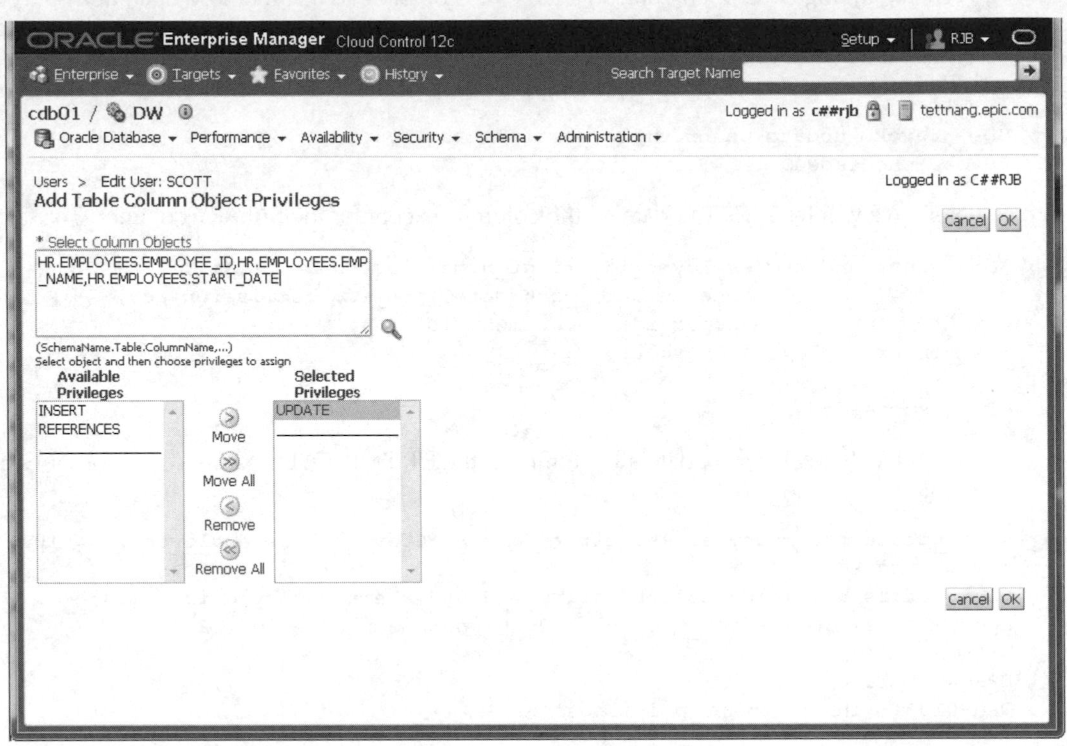

FIGURE 10-5. *Granting column privileges in Oracle Cloud Control*

A procedure with definer's rights is run as if the definer was running the procedure, with all privileges of the definer in effect against objects referenced in the procedure. This is a good way to enforce restrictions on private database objects: Other users are granted EXECUTE permissions on the procedure and no permissions on the referenced objects. As a result, the definer can control how other users access the objects.

Conversely, an invoker's rights procedure requires that the invoker have direct rights, such as SELECT and UPDATE, to any objects referenced in the procedure. The procedure could reference an unqualified table named ORDERS, and if all users of the database have an ORDERS table, the same procedure could be used by any user who has their own ORDERS table. Another advantage to using invoker's rights procedures is that roles are enabled within them. Roles are discussed in depth later in this chapter.

By default, a procedure is created with definer's rights. To specify that a procedure uses invoker's rights, you must include the keywords AUTHID CURRENT_USER in the procedure definition, as in the following example:

```
create or replace procedure process_orders (order_batch_date   date)
authid current_user as
begin
```

Data Dictionary View	Description
DBA_TAB_PRIVS	Table privileges granted to roles and users. Includes the user who granted the privilege to the role or user, with or without GRANT OPTION.
DBA_COL_PRIVS	Column privileges granted to roles or users, containing the column name and the type of privilege on the column.
SESSION_PRIVS	All system privileges in effect for this user for the session, granted directly or via a role.
ROLE_TAB_PRIVS	For the current session, privileges granted on tables via roles.

TABLE 10-9. *Object Privilege Data Dictionary Views*

```
    -- process user's ORDERS table here using invoker's rights,
    -- all roles are in effect
end;
```

To create a procedure, a user must have either the CREATE PROCEDURE or CREATE ANY PROCEDURE system privilege. For the procedure to compile correctly, the user must have direct privileges against all objects referenced in the procedure, even though roles are enabled at runtime in an invoker's rights procedure to obtain these same privileges. To allow other users to access a procedure, you grant EXECUTE privileges on the procedure or package.

Object Privilege Data Dictionary Views

A number of data dictionary views contain information about object privileges assigned to users. Table 10-9 lists the most important views containing object privilege information.

Creating, Assigning, and Maintaining Roles

A *role* is a named group of privileges, either system privileges or object privileges or a combination of the two, that helps to ease the administration of privileges. Rather than granting system or object privileges individually to each user, you can grant the group of system or object privileges to a role, and in turn the role can be granted to the user instead. This reduces tremendously the amount of administrative overhead involved in maintaining privileges for users. Figure 10-6 shows how a role can reduce the number of grant commands (and ultimately revoke commands) that need to be executed when roles are used to group privileges.

If the privileges for a group of people authorized by a role need to change, only the privileges of the role need to be changed, and the capabilities of the users with that role automatically use the new or changed privileges. Roles may selectively be enabled by a user; some roles may automatically be enabled at login. In addition, passwords can be used to protect a role, adding another level of authentication to the capabilities in the database.

In Table 10-10 are the most common roles that are automatically provided with the database, along with a brief description of what privileges come with each role.

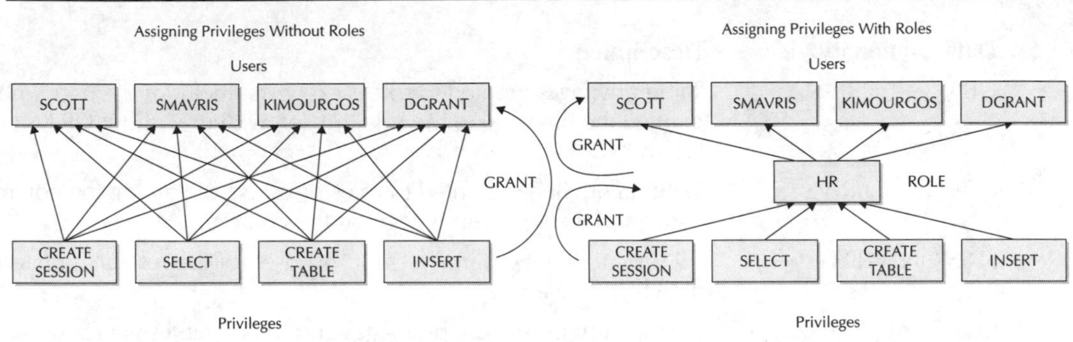

FIGURE 10-6. *Using roles to manage privileges*

The roles CONNECT, RESOURCE, and DBA are provided mainly for compatibility with previous versions of Oracle; they may not exist in future versions of Oracle. The DBA should create custom roles using the privileges granted to these roles as a starting point.

Creating or Dropping a Role

To create a role, you use the CREATE ROLE command, and you must have the CREATE ROLE system privilege. Typically, this is granted only to database administrators or application administrators. Here's an example:

```
SQL> create role hr_admin not identified;
Role created.
```

By default, no password or authentication is required to enable or use an assigned role; therefore, the NOT IDENTIFIED clause is optional.

As with creating users, you can authorize use of a role by a password (database authorization with IDENTIFIED BY *password*), by the operating system (IDENTIFIED EXTERNALLY), or by the network or directory service (IDENTIFIED GLOBALLY).

In addition to these familiar methods, a role can be authorized by the use of a package: This is known as using a *secure application role*. This type of role uses a procedure within the package to enable the role. Typically, the role is enabled only under certain conditions: The user is connecting via a web interface or from a certain IP address, or it's a certain time of day. Here is a role that is enabled using a procedure:

```
SQL> create role hr_clerk identified using hr.clerk_verif;
Role created.
```

The procedure HR.CLERK_VERIF need not exist when the role is created; however, it must be compiled and valid when a user who is granted this role needs to enable it. Typically, with secure application roles, the role is not enabled by default for the user. To specify that all roles are enabled by default, except for the secure application role, use the following command:

```
SQL> alter user klynne default role all except hr_clerk;
User altered.
```

Role Name	Privileges
CONNECT	Previous to Oracle Database 10*g* Release 2: ALTER SESSION, CREATE CLUSTER, CREATE DATABASE LINK, CREATE SEQUENCE, CREATE SESSION, CREATE SYNONYM, CREATE TABLE, CREATE VIEW. These privileges are typically those given to a general user of the database, allowing them to connect and create tables, indexes, and views. Oracle Database 10*g* Release 2 and later: CREATE SESSION only.
RESOURCE	CREATE CLUSTER, CREATE INDEXTYPE, CREATE OPERATOR, CREATE PROCEDURE, CREATE SEQUENCE, CREATE TABLE, CREATE TRIGGER, CREATE TYPE. These privileges are typically used for application developers who may be coding PL/SQL procedures and functions.
DBA	All system privileges WITH ADMIN OPTION. Allows a person with the DBA role to grant system privileges to others.
DELETE_CATALOG_ROLE	Does not have any system privileges, but only object privileges (DELETE) on SYS.AUD$ and FGA_LOG$. In other words, this role allows a user to remove audit records from the audit trail for regular or fine-grained auditing.
EXECUTE_CATALOG_ROLE	Execute privileges on various system packages, procedures, and functions, such as DBMS_FGA and DBMS_RLS.
SELECT_CATALOG_ROLE	SELECT object privilege on 1638 data dictionary tables.
EXP_FULL_DATABASE	EXECUTE_CATALOG_ROLE, SELECT_CATALOG_ROLE, and system privileges such as BACKUP ANY TABLE and RESUMABLE. Allows a user with this role to export all objects in the database.
IMP_FULL_DATABASE	Similar to EXP_FULL_DATABASE, with many more system privileges, such as CREATE ANY TABLE, to allow the import of a previously exported full database.
AQ_USER_ROLE	Execute access for routines needed with Advanced Queuing, such as DBMS_AQ.
AQ_ADMINISTRATOR_ROLE	Manager for Advanced Queuing queues.
SNMPAGENT	Used by the Cloud Control Intelligent Agent.
RECOVERY_CATALOG_OWNER	Used to create a user who owns a recovery catalog for RMAN backup and recovery.
HS_ADMIN_ROLE	Provides access to the tables HS_* and the package DBMS_HS for administering Oracle Heterogeneous Services.
SCHEDULER_ADMIN	Provides access to the DBMS_SCHEDULER package, along with privileges to create batch jobs.

TABLE 10-10. *Predefined Oracle Roles*

In this way, when the HR application starts, it can enable the role by performing a SET ROLE HR_CLERK command, thus calling the procedure HR.CLERK_VERIF. The user need not know about the role or the procedure that enables the role; therefore, no access to the objects and privileges provided by the role are available to the user outside of the application.

Dropping a role is just as easy as creating a role:

```
SQL> drop role keypunch_operator;
Role dropped.
```

Any users assigned to this role will lose the privileges assigned to this role the next time they connect to the database. If they are currently logged in, they will retain the privileges until they disconnect from the database.

Granting Privileges to a Role

Assigning a privilege to a role is very straightforward; you use the GRANT command to assign the privilege to a role, just as you would assign a privilege to a user:

```
SQL> grant select on hr.employees to hr_clerk;
Grant succeeded.
SQL> grant create table to hr_clerk;
Grant succeeded.
```

In this example, we've assigned an object privilege and a system privilege to the HR_CLERK role. In Figure 10-7, we can use Cloud Control to add more object or system privileges to the role.

Assigning or Revoking Roles

Once we have the desired system and object privileges assigned to the role, we can assign the role to a user, using familiar syntax:

```
SQL> grant hr_clerk to smavris;
Grant succeeded.
```

Any other privileges granted to the HR_CLERK role in the future will automatically be usable by SMAVRIS because SMAVRIS has been granted the role.

Roles may be granted to other roles; this allows a DBA to have a hierarchy of roles, making role administration easier. For example, we may have roles named DEPT30, DEPT50, and DEPT100, each having object privileges to tables owned by each of those departments. An employee in department 30 would be assigned the DEPT30 role, and so forth. The president of the company would like to see tables in all departments; but rather than assigning individual object privileges to the role ALL_DEPTS, we can assign the individual department roles to ALL_DEPTS:

```
SQL> create role all_depts;
Role created.
SQL> grant dept30, dept50, dept100 to all_depts;
Grant succeeded.
SQL> grant all_depts to KLYNNE;
Grant succeeded.
```

The role ALL_DEPTS may also contain individual object and system privileges that do not apply to individual departments, such as object privileges on order entry tables or accounts receivable tables.

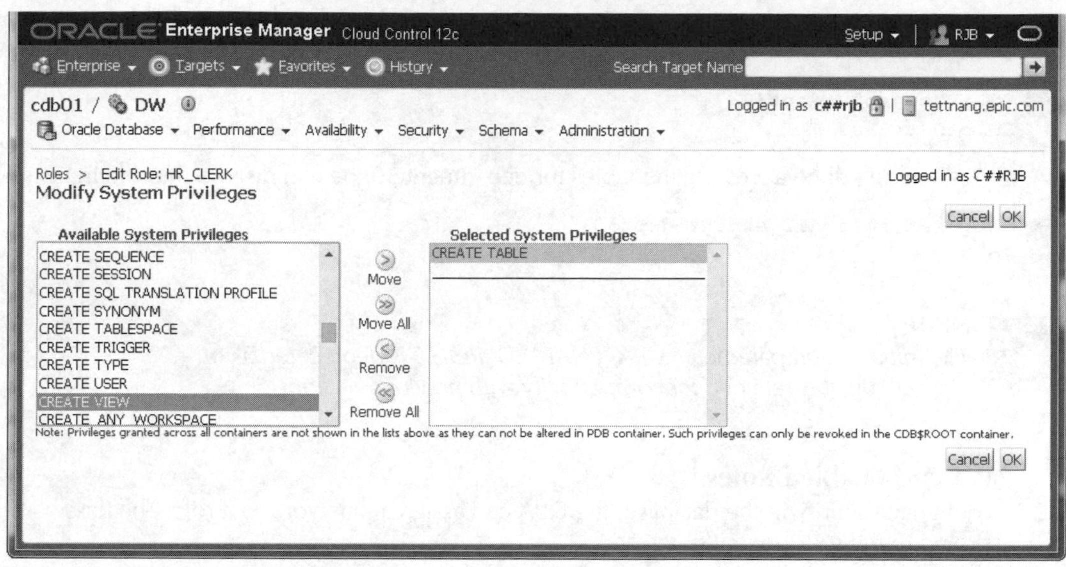

FIGURE 10-7. *Granting privileges to roles with Cloud Control*

Revoking a role from a user is very similar to revoking privileges from a user:

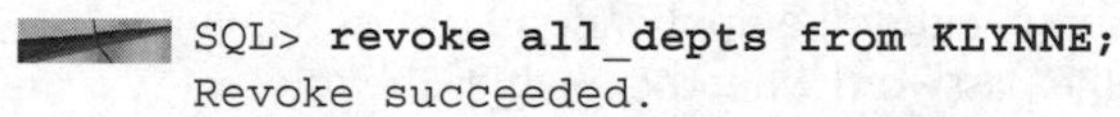

```
SQL> revoke all_depts from KLYNNE;
Revoke succeeded.
```

The privileges revoked will no longer be available to the user the next time they connect to the database. However, it is worth noting that if another role contains privileges on the same objects as the dropped role, or privileges on the objects are granted directly, the user retains these privileges on the objects until these and all other grants are explicitly revoked.

Default Roles

By default, all roles granted to a user are enabled when the user connects. If a role is going to be used only within the context of an application, the role can start out disabled when the user is logged in; then it can be enabled and disabled within the application. If the user SCOTT has CONNECT, RESOURCE, HR_CLERK, and DEPT30 roles, and we want to specify that HR_CLERK and DEPT30 are not enabled by default, we can use something like the following:

```
SQL> alter user scott default role all
  2>     except hr_clerk, dept30;
User altered.
```

When SCOTT connects to the database, he automatically has all privileges granted with all roles except for HR_CLERK and DEPT30. SCOTT may explicitly enable a role in his session by using SET ROLE:

```
SQL> set role dept30;
Role set.
```

When he's done accessing the tables for department 30, he can disable the role in his session:

```
SQL> set role all except dept30;
Role set.
```

NOTE
The initialization parameter MAX_ENABLED_ROLES is deprecated as of Oracle 10g. It is retained for compatibility with previous versions only.

Password-Enabled Roles

To enhance security in the database, the DBA can assign a password to a role. The password is assigned to the role when it's created:

```
SQL> create role dept99 identified by d99secretpw;
Role created.
SQL> grant dept99 to scott;
Grant succeeded.
SQL> alter user scott default role all except hr_clerk, dept30, dept99;
User altered.
```

When the user SCOTT is connected to the database, either the application he is using will provide or prompt for a password, or he can enter the password when he enables the role:

```
SQL> set role dept99 identified by d99secretpw;
Role set.
```

Role Data Dictionary Views

Table 10-11 lists and describes the data dictionary views related to roles.

Data Dictionary View	Description
DBA_ROLES	All roles and whether they require a password.
DBA_ROLE_PRIVS	Roles granted to users or other roles.
ROLE_ROLE_PRIVS	Roles granted to other roles.
ROLE_SYS_PRIVS	System privileges that have been granted to roles.
ROLE_TAB_PRIVS	Table and table column privileges that have been granted to roles.
SESSION_ROLES	Roles currently in effect for the session. Available to every user session.

TABLE 10-11. *Role-Related Data Dictionary Views*

The view DBA_ROLE_PRIVS is a good way to find out what roles are granted to a user as well as whether they can pass this role to another user (ADMIN_OPTION) and whether this role is enabled by default (DEFAULT_ROLE):

```
SQL> select * from dba_role_privs
  2  where grantee = 'SCOTT';

GRANTEE      GRANTED_ROLE         ADMIN_OPTION DEFAULT_ROLE
------------ -------------------- ------------ ------------
SCOTT        DEPT30               NO           NO
SCOTT        DEPT50               NO           YES
SCOTT        DEPT99               NO           YES
SCOTT        CONNECT              NO           YES
SCOTT        HR_CLERK             NO           NO
SCOTT        RESOURCE             NO           YES
SCOTT        ALL_DEPTS            NO           YES
SCOTT        DELETE_CATALOG_ROLE  NO           YES

8 rows selected.
```

Similarly, we can find out which roles we assigned to the ALL_DEPTS role:

```
SQL> select * from dba_role_privs
  2> where grantee = 'ALL_DEPTS';

GRANTEE      GRANTED_ROLE         ADMIN_OPTION DEFAULT_ROLE
------------ -------------------- ------------ ------------
ALL_DEPTS    DEPT30               NO           YES
ALL_DEPTS    DEPT50               NO           YES
ALL_DEPTS    DEPT100              NO           YES

3 rows selected.
```

The data dictionary view ROLE_ROLE_PRIVS can also be used to get this information; it only contains information about roles assigned to roles, and it does not have the DEFAULT_ROLE information.

To find out privileges granted to users on a table or table columns, we can write two queries: one to retrieve privileges granted directly, and another to retrieve privileges granted indirectly via a role. Retrieving privileges granted directly is straightforward:

```
SQL> select dtp.grantee, dtp.owner, dtp.table_name,
  2         dtp.grantor, dtp.privilege, dtp.grantable
  3  from dba_tab_privs dtp
  4  where dtp.grantee = 'SCOTT';

GRANTEE      OWNER      TABLE_NAME       GRANTOR      PRIVILEGE    GRANTABLE
------------ ---------- ---------------- ------------ ------------ ----------
SCOTT        HR         EMPLOYEES        HR           SELECT       YES
SCOTT        HR         EMPLOYEES        HR           DELETE       NO
SCOTT        HR         EMPLOYEES        HR           INSERT       NO

4 rows selected.
```

To retrieve table privileges granted via roles, we need to join DBA_ROLE_PRIVS and ROLE_TAB_PRIVS. DBA_ROLE_PRIVS has the roles assigned to the user, and ROLE_TAB_PRIVS has the privileges assigned to the roles:

```
SQL> select drp.grantee, rtp.owner, rtp.table_name,
          rtp.privilege, rtp.grantable, rtp.role
     from role_tab_privs rtp
          join dba_role_privs drp on rtp.role = drp.granted_role
     where drp.grantee = 'SCOTT';

GRANTEE    OWNER    TABLE_NAME      PRIVILEGE    GRANTABLE  ROLE
---------- -------- --------------- ------------ ---------- ---------------
SCOTT      HR       EMPLOYEES       SELECT       NO         HR_CLERK
SCOTT      HR       JOBS            SELECT       NO         JOB_MAINT
SCOTT      HR       JOBS            UPDATE       NO         JOB_MAINT
SCOTT      SYS      AUD$            DELETE       NO         DELETE_CATA
                                                            LOG_ROLE
SCOTT      SYS      FGA_LOG$        DELETE       NO         DELETE_CATA
                                                            LOG_ROLE

5 rows selected.
```

In the case of SCOTT's privileges, notice that he has the SELECT privilege on the HR.EMPLOYEES table both via a direct GRANT and via a role. Revoking either one of the privileges will still leave him with access to the HR.EMPLOYEES table until both privileges have been removed.

Using a VPD to Implement Application Security Policies

A Virtual Private Database (VPD) combines server-enforced fine-grained access control with a secure application context. The context-aware functions return a predicate—a WHERE clause—that is automatically appended to all SELECT statements or other DML statements. In other words, a SELECT statement on a table, view, or synonym controlled by a VPD will return a subset of rows based on a WHERE clause generated automatically by the security policy function in effect by the application context. The major component of a VPD is row-level security (RLS), also known as fine-grained access control (FGAC).

Because a VPD generates the predicates transparently during statement parse, the security policy is enforced consistently regardless of whether the user is running ad hoc queries, retrieving the data from an application, or viewing the data from Oracle Forms. Because the Oracle server applies the predicate to the statement at parse time, the application need not use special tables, views, and so forth to implement the policy. As a result, Oracle can optimize the query using indexes, materialized views, and parallel operations where it otherwise might not be able. Therefore, using a VPD may incur less overhead than a query whose results are filtered using applications or other means.

From a maintenance point of view, security policies can be defined within a policy function that would be difficult to create using roles and privileges. Similarly, an Application Server Provider (ASP) may only need to set up one database to service multiple customers for the same application, with a VPD policy to ensure that employees of one customer can see only their data. The DBA can maintain one larger database with a small number of VPD policies instead of an individual database for each customer.

Using column-level VPD, a DBA can restrict access to a particular column or columns in a table. The query returns the same number of rows, but if the user's context does not allow access to the column or columns, NULL values are returned in the restricted column or columns.

VPD policies can be static, context sensitive, or dynamic. Static and context-sensitive policies can improve performance dramatically because they do not need to call the policy function every time a query is run, because it is cached for use later in the session. Before Oracle Database 10*g*, all policies were dynamic; in other words, the policy function was run every time a SQL statement containing the target VPD table was parsed. Static policies are evaluated once during login and remain cached throughout the session, regardless of application context. With context-sensitive policies, the policy function is called at statement parse time if the application context changes—for example, a policy that enforces the business rule that "employees only see their own salary history, but managers can see all the salaries of their employees." If the employee executing the statement has not changed, the policy function need not be called again, thus reducing the amount of overhead due to VPD policy enforcement.

You create application contexts using the CREATE CONTEXT command, and the package DBMS_RLS manages VPD policies. The function used to return the predicates to enforce the policy is created like any other function, except that the function has two required parameters and returns a VARCHAR2. Later in this chapter, I'll go into more detail on these functions and we'll step through a VPD example using the sample schemas provided during the installation of the Oracle database.

Application Context

Using the CREATE CONTEXT command, you can create the name of application-defined attributes that will be used to enforce your security policy, along with the package name for the functions and procedures used to set the security context for the user session. Here's an example:

```
create context hr_security using vpd.emp_access;

create or replace package emp_access as
   procedure set_security_parameters;
end;
```

In this example, the context name is HR_SECURITY, and the package used to set up the characteristics or attributes for the user during the session is called EMP_ACCESS. The procedure SET_SECURITY_PARAMETERS will be called in the logon trigger. Because the context HR_SECURITY is bound only to EMP_ACCESS, no other procedures can change the session attributes. This ensures a secure application context that can't be changed by the user or any other process after connecting to the database.

In a typical package used to implement application context, you use the built-in context USERENV to retrieve information about the user session itself. In Table 10-12 are a few of the more common parameters in the USERENV context.

For example, the following calls to SYS_CONTEXT will retrieve the username and IP_ADDRESS of the database session:

```
declare
    username        varchar2(30);
    ip_addr         varchar2(30);
begin
    username := SYS_CONTEXT('USERENV','SESSION_USER');
```

Parameter	Return Value
CURRENT_SCHEMA	The default schema for the session
DB_NAME	The name of the database as specified in the initialization parameter DB_NAME
HOST	The name of the host machine from which the user connected
IP_ADDRESS	The IP address from which the user connected
OS_USER	The operating system account that initiated the database session
SESSION_USER	The authenticated database user's name

TABLE 10-12. *Common USERENV Context Parameters*

```
    ip_addr := SYS_CONTEXT('USERENV','IP_ADDRESS');
    -- other processing here
end;
```

Similarly, the SYS_CONTEXT function can be used within a SQL SELECT statement:

```
SQL> select SYS_CONTEXT('USERENV','SESSION_USER') username from dual;

USERNAME
-------------------------
KLYNNE
```

Using some combination of the USERENV context and authorization information in the database, we use DBMS_SESSION.SET_CONTEXT to assign values to parameters in the application context that we create:

```
dbms_session.set_context('HR_SECURITY','SEC_LEVEL','HIGH');
```

In this example, the application context variable SEC_LEVEL is set to HIGH in the HR_SECURITY context. The value can be assigned based on a number of conditions, including a mapping table that assigns security levels based on user ID.

To ensure that the context variables are set for each session, we can use a logon trigger to call the procedure associated with the context. As mentioned earlier, the variables in the context can only be set or changed within the assigned package. Here is a sample logon trigger that calls the procedure to set up the context:

```
create or replace trigger vpd.set_security_parameters
    after logon on database
begin
    vpd.emp_access.set_security_parameters;
end;
```

In this example, the procedure SET_SECURITY_PARAMETERS would make the necessary calls to DBMS_SESSION.SET_CONTEXT.

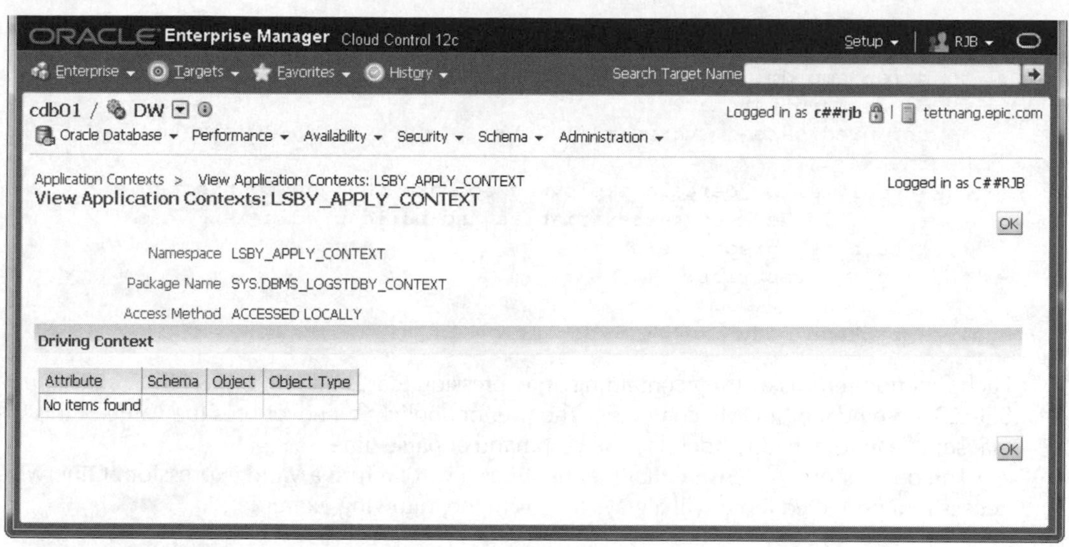

FIGURE 10-8. *Oracle Policy Manager*

Within Oracle Cloud Control, you can navigate to Application Contexts under the Security dropdown to set up contexts and policy groups, as demonstrated in Figure 10-8.

Security Policy Implementation

Once the infrastructure is in place to set up the security environment, the next step is to define the function or functions used to generate the predicate that will be attached to every SELECT statement or DML command against the protected tables. The function used to implement the predicate generation has two arguments: the owner of the object being protected, and the name of the object within the owner's schema. One function may handle predicate generation for just one type of operation, such as SELECT, or may be applicable to all DML commands, depending on how this function is associated with the protected table. The following example shows a package body containing two functions—one that will be used to control access from SELECT statements, and the other for any other DML statements:

```
create or replace package body get_predicates is

  function emp_select_restrict(owner varchar2, object_name varchar2)
          return varchar2 is
    ret_predicate    varchar2(1000);  -- part of WHERE clause
  begin
    -- only allow certain employees to see rows in the table
    -- . . . check context variables and build predicate
```

```
      return ret_predicate;
   end emp_select_restrict;

   function emp_dml_restrict(owner varchar2, object_name varchar2)
         return varchar2 is
      ret_predicate    varchar2(1000);  -- part of WHERE clause
   begin
      -- only allow certain employees to make changes to the table
      -- . . . check context variables and build predicate
      return ret_predicate;
   end emp_dml_restrict;

end; -- package body
```

Each function returns a string containing an expression that is added to a WHERE clause for a SELECT statement or a DML command. The user or application never sees the value of this WHERE clause; it is automatically added to the command at parse time.

The developer must ensure that the functions always return a valid expression. Otherwise, any access to a protected table will always fail, as in the following example:

```
SQL> select * from hr.employees;
select * from hr.employees
                 *
ERROR at line 1:
ORA-28113: policy predicate has error
```

The error message does not say what the predicate is, and all users are locked out of the table until the predicate function is fixed. Tips on how to debug a predicate function are presented later in this chapter.

Using DBMS_RLS

The built-in package DBMS_RLS contains a number of subprograms that a DBA uses to maintain the security policies associated with tables, views, and synonyms. In Table 10-13 are the subprograms available in the DBMS_RLS package. Any user who needs to create or administer policies must have EXECUTE privileges granted on the package SYS.DBMS_RLS.

In this chapter, we'll cover the most commonly used subprograms, ADD_POLICY and DROP_POLICY. The syntax of ADD_POLICY follows:

```
DBMS_RLS.ADD_POLICY
(
    object_schema           IN varchar2 null,
    object_name             IN varchar2,
    policy_name             IN varchar2,
    function_schema         IN varchar2 null,
    policy_function         IN varchar2,
    statement_types         IN varchar2 null,
    update_check            IN boolean false,
    enable                  IN boolean true,
    static_policy           IN boolean false,
    policy_type             IN binary_integer null,
```

Subprogram	Description
ADD_POLICY	Adds a fine-grained access control policy to an object
DROP_POLICY	Drops an FGAC policy from an object
REFRESH_POLICY	Reparses all cached statements associated with the policy
ENABLE_POLICY	Enables or disables an FGAC policy
CREATE_POLICY_GROUP	Creates a policy group
ADD_GROUPED_POLICY	Adds a policy to a policy group
ADD_POLICY_CONTEXT	Adds the context for the current application
DELETE_POLICY_GROUP	Deletes a policy group
DROP_GROUPED_POLICY	Drops a policy from a policy group
DROP_POLICY_CONTEXT	Drops a context for the active application
ENABLE_GROUPED_POLICY	Enables or disables a group policy
DISABLE_GROUPED_POLICY	Disables a group policy
REFRESH_GROUPED_POLICY	Reparses all cached statements associated with the policy group

TABLE 10-13. *DBMS_RLS Package Subprograms*

```
    long_predicate          IN in Boolean false,
    sec_relevant_cols       IN varchar2,
    sec_relevant_cols_opt   IN binary_integer null
);
```

Note that some of the parameters have BOOLEAN default values and that the less commonly used parameters are near the end of the argument list. This makes the syntax for any particular call to DBMS_RLS.ADD_POLICY easier to write and understand for the vast majority of cases. The description and usage for each parameter are provided in Table 10-14.

Using the parameter **sec_relevant_cols** is handy when you don't mind if users see part of a row, just not the columns that might contain confidential information, such as a Social Security Number or a salary. In our example later in this chapter, we'll build on the first security policy we define to filter out sensitive data for most employees of the company.

In the following example, we're applying a policy named EMP_SELECT_RESTRICT to the table HR.EMPLOYEES. The schema VPD owns the policy function GET_PREDICATES.EMP_SELECT_RESTRICT. The policy explicitly applies to SELECT statements on the table; however, with UPDATE_CHECK set to TRUE, UPDATE, or DELETE commands will also be checked when rows are updated or inserted into the table.

```
dbms_rls.add_policy (
        object_schema =>   'HR',
        object_name =>     'EMPLOYEES',
        policy_name =>     'EMP_SELECT_RESTRICT',
        function_schema => 'VPD',
```

Parameter	Description
object_schema	The schema containing the table, view, or synonym to be protected by the policy. If this value is NULL, the schema of the user calling the procedure is used.
object_name	The name of the table, view, or synonym to be protected by the policy.
policy_name	The name of the policy to be added to this object. It must be unique for each object being protected.
function_schema	The schema that owns the policy function; if this value is NULL, the schema of the user calling the procedure is used.
policy_function	The name of the function that will generate the predicate for the policy against the object_name. If the function is part of the package, the package name must also be specified here to qualify the policy function name.
statement_types	The statement types to which the policy applies. The allowable values, separated by commas, can be any combination of SELECT, INSERT, UPDATE, DELETE, and INDEX. By default, all types are applied except for INDEX.
update_check	For INSERT or UPDATE types, this parameter is optional, and it defaults to FALSE. If it is TRUE, the policy is also checked for INSERT or UPDATE statements when a SELECT or DELETE operation is being checked.
enable	This parameter defaults to TRUE and indicates if the policy is enabled when it is added.
static_policy	If this parameter is TRUE, the policy produces the same predicate string for anyone accessing the object, except for the SYS user or any user with the EXEMPT ACCESS POLICY privilege. The default is FALSE.
policy_type	Overrides static_policy if this value is not NULL. Allowable values are STATIC, SHARED_STATIC, CONTEXT_SENSITIVE, SHARED_CONTEXT_SENSITIVE, and DYNAMIC.
long_predicate	This parameter defaults to FALSE. If it is TRUE, the predicate string can be up to 32,000 bytes long. Otherwise, the limit is 4000 bytes.
sec_relevant_cols	Enforces column-level VPD, new as of Oracle 10*g*. Applies to tables and views only. Protected columns are specified in a list with either commas or spaces as delimiters. The policy is applied only if the specified sensitive columns are in the query or DML statement. By default, all columns are protected.
sec_relevant_cols_opt	Allows rows in a column-level VPD filtered query to still appear in the result set, with NULL values returned for the sensitive columns. The default for this parameter is NULL; otherwise, you must specify DBMS_RLS.ALL_ROWS to show all columns with NULLs for the sensitive columns.

TABLE 10-14. *DBMS_RLS.ADD_POLICY Parameters*

```
        policy_function => 'get_predicates.emp_select_restrict',
        statement_types => 'SELECT',
        update_check =>    TRUE,
        enable =>          TRUE
);
```

Because we did not set **static_policy**, it defaults to FALSE, meaning that the policy is dynamic and is checked every time a SELECT statement is parsed. This is the only behavior available before Oracle Database 10*g*.

Using the subprogram ENABLE_POLICY is an easy way to disable the policy temporarily without having to rebind the policy to the table later:

```
dbms_rls.enable_policy(
        object_schema =>   'HR',
        object_name =>     'EMPLOYEES',
        policy_name =>     'EMP_SELECT_RESTRICT',
        enable =>          FALSE
);
```

If multiple policies are specified for the same object, an AND condition is added between each predicate. If you need to have an OR condition between predicates for multiple policies instead, the policy most likely needs to be revised. The logic for each policy needs to be combined within a single policy with an OR condition between each part of the predicate.

Creating a VPD

In this section, we'll step through a complete implementation of a VPD from beginning to end. This example relies on the sample schemas installed with Oracle Database 12*c*. To be specific, we are going to implement an FGAC policy on the HR.EMPLOYEES table to restrict access based on manager status and the employee's department number. If you are an employee, you can see your own row in HR.EMPLOYEES; if you are a manager, you can see the rows for all the employees who report directly to you.

TIP
If you do not have the sample schemas installed in your database, you can create them using the scripts found in ***$ORACLE_HOME/demo/schema***.

Once the sample schemas are in place, we need to create some users in the database who want to see rows from the table HR.EMPLOYEES.

```
create user smavris identified by smavris702;
grant connect, resource to smavris;

create user dgrant identified by dgrant507;
grant connect, resource to dgrant;

create user kmourgos identified by kmourgos622;
grant connect, resource to kmourgos;
```

The user KMOURGOS is the manager for all the stocking clerks, and DGRANT is one of KMOURGOS's employees. The user SMAVRIS is the HR representative for the company.

In the following three steps, we will grant SELECT privileges on the HR.EMPLOYEES table to everyone in the database, and we will create a lookup table that maps employee ID numbers to their database account. The procedure that sets the context variables for the user session will use this table to assign the employee ID number to the context variable that will be used in the policy function to generate the predicate.

```
grant select on hr.employees to public;

create table hr.emp_login_map (employee_id, login_acct)
   as select employee_id, email from hr.employees;

grant select on hr.emp_login_map to public;
```

Next, we will create a user account called VPD that has the privileges to create contexts and maintain the policy functions:

```
create user vpd identified by vpd439;
grant connect, resource, create any context, create public synonym to vpd;
```

Connecting to the VPD schema, we will create a context called HR_SECURITY and define the package and procedure used to set the context for the application:

```
connect vpd/vpd439@dw;

create context hr_security using vpd.emp_access;

create or replace package vpd.emp_access as
    procedure set_security_parameters;
end;
```

Remember that the procedures in the package VPD.EMP_ACCESS are the only procedures that can set the context variables. The package body for VPD.EMP_ACCESS follows:

```
create or replace package body vpd.emp_access is

--
-- At user login, run set_security_parameters to
-- retrieve the user login name, which corresponds to the EMAIL
-- column in the table HR.EMPLOYEES.

--
-- context USERENV is pre-defined for user characteristics such
-- as username, IP address from which the connection is made,
-- and so forth.
--
-- for this procedure, we are only using SESSION_USER
-- from the USERENV context.
--

   procedure set_security_parameters is
      emp_id_num      number;
```

```
      emp_login        varchar2(50);
   begin

      -- database username corresponds to email address in HR.EMPLOYEES
      emp_login := sys_context('USERENV','SESSION_USER');

      dbms_session.set_context('HR_SECURITY','USERNAME',emp_login);

      -- get employee id number, so manager rights can be established
      -- but don't restrict access for other DB users who are not in the
      -- EMPLOYEES table
      begin
         select employee_id into emp_id_num
            from hr.emp_login_map where login_acct = emp_login;

         dbms_session.set_context('HR_SECURITY','EMP_ID',emp_id_num);
      exception
         when no_data_found then
            dbms_session.set_context('HR_SECURITY','EMP_ID',0);
      end;

      -- Future queries will restrict rows based on emp_id

   end; -- procedure

end; -- package body
```

A few things are worth noting about this procedure. We retrieve the user's schema by looking in the USERENV context, which is enabled by default for all users, and assigning it to the variable USERNAME in the newly created context HR_SECURITY. The other HR_SECURITY context variable EMP_ID is determined by doing a lookup in the mapping table HR.EMP_LOGIN_MAP. We don't want the procedure to terminate with an error if the logged-in user is not in the mapping table; instead, we assign an EMP_ID of 0, which will result in no access to the table HR.EMPLOYEES when the predicate is generated in the policy function.

In the next steps, we grant everyone in the database EXECUTE privileges on the package, and we create a synonym for it to save a few keystrokes any time we need to call it:

```
grant execute on vpd.emp_access to PUBLIC;
create public synonym emp_access for vpd.emp_access;
```

To ensure that the context is defined for each user when they log on, we will connect as SYSTEM and create a logon trigger to set up the variables in the context:

```
connect system/nolongermanager@dw as sysdba;

create or replace trigger vpd.set_security_parameters
   after logon on database
begin
   vpd.emp_access.set_security_parameters;
end;
```

Because this trigger is fired for every user who connects to the database, it is vitally important that the code be tested for every class of user, if not every user in the database! If the trigger fails with an error, regular users cannot log in.

So far, we have our context defined, the procedure used to set up the context variables, and a trigger that automatically calls the procedure. Logging in as one of our three users defined previously, we can query the contents of the context:

```
SQL> connect smavris/smavris702@dw
Connected.

SQL> select * from session_context;

NAMESPACE                ATTRIBUTE                 VALUE
------------------------ ------------------------- --------------------
HR_SECURITY              USERNAME                  SMAVRIS
HR_SECURITY              EMP_ID                    203

2 rows selected.
```

Notice what happens when SMAVRIS tries to impersonate another employee:

```
SQL> begin
  2     dbms_session.set_context('HR_SECURITY','EMP_ID',100);
  3  end;

begin
*
ERROR at line 1:
ORA-01031: insufficient privileges
ORA-06512: at "SYS.DBMS_SESSION", line 94
ORA-06512: at line 2
```

Only the package VPD.EMP_ACCESS is allowed to set or change variables in the context.

The final steps include defining the procedures that will generate the predicate and assigning one or more of these procedures to the HR.EMPLOYEES table. As the user VPD, which already owns the context procedures, we'll set up the package that determines the predicates:

```
connect vpd/vpd439@dw;

create or replace package vpd.get_predicates as

   -- note -- security function ALWAYS has two parameters,
   -- table owner name and table name

   function emp_select_restrict
       (owner varchar2, object_name varchar2) return varchar2;

   -- other functions can be written here for INSERT, DELETE, and so forth.

end get_predicates;
```

```
create or replace package body vpd.get_predicates is

   function emp_select_restrict
      (owner varchar2, object_name varchar2) return varchar2 is

      ret_predicate    varchar2(1000);  -- part of WHERE clause

   begin
      -- only allow employee to see their row or immediate subordinates
      ret_predicate := 'EMPLOYEE_ID = ' ||
                          sys_context('HR_SECURITY','EMP_ID') ||
                          ' OR MANAGER_ID = ' ||
                          sys_context('HR_SECURITY','EMP_ID');
      return ret_predicate;
   end emp_select_restrict;

end; -- package body
```

Once we attach the function to a table with DBMS_RLS, it will generate a text string that can be used in a WHERE clause every time the table is accessed. The string will always look something like this:

```
EMPLOYEE_ID = 124 OR MANAGER_ID = 124
```

As with the packages that set up the context environment, we need to allow users access to this package:

```
grant execute on vpd.get_predicates to PUBLIC;
create public synonym get_predicates for vpd.get_predicates;
```

Last, but certainly not least, we will attach the policy function to the table using the DBMS_RLS.ADD_POLICY procedure (run by the SYS user):

```
dbms_rls.add_policy (
        object_schema =>    'HR',
        object_name =>      'EMPLOYEES',
        policy_name =>      'EMP_SELECT_RESTRICT',
        function_schema => 'VPD',
        policy_function => 'get_predicates.emp_select_restrict',
        statement_types => 'SELECT',
        update_check =>     TRUE,
        enable =>           TRUE
);
```

An employee can access the HR.EMPLOYEES table as before, but they will only see their row and the rows of the employees who work for them, if any. Logging in as KMOURGOS, we try to retrieve all the rows of the HR.EMPLOYEES table, but we only see KMOURGOS and the employees who report directly to him:

```
SQL> connect kmourgos/kmourgos622@dw;
Connected.
```

```
SQL> select employee_id, first_name, last_name,
  2         email, job_id, salary, manager_id from hr.employees;

EMPLOYEE_ID FIRST_NAME LAST_NAME   EMAIL      JOB_ID      SALARY MANAGER_ID
----------- ---------- ----------- ---------- ---------- ------- ----------
        124 Kevin      Mourgos     KMOURGOS   ST_MAN        5800        100
        141 Trenna     Rajs        TRAJS      ST_CLERK      3500        124
        142 Curtis     Davies      CDAVIES    ST_CLERK      3100        124
        143 Randall    Matos       RMATOS     ST_CLERK      2600        124
        144 Peter      Vargas      PVARGAS    ST_CLERK      2500        124
        196 Alana      Walsh       AWALSH     SH_CLERK      3100        124
        197 Kevin      Feeney      KFEENEY    SH_CLERK      3000        124
        198 Donald     OConnell    DOCONNEL   SH_CLERK      2600        124
        199 Douglas    Grant       DGRANT     SH_CLERK      2600        124

9 rows selected.
```

For the user DGRANT, it's a different story:

```
SQL> connect dgrant/dgrant507@dw;
Connected.
SQL> select employee_id, first_name, last_name,
  2         email, job_id, salary, manager_id from hr.employees;

EMPLOYEE_ID FIRST_NAME LAST_NAME   EMAIL      JOB_ID      SALARY MANAGER_ID
----------- ---------- ----------- ---------- ---------- ------- ----------
        199 Douglas    Grant       DGRANT     SH_CLERK      2600        124

1 row selected.
```

DGRANT gets to see only his own row, because he does not manage anyone else in the company.

In the case of SMAVRIS, we see similar results from the query:

```
SQL> connect smavris/smavris702@dw;
Connected.
SQL> select employee_id, first_name, last_name,
  2         email, job_id, salary, manager_id from hr.employees;

EMPLOYEE_ID FIRST_NAME LAST_NAME    EMAIL      JOB_ID      SALARY MANAGER_ID
----------- ---------- ------------ ---------- ---------- ------- ----------
        203 Susan      Mavris       SMAVRIS    HR_REP        6500        101

1 row selected.
```

But wait, SMAVRIS is in the HR department and should be able to see *all* rows from the table. In addition, SMAVRIS should be the only person to see the salary information for all employees. As a result, we need to change our policy function to give SMAVRIS and other employees in the HR department full access to the HR.EMPLOYEES table; in addition, we can use column-level restrictions in the policy assignment to return the same number of rows, but with the sensitive data returned as NULL values.

To facilitate access to the HR.EMPLOYEES table by HR department employees, we first need to change our mapping table to include the JOB_ID column. If the JOB_ID column has a value of HR_REP, the employee is in the HR department. We will first disable the policy in effect and create the new mapping table:

```
SQL> begin
    dbms_rls.enable_policy(
          object_schema =>    'HR',
          object_name =>      'EMPLOYEES',
          policy_name =>      'EMP_SELECT_RESTRICT',
          enable =>           FALSE
       );
  end;
  /
PL/SQL procedure successfully completed.

SQL> drop table hr.emp_login_map;
Table dropped.

SQL> create table hr.emp_login_map (employee_id, login_acct, job_id)
    as select employee_id, email, job_id from hr.employees;
Table created.
```

```
SQL> grant select on hr.emp_login_map to public;
Grant succeeded.
```

The procedure we're using to set up the context variables, VPD.EMP_ACCESS, needs another context variable added that indicates the security level of the user accessing the table. We will change the SELECT statement and make another call to DBMS_SESSION.SET_CONTEXT, as follows:

```
. . .
    emp_job_id      varchar2(50);
. . .
        select employee_id, job_id into emp_id_num, emp_job_id
           from hr.emp_login_map where login_acct = emp_login;

        dbms_session.set_context('HR_SECURITY','SEC_LEVEL',
            case emp_job_id when 'HR_REP' then 'HIGH' else 'NORMAL' end );
. . .
```

Whenever the employee has a job title of HR_REP, the context variable SEC_LEVEL is set to HIGH instead of NORMAL. In our policy function, we need to check for this new condition as follows:

```
create or replace package body vpd.get_predicates is

   function emp_select_restrict
      (owner varchar2, object_name varchar2) return varchar2 is

      ret_predicate    varchar2(1000);  -- part of WHERE clause
```

```
    begin
       -- only allow employee to see their row or immediate subordinates,
       -- unless they have high security clearance
       if sys_context('HR_SECURITY','SEC_LEVEL') = 'HIGH' then
          ret_predicate := '';  -- no restrictions in WHERE clause
       else
          ret_predicate := 'EMPLOYEE_ID = ' ||
                           sys_context('HR_SECURITY','EMP_ID') ||
                           ' OR MANAGER_ID = ' ||
                           sys_context('HR_SECURITY','EMP_ID');
       end if;
       return ret_predicate;
    end emp_select_restrict;

end; -- package body
```

Because the policy is dynamic, the predicate is generated each time a SELECT statement is executed, so we don't have to do a policy refresh. When the user SMAVRIS, the HR representative, runs the query now, she sees all rows in the HR.EMPLOYEES table:

```
SQL> connect smavris/smavris702@dw;
Connected.
SQL> select employee_id, first_name, last_name,
  2          email, job_id, salary, manager_id from hr.employees;

EMPLOYEE_ID FIRST_NAME  LAST_NAME   EMAIL      JOB_ID       SALARY MANAGER_ID
----------- ----------- ----------- ---------- ---------- -------- ----------
        100 Steven      King        KLYNNE      AD_PRES      24000
        101 Neena       Kochhar     NKOCHHAR   AD_VP        17000        100
. . .
        204 Hermann     Baer        HBAER      PR_REP       10000        101
        205 Shelley     Higgins     SHIGGINS   AC_MGR       12000        101
        206 William     Gietz       WGIETZ     AC_ACCOUNT    8300        205

107 rows selected.
```

As you might expect, SMAVRIS's security level within the HR_SECURITY context is HIGH:

```
SQL> connect smavris/smavris702
Connected.

SQL> select sys_context('HR_SECURITY','SEC_LEVEL') from dual;

SYS_CONTEXT('HR_SECURITY','SEC_LEVEL')
--------------------------------------------------------------
HIGH

SQL>
```

However, DGRANT can still only see his row in the table because his security level within the HR_SECURITY context is NORMAL:

```
SQL> connect dgrant/dgrant507@dw;
Connected.

SQL> select employee_id, first_name, last_name,
  2         email, job_id, salary, manager_id from hr.employees;

EMPLOYEE_ID FIRST_NAME LAST_NAME   EMAIL      JOB_ID      SALARY MANAGER_ID
----------- ---------- ----------- ---------- ---------- ------- ----------
        199 Douglas    Grant       DGRANT     SH_CLERK      2600        124

1 row selected.

SQL> select sys_context('HR_SECURITY','SEC_LEVEL') from dual;

SYS_CONTEXT('HR_SECURITY','SEC_LEVEL')
----------------------------------------------------------------
NORMAL
```

To enforce the requirement that only HR employees can see salary information, we would need to make a slight change to the policy function and enable the policy with column-level restrictions. First, drop the current policy before creating the new one:

```
DBMS_RLS.DROP_POLICY (
         object_schema =>   'HR',
         object_name =>     'EMPLOYEES',
         policy_name =>     'EMP_SELECT_RESTRICT');

dbms_rls.add_policy (
         object_schema =>   'HR',
         object_name =>     'EMPLOYEES',
         policy_name =>     'EMP_SELECT_RESTRICT',
         function_schema => 'VPD',
         policy_function => 'get_predicates.emp_select_restrict',
         statement_types => 'SELECT',
         update_check =>    TRUE,
         enable =>          TRUE,
         sec_relevant_cols => 'SALARY',
         sec_relevant_cols_opt => dbms_rls.all_rows
);
```

The last parameter, SEC_RELEVANT_COLS_OPT, specifies the package constant DBMS_RLS.ALL_ROWS to indicate that we still want to see all rows in our query results, but with the relevant columns (in this case SALARY) returning NULL values. Otherwise, we would not see any rows from queries that contain the SALARY column.

Debugging a VPD Policy

Even if you're not getting an "ORA-28113: policy predicate has error" or an "ORA-00936: missing expression," it can be very useful to see the actual predicate being generated at statement parse time. There are a couple of ways to debug your predicates, and both have their advantages and disadvantages.

The first method uses the dynamic performance views V$SQLAREA and V$VPD_POLICY. As the names imply, V$SQLAREA contains the SQL statements currently in the shared pool, along with current execution statistics. The view V$VPD_POLICY lists all the policies currently being enforced in the database, along with the predicate. Joining the two tables, as in the following example, gives us the information we need to help debug any problems we're having with the query results:

```
SQL> select s.sql_text, v.object_name, v.policy, v.predicate
  2      from v$sqlarea s, v$vpd_policy v
  3      where s.hash_value = v.sql_hash;

SQL_TEXT                  OBJECT_NAM POLICY             PREDICATE
------------------------- ---------- ------------------ ------------------
select employee_id, first EMPLOYEES  EMP_SELECT_RESTRICT EMPLOYEE_ID = 199
_name, last_name, email,                                OR MANAGER_ID = 199
job_id, salary, manager_i
d from hr.employees

select employee_id, first EMPLOYEES  EMP_SELECT_RESTRICT
_name, last_name, email,
job_id, salary, manager_i
d from hr.employees

SQL>
```

If we add a join to V$SESSION in this query, we can identify which user was running the SQL. This is especially important in the second SQL statement: there is no predicate applied to the SQL statement; therefore, all we can infer is that one of the HR employees ran the query. There is a downside to this method: If the database is extremely busy, the SQL commands may be flushed from the shared pool for other SQL commands before you get a chance to run this query.

The other method uses the ALTER SESSION command to generate a plain-text trace file containing much of the information from the previous query. Here are the commands to set up tracing:

```
SQL> begin
  2      dbms_rls.refresh_policy;
  3  end;
  4  /
PL/SQL procedure successfully completed.

SQL> alter session set events '10730 trace name context forever, level 12';
Session altered.
```

Event 10730 is defined for tracing RLS policy predicates. Other common events that can be traced are 10029 and 10030 for session logon/logoff, 10710 to trace bitmap index access, and

10253 for simulating write errors to the redo log, among others. Once the session is altered, the user DGRANT runs his query:

```
SQL> select employee_id, first_name, last_name,
  2        email, job_id, salary, manager_id from hr.employees;

EMPLOYEE_ID FIRST_NAME  LAST_NAME   EMAIL      JOB_ID      SALARY MANAGER_ID
----------- ----------- ----------- ---------- ---------- ------- ----------
        199 Douglas     Grant       DGRANT     SH_CLERK      2600        124

1 row selected.
```

Here's a look at the bottom part of the trace file located in the directory specified by the initialization parameter DIAGNOSTIC_DEST in Oracle Database 11*g* and 12*c*, USER_DUMP_DEST in Oracle Database 10*g* and earlier.

```
Trace file
/u01/app/oracle/diag/rdbms/dw/dw/trace/dw_ora_31128.trc
Oracle Database 12c Enterprise Edition
                   Release 12.1.0.2.0 - Production
With the Partitioning, OLAP, Data Mining and
                   Real Application Testing options
ORACLE_HOME = /u01/app/oracle/product/12.1.0.2/db_1
System name:    Linux
Node name:      dw
Release:        2.6.9-55.0.2.0.1.EL
Version:        #1 Mon Jun 25 14:24:38 PDT 2014
Machine:        i686
Instance name: dw
Redo thread mounted by this instance: 1
Oracle process number: 40
Unix process pid: 31128, image: oracle@dw (TNS V1-V3)

*** 2014-08-12 12:48:37.852
*** SESSION ID:(120.9389) 2014-08-12 12:48:37.852
*** CLIENT ID:() 2014-08-12 12:48:37.852
*** SERVICE NAME:(SYS$USERS) 2014-08-12 12:48:37.852
*** MODULE NAME:(SQL*Plus) 2014-08-12 12:48:37.852
*** ACTION NAME:() 2014-08-12 12:48:37.852

-------------------------------------------------------------
Logon user      : DGRANT
Table/View      : HR.EMPLOYEES
Policy name     : EMP_SELECT_RESTRICT
Policy function: VPD.GET_PREDICATES.EMP_SELECT_RESTRICT
RLS view :
SELECT  "EMPLOYEE_ID","FIRST_NAME","LAST_NAME",
"EMAIL","PHONE_NUMBER",
"HIRE_DATE","JOB_ID","SALARY","COMMISSION_PCT","MANAGER_ID",
"DEPARTMENT_ID" FROM "HR"."EMPLOYEES"
"EMPLOYEES" WHERE (EMPLOYEE_ID = 199 OR MANAGER_ID = 199)
-------------------------------------------------------------
```

The user's original SQL statement plus the appended predicate are clearly shown in the trace file. The downside to using this method is that while a user may be able to access dynamic performance views, a developer might not normally have access to the user dump directory on the server itself. As a result, the DBA may need to be involved when trying to debug predicate problems.

Be sure to turn off tracing when you're done debugging to reduce the overhead and disk space associated with tracing operations (or just log off!):

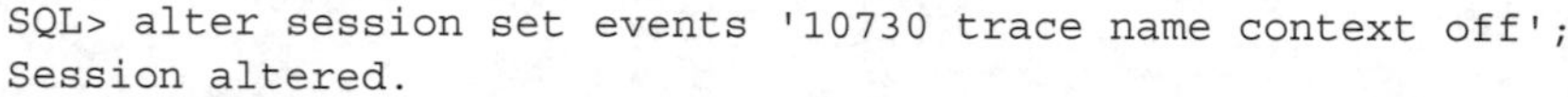

```
SQL> alter session set events '10730 trace name context off';
Session altered.
```

Auditing

Oracle uses a number of different auditing methods to monitor what kinds of privileges are being used as well as what objects are being accessed. Auditing does not prevent the use of these privileges, but it can provide useful information to uncover abuse or misuse of privileges.

Table 10-15 summarizes the different types of auditing in an Oracle database.

In the next few sections, we'll review how a DBA can manage audits of both system and object privilege use. When the granularity is required, a DBA can use fine-grained auditing to monitor access to certain rows or columns of a table, not just whether the table was accessed.

Auditing Locations

Audit records can be sent to either the SYS.AUD$ database table or an operating system file. To enable auditing and specify the location where audit records are recorded, the initialization parameter AUDIT_TRAIL is set to one of the following values:

Parameter Value	Action
NONE, FALSE	Disable auditing.
OS	Enable auditing. Send audit records to an operating system file.
DB, TRUE	Enable auditing. Send audit records to the SYS.AUD$ table.
DB_EXTENDED	Enable auditing. Send audit records to the SYS.AUD$ table, and record additional information in the CLOB columns SQLBIND and SQLTEXT.
XML	Enable auditing and write all audit records in XML format.
EXTENDED	Enable auditing and record all columns in the audit trail, including SQLTEXT and SQLBIND values.

The parameter AUDIT_TRAIL is not dynamic; the database must be shut down and restarted for a change in the AUDIT_TRAIL parameter to take effect. When auditing to the SYS.AUD$ table, the size of the table should be carefully monitored so as not to impact the space requirements for other objects in the SYS tablespace. It is recommended that the rows in SYS.AUD$ be periodically archived and the table truncated. Oracle provides the role DELETE_CATALOG_ROLE to use with a special account in a batch job to archive and truncate the audit table.

Auditing Type	Description
Statement auditing	Audits SQL statements by the type of statement regardless of the specific schema objects being accessed. One or more users can also be specified in the database to be audited for a particular statement.
Privilege auditing	Audits system privileges, such as CREATE TABLE or ALTER INDEX. As with statement auditing, privilege auditing can specify one or more particular users as the target of the audit.
Schema object auditing	Audits specific statements operating on a specific schema object (for example, UPDATE statements on the DEPARTMENTS table). Schema object auditing always applies to all users in the database.
Fine-grained auditing	Audits table access and privileges based on the content of the objects being accessed. Uses the package DBMS_FGA to set up a policy on a particular table.

TABLE 10-15. *Auditing Types*

As of Oracle Database 12*c*, system security administration is simplified by a unified audit data trail. In previous releases, you would have to go to each of the following tables to get audit information:

- **SYS.AUD$** Database audit trail
- **SYS.FGA_LOG$** Fine-grained auditing
- **DVSYS.AUDIT_TRAIL$** Database Vault audit trail

The new unified audit trail is named, not surprisingly, UNIFIED_AUDIT_TRAIL. This new audit trail has its own schema as well: the AUDSYS schema is used exclusively for the unified audit trail. In addition, two new roles, AUDIT_ADMIN and AUDIT_VIEWER, further refine separation of duties.

```
SQL> describe unified_audit_trail
 Name                                      Null?    Type
 ----------------------------------------- -------- ---------------------------
--
 AUDIT_TYPE                                         VARCHAR2(64)
 SESSIONID                                          NUMBER
 PROXY_SESSIONID                                    NUMBER
 OS_USERNAME                                        VARCHAR2(30)
 USERHOST                                           VARCHAR2(128)
 TERMINAL                                           VARCHAR2(30)
 INSTANCE_ID                                        NUMBER
 DBID                                               NUMBER
 AUTHENTICATION_TYPE                                VARCHAR2(1024)
 DBUSERNAME                                         VARCHAR2(30)
. . .
RMAN_OPERATION                                     VARCHAR2(20)
 RMAN_OBJECT_TYPE                                   VARCHAR2(20)
```

```
 RMAN_DEVICE_TYPE                                  VARCHAR2(5)
 DP_TEXT_PARAMETERS1                               VARCHAR2(512)
 DP_BOOLEAN_PARAMETERS1                            VARCHAR2(512)
 DIRECT_PATH_NUM_COLUMNS_LOADED                    NUMBER
SQL>
```

The columns in UNIFIED_AUDIT_TRAIL are much what you'd expect as an amalgam of the existing individual audit tables. There is no CON_ID column as you might see for a data dictionary view in a multitenant environment; however, auditing-related procedures such as DBMS_AUDIT_MGMT.CLEAN_AUDIT_TRAIL and FLUSH_UNIFIED_AUDIT_TRAIL let you specify a single container or all containers when operating on the audit trail rows.

Statement Auditing

All types of auditing use the AUDIT command to turn on auditing and NOAUDIT to turn off auditing. For statement auditing, the format of the AUDIT command looks something like the following:

```
AUDIT sql_statement_clause BY {SESSION | ACCESS}
    WHENEVER [NOT] SUCCESSFUL;
```

The ***sql_statement_clause*** contains a number of different pieces of information, such as the type of SQL statement we want to audit and who we are auditing.

In addition, we want to either audit the action every time it happens (BY ACCESS) or only once (BY SESSION). The default is BY SESSION.

Sometimes we want to audit successful actions—statements that did not generate an error message. For these statements, we add WHENEVER SUCCESSFUL. Other times we only care if the commands using the audited statements fail, either due to privilege violations, running out of space in the tablespace, or syntax errors. For these we use WHENEVER NOT SUCCESSFUL.

For most categories of auditing methods, we can specify ALL instead of individual statement types or objects if we truly want all types of access to a table or any privileges by a certain user to be audited.

The types of statements we can audit, with a brief description of what statements are covered in each category, are listed in Table 10-16. If ALL is specified, any statement in this list is audited. However, the types of statements in Table 10-17 do not fall into the ALL category when enabling auditing; they must be explicitly specified in any AUDIT commands.

Some examples will help make all these options a lot clearer. In our sample database, the user KLYNNE has privileges on all of the tables in the HR schema and other schemas. KLYNNE is allowed to create indexes on some of these tables, but we want to know when the indexes are created in case we have some performance issues related to execution plans changing. We can audit index creation by KSHELTON with the following command:

```
SQL> audit index by klynne;
Audit succeeded.
```

Later that day, KLYNNE creates an index on the HR.JOBS table:

```
SQL> create index job_title_idx on hr.jobs(job_title);
Index created.
```

Statement Option	SQL Operations
ALTER SYSTEM	All ALTER SYSTEM options such as dynamically altering instance parameters, switching to the next log file group, and terminating user sessions.
CLUSTER	CREATE, ALTER, DROP, or TRUNCATE a cluster.
CONTEXT	CREATE or DROP a CONTEXT.
DATABASE LINK	CREATE or DROP a database link.
DIMENSION	CREATE, ALTER, or DROP a dimension.
DIRECTORY	CREATE or DROP a directory object.
INDEX	CREATE, ALTER, or DROP an index.
MATERIALIZED VIEW	CREATE, ALTER, or DROP a materialized view.
NOT EXISTS	Failure of SQL statement due to nonexistent referenced objects.
PROCEDURE	CREATE or DROP FUNCTION, LIBRARY, PACKAGE, PACKAGE BODY, or PROCEDURE.
PROFILE	CREATE, ALTER, or DROP a profile.
PUBLIC DATABASE LINK	CREATE or DROP a public database link.
PUBLIC SYNONYM	CREATE or DROP a public synonym.
ROLE	CREATE, ALTER, DROP, or SET a role.
ROLLBACK SEGMENT	CREATE, ALTER, or DROP a rollback segment.
SEQUENCE	CREATE or DROP a sequence.
SESSION	Logons and logoffs.
SYNONYM	CREATE or DROP synonyms.
SYSTEM AUDIT	AUDIT or NOAUDIT of system privileges.
SYSTEM GRANT	GRANT or REVOKE system privileges and roles.
TABLE	CREATE, DROP, or TRUNCATE a table.
TABLESPACE	CREATE, ALTER, or DROP a tablespace.
TRIGGER	CREATE, ALTER (enable/disable), DROP triggers; ALTER TABLE with either ENABLE ALL TRIGGERS or DISABLE ALL TRIGGERS.
TYPE	CREATE, ALTER, and DROP types and type bodies.
USER	CREATE, ALTER, or DROP a user.
VIEW	CREATE or DROP a view.

TABLE 10-16. *Auditable Statements Included in the ALL Category*

Statement Option	SQL Operations
ALTER SEQUENCE	Any ALTER SEQUENCE command.
ALTER TABLE	Any ALTER TABLE command.
COMMENT TABLE	Add a comment to a table, view, materialized view, or any of their columns.
DELETE TABLE	Delete rows from a table or view.
EXECUTE PROCEDURE	Execute a procedure, function, or any variables or cursors within a package.
GRANT DIRECTORY	GRANT or REVOKE a privilege on a DIRECTORY object.
GRANT PROCEDURE	GRANT or REVOKE a privilege on a procedure, function, or package.
GRANT SEQUENCE	GRANT or REVOKE a privilege on a sequence.
GRANT TABLE	GRANT or REVOKE a privilege on a table, view, or materialized view.
GRANT TYPE	GRANT or REVOKE a privilege on a TYPE.
INSERT TABLE	INSERT INTO a table or view.
LOCK TABLE	LOCK TABLE command on a table or view.
SELECT SEQUENCE	Any command referencing the sequence's CURRVAL or NEXTVAL.
SELECT TABLE	SELECT FROM a table, view, or materialized view.
UPDATE TABLE	Execute UPDATE on a table or view.

TABLE 10-17. *Explicitly Specified Statement Types*

Checking the audit trail in the data dictionary view DBA_AUDIT_TRAIL, we see that KSHELTON did indeed create an index at 5:15 P.M. on August 12th:

```
SQL> select username, to_char(timestamp,'MM/DD/YY HH24:MI') Timestamp,
  2       obj_name, action_name, sql_text from dba_audit_trail
  3  where username = 'KLYNNE';

USERNAME   TIMESTAMP      OBJ_NAME         ACTION_NAME      SQL_TEXT
---------- -------------- ---------------- ---------------- ----------------
KSHELTON   08/12/14 17:15 JOB_TITLE_IDX    CREATE INDEX     create index hr.
                                                            job_title_idx on
                                                            hr.jobs(job_title)

1 row selected.
```

NOTE
Starting with Oracle Database 11g, the columns SQL_TEXT and SQL_BIND in DBA_AUDIT_TRAIL are populated only if the initialization parameter AUDIT_TRAIL is set to DB_EXTENDED. By default, the value of AUDIT_TRAIL is DB.

To turn off auditing for KLYNNE on the HR.JOBS table, we use the NOAUDIT command, as follows:

```
SQL> noaudit index by klynne;
Noaudit succeeded.
```

We also may wish to routinely audit both successful and unsuccessful logins. This requires two AUDIT commands:

```
SQL> audit session whenever successful;
Audit succeeded.
SQL> audit session whenever not successful;
Audit succeeded.
```

Reviewing the audit trail reveals one failed login attempt by the user RJB on August 10th:

```
SQL> select username, to_char(timestamp,'MM/DD/YY HH24:MI') Timestamp,
  2       obj_name, returncode, action_name, sql_text from dba_audit_trail
  3  where action_name in ('LOGON','LOGOFF')
  4       and username in ('SCOTT','RJB','KLYNNE')
  5  order by timestamp desc;

USERNAME   TIMESTAMP      OBJ_NAME   RETURNCODE ACTION_NAME      SQL_TEXT
---------- -------------- ---------- ---------- ---------------- ----------
KSHELTON   08/12/14 17:04                     0 LOGON
SCOTT      08/12/14 16:10                     0 LOGOFF
RJB        08/12/14 11:35                     0 LOGON
RJB        08/12/14 11:35                     0 LOGON
RJB        08/11/14 22:51                     0 LOGON
RJB        08/11/14 22:51                     0 LOGOFF
RJB        08/11/14 21:55                     0 LOGOFF
RJB        08/11/14 21:40                     0 LOGOFF
RJB        08/10/14 22:52                     0 LOGOFF
RJB        08/10/14 22:52                     0 LOGOFF
RJB        08/10/14 22:52                  1017 LOGON
RJB        08/10/14 12:23                     0 LOGOFF
SCOTT      08/03/14 04:18                     0 LOGOFF

13 rows selected.
```

The RETURNCODE represents the ORA error message. An ORA-1017 message indicates that an incorrect password was entered. Note that if we are just interested in logons and logoffs, we could use the DBA_AUDIT_SESSION view instead.

Statement auditing also includes startup and shutdown operations. Although we can audit the command SHUTDOWN IMMEDIATE in the SYS.AUD$ table, it is not possible to audit the startup command in SYS.AUD$ because the database has to be started before rows can be added to this table. For these cases, we can look in the directory specified in the initialization parameter AUDIT_FILE_DEST to see a record of a startup operation performed by a system administrator (by default this parameter contains **$ORACLE_HOME/admin/dw/adump**). Here is a text file created when the database was started with the startup command:

```
Oracle Database 12c Enterprise Edition Release 12.1.0.2.0 - Production
With the Partitioning, OLAP, Data Mining
                       and Real Application Testing options
ORACLE_HOME = /u01/app/oracle/product/12.1.0/db_1
System name:    Linux
Node name:      dw
Release:        2.6.9-55.0.2.0.1.EL
Version:        #1 Mon Jun 25 14:24:38 PDT 2014
Machine:        i686
Instance name: dw
Redo thread mounted by this instance: 1
Oracle process number: 44
Unix process pid: 28962, image: oracle@dw (TNS V1-V3)

Sun Aug 12 11:57:36 2014
ACTION : 'CONNECT'
DATABASE USER: '/'
PRIVILEGE : SYSDBA
CLIENT USER: oracle
CLIENT TERMINAL: pts/2
STATUS: 0
```

In this example, the database was started by a user connected as **oracle** on the host system and connected to the instance with operating system authentication. We will cover additional system administrator auditing issues in the next section.

Privilege Auditing

Auditing system privileges has the same basic syntax as statement auditing, except that system privileges are specified in the ***sql_statement_clause*** instead of statements.

For example, we may wish to grant the ALTER TABLESPACE privilege to all our DBAs, but we want to generate an audit record when this happens. The command to enable auditing on this privilege looks similar to statement auditing:

```
SQL> audit alter tablespace by access whenever successful;
Audit succeeded.
```

Every time the ALTER TABLESPACE privilege is successfully used, a row is added to SYS.AUD$.

Special auditing is available for system administrators who use the SYSDBA and SYSOPER privileges or connect with the SYS user. To enable this extra level of auditing, set the initialization parameter AUDIT_SYS_OPERATIONS to TRUE. The audit records are sent to the same location as the operating system audit records; therefore, this location is operating system dependent. All SQL statements executed while using one of these privileges, as well as any SQL statements executed as the user SYS, are sent to the operating system audit location.

Object Option	Description
ALTER	Alters a table, sequence, or materialized view
AUDIT	Audits commands on any object
COMMENT	Adds comments to tables, views, or materialized views
DELETE	Deletes rows from a table, view, or materialized view
EXECUTE	Executes a procedure, function, or package
FLASHBACK	Performs flashback operation on a table or view
GRANT	Grants privileges on any type of object
INDEX	Creates an index on a table or materialized view
INSERT	Inserts rows into a table, view, or materialized view
LOCK	Locks a table, view, or materialized view
READ	Performs a read operation on the contents of a DIRECTORY object
RENAME	Renames a table, view, or procedure
SELECT	Selects rows from a table, view, sequence, or materialized view
UPDATE	Updates a table, view, or materialized view

TABLE 10-18. *Object Auditing Options*

Schema Object Auditing

Auditing access to various schema objects looks similar to statement and privilege auditing:

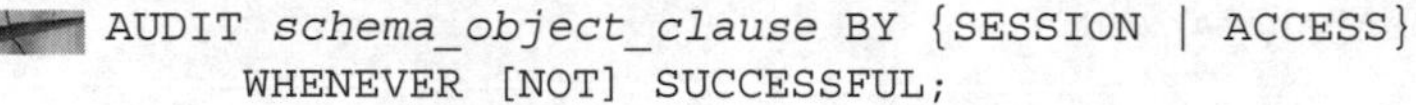

```
AUDIT schema_object_clause BY {SESSION | ACCESS}
   WHENEVER [NOT] SUCCESSFUL;
```

The ***schema_object_clause*** specifies a type of object access and the object being accessed. Fourteen different types of operations on specific objects can be audited; they are listed in Table 10-18.

If we wish to audit all INSERT and UPDATE commands on the HR.JOBS table, regardless of who is doing the update, and every time the action occurs, we can use the AUDIT command as follows:

```
SQL> audit insert, update on hr.jobs by access whenever successful;
Audit successful.
```

The user KLYNNE decides to add two new rows to the HR.JOBS table:

```
SQL> insert into hr.jobs (job_id, job_title, min_salary, max_salary)
  2  values ('IN_CFO','Internet Chief Fun Officer', 7500, 50000);
1 row created.

SQL> insert into hr.jobs (job_id, job_title, min_salary, max_salary)
```

```
  2  values ('OE_VLD','Order Entry CC Validation', 5500, 20000);
1 row created.
```

Looking in the DBA_AUDIT_TRAIL view, we see the two INSERT commands in KLYNNE's session:

```
USERNAME   TIMESTAMP      OWNER    OBJ_NAME   ACTION_NAME
SQL_TEXT
---------- -------------- -------- ---------- ---------------
---------------------------------------------------------------------
KLYNNE     08/12/14 22:54 HR       JOBS       INSERT
insert into hr.jobs (job_id, job_title, min_salary, max_salary)
 values ('IN_CFO','Internet Chief Fun Officer', 7500, 50000);
KSHELTON   08/12/14 22:53 HR       JOBS       INSERT
insert into hr.jobs (job_id, job_title, min_salary, max_salary)
 values ('OE_VLD','Order Entry CC Validation', 5500, 20000);
KSHELTON   08/12/14 22:51                     LOGON

3 rows selected.
```

Fine-Grained Auditing

Introduced in Oracle9*i,* auditing became much more focused and precise with the introduction of fine-grained object auditing, or FGA. FGA is implemented by a PL/SQL package called DBMS_FGA.

With standard auditing, you can easily find out what objects were accessed and by whom, but you don't know which columns or rows were accessed. Fine-grained auditing addresses this problem by not only specifying a predicate, or WHERE clause, for which rows need to be accessed, but also by specifying a column or columns in the table being accessed. This can dramatically reduce the number of audit table entries by only auditing access to the table if it accesses certain rows and columns.

The package DBMS_FGA has four procedures:

- **ADD_POLICY** Adds an audit policy using a predicate and audit column
- **DROP_POLICY** Drops the audit policy
- **DISABLE_POLICY** Disables the audit policy but keeps the policy associated with the table or view
- **ENABLE_POLICY** Enables a policy

The user TAMARA usually accesses the HR.EMPLOYEES table on a daily basis to look up employee e-mail addresses. The system administrators suspect that TAMARA is viewing salary information for managers, so they set up an FGA policy to audit any access to the SALARY column for anyone who is a manager:

```
begin
    dbms_fga.add_policy(
        object_schema =>   'HR',
        object_name =>     'EMPLOYEES',
```

```
         policy_name =>       'SAL_SELECT_AUDIT',
         audit_condition => 'instr(job_id,''_MAN'') > 0',
         audit_column =>      'SALARY'
      );
end;
```

Audit records for fine-grained auditing can be accessed with the data dictionary view DBA_FGA_AUDIT_TRAIL. If you typically need to see both standard audit rows and FGA rows, the data dictionary view DBA_COMMON_AUDIT_TRAIL combines rows from both types of audits.

To continue our example, the user TAMARA runs two SQL queries as follows:

```
SQL> select employee_id, first_name, last_name, email from hr.employees
  2      where employee_id = 114;

EMPLOYEE_ID FIRST_NAME           LAST_NAME                 EMAIL
----------- -------------------- ------------------------- -------------
        114 Den                  Raphaely                  DRAPHEAL

1 row selected.

SQL> select employee_id, first_name, last_name, salary from hr.employees
  2      where employee_id = 114;

EMPLOYEE_ID FIRST_NAME           LAST_NAME                     SALARY
----------- -------------------- ------------------------- ----------
        114 Den                  Raphaely                       11000

1 row selected.
```

The first query accesses a manager, but not the SALARY column. The second query is the same as the first, but does access the SALARY column and therefore triggers the FGA policy, thus generating one, and only one, row in the audit trail:

```
SQL> select to_char(timestamp,'mm/dd/yy hh24:mi') timestamp,
  2     object_schema, object_name, policy_name, statement_type
  3  from dba_fga_audit_trail
  4  where db_user = 'TAMARA';

TIMESTAMP      OBJECT_SCHEMA  OBJECT_NAME   POLICY_NAME      STATEMENT_TYPE
-------------- -------------- ------------- ---------------- --------------
08/12/14 18:07 HR             EMPLOYEES     SAL_SELECT_AUDIT SELECT

1 row selected.
```

Because we set up fine-grained access control in our VPD example earlier in this chapter to prevent unauthorized use of the SALARY column, we need to double-check our policy functions to make sure that SALARY information is still being restricted correctly. Fine-grained auditing, along with standard auditing, is a good way to ensure that our authorization policies are set up correctly in the first place.

Data Dictionary View	Description
AUDIT_ACTIONS	Contains descriptions for audit trail action type codes, such as INSERT, DROP VIEW, DELETE, LOGON, and LOCK.
DBA_AUDIT_OBJECT	Audit trail records related to objects in the database.
DBA_AUDIT_POLICIES	Fine-grained auditing policies in the database.
DBA_AUDIT_SESSION	All audit trail records related to CONNECT and DISCONNECT.
DBA_AUDIT_STATEMENT	Audit trail entries related to GRANT, REVOKE, AUDIT, NOAUDIT, and ALTER SYSTEM commands.
DBA_AUDIT_TRAIL	Contains standard audit trail entries. USER_AUDIT_TRAIL contains audit rows for connected user only.
DBA_FGA_AUDIT_TRAIL	Audit trail entries for fine-grained auditing policies.
DBA_COMMON_AUDIT_TRAIL	Combines standard and fine-grained auditing rows into one view.
DBA_OBJ_AUDIT_OPTS	Auditing options in effect for database objects.
DBA_PRIV_AUDIT_OPTS	Auditing options in effect for system privileges.
DBA_STMT_AUDIT_OPTS	Auditing options in effect for statements.

TABLE 10-19. *Auditing-Related Data Dictionary Views*

Auditing-Related Data Dictionary Views

Table 10-19 contains the data dictionary views related to auditing.

Protecting the Audit Trail

The audit trail itself needs to be protected, especially if non-system users must access the table SYS.AUD$. The built-in role DELETE_ANY_CATALOG is one of the ways that non-SYS users can have access to the audit trail (for example, to archive and truncate the audit trail to ensure that it does not impact the space requirements for other objects in the SYS tablespace).

To set up auditing on the audit trail itself, connect as SYSDBA and run the following command:

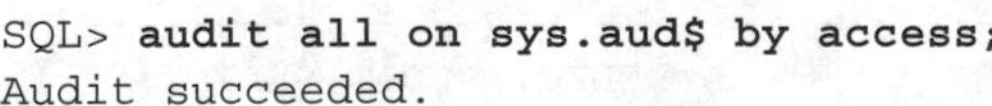

```
SQL> audit all on sys.aud$ by access;
Audit succeeded.
```

Now, all actions against the table SYS.AUD$, including SELECT, INSERT, UPDATE, and DELETE, will be recorded in SYS.AUD$ itself. But, you may ask, what if someone deletes the audit records identifying access to the table SYS.AUD$? The rows in the table are deleted, but then another row is inserted, recording the deletion of the rows. Therefore, there will always be some evidence of activity, intentional or accidental, against the SYS.AUD$ table. In addition, if AUDIT_SYS_OPERATIONS is set to TRUE, any sessions using AS SYSDBA, AS SYSOPER, or connecting as SYS itself will be logged in the operating system audit location, which presumably even the

Oracle DBAs would not have access to. As a result, we have many safeguards in place to ensure that we record all privileged activity in the database, along with any attempts to hide this activity!

Data Encryption Techniques

Data encryption can enhance security both inside and outside the database. A user may have a legitimate need for access to most columns of a table, but if one of the columns is encrypted and the user does not know the encryption key, the information is not usable. The same concern is true for information that needs to be sent securely over a network. The techniques I presented so far in this chapter, including authentication, authorization, and auditing, ensure legitimate access to data from a database user but do not prevent access to an operating system user that may have access to the operating system files that compose the database itself.

Users can leverage one of two methods for data encryption: using the package DBMS_CRYPTO, an Oracle Database 10*g* replacement for the package DBMS_OBFUSCATION_TOOLKIT found in Oracle9*i*, and transparent data encryption, which stores encryption keys globally and includes methods for encrypting entire tablespaces.

DBMS_CRYPTO Package

Introduced in Oracle 10*g*, the package DBMS_CRYPTO replaces DBMS_OBFUSCATION_TOOLKIT and includes the Advanced Encryption Standard (AES) encryption algorithm, which replaces the Data Encryption Standard (DES).

Procedures within DBMS_CRYPTO can generate private keys for you, or you can specify and store the key yourself. In contrast to DBMS_OBFUSCATION_TOOLKIT, which could only encrypt RAW or VARCHAR2 datatypes, DBMS_CRYPTO can encrypt BLOB and CLOB types.

Transparent Data Encryption

Transparent data encryption is a key-based access control system that relies on an external module for enforcing authorization. Each table with encrypted columns has its own encryption key, which in turn is encrypted by a master key created for the database and stored encrypted within the database; the master key is not stored in the database itself. The emphasis is on the word *transparent*—authorized users do not have to specify passwords or keys when accessing encrypted columns in a table or in an encrypted tablespace.

Although transparent data encryption has been significantly enhanced in Oracle Database 11*g*, there are still a few restrictions on its use; for example, you cannot encrypt columns using foreign key constraints, since every table has a unique column encryption key. This should typically not be an issue, since keys used in foreign key constraints should be system-generated, unique, and unintelligent. Business keys and other business attributes of a table are more likely candidates for encryption and usually do not participate in foreign key relationships with other tables. Other database features and types are also not eligible for transparent data encryption:

- Index types other than B-tree
- Range-scan searching of indexes
- BFILEs (external objects)
- Materialized view logs
- Synchronous Change Data Capture

- Transportable tablespaces
- Original import/export utilities (Oracle9*i* and earlier)

Alternatively, you can use DBMS_CRYPTO to manually encrypt these types and features.

NOTE
As of Oracle Database 11g, internal large objects such as BLOB and CLOB types can now be encrypted.

Summary

Auditing database access effectively and efficiently is key to a secure and accountable database environment. The database administrator (or security administrator in an enterprise with fine-grained separation of duties) needs to know who accessed the database, when they accessed it, and what they did. More importantly, the DBA must ensure that the wrong people can't get into the database in the first place.

If the database user has already authenticated with the operating system, the network, and the firewall, then the database settings will determine if they are authorized to connect to the database and access a particular schema, table, or column.

Permissions on the database can be as coarse as granting some users blanket permissions to view or modify any table; however, you'll more likely want those permissions to be much more granular. Therefore, you can control access to database objects in an application schema with literally hundreds of privileges and control over which columns a database user can see in a table. To further refine (and audit) access to rows of a table, you can leverage Oracle's Virtual Private Database (VPD) and transparently limit and control access to sensitive data regardless of how the table is accessed.

Once a user is authenticated and authorized to access a database object, you still might want to know what they accessed and when. With each new feature of Oracle Database comes a new auditing method and its associated audit trail location. Oracle Database 12*c* simplifies the navigation of the plethora of audit trails by introducing a unified audit trail—one-stop shopping for all your security auditing needs.

CHAPTER 11

Multitenant Database Architecture

Using a database appliance such as Oracle Exadata helps database administrators consolidate dozens, if not hundreds, of databases in one server room rack. Managing each of these databases separately, however, is still a challenge from a resource management perspective. Instances for each of the databases may use their memory and CPU resources inefficiently, preventing even more databases from being deployed to the server. With pluggable databases (PDBs), introduced in Oracle Database 12*c*, you can leverage your database resources more efficiently because many different databases (each consisting of a collection of schemas) can coexist within a single container database (CDB). A CDB is also known as a *multitenant* container database.

Pluggable databases make database administration simpler for a DBA. Performance metrics are gathered for all PDBs as a whole. In addition, the DBA needs to manage only one SGA, and not one for each PDB. Fewer database patches need to be applied as well: Only one CDB needs to be patched instead of having to patch each PDB within the CDB. With PDBs, hardware is used more efficiently, and the DBA can manage many more databases in the same amount of time.

Developers, network administrators, storage administrators, and database application users will rarely interact with a PDB or know they are using a PDB. One day the PDB may be plugged into container database CDB01 and the next day into container database CDB02, which is the point: A CDB acts just like any other database except that it decreases the maintenance effort for the DBA and provides generally higher availability for database users.

Even though the complexity of a CDB is higher than that of a traditional (pre-12*c*) database, the tools to manage CDBs and PDBs keep up with the complexity. Enterprise Manager Cloud Control 12*c* Release 3 fully supports the monitoring of CDBs and PDBs; Oracle SQL Developer version 4.0 and newer have a DBA module to perform most if not all of the operations you'll typically perform in a CDB environment.

This chapter covers several high-level topics; specifically, it gives an overview of the multitenant architecture and explains how PDBs are provisioned, how you manage security, and how you perform backup and recovery using RMAN. Your first decision will be whether you want to create a multitenant container at all—in most cases, you will. It's easy to fix any mistakes you make by over-provisioning a CDB: Just unplug one or more PDBs from the over-provisioned CDB and plug it or them back into another CDB on the same or different server. In addition to moving a PDB to another container, I'll show you how to create a new one from a seed template and clone an existing PDB.

The first part of the chapter sounds a lot like an introductory Oracle database administration course. You will find out how to set up the connections to a database, start up and shut down a database, and set the parameters for a database. The difference is that you're doing those things for the container (CDB) as a whole and differently for each PDB within the CDB. You'll find out that some database parameters apply only at the CDB level, whereas other parameters can be set at the PDB level. Once you start up a CDB, you can have each PDB in a different state. Some PDBs will remain in the MOUNT state while the rest can be OPEN as READ ONLY or READ WRITE.

Managing permanent and temporary tablespaces in a multitenant environment is similar to managing those tablespace types in a non-CDB environment. The SYSTEM and SYSAUX tablespaces exist in the CDB (CDB$ROOT) and in each PDB with some SYSTEM and SYSAUX objects shared from the CDB to the individual PDBs. Otherwise, the CDB and each PDB can have its own segregated permanent tablespaces. For temporary tablespaces, every PDB can use the temporary tablespace in the CDB. However, if a particular PDB has specific temporary tablespace requirements that might not operate efficiently with the CDB's shared temporary tablespace, then that PDB can have its own temporary tablespace.

Security is important in any database environment, and a multitenant database environment is no exception. A DBA in a multitenant environment must understand the distinction between common and local users along with the roles and privileges assigned to each. Much like an application user has no knowledge of whether a database is a PDB or a non-CDB, a DBA can have a local user account in a PDB and manage that PDB with no privileges or visibility outside of the PDB.

In a multitenant environment, you still need to perform backups and recoveries, but you'll use the same tools as in a non-CDB environment and be able to back up more databases in less time than in a non-CDB environment. As in any database environment, you need to back up and recover a CDB or PDB. The methods you use to back up the entire CDB or just a PDB are slightly different and, as you'd expect, have different impacts.

Understanding the Multitenant Architecture

In this section, I'll expand on some of the concepts outlined in the chapter introduction and demonstrate the mechanics of creating a new CDB using several different tools. Once the CDB is in place, you can create a new PDB by cloning the seed database (PDB$SEED).

Databases created in Oracle 11*g* are not left out, though. You can either upgrade the pre-12*c* database to 12.1 and then plug it into an existing CDB or use Data Pump export (**expdp**) on the 11*g* database and then use Data Pump import (**impdp**) on a new PDB.

In a multitenant environment, a database can be one of three types: a standalone database (non-CDB), a container database, or a pluggable database. In the following sections, I'll describe the multitenant architecture in greater detail along with the many advantages of using a multitenant environment.

Leveraging Multitenant Databases

Previous to Oracle Database 12*c*, the only type of database you could create was a non-CDB (as it's called now; the concept of a CDB or PDB had not yet been conceived then) either as a standalone database or as part of a cluster (Real Applications Cluster). Even if you ran multiple non-CDB instances on the same server, each instance would have its own memory structures (SGA, PGA, and so forth) and database files (storage structures).

Even with the efficient management of memory and disk space within each database, there is a duplication of memory structures and database objects. In addition, when upgrading a database version, at least one software upgrade must be performed on each server containing an application. With more efficient use of memory and disk via multitenant databases, more applications can be consolidated onto a much smaller number of servers or even one server.

In addition to consolidating multiple data dictionaries into a single CDB, new databases can be provisioned quickly within the container by copying a subset of objects specific to the PDB. If you want to upgrade only one PDB to a new version of the database, you can unplug the database from the current CDB and plug it into a new CDB that is at the correct version in the time it takes to export and import the PDB's metadata.

Using PDBs makes efficient use of resources while still maintaining a separation of duties and application isolation.

NOTE
The multitenant architecture includes both the container database and the pluggable databases that run inside the container database. A non-CDB does not *mean a pluggable database but instead a single traditional Oracle database regardless of version, sometimes referred to as a* standalone *database. Oracle's documentation may refer to a* user container, *which is the same as a PDB. A PDB can be either plugged in or unplugged and will always be a PDB.*

Understanding Multitenant Configurations

Given the multitenant architecture of Oracle Database 12*c*, you can leverage CDBs and PDBs in a number of ways:

- **Multitenant configuration** A single CDB that contains zero, one, or more PDBs at any given time
- **Single-tenant configuration** A single CDB with a single PDB (licensing for the multitenant option is not required)
- **Non-CDB** Oracle 11*g* architecture (standalone database and instance)

Figure 11-1 shows a sample of a multitenant configuration with one CDB and one non-CDB instance. The CDB instance has three PDBs.

The following sections describe the three types of containers and databases: system containers (CDBs), user containers (PDBs), and standalone databases (non-CDBs).

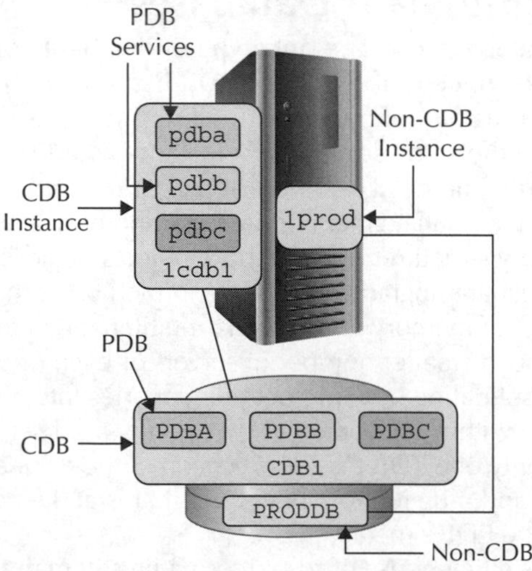

FIGURE 11-1. *Multitenant architecture with a CDB and a non-CDB*

System Container Database Architecture

Creating a system container (in other words, a CDB) is as easy as checking a radio button in the Database Configuration Assistant (DBCA). The resulting database is only the container for new databases that can be provisioned either by copying the seed database or by plugging in a database that was previously a tenant of this CDB or unplugged from a different CDB. Figure 11-2 shows a typical CDB configuration.

The single CDB in Figure 11-2 has three PDBs: DW, SALES, and HR. All three PDBs share a single instance and its process structures. The root container has the control files and redo log files shared by all PDBs along with datafiles that contain system metadata common to all databases. The individual applications have their own datafiles isolated from all other PDBs within the container. A SYS user is owned by the root container and can manage the root container and all PDBs.

As noted earlier, a CDB has a single database instance and set of related datafiles regardless of the number of PDBs in the CDB. The definition and usage of tablespaces and objects in a non-CDB or pre-12*c* database are mostly the same, with the following exceptions and qualifications:

- **Redo log files** The redo log files are shared with the root container and all PDBs. Entries in the redo log files identify the source of the redo (which PDB or the root container). All user containers share the same ARCHIVELOG mode as well.
- **Undo tablespace** All containers share the same undo tablespace.
- **Control files** The control files are shared. Datafiles added from any PDB are recorded in the common control file.

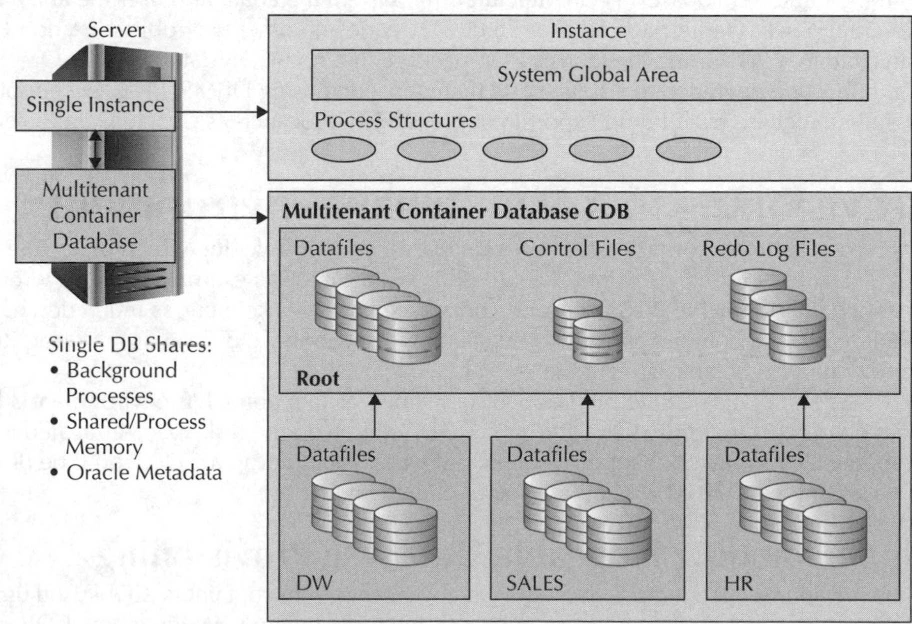

FIGURE 11-2. *Typical container database*

- **Temporary tablespaces** One temporary tablespace is required in the CDB and is the initial default temporary tablespace for each PDB. However, based on application requirements, each PDB may have its own temporary tablespace.
- **Data dictionary** Each user container has its own data dictionary in its copy of the SYSTEM tablespace (common objects have pointers to the SYSTEM tablespace in the system container database) with its private metadata.
- **SYSAUX tablespace** Each PDB has its own copy of the SYSAUX tablespace.

Tablespaces can be created within each PDB specific to the application. Each tablespace's datafile is identified in the CDB's data dictionary with a container ID in the column CON_ID. Further information about container metadata is presented later in the chapter.

User Container Databases

User containers (in other words, PDBs) have SYSTEM tablespaces just like non-CDBs do but have links to the common metadata across the entire container. Only the user metadata specific to the PDB is stored in the PDB's SYSTEM tablespace. The object names are the same in a PDB as in a non-CDB or the CDB, such as OBJ$, TAB$, and SOURCE$. Thus, the PDB appears to an application as a standalone database. A DBA can be assigned to manage only that application with new roles and privileges created in Oracle Database 12*c* (discussed later in "Leveraging CDB Security Features"). The DBA for an application in a PDB is also not aware that there may be one or many other PDBs sharing resources in the CDB.

Non-CDB Databases

Standalone (in other words, non-CDB) databases can still be created in Oracle Database 12*c* (with the Oracle Database 11*g* architecture). The system metadata and user metadata are stored in the same SYSTEM tablespace along with PL/SQL code and other user objects. A non-CDB can be converted to a PDB using the DBMS_PDB package. If a non-CDB database is at Oracle Database 11*g*, it must be upgraded to 12*c* first and then converted using DBMS_PDB. Other options for upgrading include Data Pump Export/Import or an ETL tool such as Oracle Data Integrator (ODI).

Provisioning in a Multitenant Environment

Once you create one or more container databases, you must decide which pluggable databases will be created in each container. Initial resource consumption estimates may be wrong, but given the flexibility of moving PDBs between containers. you will not incur as much downtime moving a PDB to a new container as you would creating a new non-CDB database or using RMAN to clone or move a database to another server.

CDBs and PDBs need to be dropped sometimes, as in a non-CDB environment. I'll cover the two-step process to remove a PDB from a CDB and free up the disk space allocated to the PDB. Dropping CDBs may not happen as often, but when you do drop a CDB, you'll be dropping all PDBs within the CDB as well unless you unplug them first.

Understanding Pluggable Database Provisioning

In the previous section, I made the distinction between system containers (CDBs) and user containers (PDBs). The system container is also known as the *root* container. When a new CDB is created, a *seed* container is the template for a new PDB and makes it easy to create a new PDB within a CDB.

Understanding Root Containers

The root container within a CDB contains global Oracle metadata only. This metadata includes CDB users such as SYS, which is global to all current and future PDBs within the CDB. Once a new PDB is provisioned, all user data resides in datafiles owned by the PDB. No user data resides in the root container. The root container is named CDB$ROOT, and you'll see where this metadata is stored later in this chapter.

Leveraging Seed PDBs

When you create a new CDB, one PDB is created: the seed PDB. It has the structure or template for a PDB that will contain the user data for a new application database. The seed database is named PDB$SEED. This provisioning operation is fast because it primarily consists of creating a couple of small tablespaces and empty tables for user metadata.

Using Intra-CDB Links

When databases are deployed as non-CDB databases in Oracle Database 11*g* or as a non-CDB in Oracle Database 12*c*, you often have reasons to share data between databases, whether the databases are on separate servers or even on the same server. In both Oracle Database 12*c* and many previous versions of Oracle, you use database links to access tables in other databases. You use database links to access tables from other PDBs within the same CDB as well. But since the objects in two PDBs reside within the same container, you are using a fast version of a database link under the covers. Remember that a PDB does not know where another PDB or non-CDB database resides, so the definition and use of a database link are the same regardless of where both databases reside.

Querying V$CONTAINERS

The system container's dynamic performance view V$CONTAINERS has just about everything you want to know about the user containers and the system container in your CDB. In the following example, you view the available PDBs and then open the PDB DW_01 to make it available to users:

```
[oracle@kthanid ~]$ . oraenv
ORACLE_SID = [orcl] ? qa
The Oracle base remains unchanged with value /u01/app/oracle
[oracle@kthanid ~]$ sqlplus / as sysdba

SQL*Plus: Release 12.1.0.2.0 Production on Fri Nov 14 10:08:00 2014
Copyright (c) 1982, 2014, Oracle.  All rights reserved.

Connected to:
Oracle Database 12c Enterprise Edition Release 12.1.0.2.0 - 64bit Production
With the Partitioning, Automatic Storage Management, OLAP, Advanced Analytics
and Real Application Testing options

SQL> select con_id,name,open_mode,total_size
  2  from v$containers;

    CON_ID NAME                           OPEN_MODE  TOTAL_SIZE
---------- ------------------------------ ---------- ----------
         1 CDB$ROOT                       READ WRITE  975175680
         2 PDB$SEED                       READ ONLY   283115520
```

```
         3 CCREPOS                          MOUNTED          0
         4 DW_01                            MOUNTED          0
         5 QA_2014                          MOUNTED          0

SQL> alter pluggable database dw_01 open read write;

Pluggable database altered.
SQL> select con_id,name,open_mode,total_size
  2  from v$containers;

    CON_ID NAME                           OPEN_MODE  TOTAL_SIZE
---------- ------------------------------ ---------- ----------
         1 CDB$ROOT                       READ WRITE  975175680
         2 PDB$SEED                       READ ONLY   283115520
         3 CCREPOS                        MOUNTED             0
         4 DW_01                          READ WRITE  283115520
         5 QA_2014                        MOUNTED             0
SQL>
```

A system container (in other words, a CDB) has one and only one seed database and one root container; user containers are optional (but you will eventually have one or more). A CDB can contain up to 253 user containers (in other words, PDBs), which includes the seed database. Both the root container (CDB$ROOT) and the seed database (PDB$SEED) are displayed in V$CONTAINERS along with the PDBs.

Leveraging CDB Security Features

The multitenant architecture necessarily requires new security objects and a new security hierarchy because you must be able to maintain the same separation of duties and application partitioning that existed when each application was stored in its own database.

To administer the entire CDB and all of the PDBs within the system container, you need one "superuser" also known as the *container database administrator (CDBA).* Each PDB within a CDB has DBA privileges within the CDB and is known as the *pluggable database administrator (PDBA).* In a non-CDB, the DBA role works the same as in Oracle Database 11*g*.

Users (privileged or otherwise) are of two types in a multitenant environment: common or local. As the name implies, a *common user* has access to all PDBs within a CDB, and a *local user* has access only within a specific PDB. Privileges are granted the same way. Privileges can be granted across all containers or local to only one PDB.

The new data dictionary table, CDB_USERS, contains users who exist in the data dictionary table DBA_USERS across all PDBs. When you add a new common user to the CDB, the user also shows up in the DBA_USERS table in each PDB. As with all other features of multitenant features, the DBA_USERS table in each PDB contains only those users specific to that PDB, and those users have the same characteristics as users created in non-CDB databases or pre-12*c* databases.

As you might expect, a common user can perform global operations such as starting up or shutting down the CDB as well as unplugging or plugging in a PDB. To unplug a database, you must first shut down the PDB and then issue the ALTER PLUGGABLE DATABASE command to create the XML metadata file so that the PDB can be plugged in later to the current or another CDB:

```
SQL> alter pluggable database dw_01
  2  unplug into '/u01/app/oracle/plugdata/dw_01.xml';
```

```
Pluggable database altered.

SQL>
```

In addition to new data dictionary views like CDB_USERS, a CDB contains corollaries to other DBA_ views you would see in a non-CDB database, such as CDB_TABLESPACES and CDB_PDBS:

```
SQL> select con_id,tablespace_name,status
  2  from cdb_tablespaces;

    CON_ID TABLESPACE_NAME                STATUS
---------- ------------------------------ ---------
         1 SYSTEM                         ONLINE
         1 SYSAUX                         ONLINE
         1 UNDOTBS1                       ONLINE
         1 TEMP                           ONLINE
         1 USERS                          ONLINE
         2 SYSTEM                         ONLINE
         2 SYSAUX                         ONLINE
         2 TEMP                           ONLINE
         5 SYSTEM                         ONLINE
         5 SYSAUX                         ONLINE
         5 TEMP                           ONLINE

11 rows selected.

SQL>
```

From a PDB local user's perspective, all of the DBA_ views behave just as they would in a non-CDB database.

Configuring and Creating a CDB

Creating a multitenant container database has many uses and many configurations. Compared to previous versions of Oracle Database, the flexibility of grouping or consolidating databases using the multitenant architecture (compared to using RAC or multiple non-CDB databases on the same server) has increased dramatically while at the same time not increasing the complexity of managing multiple databases within a CDB. In fact, managing multiple PDBs within a CDB not only makes more efficient use of memory and CPU resources but makes it easier to manage multiple databases. As mentioned in previous chapters, you'll be able to do things like perform upgrades on the CDB, which in turn automatically upgrades the PDBs that reside in the CDB.

Container databases can be used by developers, by testers, and of course in a production environment. For a new application, you can clone an existing database or create a new database using the seed database in a fraction of the time it takes to create a new standalone database. For testing applications in new hardware and software environments, you can easily unplug a database from one CDB and plug it into another CDB on the same or different server.

In the following sections, I'll show you how to create a new CDB using either SQL*Plus or the Database Configuration Assistant (DBCA). To view and manage the diagnostic information in a multitenant environment, I'll review how the Automatic Diagnostic Repository (ADR) is structured. To close out this section, you'll get a recap of the new data dictionary views available at the container level.

Operation/Tool	SQL*Plus	OUI	DBCA	EM Cloud Control 12c	SQL Developer	DBUA	EMDE
Create new CDB or PDB	✔	✔	✔	✔ (PDB only)	✔ (PDB only)		
Browse CDB or PDB	✔			✔	✔		✔ (PDB only)
Upgrade 12.1 non-CDB to CDB	✔					✔	

TABLE 11-1. *CDB- and PDB-Compatible Oracle Tools*

Creating a CDB Using Different Methods

As with many Oracle features, you have many tools at your disposal to create and maintain objects, which in this case means CDBs and PDBs. What tool you use depends on the level of control you need when creating these objects as well as whether you need to script the operation in a batch environment. Table 11-1 shows the tools you can use to perform various operations on CDBs and PDBs.

To create a new CDB, you have three options: SQL*Plus, the Database Configuration Assistant, and the Oracle Universal Installer (OUI). Enterprise Manager Database Express (EMDE) cannot create a CDB or browse the CDB or PDB architecture. However, EMDE can view any PDB as if it were a standalone database (non-CDB).

Using SQL*Plus to Create a CDB Using SQL*Plus to create a CDB is similar in many ways to creating a new standalone database instance. The differences are apparent when you use some of the new keywords available with the CREATE DATABASE command such as ENABLE PLUGGABLE DATABASE and SEED FILE_NAME_CONVERT. Once the initial CDB is created, you run the same post-creation scripts as you would in an Oracle 11*g* database or non-CDB 12*c* database.

The steps to create the CDB are as follows:

1. Create an **init.ora** file with the typical parameters for any instance, such as DB_NAME, CONTROL_FILES, and DB_BLOCK_SIZE, plus the new parameter ENABLE_PLUGGABLE_DATABASE.
2. Set the ORACLE_SID environment variable.
3. Create the CDB using the CREATE DATABASE command with the ENABLE PLUGGABLE DATABASE keywords.
4. Set a special session parameter to indicate that this is a new CDB:

   ```
   alter session set "_oracle_script"=true;
   ```
5. Close and open the seed PDB.
6. Run the post-creation scripts, including the following:

   ```
   ?/rdbms/admin/catalog.sql
   ?/rdbms/admin/catblock.sql
   ?/rdbms/admin/catproc.sql
   ```

```
?/rdbms/admin/catoctk.sql
?/rdbms/admin/owminst.plb
?/sqlplus/admin/pupbld.sql
```

Using SQL*Plus to create a new CDB is the ultimate in control, but as you can see, it can be quite convoluted. Unless you want to create many databases at once with slight changes in parameters or the same set of databases on several servers, then using DBCA (discussed in the next section) might be an easier and less error-prone method for creating a CDB.

Using DBCA to Create a CDB

The Database Configuration Assistant tool is likely the tool you'll use to create a new CDB. In fact, it gives you the options to create a non-CDB database (much like a pre-12.1 database), just a CDB, or a CDB with a new PDB. In Figure 11-3, I am using the "express" method to create a new container database called CDB58, which will reside in the existing Automatic Storage Management (ASM) disk group +DATA. The recovery files will reside in +RECOV. An initial PDB called RPTQA10 will be created along with the container.

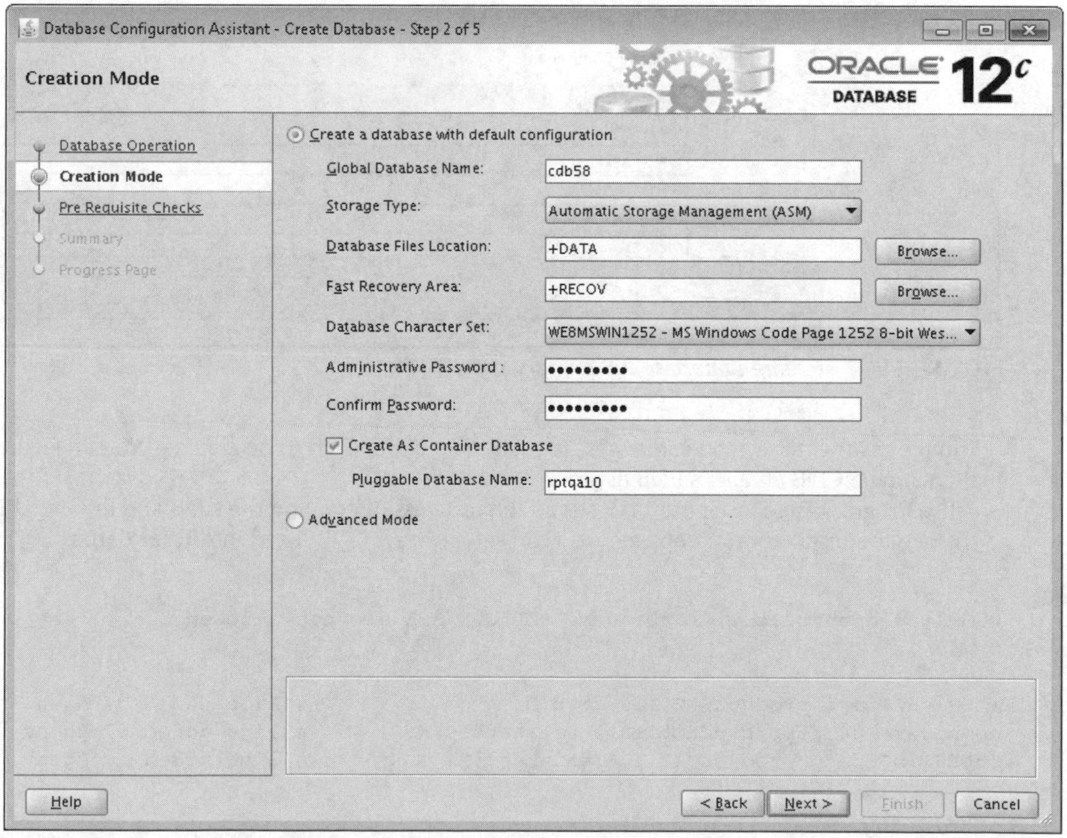

FIGURE 11-3. *Creating a container database using DBCA*

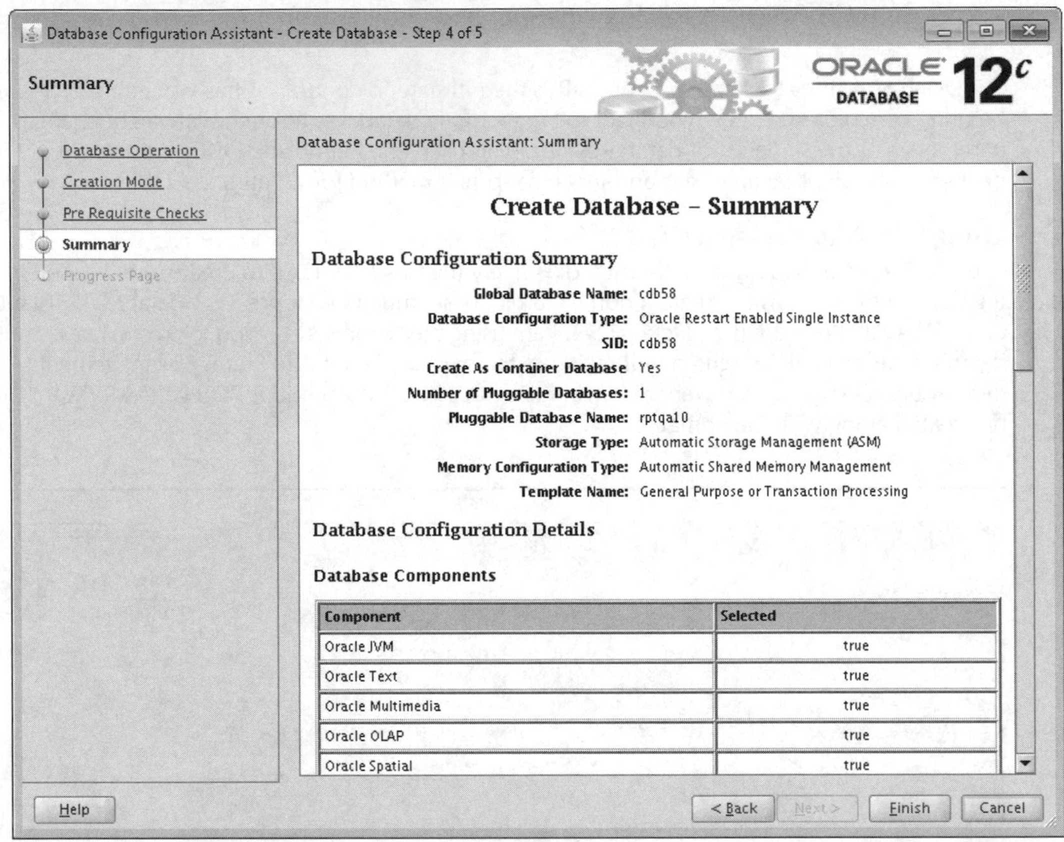

FIGURE 11-4. *Create Database – Summary page*

In the next window, you can review the summary of the CDB to be created. Note in Figure 11-4 that creating a CDB creates a PDB as well.

The Progress Page in Figure 11-5 shows the progress of creating the CDB and the initial PDB.

Once the installation completes, you can see the new CDB listed in **/etc/oratab**:

```
#
# Multiple entries with the same $ORACLE_SID are not allowed.
#
#
+ASM:/u01/app/product/12.1.0/grid:N:                # line added by Agent
complref:/u01/app/product/12.1.0/database:N:        # line added by Agent
cdb58:/u01/app/product/12.1.0/database:N:           # line added by Agent
```

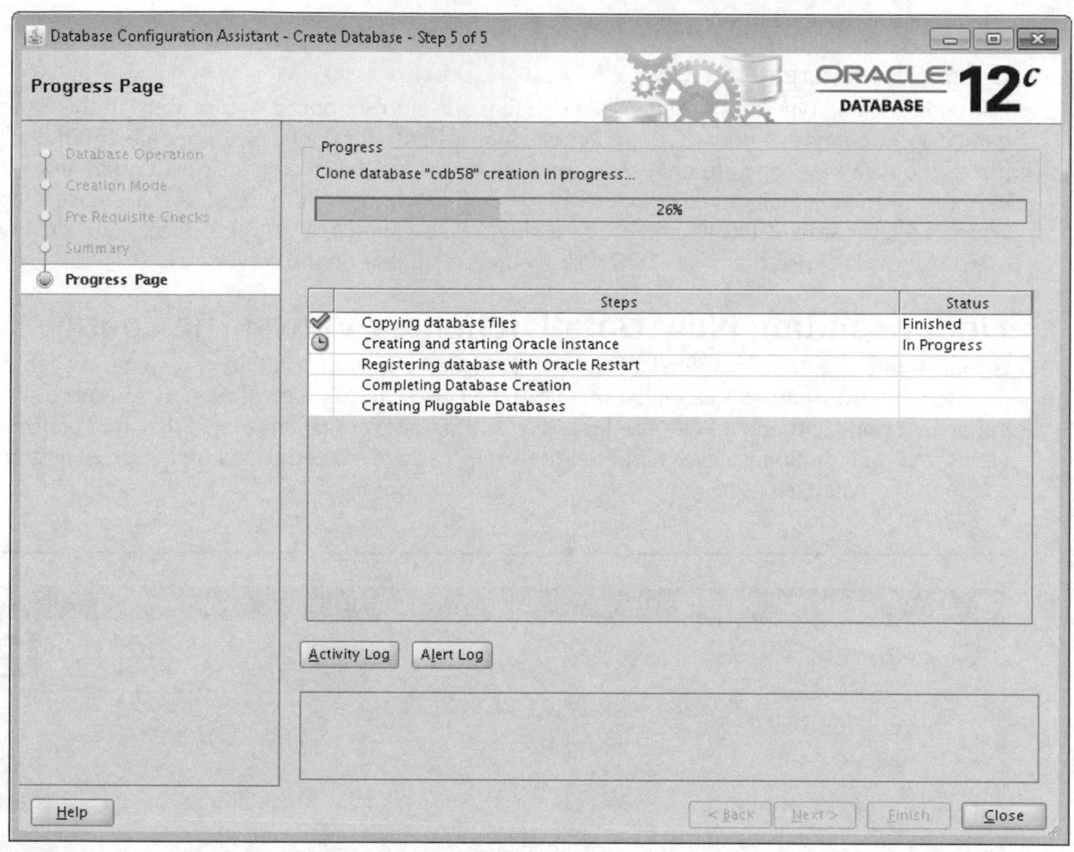

FIGURE 11-5. *Container database Progress Page*

But where is the initial PDB? For clues you can check the listener:

```
[oracle@oel63 ~]$ lsnrctl status
LSNRCTL for Linux: Version 12.1.0.1.0 - Production on 27-MAY-2013 20:47:02
. . .
Service "cdb58" has 1 instance(s).
  Instance "cdb58", status READY, has 1 handler(s) for this service...
. . .
Service "complrefXDB" has 1 instance(s).
  Instance "complref", status READY, has 1 handler(s) for this service...
Service "rptqa10" has 1 instance(s).
  Instance "cdb58", status READY, has 1 handler(s) for this service...
The command completed successfully
[oracle@oel63 ~]$
```

The listener hands off any requests for service **rptqa10** to the PDB with the same name in the container database CDB58.

Using OUI to Create a CDB

Using the Oracle Universal Installer is much like one-stop shopping. You can install the Oracle database files, create a new CDB, and create a new PDB all in one session. Since you'll likely install the database software only once on a server, using OUI to create a new container or PDB happens only once per server. In Figure 11-6 I am launching OUI to install the database software, create a CDB named CDB99, and create a single PDB called QAMOBILE. By default, OUI will use ASM for database files if an ASM disk group is available on the server.

Understanding New Data Dictionary Views: The Sequel

Earlier in this chapter I presented a brief overview of the new data dictionary views available in a multitenant environment. Remember that from the perspective of a local user, there is no distinction between a non-CDB and a PDB. The local user still sees the container-related dynamic performance views and data dictionary views, but the rows returned are filtered based on the privileges and scope of the database user.

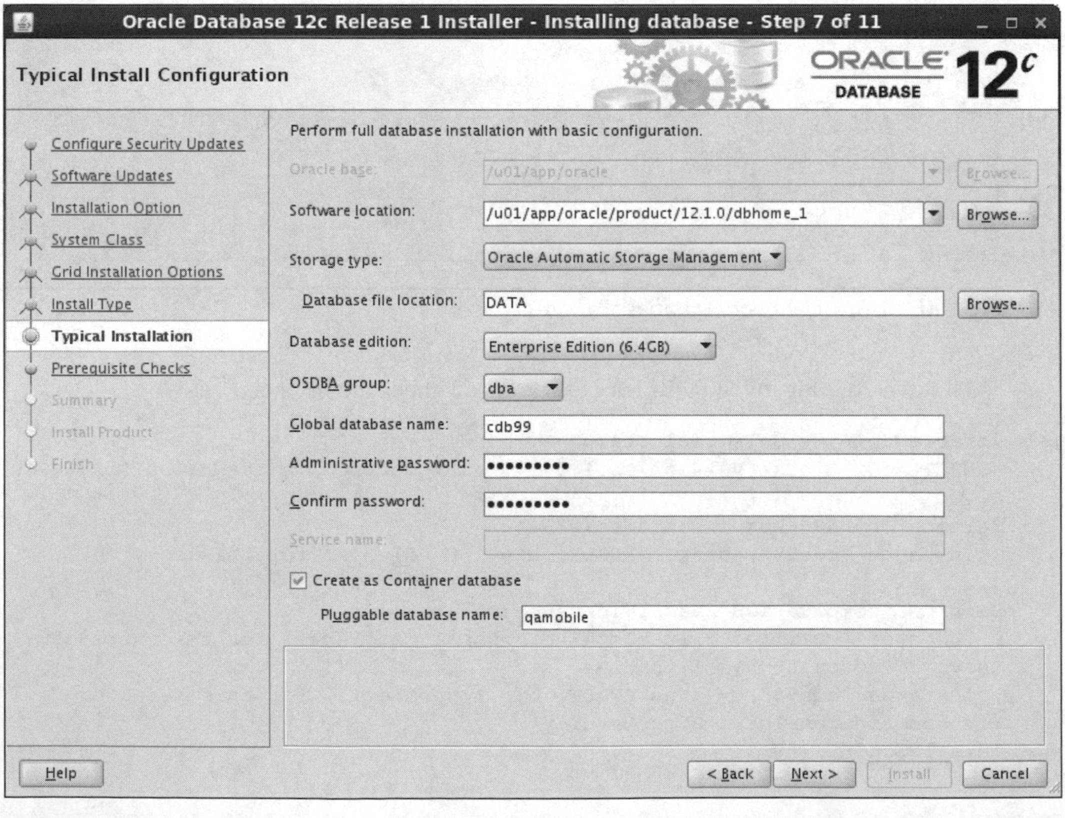

FIGURE 11-6. *Installing Oracle Database software and container database using OUI*

For example, a common user with DBA privileges (particularly the SELECT ANY DICTIONARY system privilege) can see all PDBs in the CDB:

```
[oracle@oel63 ~]$ sqlplus c##rjb/rjb@oel63/cdb01
SQL*Plus: Release 12.1.0.1.0 Production on Tue May 27 23:46:10 2014
Copyright (c) 1982, 2013, Oracle.  All rights reserved.
Last Successful login time: Tue May 27 2014 23:15:45 -05:00
Connected to:
Oracle Database 12c Enterprise Edition Release 12.1.0.1.0 - 64bit Production
With the Partitioning, Automatic Storage Management, OLAP, Advanced Analytics
and Real Application Testing options
SQL> select pdb_id,pdb_name from cdb_pdbs;

    PDB_ID PDB_NAME
---------- ------------------------
         3 QATEST1
         2 PDB$SEED
         4 QATEST2

SQL>
```

A nonprivileged common user won't even see that data dictionary view:

```
SQL> connect c##klh
Enter password:
Connected.
SQL> select pdb_id,pdb_name from cdb_pdbs;
select pdb_id,pdb_name from cdb_pdbs
                            *
ERROR at line 1:
ORA-00942: table or view does not exist

SQL>
```

Local users, even with DBA privileges, will see data dictionary views like CDB_PDBS but won't see any PDBs:

```
[oracle@oel63 ~]$ sqlplus rjb/rjb@oel63/qatest1

SQL*Plus: Release 12.1.0.1.0 Production on Tue May 27 23:53:19 2014

Copyright (c) 1982, 2013, Oracle.  All rights reserved.

Last Successful login time: Tue May 27 2014 23:37:44 -05:00

Connected to:
Oracle Database 12c Enterprise Edition Release 12.1.0.1.0 - 64bit Production
With the Partitioning, Automatic Storage Management, OLAP, Advanced Analytics
and Real Application Testing options
```

```
SQL> select pdb_id,pdb_name from cdb_pdbs;

no rows selected

SQL>
```

In previous versions of Oracle Database, the USER_ views show objects owned by the user accessing the view, the ALL_ views show objects accessible to the user accessing the view, and the DBA_ views show all objects in the database and are accessible to users with the SELECT ANY DICTIONARY system privilege, which is usually granted via the DBA role. Whether the database is a non-CDB, a CDB, or a PDB, the DBA_ views show the objects relative to where the view is accessed. For example, in a PDB, the DBA_TABLESPACES view shows tablespaces that exist only in that PDB.

If you are in the root container, DBA_USERS shows only common users, since in the root container only common users exist. In a PDB, DBA_USERS shows both common and local users.

For databases created in Oracle Database 12*c*, the CDB_ data dictionary views show object information across all PDBs and all of the CDB_ views even exist for non-CDBs. For local users and non-CDBs, the CDB_ views show the same information as the equivalent DBA_ view: the visibility does not go past the PDB or non-CDB even if the local user has the DBA role. Here are some CDB_ data dictionary views, including the new data dictionary view CDB_PDBS:

- **CDB_PDBS** All PDBs within the CDB
- **CDB_TABLESPACES** All tablespaces within the CDB
- **CDB_DATA_FILES** All datafiles within the CDB
- **CDB_USERS** All users within the CDB (common and local)

Figure 11-7 shows the hierarchy of data dictionary views in a multitenant environment. At the CDB_ view level, the main difference in the structure of the table is the new column CON_ID, which is the container ID that owns the objects. The root container and the seed container are containers as well, of course, and have their own CON_ID.

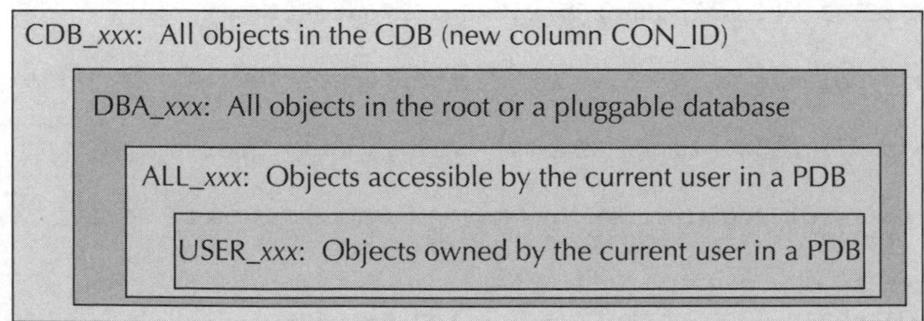

FIGURE 11-7. *Multitenant data dictionary view hierarchy*

Note that even common users (whose names are prefixed with C##) cannot access the CDB_ views unless they have the SELECT ANY DICTIONARY system privilege or have that privilege granted via a role such as the DBA role.

Creating PDBs

Once you have created the container database, you can add a new PDB regardless of whether or not you created a new PDB when you created the CDB. There are four methods: creating a PDB by cloning the seed PDB, cloning an existing PDB, plugging in a previously unplugged PDB, or plugging in a non-CDB.

Using PDB$SEED to Create a New PDB

Every container database has a read-only seed database container called PDB$SEED that is used for quickly creating a new pluggable database. When you create a new PDB from PDB$SEED, the following things happen, regardless of whether you use SQL*Plus, SQL Developer, or Enterprise Manager Cloud Control 12*c*. Each of these steps is performed with a CREATE PLUGGABLE DATABASE statement, either manually or via DBCA:

- Datafiles in PDB$SEED are copied to the new PDB.
- Local versions of the SYSTEM and SYSAUX tablespaces are created.
- Local metadata catalog is initialized (with pointers to common read-only objects in the root container).
- The common users SYS and SYSTEM are created.
- A local user is created and is granted the local PDB_DBA role.
- A new default service for the PDB is created and is registered with the listener.

Given the relatively small amount of data creation and movement in those steps, the creation of the PDB is very fast.

Cloning a PDB to Create a New PDB

If you need a new database that's similar to one that already exists, you can clone an existing database within the CDB. The new PDB will be identical to the source except for the PDB name and the DBID. In this example, you'll use the DBA features of SQL Developer to clone the PDB. No worries about what's going on under the covers; each step of the way you can see the DDL that SQL Developer runs to create the clone.

Before cloning an existing PDB, you must close it and reopen it in READ ONLY mode:

```
SQL> alter pluggable database qa_2014 close;

Pluggable database altered.
SQL> alter pluggable database qa_2014 open read only;

Pluggable database altered.

SQL>
```

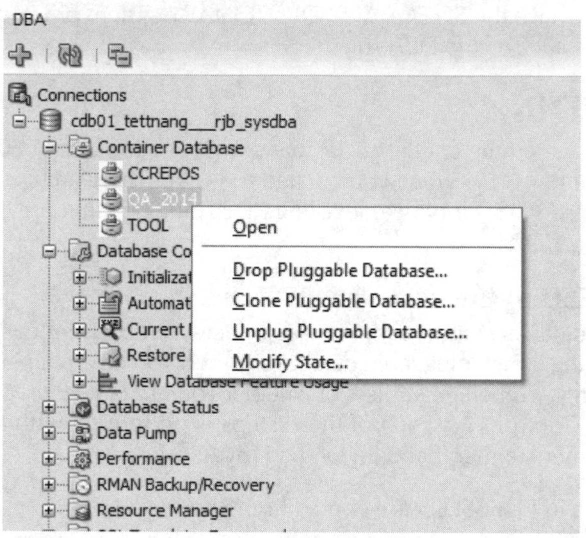

FIGURE 11-8. *Selecting a database to clone in SQL Developer*

You can browse the DBA connections for the container database CDB01 and its PDBs. Right-click the QA_2014 PDB and select Clone Pluggable Database, as shown in Figure 11-8.

In the dialog box that opens, as shown in Figure 11-9, change the database name to **QA_2015**. All other features and options of QA_2014 are retained for QA_2015.

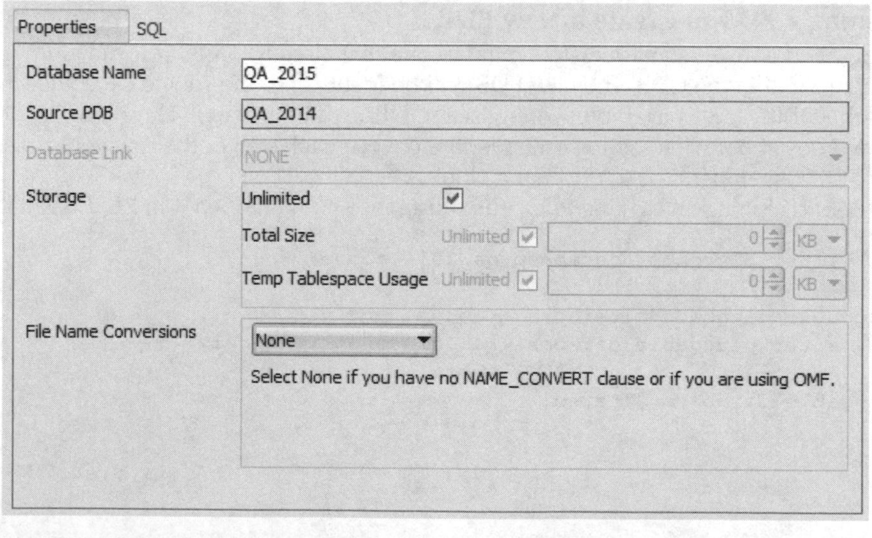

Properties SQL
Database Name QA_2015
Source PDB QA_2014
Database Link NONE
Storage Unlimited
Total Size Unlimited 0 KB
Temp Tablespace Usage Unlimited 0 KB
File Name Conversions None
Select None if you have no NAME_CONVERT clause or if you are using OMF.

FIGURE 11-9. *Specifying PDB clone characteristics*

The SQL tab shows the command that SQL Developer will run to clone the database:

```
CREATE PLUGGABLE DATABASE QA_2015 FROM QA_2014
 STORAGE UNLIMITED
 FILE_NAME_CONVERT=NONE;
```

Once you click the Apply button, the cloning operation proceeds and creates the new PDB. As with the SQL*Plus method of creating a new PDB, you have to open the new PDB as READ WRITE:

```
SQL> alter pluggable database qa_2015 open read write;

Pluggable database altered.

SQL>
```

Finally, you need to open the QA_2014 database as READ WRITE again since it was set to READ ONLY for the clone operation:

```
SQL> alter pluggable database qa_2014 close;

Pluggable database altered.

SQL> alter pluggable database qa_2014 open read write;

Pluggable database altered.

SQL>
```

Plugging a Non-CDB into a CDB

You may have a standalone (non-CDB) Oracle 12*c* database that you'd like to consolidate into an existing CDB. If you have a pre-12*c* database, you must upgrade it to 12*c* first or use an alternate method to move that database (see the "Unplugging a PDB Using Different Methods" section of this chapter). For an existing non-CDB 12*c* database, it's a straightforward process involving the PL/SQL procedure DBMS_PDB.DESCRIBE.

Using DBMS_PDB.DESCRIBE, you can quickly export the metadata for a non-CDB to an XML OS file. On the **tettnang** server, there are three instances, ASM, CDB01, and RPTQA12C:

```
 [oracle@tettnang ~]$ cat /etc/oratab
. . .
#
+ASM:/u01/app/oracle/product/12.1.0/grid:N:
cdb01:/u01/app/oracle/product/12.1.0/dbhome_1:N:
rptqa12c:/u01/app/oracle/product/12.1.0/dbhome_1:N:
```

Here is how you would export the metadata for the RPTQA12C database. Connect to the target database (the database that will be assimilated into CDB01), change its status to READ ONLY, and run the procedure:

```
SQL> startup mount
ORACLE instance started.

Total System Global Area 2622255104 bytes
Fixed Size                  2685024 bytes
```

```
Variable Size             1644169120 bytes
Database Buffers           956301312 bytes
Redo Buffers                19099648 bytes
Database mounted.
SQL> alter database open read only;

Database altered.

SQL> exec dbms_pdb.describe('/tmp/rptqa12c.xml');

PL/SQL procedure successfully completed.

SQL>
```

The XML looks like this:

```
<?xml version="1.0" encoding="UTF-8"?>
<PDB>
  <pdbname>rptqa12c</pdbname>
  <cid>0</cid>
  <byteorder>1</byteorder>
  <vsn>202375168</vsn>
  <dbid>1288637549</dbid>
  <cdbid>1288637549</cdbid>
  <guid>F754FCD8744A55AAE043E3A0080A3B17</guid>
  <uscnbas>3905844</uscnbas>
  <uscnwrp>0</uscnwrp>
  <rdba>4194824</rdba>
  <tablespace>
    <name>SYSTEM</name>
    <type>0</type>
    <tsn>0</tsn>
    <status>1</status>
    <issft>0</issft>
    <file>
      <path>+DATA/RPTQA12C/DATAFILE/system.261.845207525</path>
. . .
    </options>
    <olsoid>0</olsoid>
    <dv>0</dv>
    <ncdb2pdb>1</ncdb2pdb>
    <APEX>4.2.0.00.27:1</APEX>
    <parameters>
      <parameter>processes=300</parameter>
      <parameter>shared_pool_size=805306368</parameter>
      <parameter>sga_target=2634022912</parameter>
      <parameter>db_block_size=8192</parameter>
      <parameter>compatible=12.1.0.0.0</parameter>
      <parameter>shared_servers=0</parameter>
      <parameter>open_cursors=300</parameter>
      <parameter>star_transformation_enabled=TRUE</parameter>
```

```
      <parameter>pga_aggregate_target=524288000</parameter>
    </parameters>
    <tzvers>
      <tzver>primary version:18</tzver>
      <tzver>secondary version:0</tzver>
    </tzvers>
    <walletkey>0</walletkey>
  </optional>
</PDB>
```

Next, connect to the container database CDB01 and import the XML for RPTQA12C:

```
[oracle@tettnang ~]$ . oraenv
ORACLE_SID = [rptqa12c] ? cdb01
The Oracle base remains unchanged with value /u01/app/oracle
[oracle@tettnang ~]$ sqlplus / as sysdba

SQL*Plus: Release 12.1.0.1.0 Production on Wed May 28 12:40:34 2014

Copyright (c) 1982, 2013, Oracle.  All rights reserved.


Connected to:
Oracle Database 12c Enterprise Edition Release 12.1.0.1.0 - 64bit Production
With the Partitioning, Automatic Storage Management, OLAP, Advanced Analytics
and Real Application Testing options

SQL> create pluggable database rptqa12c using '/tmp/rptqa12c.xml';

Pluggable database created.

SQL>
```

The plugging operation may take as little as a minute or two if the datafiles for the non-CDB database are in the same ASM disk group as the destination CDB. Some final cleanup and configuration is needed before the plugged-in database can be used. The script **noncdb_to_pdb .sql** cleans up unnecessary metadata in a multitenant environment. In addition, you must open the newly plugged-in database just as you would with a clone operation:

```
SQL> alter session set container=rptqa12c;
SQL> @$ORACLE_HOME/rdbms/admin/noncdb_to_pdb.sql
. . .
  6      IF (sqlcode <> -900) THEN
  7        RAISE;
  8      END IF;
  9    END;
 10  END;
 11  /

PL/SQL procedure successfully completed.
```

```
SQL>
SQL> WHENEVER SQLERROR CONTINUE;
SQL> alter pluggable database rptqa12c open read write;

Pluggable database altered.

SQL>
```

Plugging an Unplugged PDB into a CDB

You may have several unplugged databases at any given time. Usually you're in the process of migrating a PDB from one container to another on the same or a different server. In any case, an unplugged database can't be opened outside of a CDB, so you'll likely plug an unplugged database (PDB) back into a CDB. In this example, the PDB CCREPOS is currently unplugged and has its XML file located in **/tmp/ccrepos.xml** on the server. The steps to plug a currently unplugged PDB into a CDB are both straightforward and finish quickly—just as most multitenant operations do! All you have to do is run one command to plug it in and another command to open it. Connect as a common user with the ALTER PLUGGABLE DATABASE privilege as follows (connecting as SYSDBA to CDB01 with OS authentication works great):

```
SQL> create pluggable database ccrepos using '/tmp/ccrepos.xml' nocopy;

Pluggable database created.

SQL> alter pluggable database ccrepos open read write;

Pluggable database altered.

SQL>
```

Note that a PDB must be dropped, and not just unplugged, from a CDB before it can be plugged back in. Using the NOCOPY option saves time if the PDB's datafiles are already in the correct location.

Unplugging and Dropping a PDB

Since a PDB is by nature highly mobile, it's likely that you'll move it to another CDB on the same server or another server. You may just unplug it to make it unavailable to users (and prevent common users from opening it inadvertently). You may also unplug it to drop it completely. There are a few different ways to unplug and then drop a PDB.

Unplugging a PDB Using Different Methods

You can unplug a PDB using either SQL*Plus or SQL Developer. Both methods are easy and fast. Which one you should use depends on your comfort level and which tool you happen to have open at the time.

Unplugging a PDB Using SQL*Plus When you unplug a PDB from a CDB, you make the PDB unavailable to users, but its status remains UNPLUGGED. To drop the PDB from the CDB, see the next section, "Dropping a PDB." Before you can unplug a PDB, you must first close it, as shown next. When you unplug it, you specify the location of an XML file for the PDB's metadata. This metadata will ensure that the PDB will be pluggable later, either into the same or another CDB.

```
SQL> alter pluggable database ccrepos close;

Pluggable database altered.

SQL> alter pluggable database ccrepos unplug into '/tmp/ccrepos.xml';

Pluggable database altered.

SQL>
```

Unplugging a PDB Using SQL Developer Using SQL Developer to unplug a PDB is even easier than using SQL*Plus. From the CDB's connection in the DBA window, expand the Container Database branch and right-click the PDB to be unplugged. Select Unplug Pluggable Database from the context menu, as shown in Figure 11-10.

The Unplug dialog box gives you the opportunity to specify the name and location of the XML file containing the PDB's metadata, as you can see in Figure 11-11.

Dropping a PDB

As with most CDB and PDB operations, you can use both SQL*Plus and SQL Developer to drop a PDB. In addition, you can use DBCA and Enterprise Manager Cloud Control 12*c* to drop a PDB. When you drop a PDB, all references to the PDB are removed from the CDB's control file. By default,

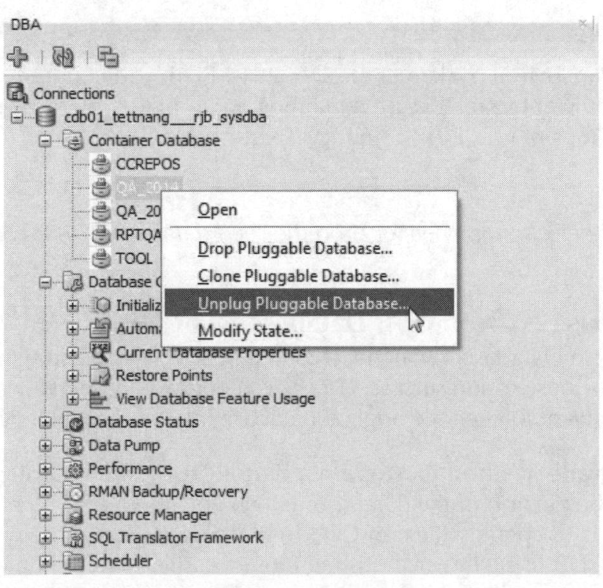

FIGURE 11-10. *Unplugging a PDB from SQL Developer*

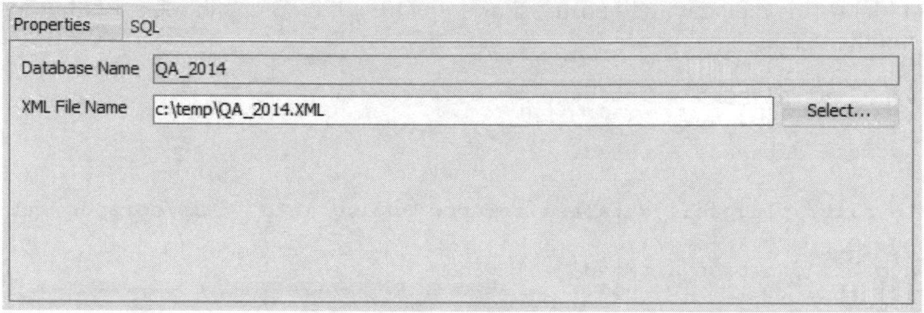

FIGURE 11-11. *Specifying the location for the unplugged PDB's XML file*

the datafiles are retained; therefore, if you had previously unplugged that PDB, you can use the XML file to plug that PDB back into the same or another CDB. In this example, you will drop the QA_2014 PDB along with its datafiles. It will no longer be available to plug into another database even if you still have the XML metadata.

```
SQL> alter pluggable database qa_2014 close;

Pluggable database altered.

SQL> drop pluggable database qa_2014 including datafiles;

Pluggable database dropped.

SQL>
```

If you have an RMAN backup of the QA_2014 PDB, you could restore it from there. Otherwise, if you want to remove all remaining traces of QA_2014, you'll have to manually remove the backups of QA_2014 using RMAN.

NOTE

You can neither unplug, open, or drop the seed database PDB$SEED.

Migrating a Pre-12.1 Non-CDB Database to a CDB

Converting Oracle Database 12*c* non-CDBs to a PDB is fast and straightforward, but what if your database is a previous version such as 11*g* or even 10*g*? You have a few options available depending on whether you want to keep the original database intact for some length of time.

Using the Upgrade Method to Migrate a Non-CDB If your application is not sensitive or dependent on the version of the database (which you should have verified by now), then your cleanest option is to upgrade the non-CDB in place up to version 12*c* (12.1.0.1 or later) and then plug it into the CDB using the methods mentioned earlier in this chapter. The biggest advantage to this method is that you don't need to allocate any extra space for the migration as you would for the other two methods.

Using the Data Pump Method to Migrate a Non-CDB To use the Data Pump method, you'll use Data Pump Export/Import as you would in a non-CDB environment. Create a new PDB from the seed database in the CDB and adjust the initialization parameters to be comparable to those in the existing database.

One of the advantages with this method is that you can leave the current non-CDB in place to ensure compatibility with Oracle Database 12*c* before dropping the original database.

Using the Database Link Method to Migrate a Non-CDB Using database links, you create a new PDB from the seed database and copy over the application's tables using database links. This is the most labor-intensive option but is probably the easiest if the number of tables in an application is small. A table migration would look like this:

```
SQL> insert into hr.employee_hist select * from employee_hist@HR11gDB;
```

Managing CDBs and PDBs

You connect to a PDB or CDB much like you connect to a non-CDB. You can connect to a CDB via OS authentication and the common user SYS. Otherwise, you will connect to either a CDB or one of the PDBs within the CDB using a service name. The service name is referenced either using an EasyConnect string or within a **tnsnames.ora** entry. This method is the same whether you are using SQL*Plus or SQL Developer.

By default a service name is created for each new, cloned, or plugged-in PDB. If that is not sufficient in your environment, you'll use the DBMS_SERVICE package to create additional services for the PDB.

Understanding CDB and PDB Service Names

In a non-CDB environment, a database instance is associated with at least one service managed by at least one listener. One listener can manage a combination of non-CDB and PDB services. The database server **oel63** has two databases: DBAHANDBOOK and CDB01. As you might suspect, the database CDB01 is a multitenant database, and DBAHANDBOOK is a non-CDB, but they are both Oracle Database version 12*c* and are managed by a single listener called LISTENER:

```
[oracle@oel63 ~]$ lsnrctl status

LSNRCTL for Linux: Version 12.1.0.1.0 - Production on 02-JUL-2014 22:47:35

Copyright (c) 1991, 2013, Oracle.  All rights reserved.
. . .
Services Summary...
Service "+ASM" has 1 instance(s).
  Instance "+ASM", status READY, has 1 handler(s) for this service...
Service "cdb01" has 1 instance(s).
  Instance "cdb01", status READY, has 1 handler(s) for this service...
Service "cdb01XDB" has 1 instance(s).
  Instance "cdb01", status READY, has 1 handler(s) for this service...
Service "dbahandbook" has 1 instance(s).
  Instance "dbahandbook", status READY, has 1 handler(s) for this service...
Service "dbahandbookXDB" has 1 instance(s).
```

```
  Instance "dbahandbook", status READY, has 1 handler(s) for this service...
Service "dw17" has 1 instance(s).
  Instance "cdb01", status READY, has 1 handler(s) for this service...
Service "qatest1" has 1 instance(s).
  Instance "cdb01", status READY, has 1 handler(s) for this service...
The command completed successfully
[oracle@oel63 ~]$
```

The container database CDB01 has two PDBs, DW17 and QATEST1, and the same listener manages connections for both PDBs.

Every container in a CDB has its own service name. The CDB itself has the default service name, which is the same as the container name plus the domain, if any. For each PDB created or cloned, a new service is created and managed by the default listener unless otherwise specified. As you might expect, the only exception to this rule is the seed container (PDB$SEED). Since it is read-only and used only to create new PDBs, there is no reason to create a service and connect to it.

In addition to using the service name to connect to the CDB or any PDBs contained within, you can use OS authentication and connect as SYSDBA just as you would with a non-CDB. You'll be connected as the SYS user—a common user with privileges to maintain all PDBs within the CDB.

The transparency of a PDB and how it appears as a non-CDB to nonprivileged users extends to how you connect using entries in **tnsnames.ora** or using Oracle EasyConnect. As you may recall, the format for an EasyConnect connect string is as follows:

```
<username>/<password>@<hostname>:<port_number>/<service_name>
```

Therefore, for connecting to the user RJB in the PDB named DW17 in the CDB named CDB01 on the server **oel63**, you would use the following when starting SQL*Plus:

```
[oracle@oel63 ~]$ sqlplus rjb/rjb@oel63:1521/dw17

SQL*Plus: Release 12.1.0.1.0 Production on Thu Jul 3 21:56:44 2014

Copyright (c) 1982, 2013, Oracle.  All rights reserved.


Connected to:
Oracle Database 12c Enterprise Edition Release 12.1.0.1.0 - 64bit Production
With the Partitioning, Automatic Storage Management, OLAP, Advanced Analytics
and Real Application Testing options

SQL>
```

Notice that no reference to CDB01 is necessary. The PDB's service name masks the existence of the CDB or any other PDBs in the CDB.

Connecting to a CDB or PDB Using SQL Developer

Connecting to the root container or any PDB within a container using SQL Developer is just as easy. You use the username (common or local), server name, port, and service name. In other words, this is EasyConnect format. Figure 11-12 shows several connections to CDB01 plus a connection to a non-CDB.

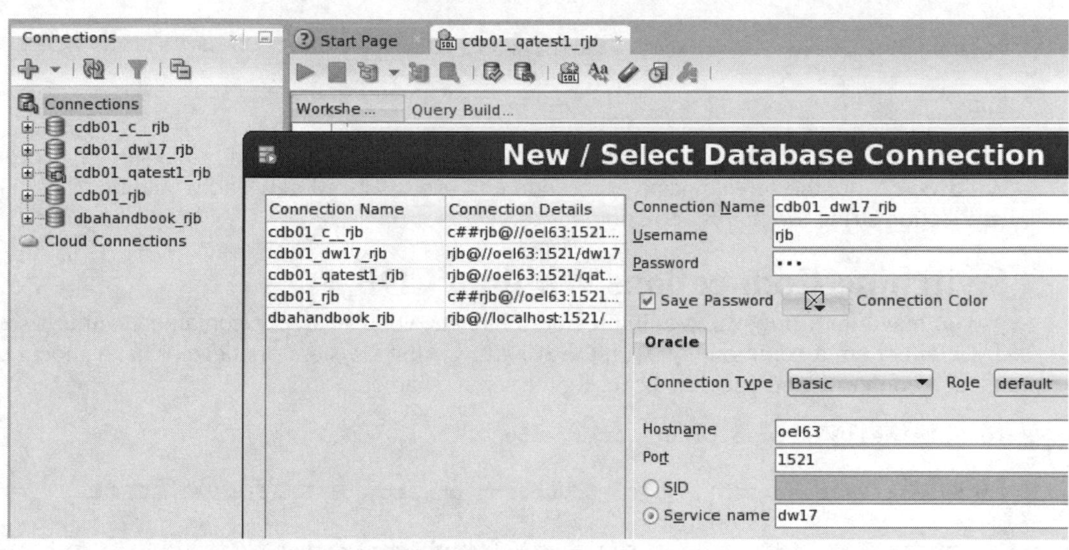

FIGURE 11-12. *Connecting to CDBs and PDBs in SQL Developer*

Creating Services for CDBs or PDBs

If you're using a standalone server environment with Oracle Restart or a clustered environment using Oracle Clusterware, you'll automatically get a new service created with every new or cloned PDB or non-CDB (database instance). If you want additional services for a PDB, use the **srvctl** command like this:

```
[oracle@oel63 ~]$ srvctl add service -db cdb01 -service dwsvc2 -pdb dw17
[oracle@oel63 ~]$ srvctl start service -db cdb01 -service dwsvc2
[oracle@oel63 ~]$ lsnrctl status
. . .
Service "dwsvc2" has 1 instance(s).
  Instance "cdb01", status READY, has 1 handler(s) for this service...
. . .
[oracle@oel63 ~]$
```

In a non-Oracle Restart or non-clustered environment, you can use the DBMS_SERVICE package to create and start the service. To create the same new service as in the previous example with **srvctl** but instead using DBMS_SERVICE, you would do the following:

```
SQL> begin
       dbms_service.create_service(
          service_name => 'dwsvc2',
          network_name => 'dwsvcnew');
       dbms_service.start_service(service_name => 'dwsvc2');
     end;
```

```
  7  /

PL/SQL procedure successfully completed.

SQL>
```

Note the slight difference in the example with DBMS_SERVICE: The actual service name is still **dwsvc2**, but the service name exposed to end users is **dwsvcnew** and would be used in the connection string for clients accessing this service.

Switching Connections Within a CDB

As you may infer from examples in previous chapters, you can switch containers within a session if you either are a common user with the SET CONTAINER system privilege or have a local user in each container and you connect using the service name:

```
[oracle@oel63 ~]$ sqlplus / as sysdba

SQL*Plus: Release 12.1.0.1.0 Production on Sat Jul 5 22:09:41 2014

Copyright (c) 1982, 2013, Oracle.  All rights reserved.


Connected to:
Oracle Database 12c Enterprise Edition Release 12.1.0.1.0 - 64bit Production
With the Partitioning, Automatic Storage Management, OLAP, Advanced Analytics
and Real Application Testing options

SQL> show con_name

CON_NAME
------------------------------
CDB$ROOT
SQL> alter session set container=qatest1;

Session altered.

SQL> show con_name

CON_NAME
------------------------------
QATEST1
SQL> connect rjb/rjb@oel63/dw17
Connected.
SQL> show con_name

CON_NAME
------------------------------
DW17
SQL>
```

You can have a pending transaction in the first PDB, switch to a different PDB, and then switch back to the first PDB, and you still have the option to COMMIT or ROLLBACK the pending transaction.

NOTE
Common users who have the SET CONTAINER system privilege or local users who switch containers using CONNECT local_user@ PDB_NAME *do not automatically commit pending transactions when switching containers.*

Starting Up and Shutting Down CDBs and PDBs

Starting up and shutting down a CDB or opening and closing a PDB will seem familiar to any Oracle DBA who starts up and shuts down a non-CDB. The point that is often missed is that a CDB is ultimately a single database instance, and each PDB shares the resources of the CDB's instance. This is to be expected since each PDB is logically partitioned from each other PDB using the CON_ID column in every table that is shared among the root and each PDB. This logical partitioning extends to user accounts and security as well; thus, it appears to non-common users that the PDB has its own dedicated instance.

NOTE
As you might expect, in a clustered (RAC) environment a CDB has one instance on each node of the cluster.

Since the CDB is a database instance, anything running within the CDB is shut down or disconnected when the CDB is shut down. This means that a PDB is not open for users until the CDB has been started and explicitly opened (either manually by the DBA or via a trigger), and similarly the PDB is closed when the CDB instance is shut down.

In the following sections, I'll show you how CDBs and PDBs are started up and shut down as well as how to automate the process. You'll also want to know how to change parameters that are specific to a PDB as well as create PDB-specific versions of database objects such as temporary tablespaces if the default global temporary tablespace does not meet the needs of the PDB's application.

CDB Instance Startup

The CDB instance is most like a traditional non-CDB instance. Figure 11-13 shows the five possible states for CDBs and PDBs in a multitenant environment.

From the shutdown state, you can perform a STARTUP NOMOUNT (connecting AS SYSDBA using OS authentication) to start a CDB instance by opening the SPFILE, creating the processes and memory structures, but not yet opening the control file:

```
SQL> startup nomount
ORACLE instance started.

Total System Global Area 2622255104 bytes
Fixed Size              2291808 bytes
Variable Size                1140852640 bytes
Database Buffers     1459617792 bytes
```

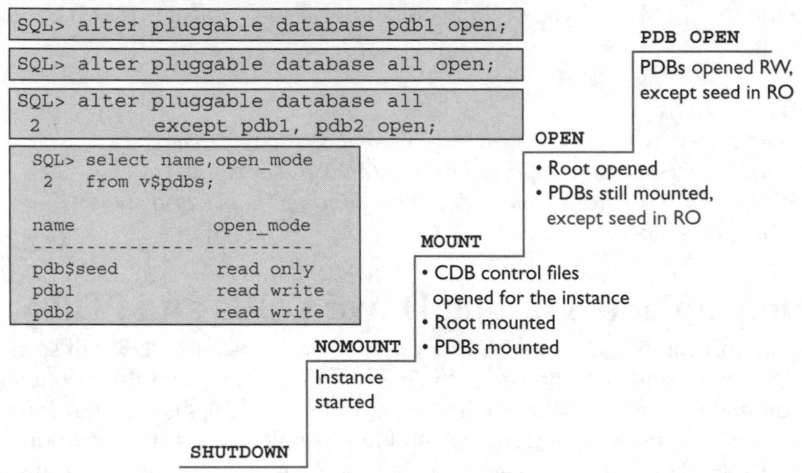

FIGURE 11-13. *CDB and PDB states*

```
Redo Buffers                    19492864 bytes
SQL> select con_id,name,open_mode from v$pdbs;

no rows selected

SQL>
```

At this point in the startup process, the instance has no information about the PDBs within the CDB yet. You would typically perform a STARTUP NOMOUNT when you need to re-create or restore a missing control file for the CDB instance.

A lot of things happen when you move a CDB to the MOUNT state, as you can see in Figure 11-13. Not only are the CDB's control files opened for the instance, but both the CDB$ROOT and all PDBs are changed to the MOUNT state:

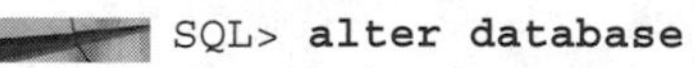

```
SQL> alter database mount;

Database altered.

SQL> select con_id,name,open_mode from v$pdbs;

    CON_ID NAME                           OPEN_MODE
---------- ------------------------------ ----------
         2 PDB$SEED                       MOUNTED
         3 QATEST1                        MOUNTED
         5 DW17                           MOUNTED

SQL>
```

If any datafile operations are necessary (restore and recovery, for example), this is where you would perform those, especially if those operations are required on the PDB's SYSTEM tablespace.

The final step to make the root container available for opening PDBs is to change the CDB's state to OPEN. After CDB$ROOT is OPEN, it's available for read and write operations. The PDBs are still mounted with the seed database PDB$SEED mounted as READ ONLY:

```
SQL> alter database cdb01 open;

Database altered.

SQL> select con_id,name,open_mode from v$pdbs;

    CON_ID NAME               OPEN_MODE
---------- ---------------- ----------
         2 PDB$SEED           READ ONLY
         3 QATEST1            MOUNTED
         5 DW17               READ WRITE

SQL>
```

Because I created a second service for the PDB named DW17 earlier in the chapter and Oracle Restart is installed in this environment, DW17 is automatically opened in READ WRITE mode. The seed database PDB$SEED is always opened READ ONLY.

Once the CDB is opened (in other words, the root's datafiles are available along with the global temporary tablespace and the online redo log files), the PDBs are mounted but not yet open and available to users. Unless a PDB is opened with a trigger or via Oracle Restart, it remains in the MOUNTED state.

At this point, the CDB instance behaves much like a non-CDB instance. In the next section, you'll see how individual PDBs are opened and closed.

Opening and Closing a PDB

Once you have the root (CDB$ROOT) container of a CDB open, you can perform all desired operations on the PDBs within the CDB, including but not limited to cloning PDBs, creating a new PDB from the seed, unplugging a PDB, or plugging in a previously unplugged PDB. Remember that the seed container, PDB$SEED, is always open when CDB$ROOT is open but with an OPEN_MODE of READ ONLY.

There are quite a few options when you want to open or close a PDB. You can use ALTER PLUGGABLE DATABASE when connected as SYSDBA or SYSOPER, or if you're connected as SYSDBA within a PDB, you can use the same commands without having to specify the PDB name. In addition, you can selectively open or close one or more PDBs with the ALL or EXCEPT ALL option.

Using the ALTER PLUGGABLE DATABASE Command You can open or close a PDB from any container by specifying the PDB name; alternatively, you can change the session context to a specific PDB and perform multiple operations on that PDB without qualifying it, as in these examples.

Regardless of the current container, you can open and close any PDB by explicitly specifying the PDB name:

```
SQL> select con_id,name,open_mode from v$pdbs;

    CON_ID NAME                           OPEN_MODE
---------- ------------------------------ ----------
         2 PDB$SEED                       READ ONLY
         3 QATEST1                        MOUNTED
         5 DW17                           READ WRITE

SQL> alter pluggable database dw17 close;

Pluggable database altered.

SQL> alter pluggable database dw17 open read only;

Pluggable database altered.

SQL> alter pluggable database qatest1 open;

Pluggable database altered.

SQL>
```

Alternatively, you can set the default PDB name at the session level:

```
SQL> alter session set container=dw17;

Session altered.

SQL> alter pluggable database close;

Pluggable database altered.

SQL> alter pluggable database open read write;

Pluggable database altered.

SQL>
```

To set the default container back to the root container, use CONTAINER=CDB$ROOT in the ALTER SESSION command.

Selectively Opening or Closing PDBs Even if you configure the PDBs in your CDB to open automatically with triggers, what if you have dozens of PDBs in your CDB and you want to open all of them except for one? You can use ALL EXCEPT to accomplish this in one command:

```
SQL> select con_id,name,open_mode from v$pdbs;

    CON_ID NAME                           OPEN_MODE
---------- ------------------------------ ----------
```

```
         2 PDB$SEED                         READ ONLY
         3 QATEST1                          MOUNTED
         4 DEV2015                          MOUNTED
         5 DW17                             MOUNTED

SQL> alter pluggable database all except qatest1 open;

Pluggable database altered.

SQL> select con_id,name,open_mode from v$pdbs;

    CON_ID NAME                             OPEN_MODE
---------- ------------------------------ ----------
         2 PDB$SEED                         READ ONLY
         3 QATEST1                          MOUNTED
         4 DEV2015                          READ WRITE
         5 DW17                             READ WRITE

SQL>
```

If you want to close all PDBs at once, just use ALL:

```
SQL> alter pluggable database all close;

Pluggable database altered.

SQL> select con_id,name,open_mode from v$pdbs;

    CON_ID NAME                             OPEN_MODE
---------- ------------------------------ ----------
         2 PDB$SEED                         READ ONLY
         3 QATEST1                          MOUNTED
         4 DEV2015                          MOUNTED
         5 DW17                             MOUNTED

SQL>
```

Opening or closing all PDBs leaves the root container in its current state, and, as noted earlier, the seed container PDB$SEED is always READ ONLY and is in the MOUNT state only when the CDB is in the MOUNT state.

NOTE

For a specific PDB, you can use either SHUTDOWN or SHUTDOWN IMMEDIATE. There is no PDB equivalent to the TRANSACTIONAL or ABORT options for a CDB instance or a non-CDB instance.

When you close one or more PDBs, you can add the IMMEDIATE keyword to roll back any pending transactions within the PDB. If you leave off the IMMEDIATE keyword, the PDB is not shut down until all pending transactions have been either committed or rolled back, just as in a non-CDB database instance, and all user sessions are disconnected by the user. If your session context is in a specific PDB, you can also use the SHUTDOWN IMMEDIATE statement to close the PDB, but note that this does not affect any other PDBs and that the root container's instance is still running.

CDB Instance Shutdown When you are connected to the root container, you can shut down the CDB instance and close all PDBs with one command, much like you would shut down a non-CDB database instance:

```
SQL> shutdown immediate
Database closed.
Database dismounted.
ORACLE instance shut down.
SQL>
```

When specifying IMMEDIATE, the CDB instance does not wait for a COMMIT or ROLLBACK of pending transactions, and all user sessions to any PDB are disconnected. Using TRANSACTIONAL waits for all pending transactions to complete and then disconnects all sessions before terminating the instance.

As described in the previous section, you can use the same command to shut down a specific PDB, but only that PDB's datafiles are closed, and its services will no longer accept connection requests until it is opened again.

Automating PDB Startup There are new options available in database event triggers for a multitenant environment. One of these triggers is persistent, while two others are not; the reason for this will be clear shortly.

By default, after a CDB instance starts, all PDBs within the CDB are in MOUNT mode. If your PDB is not automatically opened by any other method (such as Oracle Restart), you can create a database trigger to start up all PDBs, just a few, or just one. In the container database CDB01, the pluggable database DW17 starts up automatically via Oracle Restart; for the DEV2015 pluggable database, you'll create a trigger to change its status to OPEN READ WRITE when the container database is open, as shown here:

```
SQL> select con_id,name,open_mode from v$pdbs;

    CON_ID NAME                           OPEN_MODE
---------- ------------------------------ ----------
         2 PDB$SEED                       READ ONLY
         3 QATEST1                        MOUNTED
         4 DEV2015                        MOUNTED
         5 DW17                           READ WRITE

SQL> create trigger open_dev
  2     after startup on database
  3  begin
  4     execute immediate 'alter pluggable database dev2015 open';
  5  end;
  6  /

Trigger created.

SQL>
```

Next, shut down and restart the container CDB01 and see what happens:

```
SQL> shutdown immediate
Database closed.
Database dismounted.
ORACLE instance shut down.
SQL> startup
ORACLE instance started.

Total System Global Area 2622255104 bytes
Fixed Size                   291808 bytes
Variable Size             1140852640 bytes
Database Buffers    1459617792 bytes
Redo Buffers                19492864 bytes
Database mounted.
Database opened.
SQL> select con_id,name,open_mode from v$pdbs;

    CON_ID NAME                           OPEN_MODE
---------- ------------------------------ ----------
         2 PDB$SEED                       READ ONLY
         3 QATEST1                        MOUNTED
         4 DEV2015                        READ WRITE
         5 DW17                           READ WRITE

SQL>
```

The AFTER STARTUP ON DATABASE trigger is persistent unless you drop or disable it. Two new database event triggers for Oracle Database 12*c*, AFTER CLONE and BEFORE UNPLUG, are more dynamic. Both of those triggers must be specified with ON PLUGGABLE DATABASE; otherwise, the trigger will be invalid and not fire.

You would use a trigger such as AFTER CLONE for a PDB that you'll frequently clone in a testing or development environment. The trigger itself exists in the source PDB and will persist unless you explicitly drop it. However, when you create a new PDB by cloning the existing PDB that contains this trigger, you can perform one-time initialization tasks in the cloned PDB right after it is cloned. Once those tasks are completed, the trigger is deleted so that any clones of the already cloned database won't perform those initialization tasks.

Changing PDB Status In a non-CDB environment you often have reason to restrict access to a database either for maintenance tasks or to prepare it for a transportable tablespace or database operation. This is also true in a CDB environment. Previously in this chapter you saw how to open a PDB as READ ONLY. For any PDB that you want restricted to users with SYSDBA privileges (granted to either a global user or a local user), use the RESTRICTED clause just as you would in a non-CDB environment:

```
SQL> alter pluggable database qatest1 close;

Pluggable database altered.

SQL> alter pluggable database qatest1 open restricted;
```

```
Pluggable database altered.

SQL> select con_id,name,open_mode from v$pdbs;

    CON_ID NAME                           OPEN_MODE
---------- ------------------------------ ----------
         2 PDB$SEED                       READ ONLY
         3 QATEST1                        RESTRICTED
         4 DEV2015                        READ WRITE
         5 DW17                           READ WRITE

SQL>
```

To turn off RESTRICTED mode, close and reopen the PDB without the RESTRICTED keyword.

There are several operations you can perform on a PDB that do not require restarting the PDB in RESTRICTED mode:

- Take PDB datafiles offline or bring them back online
- Change the PDB's default tablespace
- Change the PDB's default temporary tablespace (local tablespace)
- Change the maximum size of a PDB:

  ```
  alter pluggable database storage (maxsize 50g);
  ```

- Change the name of a PDB

These dynamic settings help to maximize the availability of a PDB and allow you to make changes to a PDB much more quickly because you would not have to shut down and restart the database as in a non-CDB environment.

Changing Parameters in a CDB

Although the application developer or database user of a PDB will not see any difference in how a PDB operates compared to a non-CDB, some of the differences require careful consideration by the global and local DBAs. A subset of parameters can be changed at the PDB level, but for the most part, a PDB inherits the parameter settings of the CDB. In addition, some ALTER SYSTEM commands behave slightly differently depending on the context in which they are run by the DBA.

Understanding the Scope of Parameter Changes

Because a CDB is a database instance and PDBs share this instance, some of the CDB's parameters (stored in an SPFILE, of course) apply to the CDB and all PDBs and cannot be changed for any given PDB. You can identify the parameters that can be changed at the PDB level by looking at the ISPDB_MODIFIABLE column of V$PARAMETER. The data dictionary view PDB_SPFILE$ shows the non-default values for specific parameters across all PDBs:

```
SQL> select pdb_uid,name,value$
  2  from pdb_spfile$
  3  where name='star_transformation_enabled';

   PDB_UID NAME                                VALUE$
---------- ----------------------------------- --------------------
```

```
2557165657 star_transformation_enabled          'FALSE'
3994587631 star_transformation_enabled          'TRUE'

SQL>
```

The settings local to a PDB stay with the PDB even when the PDB has been cloned or unplugged.

Using ALTER SYSTEM in a Multitenant Environment

Many of the ALTER SYSTEM commands you would use in a non-CDB environment work as you'd expect in a multitenant environment, with a few caveats and exceptions. Some of the ALTER SYSTEM commands affect only the PDB or the CDB in which they are run. In contrast, some ALTER SYSTEM commands can be run only in the root container.

Using PDB-Specific ALTER SYSTEM Commands Within a PDB (as a local DBA or a global DBA with a PDB as the current container), the following ALTER SYSTEM commands affect objects, parameters, or sessions specific to the PDB with no effect on any other PDBs or the root container:

- ALTER SYSTEM FLUSH SHARED_POOL
- ALTER SYSTEM FLUSH BUFFER_CACHE
- ALTER SYSTEM ENABLE RESTRICTED SESSION
- ALTER SYSTEM KILL SESSION
- ALTER SYSTEM SET *<parameter>*

As you might expect, if flushing the shared pool in a PDB affected the shared pool of any other PDB, the side effects would be dramatic and unacceptable!

Understanding ALTER SYSTEM Commands with Side Effects in a PDB There are a few ALTER SYSTEM commands that you can run at the PDB level but affect the entire CDB. For example, running ALTER SYSTEM CHECKPOINT affects datafiles across the entire container unless the datafiles belong to a PDB that is opened as READ ONLY or are OFFLINE.

Using CDB-Specific ALTER SYSTEM Commands Some ALTER SYSTEM commands are valid only for the entire container *and* must be run by a common user with SYSDBA privileges in the root container. For example, running ALTER SYSTEM SWITCH LOGFILE switches to the next online redo log file group. Since the online redo log files are common to all containers, this is the expected behavior.

Manage Permanent and Temporary Tablespaces in CDB and PDBs

In a multitenant environment, tablespaces and the datafiles that comprise them belong to either the root container or one of the PDBs within the CDB. Of course, some objects are shared across all PDBs, and these objects are stored in the root container's tablespaces and shared with the PDB via database links. There are some syntax changes to the CREATE DATABASE command as well as behavior changes to CREATE TABLESPACE and other tablespace-related commands within a PDB.

Using CREATE DATABASE

The CREATE DATABASE statement for a CDB is nearly identical to that for a non-CDB, with a couple of exceptions. Oracle recommends that you use the DBCA to create a new CDB, but if you must use a CREATE DATABASE command (for example, to create dozens of CDBs in a script), you will use the USER_DATA TABLESPACE clause to specify a default tablespace for user objects for all PDBs created in this CDB. This tablespace is *not* used in the root container.

Using CREATE TABLESPACE

Creating a new tablespace in a CDB (root) container with CREATE TABLESPACE looks the same as creating a tablespace in any PDB. If you are connected to CDB$ROOT, then the tablespace is visible and usable only in the root container; similarly, a tablespace created when connected to a PDB is visible only to that PDB and cannot be used by any other PDB unless connected with a database link.

For ease of management, Oracle recommends using separate directories to store datafiles for each PDB and the CDB. Even better, if you use ASM, you'll automatically get your datafiles and other database objects segregated into separate directories by container ID. Here is how the datafiles for the container database CDB01 are stored in an ASM disk group:

```
SQL> select con_id,name,open_mode from v$pdbs;

    CON_ID NAME                                     OPEN_MODE
---------- ---------------------------------------- ----------
         2 PDB$SEED                                 READ ONLY
         3 QATEST1                                  READ WRITE
         4 DEV2015                                  READ WRITE
         5 DW17                                     READ WRITE

SQL> quit
Disconnected from Oracle Database 12c Enterprise Edition
     Release 12.1.0.1.0 - 64bit Production
With the Partitioning, Automatic Storage Management, OLAP, Advanced Analytics
and Real Application Testing options
[oracle@oel63 ~]$ . oraenv
ORACLE_SID = [cdb01] ? +ASM
The Oracle base has been changed from /u01/app/oracle to /u01/app
[oracle@oel63 ~]$ asmcmd
ASMCMD> ls
DATA/
RECOV/
ASMCMD> cd data
ASMCMD> ls
ASM/
CDB01/
DBAHANDBOOK/
orapwasm
ASMCMD> cd cdb01
ASMCMD> ls
CONTROLFILE/
DATAFILE/
DD7C48AA5A4404A2E04325AAE80A403C/
EA128C7783417731E0434702A8C08F56/
EA129627ACA47C9DE0434702A8C0836F/
```

```
FAE6382E325C40D8E0434702A8C03802/
FD8E768DE1094F9AE0434702A8C03E94/
ONLINELOG/
PARAMETERFILE/
TEMPFILE/
spfilecdb01.ora
ASMCMD> cd datafile
ASMCMD> ls
SYSAUX.272.830282801
SYSTEM.273.830282857
UNDOTBS1.275.830282923
USERS.274.830282921
ASMCMD>
```

The container's datafiles are stored in the DATAFILE subdirectory; each of the PDBs has its own set of datafiles in one of those subdirectories with the long string of hexadecimal digits. You use Oracle Managed Files (OMF) with ASM in this scenario; you don't need to know or care what those hexadecimal characters are since the locations of the datafiles are managed automatically.

Changing the Default Tablespace in a PDB

Changing the default tablespace in a CDB or PDB is identical to changing the default tablespace in a non-CDB. For both CDBs and PDBs, you use the ALTER DATABASE DEFAULT TABLESPACE command. If you're changing the default tablespace for a PDB, you should add the PLUGGABLE keyword because the ALTER DATABASE command within a PDB will be deprecated in a future release. In this example, you set the container to QATEST1, create a new tablespace within QATEST1, and change the default tablespace to be the tablespace you just created:

```
SQL> alter session set container=qatest1;

Session altered.

SQL> create tablespace qa_dflt datafile size 100m
  2       autoextend on next 100m maxsize 1g;

Tablespace created.

SQL> alter pluggable database
  2       default tablespace qa_dflt;

Pluggable database altered.

SQL>
```

Going forward, any new local users within QATEST1 that don't have a specific default permanent tablespace will use the tablespace QA_DFLT.

Using Local Temporary Tablespaces

For any CDB, you can have one default temporary tablespace or temporary tablespace group defined at the CDB level that can be used for all PDBs as their temporary tablespace. You can, however, create a temporary tablespace for a PDB that is used only by that PDB. In this example, you create a new temporary tablespace called QA_DFLT_TEMP in the PDB QATEST1 and make it the default temporary tablespace for QATEST1:

```
SQL> create temporary tablespace qa_dflt_temp
  2  tempfile size 100m autoextend on
  3  next 100m maxsize 500m;

Tablespace created.

SQL> alter pluggable database
  2  default temporary tablespace qa_dflt_temp;

Pluggable database altered.

SQL>
```

A temporary tablespace created within a PDB stays with that PDB when it's unplugged and plugged back into the same or a different CDB. If a user is not assigned a specific temporary tablespace, then that user is assigned the default temporary tablespace for the PDB. If there is no default temporary tablespace for the PDB, then the default temporary tablespace for the CDB applies.

Multitenant Security

As described earlier in the chapter, in a multitenant environment, there are two types of users: *common* users and *local* users. A common user in a CDB (root container) has visibility and an account available in the root container and automatically in each PDB within the CDB. Common users do not automatically have the same privileges in every PDB; this flexibility simplifies your authentication processes but makes it easy to fine-tune the authorization in each PDB.

Managing Common and Local Users

The names of common users start with C##, which makes it easy to distinguish a common user from a local user in each PDB. Creating a local user is exactly like creating a user in a non-CDB. You can create a local user either with a common user or with another local user with the CREATE USER privileges:

```
SQL> alter session set container=qatest1;

Session altered.

SQL> create user qa_fnd1 identified by qa901;

User created.

SQL> grant create session to qa_fnd1;

Grant succeeded.

SQL> connect qa_fnd1/qa901@oel63:1521/qatest1
Connected.
SQL>
```

The root container (CDB$ROOT) cannot have local users, only common users. Common users have the same identity and password in the root container and every PDB, both current and future. Having a common user account doesn't automatically mean you have the same privileges across every PDB including the root container. The accounts SYS and SYSTEM are common users who can set any PDB as their default container. For new common users, the username must begin with C## or c##, although creating a username with lowercase letters by using double quotation marks around the username is highly discouraged.

When you create a common user with the CREATE USER command, you typically add CONTAINER=ALL to the command, as in this example:

```
SQL> create user c##secadmin identified by sec404 container=all;

User created.

SQL> grant dba to c##secadmin;

Grant succeeded.

SQL>
```

If you are connected to the root container and have the CREATE USER privilege, the CONTAINER=ALL clause is optional. The same applies to a local user and the CONTAINER=CURRENT clause. The C##SECADMIN user now has DBA privileges in the root container. This user has an account set up in each PDB but no privileges in any PDB unless explicitly assigned:

```
SQL> connect c##secadmin/sec404@oel63:1521/cdb01
Connected.
SQL> alter session set container=qatest1;
ERROR:
ORA-01031: insufficient privileges


SQL>
```

To allow the user C##SECADMIN to at least connect to the QATEST1 database, grant the appropriate privileges as follows:

```
SQL> grant create session, set container to c##secadmin;

Grant succeeded.

SQL> connect c##secadmin/sec404@oel63:1521/cdb01
Connected.
SQL> alter session set container=qatest1;

Session altered.

SQL>
```

When using CREATE USER, you can optionally specify the default tablespace, the default temporary tablespace, and the profile. These three attributes must exist in each PDB; otherwise, those values will be set to the PDB defaults for those items.

What if a common user is created while one of the PDBs is currently not OPEN, in RESTRICTED mode, or in READ ONLY mode? The new common user's attributes are synced the next time the other PDBs are opened.

Managing Common and Local Privileges

Common and local privileges apply to common and local users. If a privilege is granted across all containers to a common user, it's a common privilege. Similarly, a privilege granted in the context of a single PDB is a local privilege regardless of whether the user is local or common.

In the previous section, the user C##SECADMIN, a common user, was granted the CREATE SESSION privilege but only on the QATEST1 container. If C##SECADMIN needs access to all PDBs by default, use the CONTAINER=ALL keyword to grant that privilege across all current and new PDBs in the CDB:

```
SQL> connect / as sysdba
Connected.
SQL> show con_id

CON_ID
------------------------------
1
SQL> grant create session to c##secadmin container=all;

Grant succeeded.

SQL> connect c##secadmin/sec404@oel63:1521/dw17
Connected.
SQL>
```

From a security perspective, you can grant common users privileges in the root container but no other containers. Remember that only common users can connect to the root container regardless of the privileges granted; for a common user to connect to the root container, the user will need the CREATE SESSION privilege in the context of the root container, as you can see in this example:

```
SQL> connect / as sysdba
Connected.
SQL> alter session set container=cdb$root;

Session altered.

SQL> create user c##rootadm identified by adm580;

User created.

SQL> connect c##rootadm/adm580@oel63:1521/cdb01
ERROR:
```

```
ORA-01045: user C##ROOTADM lacks CREATE SESSION privilege; logon denied


Warning: You are no longer connected to ORACLE.
SQL>
```

To fix this issue for C##ROOTADM, you need to grant the CREATE SESSION privilege in the context of the root container:

```
SQL> grant create session to c##rootadm container=current;

Grant succeeded.

SQL> connect c##rootadm/adm580@oel63:1521/cdb01
Connected.
SQL>
```

You revoke privileges from users and roles using the REVOKE command as in previous releases and non-CDBs. The key difference of using GRANT and REVOKE in a multitenant environment is the addition of the CONTAINER clause where you specify the context of the GRANT or REVOKE. Here are some examples of the CONTAINER clause:

- CONTAINER=QATEST1 (privileges valid only in the PDB QATEST1)
- CONTAINER=ALL (privileges valid across all PDBs, current and future)
- CONTAINER=CURRENT (privileges granted or revoked in the current container)

To grant a privilege with CONTAINER=ALL, the grantor must have the SET CONTAINER privilege along with the GRANT ANY PRIVILEGE system privilege.

Managing Common and Local Roles

Roles, just like system and object privileges, work much the same in a multitenant environment as they do in a non-CDB environment. Common roles use the same conventions as common users and start with C##; a common role can have the same privileges across all containers or specific privileges or no privileges in a subset of containers. You use the CONTAINER clause to specify the context of the role:

```
SQL> connect / as sysdba
Connected.
SQL> create role c##mv container=all;

Role created.

SQL> alter session set container=dw17;

Session altered.

SQL> create user dw_repl identified by dw909;

User created.
```

```
SQL> grant c##mv to dw_repl;

Grant succeeded.

SQL>
```

Note in the example that a common role (C##MV) was granted to a local user (DW_REPL) in DW17. The user DW_REPL inherits all the privileges in the role C##MV but only in the DW17 PDB. The reverse is also possible: A common user (such as C##RJB) can be granted a local role (such as LOCAL_ADM) in a specific PDB (such as QATEST1), and therefore the privileges granted via LOCAL_ADM are available only in QATEST1 for C##RJB.

Enabling Common Users to Access Data in Specific PDBs

Just as in a non-CDB environment, you may want to share objects with users in other PDBs. By default, any tables created by a common or local user are nonshared and are accessible only in the PDB where they were created.

Shared tables, on the other hand, have some restrictions. Only Oracle-supplied common users (such as SYS or SYSTEM) can create shared tables; common users that the DBA creates (even with DBA privileges such as CREATE USER, DROP ANY TABLE, and so forth) cannot create shared tables.

The two types of shared objects are "links": Object Links and Metadata Links. Object Links connect every PDB to a table in the root container, and each PDB sees the same rows. A good example of this is Automatic Workload Repository (AWR) data in tables like DBA_HIST_ACTIVE_SESS_HISTORY, which has the column CON_ID so you can identify which container the row in DBA_HIST_ACTIVE_SESSION_HISTORY applies to.

In contrast, Metadata Links allow access to tables in the root container plus their own private copies of the data. Most of the DBA_ views use this method. For example, looking at the DBA_USERS view in the PDB QATEST1, there is no CON_ID column from the PDB perspective:

```
SQL> select username, common from dba_users;

USERNAME                       COMMON
------------------------------ ----------
C##KLH                         YES
PDBADMIN                       NO
AUDSYS                         YES
GSMUSER                        YES
SPATIAL_WFS_ADMIN_USR          YES
C##RJB                         YES
SPATIAL_CSW_ADMIN_USR          YES
APEX_PUBLIC_USER               YES
RJB                            NO
SYSDG                          YES
DIP                            YES
QA_FND1                        NO
```

However, from the same table in the root container, you can look at CDB_USERS and see the local and common users across all containers:

```
SQL> select con_id,username,common from cdb_users
  2  order by username,con_id;

    CON_ID USERNAME                       COMMON
---------- ------------------------------ ----------
         1 ANONYMOUS                      YES
. . .
         5 AUDSYS                         YES
         1 C##KLH                         YES
         3 C##KLH                         YES
         4 C##KLH                         YES
         5 C##KLH                         YES
         1 C##RJB                         YES
         3 C##RJB                         YES
         4 C##RJB                         YES
         5 C##RJB                         YES
         1 C##ROOTADM                     YES
         3 C##ROOTADM                     YES
. . .
         4 DVSYS                          YES
         5 DVSYS                          YES
         5 DW_REPL                        NO
         1 FLOWS_FILES                    YES
         2 FLOWS_FILES                    YES
. . .
         5 OUTLN                          YES
         3 PDBADMIN                       NO
         3 QAFRED                         NO
         3 QA_FND1                        NO
         3 RJB                            NO
         4 RJB                            NO
         5 RJB                            NO
         1 SI_INFORMTN_SCHEMA             YES
         2 SI_INFORMTN_SCHEMA             YES
. . .
198 rows selected.

SQL>
```

The common users such as C##RJB exist for every PDB (other than the seed database). Users such as QAFRED exist only in the PDB with CON_ID=3 (QATEST1). Note also that the common users you create must start with C##; Oracle-supplied common users do not need this prefix.

By default, common users cannot see information about specific PDBs. This follows the *principle of least privilege* required to accomplish a task; a common user won't automatically be able to connect to a specific PDB nor see metadata about any PDB unless explicitly granted.

To leverage the granularity of data dictionary views by common users, you'll use the ALTER USER command to specify a common user, what container data they can access, and what container they can access it from. For example, you may want only the common user C##RJB to see rows in V$SESSION for the PDB DW17 when connected to the PDB QATEST1. You would use the following command to accomplish this:

```
SQL> alter user c##rjb
  2      set container_data=(cdb$root,dw17)
  3      for v$session container=current;

User altered.

SQL>
```

To view the list of users and the container objects accessible to them, look in DBA_CONTAINER_DATA:

```
SQL> select username,owner,object_name,
  2      all_containers,container_name
  3  from dba_container_data
  4  where username='C##RJB';

USERNAME     OWNER        OBJECT_NAME    A CONTAINER_NAME
------------ ------------ -------------- - -------------------------
C##RJB       SYS          V$SESSION      N DW17
C##RJB       SYS          V$SESSION      N CDB$ROOT

SQL>
```

The common user C##RJB will be able to see only rows in V$SESSION for the container DW17.

Backup and Recovery in Multitenant Environments

There are several backup and recovery options for a CDB or a PDB. Using ARCHIVELOG mode enhances the recoverability of a database, but in a multitenant environment you can enable ARCHIVELOG mode only at the CDB level since the redo log files are only at the CDB level. Otherwise, you can still back up your database in much the same way as in a non-CDB environment. You can back up the entire CDB, a single PDB, a tablespace, a datafile, or even a single block anywhere in the container.

The Data Recovery Advisor works much the same way as it did in previous releases of Oracle Database: When a failure occurs, the Data Recovery Advisor gathers failure information into the Automatic Diagnostic Repository (ADR). The Data Recovery Advisor also has proactive features to check for failures before they are detected by a user session.

You can also easily duplicate a PDB using RMAN. Using RMAN gives you more flexibility when copying a PDB compared to using the CREATE PLUGGABLE DATABASE . . . FROM . . . option. For example, you can use the RMAN DUPLICATE command to copy all PDBs within its CDB to a new CDB with the same PDBs plus the root and seed databases.

Performing Backups of a CDB and All PDBs

For multitenant databases, the RMAN syntax has been modified and new clauses have been added. At the OS level, the environment variable ORACLE_SID was previously set at the instance level, but now that all databases within a CDB are running in the same database instance, you can connect to a single PDB with RMAN using the service name and not the instance name. Here's an example:

```
[oracle@tettnang ~]$ echo $ORACLE_SID
cdb01
[oracle@tettnang ~]$ rman target rjb/rjb@tettnang/tool

Recovery Manager: Release 12.1.0.1.0 - Production on Tue Jun 3 07:50:06 2014

Copyright (c) 1982, 2013, Oracle and/or its affiliates.  All rights reserved.

connected to target database: CDB01 (DBID=1382179355)

RMAN>
```

As in previous releases, you can connect to the CDB with RMAN using the syntax you're familiar with:

```
[oracle@tettnang ~]$ rman target /

Recovery Manager: Release 12.1.0.1.0 - Production on Tue Jun 3 07:52:33 2014

Copyright (c) 1982, 2013, Oracle and/or its affiliates.  All rights reserved.

connected to target database: CDB01 (DBID=1382179355)

RMAN>
```

Note, however, that the target database is displayed as CDB01 in both cases. How else would you know that you're connected to a specific PDB instead of the CDB? To find out, just use the REPORT SCHEMA command:

```
[oracle@tettnang ~]$ rman target /

Recovery Manager: Release 12.1.0.1.0 - Production on Tue Jun 3 10:00:38 2014

Copyright (c) 1982, 2013, Oracle and/or its affiliates.  All rights reserved.

connected to target database: CDB01 (DBID=1382179355)

RMAN> report schema;

using target database control file instead of recovery catalog
Report of database schema for database with db_unique_name CDB01

List of Permanent Datafiles
===========================
File Size(MB) Tablespace           RB segs Datafile Name
---- -------- -------------------- ------- ------------------------
1    790      SYSTEM               ***     +DATA/CDB01/DATAFILE/system.268.845194003
3    1460     SYSAUX               ***     +DATA/CDB01/DATAFILE/sysaux.267.845193957
```

```
4    735      UNDOTBS1             ***      +DATA/CDB01/DATAFILE/undotbs1.270.845194049
5    250      PDB$SEED:SYSTEM      ***      +DATA/CDB01/
DD7C48AA5A4404A2E04325AAE80A403C/DATAFILE/system.277.845194085
6    5        USERS                ***      +DATA/CDB01/DATAFILE/users.269.845194049
7    590      PDB$SEED:SYSAUX      ***      +DATA/CDB01/
DD7C48AA5A4404A2E04325AAE80A403C/DATAFILE/sysaux.276.845194085
18   260      TOOL:SYSTEM          ***      +DATA/CDB01/
FA782A61F8447D03E043E3A0080A9E54/DATAFILE/system.286.848743627
. . .
27   5        CCREPOS:USERS        ***      +DATA/CDB01/
F751E0E9988D6064E043E3A0080A6DC5/DATAFILE/users.283.845194257
28   100      UNDOTBS1             ***      +DATA/CDB01/DATAFILE/undotbs1.263.848922747
29   100      TOOL:PROCREPO        ***      +DATA/CDB01/
FA782A61F8447D03E043E3A0080A9E54/DATAFILE/procrepo.257.849257047

List of Temporary Files
=======================
File Size(MB) Tablespace           Maxsize(MB) Tempfile Name
---- -------- -------------------- ----------- --------------------
1    521      TEMP                 32767       +DATA/CDB01/TEMPFILE/temp.275.845194083
2    20       PDB$SEED:TEMP        32767       +DATA/CDB01/
DD7C48AA5A4404A2E04325AAE80A403C/DATAFILE/pdbseed_temp01.dbf
3    20       CCREPOS:TEMP         32767       +DATA/CDB01/
F751E0E9988D6064E043E3A0080A6DC5/TEMPFILE/temp.282.848755025
4    20       TOOL:TEMP            32767       +DATA/CDB01/
FA782A61F8447D03E043E3A0080A9E54/TEMPFILE/temp.299.848743629
6    20       QA_2015:TEMP         32767       +DATA/CDB01/
FA787E0038B26FFBE043E3A0080A1A75/TEMPFILE/temp.291.848745313
7    60       RPTQA12C:TEMP        32767       +DATA/CDB01/
F754FCD8744A55AAE043E3A0080A3B17/TEMPFILE/temp.300.848752943
8    100      TEMP                 1000        +DATA/CDB01/TEMPFILE/temp.258.848922745

RMAN> quit

Recovery Manager complete.
```

Note that connecting to the CDB shows all tablespaces, including those of the seed and root containers. Connecting to an individual PDB returns different (but expected) results for the REPORT SCHEMA command:

```
[oracle@tettnang ~]$ rman target rjb/rjb@tettnang/tool

Recovery Manager: Release 12.1.0.1.0 - Production on Tue Jun 3 10:00:50 2014

Copyright (c) 1982, 2013, Oracle and/or its affiliates.  All rights reserved.

connected to target database: CDB01 (DBID=1382179355)
```

```
RMAN> report schema;

using target database control file instead of recovery catalog
Report of database schema for database with db_unique_name CDB01

List of Permanent Datafiles
===========================
File Size(MB) Tablespace           RB segs Datafile Name
---- -------- -------------------- ------- ------------------------
18   260      SYSTEM               ***     +DATA/CDB01/
FA782A61F8447D03E043E3A0080A9E54/DATAFILE/system.286.848743627
19   620      SYSAUX               ***     +DATA/CDB01/
FA782A61F8447D03E043E3A0080A9E54/DATAFILE/sysaux.303.848743627
29   100      PROCREPO             ***     +DATA/CDB01/
FA782A61F8447D03E043E3A0080A9E54/DATAFILE/procrepo.257.849257047

List of Temporary Files
=======================
File Size(MB) Tablespace           Maxsize(MB) Tempfile Name
---- -------- -------------------- ----------- --------------------
4    20       TEMP                 32767       +DATA/CDB01/
FA782A61F8447D03E043E3A0080A9E54/TEMPFILE/temp.299.848743629

RMAN>
```

The RMAN BACKUP, RESTORE, and RECOVER commands have been enhanced to include the PLUGGABLE keyword when operating on one or more PDBs:

```
RMAN> backup pluggable database rptqa12c;
```

In addition, you can qualify a tablespace backup with a PDB name to back up one specific tablespace within the PDB:

```
[oracle@tettnang ~]$ rman target /

Recovery Manager: Release 12.1.0.1.0 - Production on Tue Jun 3 08:44:15 2014

Copyright (c) 1982, 2013, Oracle and/or its affiliates.  All rights reserved.

connected to target database: CDB01 (DBID=1382179355)

RMAN> backup tablespace tool:procrepo;

Starting backup at 03-JUN-14
using target database control file instead of recovery catalog
allocated channel: ORA_DISK_1
channel ORA_DISK_1: SID=258 device type=DISK
```

```
channel ORA_DISK_1: starting full datafile backup set
channel ORA_DISK_1: specifying datafile(s) in backup set
input datafile file number=00029 name=+DATA/CDB01
    /FA782A61F8447D03E043E3A0080A9E54
    /DATAFILE/procrepo.257.849257047
channel ORA_DISK_1: starting piece 1 at 03-JUN-14
channel ORA_DISK_1: finished piece 1 at 03-JUN-14
piece handle=+RECOV/CDB01
    /FA782A61F8447D03E043E3A0080A9E54
    /BACKUPSET/2014_06_03/nnndf0_tag20140603t084425_0.256.849257065
tag=TAG20140603T084425 comment=NONE
channel ORA_DISK_1: backup set complete, elapsed time: 00:00:01
Finished backup at 03-JUN-14

Starting Control File and SPFILE Autobackup at 03-JUN-14
piece handle=+RECOV/CDB01/AUTOBACKUP/2014_06_03/s_849257066.257.849257067
comment=NONE
Finished Control File and SPFILE Autobackup at 03-JUN-14

RMAN>
```

Without any qualification, when connected to the CDB, any RMAN commands operate on the root container and all PDBs. To back up just the root container, use the name CDB$ROOT, which as you know from Chapter 11 is the name of the root container within the CDB.

Backing Up CDBs

As mentioned in the previous section, you can back up the entire CDB as a full backup, a single PDB within the CDB, or individual tablespaces in any of the PDBs or root container. To run RMAN and back up a container, the user must have a common account with either the SYSDBA or SYSBACKUP privilege in the root container. To accommodate separation of duties, Oracle recommends assigning only the SYSBACKUP privilege to a database user who is responsible only for database backups and recovery.

Since a CDB is most similar to a pre-12*c* database (non-CDB), your backups will look similar to RMAN backups you created in Oracle Database 11*g*. You can create backupsets or image copies along with the control file, SPFILE, and optionally the archived redo log files.

Backing up the CDB (and all PDBs) with the container open requires ARCHIVELOG mode as in previous releases; if the CDB is in NOARCHIVELOG mode, then the container must be open in MOUNT mode (and therefore no PDBs are open as well). Here is an example:

```
[oracle@tettnang ~]$ rman target /

Recovery Manager: Release 12.1.0.1.0 - Production on Tue Jun 3 12:13:26 2014

Copyright (c) 1982, 2013, Oracle and/or its affiliates.  All rights reserved.

connected to target database: CDB01 (DBID=1382179355)

RMAN> backup database;
```

```
Starting backup at 03-JUN-14
using target database control file instead of recovery catalog
allocated channel: ORA_DISK_1
channel ORA_DISK_1: SID=6 device type=DISK
allocated channel: ORA_DISK_2
channel ORA_DISK_2: SID=1021 device type=DISK
allocated channel: ORA_DISK_3
channel ORA_DISK_3: SID=1281 device type=DISK
allocated channel: ORA_DISK_4
channel ORA_DISK_4: SID=1025 device type=DISK
channel ORA_DISK_1: starting compressed full datafile backup set
channel ORA_DISK_1: specifying datafile(s) in backup set
input datafile file number=00003 name=+DATA/CDB01/DATAFILE/sysaux.267.845193957
channel ORA_DISK_1: starting piece 1 at 03-JUN-14
channel ORA_DISK_2: starting compressed full datafile backup set
channel ORA_DISK_2: specifying datafile(s) in backup set
input datafile file number=00023 name=+DATA/CDB01/
F754FCD8744A55AAE043E3A0080A3B17/DATAFILE/sysaux.302.848752939
channel ORA_DISK_2: starting piece 1 at 03-JUN-14
channel ORA_DISK_3: starting compressed full datafile backup set
channel ORA_DISK_3: specifying datafile(s) in backup set
input datafile file number=00004 name=+DATA/CDB01/DATAFILE/undotbs1.270.845194049
input datafile file number=00028 name=+DATA/CDB01/DATAFILE/undotbs1.263.848922747
. . .
channel ORA_DISK_2: backup set complete, elapsed time: 00:00:00
channel ORA_DISK_3: finished piece 1 at 03-JUN-14
piece handle=+RECOV/CDB01/F751E0E9988D6064E043E3A0080A6DC5/
BACKUPSET/2014_06_03/nnndf0_tag20140603t121337_0.280.849269683
tag=TAG20140603T121337 comment=NONE
channel ORA_DISK_3: backup set complete, elapsed time: 00:00:01
Finished backup at 03-JUN-14

Starting Control File and SPFILE Autobackup at 03-JUN-14
piece handle=+RECOV/CDB01/AUTOBACKUP/2014_06_03/s_849269683.281.849269683
comment=NONE
Finished Control File and SPFILE Autobackup at 03-JUN-14

RMAN>
```

Note the references to tablespaces and datafiles like this:

```
name=+DATA/CDB01/F754FCD8744A55AAE043E3A0080A3B17/
         DATAFILE/sysaux.302.848752939
```

It's the datafile for the SYSAUX tablespace in one of the PDBs. To find out which one, you can look in the dynamic performance view V$PDBS at the column GUID. The globally unique identifier (GUID) value is a long hexadecimal string that uniquely identifies the container even when it's unplugged from one CDB and plugged back into another.

```
SQL> select con_id,dbid,guid,name from v$pdbs;

  CON_ID       DBID GUID                             NAME
-------- ---------- -------------------------------- --------------------
       2 4087805696 F751D8C27D475B57E043E3A0080A2A47 PDB$SEED
       3 1248256969 F751E0E9988D6064E043E3A0080A6DC5 CCREPOS
       4 1258510409 FA782A61F8447D03E043E3A0080A9E54 TOOL
       6 2577431197 FA787E0038B26FFBE043E3A0080A1A75 QA_2015
       7 1288637549 F754FCD8744A55AAE043E3A0080A3B17 RPTQA12C

SQL>
```

In this case, the SYSAUX datafile belongs to the RPTQA12C PDB.

If you want to perform a *partial CDB backup,* you connect to the container (CDB) with RMAN and back up one or more containers in a single command along with the root container using the PLUGGABLE DATABASE clause, as in this example:

```
RMAN> backup pluggable database tool,rptqa12c,"CDB$ROOT";
```

In a recovery scenario, you can restore and recover the TOOL PDB separately from the RPTQA12C PDB or just the root container.

Backing Up PDBs

Backing up a PDB is also similar to backing up a non-CDB in Oracle Database 12c or previous releases. Note that backing up a PDB is identical to backing up part of a CDB but without the root container (CDB$ROOT). For separation of duties, you can have a user with SYSBACKUP privileges in only one PDB. They will connect only to the PDB and then back it up as if it were a non-CDB. This example shows a backup administrator connecting to only the CCREPOS PDB as a local user and performing a full RMAN backup:

```
[oracle@tettnang ~]$ rman target rjb/rjb@tettnang/ccrepos

Recovery Manager: Release 12.1.0.1.0 - Production on Tue Jun 3 21:00:27 2014

Copyright (c) 1982, 2013, Oracle and/or its affiliates.  All rights reserved.

connected to target database: CDB01 (DBID=1382179355)

RMAN> backup database;

Starting backup at 03-JUN-14
using target database control file instead of recovery catalog
allocated channel: ORA_DISK_1
channel ORA_DISK_1: SID=1027 device type=DISK
allocated channel: ORA_DISK_2
channel ORA_DISK_2: SID=1283 device type=DISK
```

```
allocated channel: ORA_DISK_3
channel ORA_DISK_3: SID=1028 device type=DISK
allocated channel: ORA_DISK_4
channel ORA_DISK_4: SID=13 device type=DISK
channel ORA_DISK_1: starting compressed full datafile backup set
channel ORA_DISK_1: specifying datafile(s) in backup set
input datafile file number=00026 name=+DATA/CDB01/
F751E0E9988D6064E043E3A0080A6DC5
    /DATAFILE/sysaux.281.845194249
channel ORA_DISK_1: starting piece 1 at 03-JUN-14
channel ORA_DISK_2: starting compressed full datafile backup set
channel ORA_DISK_2: specifying datafile(s) in backup set
input datafile file number=00025 name=+DATA/CDB01/
F751E0E9988D6064E043E3A0080A6DC5
    /DATAFILE/system.280.845194249
channel ORA_DISK_2: starting piece 1 at 03-JUN-14
channel ORA_DISK_3: starting compressed full datafile backup set
channel ORA_DISK_3: specifying datafile(s) in backup set
input datafile file number=00027 name=+DATA/CDB01/
F751E0E9988D6064E043E3A0080A6DC5
    /DATAFILE/users.283.845194257
channel ORA_DISK_3: starting piece 1 at 03-JUN-14
channel ORA_DISK_3: finished piece 1 at 03-JUN-14
piece handle=+RECOV/CDB01/F751E0E9988D6064E043E3A0080A6DC5
    /BACKUPSET/2014_06_03/nnndf0_tag20140603t210035_0.284.849301235
tag=TAG20140603T210035 comment=NONE
channel ORA_DISK_3: backup set complete, elapsed time: 00:00:01
channel ORA_DISK_2: finished piece 1 at 03-JUN-14
piece handle=+RECOV/CDB01/F751E0E9988D6064E043E3A0080A6DC5
    /BACKUPSET/2014_06_03/nnndf0_tag20140603t210035_0.285.849301235
tag=TAG20140603T210035 comment=NONE
channel ORA_DISK_2: backup set complete, elapsed time: 00:00:07
channel ORA_DISK_1: finished piece 1 at 03-JUN-14
piece handle=+RECOV/CDB01/F751E0E9988D6064E043E3A0080A6DC5
    /BACKUPSET/2014_06_03/nnndf0_tag20140603t210035_0.283.849301235
tag=TAG20140603T210035 comment=NONE
channel ORA_DISK_1: backup set complete, elapsed time: 00:00:25
Finished backup at 03-JUN-14

Starting Control File and SPFILE Autobackup at 03-JUN-14
piece handle=+RECOV/CDB01/F751E0E9988D6064E043E3A0080A6DC5
    /AUTOBACKUP/2014_06_03/s_849301260.286.849301261 comment=NONE
Finished Control File and SPFILE Autobackup at 03-JUN-14

RMAN>
```

Note that you do not need to specify the PLUGGABLE keyword since you're doing the backup from the perspective of a single PDB. Even though you're backing up a single PDB, the control file is included in the full backup despite the fact that the control file is shared across the entire container along with the SPFILE.

Recovering from PDB Datafile Loss

As with non-CDB databases, both PDBs and a CDB can suffer from instance failure or media failure requiring some kind of recovery operation. The recovery can occur at the CDB level, the PDB level, a tablespace within a PDB, a datafile, or even an individual block. The one major difference is instance recovery: Since all PDBs and the CDB share a single instance, all PDBs go down if the CDB goes down, and thus crash recovery for the instance occurs only at the CDB level. Similarly, any objects that are global and exist at the CDB level, such as the control files, redo log files, or datafiles from the root's SYSTEM or UNDO tablespaces, require media recovery at the CDB level only.

In the following sections, I'll review the types of media failure and how to recover from them. Many of the scenarios have the same recovery solution as a non-CDB, and in the case of a single PDB, the recovery of that PDB can occur with little or no disruption to other PDBs that may be open at the time.

Tempfile Recovery

Recall from earlier in this chapter that a temporary tablespace (with one or more tempfiles) exists at the CDB level, but each PDB can have its own temporary tablespace if the application has different requirements. If a PDB's DML or SELECT statements require the TEMP tablespace at the CDB level and it is suddenly lost because of media failure, the statement will fail. In this example, one of the ASM administrators accidentally deletes one of the tempfiles belonging to the CDB:

```
[oracle@tettnang ~]$ asmcmd
ASMCMD> cd +data/cdb01/tempfile
ASMCMD> ls -l
Type      Redund  Striped  Time             Sys  Name
TEMPFILE  UNPROT  COARSE   JUN 03 08:00:00  Y    TEMP.258.848922745
TEMPFILE  UNPROT  COARSE   JUN 03 08:00:00  Y    TEMP.275.845194083
ASMCMD> rm TEMP.258.848922745
ASMCMD> quit
[oracle@tettnang ~]$
```

The easy but draconian solution to fix the problem would be to restart the entire CDB. Instead, you can just add another tempfile to the TEMP tablespace and drop the one that no longer exists:

```
SQL> alter tablespace temp add tempfile '+DATA'
  2      size 100m autoextend on next 100m maxsize 2g;

Tablespace altered.

SQL> alter tablespace temp drop tempfile
  2     '+DATA/CDB01/TEMPFILE/temp.258.848922745';

Tablespace altered.

SQL>
```

As with non-CDBs, if a temporary tablespace (at either the CDB or PDB level) is missing at container startup, it is re-created automatically.

Recovering from Control File Loss

Losing one or all control files is just as serious as losing a control file in a non-CDB. Oracle best practices dictate that you have at least three copies of the control file available. If you lose all copies of the control file, you can get them from the latest RMAN autobackup. In this example, the copy of the control file in the +RECOV disk group is missing, and the CDB will not start (and as a result, none of the PDBs can start):

```
[oracle@tettnang ~]$ . oraenv
ORACLE_SID = [+ASM] ? cdb01
The Oracle base remains unchanged with value /u01/app/oracle
[oracle@tettnang ~]$ sqlplus / as sysdba

SQL*Plus: Release 12.1.0.1.0 Production on Tue Jun 3 23:03:52 2014

Copyright (c) 1982, 2013, Oracle.  All rights reserved.

Connected to an idle instance.

SQL> startup
ORACLE instance started.

Total System Global Area 5027385344 bytes
Fixed Size                  2691952 bytes
Variable Size            1241517200 bytes
Database Buffers         3774873600 bytes
Redo Buffers                8302592 bytes
ORA-00205: error in identifying control file, check alert log for more info


SQL>
```

Shut down the instance and recover the control file from the last RMAN backup:

```
SQL> shutdown immediate
ORA-01507: database not mounted


ORACLE instance shut down.
SQL> quit
Disconnected from Oracle Database 12c Enterprise Edition Release 12.1.0.1.0 -
64bit Production
With the Partitioning, OLAP, Advanced Analytics and Real Application Testing
options
[oracle@tettnang ~]$ rman target /

Recovery Manager: Release 12.1.0.1.0 - Production on Tue Jun 3 23:07:30 2014

Copyright (c) 1982, 2013, Oracle and/or its affiliates.  All rights reserved.

connected to target database (not started)
```

```
RMAN> startup nomount;

Oracle instance started

Total System Global Area    5027385344 bytes

Fixed Size                     2691952 bytes
Variable Size               1241517200 bytes
Database Buffers            3774873600 bytes
Redo Buffers                   8302592 bytes

RMAN> restore controlfile from autobackup;

Starting restore at 03-JUN-14
using target database control file instead of recovery catalog
allocated channel: ORA_DISK_1
channel ORA_DISK_1: SID=1021 device type=DISK

recovery area destination: +RECOV
database name (or database unique name) used for search: CDB01
channel ORA_DISK_1: AUTOBACKUP +RECOV/CDB01/AUTOBACKUP/2014_06_03
/s_849308463.289.849308463 found in the recovery area
AUTOBACKUP search with format "%F" not attempted because DBID was not set
channel ORA_DISK_1: restoring control file from AUTOBACKUP +RECOV/CDB01/AUTOBA
CKUP/2014_06_03/s_849308463.289.849308463
channel ORA_DISK_1: control file restore from AUTOBACKUP complete
output file name=+DATA/CDB01/CONTROLFILE/current.271.849308871
output file name=+RECOV/CDB01/CONTROLFILE/current.260.845194075
Finished restore at 03-JUN-14

RMAN>
```

Even though only one copy of the control file was lost, the RMAN recovery operation restores both copies; the remaining control file is almost certainly out of sync with the autobackup version:

```
RMAN> alter database mount;

Statement processed
released channel: ORA_DISK_1

RMAN> recover database;

Starting recover at 03-JUN-14
Starting implicit crosscheck backup at 03-JUN-14
allocated channel: ORA_DISK_1
channel ORA_DISK_1: SID=1021 device type=DISK
allocated channel: ORA_DISK_2
channel ORA_DISK_2: SID=260 device type=DISK
allocated channel: ORA_DISK_3
channel ORA_DISK_3: SID=514 device type=DISK
```

```
allocated channel: ORA_DISK_4
channel ORA_DISK_4: SID=769 device type=DISK
Crosschecked 25 objects
Finished implicit crosscheck backup at 03-JUN-14

Starting implicit crosscheck copy at 03-JUN-14
using channel ORA_DISK_1
using channel ORA_DISK_2
using channel ORA_DISK_3
using channel ORA_DISK_4
Finished implicit crosscheck copy at 03-JUN-14

searching for all files in the recovery area
cataloging files...
cataloging done

List of Cataloged Files
=======================
File Name: +RECOV/CDB01/AUTOBACKUP/2014_06_03/s_849308463.289.849308463

using channel ORA_DISK_1
using channel ORA_DISK_2
using channel ORA_DISK_3
using channel ORA_DISK_4

starting media recovery

archived log for thread 1 with sequence 215 is already on disk as file +DATA/
CDB01/ONLINELOG/group_2.273.845194077
archived log file name=+DATA/CDB01/ONLINELOG/group_2.273.845194077 thread=1
sequence=215
media recovery complete, elapsed time: 00:00:00
Finished recover at 03-JUN-14

RMAN> alter database open resetlogs;

Statement processed

RMAN> alter pluggable database all open;

Statement processed

RMAN>
```

Data loss will not occur unless you have objects defined in the recovered control file that were created after the last RMAN autobackup of the control file.

Recovering from Redo Log File Loss

Redo log files are only at the CDB level and therefore are recovered in much the same way as in a non-CDB. Redo log files should be multiplexed with at least two copies. If one copy of a redo log group is lost or corrupted, the database writes to the remaining log group members, and an alert is issued. No database recovery is required, but the missing or corrupted redo log group member should be replaced as soon as possible to avoid possible data loss.

If all members of a redo log file group go missing or become corrupted, the database shuts down, and media recovery will likely be required since there are committed transactions in the lost redo log file group that have not yet been written to the datafiles. If the entire log file group was on a disk that was temporarily offline, just changing the status of the log file group to ONLINE will trigger an automatic instance recovery, and no data should be lost.

Recovering from Root Datafile Loss

Losing the critical SYSTEM or UNDO tablespace datafiles is just as serious as losing them in a non-CDB. If the instance does not shut down automatically, you'll have to shut down the CDB and perform media recovery. The media recovery will also affect any PDBs that were open at the time of datafile loss or corruption.

The recovery process is the same as in a non-CDB for the loss of SYSTEM or UNDO. Losing a noncritical tablespace (such as an application-specific tablespace) does allow the CDB to remain open along with all PDBs while you perform media recovery.

Recovering the SYSTEM or UNDO Tablespace

As an example, suppose the datafiles for the CDB's SYSTEM tablespace are accidentally deleted while the CDB is down. Starting it up gives the expectedly ominous message:

```
[oracle@tettnang ~]$ . oraenv
ORACLE_SID = [+ASM] ? cdb01
The Oracle base remains unchanged with value /u01/app/oracle
[oracle@tettnang ~]$ sqlplus / as sysdba

SQL*Plus: Release 12.1.0.1.0 Production on Wed Jun 4 07:37:25 2014

Copyright (c) 1982, 2013, Oracle.  All rights reserved.

Connected to an idle instance.

SQL> startup
ORACLE instance started.

Total System Global Area 5027385344 bytes
Fixed Size                  2691952 bytes
Variable Size            1241517200 bytes
Database Buffers         3774873600 bytes
Redo Buffers                8302592 bytes
Database mounted.
ORA-01157: cannot identify/lock data file 1 - see DBWR trace file
ORA-01110: data file 1: '+DATA/CDB01/DATAFILE/system.268.845194003'


SQL>
```

Since you're in ARCHIVELOG mode and you did a recent full backup, you can restore and recover the CDB's SYSTEM tablespace up to the point in time when the CDB was shut down last. Stop the instance and initiate recovery as you would with a non-CDB:

```
SQL> shutdown immediate
ORA-01109: database not open


Database dismounted.
ORACLE instance shut down.
SQL> quit
Disconnected from Oracle Database 12c Enterprise Edition Release 12.1.0.1.0 -
64bit Production
With the Partitioning, Automatic Storage Management, OLAP, Advanced Analytics
and Real Application Testing options
[oracle@tettnang ~]$ rman target /

Recovery Manager: Release 12.1.0.1.0 - Production on Wed Jun 4 07:39:44 2014

Copyright (c) 1982, 2013, Oracle and/or its affiliates.  All rights reserved.

connected to target database (not started)

RMAN> startup mount

Oracle instance started
database mounted

Total System Global Area    5027385344 bytes

Fixed Size                     2691952 bytes
Variable Size               1241517200 bytes
Database Buffers            3774873600 bytes
Redo Buffers                   8302592 bytes

RMAN> restore tablespace system;

Starting restore at 04-JUN-14
using target database control file instead of recovery catalog
allocated channel: ORA_DISK_1
. . .
channel ORA_DISK_1: restoring datafile 00001 to +DATA/CDB01/DATAFILE/
system.268.845194003
channel ORA_DISK_1: reading from backup piece +RECOV/CDB01/
BACKUPSET/2014_06_04/nnndf0_tag20140604t073433_0.302.849339275
channel ORA_DISK_1: piece handle=+RECOV/CDB01/BACKUPSET
   /2014_06_04/nnndf0_tag20140604t073433_0.302.849339275
tag=TAG20140604T073433
channel ORA_DISK_1: restored backup piece 1
channel ORA_DISK_1: restore complete, elapsed time: 00:00:25
Finished restore at 04-JUN-14
```

```
RMAN> recover tablespace system;

Starting recover at 04-JUN-14
using channel ORA_DISK_1
using channel ORA_DISK_2
using channel ORA_DISK_3
using channel ORA_DISK_4

starting media recovery
media recovery complete, elapsed time: 00:00:00

Finished recover at 04-JUN-14

RMAN> alter database open;

Statement processed

RMAN> alter pluggable database all open;

Statement processed

RMAN>
```

Note that in Oracle Database 12*c*, nearly all commands you would run in SQL*Plus are now available in RMAN without having to qualify them with the SQL keyword.

Recovering the SYSAUX or Other Root Tablespace

Restoring and recovering a missing noncritical root container tablespace other than SYSTEM or UNDO (such as SYSAUX) is even easier; there is no need to shut down the database (if it's not down already). You merely have to take the tablespace with the missing datafiles offline, perform a tablespace restore and recovery, and then bring the tablespace online. All PDBs and the root container can remain online during this operation since root-specific tablespaces other than SYSTEM, TEMP, and UNDO are not shared with any PDB (other than TEMP if the PDB does not have its own TEMP tablespace). The series of commands looks something like this:

```
RMAN> alter tablespace sysaux offline immediate;
RMAN> restore tablespace sysaux;
RMAN> recover tablespace sysaux;
RMAN> alter tablespace sysaux online;
```

Recovering PDB Datafiles

Since all PDBs operate independently as if they were a non-CDB, any failure or datafile loss in a PDB has no effect on the root container or other PDBs unless the datafiles in the PDB's SYSTEM tablespace are lost or damaged. Otherwise, restoring/recovering datafiles in a PDB is much the same as restoring and recovering datafiles in a CDB or non-CDB.

PDB SYSTEM Datafile Loss The loss of the SYSTEM tablespace in an open PDB is one of the few cases where the entire CDB must be shut down to recover the PDB's SYSTEM tablespace. Otherwise, if the PDB is closed and won't open because of a damaged or missing SYSTEM datafile, the CDB and other PDBs can remain open during the PDB's restore and recovery operation.

In this example, the SYSTEM datafile for the PDB CCREPOS is accidentally dropped while CCREPOS is closed. Trying to open CCREPOS fails as expected:

```
SQL> alter pluggable database ccrepos open;
alter pluggable database ccrepos open
*
ERROR at line 1:
ORA-01157: cannot identify/lock data file 30 - see DBWR trace file
ORA-01110: data file 30:
'+DATA/CDB01/FB03AEEBB6F60995E043E3A0080AEE85/DATAFILE/system.258.849342981'
SQL>
```

Next, start RMAN and initiate a recovery on the SYSTEM tablespace. Be sure to qualify the tablespace name with the PDB name in the RESTORE command:

```
RMAN> restore tablespace ccrepos:system;

Starting restore at 04-JUN-14
using target database control file instead of recovery catalog
allocated channel: ORA_DISK_1
channel ORA_DISK_1: SID=774 device type=DISK
allocated channel: ORA_DISK_2
channel ORA_DISK_2: SID=1028 device type=DISK
allocated channel: ORA_DISK_3
channel ORA_DISK_3: SID=1279 device type=DISK
allocated channel: ORA_DISK_4
channel ORA_DISK_4: SID=9 device type=DISK

channel ORA_DISK_1: starting datafile backup set restore
channel ORA_DISK_1: specifying datafile(s) to restore from backup set
channel ORA_DISK_1: restoring datafile 00030 to +DATA/CDB01/
FB03AEEBB6F60995E043E3A0080AEE85/DATAFILE/system.258.849342981
channel ORA_DISK_1: reading from backup piece +RECOV/CDB01/
FB03AEEBB6F60995E043E3A0080AEE85
    /BACKUPSET/2014_06_04/nnndf0_tag20140604t084003_0.316.849343205
channel ORA_DISK_1: piece handle=+RECOV/CDB01/FB03AEEBB6F60995E043E3A0080AEE85
    /BACKUPSET/2014_06_04/nnndf0_tag20140604t084003_0.316.849343205
tag=TAG20140604T084003
channel ORA_DISK_1: restored backup piece 1
channel ORA_DISK_1: restore complete, elapsed time: 00:00:07
Finished restore at 04-JUN-14

RMAN> recover tablespace ccrepos:system;

Starting recover at 04-JUN-14
using channel ORA_DISK_1
using channel ORA_DISK_2
using channel ORA_DISK_3
using channel ORA_DISK_4

starting media recovery
```

```
media recovery complete, elapsed time: 00:00:00

Finished recover at 04-JUN-14

RMAN> alter pluggable database ccrepos open;

Statement processed

RMAN>
```

PDB Non-SYSTEM Datafile Loss Recovering a non-SYSTEM datafile in a PDB uses the same steps as recovering a non-SYSTEM datafile or tablespace in a CDB: offline the tablespace and then restore and recover. The only difference is that you qualify the tablespace name with the PDB name, like this:

```
RMAN> restore tablespace tool:fishinv;
RMAN> recover tablespace tool:fishinv;
. . .
SQL> connect rjb/rjb@tettnang/tool
SQL> alter tablespace fishinv online;
```

Using the Data Recovery Advisor

The Data Recovery Advisor (DRA) can both proactively and reactively analyze failures. In both scenarios, it does not automatically fix problems it finds but instead provides one or more possible fixes and gives you the option and the commands to perform the fix. As of Oracle Database 12c release 1 (12.1.0.1), only non-CDBs and single-instance CDBs are supported (non-RAC environments).

In previous releases of Oracle RMAN, you could perform proactive checks of the database's datafiles with the VALIDATE command. In a CDB environment, the VALIDATE command has been enhanced to analyze individual PDBs or the entire CDB.

Data Failures

In one of the scenarios presented earlier, the SYSTEM tablespace's datafiles of the CCREPOS PDB were lost. You might come to that conclusion after viewing the alert log or, more likely, after a user submits a help-desk ticket saying she can't get into the CCREPOS database. You suspect that there might be more failures, so you start RMAN and use the DRA commands LIST FAILURE, ADVISE FAILURE, and REPAIR FAILURE to fix one or more issues.

To view and repair any issues with the CDB containing the CCREPOS PDB, start RMAN from the root container and run the LIST FAILURE DETAIL command:

```
RMAN> list failure detail;

using target database control file instead of recovery catalog
Database Role: PRIMARY

List of Database Failures
=========================

Failure ID Priority Status    Time Detected Summary
---------- -------- --------- ------------- -------
1562       CRITICAL OPEN      04-JUN-14     System datafile 30: '+DATA/CDB01/
```

```
FB03AEEBB6F60995E043E3A0080AEE85/DATAFILE/system.258.849343395' is missing
  Impact: Database cannot be opened

Failure ID Priority Status    Time Detected Summary
---------- -------- --------- ------------- -------
1542       CRITICAL OPEN      04-JUN-14     System datafile 30: '+DATA/CDB01/
FB03AEEBB6F60995E043E3A0080AEE85/DATAFILE/system.258.849342981' is missing
  Impact: Database cannot be opened

RMAN>
```

It looks like the SYSTEM datafile was lost once already (and recovered) earlier in the chapter! But the failure was not cleared from RMAN, so use CHANGE FAILURE to clear the earlier event:

```
RMAN> change failure 1542 closed;

Database Role: PRIMARY

List of Database Failures
=========================

Failure ID Priority Status    Time Detected Summary
---------- -------- --------- ------------- -------
1542       CRITICAL OPEN      04-JUN-14     System datafile 30: '+DATA/CDB01/
FB03AEEBB6F60995E043E3A0080AEE85/DATAFILE/system.258.849342981' is missing

Do you really want to change the above failures (enter YES or NO)? yes
closed 1 failures

RMAN>
```

Next, let's see what RMAN recommends to fix the problem:

```
RMAN> advise failure 1562;

Database Role: PRIMARY

List of Database Failures
=========================

Failure ID Priority Status    Time Detected Summary
---------- -------- --------- ------------- -------
1562       CRITICAL OPEN      04-JUN-14     System datafile 30: '+DATA/CDB01/
FB03AEEBB6F60995E043E3A0080AEE85/DATAFILE/system.258.849343395' is missing

analyzing automatic repair options; this may take some time
allocated channel: ORA_DISK_1
channel ORA_DISK_1: SID=774 device type=DISK
allocated channel: ORA_DISK_2
channel ORA_DISK_2: SID=1028 device type=DISK
allocated channel: ORA_DISK_3
channel ORA_DISK_3: SID=1276 device type=DISK
allocated channel: ORA_DISK_4
channel ORA_DISK_4: SID=10 device type=DISK
```

```
analyzing automatic repair options complete

Mandatory Manual Actions
========================
no manual actions available

Optional Manual Actions
=======================
1. If file +DATA/CDB01/FB03AEEBB6F60995E043E3A0080AEE85/DATAFILE/system.258.849343395
was unintentionally renamed or moved, restore it
2. Automatic repairs may be available if you shut down the database and restart it in
mount mode

Automated Repair Options
========================
Option Repair Description
------ ------------------
1      Restore and recover datafile 30
  Strategy: The repair includes complete media recovery with no data loss
  Repair script: /u01/app/oracle/diag/rdbms/cdb01/cdb01/hm/reco_461168804.hm

RMAN>
```

The repair script generated by RMAN is as follows:

```
# restore and recover datafile
sql 'CCREPOS' 'alter database datafile 30 offline';
restore ( datafile 30 );
recover datafile 30;
sql 'CCREPOS' 'alter database datafile 30 online';
```

The script is generated to run as is in RMAN. Knowing that the CCREPOS PDB is closed, however, means you can skip the first and last commands and just run the RESTORE and RECOVER commands:

```
RMAN> restore (datafile 30);

Starting restore at 04-JUN-14
using channel ORA_DISK_1
using channel ORA_DISK_2
using channel ORA_DISK_3
using channel ORA_DISK_4

channel ORA_DISK_1: starting datafile backup set restore
channel ORA_DISK_1: specifying datafile(s) to restore from backup set
channel ORA_DISK_1: restoring datafile 00030 to +DATA/CDB01/
FB03AEEBB6F60995E043E3A0080AEE85/DATAFILE/system.258.849343395
channel ORA_DISK_1: reading from backup piece +RECOV/CDB01/
FB03AEEBB6F60995E043E3A0080AEE85/BACKUPSET/2014_06_04/nnndf0_tag2014060
4t084003_0.316.849343205
channel ORA_DISK_1: piece handle=+RECOV/CDB01/FB03AEEBB6F60995E043E3A0080AEE85/
BACKUPSET/2014_06_04/nnndf0_tag20140604t084003_0.316.849343205 tag=TAG20140604T084003
channel ORA_DISK_1: restored backup piece 1
channel ORA_DISK_1: restore complete, elapsed time: 00:00:07
Finished restore at 04-JUN-14
```

```
RMAN> recover datafile 30;

Starting recover at 04-JUN-14
using channel ORA_DISK_1
using channel ORA_DISK_2
using channel ORA_DISK_3
using channel ORA_DISK_4

starting media recovery
media recovery complete, elapsed time: 00:00:01

Finished recover at 04-JUN-14

RMAN>
```

Finally, open the PDB and see whether all is well:

```
RMAN> alter pluggable database ccrepos open;
Statement processed
RMAN>
```

Since CCREPOS starts fine now, you can clear the failure in RMAN:

```
RMAN> change failure 1562 closed;

Database Role: PRIMARY

List of Database Failures
=========================

Failure ID Priority Status    Time Detected Summary
---------- -------- --------- ------------- -------
1562       CRITICAL OPEN      04-JUN-14     System datafile 30: '+DATA/CDB01/
FB03AEEBB6F60995E043E3A0080AEE85/DATAFILE/system.258.849343395' is missing

Do you really want to change the above failures (enter YES or NO)? yes
closed 1 failures

RMAN>
```

PITR Scenarios

There are occasions where you want to roll the entire database back to a point in time before a logical corruption occurred. If the flashback retention is not sufficient to rewind back as far as you would like, then you have to resort to restoring the entire database and applying incremental backups and archived redo logs to a point in time right before the logical corruption occurred (for example, dropping several large tables or updating hundreds of tables with the wrong date).

Therefore, point-in-time recovery (PITR) is a good solution for a PDB tablespace or the entire PDB. As you might expect, all other PDBs and the CDB are unaffected when performing PITR for a PDB. As with a non-CDB PITR, when you perform an incomplete recovery, you have to open the PDB with RESETLOGS. For a tablespace within the PDB, the PDB remains open for the duration of the tablespace PITR.

In the following example, in the PDB named TOOL, you have a series of routine transactions and a logically consistent database as of SCN 4759498:

```
SQL> select current_scn from v$database;

CURRENT_SCN
-----------
    4759498
SQL>
```

Later in the day, at SCN=4767859, all of the rows in the table BIG_IMPORT are accidentally deleted, and neither the flashback data for that table nor UNDO data is available. The only viable option is to recover the tablespace USERS to SCN=4759498 using PITR:

```
RMAN>  recover tablespace tool:users until scn 4759498
2>          auxiliary destination '+RECOV';
. . .
SQL> alter tablespace tool:users online;
```

If this PDB did not use a flash recovery area, the AUXILIARY DESTINATION clause would specify the location to hold temporary files for the auxiliary instance, including the datafiles, control files, and online log files.

Using Flashback CDB

If you do have enough space for flashback logs for a specific recovery window across all PDBs in a CDB, then using Flashback CDB is another good option for recovery when doing a full CDB restore and recovery operation would take significantly longer. Even if you have plenty of disk space for flashback logs, the flashback operation is across all PDBs and the CDB. If an individual PDB needs to be flashed back, you would instead use PDB PITR and leave the rest of the PDBs and CDB at their current SCN.

To configure the fast recovery area, enable ARCHIVELOG mode, set your flashback retention target, and turn on flashback:

```
SQL> alter system set db_flashback_retention_target=4000;

System altered.

SQL> alter database flashback on;

Database altered.

SQL>
```

One other caveat to using Flashback CDB is that you won't be able to flash back the CDB to a point in time earlier than any PDB that has been rewound with database PITR.

Identifying Block Corruption

The RMAN VALIDATE command works in a CDB environment much like it did in previous releases of Oracle with the expected granularity in Oracle Database 12c to validate individual PDBs, the root container, or the entire CDB. Connecting to the root container in RMAN, you can use the

VALIDATE command as in this example to check the existence of all datafiles in the TOOL and CCREPOS PDBs as well as check for any block corruptions:

```
[oracle@tettnang ~]$ rman target /

Recovery Manager: Release 12.1.0.1.0 - Production on Wed Jun 4 21:09:02 2014

Copyright (c) 1982, 2013, Oracle and/or its affiliates.  All rights reserved.

connected to target database: CDB01 (DBID=1382179355)

RMAN> validate pluggable database tool,ccrepos;

Starting validate at 04-JUN-14
using target database control file instead of recovery catalog
allocated channel: ORA_DISK_1
channel ORA_DISK_1: SID=1276 device type=DISK
allocated channel: ORA_DISK_2
channel ORA_DISK_2: SID=517 device type=DISK
allocated channel: ORA_DISK_3
channel ORA_DISK_3: SID=1277 device type=DISK
allocated channel: ORA_DISK_4
channel ORA_DISK_4: SID=1025 device type=DISK
channel ORA_DISK_1: starting validation of datafile
channel ORA_DISK_1: specifying datafile(s) for validation
input datafile file number=00033 name=+DATA/CDB01/
FA782A61F8447D03E043E3A0080A9E54/DATAFILE/users.283.849369565
. . .
channel ORA_DISK_3: validation complete, elapsed time: 00:00:01
List of Datafiles
=================
File Status Marked Corrupt Empty Blocks Blocks Examined High SCN
---- ------ -------------- ------------ --------------- ----------
31   OK     0              20112        80685           4769786
  File Name: +DATA/CDB01/FB03AEEBB6F60995E043E3A0080AEE85/DATAFILE/
sysaux.282.849342981
  Block Type Blocks Failing Blocks Processed
  ---------- -------------- ----------------
  Data       0              14367
  Index      0              7673
  Other      0              38488

Finished validate at 04-JUN-14

RMAN>
```

Duplicating PDBs Using RMAN

Earlier in this chapter I showed you how to clone a PDB using the CREATE PLUGGABLE DATABASE . . . FROM command. RMAN gives you more flexibility and scalability when duplicating one or more PDBs within a CDB or the entire CDB.

As in any RMAN DUPLICATE operation, you must create an auxiliary instance for the destination CDB and PDBs. Even when duplicating a PDB, the auxiliary instance must be started with the initialization parameter ENABLE_PLUGGABLE_DATABASE=TRUE, and therefore the target is a complete CDB with the root container (CDB$ROOT) and the seed database (PDB$SEED).

To duplicate a single PDB called TOOL to a new CDB called NINE, the RMAN DUPLICATE command would look like this:

```
RMAN> duplicate database to nine pluggable database tool;
```

If you want to copy two or more PDBs, you just add them to the end of the DUPLICATE command:

```
RMAN> duplicate database to nine pluggable database qa_2015,tool;
```

Exclusions are allowed in the DUPLICATE command. If you want to clone an entire CDB but without the CCREPOS PDB, do this:

```
RMAN> duplicate database to nine skip pluggable database ccrepos;
```

Finally, you can duplicate not only PDBs but also individual tablespaces to a new CDB:

```
RMAN> duplicate database to nine
2>        pluggable databases qa_2015,ccrepos tablespace tool:users;
```

In this example you want a new CDB with a new PDB called QA_2015_CCREPOS with only the USERS tablespace from the existing PDB called TOOL.

Summary

Oracle's multitenant architecture, new to Oracle Database 12*c*, gives the database administrator an entire range of new capabilities to simplify and reduce maintenance activities as well as respond to changing resource needs and maximize utilization of existing infrastructure.

Creating a new database or even cloning an existing database occurs in a fraction of the time as in previous releases of Oracle: One reason is that the shared resources in a container database, such as the base data dictionary, make up the bulk of the metadata in a new database and do not need to be copied for each individual pluggable database. The temporary and undo tablespaces are already in place along with the online redo log files—a PDB can, however, have its own temporary tablespace if desired to accommodate a specific application workload that might be different from that of other PDBs sharing the same CDB.

Moving a PDB to another container either on the same server or on a different server is as easy as shutting down the database, creating an XML file with the PDB's metadata, and moving the database files themselves to a location where the new CDB can access them.

The best part of using this feature is that you can use the same tools you used before. You'll still use RMAN to back up and recover a PDB, the initialization parameters will for the most part behave as they did in previous releases, and users will not have to make any changes to their applications to run efficiently in a multitenant environment.

PART III

High Availability

CHAPTER 12

Real Application Clusters

Chapter 4 presented an overview of Automatic Storage Management (ASM) and Oracle Managed Files (OMF) and how they can ease administration, enhance performance, and improve availability. You can add one or more disk volumes to a rapidly growing database without bringing down the instance.

Chapter 6 discussed bigfile tablespaces and how they not only allow the total size of the database to be much larger than in previous versions of Oracle, but also ease administration by moving the maintenance point from the datafile to the tablespace. Chapter 17 will focus on Oracle Net, providing you with the basics for ensuring that your clients can reach the database servers in an efficient and prompt manner. Chapter 16 will expand our coverage of bigfile tablespaces in addition to presenting other tools to make large database management easier, such as partitioned table support, transportable tablespaces, and Oracle Data Pump introduced in Oracle Database 10*g*.

As your databases get larger, and the number of users increases, the need for availability becomes even more critical. Real Application Clusters (RAC) will tie together OMF, bigfile tablespaces, a robust network infrastructure, and ASM into key elements of the RAC architecture. In this chapter, we will revisit many of these database features, but with an emphasis on how they can be leveraged in a RAC environment.

This chapter focuses on some key RAC topics, including the differences between the hardware, software, and network configuration in a RAC environment compared to a single-server database environment. I'll also touch upon how a single SPFILE controls the initialization parameters for one, many, or all instances in your RAC database. Finally, I'll give some examples of how RAC can give you scalability and availability features not available in most single-database environments.

During the installation of a RAC, you can configure the Enterprise Manager agent and Enterprise Manager Cloud Control 12*c* to manage your cluster. Cloud Control 12*c* extends the functionality available to manage a single instance by providing a cluster-aware layer; you can manage both the Oracle instances and the underlying cluster configuration from a single web interface.

Subsequent chapters present other ways to ensure high database availability and recoverability: Chapter 15 will give a detailed look at Oracle Data Guard for near-real-time failover capabilities, and Chapter 19 will cover Oracle Streams for advanced replication. In Chapter 16, we'll finish up our discussion on Oracle Flashback options started in Chapter 7 by examining how to perform Flashback Drop and Flashback Database as well as how to use LogMiner to undo individual transactions.

Overview of Real Application Clusters

A Real Application Cluster is highly available and scalable. The failure of one node in the cluster does not affect client sessions or the availability of the cluster itself until the last node in the cluster fails; the only impact a lost node has on the cluster is a slight degradation in response time, depending on the total number of nodes in the cluster.

A RAC database has a few disadvantages. Licensing costs are higher, because each node in the cluster has to have its own Oracle license plus the license for the RAC option. The close physical proximity of the nodes in the cluster due to the high-speed requirements of the cluster interconnect means that a natural disaster can take out the entire cluster; using a remote standby database can help alleviate some of these concerns. You will have to weigh the cost of high availability (or the lack thereof) compared to the increased cost and slight increase in maintenance of a RAC.

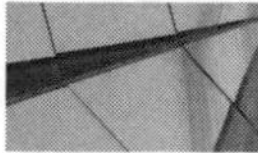

NOTE
A stretch cluster, or a cluster using RAC technology over a wide-area network (WAN), protects against the loss of an entire data center, but it increases the cost of the infrastructure, since the already-redundant storage systems must be duplicated across the sites and the network bandwidth must be high enough to keep up with synchronization tasks during peak transaction periods.

In the next few sections, I'll cover some of the hardware and software requirements for a RAC database as well as detail the network configuration and disk storage requirements to build a successful cluster.

Hardware Configuration

A complete discussion of all possible RAC hardware configurations is beyond the scope of this book. You want to have at least two and preferably three nodes for a RAC, each with redundant power supplies, network cards, dual CPUs, and error-correcting memory; these are desirable characteristics for any type of server, not just an Oracle server! The higher the number of nodes configured in the cluster, the lower the performance hit you will take when one of the cluster's nodes fails.

The shared disk subsystem should also have hardware redundancy built in—multiple power supplies, RAID-enabled disks (or just leverage an engineered system such as Oracle Exadata!), and so forth. You will balance the redundancy built into the shared disk with the types of disk groups you will create for the RAC. The higher redundancy built into the disk subsystem hardware can potentially reduce the amount of software redundancy you specify when you create the database's disk groups.

Software Configuration

Although Oracle clustering solutions have been available since version 6, not until version 10*g* has there been a native clusterware solution that more tightly couples the database to the volume management solution. Cluster Ready Services (CRS) is the clustering solution that can be used on all major platforms instead of an OS vendor or third-party clusterware.

CRS is installed before the RDBMS and must be in its own home directory, referred to as the CRS_HOME. If you are only using a single instance in the near future but plan to cluster at a later date, it is useful to install CRS first so that the components of CRS that are needed for ASM and RAC are in the RDBMS directory structure. If you do not install CRS first, you will have to perform some extra steps later to remove the CRS-related process executables from the RDBMS home directory.

After CRS is installed, you install the database software in the home directory, referred to as the ORACLE_HOME. On some platforms, such as Microsoft Windows, this directory can be a directory common to all nodes, whereas other platforms, such as Linux, require OCFS version 2.*x* or later. Otherwise, each node will have its own copy of the binary executables.

Network Configuration

Each node in a RAC has a minimum of three IP addresses: one for the public network, one for the private network interconnect, and a virtual IP address to support faster failover in the event of a node failure. As a result, a minimum of two physical network cards are required to support RAC;

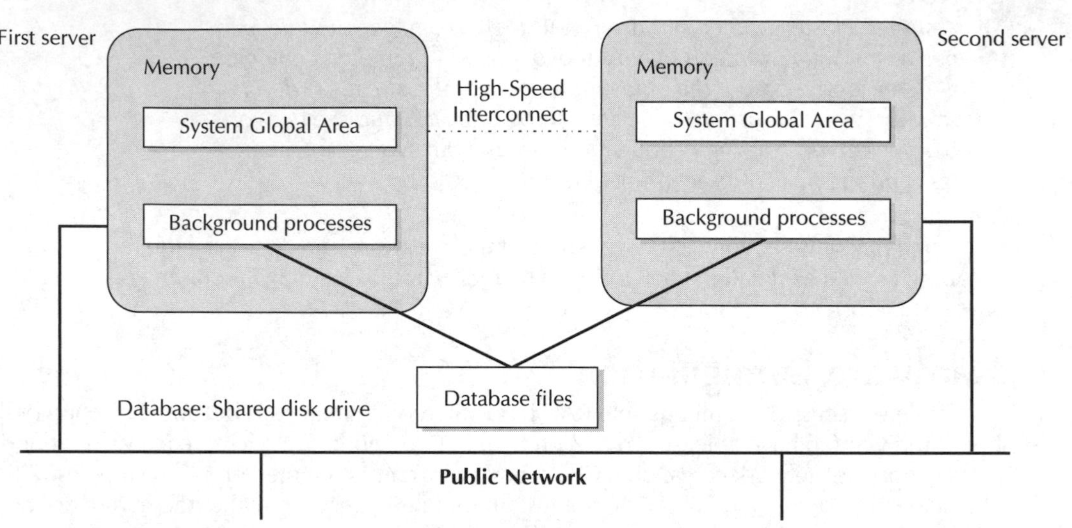

FIGURE 12-1. *RAC network configuration*

additional network cards are used to provide redundancy on the public network and thus an alternate network path for incoming connections. For the private network, additional network cards can boost performance by providing more total bandwidth for interconnect traffic. Figure 12-1 shows a two-node RAC with one network card on each node for the private interconnect and one network card on each node to connect to the public network.

The public network is used for all routine connections to and from the server; the interconnect network, or private network, supports communication between the nodes in the cluster, such as node status information and the actual data blocks shared between the nodes. This interface should be as fast as possible, and no other types of communication between the nodes should occur on the private interface; otherwise, the performance of the RAC may suffer.

The virtual IP address is the address assigned to the Oracle listener process and supports *rapid connect-time failover,* which is able to switch the network traffic and Oracle connection to a different instance in the RAC much faster than a third-party, high-availability solution.

Disk Storage

The shared disk drive may or may not be a RAID device to support redundancy; more importantly, the disk controllers and connections to the shared storage should be multiplexed to ensure high availability. If the disks in the shared drive are not mirrored, you can use the mirroring capabilities of ASM to provide performance and availability benefits.

RAC Characteristics

A RAC instance is different in many ways from a standalone instance; in this section, I will review some of the initialization parameters that are specific to a RAC database. In addition, I'll show you some of the data dictionary views and dynamic performance views that are either unique to a RAC or have columns that are only populated when the instance is part of a RAC.

Server Parameter File Characteristics

The server parameter file (SPFILE) typically resides on an ASM disk group and therefore is shared by each node in the cluster. Within the SPFILE, you can assign different values for given parameters on an instance-by-instance basis; in other words, the value for an initialization parameter can differ between instances. If an initialization parameter is the same for all nodes in the cluster, it is prefixed with "***.**"; otherwise, it is prefixed with the node name.

In this example, the physical memory on the cluster server **oc2** is temporarily reduced due to other applications that are currently running on the server (ideally, though, you have no other applications running on the server except for Oracle!). Therefore, to reduce the demands of the instance on the server, you will change the value of MEMORY_TARGET for the instance **rac2**:

```
SQL> select sid, name, value
  2  from v$spparameter where name = 'memory_target';

SID        NAME                 VALUE
---------- -------------------- ----------------
*          memory_target        17179869184

SQL> alter system set memory_target = 12g sid='rac2';

System altered.

SQL> select sid, name, value
  2  from v$spparameter where name = 'memory_target';

SID        NAME                 VALUE
---------- -------------------- ----------------
*          memory_target        17179869184
rac2       memory_target        12884901888
```

Depending on your hardware and the amount of memory you're allocating or deallocating, the memory resize operation might take a few seconds or possibly a few minutes depending on the current system load. Once the memory issue has been resolved, you can restore the size of the SGA on the **rac2** instance as follows:

```
SQL> alter system set memory_target = 16g sid='rac2';

System altered.
SQL>
```

Alternatively, and usually more simply, you want to reset the value to the same value for the rest of the cluster; in this situation, you can use the RESET option of the ALTER SYSTEM command:

```
SQL> alter system reset memory_target sid = 'rac2';

System altered.

SQL> select sid, name, value
  2  from v$spparameter where name = 'memory_target';
```

```
SID        NAME                 VALUE
---------- -------------------- ---------------
*          memory_target        17179869184

SQL>
```

RAC-Related Initialization Parameters

A number of initialization parameters are used only in a RAC environment. Although these initialization parameters exist in any instance, in a single-instance environment they are either null or have a value of 1 (for example, INSTANCE_NUMBER). Table 12-1 provides an overview of some of the key RAC-related initialization parameters.

Dynamic Performance Views

In a single-instance environment, all dynamic performance views that begin with V$ have a corresponding view beginning with GV$, with the additional column INST_ID always set to 1. For a RAC environment with two nodes, the GV$ views have twice as many rows as the corresponding V$ views; for a three-node RAC, there are three times as many rows, and so forth. In the sections that follow, we'll review some of the V$ dynamic performance views that show the same contents regardless of the node you are connected to, along with some of the GV$ views that can show you the contents of the V$ views on each node without connecting to each node explicitly.

Common Database File Views

Some dynamic performance views are the same whether you're in a RAC environment or a single-instance environment; the ASM configuration is a perfect example of this. In this query run on any database instance in the cluster, you want to verify that all your database files are stored in one of the two ASM disk groups, +DATA1 or +RECOV1:

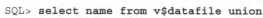

```
SQL> select name from v$datafile union
  2  select name from v$tempfile union
  3  select member from v$logfile union
```

Initialization Parameter	Description
INSTANCE_NUMBER	Unique number identifying this instance in the cluster.
INSTANCE_NAME	The unique name of this instance within the cluster; typically the cluster name with a numeric suffix.
CLUSTER_DATABASE	This parameter is TRUE if this instance is participating in a RAC environment.
CLUSTER_DATABASE_INSTANCES	The number of instances configured for this cluster, whether each instance is active or not. If INSTANCE_TYPE is ASM, then this parameter has a value of 4.
CLUSTER_INTERCONNECTS	Specifies the network used for the cluster's IPC traffic.

TABLE 12-1. *RAC-Related Initialization Parameters*

```
  4  select name from v$controlfile union
  5  select name from v$flashback_database_logfile;

NAME
---------------------------------------------------------
+DATA1/rac/controlfile/current.260.631034951
+DATA1/rac/datafile/example.264.631035151
+DATA1/rac/datafile/sysaux.257.631034659
+DATA1/rac/datafile/system.256.631034649
+DATA1/rac/datafile/undotbs1.258.631034665
+DATA1/rac/datafile/undotbs2.265.631035931
+DATA1/rac/datafile/undotbs3.266.631035935
+DATA1/rac/datafile/users.259.631034665
+DATA1/rac/onlinelog/group_1.261.631034959
+DATA1/rac/onlinelog/group_2.262.631034973
+DATA1/rac/onlinelog/group_3.269.631036295
+DATA1/rac/onlinelog/group_4.270.631036303
+DATA1/rac/onlinelog/group_5.267.631036273
+DATA1/rac/onlinelog/group_6.268.631036281
+DATA1/rac/tempfile/temp.263.631035129
+RECOV1/rac/controlfile/current.256.631034953
+RECOV1/rac/onlinelog/group_1.257.631034965
+RECOV1/rac/onlinelog/group_2.258.631034977
+RECOV1/rac/onlinelog/group_3.261.631036301
+RECOV1/rac/onlinelog/group_4.262.631036307
+RECOV1/rac/onlinelog/group_5.259.631036277
+RECOV1/rac/onlinelog/group_6.260.631036285

22 rows selected.

SQL> show parameter spfile

NAME                    TYPE        VALUE
---------------------- ----------- ----------------------------
spfile                  string      +DATA1/rac/spfilerac.ora
SQL>
```

Cluster-Aware Dynamic Performance Views

The GV$ views make it easy to view each instance's characteristics in a single SELECT statement, while at the same time filtering out nodes that you do not want to see; these views also make it easier to aggregate totals from some or all of the nodes in the cluster, as in this example:

```
SQL> select nvl(to_char(inst_id),'TOTAL') INST#,
  2       count(inst_id) sessions from gv$session
  3       group by rollup(inst_id)
  4       order by inst_id;

INST#      SESSIONS
-------- ----------
1                48
```

```
2                48
3                44
TOTAL           140

4 rows selected.
```

From this query, you can see the number of sessions per instance and the total number of instances for the cluster using the view GV$SESSION.

RAC Maintenance

Most of the maintenance operations you perform on a single-node instance apply directly to a multiple-node RAC environment. In this section, I will review the basics for maintaining a RAC—including how to start up a RAC and how redo logs and undo tablespaces work—and then work through an example of an instance failure scenario using Transparent Application Failover (TAF).

Starting Up a RAC

Starting up a RAC is not much different from starting up a standalone instance; the nodes in a RAC can start up in any order, and they can be shut down and started up at any time with minimal impact to the rest of the cluster. During database startup, first the ASM instance starts and mounts the shared disk groups; next, the RDBMS instance starts and joins the cluster.

On Linux, the file **/etc/oratab** can be modified to auto-start the instances (both the ASM instance and the RDBMS instance) on each cluster:

```
# This file is used by ORACLE utilities.  It is created by root.sh
# and updated by the Database Configuration Assistant when creating
# a database.

# A colon, ':', is used as the field terminator.  A new line terminates
# the entry.  Lines beginning with a pound sign, '#', are comments.
#
# Entries are of the form:
#   $ORACLE_SID:$ORACLE_HOME:<N|Y>:
#
# The first and second fields are the system identifier and home
# directory of the database respectively.  The third field indicates
# to the dbstart utility that the database should , "Y", or should not,
# "N", be brought up at system boot time.
#
# Multiple entries with the same $ORACLE_SID are not allowed.
#
#
+ASM1:/u01/app/oracle/product/11.1.0/db_1:Y
rac:/u01/app/oracle/product/11.1.0/db_1:Y
```

Redo Logs in a RAC Environment

As with a single-node instance, online redo logs are used for instance recovery in a RAC environment; each instance in a RAC environment has its own set of online redo log files that are used to roll forward all information in the redo logs and then roll back any uncommitted transactions initiated on that node using the undo tablespace.

Even before the failed instance has restarted, one of the surviving instances detects the instance failure and uses the online redo log files to ensure that no committed transactions are lost; if this process completes before the failed instance restarts, the restarted instance does not need instance recovery. Even if more than one instance fails, all that is required for instance recovery is one remaining node. If all instances in a RAC fail, the first instance that starts up will perform instance recovery for the database using the online redo log files from all instances in the cluster.

If media recovery is required and the entire database must be recovered, all instances except for one must be shut down and media recovery is performed from a single instance. If you are recovering noncritical database files, all nodes may be up as long as the tablespaces containing the files to be recovered are marked as OFFLINE.

Undo Tablespaces in a RAC Environment

As with redo logs, each instance in a RAC environment must have its own undo tablespace on a shared drive or disk group. This undo tablespace is used for rolling back transactions during normal transactional operations or during instance recovery. In addition, the undo tablespace is used by other nodes in the cluster to support read consistency for transactions that are reading rows from a table on node **rac2** while a data-entry process on node **rac1** makes updates to the same table and has not yet committed the transaction. The user on **rac2** needs to see the before-image data stored in **rac1**'s undo tablespace. This is why all undo tablespaces must be visible to all nodes in the cluster.

Failover Scenarios and TAF

If you have configured your client correctly and the instance to which the client is connected to fails, the client connection is rapidly switched to another instance in the cluster and processing can continue with only a slight delay in response time.

Here is the **tnsnames.ora** entry for the service **racsvc**:

```
racsvc =
  (description =
    (address = (protocol = tcp)(host = voc1)(port = 1521))
    (address = (protocol = tcp)(host = voc2)(port = 1521))
    (address = (protocol = tcp)(host = voc3)(port = 1521))
    (load_balance = yes)
    (connect_data =
      (server = dedicated)
      (service_name = racsvc.world)
      (failover_mode =
        (type = select)
        (method = basic)
        (retries = 180)
        (delay = 5)
      )
    )
  )
```

This will show you what happens and how you will know if a session is connected to the cluster and its instance fails. First, you connect to the cluster via **racsvc** and find out the node and instance that you are connected to:

```
SQL> connect rjb/rjb@racsvc;
Connected.
SQL> select instance_name, host_name, failover_type,
  2        failover_method, failed_over
  3   from v$instance
  4   cross join
  5   (select failover_type, failover_method, failed_over
  6    from v$session
  7    where username = 'RJB');

INSTANCE_NAME HOST_NAME FAILOVER_TYPE FAILOVER_METHOD FAILED_OVER
------------- --------- ------------- --------------- -----------
rac1          oc1       SELECT        BASIC           NO

SQL>
```

You are using the columns from V$INSTANCE to give you the instance name and host name that you are connected to and then joining this to V$SESSION and retrieving the columns related to failover, which are only populated in a RAC environment. In this case, the session has not yet failed over, and the failover type is BASIC, as specified when the service was created.

Next, you will shut down instance **rac1** from another session while you are still connected to the first session:

```
SQL> connect system@rac1 as sysdba
Connected.
SQL> shutdown immediate
Database closed.
Database dismounted.
ORACLE instance shut down.
SQL>
```

Back at your user session, you rerun the query to find out what node you are connected to:

```
SQL> select instance_name, host_name, failover_type,
  2        failover_method, failed_over
  3   from v$instance
  4   cross join
  5   (select failover_type, failover_method, failed_over
  6    from v$session
  7    where username = 'RJB');

INSTANCE_NAME HOST_NAME FAILOVER_TYPE FAILOVER_METHOD FAILED_OVER
------------- --------- ------------- --------------- -----------
rac3          oc3       SELECT        BASIC           YES

SQL>
```

RAC Statistics Summary

	Begin	End
1st Number of Instances:	2	2
2nd Number of Instances:	2	2

Global Cache Load Profile

	Total Per Second			Total Per Txn			Avg Per Second		
	1st	2nd	%Diff	1st	2nd	%Diff	1st	2nd	%Diff
Global Cache blocks received	35.56	22.20	-37.57	3.91	3.82	-2.30	17.78	11.10	-37.57
Global Cache blocks served	35.56	22.19	-37.60	3.91	3.82	-2.30	17.78	11.09	-37.63
GCS/GES messages received	2,311.64	1,295.91	-43.94	254.45	223.00	-12.36	1,155.82	647.96	-43.94
GCS/GES messages sent	2,311.64	1,295.82	-43.94	254.45	222.99	-12.36	1,155.82	647.91	-43.94
DBWR Fusion Writes sent	4.67	3.56	-23.77	0.51	0.61	19.61	2.33	1.78	-23.61

	Min Per Second		Max Per Second		Avg Per Txn			Min Per Txn		Max Per Txn	
	1st	2nd	1st	2nd	1st	2nd	%Diff	1st	2nd	1st	2nd
Global Cache blocks received	11.04	7.39	24.52	14.81	4.24	4.00	-5.66	2.11	3.58	6.37	4.41
Global Cache blocks served	11.04	7.41	24.52	14.78	3.78	5.30	40.21	2.87	1.79	4.68	8.81
GCS/GES messages received	847.63	492.99	1,464.01	802.92	249.92	299.06	19.66	220.23	119.24	279.60	478.87
GCS/GES messages sent	847.62	492.66	1,464.03	803.16	271.13	244.05	-9.99	161.88	194.26	380.39	293.83
DBWR Fusion Writes sent	1.20	0.75	3.46	2.81	0.56	0.56	0.00	0.23	0.45	0.90	0.68

Global Cache and Enqueue Services - Workload Characteristics

	Average Time (ms)			Max Average Time (ms)			Max Instance #	
	1st	2nd	%Diff	1st	2nd	%Diff	1st	2nd
Global Enqueue Get	2.23	2.19	-1.79	2.37	2.28	-3.80	1	2
Global Cache CR Block Receive	3.13	2.38	-23.96	3.19	2.76	-13.48	1	1
Global Cache Current Block Receive	1.76	2.43	38.07	4.58	7.52	64.19	2	2
Global Cache CR Block Build	0.00	0.00	0.00	0.00	0.00	0.00	1	1
Global Cache CR Block Send	0.00	0.00	0.00	0.00	0.00	0.00	1	1
Global Cache CR Block Flush	22.98	11.27	-50.96	29.08	16.78	-42.30	2	2
Global Cache Current Block Pin	0.63	1.15	82.54	3.30	4.54	37.58	1	1
Global Cache Current Block Send	0.00	0.00	0.00	0.00	0.00	0.00	1	1
Global Cache Current Block Flush	33.60	53.10	58.04	41.43	71.21	71.88	1	1

	First	Second	Diff
Global cache log flushes for cr blocks served %:	2.4	4.3	1.9
Global cache log flushes for current blocks served %:	0.8	0.7	-0.2

FIGURE 12-2. *Cloud Control 12c RAC cache statistics*

If you were running a query at the time the instance was shut down, your query would pause for a brief moment and then continue as if nothing happened. If your result set is quite large and you already retrieved most of the result set, the pause will be slightly longer since the first part of the result set must be re-queried and discarded.

Tuning a RAC Node

The first step in tuning a RAC is to tune the instance. If an individual instance is not tuned correctly, the performance of the entire RAC will not be optimal. You can use the Automatic Workload Repository (AWR) to tune an instance as if it was not part of a cluster.

Using Cloud Control 12*c*, you can further leverage the statistics from the AWR to produce reports on a RAC-wide basis. In Figure 12-2, you can see how Cloud Control 12*c* makes it easy to analyze the performance of the shared global cache as well as the cache performance on an instance-by-instance basis, even comparing the cluster-wide performance for a given day to a similar time period in the past.

Summary

In this chapter I provided a brief but informative summary of Oracle's primary availability and scalability solution: Real Application Clusters. Managing the components of RAC is much the same as managing a single-instance database: you use many of the same tools to manage users, tablespaces, and other server resources. Using RAC makes it easier for the users too: in virtually all cases, a failure of any node in the cluster is completely transparent to any user who is running a query or DML statement. The processing for that SQL statement continues to completion without the user having to resubmit the statement.

CHAPTER 13

Backup and Recovery Options

Oracle provides a variety of backup procedures and options that help protect an Oracle database. If they are properly implemented, these options will allow you to effectively back up your databases and recover them easily and efficiently.

Oracle's backup capabilities include logical and physical backups, both of which have a number of options available. This chapter will not detail every possible option and recovery scenario; rather, I will focus on using the best options in the most effective manner possible. You will see how to best integrate the available backup procedures with each other and with the operating system backups. You will also see details on the options for Data Pump Export and Import, which were introduced in Oracle Database 10*g*.

Backup Capabilities

There are three standard methods of backing up an Oracle database: exports, offline backups, and online backups. An export is a *logical* backup of the database; the other two backup methods are *physical* file backups. In the following sections, you will see each of these options described. The standard (and preferred) tool for physical backups is Oracle's Recovery Manager (RMAN) utility; see Chapter 14 for details on the implementation and usage of RMAN.

A robust backup strategy includes both physical and logical backups. In general, production databases rely on physical backups as their primary backup method, and logical backups serve as the secondary method. For development databases and for some small data movement processing, logical backups offer a viable solution. You should understand the implications and uses of both physical and logical backups in order to develop the most appropriate solution for your applications.

Logical Backups

A *logical backup* of a database involves reading a set of database records and writing them to a file. These records are read independently of their physical location. In Oracle, the Data Pump Export utility performs this type of database backup. To recover using the file generated from a Data Pump Export, you use Data Pump Import.

NOTE

*The Import utility (**imp**) of Oracle's original Import and Export utilities, available prior to Oracle Database 10g, is still provided as part of the Oracle 12c installation to read dump files created in previous versions. Users of the old Export and Import utilities are encouraged to replace their usage with Data Pump Export and Data Pump Import.*

Oracle's Data Pump Export utility queries the database, including the data dictionary, and writes the output to an XML file called an *export dump file*. You can export the full database, specific users, tablespaces, or specific tables. During exports, you may choose whether or not to export the data dictionary information associated with tables, such as grants, indexes, and constraints. The file written by Data Pump Export will contain the commands necessary to completely re-create all the chosen objects and data.

Once data has been exported via Data Pump Export, it may be imported via the Data Pump Import utility. Data Pump Import reads the dump file created by Data Pump Export and executes the commands found there. For example, these commands may include a CREATE TABLE command, followed by an INSERT command to load data into the table.

NOTE
Data Pump Export and Import can use a network connection for a simultaneous export and import operation, avoiding the use of intermediate operating system files and reducing total export and import time. You can also leverage parallelism if your network bandwidth is high enough.

The data that has been exported does not have to be imported into the same database, or the same schema, as was used to generate the export dump file. You may use the export dump file to create a duplicate set of the exported objects under a different schema or in a separate database.

You can import either all or part of the exported data. If you import the entire export dump file from a full export, then the entire set of database objects, including tablespaces, datafiles, and users, will be created during the import. However, it is often useful to pre-create tablespaces and users in order to specify the physical distribution of objects in the database or provide different attributes for those tablespaces. This advice is also applicable even in an ASM storage environment.

If you are only going to import part of the data from the export dump file, the tablespaces, datafiles, and users that will own and store that data should be set up prior to the import.

Physical Backups

Physical backups involve copying the files that constitute the database. These backups are also referred to as *file system backups* because they involve using operating system file backup commands. Oracle supports two different types of physical file backups: *offline backups* and *online backups* (also known as *cold* and *hot backups,* respectively). You can use the RMAN utility (see Chapter 14) to perform all physical backups. You may optionally choose to write your own scripts to perform physical backups, but doing so will prevent you from obtaining many of the benefits of the RMAN approach.

Offline Backups

Consistent offline backups occur when the database has been shut down normally (that is, not due to instance failure) using the NORMAL, IMMEDIATE, or TRANSACTIONAL option of the SHUTDOWN command. While the database is "offline," the following files should be backed up:

- All datafiles
- All control files
- All archived redo log files
- The **init.ora** file or server parameter file (SPFILE)

CAUTION
You should never, ever, want or need to back up online redo log files. Although there is a slight time-savings for restoring from a cold backup after a clean shutdown, the risk of losing committed transactions outweighs the convenience. Your online redo logs should be mirrored and multiplexed so that you should never lose the current online log file.

Having all these files backed up while the database is closed provides a complete image of the database as it existed at the time it was closed. The full set of these files could be retrieved from the backups at a later date, and the database would be able to function. It is *not* valid to perform a file system backup of the database while it is open unless an online backup is being performed. Offline backups that occur following database aborts will also be considered inconsistent and may require more effort to use during recoveries if they are usable.

Online Backups

You can use online backups for any database that is running in ARCHIVELOG mode. In this mode, the online redo logs are archived, creating a log of all transactions within the database.

Oracle writes to the online redo log files in a cyclical fashion: After filling the first log file, it begins writing to the second, until that one fills, and then it begins writing to the third. Once the last online redo log file is filled, the LGWR (Log Writer) background process begins to overwrite the contents of the first redo log file.

When Oracle is run in ARCHIVELOG mode, the archiver background processes (ARC0–ARC9 and ARCa–ARCt) make a copy of each redo log file before overwriting it. These archived redo log files are usually written to a disk device. The archived redo log files may also be written directly to a tape device, but disk space is getting cheap enough that the additional cost of archiving to disk is offset by the time and labor savings when a disaster recovery operation must occur.

NOTE
Most production databases, particularly those that support transaction-processing applications, should be run in ARCHIVELOG mode to ensure recoverability in case of media failure.

You can perform file system backups of a database while that database is open, provided the database is running in ARCHIVELOG mode. An online backup involves setting each tablespace into a backup state, backing up its datafiles, and then restoring the tablespace to its normal state.

NOTE
When using the Oracle-supplied RMAN utility, you do not have to manually place each tablespace into a backup state. RMAN reads the data blocks in the same manner Oracle uses for queries.

The database can be fully recovered from an online backup, and it can, via the archived redo logs, be rolled forward to any point in time before the failure. When the database is then opened, any committed transactions that were in the database at the time of the failure will have been restored, and any uncommitted transactions will have been rolled back.

While the database is open, the following files can be backed up:

- All datafiles
- All archived redo log files
- One control file, via the ALTER DATABASE BACKUP CONTROLFILE command
- The server parameter file (SPFILE)

NOTE
RMAN automatically backs up the control file and SPFILE whenever the entire database or the SYSTEM tablespace are backed up and when you have CONTROLFILE AUTOBACKUP set as the default in RMAN.

Online backup procedures are very powerful for two reasons. First, they provide full point-in-time recovery. Second, they allow the database to remain open during the file system backup. Even databases that cannot be shut down due to user requirements can still have file-system backups. Keeping the database open also keeps the System Global Area (SGA) of the database instance from being cleared when the database is shut down and restarted. Keeping the SGA memory from being cleared will improve the database's performance because it will reduce the number of physical I/Os required by the database.

NOTE
You can use the Flashback Database option, introduced in Oracle Database 10g, to roll the database backward in time without relying on physical backups. To use the FLASHBACK DATABASE command, you must have a fast recovery area defined, be running in ARCHIVELOG mode, and must have issued the ALTER DATABASE FLASHBACK ON command while the database was mounted but not open. Logs written to the fast recovery area are used by Oracle during the Flashback Database operation.

Using Data Pump Export and Import

Introduced with Oracle Database 10*g*, Data Pump provides a server-based data-extraction and data-import utility. Its features include significant architectural and functional enhancements over the original Import and Export utilities. Data Pump allows you to stop and restart jobs, see the status of running jobs, and restrict the data that is exported and imported.

NOTE
Data Pump files are incompatible with those generated from the original Export utility.

Data Pump runs as a server process, benefiting users in many ways. The client process that starts the job can disconnect and later reattach to the job. Performance is enhanced (as compared to the original Export/Import) because the data no longer has to be processed by a client program. Data Pump extractions and loads can be parallelized, further enhancing performance.

In this section, you will see how to use Data Pump, along with descriptions and examples of its major options. This includes how Data Pump uses directory objects, specifying options on the command line, and how to stop and restart jobs within the Data Pump command-line interface.

Creating a Directory

Data Pump requires you to create directories for the datafiles and log files it will create and read. Use the CREATE DIRECTORY command to create the directory pointer within Oracle to the external directory you will use. Users who will access the Data Pump files must have the READ and WRITE privileges on the directory.

Before you start, verify that the external directory exists and that the user who will be issuing the CREATE DIRECTORY command has the CREATE ANY DIRECTORY system privilege.

NOTE

In a default installation of Oracle Database 12c, a directory object called DATA_PUMP_DIR is created and points to the directory **$ORACLE_BASE/admin/*database_name*/dpdump** *in a non-multitenant environment.*

The following example creates a directory object called DPXFER in the Oracle instance **dw** referencing the file system directory **/u01/app/oracle/DataPumpXfer** and grants READ and WRITE access to the user RJB:

```
SQL> create directory dpxfer as '/u01/app/oracle/DataPumpXfer';

Directory created.

SQL> grant read, write on directory dpxfer to rjb;

Grant succeeded.

SQL>
```

The RJB user can now use the DPXFER directory for Data Pump jobs. The file system directory **/u01/app/oracle/DataPumpXfer** can exist on the source server, the target server, or any server on the network, as long as each server can access the directory and the permissions on the directory allow read/write access by the **oracle** user (the user that owns the Oracle executable files).

On the server **oc1**, the administrator creates a directory with the same name that references the same network file system, except that privileges on the directory are granted to the HR user instead:

```
SQL> create directory dpxfer as '/u01/app/oracle/DataPumpXfer';

Directory created.

SQL> grant read,write on directory dpxfer to hr;

Grant succeeded.

SQL>
```

Data Pump Export Options

Oracle provides the OS utility **expdp** that serves as the interface to Data Pump. If you have previous experience with the Export utility, some of the options will be familiar. However, some significant features are available only via Data Pump. Table 13-1 shows the command-line input parameters for **expdp** when a job is created. These parameters can be specified in a parameter file unless otherwise noted.

Parameter	Description
ACCESS_METHOD	Defaults to AUTOMATIC but you can specify DIRECT_PATH or EXTERNAL_TABLE if AUTOMATIC doesn't choose the right value.
ATTACH	Connects a client session to a currently running Data Pump Export job.
CLUSTER	Defaults to YES. Enables Data Pump to use resources on multiple nodes in a RAC environment.
COMPRESSION	Specifies which data to compress: ALL, DATA_ONLY, METADATA_ONLY, NONE.
COMPRESSION_ALGORITHM	BASIC, LOW, MEDIUM, or HIGH. Using BASIC balances speed and size. Values of LOW, MEDIUM, or HIGH require the Advanced Compression license.
CONTENT	Filters what is exported: DATA_ONLY, METADATA_ONLY, or ALL.
DATA_OPTIONS	If set to XML_CLOBS, then XMLType columns are exported uncompressed.
DIRECTORY	Specifies the destination directory for the log file and the dump file set.
DUMPFILE	Specifies the names and directories for dump files.
ENCRYPTION	Encryption level of the output: ALL, DATA_ONLY, ENCRYPTED_COLUMNS_ONLY, METADATA_ONLY, NONE.
ENCRYPTION_ALGORITHM	The encryption method to perform the encryption: AES128, AES192, AES256.
ENCRYPTION_MODE	Uses a password or Oracle wallet or both: values are DUAL, PASSWORD, TRANSPARENT.
ENCRYPTION_PASSWORD	Encryption key required to encrypt and decrypt the backup files.
ESTIMATE	Determines the method used to estimate the dump file size (BLOCKS or STATISTICS).
ESTIMATE_ONLY	A YES/NO flag used to instruct Data Pump whether the data should be exported or just estimated.
EXCLUDE	Specifies the criteria for excluding objects and data from being exported.
FILESIZE	Specifies the maximum file size of each export dump file.
FLASHBACK_SCN	The SCN for the database to flash back to during the export.
FLASHBACK_TIME	The timestamp for the database to flash back to during the export. FLASHBACK_TIME and FLASHBACK_SCN are mutually exclusive.

TABLE 13-1. *Command-Line Input Parameters for expdp*

Parameter	Description
FULL	Tells Data Pump to export all data and metadata in a Full mode export.
HELP	Displays a list of available commands and options.
INCLUDE	Specifies the criteria for which objects and data will be exported.
JOB_NAME	Specifies a name for the job; the default is system-generated.
KEEP_MASTER	YES/NO flag to indicate whether to keep the master metadata table at the end of an export or import job.
LOGFILE	The name and optional directory name for the export log.
LOGTIME	Adds timestamps to each step in the log file.
METRICS	YES/NO flag to indicate whether to add more metadata to the log file such as the number of objects and elapsed time.
NETWORK_LINK	Specifies the source database link for a Data Pump job exporting a remote database.
NOLOGFILE	A YES/NO flag is used to suppress log file creation.
PARALLEL	Sets the number of workers for the Data Pump Export job.
PARFILE	Names the parameter file to use, if any.
QUERY	Filters rows from tables during the export.
REMAP_DATA	Specifies a function that can transform a column or columns in the data, for testing or masking sensitive data.
REUSE_DUMPFILES	Overwrites existing dump files.
SAMPLE	Specifies a percentage of the data blocks to easily select a percentage of the rows in each table.
SCHEMAS	Names the schemas to be exported for a Schema mode export.
STATUS	Displays detailed status of the Data Pump job.
TABLES	Lists the tables and partitions to be exported for a Table mode export.
TABLESPACES	Lists the tablespaces to be exported in tablespace mode.
TRANSPORT_FULL_CHECK	Specifies whether the tablespaces being exported should first be verified as a self-contained set.
TRANSPORT_TABLESPACES	Specifies a Transportable Tablespace mode export.
TRANSPORTABLE	Exports metadata only for a Table mode export.
VERSION	Specifies the version of database objects to be created so the dump file set may be compatible with earlier releases of Oracle. The options are COMPATIBLE, LATEST, and database version numbers (not lower than 9.2).

TABLE 13-1. *Command-Line Input Parameters for expdp* (Continued)

As detailed in Table 13-1, five modes of Data Pump exports are supported:

- **Full** Export all database data and metadata
- **Schema** Export data and metadata for specific user schemas
- **Tablespace** Export data and metadata for tablespaces
- **Table** Export data and metadata for tables and table partitions
- **Transportable Tablespace** Export metadata for specific tablespaces in preparation for transporting a tablespace from one database to another

NOTE
You must have the EXP_FULL_DATABASE system privilege in order to perform a Full export or a Transportable Tablespace export.

When you submit a job, Oracle will give the job a system-generated name. If you specify a name for the job via the JOB_NAME parameter, you must be certain that the job name will not conflict with the name of any table or view in your schema. During Data Pump jobs, Oracle will create and maintain a master table for the duration of the job. The master table will have the same name as the Data Pump job, so its name cannot conflict with existing objects.

While a job is running, you can execute the commands listed in Table 13-2 via Data Pump's interface.

Parameter	Description
ADD_FILE	Adds dump files.
CONTINUE_CLIENT	Exits the interactive mode and enters logging mode.
EXIT_CLIENT	Exits the client session but leaves the server Data Pump Export job running.
FILESIZE	Redefines the default size for subsequent dump files.
HELP	Displays online help for the import.
KILL_JOB	Kills the current job and detaches related client sessions.
PARALLEL	Alters the number of workers for the Data Pump Export job.
START_JOB	Restarts the attached job.
STATUS	Displays a detailed status of the Data Pump job.
STOP_JOB	Stops the job for later restart.

TABLE 13-2. *Parameters for Interactive Mode Data Pump Export*

Starting a Data Pump Export Job

You can store your job parameters in a parameter file, referenced via the PARFILE parameter of **expdp**. For example, you can create a file named **dp_rjb.par** with the following entries:

```
directory=dpxfer
dumpfile=metadata_only.dmp
content=metadata_only
```

The logical Data Pump directory is DPXFER, the one created earlier in the chapter. The Data Pump Export will only have metadata; the name of the dump file, **metadata_only.dmp**, reflects the contents of the dump file. Here's how you initiate a Data Pump job using this parameter file:

```
expdp rjb/rjb parfile=dp_rjb.par
```

Oracle will then pass the **dp_rjb.par** entries to the Data Pump Export job. A schema-type Data Pump Export (which is the default) will be executed, and the output (metadata only, no table rows) will be written to a file in the DPXFER directory. Here is the output from the **expdp** command:

```
[oracle@dw ~]$ expdp rjb/rjb parfile=dp_rjb.par

Export: Release 12.1.0.2.0 - Production on Thu Nov 13 09:13:10 2014

Copyright (c) 1982, 2014, Oracle and/or its affiliates.  All rights reserved.

Connected to: Oracle Database 12c Enterprise Edition Release 12.1.0.2.0 -
64bit Production
With the Partitioning, Automatic Storage Management, OLAP, Advanced Analytics
and Real Application Testing options

Starting "RJB"."SYS_EXPORT_SCHEMA_01":  rjb/******** parfile=dp_rjb.par
Processing object type SCHEMA_EXPORT/USER
Processing object type SCHEMA_EXPORT/SYSTEM_GRANT
Processing object type SCHEMA_EXPORT/ROLE_GRANT
Processing object type SCHEMA_EXPORT/DEFAULT_ROLE
Processing object type SCHEMA_EXPORT/PRE_SCHEMA/PROCACT_SCHEMA
Processing object type SCHEMA_EXPORT/TABLE/TABLE
Processing object type SCHEMA_EXPORT/TABLE/COMMENT
Processing object type SCHEMA_EXPORT/TABLE/INDEX/INDEX
Processing object type SCHEMA_EXPORT/TABLE/CONSTRAINT/CONSTRAINT
Processing object type SCHEMA_EXPORT/TABLE/INDEX/STATISTICS/INDEX_STATISTICS
Processing object type SCHEMA_EXPORT/TABLE/STATISTICS/TABLE_STATISTICS
Processing object type SCHEMA_EXPORT/STATISTICS/MARKER
Master table "RJB"."SYS_EXPORT_SCHEMA_01" successfully loaded/unloaded
******************************************************************************
Dump file set for RJB.SYS_EXPORT_SCHEMA_01 is:
  /u01/app/oracle/DataPumpXfer/metadata_only.dmp
Job "RJB"."SYS_EXPORT_SCHEMA_01" successfully completed at Thu Nov 13 09:13:50
2014 elapsed 0 00:00:27 [oracle@dw ~]$
```

The output file, as shown in the listing, is named **metadata_only.dmp**. The output dump file contains a binary header and XML entries for re-creating the structures for the RJB schema. During the export, Data Pump created and used an external table called SYS_EXPORT_SCHEMA_01.

NOTE
Dump files will not overwrite previously existing dump files in the same directory unless you use the REUSE_DUMPFILES parameter.

You can use multiple directories and dump files for a single Data Pump Export. Within the DUMPFILE parameter setting, list the directory along with the filename, in this format:

```
DUMPFILE=directory1:file1.dmp,
         directory2:file2.dmp
```

Using multiple directories in the DUMPFILE parameter has two benefits: the Data Pump job can use parallel processes (using the PARALLEL parameter), in addition to spreading out the dump file to wherever disk space is available. You can also use the substitution variable **%U** in the filename specification to automatically create multiple dump files that can be written to by multiple processes automatically. Even if only one process is writing the dump file, using the **%U** substitution variable in combination with the FILESIZE parameter will limit the size of each dump file.

Stopping and Restarting Running Jobs

After you have started a Data Pump Export job, you can close the client window you used to start the job. Because it is server based, the export will continue to run. You can then attach to the job, check its status, and alter it. For example, you can start the job via **expdp**:

```
expdp rjb/rjb parfile=dp_rjb.par
```

Press CTRL-C to leave the log display, and Data Pump will return you to the **expdb** prompt:

```
Export>
```

Exit to the client using the **exit_client** command:

```
Export> exit_client
```

Later, you can restart the client and attach to the currently running job under your schema:

```
expdp rjb/rjb attach
```

If you gave a name to your Data Pump Export job (or you identified the job name in the log file when the job started), specify the name as part of the **attach** parameter. For example, if you had named the job RJB_JOB, attach to the job by name:

```
expdp rjb/rjb attach=RJB_JOB
```

When you attach to a running job, Data Pump will display the status of the job: its basic configuration parameters and its current status. You can then issue the **continue_client** command to see the log entries as they are generated, or you can alter the running job:

```
Export> continue_client
```

In addition, you can stop a job using the **stop_job** command:

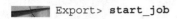

```
Export> stop_job
```

The job is not canceled, only suspended. With the job stopped, you can then add additional dump files in new directories via the ADD_FILE option. You can then restart the job using **start_job**:

```
Export> start_job
```

You can specify a log file location for the export log file via the LOGFILE parameter. If you do not specify a value for LOGFILE, the log file will be written to the same directory as the dump file.

Exporting from Another Database

You can use the NETWORK_LINK parameter to export data from a different database. If you are logged into the HQ database and you have a database link to the DW database, Data Pump can use that link to connect to the DW database and extract its data.

NOTE
If the source database is read-only, the user on the source database must have a locally managed tablespace assigned as the temporary tablespace; otherwise, the job will fail.

In your parameter file or on the **expdp** command line, set the NETWORK_LINK parameter to the name of the database link. The Data Pump Export job will write the data from the remote database to the directory defined in your local database.

Using EXCLUDE, INCLUDE, and QUERY

You can exclude or include sets of tables from the Data Pump Export via the EXCLUDE and INCLUDE options. You can exclude objects by type and by name. If an object is excluded, all its dependent objects are also excluded. The format for the EXCLUDE option is

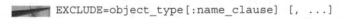

```
EXCLUDE=object_type[:name_clause] [, ...]
```

NOTE
You cannot specify EXCLUDE if you specify CONTENT=DATA_ONLY.

For example, to exclude the ANGUSP schema from a full export, the format of the EXCLUDE option is as follows:

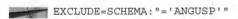

```
EXCLUDE=SCHEMA:"='ANGUSP'"
```

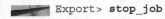

NOTE
You can specify more than one EXCLUDE option within the same Data Pump Export job.

The EXCLUDE option in the preceding example contains a limiting condition within a set of double quotes. The *object_type* variable can be any Oracle object type, including a grant, index, or table. The *name_clause* variable restricts the value returned. For example, to exclude from the export all tables whose names begin with TEMP, use the following EXCLUDE clause:

```
EXCLUDE=TABLE:"LIKE 'TEMP%'"
```

When you enter this at the command line on Linux, you may need to use escape characters so the quotation marks and other special characters are properly passed to Oracle. Your **expdp** command will look similar to this:

```
expdp rjb/rjb EXCLUDE=TABLE:\"LIKE \'TEMP%\'\"
```

NOTE
This example shows part of the syntax, not the full syntax for the command.

If you do not provide a *name_clause* value, all objects of the specified type are excluded. For example, to exclude all indexes, you would use an EXCLUDE clause similar to the following:

```
expdp rjb/rjb EXCLUDE=INDEX
```

For a listing of the objects you can filter, query the DATABASE_EXPORT_OBJECTS, SCHEMA_EXPORT_OBJECTS, and TABLE_EXPORT_OBJECTS data dictionary views. If the *object_type* value is CONSTRAINT, all constraints will be excluded except for NOT NULL. Additionally, constraints needed for a table to be created successfully, such as a primary key constraint for an index-organized table, cannot be excluded. If the *object_type* value is USER, the user definitions are excluded, but the objects within the user schemas will still be exported. Use the SCHEMA *object_type*, as shown in an earlier example, to exclude a user and all of the user's objects. If the *object_type* value is GRANT, all object grants and system privilege grants are excluded.

A second option, INCLUDE, is also available. When you use INCLUDE, only those objects that pass the criteria are exported; all others are excluded. INCLUDE and EXCLUDE are mutually exclusive. The format for INCLUDE is

```
INCLUDE = object_type[:name_clause] [, ...]
```

NOTE
You cannot specify INCLUDE if you specify CONTENT=DATA_ONLY.

For example, to export two specific tables and all procedures, your parameter file will include two lines similar to the following:

```
INCLUDE=TABLE:"IN ('BOOKSHELF','BOOKSHELF_AUTHOR')"
INCLUDE=PROCEDURE
```

What rows will be exported for the objects that meet the EXCLUDE or INCLUDE criteria? By default, all rows are exported for each table. You can use the QUERY option to limit the rows returned. Here is the format for the QUERY parameter:

```
QUERY = [schema.][table_name:] query_clause
```

If you do not specify values for the *schema* and *table_name* variables, the *query_clause* will be applied to all the exported tables. Because *query_clause* will usually include specific column names, you should be very careful when selecting the tables to include in the export. You can specify a QUERY value for a single table, as shown in the following example:

```
QUERY=BOOKSHELF:'"where rating > 2"'
```

As a result, the dump file will only contain rows from the BOOKSHELF table that meet the QUERY criterion as well as any INCLUDE or EXCLUDE criteria. You can also apply these filters during a subsequent Data Pump Import job, as described in the next section.

Data Pump Import Options

To import a dump file exported via Data Pump Export, use Data Pump Import. As with the export process, the import process runs as a server-based job you can manage as it executes. You can interact with Data Pump Import via the command-line interface, a parameter file, and an interactive interface. Table 13-3 lists the parameters for the command-line interface.

Parameter	Description
ACCESS_METHOD	Defaults to AUTOMATIC but you can specify one of DIRECT_PATH, EXTERNAL_TABLE, or CONVENTIONAL if Data Pump Import does not choose the best option.
ATTACH	Attaches the client to a server session and places you in interactive mode.
CLUSTER	Defaults to YES. Enables Data Pump to use resources on multiple nodes in a RAC environment.
CONTENT	Filters what is imported: ALL, DATA_ONLY, or METADATA_ONLY.
DATA_OPTIONS	Specifies how to handle certain exceptions. Possible values are DISABLE_APPEND_HINT, SKIP_CONSTRAINT_ERRORS, and REJECT_ROWS_WITH_REPL_CHAR. Using DISABLE_APPEND_HINT is useful if other sessions may be accessing the table during the import and you don't want to block them or vice versa.
DIRECTORY	Specifies the location of the dump file set and the destination directory for the log and SQL files.
DUMPFILE	Specifies the names and, optionally, the directories for the dump file set.
ENCRYPTION_PASSWORD	Specifies the password used to encrypt the export during a Data Pump Export.
ESTIMATE	Determines the method used to estimate the dump file size (BLOCKS or STATISTICS).

TABLE 13-3. *Data Pump Import Command-Line Parameters*

Parameter	Description
EXCLUDE	Excludes objects and data from being exported.
FLASHBACK_SCN	The SCN for the database to flash back to during the import.
FLASHBACK_TIME	The timestamp for the database to flash back to during the import.
FULL	A YES/NO flag is used to specify whether you want to import the full dump file.
HELP	Displays online help for the import.
INCLUDE	Specifies the criteria for objects to be imported.
JOB_NAME	Specifies a name for the job; the default is system-generated.
KEEP_MASTER	Specify whether to keep or delete (YES or NO) the master table after the job completes. The master table is always kept if there are errors in the job.
LOGFILE	The name and optional directory name for the import log.
LOGTIME	Choose when to attach timestamps to each log entry during the import. Values are NONE (the default), STATUS (timestamps on status messages only), LOGFILE (timestamps on log file messages only), or ALL.
METRICS	Adds more information about the job to the log file.
NETWORK_LINK	Specifies the source database link for a Data Pump job importing a remote database.
NOLOGFILE	A Y/N flag is used to suppress log file creation.
PARALLEL	Sets the number of workers for the Data Pump Import job.
PARFILE	Names the parameter file to use, if any.
PARTITION_OPTIONS	NONE creates the partitions with the same characteristics as the source. MERGE merges partitions into one table, and DEPARTITION creates a new table for each source partition.
QUERY	Filters rows from tables during the import.
REMAP_DATA	Remaps column contents using a user-defined function before it's inserted into the target database.
REMAP_DATAFILE	Changes the name of the source datafile to the target datafile in the CREATE LIBRARY, CREATE TABLESPACE, and CREATE DIRECTORY commands during the import.
REMAP_SCHEMA	Imports data exported from the source schema into the target schema.
REMAP_TABLE	Renames a table during import.

TABLE 13-3. *Data Pump Import Command-Line Parameters* (Continued)

Parameter	Description
REMAP_TABLESPACE	Imports data exported from the source tablespace into the target tablespace.
REUSE_DATAFILES	Specifies whether existing datafiles should be reused by CREATE TABLESPACE commands during Full mode imports.
SCHEMAS	Names the schemas to be exported for a Schema mode import.
SKIP_UNUSABLE_INDEXES	A Y/N flag. If set to Y, the import does not load data into tables whose indexes are set to the Index Unusable state.
SQLFILE	Names the file to which the DDL for the import will be written. The data and metadata will not be loaded into the target database.
STATUS	Displays a detailed status of the Data Pump job.
STREAMS_ CONFIGURATION	A YES/NO flag is used to specify whether Streams configuration information should be imported.
TABLE_EXISTS_ACTION	Instructs Import how to proceed if the table being imported already exists. Values include SKIP, APPEND, TRUNCATE, and REPLACE. The default is APPEND if CONTENT=DATA_ONLY; otherwise, the default is SKIP.
TABLES	Lists tables for a Table mode import.
TABLESPACES	Lists tablespaces for a Tablespace mode import.
TRANSFORM	Directs changes to the segment attributes or storage during import.
TRANSPORT_DATAFILES	Lists the datafiles to be imported during a Transportable Tablespace mode import.
TRANSPORT_FULL_CHECK	Specifies whether the tablespaces being imported should first be verified as a self-contained set.
TRANSPORT_TABLESPACES	Lists the tablespaces to be imported during a Transportable Tablespace mode import.
TRANSPORTABLE	Specifies whether the transportable option should be used with a table mode import (ALWAYS or NEVER).
VERSION	Specifies the version of database objects to be created so the dump file set may be compatible with earlier releases of Oracle. The options are COMPATIBLE, LATEST, and database version numbers (not lower than 10.1). Only valid for NETWORK_LINK and SQLFILE.
VIEWS_AS_TABLES	Converts views in the dump file to permanent tables.

TABLE 13-3. *Data Pump Import Command-Line Parameters* (Continued)

As with Data Pump Export, five modes are supported in Data Pump Import:

- **Full** Import all database data and metadata
- **Schema** Import data and metadata for specific user schemas
- **Tablespace** Import data and metadata for tablespaces
- **Table** Import data and metadata for tables and table partitions
- **Transportable Tablespace** Import metadata for specific tablespaces in preparation for transporting a tablespace from the source database

If no mode is specified, Data Pump Import attempts to load the entire dump file.

NOTE
The directory for the dump file and log file must already exist; see the prior section on the CREATE DIRECTORY command, "Creating a Directory."

Table 13-4 lists the parameters that are valid in the interactive mode of Data Pump Import. Many of the Data Pump Import parameters are the same as those available for the Data Pump Export. In the following sections, you'll see how to start an import job, along with descriptions of the major options unique to Data Pump Import.

Starting a Data Pump Import Job

You can start a Data Pump Import job via the **impdp** OS executable provided with Oracle Database 12*c*. Use the command-line parameters to specify the import mode and the locations for all the files. You can store the parameter values in a parameter file and then reference the file via the PARFILE option.

Parameter	Description
CONTINUE_CLIENT	Exits the interactive mode and enters logging mode. The job will be restarted if idle.
EXIT_CLIENT	Exits the client session but leaves the server Data Pump Import job running.
HELP	Displays online help for the import.
KILL_JOB	Kills the current job and detaches related client sessions.
PARALLEL	Alters the number of workers for the Data Pump Import job.
START_JOB	Restarts the attached job.
STATUS	Displays detailed status of the Data Pump job.
STOP_JOB	Stops the job for later restart.

TABLE 13-4. *Interactive Parameters for Data Pump Import*

In the first export example of this chapter, using the RJB schema, the parameter file named **dp_rjb.par** has been copied to the destination and renamed to **rjb_dp_imp.par**. It contains the following entries:

```
directory=dpxfer
dumpfile=metadata_only.dmp
content=metadata_only
```

If the Oracle directory object has the same name on the target database, you can reuse the same parameter file. To create the RJB schema's objects in a different schema on the target database, use the REMAP_SCHEMA parameter as follows:

```
REMAP_SCHEMA=source_schema:target_schema
```

You can change the destination tablespace as well using the REMAP_TABLESPACE option. Before starting the import, create a new user KFC as follows:

```
SQL> grant create session, unlimited tablespace to kfc identified by kfc;
Grant succeeded.
SQL>
```

Next, add the REMAP_SCHEMA parameter to the end of the parameter file you copied from the source database:

```
directory=dpxfer
dumpfile=metadata_only.dmp
content=metadata_only
remap_schema=RJB:KFC
```

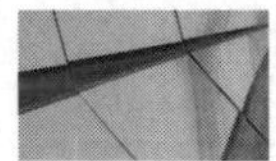

NOTE
All dump files must be specified at the time the job is started.

You are now ready to start the import job. Because you are changing the original owner of the schema, you must have the IMP_FULL_DATABASE system privilege. Data Pump Import jobs are started using the **impdp** utility; here is the command, including the revised parameter file:

```
impdp user/password parfile=rjb_dp_imp.par
```

Data Pump Import will now perform the import and display its progress. Because the NOLOGFILE option was not specified, the log file for the import will be placed in the same directory as the dump file and will be given the name **import.log**. You can verify the success of the import by logging into the KFC schema and reviewing the objects. Here is the log file from the **impdp** command:

```
[oracle@oc1 ~]$ impdp rjb/rjb parfile=rjb_dp_imp.par

Import: Release 12.1.0.2.0 - Production on Thu Nov 13 10:15:40 2014

Copyright (c) 1982, 2014, Oracle and/or its affiliates.  All rights reserved.
Password:
```

```
Connected to: Oracle Database 12c Enterprise Edition Release 12.1.0.2.0 -
64bit Production
With the Partitioning, Automatic Storage Management, OLAP, Advanced Analytics
and Real Application Testing options
Master table "RJB"."SYS_IMPORT_FULL_01" successfully loaded/unloaded
Starting "RJB"."SYS_IMPORT_FULL_01":  rjb/******** parfile=rjb_dp_imp.par
Processing object type SCHEMA_EXPORT/USER
ORA-31684: Object type USER:"KFC" already exists
Processing object type SCHEMA_EXPORT/SYSTEM_GRANT
Processing object type SCHEMA_EXPORT/ROLE_GRANT
Processing object type SCHEMA_EXPORT/DEFAULT_ROLE
Processing object type SCHEMA_EXPORT/PRE_SCHEMA/PROCACT_SCHEMA
Job "RJB"."SYS_IMPORT_FULL_01" completed with 1 error(s) at Thu Nov 13
10:15:48 2014 elapsed 0 00:00:03

[oracle@oc1 ~]$
```

The only error during the **impdp** command was that the KFC user already exists; I created it explicitly earlier, and this error message can safely be ignored.

What if a table being imported already exists? In this example, with the CONTENT option set to METADATA_ONLY, the table would be skipped by default. If the CONTENT option was set to DATA_ONLY, the new data would be appended to the existing table data. To alter this behavior, use the TABLE_EXISTS_ACTION option. Valid values for TABLE_EXISTS_OPTION are SKIP, APPEND, TRUNCATE, and REPLACE.

Stopping and Restarting Running Jobs After you have started a Data Pump Import job, you can close the client window you used to start the job. Because it is server based, the import will continue to run. You can then attach to the job, check its status, and alter it:

```
impdp rjb/rjb parfile=rjb_dp_imp.par
```

Press CTRL-C to leave the log display, and Data Pump Import will return you to the **impdp** prompt:

```
Import>
```

Exit to the operating system using the **exit_client** command:

```
Import> exit_client
```

Later, you can restart the client and attach to the currently running job under your schema:

```
impdp rjb/rjb attach
```

If you gave a name to your Data Pump Import job, specify the name as part of the **attach** parameter. When you attach to a running job, Data Pump Import will display the status of the job—its basic configuration parameters and its current status. You can then issue the **continue_client** command to see the log entries as they are generated, or you can alter the running job:

```
Import> continue_client
```

Not surprisingly, you can temporarily stop a job using the **stop_job** command:

```
Import> stop_job
```

While the job is stopped, you can increase its parallelism via the **parallel** option, and then restart the job:

```
Import> start_job
```

EXCLUDE, INCLUDE, and QUERY Data Pump Import, like Data Pump Export, allows you to restrict the data processed via the use of the EXCLUDE, INCLUDE, and QUERY options, as described earlier in this chapter. Because you can use these options on both the export and the import, you can be very flexible in your imports. For example, you may choose to export an entire table but only import the rows that match your QUERY criteria. You could choose to export an entire schema but, when recovering the database via import, include only the most necessary tables so that the application downtime can be minimized. EXCLUDE, INCLUDE, and QUERY provide powerful capabilities to developers and database administrators during both export and import jobs.

Transforming Imported Objects In addition to changing or selecting schemas, tablespaces, datafiles, and rows during the import, you can change the segment attributes and storage requirements during import via the TRANSFORM option. The format for TRANSFORM is as follows:

```
TRANSFORM = transform_name:value[:object_type]
```

The *transform_name* variable can have a value of SEGMENT_ATTRIBUTES or STORAGE. You can use the *value* variable to include or exclude segment attributes (physical attributes such as storage attributes, tablespaces, and logging). The *object_type* variable is optional, but if specified, it must be one of these values:

- CLUSTER
- CONSTRAINT
- INC_TYPE
- INDEX
- ROLLBACK_SEGMENT
- TABLE
- TABLESPACE
- TYPE

For example, object storage requirements may change during an export/import; you may be using the QUERY option to limit the rows imported, or you may be importing only the metadata, without the table data. To eliminate the exported storage clauses from the imported tables, add the following to the parameter file:

```
transform=storage:n:table
```

To eliminate the exported tablespace and storage clauses from all tables and indexes, use the following:

```
transform=segment_attributes:n
```

When the objects are imported, they will be assigned to the user's default tablespace and will use the default tablespace's storage parameters.

Generating SQL Instead of importing the data and objects, you can generate the SQL for the objects (without the data) and store it in a file on your operating system. The file will be written to the directory and filename specified via the SQLFILE option. The SQLFILE option format is as follows:

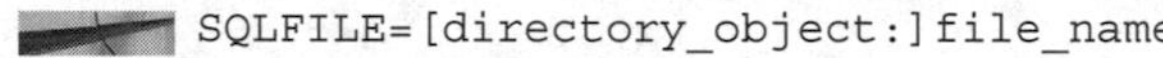

```
SQLFILE=[directory_object:]file_name
```

NOTE
If you do not specify a value for the directory_object variable, the file will be created in the dump file directory.

Here is the same parameter file used for the import earlier in this chapter, modified to create the SQL only:

```
directory=dpxfer
dumpfile=metadata_only.dmp
sqlfile=sql.txt
```

Notice that we do not need the **content=metadata_only** or the **remap_schema** parameters, since all we want to do is to create SQL statements:

```
impdp rjb/rjb parfile=rjb_dp_imp_sql.par
```

In the **sql.txt** file that the import process creates, you will see entries for each of the object types within the schema. Here is an excerpt from the file:

```
-- CONNECT RJB
. . .
-- new object type path: SCHEMA_EXPORT/USER
-- CONNECT SYSTEM
 CREATE USER "RJB" IDENTIFIED BY VALUES 'S:46. . .569A6174D117AAC'
      DEFAULT TABLESPACE "USERS"
      TEMPORARY TABLESPACE "TEMP";
-- new object type path: SCHEMA_EXPORT/SYSTEM_GRANT
GRANT UNLIMITED TABLESPACE TO "RJB";
-- new object type path: SCHEMA_EXPORT/ROLE_GRANT
 GRANT "CONNECT" TO "RJB";
 GRANT "RESOURCE" TO "RJB";
 GRANT "DBA" TO "RJB";
-- new object type path: SCHEMA_EXPORT/DEFAULT_ROLE
 ALTER USER "RJB" DEFAULT ROLE ALL;
-- new object type path: SCHEMA_EXPORT/PRE_SCHEMA/PROCACT_SCHEMA
-- CONNECT RJB
BEGIN
sys.dbms_logrep_imp.instantiate_schema(schema_name=>SYS_
CONTEXT('USERENV','CURRENT_SCHEMA'), export_db_name=>'BOB', inst_
scn=>'1844409');
COMMIT;
END;
/
```

```
-- new object type path: SCHEMA_EXPORT/TABLE/TABLE
CREATE TABLE "RJB"."EMPLOYEE_ARCHIVE"
   (    "EMPLOYEE_ID" NUMBER(6,0),
        "FIRST_NAME" VARCHAR2(20 BYTE),
        "LAST_NAME" VARCHAR2(25 BYTE) NOT NULL ENABLE,
        "EMAIL" VARCHAR2(25 BYTE) NOT NULL ENABLE,
        "PHONE_NUMBER" VARCHAR2(20 BYTE),
        "HIRE_DATE" DATE NOT NULL ENABLE,
        "JOB_ID" VARCHAR2(10 BYTE) NOT NULL ENABLE,
        "COMMISSION_PCT" NUMBER(2,2),
        "MANAGER_ID" NUMBER(6,0),
        "DEPARTMENT_ID" NUMBER(4,0)
   ) SEGMENT CREATION DEFERRED
  PCTFREE 10 PCTUSED 40 INITRANS 1 MAXTRANS 255
 NOCOMPRESS LOGGING
  STORAGE( INITIAL 65536 NEXT 1048576 MINEXTENTS 1 MAXEXTENTS 2147483645
  PCTINCREASE 0 FREELISTS 1 FREELIST GROUPS 1
  BUFFER_POOL DEFAULT FLASH_CACHE DEFAULT CELL_FLASH_CACHE DEFAULT)
  TABLESPACE "USERS" ;
-- new object type path: SCHEMA_EXPORT/TABLE/STATISTICS/TABLE_STATISTICS
-- new object type path: SCHEMA_EXPORT/STATISTICS/MARKER
```

The SQLFILE output is a plain-text file, so you can edit the file, use it with SQL*Plus or SQL Developer, or keep it as documentation of your application's database structures.

Implementing Offline Backups

An offline backup is a physical backup of the database files made after the database has been shut down cleanly via a SHUTDOWN NORMAL, a SHUTDOWN IMMEDIATE, or a SHUTDOWN TRANSACTIONAL command. While the database is shut down, each of the files actively used by the database is backed up. These files provide a complete image of the database as it existed at the moment it was shut down.

NOTE
You should not rely on an offline backup performed following a SHUTDOWN ABORT, because it may be inconsistent. If you must perform a SHUTDOWN ABORT, you should restart the database and perform a normal SHUTDOWN or a SHUTDOWN IMMEDIATE or a SHUTDOWN TRANSACTIONAL prior to beginning your offline backup.

The following files should be backed up during a cold backup:

- All datafiles
- All control files
- All archived redo log files
- Initialization parameter file or server parameter file (SPFILE)
- Password file

If you are using raw devices for database storage, with or without ASM, you'll have to back up these devices as well using operating system commands such as **dd** in combination with a compression utility, as in this example:

```
dd if=/dev/sdb | gzip > /mnt/bkup/dw_sdb_backup.img.gz
```

During a recovery, an offline backup can restore the database to the point in time at which the database was shut down. Offline backups commonly play a part in disaster recovery planning, because they are self-contained and may be simpler to restore on a disaster recovery server than other types of backups. If the database is running in ARCHIVELOG mode, you can apply more recent archived redo logs to the restored offline backup to bring the database back to the point in time of a media failure or a complete loss of the database. As I've emphasized throughout this book, the need for cold backups is minimized or eliminated if you use RMAN; your database may never need to be shut down for a cold backup (unless disaster strikes—in which case, be sure to create a RAC database as well!).

Implementing Online Backups

Consistent offline backups can only be performed while the database is shut down. However, you can perform physical file backups of a database while the database is open, provided the database is running in ARCHIVELOG mode and the backup is performed correctly. These backups are referred to as *online backups*.

Oracle writes to the online redo log files in a cyclical fashion: After filling the first log file, it begins writing to the second, until that one fills, and it then begins writing to the third. Once the last online redo log file is filled, the LGWR (Log Writer) background process begins to overwrite the contents of the first redo log file.

When Oracle is run in ARCHIVELOG mode, the archiver background processes (ARC0–ARC9 and ARCa–ARCt) make a copy of each redo log file after the LGWR process finishes writing to it. These archived redo log files are usually written to a disk device. They may instead be written directly to a tape device, but this tends to be very operator intensive.

Getting Started

To make use of the ARCHIVELOG capability, you must first place the database in ARCHIVELOG mode. Before starting the database in ARCHIVELOG mode, make sure you are using one of the following configurations, listed from most to least recommended:

- Enable archiving to the fast recovery area only; use disk mirroring on the disks containing the fast recovery area. The DB_RECOVERY_FILE_DEST parameter specifies the file system location or ASM disk group containing the fast recovery area. As an Oracle best practice, you should create the fast recovery area on a mirrored ASM disk group separate from the primary disk group.
- Enable archiving to the fast recovery area and set at least one LOG_ARCHIVE_DEST_*n* parameter to another location outside of the fast recovery area.
- Set at least two LOG_ARCHIVE_DEST_*n* parameters to archive to non–fast recovery area destinations.

NOTE
If the initialization parameter DB_RECOVERY_FILE DEST is specified and no LOG_ARCHIVE_DEST_*n parameter is specified, then LOG_ARCHIVE_DEST_10 is implicitly set to the fast recovery area.*

In the following examples, I assume that the best configuration, a single mirrored fast recovery area, has been selected. The following listing shows the steps needed to place a database in ARCHIVELOG mode; first, shut down the database, and then issue these commands:

```
SQL> startup mount;
SQL> alter database archivelog;
SQL> alter database open;
```

NOTE
To see the currently active online redo log and its sequence number, query the V$LOG dynamic view.

If you enable archiving but do not specify any archiving locations, the archived log files reside in a default, platform-dependent location; on Unix and Linux platforms the default location is **$ORACLE_HOME/dbs**.

Each of the archived redo log files contains the data from a single online redo log. They are numbered sequentially, in the order in which they were created. The size of the archived redo log files varies, but it does not exceed the size of the online redo log files.

If the destination directory of the archived redo log files runs out of space, the ARC*n* processes will stop processing the online redo log data and the database will stop itself. This situation can be resolved by adding more space to the archived redo log file destination disk or by backing up the archived redo log files and then removing them from this directory. If you are using the fast recovery area for your archived redo log files, the database issues a warning alert if the available space in the fast recovery area is less than 15 percent, and a critical alert when the available space is less than 3 percent. Taking action at the 15 percent level, such as increasing the size or changing the location of the fast recovery area, can most likely avoid any service interruptions, assuming that there are no runaway processes consuming space in the fast recovery area.

The initialization parameter DB_RECOVERY_FILE_DEST_SIZE can also assist in managing the size of the fast recovery area. While its primary purpose is to limit the amount of disk space used by the fast recovery area on the specified disk group or file system directory, it can be temporarily increased once an alert is received to give the DBA additional time to allocate more disk space to the disk group or relocate the fast recovery area.

DB_RECOVERY_FILE_DEST_SIZE helps manage space not only within a database but also across all databases that use the same ASM disk groups. Each database can have its own setting for DB_RECOVERY_FILE_DEST_SIZE.

Short of receiving a warning or critical alert, you can be a bit more proactive in monitoring the size of the fast recovery area using the dynamic performance view V$RECOVERY_FILE_DEST to see the total used and reclaimable space on the destination file system. In addition, you can use the dynamic performance view V$FLASH_RECOVERY_AREA_USAGE to see a usage breakdown by file type:

```
SQL> select * from v$recovery_file_dest;

NAME                 SPACE_LIMIT SPACE_USED SPACE_RECLAIMABLE NUMBER_OF_FILES
-------------------- ----------- ---------- ----------------- ---------------
+RECOV                8589934592 1595932672          71303168              13

SQL> select * from v$flash_recovery_area_usage;

FILE_TYPE        PERCENT_SPACE_USED PERCENT_SPACE_RECLAIMABLE NUMBER_OF_FILES
---------------- ------------------ ------------------------- ---------------
CONTROL FILE                    .12                         0               1
REDO LOG                       1.87                         0               3
ARCHIVED LOG                    .83                         1               7
BACKUP PIECE                  15.75                         0               2
IMAGE COPY                        0                         0               0
FLASHBACK LOG                     0                         0               0
FOREIGN ARCHIVE                   0                         0               0
D LOG

7 rows selected.

SQL>
```

In this example, the fast recovery area is less than 20 percent used, with the largest percentage due to RMAN backups.

Performing Online Database Backups

Once a database is running in ARCHIVELOG mode, you can back it up while it is open and available to users. This capability allows round-the-clock database availability to be achieved while still guaranteeing the recoverability of the database.

Although online backups can be performed during normal working hours, they should be scheduled for the times of the least user activity for several reasons. First, the online backups will use operating system commands to back up the physical files, and these commands will use the available I/O resources in the system (impacting the system performance for interactive users). Second, while the tablespaces are being backed up, the manner in which transactions are written to the archived redo log files changes. When you put a tablespace in "online backup" mode, the DBWR process writes all the blocks in the buffer cache that belong to any file that is part of the tablespace back to disk. When the blocks are read back into memory and then changed, they will be copied to the log buffer the first time that a change is made to them. As long as they stay in the buffer cache, they will not be recopied to the online redo log file. This will use a great deal more space in the archived redo log file destination directory.

NOTE

You can create a command file to perform your online backups, but using RMAN is preferred for several reasons: RMAN maintains a catalog of your backups, allows you to manage your backup repository, and allows you to perform incremental backups of the database.

Follow these steps to perform an online database backup or individual tablespace backups:

1. Set the database into backup state (prior to Oracle 10*g*, the only option was to enable backup on a tablespace-by-tablespace basis) by using the ALTER TABLESPACE . . . BEGIN BACKUP command for each tablespace or ALTER DATABASE BEGIN BACKUP to put all tablespaces into online backup mode.
2. Back up the datafiles using operating system commands.
3. Set the database back to its normal state by issuing ALTER TABLESPACE . . . END BACKUP for each tablespace or ALTER DATABASE END BACKUP for all tablespaces in the database.
4. Archive the unarchived redo logs so that the redo required to recover the tablespace backup is used by issuing the command ALTER SYSTEM ARCHIVE LOG CURRENT.
5. Back up the archived redo log files. If necessary, compress or delete the backed-up archived redo log files to free space on disk.
6. Back up the control file.

See Chapter 14 for details on RMAN's automation of this process.

Integration of Backup Procedures

Because there are multiple methods for backing up the Oracle database, there is no need to have a single point of failure in your backup strategy. Depending on your database's characteristics, you should choose one method, and use at least one of the remaining methods as a backup to your primary backup method.

NOTE

When considering physical backups, you should also evaluate the use of RMAN to perform incremental physical backups.

In the following sections, you will see how to choose the primary backup method for your database, how to integrate logical and physical backups, and how to integrate database backups with file system backups. For details on RMAN, see Chapter 14.

Integration of Logical and Physical Backups

Which backup method is appropriate to use as the primary backup method for your database? When deciding, you should take into account the characteristics of each method:

Method	Type	Recovery Characteristics
Data Pump Export	Logical	Can recover any database object to its status as of the moment it was exported.
Offline backups	Physical	Can recover the database to its status as of the moment it was shut down. If the database is run in ARCHIVELOG mode, you can recover the database to a status at any point in time.
Online backups	Physical	Can recover the database to its status at any point in time.

Offline backups are the least flexible method of backing up the database if the database is running in NOARCHIVELOG mode. Offline backups are a point-in-time snapshot of the database. Also, because they are a physical backup, DBAs cannot selectively recover logical objects (such as tables) from them. Although there are times when they are appropriate (such as for disaster recovery), offline backups should normally be used as a fallback in case your primary method fails. If you are running the database in ARCHIVELOG mode (strongly recommended!), you can use the offline backups as the basis for a media recovery, but an online backup would typically be easier to use for recovery in that situation.

Of the two remaining methods, which one is more appropriate? For production environments, the answer is almost always online backups. Online backups, with the database running in ARCHIVELOG mode, allow you to recover the database to the point in time immediately preceding a system fault or a user error. Using a Data Pump Export-based strategy would limit you to only being able to go back to the data as it existed the last time the data was exported.

Consider the size of the database and what objects you will likely be recovering. Given a standard recovery scenario, such as the loss of a disk, how long will it take for the data to be recovered? If a file is lost, the quickest way to recover it is usually via a physical backup, which again favors online backups over exports.

If the database is small, transaction volume is very low, and availability is not a concern, then offline backups may serve your needs. If you are only concerned about one or two tables, you could use Data Pump Export to selectively back them up. However, if the database is large, the recovery time needed for Data Pump Export/Import may be prohibitive. For large, low-transaction environments, offline backups may be appropriate.

Regardless of your choice for primary backup method, the final implementation should include a physical backup and some sort of logical backup, either via Data Pump Export or via replication. This redundancy is necessary because these methods validate different aspects of the database: Data Pump Export validates that the data is logically sound, and physical backups validate that the data is physically sound. A good database backup strategy integrates logical and physical backups. The frequency and type of backup performed will vary based on the database's usage characteristics.

Other database activities may call for ad hoc backups. Ad hoc backups may include offline backups before performing database upgrades and exports during application migration between databases.

Integration of Database and Operating System Backups

As described in this chapter, the DBA's backup activities involve a number of tasks normally assigned to a systems management group: monitoring disk usage, maintaining tapes, and so on. Rather than duplicate these efforts, it is best to integrate them; focus on a process-based alignment of your organization. The database backup strategy should be modified so that the systems management personnel's file system backups will take care of all tape handling, allowing you to centralize the production control processes in your environment.

Centralization of production control processes is usually accomplished by dedicating disk drives as destination locations for physical file backups. Instead of files being backed up to tape drives, the backups will instead be written to other disks on the same server. Those disks should be targeted for backups by the systems management personnel's regular file system backups. The DBA does not have to run a separate tape backup job. However, the DBA does need to verify that the systems management team's backup procedures executed correctly and completed successfully.

If your database environment includes files outside the database, such as datafiles for external tables or files accessed by BFILE datatypes, then you must determine how you are going to back those files up in a way that will provide consistent data in the event of a recovery. The backups of these flat files should be coordinated with your database backups and should also be integrated into any disaster recovery planning.

Summary

As with most Oracle features and tools, you have more than one if not several ways to accomplish a specific task. Performing backup and recovery is no exception. You can perform logical backups of your database using Data Pump Export and Import; physical backups of the database using RMAN in ARCHIVELOG mode; physical backups with the database shut down; or manual physical database backups of datafiles, control files, the SPFILE, and other miscellaneous files such as the password file and wallet while the database is in ARCHIVELOG mode.

Which method you should use depends on how available your database needs to be, how much storage space you can allocate for backups, and how quickly you must restore and recover the database in case of media failure. Using at least two of the methods described in this chapter ensures that your backup infrastructure doesn't become the single point of failure in your environment.

CHAPTER 14

Using Recovery Manager (RMAN)

In Chapters 11 and 13, we discussed a number of different ways in which we can back up our data and protect the database from accidental, inadvertent, or deliberate corruption. Physical backups of the database ensure that no committed transaction is lost and that we can restore the database from any previous backup to the current point in time or any point in between; logical backups allow the DBA or a user to capture the contents of individual database objects at a particular point in time, providing an alternative recovery option when a complete database-restoration operation would have too big an impact on the rest of the database.

Oracle's Recovery Manager (RMAN) takes backup and recovery to a new level of protection and ease of use. Since RMAN's appearance in Oracle version 8, there have been a number of major improvements and enhancements that can make RMAN a "one-stop shopping" solution for nearly every database environment, including those that are leveraging Oracle's multitenant architecture features first available in Oracle Database 12*c*. In addition to the RMAN command-line interface improvements in Oracle 12*c*, all the RMAN functionality has been included in the web-based Enterprise Manager Cloud Control 12*c* (EM Cloud Control) interface as well, allowing a DBA to monitor and perform backup operations when only a web browser connection is available.

In this chapter, we'll use a number of examples of RMAN operations, both using command-line syntax and the EM Cloud Control web interface. The examples will run the gamut from RMAN environment setup to backup, and the recovery and validation of the backup itself. We'll go into some detail about how RMAN manages the metadata associated with the database and its backups. Finally, we'll cover a number of miscellaneous topics, such as using RMAN to catalog backups made outside of the RMAN environment.

Oracle Database 12*c* brings even more functionality to an RMAN environment. To make database management more easily accessible from the command line, virtually all commands you would run at the SQL> prompt in SQL*Plus are now available at the RMAN> prompt without using the RMAN **sql** command. You can also now perform a restore and recovery operation at the table level—you would typically use Data Pump for logical export and import of table objects, but this gives you another option to retrieve a single table or a small number of tables using the latest RMAN backups. Finally, the DUPLICATE command can back up much faster over a network connection by leveraging a higher degree of parallelism on the auxiliary instance as well as better compression algorithms; these dramatically reduce the amount of time needed to create a copy of a database.

Due to the wide variety of tape backup management systems available, discussing any particular hardware configuration would be beyond the scope of this book. Instead, the focus in this chapter will be on using the fast recovery area, a dedicated area allocated on disk to store disk-based copies of all types of objects that RMAN can back up. The fast recovery area (formerly known as the flash recovery area) has been available since Oracle Database 10*g*.

For all the examples in this chapter, we will use a recovery catalog with RMAN. Although most of the functionality of RMAN is available by only using the control file of the target database, benefits such as being able to store RMAN scripts and additional recovery capabilities far outweigh the relatively low cost of maintaining an RMAN user account in a different database.

RMAN Features and Components

RMAN is more than just a client-side executable that can be used with a web interface. It comprises a number of other components, including the database to be backed up (the target database), an optional recovery catalog, an optional fast recovery area, and media management software to support tape backup systems. We will review each of these briefly in this section.

Many features of RMAN do not have equivalents in the backup methods presented in Chapter 13. We'll contrast the advantages and disadvantages of using RMAN versus the more traditional methods of backups.

RMAN Components

The first, and minimal, component in the RMAN environment is the RMAN executable. It is available along with the other Oracle utilities in the directory **$ORACLE_HOME/bin**, and it's installed by default with both the Standard and Enterprise Editions of Oracle Database 12*c*. From a command-line prompt, you can invoke RMAN with or without command-line arguments; in the following example, we're starting up RMAN using operating system authentication without connecting to a recovery catalog:

```
[oracle@tettnang ~]$ rman target /
RMAN>
```

The command-line arguments are optional; we can specify our target database and a recovery catalog from the RMAN> prompt also. In Figure 14-1, you can see how to access RMAN features from EM Cloud Control.

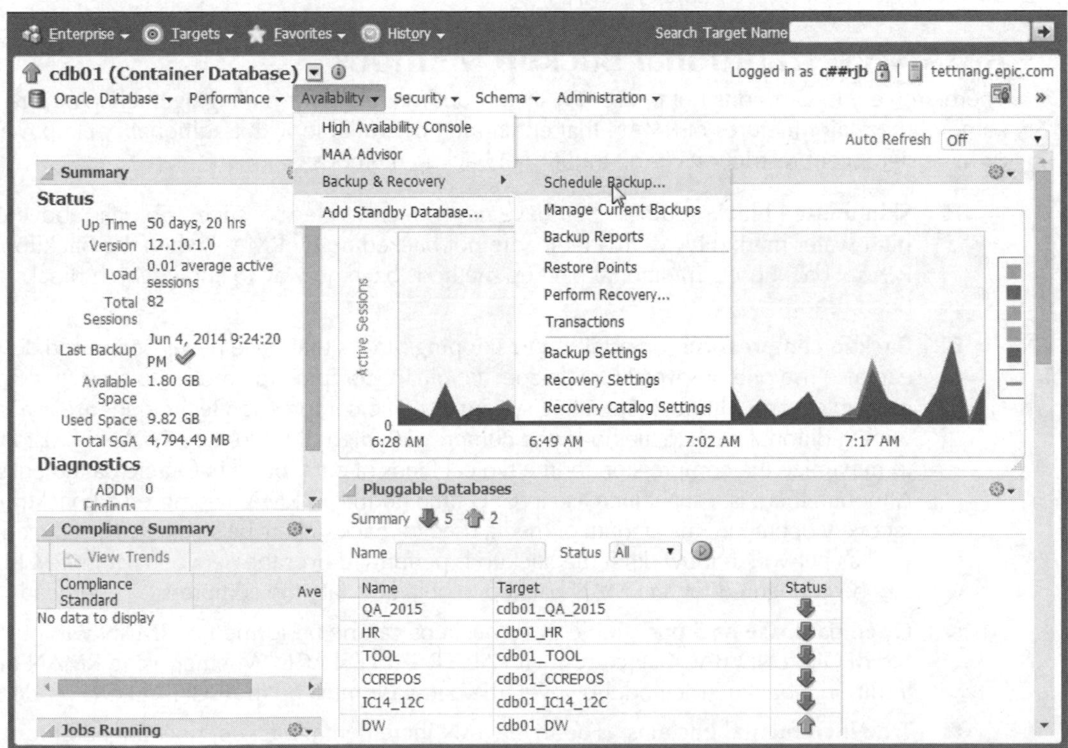

FIGURE 14-1. *Accessing RMAN functionality from EM Cloud Control*

RMAN is not of much use unless we have a database to back up. One or more target databases can be cataloged in the recovery catalog; in addition, the control file of the database being backed up contains information about backups performed by RMAN. From within the RMAN client, you can also issue SQL commands for those operations you cannot perform with native RMAN commands.

The RMAN recovery catalog, whether using the target database control file or a dedicated repository in a separate database, contains the location of recovery data, its own configuration settings, and the target database schema. At a minimum, the target database control file contains this data; to be able to store scripts and to maintain a copy of the target database control file, a recovery catalog is highly recommended. In this chapter, all examples will use a recovery catalog.

Since the release of Oracle 10*g*, the *fast recovery area* simplifies disk-based backup and recovery by defining a location on disk to hold all RMAN backups. Along with the location, the DBA can also specify an upper limit to the amount of disk space used in the fast recovery area. Once a retention policy is defined within RMAN, RMAN will automatically manage the backup files by deleting obsolete backups from both disk and tape. The initialization parameters related to the fast recovery area are covered in the next section.

To access all non-disk-based media, such as tape and BD-ROM, RMAN utilizes third-party media management software to move backup files to and from these offline and near-line devices, automatically requesting the mount and dismount of the appropriate media to support backup and restore operations. Most major media management software and hardware vendors have device drivers that directly support RMAN.

RMAN vs. Traditional Backup Methods

There are very few reasons not to use RMAN as your main tool for managing backups. Here are some of the major features of RMAN that either are not available with traditional backup methods or have significant restrictions using traditional backup methods:

- **Skip unused blocks** Blocks that have never been written to, such as blocks above the high-water mark (HWM) in a table, are not backed up by RMAN when the backup is an RMAN backupset. Traditional backup methods have no way to know which blocks have been used.
- **Backup compression** In addition to skipping blocks that have never been used, RMAN can also use one of several Oracle-specific binary compression modes to save space on the backup device. Although operating system–specific compression techniques are available with traditional backup methods, the compression algorithm used by RMAN is customized to maximize the compression for the typical kinds of data found in Oracle data blocks. Although there is a slight increase in CPU time during an RMAN compressed backup or recovery operation, the amount of media used for backup may be significantly reduced, as well as network bandwidth if the backup is performed over the network. Multiple CPUs can be configured for an RMAN backup to help alleviate the compression overhead.
- **Open database backups** Tablespace backups can be performed in RMAN without using the BEGIN/END BACKUP clause with ALTER TABLESPACE. Whether using RMAN or a traditional backup method, however, the database must be in ARCHIVELOG mode.
- **True incremental backups** For any RMAN incremental backup, unchanged blocks since the last backup will not be written to the backup file. This saves a significant amount of disk space, I/O time, and CPU time. For restore and recovery operations, RMAN supports

incrementally updated backups. Data blocks from an incremental backup are applied to a previous backup to potentially reduce the amount of time and number of files that need to be accessed to perform a recovery operation. We will cover an example of an incrementally updated backup later in this chapter.

- **Block-level recovery** To potentially avoid downtime during a recovery operation, RMAN supports *block-level recovery* for recovery operations that only need to restore or repair a small number of blocks identified as being corrupt during the backup operation. The rest of the tablespace and the objects within the tablespace can remain online while RMAN repairs the damaged blocks. The rows of a table not being repaired by RMAN are even available to applications and users.
- **Table-level recovery** When logical backups of a table aren't available or when FLASHBACK TABLE cannot bring back a table to a previous state, you can use RMAN to restore a table or tables from an RMAN backup as of any SCN since the last full RMAN backup with the database in ARCHIVELOG mode. This makes table-level recovery much easier than having to restore and recover an entire tablespace, much less the entire database, for just one table.
- **Multiple I/O channels** During a backup or recovery operation, RMAN can utilize many I/O channels, via separate operating system processes, to perform concurrent I/O. Traditional backup methods, such as a Unix **cp** command, are typically single-threaded operations.
- **Platform independence** Backups written with RMAN commands will be syntactically identical regardless of the hardware or software platform used, with the only difference being the media management channel configuration. On the other hand, a Unix script with lots of **cp** commands will not run very well if the backup script is migrated to a Windows platform!
- **Tape manager support** All major enterprise backup systems are supported within RMAN by a third-party media management driver provided by a tape backup vendor.
- **Cataloging** A record of all RMAN backups is recorded in the target database control file, and optionally in a recovery catalog stored in a different database. This makes restore and recovery operations relatively simple compared to manually tracking operating system–level backups using "copy" commands.
- **Scripting capabilities** RMAN scripts can be saved in a recovery catalog for retrieval during a backup session. The tight integration of the scripting language, the ease of maintaining scripts in RMAN, and the Oracle scheduling facility make it a better choice than storing traditional operating system scripts in an operating system directory with the operating system's native scheduling mechanisms.
- **Encrypted backups** RMAN uses backup encryption integrated into Oracle Database 12*c* (including advanced compression) to store encrypted backups. Storing encrypted backups on tape requires the Advanced Security Option.

In a few limited cases, a traditional backup method may have an advantage over RMAN; but now that RMAN supports the backup of password files and other non-database files such as **tnsnames.ora**, **listener.ora**, and **sqlnet.ora** (using Oracle Secure Backup), the case for RMAN as your single backup and recovery solution is compelling.

Backup Types

RMAN supports a number of different backup methods, depending on your availability needs, the desired size of your recovery window, and the amount of downtime you can endure while the database or a part of the database is involved in a recovery operation.

Consistent and Inconsistent Backups

A physical backup can be classified by being a *consistent* or an *inconsistent* backup. In a consistent backup, all datafiles have the same SCN; in other words, all changes in the redo logs have been applied to the datafiles. Because an open database with no uncommitted transactions may have some dirty blocks in the buffer cache, it is rare that an open database backup can be considered consistent. As a result, consistent backups are taken when the database is shut down normally or in a MOUNT state.

In contrast, an inconsistent backup is performed while the database is open and users are accessing the database. Because the SCNs of the datafiles typically do not match when an inconsistent backup is taking place, a recovery operation performed using an inconsistent backup must rely on both archived and online redo log files to bring the database into a consistent state before it is opened. As a result, a database must be in ARCHIVELOG mode to use an inconsistent backup method.

Full and Incremental Backups

Full backups include all blocks of every datafile within a tablespace or a database; it is essentially a bit-for-bit copy of one or more datafiles in the database. Either RMAN or an operating system command can be used to perform a full backup, although backups performed outside of RMAN must be cataloged with RMAN before they can be used in an RMAN recovery operation.

In Oracle 11*g* and later, incremental backups can be level 0 or level 1. A level 0 backup is a full backup of all blocks in the database that can be used in conjunction with differential, incremental, or cumulative incremental level 1 backups in a database recovery operation. A distinct advantage to using an incremental backup in a recovery strategy is that archived and online redo log files may not be necessary to restore a database or tablespace to a consistent state; the incremental backups may have some or all of the blocks needed. An example of using level 0 and level 1 incremental backups is presented later in this chapter. Incremental backups can only be performed within RMAN.

Image Copies

Image copies are full backups created by operating system commands or RMAN BACKUP AS COPY commands. Although a full backup created with a Unix **cp** command can be later registered in the RMAN catalog as a database backup, doing the same image copy backup in RMAN has the advantage of checking for corrupt blocks as they are being read by RMAN and recording the information about the bad blocks in the data dictionary. Image copies are the default backup file format in RMAN.

This is a great feature of Oracle 12*c*'s RMAN for the following reason: If you add another datafile to a tablespace, you need to also remember to add the new datafile to your Unix script **cp** command. By creating image copies using RMAN, all datafiles will automatically be included in the backup. Forgetting to add the new datafile to a Unix script will make a recovery situation extremely inconvenient at best and a disaster at worst.

Backupsets and Backup Pieces

In contrast to image copies, which can be created in most any backup environment, backupsets can be created and restored only with RMAN. A *backupset* is an RMAN backup of part or all of a database, consisting of one or more *backup pieces*. Each backup piece belongs to only one backupset, and can contain backups of one or many datafiles in the database. All backupsets and pieces are recorded in the RMAN repository, the same as any other RMAN-initiated backup.

Compressed Backups

For any Oracle 12*c* RMAN backup creating a backupset, compression is available to reduce the amount of disk space or tape needed to store the backup. Compressed backups are only usable by RMAN, and they need no special processing when used in a recovery operation; RMAN automatically decompresses the backup. Creating compressed backups is as easy as specifying AS COMPRESSED BACKUPSET and COMPRESSION ALGORITHM in the RMAN BACKUP command or as part of the default settings.

Overview of RMAN Commands and Options

In the next few sections, we'll review the basic set of commands you'll use on a regular basis. We'll look at how to make your job even easier by persisting some of the settings in an RMAN session; in addition, we'll set up the retention policy and the repository we'll use to store RMAN metadata.

At the end of this section, we'll review the initialization parameters related to RMAN backups and the fast recovery area.

Running SQL Commands in RMAN

Running SQL commands within an RMAN session becomes much easier in Oracle Database 12*c*. Unless there is an RMAN command that has the same name as a SQL or SQL*Plus command, you can just type it at the RMAN command line as if you were using SQL*Plus, as in this example:

```
[oracle@tettnang ~]$ rman target /
Recovery Manager: Release 12.1.0.1.0 - Production on Tue Aug 19 21:57:11 2014
Copyright (c) 1982, 2013, Oracle and/or its affiliates.  All rights reserved.
connected to target database: HR (DBID=3516035730)
using target database control file instead of recovery catalog
RMAN> select ts#,name,bigfile
2> from v$tablespace
3> where name like 'S%';

       TS# NAME                           BIG
---------- ------------------------------ ---
         0 SYSTEM                         NO
         1 SYSAUX                         NO
RMAN>
```

The existing method to run SQL statements in RMAN, SQL *"command"*, is still available if you want to avoid any ambiguity or don't want to change any existing RMAN scripts.

Frequently Used Commands

Table 14-1 provides a list of the most common RMAN commands you'll use on a regular basis, along with some common options and caveats for each command. For the complete list of all RMAN commands and their syntax, see the *Oracle Database Backup and Recovery Reference, 12c Release 1*.

RMAN Command	Description
@	Runs an RMAN command script at the pathname specified after the @. If no path is specified, the path is assumed to be the directory from which RMAN was invoked.
ADVISE FAILURE	Displays repair options for the failure found.
BACKUP	Performs an RMAN backup, with or without archived redo logs. Backs up datafiles or datafile copies, or performs an incremental level 0 or level 1 backup. Backs up an entire database, or a single tablespace or datafile. Validates the blocks to be backed up with the VALIDATE clause.
CATALOG	Adds information about file copies and user-managed backups to the repository.
CHANGE	Changes the status of a backup in the RMAN repository. Useful for explicitly excluding a backup from a restore or recovery operation, or to notify RMAN that a backup file was inadvertently or deliberately removed by an operating system command outside of RMAN.
CONFIGURE	Configures the persistent parameters for RMAN. The parameters configured are available during every subsequent RMAN session unless they are explicitly cleared or modified.
CONVERT	Converts datafile formats for transporting tablespaces or entire databases across platforms.
CREATE CATALOG	Creates the repository catalog containing RMAN metadata for one or more target databases. It is strongly recommended that this catalog not be stored in one of the target databases.
CROSSCHECK	Checks the record of backups in the RMAN repository against the actual files on disk or tape. Objects are flagged as EXPIRED, AVAILABLE, UNAVAILABLE, or OBSOLETE. If the object is not available to RMAN, it is marked UNAVAILABLE.
DELETE	Deletes backup files or copies and marks them as DELETED in the target database control file. If a repository is used, the record of the backup file is removed.
DROP DATABASE	Deletes the target database from disk and unregisters it.
DUPLICATE	Uses backups of the target database (or uses the live database) to create a duplicate database.

TABLE 14-1. *Common RMAN Commands*

RMAN Command	Description
FLASHBACK DATABASE	Performs a Flashback Database operation. The database is restored to a point in the past by SCN or log sequence number using flashback logs to undo changes before the SCN or log sequence number, and then archived redo logs are applied to bring the database forward to a consistent state.
LIST	Displays information about backupsets and image copies recorded in the target database control file or repository. See REPORT for identifying complex relationships between backupsets.
RECOVER	Performs a complete or incomplete recovery on a datafile, a tablespace, or the entire database. Can also apply incremental backups to a datafile image copy to roll it forward in time.
REGISTER DATABASE	Registers a target database in the RMAN repository.
REPAIR FAILURE	Repairs one or more failures recorded in the Automatic Diagnostic Repository (ADR).
REPORT	Performs a detailed analysis of the RMAN repository. For example, this command can identify which files need a backup to meet the retention policy or which backup files can be deleted.
RESTORE	Restores files from image copies or backupsets to disk, typically after a media failure. Can be used to validate a restore operation without actually performing the restore by specifying the PREVIEW option.
RUN	Runs a sequence of RMAN statements as a group between { and }. Allows you to override default RMAN parameters for the duration of the execution of the group.
SET	Sets RMAN configuration settings for the duration of the RMAN session, such as allocated disk or tape channels. Persistent settings are assigned with CONFIGURE.
SHOW	Shows all or individual RMAN configured settings.
SHUTDOWN	Shuts down the target database from within RMAN. Identical to the SHUTDOWN command within SQL*Plus.
STARTUP	Starts up the target database. This command has the same options and function as the SQL*Plus STARTUP command.
SQL	Runs SQL commands within RMAN. Rarely needed, as virtually all SQL commands will run as is from the RMAN command line as of Oracle Database 12*c*.
TRANSPORT TABLESPACE	Creates transportable tablespace sets from backup for one or more tablespaces.
VALIDATE	Examines a backupset and reports whether its data is intact and consistent.

TABLE 14-1. *Common RMAN Commands* (Continued)

If backups use a fast recovery area (presented in Chapter 13), you can back up the database without any other explicit RMAN configuration by running the following command:

```
RMAN> backup database;
```

Note that this is a full backup and can be used with archived redo log files to recover a database. However, this is not a level 0 backup and cannot be used as part of an incremental backup strategy. See the "Backup Operations" section later in this chapter.

Setting Up a Repository

Whether you use a repository for the metadata from one database or a hundred, the repository setup is very straightforward and needs to be done only once. The examples that follow assume that we have a default installation of an Oracle 12*c* database; the repository database itself can be used for other applications if there is no significant performance degradation when RMAN needs to update metadata in the repository.

CAUTION
Using an RMAN target database for the repository is strongly discouraged. Loss of the target database prevents any chance of a successful recovery of the database using RMAN because the repository metadata is lost along with the target database.

The following sequence of commands creates a tablespace and a user to maintain the metadata in the repository database. In this and all subsequent examples, a database with a SID of **rman_rep** is used for all repository operations.

The tablespace that holds the repository database requires at least 125MB to hold recovery catalog entries; here is a space requirements breakdown by tablespace:

- 90MB in the SYSTEM tablespace
- 5MB in the TEMP tablespace
- 5MB in the UNDO tablespace
- 15MB in RMAN's default tablespace for each database registered in the recovery catalog
- 1MB for each online redo log file

Starting out with available free space of 125MB will in most cases be sufficient for the first year, and enabling additional extents of 75MB each will be sufficient in the long term depending on how many databases you manage in the recovery catalog. Overall, it's a very small amount of disk space compared to your terabyte data warehouse!

Connect to the repository database with SYSDBA privileges and create the RMAN account and the recovery catalog in the RMAN tablespace as follows:

```
[oracle@kthanid ~]$ sqlplus rjb/rjb909@kthanid:1521/rman_rep

SQL*Plus: Release 12.1.0.2.0 Production on Wed Aug 20 06:58:59 2014
Copyright (c) 1982, 2014, Oracle.  All rights reserved.
Last Successful login time: Wed Aug 20 2014 06:50:11 -05:00
```

```
Connected to:
Oracle Database 12c Enterprise Edition Release 12.1.0.2.0 - 64bit Production
With the Partitioning, Automatic Storage Management, OLAP, Advanced Analytics
and Real Application Testing options

SQL> create tablespace rman datafile 'data12c'
  2      size 125m autoextend on next 75m maxsize 1g;

Tablespace created.
SQL> grant recovery_catalog_owner to rman identified by rman;
Grant succeeded.
SQL> alter user rman default tablespace rman
  2      quota unlimited on rman;
User altered.
SQL>
```

TIP
You can create a user, grant privileges, and assign a password using the GRANT command alone instead of using a separate CREATE USER command.

Now that the RMAN user account exists in the repository database, we can start RMAN, connect to the catalog, and initialize the repository with the CREATE CATALOG command from the server with the target database:

```
[oracle@tettnang ~]$ rman catalog rman/rman@kthanid/rman_rep

Recovery Manager: Release 12.1.0.1.0 - Production on Wed Aug 20 07:05:29 2014

Copyright (c) 1982, 2013, Oracle and/or its affiliates.  All rights reserved.

connected to recovery catalog database

RMAN> create catalog;

recovery catalog created

RMAN
```

From this point on, using a repository is as easy as specifying the repository username and password on the RMAN command line with the CATALOG parameter or using the CONNECT CATALOG command in an RMAN session. Within EM Cloud Control, you can persist the repository credentials as demonstrated in Figure 14-2.

In future EM Cloud Control sessions, any RMAN backup or recovery operations will automatically use the recovery catalog.

Registering a Database

For each database for which RMAN will perform a backup or recovery, we must *register* the database in the RMAN repository; this operation records information such as the target database

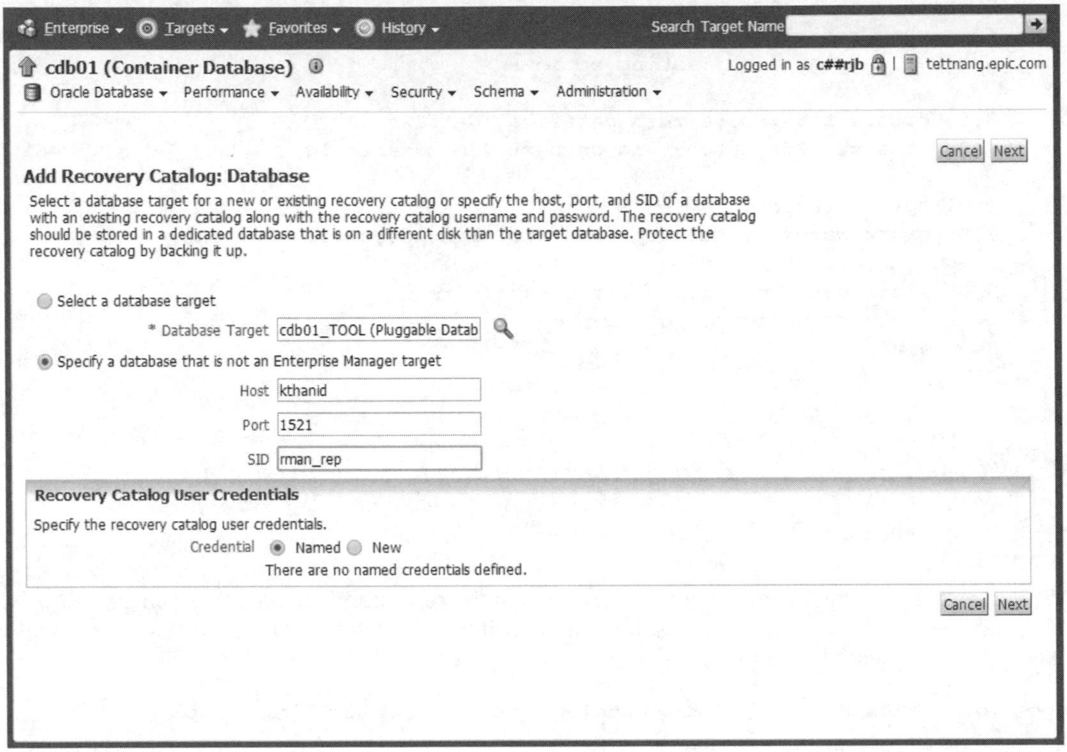

FIGURE 14-2. *Persisting RMAN repository credentials*

schema and the unique database ID (DBID) of the target database. The target database need only be registered once; subsequent RMAN sessions that connect to the target database will automatically reference the correct metadata in the repository.

```
[oracle@tettnang ~]$ rman target / catalog rman/rman@kthanid/rman_rep

Recovery Manager: Release 12.1.0.1.0 - Production on Wed Aug 20 08:44:21 2014

Copyright (c) 1982, 2013, Oracle and/or its affiliates.  All rights reserved.

connected to target database: CDB01 (DBID=1382179355)
connected to recovery catalog database

RMAN> register database;

database registered in recovery catalog
starting full resync of recovery catalog
full resync complete

RMAN>
```

In the preceding example, we connect to the target database using operating system authentication and to the repository with password authentication. Note that in this example the database CDB01 may or may not be a container database (CDB), but it doesn't matter since RMAN must connect to a CDB in the root container to perform backup and recovery operations for the entire CDB or any individual PDB.

All databases registered with the repository must have unique DBIDs; trying to register the database again yields the following error message:

```
RMAN> register database;

RMAN-00571: ===========================================================
RMAN-00569: =============== ERROR MESSAGE STACK FOLLOWS ===============
RMAN-00571: ===========================================================
RMAN-03009: failure of register command on default channel
    at 08/28/2014 21:38:44
RMAN-20002: target database already registered in recovery catalog

RMAN>
```

Persisting RMAN Settings

To make the DBA's job easier, a number of RMAN settings can be *persisted*. In other words, these settings will stay in effect between RMAN sessions. In the example that follows, we use the SHOW command to display the default RMAN settings:

```
RMAN> show all;

RMAN configuration parameters for database with db_unique_name CDB01 are:
CONFIGURE RETENTION POLICY TO REDUNDANCY 1; # default
CONFIGURE BACKUP OPTIMIZATION ON;
CONFIGURE DEFAULT DEVICE TYPE TO DISK; # default
CONFIGURE CONTROLFILE AUTOBACKUP ON; # default
CONFIGURE CONTROLFILE AUTOBACKUP FORMAT FOR DEVICE TYPE DISK TO '%F'; #
default
CONFIGURE DEVICE TYPE DISK PARALLELISM 4 BACKUP TYPE TO COMPRESSED BACKUPSET;
CONFIGURE DATAFILE BACKUP COPIES FOR DEVICE TYPE DISK TO 1; # default
CONFIGURE ARCHIVELOG BACKUP COPIES FOR DEVICE TYPE DISK TO 1; # default
CONFIGURE MAXSETSIZE TO UNLIMITED; # default
CONFIGURE ENCRYPTION FOR DATABASE OFF; # default
CONFIGURE ENCRYPTION ALGORITHM 'AES128'; # default
CONFIGURE COMPRESSION ALGORITHM 'BASIC' AS OF RELEASE 'DEFAULT'
    OPTIMIZE FOR LOAD TRUE ; # default
CONFIGURE RMAN OUTPUT TO KEEP FOR 7 DAYS; # default
CONFIGURE ARCHIVELOG DELETION POLICY TO NONE; # default
CONFIGURE SNAPSHOT CONTROLFILE NAME TO
    '/u01/app/oracle/product/12.1.0/dbhome_1/dbs/snapcf_cdb01.f'; # default

RMAN>
```

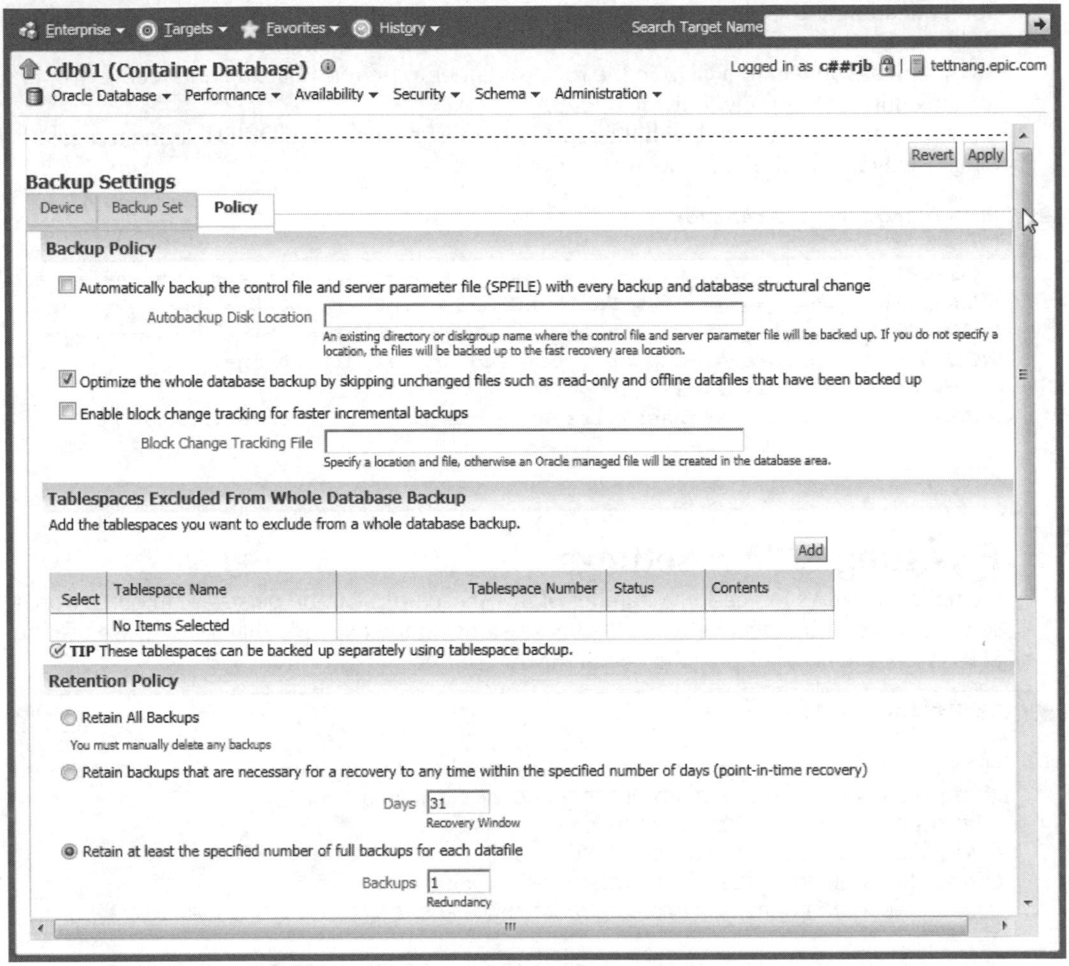

FIGURE 14-3. *Reviewing RMAN settings in EM Cloud Control*

Any parameters that are set to their default values have **# default** at the end of the configuration setting. These parameters are easy to review and change using EM Cloud Control, as demonstrated in Figure 14-3.

In the next few sections, we'll review a few of the more common RMAN persistent settings.

Retention Policy

Backups can be automatically retained and managed using one of two methods: by a *recovery window* or by *redundancy*. Using a recovery window, RMAN will retain as many backups as necessary to bring the database to any point in time within the recovery window. For example, with a recovery window of seven days, RMAN will maintain enough image copies, incremental backups, and archived redo logs to ensure that the database can be restored and recovered to any point in time within the last seven days. Any backups that are not needed to support this recovery window are marked as OBSOLETE and are automatically removed by RMAN if a fast recovery area is used and disk space is needed for new backups.

In contrast, a redundancy retention policy directs RMAN to retain the specified number of backups or copies of each datafile and control file. Any extra copies or backups beyond the number specified in the redundancy policy are marked as OBSOLETE. As with a recovery window, obsolete backups are automatically removed if disk space is needed and a fast recovery area is used. Otherwise, you can use the DELETE OBSOLETE command to remove the backup files and update the catalog.

If the retention policy is set to NONE, no backups or copies are ever considered obsolete, and the DBA must manually remove unneeded backups from the catalog and from disk.

In the following example, we will set the retention policy to a recovery window of four days (from a default redundancy policy of one copy):

```
RMAN> configure retention policy to recovery window of 4 days;

new RMAN configuration parameters:
CONFIGURE RETENTION POLICY TO RECOVERY WINDOW OF 4 DAYS;
new RMAN configuration parameters are successfully stored
RMAN>
```

Device Type

If the default device type is set to DISK and no pathname parameter is specified, RMAN uses the fast recovery area for all backups (in this case the disk group +RECOV); you can easily override the disk backup location in EM Cloud Control, as you can see in Figure 14-4. As with many of the simplified administration tasks from Oracle 12*c*, there is no need to allocate or deallocate a specific channel for backups unless you're using a tape device.

Although configuring a tape device is specific to your installation, in general terms we configure a tape device as follows:

```
RMAN> configure channel device type sbt
2>    parms='ENV=(<vendor specific arguments>)';
```

NOTE
sbt *is the device type used for any tape backup subsystem, regardless of vendor.*

Although we can use the fast recovery area to restore and recover our database entirely from disk, at some point it becomes inefficient to keep all our backups on disk, especially if we have a large recovery window. As a result, we can make copies of our backup files to tape, and RMAN will dutifully keep track of where the backups are in case we need to restore or recover the database from tape, or restore archived redo logs to roll forward an image copy in the fast recovery area.

Control File Autobackup

Because of the importance of the control file, we want to back it up at least as often as it changes due to modifications in the structure of the database. By default, the backup of the control file

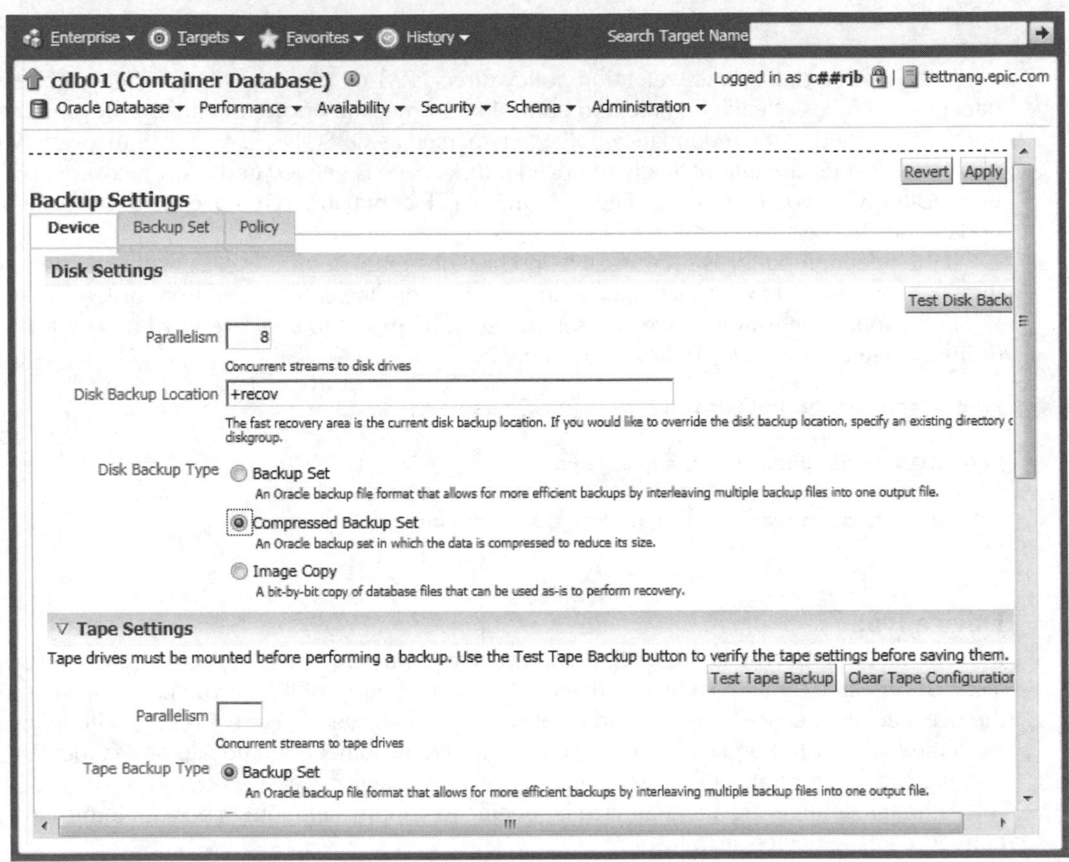

FIGURE 14-4. *Configuring backup destination using EM Cloud Control*

does not occur automatically. This is a strange default, considering the importance of the control file and how little disk space it takes to back it up. Fortunately, RMAN can easily be configured to back up the control file automatically, either any time a successful backup must be recorded in the repository or when a structural change affects the contents of the control file (in other words, cases when a control file backup must occur to ensure a successful recovery if and when a recovery operation is required):

```
RMAN> configure controlfile autobackup on;

new RMAN configuration parameters:
CONFIGURE CONTROLFILE AUTOBACKUP ON;
new RMAN configuration parameters are successfully stored

RMAN>
```

Every RMAN backup from this point on will automatically include a copy of the control file; the control file is also backed up whenever a new tablespace is created or another datafile is added to an existing tablespace.

Backup Compression

If disk space is at a premium, you have a very large database, and you have some extra CPU capacity, it makes sense to compress the backups to save space. The files are decompressed automatically during a restore or recovery operation.

```
RMAN> configure device type disk backup type to compressed backupset;

new RMAN configuration parameters:
CONFIGURE DEVICE TYPE DISK BACKUP TYPE TO
      COMPRESSED BACKUPSET PARALLELISM 8;
new RMAN configuration parameters are successfully stored

RMAN>
```

Compressing backupsets may not be necessary if the operating system's file system has compression enabled or if the tape device hardware automatically compresses backups; however, RMAN's compression algorithm is tuned to efficiently back up Oracle data blocks, and as a result it may do a better job of compressing the backupsets.

Initialization Parameters

A number of initialization parameters are used to control RMAN backups. We'll cover some of the more important parameters in this section.

CONTROL_FILE_RECORD_KEEP_TIME

A record of all RMAN backups is kept in the target control file. This parameter specifies the number of days that RMAN will attempt to keep a record of backups in the target control file. After this time, RMAN will begin to reuse records older than this retention period. If RMAN needs to write a new backup record, and the retention period has not been reached, RMAN will attempt to expand the size of the control file. Usually, this is successful because the size of the control file is relatively small compared to other database objects. However, if space is not available for the expansion of the control file, RMAN will reuse the oldest record in the control file and write a message to the alert log.

As a rule of thumb, you should set CONTROL_FILE_RECORD_KEEP_TIME to several days beyond your actual recovery window to ensure that backup records are retained in the control file. The default is seven days.

DB_RECOVERY_FILE_DEST

This parameter specifies the location of the fast recovery area. It should be located on a file system different from any database datafiles, control files, or redo log files, online or archived. If you lose the disk with the datafiles, the fast recovery area is gone too, mitigating the advantages of using a fast recovery area.

DB_RECOVERY_FILE_DEST_SIZE

The parameter DB_RECOVERY_FILE_DEST_SIZE specifies an upper limit to the amount of space used for the fast recovery area. The underlying file system may have less or more than this amount of space; the DBA should ensure that at least this amount of space is available for backups. Note that this is the amount of recovery space for this database only; if multiple databases share the same ASM disk group for their fast recovery area, the sum of all values for DB_RECOVERY_FILE_DEST_SIZE must not exceed the available space in the disk group.

In our data warehouse database, **dw**, a fast recovery area is defined in the disk group +RECOV with a maximum size of 8GB. As this limit is reached, RMAN will automatically remove obsolete backups and generate an alert in the alert log when the amount of space occupied by nonobsolete backups is within 10 percent of the value specified in DB_RECOVERY_FILE_DEST_SIZE.

The parameters DB_RECOVERY_FILE_DEST and DB_RECOVERY_FILE_DEST_SIZE are both dynamic; they can be changed on the fly while the instance is running to respond to changes in disk space availability.

Data Dictionary and Dynamic Performance Views

A number of Oracle data dictionary and dynamic performance views contain information specific to RMAN operations, on both the target database and the catalog database. In Table 14-2 are the key views related to RMAN. Each of these views will be covered in more detail later in this chapter.

View	Description
RC_*	RMAN recovery catalog views. Only exist in the RMAN repository database and contain recovery information for all target databases.
V$RMAN_STATUS	Displays finished and in-progress RMAN jobs.
V$RMAN_OUTPUT	Contains messages generated by RMAN sessions and each RMAN command executed within the session.
V$SESSION_LONGOPS	Contains the status of long-running administrative operations that run for more than six seconds; includes statistics gathering and long-running queries, in addition to RMAN recovery and backup operations.
V$DATABASE_BLOCK_CORRUPTION	Corrupted blocks detected during an RMAN session.
V$FLASH_RECOVERY_AREA_USAGE	The percentage of space used, by object type, in the fast recovery area.
V$RECOVERY_FILE_DEST	The number of files, space used, space that can be reclaimed, and space limit for the fast recovery area.
V$RMAN_CONFIGURATION	RMAN configuration parameters with non-default values for this database.

TABLE 14-2. *RMAN Data Dictionary and Dynamic Performance Views*

The RC_* views only exist in a database that is used as an RMAN repository; the V$ views exist and have rows in any database that is backed up using RMAN. To highlight this difference, we'll look at the view V$RMAN_CONFIGURATION in the target database:

```
[oracle@tettnang ~]$ sqlplus rjb/rjb@tettnang/dw

SQL*Plus: Release 12.1.0.1.0 Production on Wed Aug 20 09:06:37 2014

Copyright (c) 1982, 2013, Oracle.  All rights reserved.


Connected to:
Oracle Database 12c Enterprise Edition Release 12.1.0.1.0 - 64bit Production
With the Partitioning, Automatic Storage Management, OLAP, Advanced Analytics
and Real Application Testing options

SQL> select * from v$rman_configuration;

     CONF# NAME                     VALUE                              CON_ID
---------- ------------------------ ---------------------------------- ----------
         1 BACKUP OPTIMIZATION      ON                                          0
         2 DEVICE TYPE              DISK BACKUP TYPE TO COMPRESSED              0
                                     BACKUPSET PARALLELISM 4

         3 RETENTION POLICY         TO RECOVERY WINDOW OF 4 DAYS                0
         4 CONTROLFILE AUTOBACKUP   ON                                          0

SQL>
```

Note that these are the RMAN persistent parameters that were changed from the default. The recovery catalog database keeps these non-default values in the view RC_RMAN_CONFIGURATION for all databases registered with RMAN. Note also the CON_ID column for databases in a multitenant environment. A PDB will have CON_ID=0 (no visibility to other PDBs in the CDB), whereas CON_ID will have a unique identifier for each PDB when connected to the root container.

```
SQL> connect rman/rman@kthanid/rman_rep
Connected.
SQL> select db_key, db_unique_name, name, value
  2       from rman.rc_rman_configuration;

    DB_KEY DB_UNIQUE_NAME      NAME                       VALUE
---------- ------------------- -------------------------- ---------------
         1 CDB01               BACKUP OPTIMIZATION        ON
         1 CDB01               DEVICE TYPE                DISK BACKUP TYP
                                                          E TO COMPRESSED
                                                           BACKUPSET PARA
                                                          LLELISM 4
```

```
        1                    RETENTION POLICY          TO RECOVERY WIN
                                                       DOW OF 4 DAYS

        1 CDB01              CONTROLFILE AUTOBACKUP    ON

4 rows selected.
```

If we were using RMAN to back up another database, this view would contain other values for DB_KEY and DB_UNIQUE_NAME for other target databases with non-default RMAN parameters.

Because we are not using RMAN to back up the **rman_rep** database, the views V$RMAN_* are empty.

Backup Operations

In this section, we'll run through some examples to back up the target database in a variety of ways: We'll perform two kinds of full backups, create image copies of selected database files, investigate how incremental backups work, and discuss both incremental backup optimization and the fast recovery area.

We'll continue to use our data warehouse database, **dw**, as the target database, with the database **rman_rep** as the RMAN repository.

Full Database Backups

In our first example of a full database backup, we'll use backupsets to copy all database files, including the SPFILE, to the fast recovery area:

```
RMAN> backup as compressed backupset database spfile;
Starting backup at 20-AUG-14
starting full resync of recovery catalog
full resync complete
allocated channel: ORA_DISK_1
channel ORA_DISK_1: SID=269 device type=DISK
allocated channel: ORA_DISK_2
channel ORA_DISK_2: SID=523 device type=DISK
allocated channel: ORA_DISK_3
channel ORA_DISK_3: SID=778 device type=DISK
allocated channel: ORA_DISK_4
channel ORA_DISK_4: SID=1024 device type=DISK
skipping datafile 5; already backed up 1 time(s)
skipping datafile 7; already backed up 1 time(s)
skipping datafile 18; already backed up 1 time(s)
skipping datafile 19; already backed up 1 time(s)
. . .
piece handle=+RECOV/CDB01/F754FCD8744A55AAE043E3A0080A3B17/
BACKUPSET/2014_08_20/nnndf0_tag20140820t094015_0.758.856086089
tag=TAG20140820T094015 comment=NONE
channel ORA_DISK_2: backup set complete, elapsed time: 00:01:07
Finished backup at 20-AUG-14
Starting Control File and SPFILE Autobackup at 20-AUG-14
piece handle=+RECOV/CDB01/AUTOBACKUP/2014_08_20/s_856086157.752.856086157
comment=NONE
Finished Control File and SPFILE Autobackup at 20-AUG-14
RMAN>
```

NOTE
When using a recovery catalog, RMAN can only connect to the root container (CDB) to perform backup and recovery operations.

Files 5, 7, 18, and 19 did not need to be backed up because of the BACKUP OPTIMIZATION setting configured to ON. Note also that the SPFILE is backed up twice, the second time along with the control file. Because we set CONFIGURE CONTROLFILE AUTOBACKUP to ON, we automatically back up the control file and SPFILE whenever we do any other kind of backup or the structure of the database changes. As a result, we don't need to specify SPFILE in the BACKUP command.

Taking a peek into the fast recovery area using the **asmcmd** tool, we see a lot of cryptic filenames for the recent archived redo logs and the full database backup we just performed:

```
[oracle@tettnang ~]$ sqlplus / as sysdba

SQL*Plus: Release 12.1.0.1.0 Production on Wed Aug 20 09:46:59 2014

Copyright (c) 1982, 2013, Oracle.  All rights reserved.


Connected to:
Oracle Database 12c Enterprise Edition Release 12.1.0.1.0 - 64bit Production
With the Partitioning, Automatic Storage Management, OLAP, Advanced Analytics
and Real Application Testing options

SQL> show parameter db_recov

NAME                                 TYPE        VALUE
------------------------------------ ----------- ------------------------------
db_recovery_file_dest                string      +RECOV
db_recovery_file_dest_size           big integer 25G
SQL> select name from v$database;
NAME
---------
CDB01
SQL> exit
[oracle@tettnang ~]$ . oraenv
ORACLE_SID = [cdb01] ? +ASM
The Oracle base remains unchanged with value /u01/app/oracle
[oracle@tettnang ~]$ asmcmd
ASMCMD> ls
DATA/
RECOV/
ASMCMD> cd recov
ASMCMD> ls
CDB01/
HR/
ASMCMD> cd cdb01
ASMCMD> ls
```

```
00FF6323468C3972E053E3A0080AAFD5/
AUTOBACKUP/
BACKUPSET/
CONTROLFILE/
F754FCD8744A55AAE043E3A0080A3B17/
FA782A61F8447D03E043E3A0080A9E54/
FA787E0038B26FFBE043E3A0080A1A75/
FB03AEEBB6F60995E043E3A0080AEE85/
FBA928F391D2217DE043E3A0080AB287/
FC9588B12BBD413FE043E3A0080A5528/
ASMCMD> ls -l backupset
Type  Redund  Striped  Time             Sys  Name
                                        Y    2014_06_04/
                                        Y    2014_08_20/
ASMCMD> ls -l backupset/2014_08_20
Type       Redund  Striped  Time             Sys  Name
BACKUPSET  UNPROT  COARSE   AUG 20 09:00:00  Y    nnndf0_TAG2014082
0T094015_0.756.856086105
BACKUPSET  UNPROT  COARSE   AUG 20 09:00:00  Y    nnndf0_TAG2014082
0T094015_0.757.856086105
BACKUPSET  UNPROT  COARSE   AUG 20 09:00:00  Y    nnndf0_TAG2014082
0T094015_0.762.856086041
BACKUPSET  UNPROT  COARSE   AUG 20 09:00:00  Y    nnsnf0_TAG2014082
0T093249_0.763.856085647
BACKUPSET  UNPROT  COARSE   AUG 20 09:00:00  Y    nnsnf0_TAG2014082
0T094015_0.753.856086141
ASMCMD>
```

As an alternative, you can use RMAN's LIST command to see these backups as they are cataloged in the target database control file and the RMAN repository. There are four backupsets, one for a previous full database backup, and three others: a more recent full backup containing the datafiles themselves, one for the explicit SPFILE backup, and one for the implicit SPFILE and control file backup.

```
RMAN> list backup by backup;


List of Backup Sets
===================

BS Key  Type LV Size       Device Type Elapsed Time Completion Time
------- ---- -- ---------- ----------- ------------ ---------------
1606    Full    1.39M      DISK        00:00:00     04-JUN-14
        BP Key: 1633   Status: AVAILABLE  Compressed: YES  Tag:
TAG20140604T073433
        Piece Name: +RECOV/CDB01/BACKUPSET/2014_06_04/nnndf0_tag2014060
4t073433_0.300.849339275
  List of Datafiles in backup set 1606
  File LV Type Ckp SCN    Ckp Time  Name
  ---- -- ---- ---------- --------- ----
  4       Full 4733015    04-JUN-14 +DATA/CDB01/DATAFILE/
undotbs1.270.845194049
```

```
  28       Full 4733015     04-JUN-14 +DATA/CDB01/DATAFILE/
undotbs1.263.848922747
. . .
  126      Full 13866695    20-AUG-14 +DATA/CDB01/
F754FCD8744A55AAE043E3A0080A3B17/DATAFILE/epicixsochx.387.850144917

BS Key  Type LV Size       Device Type Elapsed Time Completion Time
------- ---- -- ---------- ----------- ------------ ---------------
2109    Full    18.39M     DISK        00:00:01     20-AUG-14
        BP Key: 2133   Status: AVAILABLE  Compressed: NO  Tag:
TAG20140820T094237
        Piece Name: +RECOV/CDB01/AUTOBACKUP/2014_08_20
/s_856086157.752.856086157
  SPFILE Included: Modification time: 20-AUG-14
  SPFILE db_unique_name: CDB01
  Control File Included: Ckp SCN: 13868824     Ckp time: 20-AUG-14

RMAN>
```

One of the full backups can be used in conjunction with the archived redo logs (stored by default in the fast recovery area residing in the ASM disk group +RECOV) to recover the database to any point in time up to the last committed transaction.

Figure 14-5 shows a whole database backup configured to run using EM Cloud Control. Notice that you can view, copy, or edit the RMAN script that EM Cloud Control generates.

Displaying the contents of the catalog is just as easy in EM Cloud Control. Figure 14-6 shows results equivalent to the LIST BACKUP BY BACKUP command.

The LIST and REPORT commands are covered in more detail later in this chapter.

Tablespace Backups

After adding a tablespace to the database, performing an immediate backup of the tablespace will shorten the time it will take to restore the tablespace later in the event of media failure. In addition, you might back up an individual tablespace in a database that is too large to back up all at once; again, creating a backupset or image copy of a tablespace at frequent intervals will reduce the amount of redo that would need to be applied to an older backup of the tablespace in the event of media failure. For example, in an environment with three large tablespaces—USERS, USERS2, and USERS3—along with the default tablespaces SYSTEM and SYSAUX, you might back up the SYSTEM and SYSAUX tablespaces on Sunday, USERS on Monday, USERS2 on Wednesday, and USERS3 on Friday. Failures of any media containing datafiles from one of these tablespaces will use a tablespace backup that is no more than a week old plus the intervening archived and online redo log files for recovery.

In our next example, we're adding a tablespace to the **dw** database (a PDB within the CDB01 container) to support a new set of star schemas:

```
SQL> create tablespace inet_star
  2  datafile '+data' size 100m
  3  autoextend on next 100m maxsize 5g;
Tablespace created.
```

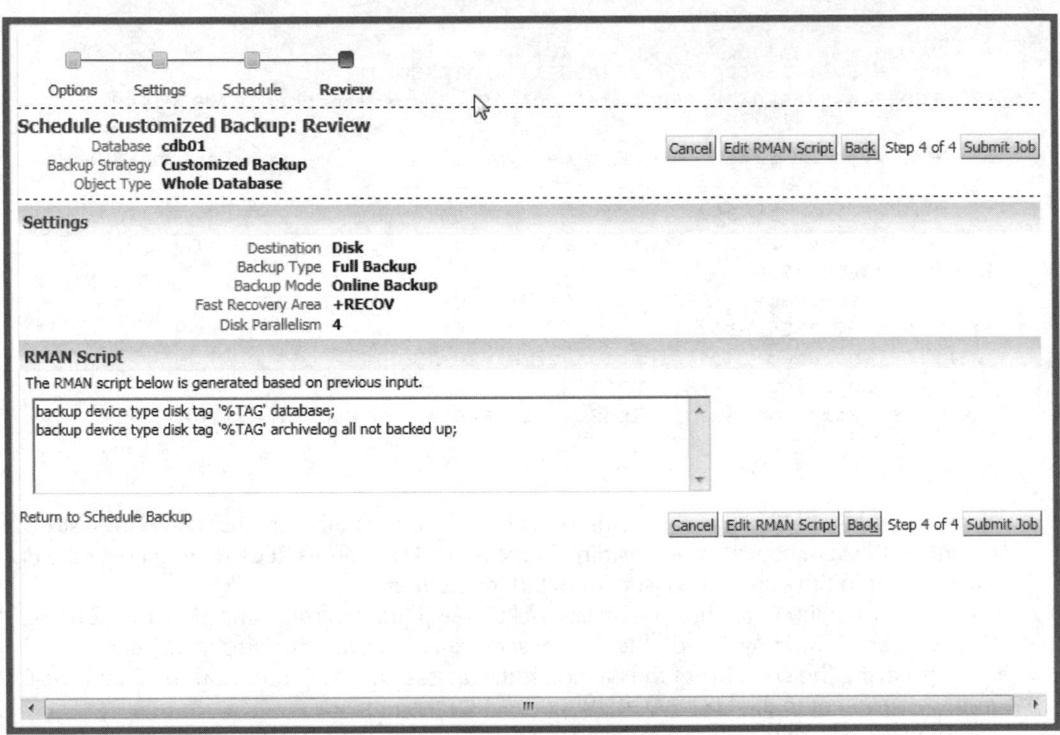

FIGURE 14-5. *Configure backup job with EM Cloud Control*

From an RMAN session, we will back up the tablespace along with the control file. In this case, it's critical that we back up the control file because it contains the definition for the new tablespace.

```
RMAN> backup tablespace dw:inet_star;
Starting backup at 20-AUG-14
allocated channel: ORA_DISK_1
channel ORA_DISK_1: SID=10 device type=DISK
allocated channel: ORA_DISK_2
channel ORA_DISK_2: SID=268 device type=DISK
allocated channel: ORA_DISK_3
channel ORA_DISK_3: SID=522 device type=DISK
allocated channel: ORA_DISK_4
channel ORA_DISK_4: SID=776 device type=DISK
channel ORA_DISK_1: starting compressed full datafile backup set
channel ORA_DISK_1: specifying datafile(s) in backup set
input datafile file number=00218 name=+DATA/CDB01/00FF6323468C3972E053E3A0080A
AFD5/DATAFILE/inet_star.493.856087357
channel ORA_DISK_1: starting piece 1 at 20-AUG-14
```

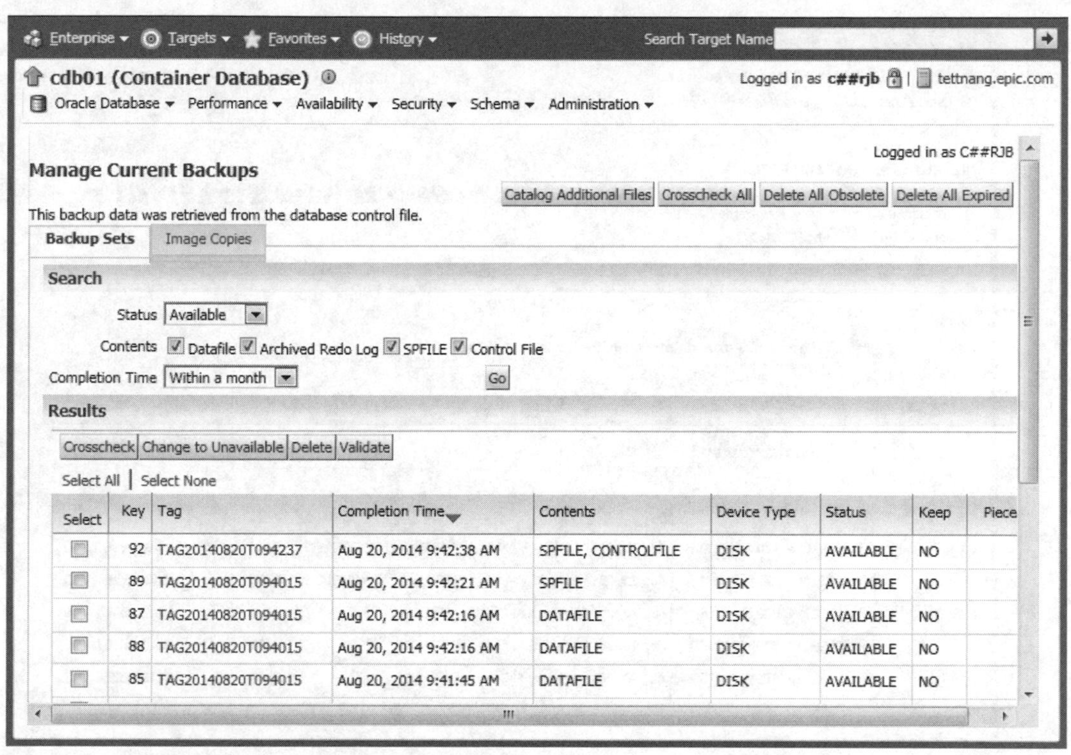

FIGURE 14-6. *Display backupset information with EM Cloud Control*

```
channel ORA_DISK_1: finished piece 1 at 20-AUG-14
piece handle=+RECOV/CDB01/00FF6323468C3972E053E3A0080AAFD5/
BACKUPSET/2014_08_20/nnndf0_tag20140820t100445_0.751.856087487
tag=TAG20140820T100445 comment=NONE
channel ORA_DISK_1: backup set complete, elapsed time: 00:00:01
Finished backup at 20-AUG-14

Starting Control File and SPFILE Autobackup at 20-AUG-14
piece handle=+RECOV/CDB01/AUTOBACKUP/2014_08_20/s_856087488.750.856087489
comment=NONE
Finished Control File and SPFILE Autobackup at 20-AUG-14

RMAN>
```

Since the **dw** database is a PDB within the CDB01 container (a feature new to Oracle Database 12*c*; see Chapter 11), you must qualify the tablespace name with the PDB name, even if there is only one PDB with a tablespace with that name.

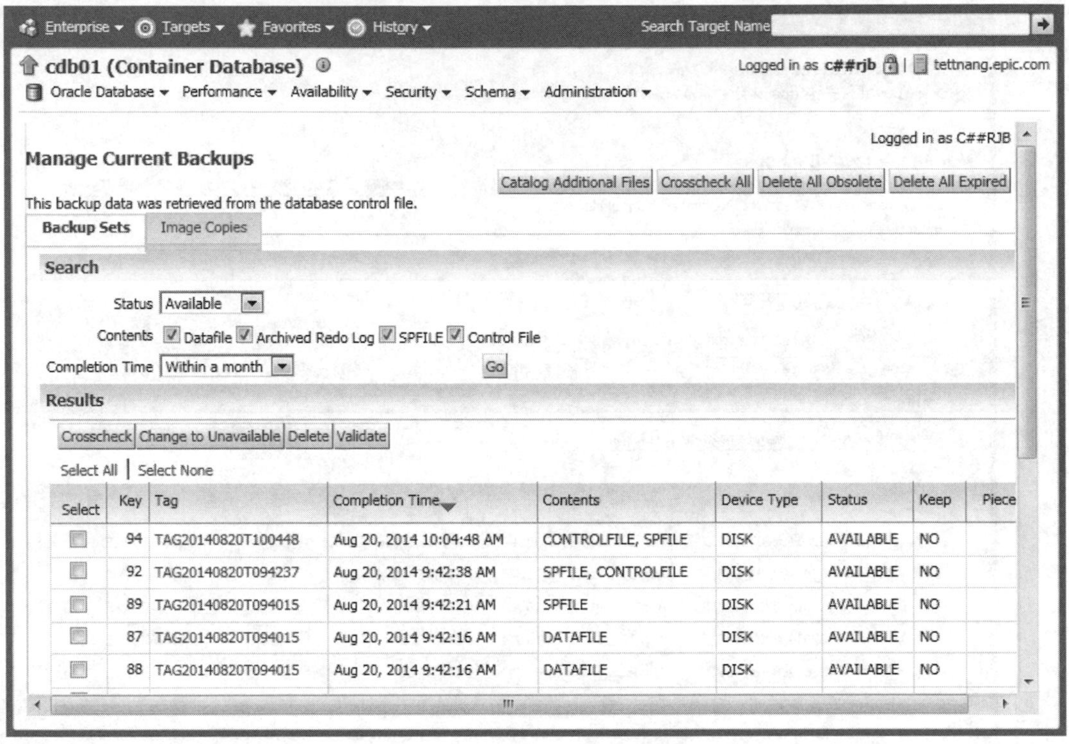

FIGURE 14-7. *Tablespace backup files in EM Cloud Control*

In Figure 14-7, you can see the new RMAN backup record in the repository (TAG20140820T100448)—a combined backupset for the tablespace and the control file/SPFILE autobackup.

Datafile Backups

Backing up individual datafiles is as easy as backing up a tablespace. If it's impractical to back up an entire tablespace within an RMAN session, you can back up individual datafiles within a tablespace over a period of days, and the archived redo log files will take care of the rest during a recovery operation. Here is an example of a datafile backup of a single datafile within a non-ASM tablespace:

```
RMAN> backup as backupset datafile
2>        '/u04/oradata/ord/oe_trans_06.dbf';
```

Image Copy Backups

Up until this point, we have been using backupset backups; in contrast, image copies make bit-for-bit copies of the specified tablespace or entire database. There are a couple of distinct advantages for using RMAN to perform image copy backups: First, the backup is automatically recorded in the RMAN repository. Second, all blocks are checked for corruption as they are read and copied to the backup destination. Another side benefit to making image copies is that the copies can be used "as is" outside of RMAN if, for some reason, a recovery operation must occur outside of RMAN.

In the example that follows, we make another backup of the INET_STAR tablespace, this time as an image copy:

```
RMAN> backup as copy tablespace dw:inet_star;
Starting backup at 20-AUG-14
using channel ORA_DISK_1
using channel ORA_DISK_2
using channel ORA_DISK_3
using channel ORA_DISK_4
channel ORA_DISK_1: starting datafile copy
input datafile file number=00218 name=+DATA/CDB01/00FF6323468C3972E053E3A0080A
AFD5/DATAFILE/inet_star.493.856087357
output file name=+RECOV/CDB01/00FF6323468C3972E053E3A0080AAFD5/DATAFILE/inet_
star.749.856087951 tag=TAG20140820T101231 RECID=3 STAMP=856087951
channel ORA_DISK_1: datafile copy complete, elapsed time: 00:00:01
Finished backup at 20-AUG-14

Starting Control File and SPFILE Autobackup at 20-AUG-14
piece handle=+RECOV/CDB01/AUTOBACKUP/2014_08_20/s_856087953.748.856087953
comment=NONE
Finished Control File and SPFILE Autobackup at 20-AUG-14
RMAN>
```

Image copies can only be created on DISK device types. In Figure 14-8, we perform an image copy of the root container's USERS tablespace with EM Cloud Control.

Because we had earlier configured the default backup type to COMPRESSED BACKUPSET, we overrode the default value in an earlier setup screen for this backup.

Control File, SPFILE Backup

To back up the control file and SPFILE manually, use the following RMAN command:

```
RMAN> backup current controlfile spfile;
Starting backup at 20-AUG-14
allocated channel: ORA_DISK_1
channel ORA_DISK_1: SID=10 device type=DISK
allocated channel: ORA_DISK_2
channel ORA_DISK_2: SID=268 device type=DISK
allocated channel: ORA_DISK_3
channel ORA_DISK_3: SID=522 device type=DISK
allocated channel: ORA_DISK_4
channel ORA_DISK_4: SID=776 device type=DISK
channel ORA_DISK_1: starting datafile copy
copying current control file
channel ORA_DISK_2: starting full datafile backup set
channel ORA_DISK_2: specifying datafile(s) in backup set
including current SPFILE in backup set
```

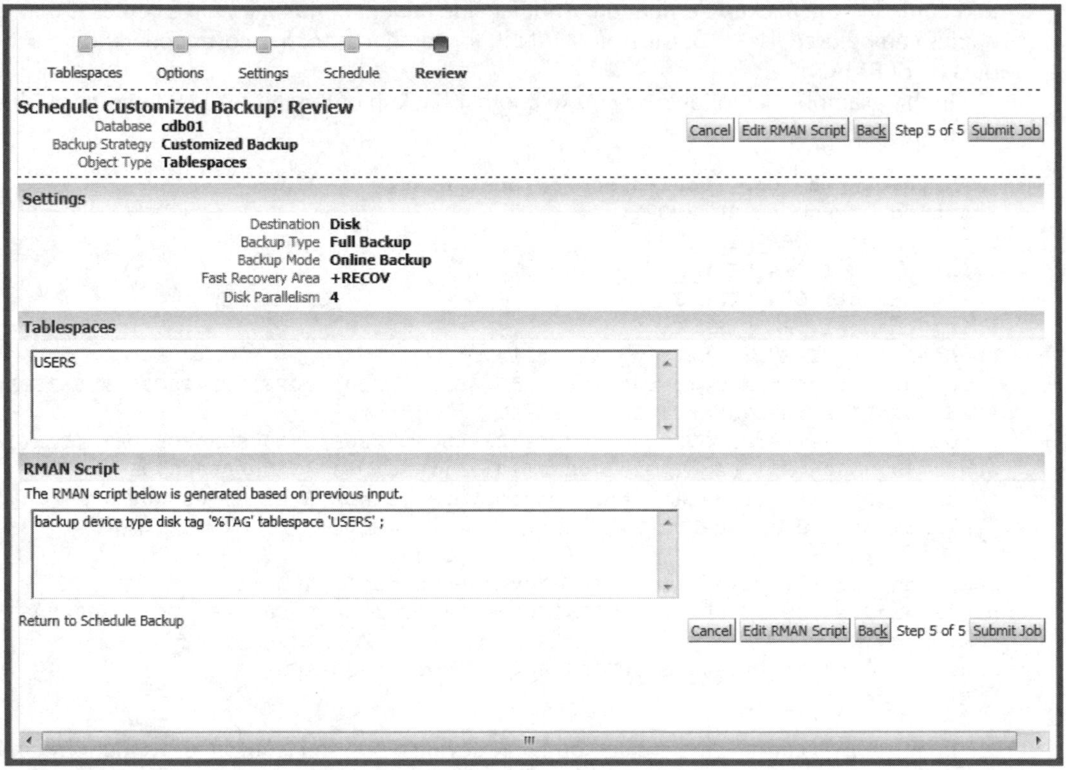

FIGURE 14-8. *Image copy backup of a tablespace using EM Cloud Control*

```
channel ORA_DISK_2: starting piece 1 at 20-AUG-14
output file name=+RECOV/CDB01/CONTROLFILE/backup.747.856089293
tag=TAG20140820T103452 RECID=4 STAMP=856089292
channel ORA_DISK_1: datafile copy complete, elapsed time: 00:00:01
channel ORA_DISK_2: finished piece 1 at 20-AUG-14
piece handle=+RECOV/CDB01/BACKUPSET/2014_08_20/nnsnf0_tag2014082
0t103452_0.746.856089293 tag=TAG20140820T103452 comment=NONE
channel ORA_DISK_2: backup set complete, elapsed time: 00:00:01
Finished backup at 20-AUG-14

Starting Control File and SPFILE Autobackup at 20-AUG-14
piece handle=+RECOV/CDB01/AUTOBACKUP/2014_08_20/s_856089294.745.856089295
comment=NONE
Finished Control File and SPFILE Autobackup at 20-AUG-14

RMAN>
```

Note that because we already had AUTOBACKUP set to ON, we actually performed two backups of the control file and the SPFILE. The second backup of the control file, however, has a record of the first control file and SPFILE backup.

Archived Redo Log Backup

Even when archived redo logs are sent to multiple destinations, including the fast recovery area, due to the critical nature of the archived redo logs, we want to back up copies of the logs to tape or another disk destination. Once the backup is completed, we have the option to leave the logs in place, to delete only the logs that RMAN used for the backup, or to delete all copies of the archived logs that were backed up to tape.

In the following example, we back up all the archived log files in the fast recovery area and then remove them from disk:

```
RMAN> backup device type sbt archivelog all delete input;
```

If archived log files are being sent to multiple locations, then only one set of the archived redo log files is deleted. If we want all copies to be deleted, we use DELETE ALL INPUT instead of DELETE INPUT. As of Oracle Database 11*g*, corrupt or missing archived log files do not prevent a successful RMAN backup of the archived logs as in previous releases; as long as one of the archive log file destinations has a valid log file for a given log sequence number, the backup is successful.

Backing up and deleting only older archived redo log files can be accomplished by specifying a date range in the BACKUP ARCHIVELOG command:

```
RMAN> backup device type sbt
2>       archivelog from time 'sysdate-30' until time 'sysdate-7'
3>       delete all input;
```

In the preceding example, all archived redo logs older than one week, going back for three weeks, are copied to tape and deleted from disk. In addition, you can specify a range using SCNs or log sequence numbers.

Incremental Backups

An alternative strategy to relying on full backups with archived redo logs is to use *incremental backups* along with archived redo logs for recovery. The initial incremental backup is known as a *level 0* incremental backup. Each incremental backup after the initial incremental backup (also known as a *level 1* incremental backup) contains only changed blocks and as a result takes less time and space. Incremental level 1 backups can either be *cumulative* or *differential*. A cumulative backup records all changed blocks since the initial incremental backup; a differential backup records all changed blocks since the last incremental backup, whether it was a level 0 or a level 1 incremental backup.

When a number of different types of backups exist in the catalog, such as image copies, tablespace backupsets, and incremental backups, RMAN will choose the best combination of backups to most efficiently recover and restore the database. The DBA still has the option to prevent RMAN from using a particular backup (for example, if the DBA thinks that a particular backup is corrupt and will be rejected by RMAN during the recovery operation).

The decision whether to use cumulative or differential backups is based partly on where you want to spend the CPU cycles, and how much disk space you have available. Using cumulative backups means that each incremental backup will become progressively larger and take longer until another level 0 incremental backup is performed, but during a restore and recovery operation, only two backupsets will be required. On the other hand, differential backups only record the changes since the last backup, so each backupset might be smaller or larger than the previous one, with no overlap in data blocks backed up. However, a restore and recovery operation may take longer if you have to restore from several backupsets instead of just two.

Following our example with the **dw** database, we have changed the retention policy to a window of eight days. Therefore, we will likely need to perform a backup to satisfy that policy:

```
RMAN> report need backup;

RMAN retention policy will be applied to the command
RMAN retention policy is set to recovery window of 8 days
Report of files whose recovery needs more than 8 days of archived logs

File #bkps Name
---- ----- -----------------------------------------------------
5    1     +DATA/CDB01/DD7C48AA5A4404A2E04325AAE80A403C/DATAFILE/
system.277.845194085
7    1     +DATA/CDB01/DD7C48AA5A4404A2E04325AAE80A403C/DATAFILE/
sysaux.276.845194085
34   1
. . .
216  1     +DATA/CDB01/00FF6323468C3972E053E3A0080AAFD5/DATAFILE/
system.490.856007869
217  1     +DATA/CDB01/00FF6323468C3972E053E3A0080AAFD5/DATAFILE/
sysaux.491.856007871

RMAN>
```

To remedy this situation, we can do another full backup, or we can pursue an incremental backup policy, which might be easier to implement and maintain. To set up our incremental policy, we need to perform a level 0 incremental backup first:

```
RMAN> backup incremental level 0
2>       as compressed backupset database;

Starting backup at 20-AUG-14
allocated channel: ORA_DISK_1
channel ORA_DISK_1: SID=10 device type=DISK
allocated channel: ORA_DISK_2
channel ORA_DISK_2: SID=268 device type=DISK
allocated channel: ORA_DISK_3
channel ORA_DISK_3: SID=522 device type=DISK
allocated channel: ORA_DISK_4
channel ORA_DISK_4: SID=776 device type=DISK
. . .
Finished backup at 20-AUG-14

Starting Control File and SPFILE Autobackup at 20-AUG-14
```

```
piece handle=+RECOV/CDB01/AUTOBACKUP/2014_08_20/s_856090305.314.856090305
comment=NONE
Finished Control File and SPFILE Autobackup at 20-AUG-14

RMAN>
```

At any point in the future after this level 0 backup, we can perform an incremental level 1 differential backup:

```
RMAN> backup as compressed backupset
2>     incremental level 1 database;
```

The default incremental backup type is differential; the keyword DIFFERENTIAL is neither needed nor allowed. However, to perform a cumulative backup, we add the CUMULATIVE keyword:

```
RMAN> backup as compressed backupset
2>      incremental level 1 cumulative database;
```

How much database activity is performed may also dictate whether you use cumulative or differential backups. In an OLTP environment with heavy insert and update activity, incremental backups may be more manageable in terms of disk space usage. For a data warehouse environment with infrequent changes, a differential backup policy may be more suitable. Compared to using redo log files, both types of incremental backups are far superior in terms of the time to recover a database. In any case, we have addressed RMAN's retention policy:

```
RMAN> report need backup;
RMAN retention policy will be applied to the command
RMAN retention policy is set to recovery window of 8 days
Report of files that must be backed up to satisfy 8 days recovery window
File Days  Name
---- ----- -----------------------------------------------------

RMAN>
```

Incrementally Updated Backups

An *incrementally updated* backup can potentially make a restore and recovery operation even more efficient by rolling the changes from a level 1 incremental backup to a level 0 incremental image backup. If the incrementally updated backup is run on a daily basis, then any recovery operation would require at most the updated image copy, one incremental level 1 backup, and the most recent archived and online redo logs. The following example uses an RMAN script that can be scheduled to run at the same time every day to support an incrementally updated backup strategy:

```
run
{
    recover copy of database with tag 'incr_upd_img';
    backup incremental level 1
          for recover of copy with tag 'incr_upd_img' database;
}
```

The key part of both commands within the RUN script is the RECOVER COPY clause. Rather than doing a recovery of the actual database datafiles, we are recovering a *copy* of a database datafile by applying incremental backups. Using a *tag* with an RMAN backup allows us to apply the incremental backup to the correct image copy. Tags allow DBAs to easily refer to a specific backup for recovery or catalog cleanup operations; if the BACKUP command does not provide a tag, one is automatically generated for the backupset and is unique within the backupsets for the target database.

The basics of standard recovery operations and RMAN scripting capabilities are covered later in this chapter.

The EM Cloud Control backup wizards make it easy to automate an incrementally updated backup strategy. In the figures that follow, we'll cover the steps needed to configure this strategy within EM Cloud Control.

In Figure 14-9, we're specifying the strategy for backing up our database.

The database is open, ARCHIVELOG mode is enabled, and backups will follow the Oracle-suggested guidelines for a backup strategy. Figure 14-10 shows the next step in the backup configuration process: a summary of the database name, the selected strategy, where the backups will be sent, the recovery catalog in use, and a brief explanation as to how the backup will be performed.

In Figure 14-11, we specify when the backups will start, and what time of day they will run. Although the backup job can run any time during the day, because we are performing a hot backup (the database is open and users can process transactions), we want to minimize the

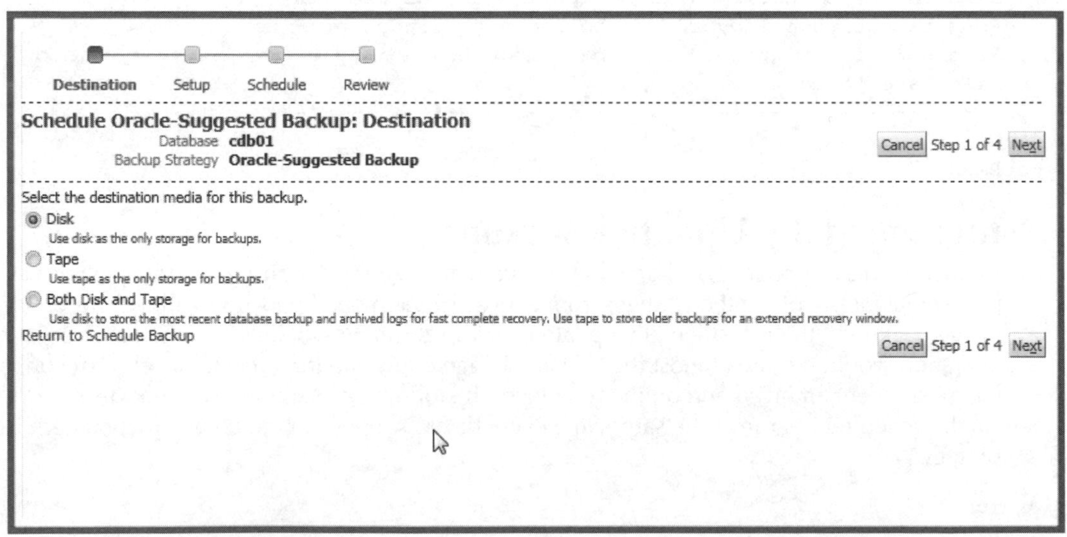

FIGURE 14-9. *EM Cloud Control backup strategy selection*

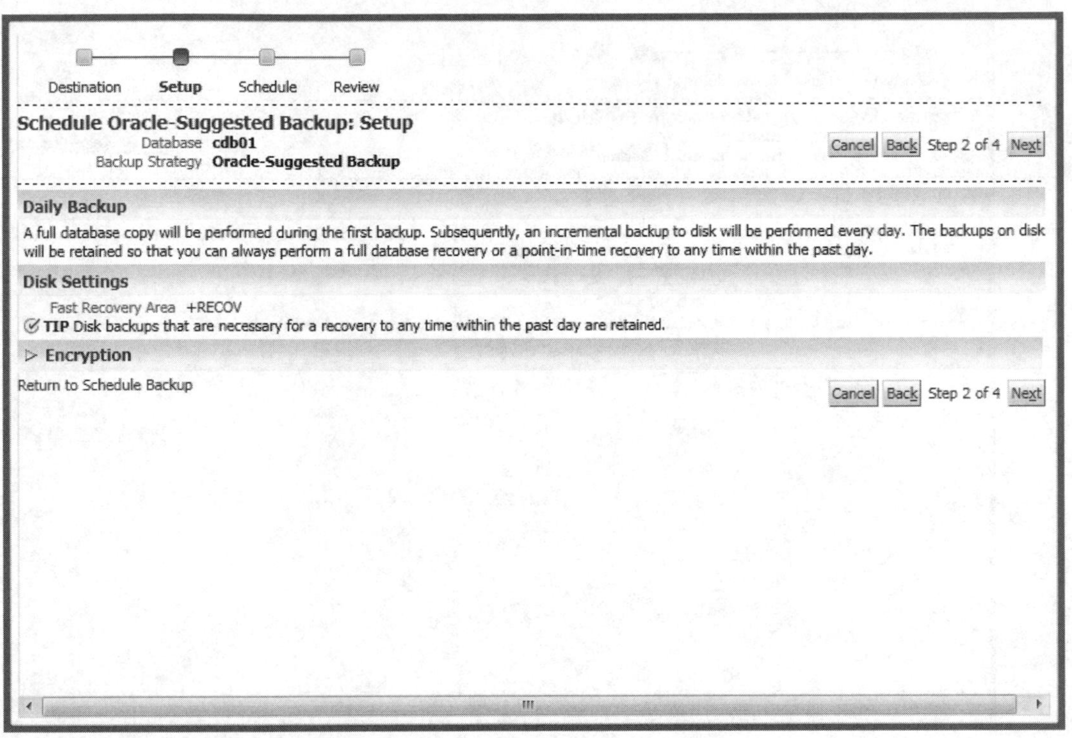

FIGURE 14-10. *EM Cloud Control backup setup summary*

possible impact on query and DML response time by scheduling the job during a time period with low activity.

Figure 14-12 gives us one more chance to review how the backup will be performed and where it will reside.

At the bottom of the browser window is the actual RMAN script that will be scheduled to run on a daily basis (see Figure 14-12). Coincidentally, it strongly resembles the RMAN script we presented earlier in this section.

Incremental Backup Block Change Tracking

Another way to improve the performance of incremental backups is to enable *block change tracking*. For a traditional incremental backup, RMAN must inspect every block of the tablespace or datafile to be backed up to see if the block has changed since the last backup. For a very large database, the time it takes to scan the blocks in the database can easily exceed the time it takes to perform the actual backup.

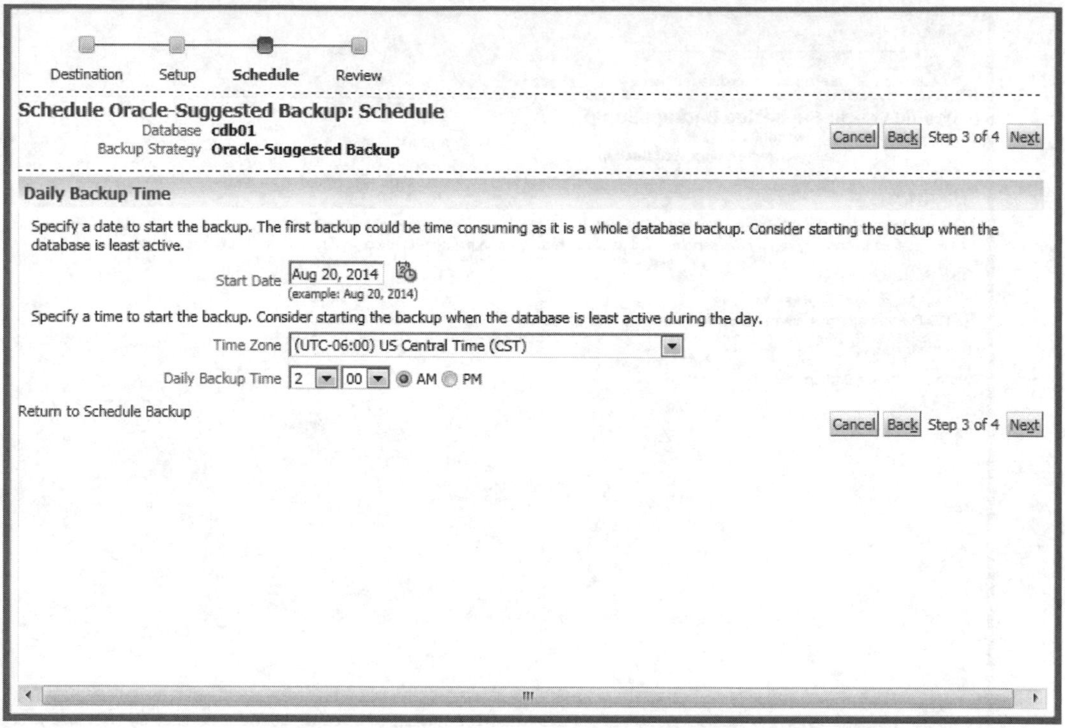

FIGURE 14-11. *EM Cloud Control backup schedule*

By enabling block change tracking, RMAN knows which blocks have changed by using a *change tracking file*. Although there is some slight overhead in space usage and maintenance of the tracking file every time a block is changed, the tradeoff is well worth it if frequent incremental backups are performed on the database. In the following example, we create a block change tracking file in the DATA disk group and enable block change tracking:

```
RMAN> alter database enable block change tracking using file '+data';
Statement processed
RMAN>
```

The next time a backup is performed, RMAN will only have to use the contents of an OMF-named file in the DW/CHANGETRACKING directory of the DATA disk group to determine which blocks need to be backed up. The space needed for the block change tracking file is approximately 1/250,000 the size of the database.

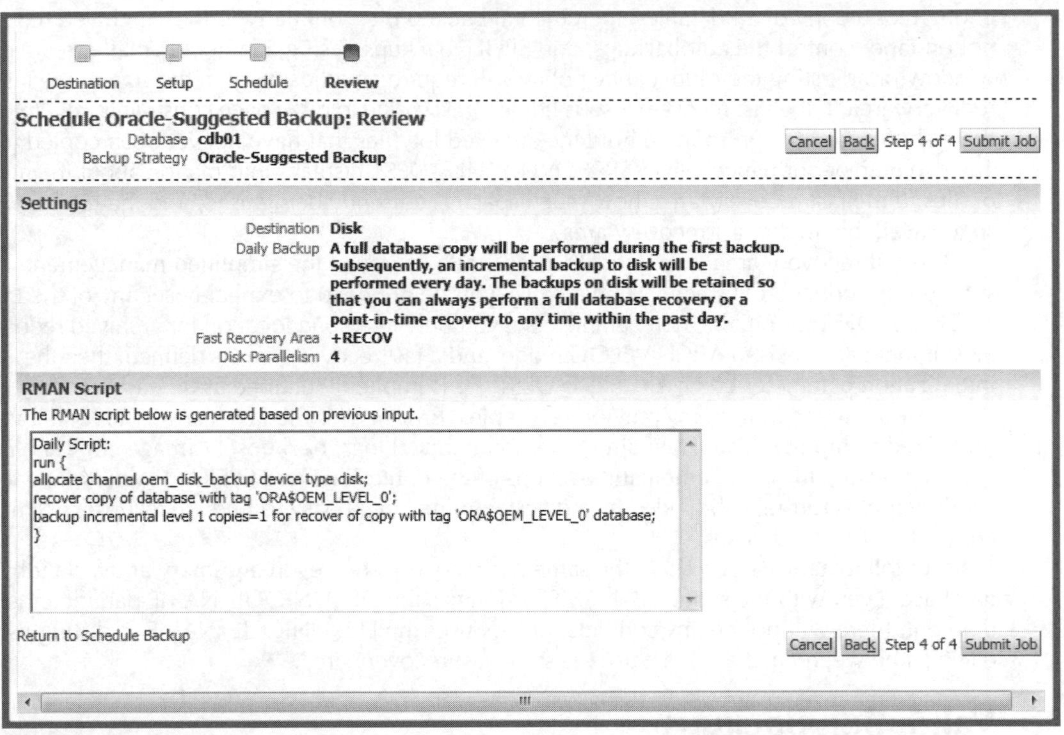

FIGURE 14-12. *EM Cloud Control backup summary*

The dynamic performance view V$BLOCK_CHANGE_TRACKING contains the name and size of the block change tracking file as well as whether change tracking is enabled:

```
SQL> select filename, status, bytes from v$block_change_tracking;

FILENAME                                        STATUS          BYTES
----------------------------------------------- --------- ----------
+DATA/ CDB01/CHANGETRACKING/ctf.494.856091195   ENABLED     11599872
SQL>
```

Using a Fast Recovery Area

Earlier in this chapter, we covered the initialization parameters required to set up the fast recovery area: DB_RECOVERY_FILE_DEST and DB_RECOVERY_FILE_DEST_SIZE. Both of these parameters are dynamic, allowing the DBA to change either the RMAN destination for backups or the amount of space allowed for backups in the fast recovery area without restarting the instance.

To facilitate a completely disk-based recovery scenario, the fast recovery area should be big enough for a copy of all datafiles, incremental backup files, online redo logs, archived redo logs not on tape, control file autobackups, and SPFILE backups. Using a larger or smaller recovery window or adjusting the redundancy policy will require an adjustment in the size of the fast recovery area. If the fast recovery area is limited in size due to disk space constraints, at a minimum there should be enough room to hold the archived log files that have not yet been copied to tape. The dynamic performance view V$RECOVERY_FILE_DEST displays information about the number of files in the fast recovery area, how much space is currently being used, and the total amount of space available in the fast recovery area.

The fast recovery area automatically uses OMF. As part of the simplified management structure introduced in Oracle Database 11*g*, you do not need to explicitly set any of the LOG_ARCHIVE_DEST_*n* initialization parameters if you only need one location for archived redo log files; if the database is in ARCHIVELOG mode, and a fast recovery area is defined, then the initialization parameter LOG_ARCHIVE_DEST_10 is implicitly defined as the fast recovery area.

As you have seen in many previous examples, RMAN uses the fast recovery area in a very organized fashion with separate directories for archived logs, backupsets, image copies, block change tracking files, and automatic backups of the control file and SPFILE. In addition, each subdirectory is further subdivided by a datestamp, making it easy to find a backupset or image copy when the need arises.

Multiple databases can share the same fast recovery area, even a primary and a standby database. Even with the same DB_NAME, as long as the DB_UNIQUE_NAME parameter is different, there will not be any conflicts. RMAN uses the DB_UNIQUE_NAME to distinguish backups between databases that use the same fast recovery area.

Validating Backups

Having multiple image backups or enough archived redo log files to support a recovery window is of less value if there are problems with the live database files or control files. The RMAN command BACKUP VALIDATE DATABASE will simulate a backup, checking for the existence of the specified files, ensuring that they are not corrupted. No backup files are created. This command would be useful in a scenario where you can check for problems with the database or archived redo logs proactively, giving you an opportunity to fix problems before the actual backup operation or for scheduling additional time overnight to repair problems found during the day.

In the following example, we will validate the entire database along with the archived redo logs after some logs are accidentally deleted:

```
[oracle@tettnang ~]$ asmcmd
ASMCMD> ls
DATA/
RECOV/
ASMCMD> cd recov
ASMCMD> ls
CDB01/
HR/
ASMCMD> cd cdb01
ASMCMD> ls
00FF6323468C3972E053E3A0080AAFD5/
ARCHIVELOG/
```

```
AUTOBACKUP/
BACKUPSET/
CONTROLFILE/
F751D8C27D475B57E043E3A0080A2A47/
F754FCD8744A55AAE043E3A0080A3B17/
FA782A61F8447D03E043E3A0080A9E54/
FA787E0038B26FFBE043E3A0080A1A75/
FB03AEEBB6F60995E043E3A0080AEE85/
FBA928F391D2217DE043E3A0080AB287/
FC9588B12BBD413FE043E3A0080A5528/
ONLINELOG/
ASMCMD> cd backupset
ASMCMD> ls
2014_06_04/
2014_08_20/
ASMCMD> cd 2014_06_04
ASMCMD> ls
nnndf0_TAG20140604T073433_0.298.849339275
nnndf0_TAG20140604T073433_0.300.849339275
nnndf0_TAG20140604T073433_0.302.849339275
ASMCMD> rm *275
You may delete multiple files and/or directories.
Are you sure? (y/n) y
ASMCMD>
. . .
RMAN> backup validate database archivelog all;

Starting backup at 20-AUG-14
allocated channel: ORA_DISK_1
channel ORA_DISK_1: SID=10 device type=DISK
allocated channel: ORA_DISK_2
channel ORA_DISK_2: SID=4 device type=DISK
allocated channel: ORA_DISK_3
channel ORA_DISK_3: SID=268 device type=DISK
allocated channel: ORA_DISK_4
channel ORA_DISK_4: SID=522 device type=DISK
. . .
RMAN-00571: ===========================================================
RMAN-00569: =============== ERROR MESSAGE STACK FOLLOWS ===============
RMAN-00571: ===========================================================
RMAN-03002: failure of backup command at 08/20/2014 11:14:30
RMAN-06059: expected archived log not found, loss of archived log compromises
recoverability
ORA-19625: error identifying file +RECOV/CDB01/ARCHIVELOG/2014_06_28/thread_1_
seq_494.780.851385617
ORA-17503: ksfdopn:2 Failed to open file +RECOV/CDB01/ARCHIVELOG/2014_06_28/
thread_1_seq_494.780.851385617
ORA-15012: ASM file '+RECOV/CDB01/ARCHIVELOG/2014_06_28/thread_1_
seq_494.780.851385617' does not exist
RMAN>
```

The BACKUP VALIDATE command has identified an archived redo log file that is no longer in the fast recovery area. It may have been archived to tape outside of RMAN, or it may have been inadvertently deleted (in this case, it appears that the log file was intentionally deleted). Looking at the datestamp of the log file, we see that it is outside of our recovery window of four days, so it is not a critical file in terms of recoverability.

Synchronizing the fast recovery area and the catalog with the CROSSCHECK command is covered later in this chapter; once we have fixed the cross-reference problem we have just discovered, we can perform the rest of the validation:

```
RMAN> backup validate database archivelog all;

Starting backup at 20-AUG-14
using channel ORA_DISK_1
using channel ORA_DISK_2
using channel ORA_DISK_3
using channel ORA_DISK_4
channel ORA_DISK_1: starting compressed full datafile backup set
channel ORA_DISK_1: specifying datafile(s) in backup set
input datafile file number=00003 name=+DATA/CDB01/DATAFILE/
sysaux.267.845193957
channel ORA_DISK_2: starting compressed full datafile backup set
channel ORA_DISK_2: specifying datafile(s) in backup set
input datafile file number=00042 name=+DATA/CDB01/
F754FCD8744A55AAE043E3A0080A3B17/DATAFILE/epicstagelarge.296.849782391
input datafile file number=00036 name=+DATA/CDB01/
F754FCD8744A55AAE043E3A0080A3B17/DATAFILE/epicstagemedium.266.849459763
input datafile file number=00057 name=+DATA/CDB01/
F754FCD8744A55AAE043E3A0080A3B17/DATAFILE/epicsmall.318.850144911. . .
List of Datafiles
=================
File Status Marked Corrupt Empty Blocks Blocks Examined High SCN
---- ------ -------------- ------------ --------------- ----------
218  OK     0              12673        12800           13871102
  File Name: +DATA/CDB01/00FF6323468C3972E053E3A0080AAFD5/DATAFILE/inet_
star.493.856087357
  Block Type Blocks Failing Blocks Processed
  ---------- -------------- ----------------
  Data       0              0
  Index      0              0
  Other      0              127

Finished backup at 20-AUG-14

RMAN>
```

No errors were found during the validation; RMAN read every block of every archived redo log file and datafile to ensure that they were readable and had no corrupted blocks. However, no backups were actually written to a disk or tape channel.

Recovery Operations

Every good backup plan includes a disaster recovery plan so that we can retrieve the datafiles and logs from the backups and recover the database files. In this section, we'll review several different aspects of RMAN recovery operations.

RMAN can perform restore and recovery operations at various levels of granularity, and most of these operations can be performed while the database is open and available to users. We can recover individual blocks, tablespaces, datafiles, or even an entire database. In addition, RMAN has various methods of validating a restore operation without performing an actual recovery on the database datafiles.

Block Media Recovery

When there are only a small handful of blocks to recover in a database, RMAN can perform *block media recovery* rather than a full datafile recovery. Block media recovery minimizes redo log application time, and it drastically reduces the amount of I/O required to recover only the block or blocks in question. While block media recovery is in progress, the affected datafiles can remain online and available to users.

NOTE
Block media recovery is only available from within the RMAN application.

There are a number of ways in which block corruption is detected. During a read or write operation from an INSERT or SELECT statement, Oracle may detect a block is corrupt, write an error in a user trace file, and abort the transaction. An RMAN BACKUP or BACKUP VALIDATE command can record corrupted blocks in the dynamic performance view V$DATABASE_BLOCK_CORRUPTION. In addition, the SQL commands ANALYZE TABLE and ANALYZE INDEX could uncover corrupted blocks.

To recover one or more data blocks, RMAN must know the datafile number and block number within the datafile. This information is available in a user trace file, as in the following example:

```
ORA-01578: ORACLE data block corrupted (file # 6, block # 403)
ORA-01110: data file 6: '/u09/oradata/ord/oe_trans01.dbf'
```

Alternatively, the block may appear in the view V$DATABASE_BLOCK_CORRUPTION after an RMAN BACKUP command; the columns FILE# and BLOCK# provide the information needed to execute the RECOVER command. The column CORRUPTION_TYPE identifies the type of corruption in the block, such as FRACTURED, CHECKSUM, or CORRUPT. Fixing the block is easily accomplished in RMAN:

```
RMAN> recover datafile 6 block 403;

Starting recover at 04-SEP-14
using channel ORA_DISK_1

starting media recovery
media recovery complete, elapsed time: 00:00:01
```

```
Finished recover at 04-SEP-14

RMAN>
```

A corrupted block must be restored completely; in other words, all redo operations up to the latest SCN against the data block must be applied before the block can be considered usable again.

NOTE
The BLOCKRECOVER command, available in previous releases of RMAN, has been deprecated as of Oracle Database 11g in favor of the RECOVER command; the syntax of the command is otherwise the same.

Restoring a Control File

In the rare event that you lose all copies of your control file, it is easy to restore the control file when a recovery catalog is used; start the instance with NOMOUNT (since we don't have a control file to read with MOUNT) and issue the following RMAN command:

```
RMAN> restore controlfile;
```

If you are not using a recovery catalog, you can add the FROM '<*FILENAME*>' clause to the command to specify where the latest control file exists:

```
RMAN> restore controlfile from '/u11/oradata/ord/bkup.ctl';
```

After restoring the control files, you must perform complete media recovery of your database and open the database with the RESETLOGS option. Complete media recovery can be performed using RMAN or the methods described in Chapter 13.

Restoring a Tablespace

If the disk containing the datafiles for a tablespace fails or becomes corrupted, recovery of the tablespace is possible while the database remains open and available. The exception to this is the SYSTEM tablespace. In our **dw** database, suppose the disk containing the datafiles for the root container's USERS2 tablespace has crashed. After the first phone call from the users (which happened even before EM Cloud Control notified us of the error), we can check the dynamic performance view V$DATAFILE_HEADER to see which datafiles need recovery:

```
SQL> select file#, status, error, tablespace_name, name
  2  from v$datafile_header
  3  where error is not null;

     FILE# STATUS  ERROR                TABLESPACE_NAME              NAME
---------- ------- ---------------- ------------------------- ---------------
       219 OFFLINE OFFLINE NORMAL

SQL>
```

Incidentally, you would have also seen this error when trying to bring the USERS2 tablespace back online:

```
SQL> alter tablespace users2 online;
alter tablespace users2 online
*
ERROR at line 1:
ORA-01157: cannot identify/lock data file 219 - see DBWR trace file
ORA-01110: data file 219: '+DATA/CDB01/DATAFILE/users2.495.856093073'
```

After replacing the disk drive, you can use also the REPORT SCHEMA command to find the tablespace associated with file number 219. To restore and recover the tablespace, we force the tablespace offline, restore and recover the tablespace, and bring it back online. If the USERS2 tablespace was not already offline, you can do that within RMAN before recovering it:

```
RMAN> alter tablespace users2 offline immediate;

Statement processed
RMAN> restore tablespace users2;

Starting restore at 20-AUG-14
allocated channel: ORA_DISK_1
channel ORA_DISK_1: SID=10 device type=DISK
allocated channel: ORA_DISK_2
channel ORA_DISK_2: SID=1280 device type=DISK
allocated channel: ORA_DISK_3
channel ORA_DISK_3: SID=14 device type=DISK
allocated channel: ORA_DISK_4
channel ORA_DISK_4: SID=522 device type=DISK
. . .
channel ORA_DISK_1: starting datafile backup set restore
channel ORA_DISK_1: specifying datafile(s) to restore from backup set
channel ORA_DISK_1: restoring datafile 00219 to +DATA/CDB01/DATAFILE/
users2.495.856093073
channel ORA_DISK_1: reading from backup piece +RECOV/CDB01/
BACKUPSET/2014_08_20/nnndf0_tag20140820t113833_0.302.856093115
channel ORA_DISK_1: piece handle=+RECOV/CDB01/BACKUPSET/2014_08_20/nnndf0_tag2
0140820t113833_0.302.856093115 tag=TAG20140820T113833
channel ORA_DISK_1: restored backup piece 1
channel ORA_DISK_1: restore complete, elapsed time: 00:00:24
Finished restore at 20-AUG-14
starting full resync of recovery catalog
full resync complete
RMAN> recover tablespace users2;

Starting recover at 20-AUG-14
using channel ORA_DISK_1
using channel ORA_DISK_2
using channel ORA_DISK_3
using channel ORA_DISK_4
```

```
starting media recovery
media recovery complete, elapsed time: 00:00:00

Finished recover at 20-AUG-14

RMAN> alter tablespace users2 online;
Statement processed
starting full resync of recovery catalog
full resync complete

RMAN>
```

The RESTORE command copied the latest image or backupset copy of the datafiles in the USERS tablespace to their original locations; the RECOVER command applied redo from either redo log files or incremental backups to bring the objects in the tablespace back up to the latest SCN. Once the tablespace is back online, it is available for use again, without the loss of any committed transactions to tables in the tablespace.

Restoring a Table

As of Oracle Database 12*c*, you can use an RMAN backup to recover a single table. This method fills the gap between the tablespace point in time recovery (TSPITR) method (which is time consuming and must involve the DBA) and methods that are available to a database user such as Flashback Table using the UNDO tablespace and possibly a Flashback Data Archive. Because the logical corruption of a table may have been discovered long after the UNDO data has expired and been purged from the UNDO tablespace, recovering a single table from an RMAN backup fills the gap between a full TSPITR and a Flashback Table or Flashback Drop operation.

Scenarios for Table Recovery from Backups

In addition to the time it takes to recover an entire tablespace versus a single table from a tablespace backup, there are several other reasons why you would use table recovery from backups (TRFB) instead of other Flashback methods.

Using TSPITR may be a reasonable option if you have many tables in a tablespace that you need to recover, but what if the tablespace is not self-contained? In that scenario, you will have to recover more than one tablespace, which makes TSPITR less attractive.

You may often rely on Flashback Drop to get back a table that might have been dropped even weeks ago, but space pressure may have already purged it or the table may have been dropped while the recycle bin was turned off.

Finally, even if your UNDO tablespace and retention period is long, there may have been a recent structural change to the table, which will prevent any Flashback operation using the UNDO tablespace.

Prerequisites and Limitations for Table Recovery from Backups

In addition to the limitations mentioned in the previous section, there are several other conditions that must be met to perform TRFB:

- The database must be in read-write mode.
- The database must be in ARCHIVELOG mode.
- COMPATIBLE must be set to 12.0 or higher.

- You cannot recover tables or table partitions from the SYS schema.
- You cannot recover objects from the SYSTEM or SYSAUX tablespace.
- Objects cannot be recovered to standby databases.

Using Table Recovery from Backups

Using TRFB is quite similar to TSPITR in many ways. In fact, you could argue that TRFB is more of an RMAN recovery method than a tool in your Flashback toolkit. The key is the scope of the objects that you are recovering or rewinding to a previous point in time or SCN.

Figure 14-13 shows the general steps and flow of the recovery operation.

Here are the steps you use in RMAN to recover a single table using TRFB:

1. Specify the RMAN parameters for the TRFB operation:
   a. Names of tables or table partitions to recover
   b. Point in time at which the objects need to be recovered to (timestamp or SCN)
   c. Whether the recovered objects must be imported into the target database
2. RMAN determines which backups will be used for the operation.
3. RMAN creates a temporary auxiliary instance.
4. RMAN recovers the table or tables into a tablespace available to this auxiliary instance.
5. RMAN creates a Data Pump Export dump file with the recovered objects.
6. If specified, RMAN will use Data Pump Import to copy the objects into the target database.

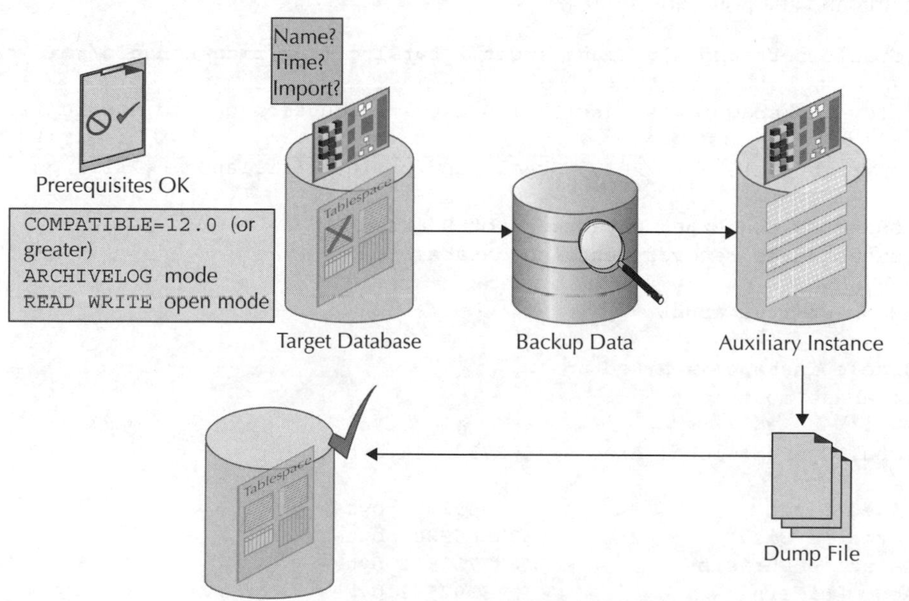

FIGURE 14-13. *Process flow for table recovery from backups*

As you may have noticed, this operation is somewhat automated compared to TSPITR, especially in versions of Oracle Database before 12c. This operation still must be performed by a DBA, however.

Restoring a Datafile

Restoring a datafile is a very similar operation to restoring a tablespace. Once the missing or corrupted datafile is identified using the V$DATAFILE_HEADER view, the RMAN commands are very similar to the previous example in the "Restoring a Tablespace" section; the tablespace is taken offline, the datafile(s) are restored and recovered, and the tablespace is brought back online. If only file number 7 was lost, the RECOVER and RESTORE commands are as simple as this:

```
RMAN> restore datafile 7;
RMAN> recover datafile 7;
```

Restoring an Entire Database

Although the loss of an entire database is a serious and disastrous event, having a solid backup and recovery policy, as described previously in this chapter, can bring the database back up to the most recent committed transaction with a minimum of effort. In the following scenario, we have lost all datafiles. However, because we have multiplexed the control file and online redo log files on many different disks, we will have them available during the RMAN restore and recovery operation. Alternatively, you can restore the control files or copy the online redo log files to the other destinations before mounting the database. If this is not feasible because the alternate disk locations are not available, you can alter your parameter file or SPFILE to indicate which files are still available.

The entire restore and recovery operation can be performed within RMAN; first, we start up RMAN and open the database in MOUNT mode, just as if we used the STARTUP MOUNT command at a SQL*Plus prompt:

```
[oracle@tettnang ~]$ rman target / catalog rman/rman@kthanid/rman_rep

Recovery Manager: Release 12.1.0.1.0 - Production on Wed Aug 20 11:58:15 2014

Copyright (c) 1982, 2013, Oracle and/or its affiliates.  All rights reserved.

connected to target database (not started)
connected to recovery catalog database

RMAN> startup mount

Oracle instance started
database mounted

Total System Global Area    5027385344 bytes

Fixed Size                     2691952 bytes
Variable Size               3338669200 bytes
Database Buffers            1677721600 bytes
Redo Buffers                   8302592 bytes
starting full resync of recovery catalog
```

```
full resync complete
RMAN> restore database;
Starting restore at 20-AUG-14
allocated channel: ORA_DISK_1
channel ORA_DISK_1: SID=1022 device type=DISK
allocated channel: ORA_DISK_2
channel ORA_DISK_2: SID=1275 device type=DISK
allocated channel: ORA_DISK_3
. . .
channel ORA_DISK_1: restored backup piece 1
channel ORA_DISK_1: restore complete, elapsed time: 00:01:50
Finished restore at 20-AUG-14
RMAN> recover database;
Starting recover at 20-AUG-14
using channel ORA_DISK_1
using channel ORA_DISK_2
using channel ORA_DISK_3
using channel ORA_DISK_4
. . .
starting media recovery
media recovery complete, elapsed time: 00:00:03

Finished recover at 20-AUG-14
RMAN> alter database open;
database opened
RMAN>
```

The database is now open and available for use. RMAN will pick the most efficient way to perform the requested operation, minimizing the number of files accessed or the number of disk I/Os to bring the database back to a consistent state in as short a time as possible. In the previous example, RMAN used a full database backupset and archived redo log files to recover the database.

During a recovery operation, RMAN may need to restore archived redo logs from tape; to limit the amount of disk space used during a recovery operation, the RECOVER command used in the previous example could use the following options instead:

```
RMAN> recover database delete archivelog maxsize 2gb;
```

The parameter DELETE ARCHIVELOG directs RMAN to remove archived log files from disk that were restored from tape for this recovery option; the MAXSIZE 2GB parameter restricts the amount of space that can be occupied by restored archived log files at any point in time to 2GB. In our **dw** database, these two parameters are not needed; all archived log files needed to recover the database are kept in the fast recovery area on disk to support the defined retention policy.

Validating Restore Operations

Earlier in this chapter, we validated the data blocks in the datafiles that we want to back up. In this section, we'll take the opposite approach and instead validate the backups that we have already made. We'll also find out from RMAN which backupsets, image copies, and archived redo logs would be used in a recovery operation without actually performing the recovery.

RESTORE PREVIEW

The command RESTORE PREVIEW will provide a list of the files that RMAN will use to perform the requested operation; the preview will also indicate if a tape volume will be requested, for example. No files are actually restored; only the recovery catalog is queried to determine which files are needed. In the following example, we want to find out what RMAN will need if we need to recover the USERS tablespace:

```
RMAN> restore tablespace users preview;
Starting restore at 20-AUG-14
using channel ORA_DISK_1
using channel ORA_DISK_2
using channel ORA_DISK_3
using channel ORA_DISK_4


List of Backup Sets
===================

BS Key  Type LV Size       Device Type Elapsed Time Completion Time
------- ---- -- ---------- ----------- ------------ ---------------
2583    Incr 0  1.48M      DISK        00:00:00     20-AUG-14
        BP Key: 2613   Status: AVAILABLE  Compressed: YES  Tag:
TAG20140820T104812
        Piece Name: +RECOV/CDB01/BACKUPSET/2014_08_20/nnndn0_tag2014082
0t104812_0.737.856090217
  List of Datafiles in backup set 2583
  File LV Type Ckp SCN    Ckp Time  Name
  ---- -- ---- ---------- --------- ----
  6    0  Incr 13878805   20-AUG-14 +DATA/CDB01/DATAFILE/users.269.845194049

List of Archived Log Copies for database with db_unique_name CDB01
=====================================================================

Key     Thrd Seq     S Low Time
------- ---- ------- - ---------
2981    1    1484    A 20-AUG-14
        Name: +RECOV/CDB01/ARCHIVELOG/2014_08_20/thread_1_
seq_1484.318.856090843
Media recovery start SCN is 13878805
Recovery must be done beyond SCN 13878805 to clear datafile fuzziness
Finished restore at 20-AUG-14
RMAN>
```

For the restore operation, RMAN will need to use one backupset for the single datafile in the tablespace; archived redo log files will be used to bring the tablespace up to the current SCN.

If a restore operation needs to be performed immediately, and one of the files that RMAN will request to perform the operation is offsite, you can use the CHANGE . . . UNAVAILABLE command to mark a backupset as unavailable and then run the RESTORE TABLESPACE . . . PREVIEW command again to see if RMAN can use disk-based backupsets to fulfill the request.

RESTORE VALIDATE

The RESTORE . . . PREVIEW command does not read the actual backupsets, only the catalog information; if we want to validate whether the backupsets themselves are readable and not corrupted, we use the RESTORE . . . VALIDATE command. As with most other RMAN commands, we can perform the validation for a datafile, a tablespace, or the entire database. In the following example, we'll perform a validation on the same backupsets that RMAN reported in the previous example for the USERS tablespace:

```
RMAN> restore tablespace users validate;
Starting restore at 20-AUG-14
using channel ORA_DISK_1
using channel ORA_DISK_2
using channel ORA_DISK_3
using channel ORA_DISK_4

channel ORA_DISK_1: starting validation of datafile backup set
channel ORA_DISK_1: reading from backup piece +RECOV/CDB01/
BACKUPSET/2014_08_20/nnndn0_tag20140820t104812_0.737.856090217
channel ORA_DISK_1: piece handle=+RECOV/CDB01/BACKUPSET/2014_08_20/nnndn0_tag2
0140820t104812_0.737.856090217 tag=TAG20140820T104812
channel ORA_DISK_1: restored backup piece 1
channel ORA_DISK_1: validation complete, elapsed time: 00:00:01
Finished restore at 20-AUG-14
RMAN>
```

All blocks of the backupsets were read to ensure that they are usable for a restore operation for the USERS tablespace.

Point-in-Time Recovery

RMAN can be used to implement *point-in-time recovery,* or restoring and recovering a database up to a timestamp or SCN before the point at which a database failure occurred. As you found out in Chapter 13, a point-in-time recovery (PITR) may be useful for recovering from a user error where a table was dropped yesterday but the error was not detected until today. Using PITR, we can recover the database to a point in time right before the table was dropped.

Using PITR has the disadvantage of losing all other changes to the database from the point at which the database was restored; this disadvantage needs to be weighed against the consequences of the dropped table. If both options are undesirable, then another method such as Flashback Table, Flashback Database, or TSPITR should be considered as an alternative for recovering from these types of user errors. If you are using Oracle Database 12*c,* you can also restore and recover a table using RMAN, as covered earlier in this chapter.

Data Recovery Advisor

The Data Recovery Advisor (DRA), enhanced in Oracle Database 12*c,* can both proactively and reactively analyze failures. In both scenarios, it will not automatically fix problems it finds but instead provide one or more possible fixes and give you the option and the commands to perform the fix. As of Oracle Database 12*c* release 1 (12.1.0.2) only non-CDBs and single-instance CDBs are supported (non-RAC environments).

In previous releases of Oracle RMAN, you could perform proactive checks of the database's datafiles with the VALIDATE command. In a CDB environment the VALIDATE command has been enhanced to analyze individual PDBs or the entire CDB.

In this scenario I'll show you how DRA works in a multitenant environment, which means it also works the same way for a pre-Oracle Database 12*c* database or a non-CDB. In the container database CDB01, the datafiles for the CCREPOS SYSTEM tablespace were lost. You might come to that conclusion after viewing the alert log or, more likely, after a user submits a help desk ticket saying they can't get into the CCREPOS database. You suspect that there might be more failures, so you start RMAN and use the DRA commands LIST FAILURE, ADVISE FAILURE, and REPAIR FAILURE to fix one or more issues.

To view and repair any issues with the CDB containing the CCREPOS PDB, start RMAN from the root container and run the LIST FAILURE DETAIL command:

```
RMAN> list failure detail;

using target database control file instead of recovery catalog
Database Role: PRIMARY

List of Database Failures
=========================

Failure ID Priority Status    Time Detected Summary
---------- -------- --------- ------------- -------
1562       CRITICAL OPEN      04-JUN-14     System datafile 30: '+DATA/CDB01/
FB03AEEBB6F60995E043E3A0080AEE85/DATAFILE/system.258.849343395' is missing
  Impact: Database cannot be opened

Failure ID Priority Status    Time Detected Summary
---------- -------- --------- ------------- -------
1542       CRITICAL OPEN      04-JUN-14     System datafile 30: '+DATA/CDB01/
FB03AEEBB6F60995E043E3A0080AEE85/DATAFILE/system.258.849342981' is missing
  Impact: Database cannot be opened
RMAN>
```

It looks like the SYSTEM datafile was lost once already (and recovered) earlier in the day! But the failure was not cleared from RMAN, so use CHANGE FAILURE to clear the earlier event:

```
RMAN> change failure 1542 closed;

Database Role: PRIMARY

List of Database Failures
=========================

Failure ID Priority Status    Time Detected Summary
---------- -------- --------- ------------- -------
1542       CRITICAL OPEN      04-JUN-14     System datafile 30: '+DATA/CDB01/
FB03AEEBB6F60995E043E3A0080AEE85/DATAFILE/system.258.849342981' is missing
```

```
Do you really want to change the above failures (enter YES or NO)? yes
closed 1 failures

RMAN>
```

Next, let's see what RMAN recommends to fix the problem:

```
RMAN> advise failure 1562;

Database Role: PRIMARY

List of Database Failures
=========================

Failure ID Priority Status    Time Detected Summary
---------- -------- --------- ------------- -------
1562       CRITICAL OPEN      04-JUN-14     System datafile 30: '+DATA/CDB01/
FB03AEEBB6F60995E043E3A0080AEE85/DATAFILE/system.258.849343395' is missing

analyzing automatic repair options; this may take some time
allocated channel: ORA_DISK_1
channel ORA_DISK_1: SID=774 device type=DISK
allocated channel: ORA_DISK_2
channel ORA_DISK_2: SID=1028 device type=DISK
allocated channel: ORA_DISK_3
channel ORA_DISK_3: SID=1276 device type=DISK
allocated channel: ORA_DISK_4
channel ORA_DISK_4: SID=10 device type=DISK
analyzing automatic repair options complete

Mandatory Manual Actions
========================
no manual actions available

Optional Manual Actions
=======================
1. If file +DATA/CDB01/FB03AEEBB6F60995E043E3A0080AEE85/DATAFILE/
system.258.849343395 was unintentionally renamed or moved, restore it
2. Automatic repairs may be available if you shut down the database and
restart it in mount mode

Automated Repair Options
========================
Option Repair Description
------ ------------------
1      Restore and recover datafile 30
  Strategy: The repair includes complete media recovery with no data loss
  Repair script: /u01/app/oracle/diag/rdbms/cdb01/cdb01/hm/reco_461168804.hm

RMAN>
```

The repair script generated by RMAN is as follows:

```
# restore and recover datafile
sql 'CCREPOS' 'alter database datafile 30 offline';
restore ( datafile 30 );
recover datafile 30;
sql 'CCREPOS' 'alter database datafile 30 online';
```

The script is generated to run as is in RMAN. Knowing that the CCREPOS PDB is closed, however, means that we can skip the first and last commands and just run the RESTORE and RECOVER commands:

```
RMAN> restore (datafile 30);

Starting restore at 04-JUN-14
using channel ORA_DISK_1
using channel ORA_DISK_2
using channel ORA_DISK_3
using channel ORA_DISK_4

channel ORA_DISK_1: starting datafile backup set restore
channel ORA_DISK_1: specifying datafile(s) to restore from backup set
channel ORA_DISK_1: restoring datafile 00030 to +DATA/CDB01/
FB03AEEBB6F60995E043E3A0080AEE85/DATAFILE/system.258.849343395
channel ORA_DISK_1: reading from backup piece +RECOV/CDB01/
FB03AEEBB6F60995E043E3A0080AEE85/BACKUPSET/2014_06_04/nnndf0_tag2014060
4t084003_0.316.849343205
channel ORA_DISK_1: piece handle=+RECOV/CDB01/
FB03AEEBB6F60995E043E3A0080AEE85/BACKUPSET/2014_06_04/nnndf0_tag2014060
4t084003_0.316.849343205 tag=TAG20140604T084003
channel ORA_DISK_1: restored backup piece 1
channel ORA_DISK_1: restore complete, elapsed time: 00:00:07
Finished restore at 04-JUN-14

RMAN> recover datafile 30;

Starting recover at 04-JUN-14
using channel ORA_DISK_1
using channel ORA_DISK_2
using channel ORA_DISK_3
using channel ORA_DISK_4

starting media recovery
media recovery complete, elapsed time: 00:00:01

Finished recover at 04-JUN-14

RMAN>
```

Finally, open the PDB and see if all is well:

```
RMAN> alter pluggable database ccrepos open;
Statement processed
RMAN>
```

Since CCREPOS starts fine now, you can clear the failure in RMAN:

```
RMAN> change failure 1562 closed;

Database Role: PRIMARY

List of Database Failures
=========================

Failure ID Priority Status    Time Detected Summary
---------- -------- --------- ------------- -------
1562       CRITICAL OPEN      04-JUN-14     System datafile 30: '+DATA/CDB01/
FB03AEEBB6F60995E043E3A0080AEE85/DATAFILE/system.258.849343395' is missing

Do you really want to change the above failures (enter YES or NO)? yes
closed 1 failures

RMAN>
```

Miscellaneous Operations

The next few sections cover some of the other capabilities of RMAN, beyond the backup, restore, and recovery operations. I'll show how to record the existence of other backups made outside of the database and perform some catalog maintenance. I'll also give a couple more examples of the LIST and REPORT commands.

Cataloging Other Backups

On occasion, we want the recovery catalog to include backups made outside of RMAN, such as image copies made with operating system commands or with the **asmcmd** command, as in this example:

```
ASMCMD> pwd
+data/cdb01/datafile
ASMCMD> ls
SYSAUX.267.845193957
SYSTEM.268.849339613
UNDOTBS1.263.848922747
UNDOTBS1.270.845194049
USERS.269.845194049
USERS2.495.856093717
ASMCMD> cp users.269.845* /u01/image_copy
copying +data/cdb01/datafile/USERS.269.845194049 ->
      /u01/image_copy/USERS.269.845194049
ASMCMD>
```

CAUTION
Image copies created with operating system commands must be performed either while the database is shut down or by using the ALTER TABLESPACE . . . BEGIN/END BACKUP commands.

Recording this image copy of the USERS tablespace is easy in RMAN using the CATALOG command:

```
[oracle@tettnang u01]$ rman target / catalog rman/rman@kthanid/rman_rep

Recovery Manager: Release 12.1.0.1.0 - Production on Wed Aug 20 12:16:24 2014

Copyright (c) 1982, 2013, Oracle and/or its affiliates.  All rights reserved.

connected to target database: CDB01 (DBID=1382179355)
connected to recovery catalog database

RMAN> catalog datafilecopy '/u01/image_copy/USERS.269.845194049';

cataloged datafile copy
datafile copy file name=/u01/image_copy/USERS.269.845194049 RECID=5
STAMP=856095390

RMAN>
```

Now that the image copy is recorded in the RMAN repository, it may be considered for use in restore and recovery operations for the USERS tablespace.

Catalog Maintenance

Earlier in this chapter, we discussed the use of the BACKUP VALIDATE command to ensure that all the files that could be used in a backup operation were available, readable, and not corrupted. In that example, we found out that we had a mismatch between what the catalog reported and the archived redo logs on disk; some old archived redo logs were inadvertently removed from disk during a cleanup operation. You can use the CROSSCHECK command to update the recovery catalog with what archived redo log files are in the fast recovery area and which ones are missing:

```
[oracle@tettnang u01]$ rman target / catalog rman/rman@kthanid/rman_rep

Recovery Manager: Release 12.1.0.1.0 - Production on Wed Aug 20 12:30:37 2014

Copyright (c) 1982, 2013, Oracle and/or its affiliates.  All rights reserved.

connected to target database: CDB01 (DBID=1382179355)
connected to recovery catalog database

RMAN> crosscheck archivelog all;

allocated channel: ORA_DISK_1
channel ORA_DISK_1: SID=260 device type=DISK
```

```
allocated channel: ORA_DISK_2
channel ORA_DISK_2: SID=6 device type=DISK
allocated channel: ORA_DISK_3
channel ORA_DISK_3: SID=1031 device type=DISK
allocated channel: ORA_DISK_4
channel ORA_DISK_4: SID=522 device type=DISK
validation succeeded for archived log
archived log file name=+RECOV/CDB01/ARCHIVELOG/2014_08_20/thread_1_
seq_1484.318.856090843 RECID=560 STAMP=856090843
. . .
validation failed for archived log
archived log file name=+RECOV/CDB01/ARCHIVELOG/2014_06_29/thread_1_
seq_546.832.851526505 RECID=559 STAMP=851526504
validation failed for archived log
archived log file name=+RECOV/CDB01/ARCHIVELOG/2014_08_20/thread_1_
seq_1485.322.856094699 RECID=561 STAMP=856094699
Crosschecked 54 objects
RMAN>
```

The missing archived redo logs are now marked as EXPIRED in the catalog, and they won't be considered when validating backups or for performing restore or recovery operations.

All other datafiles that RMAN could consider for a backup operation, including archived redo logs, are available and readable.

REPORT and LIST

All throughout this chapter, I've provided a number of examples of how to extract information from the recovery catalog, whether it resides in the target database control file or in a catalog database repository. We've used both the LIST and REPORT commands. The primary difference between these commands is in their complexity: The LIST command displays information about backupsets and image copies in the repository and lists the contents of scripts stored in the repository catalog:

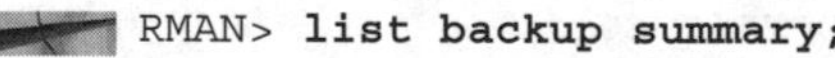

```
RMAN> list backup summary;

List of Backups
===============
Key     TY LV S Device Type Completion Time #Pieces #Copies Compressed Tag
------- -- -- - ----------- --------------- ------- ------- ---------- ---
1606    B  F  A DISK        04-JUN-14       1       1       YES
TAG20140604T073433
1607    B  F  A DISK        04-JUN-14       1       1       YES
TAG20140604T073433
1608    B  F  A DISK        04-JUN-14       1       1       YES
TAG20140604T073433
1609    B  F  A DISK        04-JUN-14       1       1       YES
TAG20140604T073433
1610    B  F  A DISK        04-JUN-14       1       1       YES
TAG20140604T073433
1611    B  F  A DISK        04-JUN-14       1       1       YES
TAG20140604T073433
```

```
. . .
3735    B  F  A DISK        20-AUG-14       1       1       NO
TAG20140820T123711
RMAN>
```

In contrast, the REPORT command performs a more detailed analysis of the information in the recovery catalog; as in one of our previous examples, we used REPORT to identify which database files needed backups to comply with our retention policy. In the following example, we find out what the datafiles looked like back on August 19, 2014:

```
RMAN> report schema at time='19-aug-2014';
Report of database schema for database with db_unique_name CDB01
List of Permanent Datafiles
===========================
File Size(MB) Tablespace           RB segs Datafile Name
---- -------- -------------------- ------- ------------------------
1    810      SYSTEM               YES     +DATA/CDB01/DATAFILE/
system.268.849339613
3    2950     SYSAUX               NO      +DATA/CDB01/DATAFILE/
sysaux.267.845193957
4    900      UNDOTBS1             YES     +DATA/CDB01/DATAFILE/
undotbs1.270.845194049
5    250      PDB$SEED:SYSTEM      NO      +DATA/CDB01/
DD7C48AA5A4404A2E04325AAE80A403C/DATAFILE/system.277.845194085
. . .
List of Temporary Files
=======================
File Size(MB) Tablespace           Maxsize(MB) Tempfile Name
---- -------- -------------------- ----------- --------------------
1    521      TEMP                 32767       +DATA/CDB01/TEMPFILE/
temp.275.845194083
2    20       PDB$SEED:TEMP        32767       +DATA/CDB01/
DD7C48AA5A4404A2E04325AAE80A403C/DATAFILE/pdbseed_temp01.dbf
3    20       CCREPOS:TEMP         32767       +DATA/CDB01/
FB03AEEBB6F60995E043E3A0080AEE85/TEMPFILE/temp.262.849342985
4    20       TOOL:TEMP            32767       . . .
. . .
14   20       HR:TEMP              32767       +DATA/CDB01/
FC9588B12BBD413FE043E3A0080A5528/TEMPFILE/temp.485.851068789
RMAN>
```

At some point between 8/19/2014 and today, we created the tablespace INET_STAR, as indicated by its omission from this report.

Summary

If you have not been using RMAN extensively since the release of Oracle Database 11*g*, you should be using it almost exclusively in Oracle Database 12*c*. RMAN can manage all aspects of physical backup and recovery for your departmental database or for hundreds of databases, including OLTP and data warehouse databases throughout an enterprise.

The features included with RMAN keep pace with the new features of the database. Backing up an entire container database or a pluggable database in Oracle 12*c* is as easy as backing up a non-CDB database in Oracle 11*g*. Other new features of RMAN, such as network support of compressed duplication of a database in parallel over a network to an auxiliary instance, means you may not need any intermediate RMAN backups on disk to support the duplication process.

Finally, having a recovery catalog makes it easy to recover an entire database even when you lose all datafiles and control files. If your environment has more than one production database, then maintaining a recovery catalog is worthwhile.

CHAPTER 15

Oracle Data Guard

Oracle Data Guard provides a solution for high availability, enhanced performance, and automated failover. You can use Oracle Data Guard to create and maintain multiple standby databases for a primary database. The standby databases can be started in read-only mode to support reporting users and then returned to standby mode. Changes to the primary database can be automatically relayed from the primary database to the standby databases with a guarantee of no data lost in the process. The standby database servers can be physically separate from the primary server.

In this chapter, you will get an overview on how to administer an Oracle Data Guard environment, along with sample configuration files for a Data Guard environment.

Data Guard Architecture

In a Data Guard implementation, a database running in ARCHIVELOG mode is designated as the primary database for an application. One or more standby databases, accessible via Oracle Net, provide for failover capabilities. Data Guard automatically transmits redo information to the standby databases, where it is applied. As a result, the standby database is transactionally consistent. Depending on how you configure the redo apply process, the standby databases may be in sync with the primary database or may lag behind it. Figure 15-1 shows a standard Data Guard implementation.

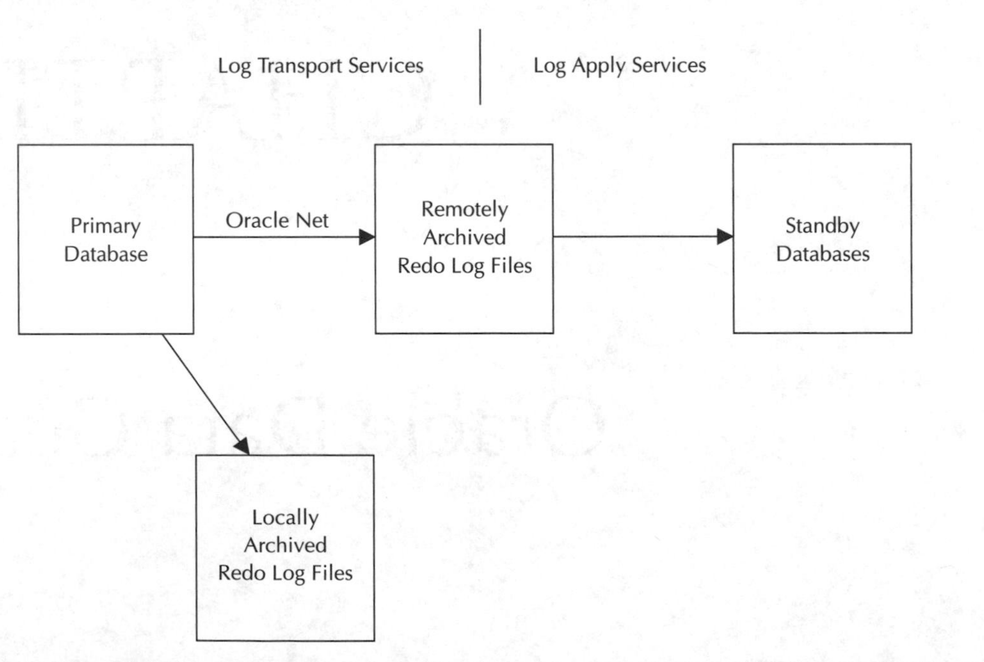

FIGURE 15-1. *Simple Data Guard configuration*

The redo log data is transferred to the standby databases via Log Transport Services, as defined via your initialization parameter settings. Log Apply Services apply the redo information to the standby databases. A third set of services, Global Data Services, simplify the process of making standby databases serve as the primary database.

NOTE
The primary database can be a single instance or a multi-instance Real Application Clusters implementation.

Physical vs. Logical Standby Databases

Two types of standby databases are supported: physical standbys and logical standbys. A *physical standby* database has the same structures as the primary database. A *logical standby* database may have different internal structures (such as additional indexes used for reporting or a different tablespace layout). You synchronize a logical standby database with the primary by transforming the redo data into SQL statements that are executed against the standby database.

Physical and logical standby databases serve different purposes. A physical standby database is a block-for-block copy of the primary database, so it can be used for database backups in place of the primary database. During disaster recovery, the physical standby looks exactly like the primary database it replaces.

A logical standby database, because it supports additional database structures, can more easily be used to support specific reporting requirements that would otherwise burden the primary database. Additionally, rolling upgrades of primary and standby databases can be performed with minimal downtime when logical standby databases are used. The type of standby to use depends on your needs; many environments start out using physical standby databases for disaster recovery and then add in additional logical standby databases to support specific reporting and business requirements.

NOTE
*The operating system and platform architecture on the primary and standby locations do not need to be identical as of Oracle Database 11*g. *The directory structures for the primary and standby databases may differ, but you should minimize the differences to simplify administration and failover processes. If the standby is located on the same server as the primary, you must use a different directory structure for the two databases, and they cannot share an archive log directory. In addition, Oracle Data Guard is available only in Oracle Enterprise Edition. Also, not all cross-platform Data Guard replication is supported, even in Oracle Database 12*c *(12.1.0.2). See My Oracle Support note* Data Guard Support for Heterogeneous Primary and Physical Standbys in Same Data Guard Configuration *(ID 413484.1).*

Data Protection Modes

When you configure the primary and standby databases, you will need to determine the level of data loss that is acceptable to the business. In the primary database, you will define its archive log destination areas, at least one of which will refer to the remote site used by the standby database. The ASYNC, SYNC, ARCH, LGWR, NOAFFIRM, and AFFIRM attributes of the LOG_ARCHIVE_DEST_*n* parameter setting (see the upcoming Table 15-1) for the standby database will direct Oracle Data Guard to select among several modes of operation:

- In *maximum protection* (or "no data loss") mode, at least one standby location must be written to before a transaction commits in the primary database. The primary database shuts down if the standby database's log location is unavailable.
- In *maximum availability* mode, at least one standby location must be written to before a transaction commits in the primary database. If the standby location is not available, the primary database does not shut down. When the fault is corrected, the redo that has been generated since the fault is transported and applied to the standby databases.
- In *maximum performance* mode (the default), transactions can commit before their redo information is sent to the standby locations. Commits in the primary database occur as soon as writes to the local online redo logs complete. The writes to the standby locations are handled by the ARC*n* processes by default (up to 30 archiver processes in Oracle Database 12*c*).

Once you have decided the type of standby and the data protection mode for your configuration, you can create your standby database.

LOG_ARCHIVE_DEST_*n* Parameter Attributes

As illustrated in the following sections, Oracle Data Guard configurations rely on a number of attributes within the LOG_ARCHIVE_DEST_*n* parameter. Table 15-1 summarizes the attributes available for this parameter. In almost all cases the attributes are paired; in some cases the second member of the pair simply serves to nullify the setting.

NOTE
LOG_ARCHIVE_DEST and LOG_ARCHIVE_DUPLEX_DEST are deprecated unless you do not *have Oracle Database 12*c *Enterprise Edition, otherwise you can still use these parameters. With Enterprise Edition, use LOG_ARCHIVE_DEST_*n *instead.*

Attribute	Description
AFFIRM and NOAFFIRM	AFFIRM ensures all disk I/O to the archived redo log files or standby redo log files at the standby destination is performed synchronously and completes successfully before the Log Writer process (LGWR) can continue. AFFIRM is required to achieve no data loss. NOAFFIRM indicates all disk I/O to archived redo log files and standby redo log files is to be performed asynchronously; online redo log files on the primary database can be reused before the disk I/O on the standby destination completes. In Oracle Database 12*c*, you can use NOAFFIRM in conjunction with the Data Guard Maximum Availability feature to acknowledge receipt of the redo in memory before it is written to the remote redo log file.

TABLE 15-1. *LOG_ARCHIVE_DEST_*n *Parameter Attributes*

Attribute	Description
ALTERNATE and NOALTERNATE	ALTERNATE specifies an alternate LOG_ARCHIVE_DEST_*n* destination to use when the original archiving destination fails.
COMPRESSION	Compress redo data before transmission to a redo transport destination. This feature is part of the Advanced Compression option, which is a separately licensed product that is available in Oracle Database 12.1.0.2 or later.
DB_UNIQUE_NAME and NODB_UNIQUE_NAME	DB_UNIQUE_NAME specifies the unique database name for the destination.
DELAY and NODELAY	DELAY specifies a time lag between archiving redo data on the standby site and applying the archived redo log file to the standby database; DELAY may be used to protect the standby database from corrupted or erroneous primary data. If neither DELAY nor NODELAY is specified, NODELAY is the default. If DELAY is specified and no value is provided, then 30 minutes is the default.
ENCRYPTION	Encrypt redo data before transmission. Only supported for a Zero Data Loss Recovery Appliance.
LOCATION and SERVICE	Each destination *must* specify either the LOCATION or the SERVICE attribute to identify either a local disk directory (via LOCATION) or a remote database destination where Log Transport Services can transmit redo data (via SERVICE).
MANDATORY and OPTIONAL	If a destination is OPTIONAL, archiving to that destination may fail, yet the online redo log file is available for reuse and may be overwritten eventually. If the archival operation of a MANDATORY destination fails, online redo log files cannot be overwritten.
MAX_CONNECTIONS	Use additional network paths to the redo transport destination.
MAX_FAILURE and NOMAX_FAILURE	MAX_FAILURE specifies the maximum number of reopen attempts before the primary database permanently gives up on the standby database.
NET_TIMEOUT and NONET_TIMEOUT	NET_TIMEOUT specifies the number of seconds the LGWR process on the primary system waits for status from the network server process before terminating the network connection. The default value is 30 seconds.
REGISTER and NOREGISTER	REGISTER indicates that the location of the archived redo log file is to be recorded at the corresponding destination.
REOPEN and NOREOPEN	REOPEN specifies the minimum number of seconds (the default is 300 seconds) before the archiver processes (ARC*n*) or the LGWR process should try again to access a previously failed destination.

TABLE 15-1. *LOG_ARCHIVE_DEST_*n *Parameter Attributes* (Continued)

Attribute	Description
SYNC and ASYNC	SYNC and ASYNC specify that network I/O is to be done synchronously or asynchronously when using the LGWR process. The default is SYNC=PARALLEL, which should be used when there are multiple destinations with the SYNC attribute. All destinations should use the same value.
TEMPLATE and NOTEMPLATE	TEMPLATE defines a directory specification and format template for names of the archived redo log files or standby redo log files at the standby destination. You can specify these attributes in either the primary or standby initialization parameter file, but the attribute applies only to the database role that is archiving.
VALID_FOR	VALID_FOR identifies when Log Transport Services can transmit redo data to destinations based on the following factors: (1) whether the database is currently running in the primary or the standby role, and (2) whether online redo log files, standby redo log files, or both are currently being archived on the database at this destination. The default value for this attribute is VALID_FOR=(ALL_LOGFILES, ALL_ROLES). Other values include PRIMARY_ROLE, STANDBY_ROLE, ONLINE_LOGFILES, and STANDBY_LOGFILE.

TABLE 15-1. *LOG_ARCHIVE_DEST_*n *Parameter Attributes* (Continued)

Creating the Standby Database Configuration

You can use SQL*Plus, Oracle Enterprise Manager (OEM), or Data Guard–specific tools to configure and administer Data Guard configurations. The parameters you set will depend on the configuration you choose.

If the primary and standby databases are on the same server, you will need to set a value for the DB_UNIQUE_NAME parameter. Because the directory structures for the two databases will be different, you must either manually rename files or define values for the DB_FILE_NAME_CONVERT and LOG_FILE_NAME_CONVERT parameters in the standby database. You must set up unique service names for the primary and standby databases via the SERVICE_NAMES initialization parameter.

If the primary and standby databases are on separate servers, you can use the same directory structures for each, avoiding the need for the filename conversion parameters. If you use a different directory structure for the database files, you will need to define the values for the DB_FILE_NAME_CONVERT and LOG_FILE_NAME_CONVERT parameters in the standby database.

In physical standby databases, all the redo comes from the primary database. When physical standby databases are opened in read-only mode, no redo is generated. Oracle Data Guard does, however, use archived redo log files to support the replication of the data and SQL commands used to update the standby databases.

NOTE
For each standby database, you should create a standby redo log file to store redo data received from the primary database.

Preparing the Primary Database

On the primary database, make sure you have set values for the following parameters, which impact the transfer of the redo log data. The first five parameters are standard for most databases; set REMOTE_LOGIN_PASSWORDFILE to EXCLUSIVE to support remote access by SYSDBA-privileged users.

DB_NAME	The database name. Use the same name for all standby databases and the primary database.
DB_UNIQUE_NAME	The unique name for the database. This value must be different for each standby database and must differ from the primary database.
SERVICE_NAMES	Service names for the databases; set separate service names for the primary and standby databases.
CONTROL_FILES	The location of the control files.
REMOTE_LOGIN_PASSWORDFILE	Set to EXCLUSIVE or SHARED. Set the same password for SYS on both the primary and standby databases.

The LOG_ARCHIVE-related parameters, listed next, will configure how the Log Transport Services work.

LOG_ARCHIVE_CONFIG	Within the DB_CONFIG parameter, list the primary and standby databases.
LOG_ARCHIVE_DEST_1	The location of the primary database's archived redo log files.
LOG_ARCHIVE_DEST_2	The remote location used for the standby redo log files.
LOG_ARCHIVE_DEST_STATE_1	Set to ENABLE.
LOG_ARCHIVE_DEST_STATE_2	Set to ENABLE to enable log transport.
LOG_ARCHIVE_FORMAT	Specify the format for the archive log file's name.

For this example, assume that the primary database has a DB_UNIQUE_NAME value of HEADQTR and the physical standby database has a DB_UNIQUE_NAME value of SALESOFC. The SERVICE_NAMES values can be the same as the DB_UNIQUE_NAME values, but this is not a requirement. In fact, the SERVICE_NAMES value may be unique to a single node in a RAC instance.

The LOG_ARCHIVE_CONFIG parameter setting may resemble the following:

```
LOG_ARCHIVE_CONFIG='DG_CONFIG=(headqtr,salesofc)'
```

There are two LOG_ARCHIVE_DEST_*n* entries—one for the local copy of the archived redo log files, and a second for the remote copy that will be shipped to the physical standby database:

```
LOG_ARCHIVE_DEST_1=
'LOCATION=/arch/headqtr/
 VALID_FOR=(ALL_LOGFILES,ALL_ROLES)
```

```
  DB_UNIQUE_NAME=headqtr'
LOG_ARCHIVE_DEST_2=
 'SERVICE=salesofc
  VALID_FOR=(ONLINE_LOGFILES,PRIMARY_ROLE)
  DB_UNIQUE_NAME=salesofc'
```

The LOG_ARCHIVE_DEST_1 parameter specifies the location of the archived redo log files for the primary database (as specified via the DB_UNIQUE_NAME parameter). The LOG_ARCHIVE_DEST_2 parameter gives the service name of the physical standby database as its location. For each of these destinations, the corresponding LOG_ARCHIVE_DEST_STATE_*n* parameter should have a value of ENABLE.

The standby role–related parameters include the FAL (Fetch Archive Log) parameters used prior to Oracle Database 10*g* to resolve gaps in the range of archive logs copied to the standby databases:

FAL_SERVER	Specify the service name of the FAL server (typically the primary database).
FAL_CLIENT	Specify the service name of the FAL client (the standby database fetching the logs).
DB_FILE_NAME_CONVERT	If the primary and standby databases use differing directory structures, specify the pathname and filename location of the primary database datafiles, followed by the standby location.
LOG_FILE_NAME_CONVERT	If the primary and standby databases use differing directory structures, specify the pathname and filename location of the primary database log files, followed by the standby location.
STANDBY_FILE_MANAGEMENT	Set to AUTO.

TIP

FAL_SERVER and FAL_CLIENT should both be defined on each node so they are ready to switch back to their original roles after a role switch.

Sample settings for these parameters are shown in the following listing:

```
FAL_SERVER=headqtr
FAL_CLIENT=salesofc
LOG_FILE_NAME_CONVERT=
'/arch/headqtr/','/arch/salesofc/','/arch1/headqtr/','/arch1/salesofc/'
STANDBY_FILE_MANAGEMENT=AUTO
```

If the primary database is not already in ARCHIVELOG mode, enable archiving by issuing the ALTER DATABASE ARCHIVELOG command while the database is mounted but not open. In addition, enable forced logging in the primary database to ensure that all unlogged direct writes will be propagated to the standby database by using the ALTER DATABASE FORCE LOGGING command.

Once the log-related parameters have been set, you can begin the process of creating the standby database.

Step 1: Back Up the Primary Database's Datafiles

First, perform a physical backup of the primary database. Oracle recommends using the RMAN utility to back up the database; you can use the DUPLICATE command within RMAN to automate the process of creating the standby database.

Step 2: Create a Control File for the Standby Database

In the primary database, issue the following command to generate a control file that will be used for the standby database:

```
alter database create standby controlfile as '/tmp/salesofc.ctl';
```

Note that you specify the directory and filename where you want the control file to be created. Also, do not use the same directory and control file name as you use for the primary database.

Step 3: Create an Initialization Parameter File for the Standby Database

In the primary database, create a parameter file from the server parameter file:

```
create pfile='/tmp/initsalesofc.ora' from spfile;
```

Edit this initialization file to set the proper values for the standby database. Set the standby database's values for DB_UNIQUE_NAME, SERVICE_NAMES, CONTROL_FILES, DB_FILE_NAME_CONVERT, LOG_FILE_NAME_CONVERT, LOG_ARCHIVE_DEST_*n*, INSTANCE_NAME, FAL_SERVER, and FAL_CLIENT. The filename conversions should be the same as in the primary database—you want to convert the filenames from the primary database to the standby database format when the redo information is applied:

```
LOG_ARCHIVE_DEST_1=
'LOCATION=/arch/salesofc/
VALID_FOR=(ALL_LOGFILES,ALL_ROLES)
DB_UNIQUE_NAME=salesofc'
LOG_ARCHIVE_DEST_2=
'SERVICE=headqtr
VALID_FOR=(ONLINE_LOGFILES,PRIMARY_ROLE)
```

In the standby environment, the LOG_ARCHIVE_DEST_1 parameter points to its local archive log destination, and LOG_ARCHIVE_DEST_2 points to the primary database's service name. If the roles of the two databases are switched, the original primary database will be able to serve as the standby database. While the standby database is running in standby mode, the LOG_ARCHIVE_DEST_2 value will be ignored.

NOTE

Set the COMPATIBLE parameter to the same value for both the primary and standby databases. To take advantage of the new features in Oracle 12c, set the COMPATIBLE value to 12.1.0 or higher. Once COMPATIBLE is set to 12.1.0, you cannot reset it to a lower value.

Step 4: Copy the Database Files to the Standby Database Location

Copy the datafiles from Step 1, the control file from Step 2, and the standby initialization file from Step 3 to the standby database location. Put the files in the proper directories (as defined by the CONTROL_FILES, DB_FILE_NAME_CONVERT, and LOG_FILE_NAME_CONVERT parameters). Alternatively, use an RMAN backup of the primary database to create the standby database files.

Step 5: Configure the Standby Database Environment

At this point, the files are in place. You need to create the proper environment variables and services to allow an instance to access the files. For example, in a Windows environment you should use the **oradim** utility to create a new service, as shown in this example:

```
oradim -new -sid salesofc -intpwd oracle -startmode manual
```

Next, create a password file for the standby database via the **orapwd** utility (see Chapter 2 for details on creating a new password file).

Next, create the Oracle Net parameters and services needed to access the standby database. In the standby environment, create an Oracle Net listener service for the standby database. In the standby server's **sqlnet.ora** file, set the SQLNET.EXPIRE_TIME parameter to 1 to activate broken-connection detection after one minute. See Chapter 17 for further details on Oracle Net connections.

Next, create a service name entry for the standby database in the **tnsnames.ora** file and then distribute that update to both the standby and primary database servers.

If the primary database has an encryption wallet, copy the wallet to the standby database system and configure the standby database to use this wallet; the wallet must be re-copied from the primary to all standby databases whenever the master encryption key is updated.

Lastly, create a server parameter file via the CREATE SPFILE FROM PFILE command, passing the name and location of the standby parameter file as input to that command.

Step 6: Start the Standby Database

From within SQL*Plus, start the standby database in MOUNT mode, as shown in the following example:

```
startup mount;
```

NOTE

You can add new temporary files to the temporary tablespaces in the standby database. Adding temporary files will support sorting operations required for reporting activity within the standby database if the standby database is going to be used for read-only operations such as reporting.

Oracle recommends that you create the same number of online redo log files on each standby database; you could create fewer to speed up the migration process, but if there are not at least two, then the instance will not open.

Start the redo application process within the standby database via the following ALTER DATABASE command:

```
alter database recover managed standby database
   using current logfile disconnect from session;
```

Step 7: Verify the Configuration

To test the configuration, go to the primary database and force a log switch to occur via the ALTER SYSTEM command, as shown here:

```
alter system switch logfile;
```

The primary database's redo log data should then be copied to the standby location.

On the standby database, you can query the V$ARCHIVED_LOG view or use the ARCHIVE LOG LIST command to see which archived logs have been applied to the database. As new logs are received from the primary database and applied to the standby, new rows will be added to the listing in V$ARCHIVED_LOG.

Creating Logical Standby Databases

Logical standby databases follow many of the same steps used to create physical standby databases. Because they rely on the re-execution of SQL commands, logical standby databases have greater restrictions on their use. If any of your tables in the primary database use the following datatypes, they will be skipped during the redo application process:

- BFILE
- ROWID, UROWID
- User-defined datatypes
- Identity columns
- Objects with nested tables and REFs
- Collections (varying arrays, nested tables)
- Spatial datatypes

NOTE

Support for logical replication of XMLtype was added in Oracle Database 12c Release 1 (12.1.0.1). Oracle's Extended Datatype Support (EDS) supports most datatypes that do not otherwise have native redo-based support.

Additionally, tables that use table compression and the schemas that are installed with the Oracle software are skipped during redo application. The DBA_LOGSTDBY_UNSUPPORTED view lists the objects that are not supported for logical standby databases. The DBA_LOGSTDBY_SKIP view lists the schemas that will be skipped. Figure 15-2 shows the processing flow for the SQL apply architecture for a logical standby database.

A logical standby database is not identical to the primary database. Each transaction that is executed in the logical standby database must be the logical equivalent of the transaction that was executed in the primary database. Therefore, you should make sure your tables have the proper constraints on them—primary keys, unique constraints, check constraints, and foreign keys—so the proper rows can be targeted for update in the logical standby database. You can query DBA_LOGSTDBY_NOT_UNIQUE to list tables that lack primary key or unique constraints in the primary database.

To create a logical standby database, follow the steps outlined in the remainder of this section.

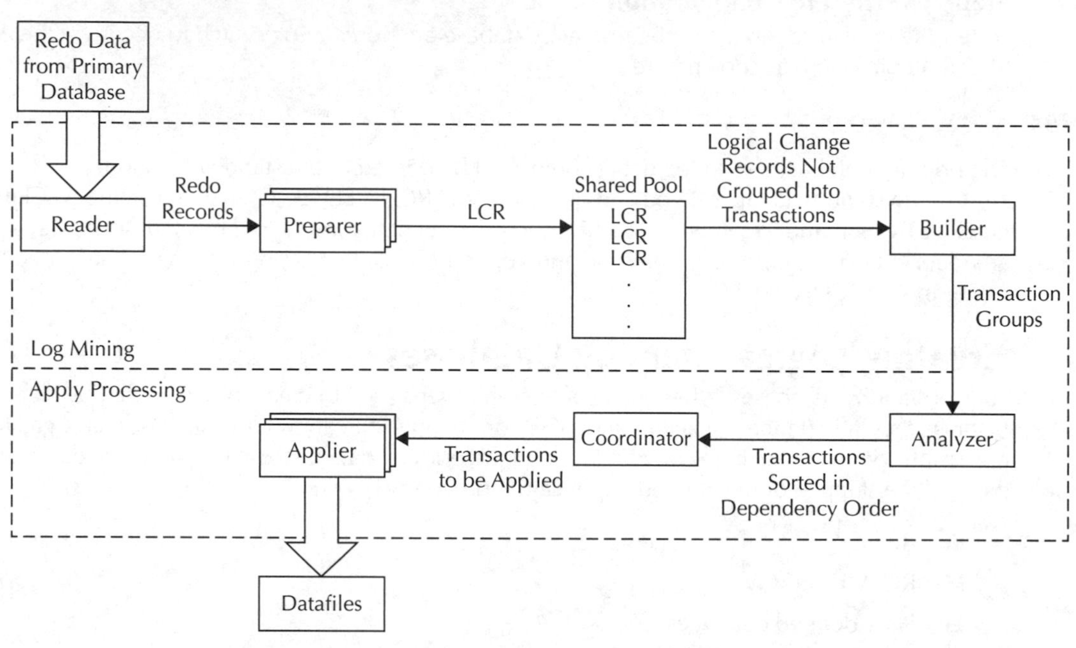

FIGURE 15-2. *SQL apply process for logical standby databases*

Step 1: Create a Physical Standby Database

Following the steps in the prior section of this chapter, create a physical standby database. After you create and start up the physical standby, stop the redo apply process on the physical standby to avoid applying changes past the redo that contains the supplemental log information:

```
alter database recover managed standby database cancel;
```

Step 2: Enable Supplemental Logging

Supplemental logging on the primary database generates additional information in the redo log. That information is then used during the redo application process in the standby database to make sure the correct rows are affected by the generated SQL. To add primary key and unique index information to the redo data, issue the following command in the primary database:

```
execute dbms_logstdby.build;
```

This procedure waits for all existing transactions to complete; if there are long-running transactions on the primary database, this process will not finish until those transactions commit or roll back.

Step 3: Transition the Physical Standby to a Logical Standby

The redo log files have the information necessary to convert your physical database to a logical database; run this command to continue redo log data application to the physical standby database until the moment you're ready to convert to a logical standby:

```
alter database recover to logical standby new_db_name;
```

Oracle automatically stores the name of your new logical standby database, ***new_db_name***, in the SPFILE. Otherwise, this command generates a message reminding you to change the DB_NAME parameter in your initialization parameter file after shutting down the database.

Physical standby databases operate in read-only mode; logical standby databases are open for writes and generate their own redo data. In the initialization file for the logical standby database, specify destinations for the logical standby database's redo data (LOG_ARCHIVE_DEST_1) and the incoming redo from the primary database (in this example, LOG_ARCHIVE_DEST_3 will be used to avoid conflicts with the earlier LOG_ARCHIVE_DEST_2 setting). You do not want a logical standby database to have the LOG_ARCHIVE_DEST_2 destination enabled and pointing back to the primary database.

Shut down and start up the database and change these parameters:

```
shutdown;
startup mount;
```

Step 4: Start the Logical Standby Database

Open the logical standby database using its new initialization parameter file or SPFILE as follows:

```
alter database open resetlogs;
```

Because this is the first time the database is opened after being converted to a standby, the database's global name is adjusted to match the new DB_NAME initialization parameter.

Step 5: Start the Redo Application Process

Within the logical standby database, you can now start the redo application process:

```
alter database start logical standby apply immediate;
```

To see the logs that have been received and applied to the logical standby database, query the DBA_LOGSTDBY_LOG view. You can query the V$LOGSTDBY view to see the activity log of the logical standby redo application process. The logical standby database is now available for use.

Using Real-Time Apply

By default, redo data is not applied to a standby database until the standby redo log file is archived. When you use the real-time apply feature, redo data is applied to the standby database as it is received, reducing the time lag between the databases and potentially shortening the time required to fail over to the standby database.

To enable real-time apply in a physical standby database, execute the following command in the standby database:

```
alter database recover managed standby database
using current logfile;
```

For a logical standby database, the command to use is

```
alter database start logical standby apply immediate;
```

The RECOVERY_MODE column of the V$ARCHIVE_DEST_STATUS view will have a value of MANAGED REAL TIME APPLY if real-time apply has been enabled.

As shown earlier in this chapter, you can enable the redo application on a physical standby database via the command:

```
alter database recover managed standby database disconnect;
```

The DISCONNECT keyword allows the command to run in the background after you disconnect from your Oracle session. When you start a foreground session and issue the same command without the DISCONNECT keyword, control is not returned to the command prompt until the recovery is cancelled by another session. To stop the redo application in a physical standby database, whether in a background session or a foreground session, use the following command:

```
alter database recover managed standby database cancel;
```

For a logical standby database, the command to stop the Log Apply Services is

```
alter database stop logical standby apply;
```

Managing Gaps in Archive Log Sequences

If the standby database has not received one or more archived logs generated by the primary database, it does not have a full record of the transactions in the primary database. Oracle Data Guard detects the gap in the archive log sequence automatically; it resolves the problem by copying the missing sequence of log files to the standby destination. In versions of Oracle Database prior to 10*g*, the FAL (Fetch Archive Log) client and server were used to resolve gaps from the primary database.

To determine if there is a gap in your physical standby database, query the V$ARCHIVE_GAP view. For each gap, that view will report the lowest and highest log sequence number of the set of logs missing from the standby database. If there is some reason why Oracle Data Guard has not been able to copy the logs, you can copy the files manually to your physical standby database environment and register them using the ALTER DATABASE REGISTER LOGFILE *filename* command; then you can start the redo apply process. After the logs have been applied, check the V$ARCHIVE_GAP view again to see if there is another gap to resolve.

Managing Roles: Switchovers and Failovers

Each database that participates in a Data Guard configuration has a role—it is either a primary database or a standby database. At some point, those roles may need to change. For example, if there is a hardware failure on the primary database's server, you may fail over to the standby database. Depending on your configuration choices, there may be some loss of data during a failover.

A second type of role change is called a *switchover*. This occurs when the primary database switches roles with a standby database, and the standby becomes the new primary database. During a switchover, there should be no data lost. Switchovers and failovers require manual intervention by a database administrator.

Switchovers

Switchovers are planned role changes, usually to allow for maintenance activities to be performed on the primary database server. A standby database is chosen to act as the new primary database, the switchover occurs, and applications now write their data to the new primary database. At some later point in time you can switch the databases back to their original roles.

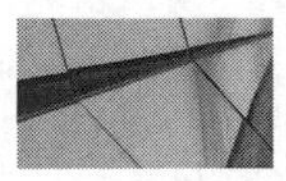

NOTE
You can perform switchovers with either a logical standby database or a physical standby database; the physical standby database is the preferred option.

What if you have defined multiple standby databases? When one of the physical standby databases becomes the new primary database, the other standby databases must be able to receive their redo log data from the new primary database. In that configuration, you must define the LOG_ARCHIVE_DEST_*n* parameters to allow those standby sites to receive data from the new primary database location.

NOTE
Verify that the database that will become the new primary database is running in ARCHIVELOG mode.

In the following sections, you will see the steps required to perform a switchover to a standby database. The standby database should be actively applying redo log data prior to the switchover, as this will minimize the time required to complete the switchover.

Switchovers to Physical Standby Databases

Switchovers are initiated on the primary database and completed on the standby database. In this section, you will see the steps for performing a switchover to a physical standby database. There is no data loss during a switchover.

Begin by verifying that the primary database is capable of performing a switchover. Query V$DATABASE for the value of the SWITCHOVER_STATUS column:

```
select switchover_status from v$database;
```

If the SWITCHOVER_STATUS column's value is anything other than TO STANDBY, it is not possible to perform the switchover (usually due to a configuration or hardware issue). If the column's value is SESSIONS ACTIVE, you should terminate active user sessions. Valid values for the SWITCHOVER_STATUS column are shown in Table 15-2.

From within the primary database, you can initiate its transition to the physical standby database role with the following command:

```
alter database commit to switchover to physical standby;
```

As part of executing this command, Oracle will back up the current primary database's control file to a trace file. At this point, you should shut down the primary database and mount it:

```
shutdown immediate;
startup mount;
```

The primary database is prepared for the switchover; you should now go to the physical standby database that will serve as the new primary database.

Value	Description
NOT ALLOWED	The current database is not a primary database with standby databases.
PREPARING DICTIONARY	This logical standby database is sending its redo data to a primary database and other standby databases to prepare for the switchover.
PREPARING SWITCHOVER	Used by logical standby configurations while redo data is being accepted for the switchover.
FAILED DESTINATION	On a primary database, indicates that one or more standby destinations are in an error state.
RECOVERY NEEDED	This standby database has not received the switchover request.
RESOLVABLE GAP	On a primary database, indicates that one or more standby destinations have a redo gap that can be automatically resolved by retrieving the missing redo log from the primary or another standby database.
UNRESOLVABLE GAP	On a primary database, indicates that one or more standby databases have a redo log gap that cannot be automatically resolved by copying the redo log from another database.
LOG SWITCH GAP	On a primary database, indicates that one or more standby databases are missing redo because of a recent log switch. This status is typically resolved quickly because the redo log ship is likely in process.
SESSIONS ACTIVE	There are active SQL sessions in the primary database; they must be disconnected before continuing.
SWITCHOVER PENDING	Valid for standby databases in which the primary database switchover request has been received but not processed.
SWITCHOVER LATENT	The switchover did not complete and went back to the primary database.
TO LOGICAL STANDBY	This primary database has received a complete dictionary from a logical standby database.
TO PRIMARY	This standby database can switch over to a primary database.
TO STANDBY	This primary database can switch over to a standby database.

TABLE 15-2. *SWITCHOVER_STATUS Values*

In the physical standby database, check the switchover status in the V$DATABASE view; its status should be TO PRIMARY (see Table 15-2). You can now switch the physical standby database to the primary via the following command:

```
alter database commit to switchover to primary;
```

If you add the WITH SESSION SHUTDOWN WAIT clause, the statement will not return to the SQL> prompt until the switchover is complete. Start up the database using the OPEN keyword:

```
alter database open;
```

The database has completed its transition to the primary database role. Next, start the redo apply services on the standby databases if they were not already running in the background:

```
alter database recover managed standby database
  using current logfile
  disconnect from session;
```

Switchovers to Logical Standby Databases

Switchovers are initiated on the primary database and completed on the standby database. In this section, you will see the steps for performing a switchover to a logical standby database.

Begin by verifying that the primary database is capable of performing a switchover. Query V$DATABASE for the value of the SWITCHOVER_STATUS column:

```
select switchover_status from v$database;
```

For the switchover to complete, the status must be either TO STANDBY, TO LOGICAL STANDBY, or SESSIONS ACTIVE.

In the primary database, issue the following command to prepare the primary database for the switchover:

```
alter database prepare to switchover to logical standby;
```

In the logical standby database, issue the following command:

```
alter database prepare to switchover to primary;
```

At this point, the logical standby database will begin transmitting its redo data to the current primary database and to the other standby databases in the configuration. The redo data from the logical standby database is sent but is not applied at this point.

In the primary database, you must now verify that the dictionary data was received from the logical standby database. The SWITCHOVER_STATUS column value in V$DATABASE must read TO LOGICAL STANDBY in the primary database before you can continue to the next step. When that status value is shown in the primary database, switch the primary database to the logical standby role:

```
alter database commit to switchover to logical standby;
```

You do not need to shut down and restart the old primary database. You should now go back to the original logical standby database and verify its SWITCHOVER_STATUS value in V$DATABASE (it should be TO PRIMARY). You can then complete the switchover; in the original logical standby database, issue the following command:

```
alter database commit to switchover to primary;
```

The original logical standby database is now the primary database. In the new logical standby database (the old primary database), start the redo apply process:

```
alter database start logical standby apply immediate;
```

The switchover is now complete.

Failovers

Failovers occur when the primary database can no longer be part of the primary database configuration. In the following section, you will see the steps required to fail over a physical standby database to the role of the primary database in a Data Guard configuration. In the subsequent section, you will see the steps required to fail over a logical standby database to the role of the primary database in a Data Guard configuration.

Failovers to Physical Standby Databases

In the standby database, you should first attempt to identify and resolve any gaps in the archived redo log files (see the section "Managing Gaps in Archive Log Sequences," earlier in this chapter). You may need to manually copy and register log files for use by the standby database.

Within the standby database, you must then finish the recovery process. If you have configured the standby database to have standby redo log files, the command to execute is

```
alter database recover managed standby database finish;
```

If there are no standby redo log files, execute the following command:

```
alter database recover managed standby database finish
    skip standby logfile;
```

Once the standby recovery operation has completed, you can perform the switchover using the following command:

```
alter database commit to switchover to primary;
```

Shut down and restart the new primary database to complete the transition. The old primary database is no longer a part of the Data Guard configuration. If you want to re-create the old primary database and use it as a standby database, you must create it as a standby database following the steps provided earlier in this chapter.

Failovers to Logical Standby Databases

In the standby database, you should first attempt to identify and resolve any gaps in the archived redo log files (see the section "Managing Gaps in Archive Log Sequences," earlier in this chapter). You may need to manually copy and register log files for use by the standby database. Query the DBA_LOGSTDBY_LOG view for details on the logs remaining to be applied. If the redo apply process was not active on the logical standby database, start it by using the following command:

```
alter database start logical standby apply nodelay finish;
```

Next, enable the remote locations for the redo log files that the logical standby database generates. You may need to update the logical standby database's settings of the LOG_ARCHIVE_DEST_STATE_*n* parameters so the other standby databases in the configuration will receive the redo generated from the original logical standby database. You can then activate the original logical standby database as the new primary database via the following command:

```
alter database activate logical standby database finish apply;
```

If there are other logical standby databases that are part of the Data Guard configuration, you may need to re-create them or use database links to add them to the new configuration. First, create a link in each of the databases that will act as a logical standby database to the new primary database. The ALTER SESSION DISABLE GUARD command allows you to bypass the Data Guard processes within your session. The database account used by the database link must have the SELECT_CATALOG_ROLE role:

```
alter session disable guard;
create database link salesofc
   connect to username identified by password using 'salesofc';
alter session enable guard;
```

You should verify the link by selecting from the DBA_LOGSTDBY_PARAMETERS view in the remote database (the new primary database).

In each logical standby database, you can now start the redo apply process based on the new primary database:

```
alter database start logical standby apply new primary salesofc;
```

Administering the Databases

In the following sections, you will see the steps required to perform standard maintenance actions on the databases that are part of the Data Guard configuration, including startup and shutdown operations.

Startup and Shutdown of Physical Standby Databases

When you start up a physical standby database, you should start the redo apply process. First, mount the database:

```
startup mount;
```

Next, start the redo apply process:

```
alter database recover managed standby database disconnect from session;
```

Use the USING CURRENT LOGFILE clause in place of the DISCONNECT FROM SESSION clause to start real-time apply.

To shut down the standby database, you should first stop the Log Apply Services. Query the V$MANAGED_STANDBY view; if Log Apply Services are listed there, cancel them using the following command:

```
alter database recover managed standby database cancel;
```

You can then shut down the database.

Opening Physical Standby Databases in Read-Only Mode

To make the physical standby database open for read operations, you should first cancel any log apply operations in the database:

```
alter database recover managed standby database cancel;
```

Next, open the database:

```
alter database open;
```

Managing Datafiles in Data Guard Environments

As noted earlier in this chapter, you should set the STANDBY_FILE_MANAGEMENT initialization parameter to AUTO. Setting this parameter simplifies the administration of the Data Guard environment, because files added to the primary environment can be automatically propagated to the physical standby databases. When this parameter is set to AUTO, any new datafiles created in the primary database are automatically created in the standby databases; when the parameter is set to MANUAL, you must manually create the new datafiles in the standby databases.

When STANDBY_FILE_MANAGEMENT is set to MANUAL, follow these steps to add a datafile to a tablespace:

1. Add the new datafile in the primary database.
2. Alter the datafile's tablespace so that it is offline.
3. Copy the datafile to the standby location.
4. Alter the datafile's tablespace so that it is once again online.

To add a new tablespace using manual file management, follow the same steps: Create the tablespace, take the tablespace offline, copy its datafiles to the standby location, and then alter the tablespace so it is online. If you are using automatic file management, you only need to create the new tablespace in the primary database for it to be propagated to the standby databases.

To drop a tablespace, simply drop it in the primary database and force a log switch via the ALTER SYSTEM SWITCH LOGFILE command. You can then drop the file at the operating system level in the primary and standby environments.

Changes to the names of datafiles are not propagated, even if you are using automatic file management. To rename a datafile in a Data Guard configuration, take the tablespace offline and rename the datafile at the operating system level on the primary server. Use the ALTER TABLESPACE RENAME DATAFILE command on the primary database to point to the new location of the datafile. Bring the tablespace back online with the ALTER TABLESPACE *tablespace_name* ONLINE command. On the standby database, query the V$ARCHIVED_LOG view to verify all logs have been applied and then shut down the redo apply services:

```
alter database recover managed standby database cancel;
```

Shut down the standby database and rename the file on the standby server. Next, use the STARTUP MOUNT command to mount the standby database. With the database mounted but not opened, use the ALTER DATABASE RENAME FILE command to point to the new file location on the standby server. Finally, restart the redo apply process:

```
alter database recover managed standby database
   disconnect from session;
```

Performing DDL on a Logical Standby Database

As illustrated earlier in this chapter, you can temporarily disable Data Guard within a logical standby database. When you need to perform DDL operations (such as the creation of new indexes to improve query performance), you will follow the same basic steps:

1. Stop the application of redo on the logical standby database.
2. Disable Data Guard.
3. Execute the DDL commands.
4. Enable Data Guard.
5. Restart the redo apply process.

For example, to create a new index, start by turning off the Data Guard features:

```
alter database stop logical standby apply; alter session disable guard;
```

At this point, you can perform your DDL operations. When you are done, reenable the Data Guard features:

```
alter session enable guard;
alter database start logical standby apply;
```

The logical standby database will then restart its redo apply process, while the index will be available to its query users.

Summary

Disasters happen. They can be physical disasters (data center fire, flood, and so forth) or logical disasters (dropped databases with no current backup). Even with a recent backup, a dropped database may take hours or days to restore and recover. Using Oracle Data Guard (and a suitable redo log file apply delay) you can be up and running in minutes instead of hours or days by having a standby database either in the same data center or on the other side of the world. While normal operations continue on the standby database, you can repair the original primary database and switch it back. A physical Data Guard destination matches the primary database bit for bit, including the physical layout of the tablespaces and datafiles.

If your standby needs are primarily as a read-only reporting database, then using a logical standby database fits the bill. The logical standby database need not have the same physical layout. In fact, the logical standby's layout may differ significantly in its role as a reporting database: You may have additional temporary tablespaces, for example, to support long-running reports with many queries having ORDER BY and GROUP BY clauses that require a big temporary tablespace. Regardless of the type of standby you need, Oracle Database 12*c* has a configuration to maintain and enhance your recoverability, scalability, and availability.

CHAPTER 16

Miscellaneous High Availability Features

In this chapter, you will see the implementation details for features that can significantly enhance the availability of your database applications. Some of these features, such as the LogMiner options, are enhancements of features available in earlier versions of Oracle. Others, such as the use of the recycle bin and the FLASHBACK DATABASE command, have been introduced in Oracle Database 10*g* and enhanced in Oracle Database 11*g* and 12*c*. Other Flashback options, such as Flashback Table and Flashback Query, which rely solely on undo data, were thoroughly covered in Chapter 7. In this chapter, you will see how to use the following features to enhance the availability of your database:

- Flashback Drop
- Flashback Database
- LogMiner
- Online object-reorganization options

Flashback Drop relies on a construct introduced in Oracle Database 10*g*, the recycle bin, which behaves much like the recycle bin on a Windows-based computer: if there is enough room in the tablespace, dropped objects can be restored to their original schema with all indexes and constraints intact. Flashback Database relies on data stored in the fast recovery area, a new storage area also introduced in Oracle Database 10*g*. LogMiner, available since Oracle9*i*, relies on archived redo log files to see the changes made to tables, indexes, and other database structures (DDL operations) over time.

Recovering Dropped Tables Using Flashback Drop

When you drop a table (and its associated indexes, constraints, and nested tables), Oracle does not immediately release the table's disk space for use by other objects in the tablespace. Instead, the objects are retained in the recycle bin until purged by the owner or the space occupied by the dropped objects is needed for new objects.

TIP
To leverage the features of the recycle bin, you must set the initialization parameter RECYCLEBIN to ON.

In this example, consider the AUTHOR table, defined as follows:

```
SQL> describe author

Name                     Null?    Type
------------------------ -------- ----------------------------
AUTHORNAME               NOT NULL VARCHAR2(50)
COMMENTS                          VARCHAR2(100)
```

Now, assume that the table is dropped accidentally. This can happen when a user with privileges on a table that exists in multiple environments intends to drop a table in a development environment but is pointing to the production database when the command is executed.

```
SQL> drop table author cascade constraints;

Table dropped.
```

How can the table be recovered? As of Oracle Database 10*g*, a dropped table does not fully disappear. Its blocks are still maintained in its tablespace, and it still counts against your space quota. You can see the dropped objects by querying the RECYCLEBIN data dictionary view. Note that the format for the OBJECT_NAME column may differ between versions:

```
SQL> select object_name, original_name, operation, type, user,
  2  can_undrop, space from recyclebin;

OBJECT_NAME                   ORIGINAL_NAME        OPERATION
----------------------------- -------------------- ---------
TYPE                      USER                          CAN_UNDROP      SPACE
------------------------- ------------------------------ ---------- ----------
BIN$AWo20R+6ce3gU8pnCAoT4Q==$0 SYS_C0010718         DROP
INDEX                     RJB                            NO                  8

BIN$AWo20R+7ce3gU8pnCAoT4Q==$0 AUTHOR               DROP
TABLE                     RJB                            YES                 8


SQL>
```

RECYCLEBIN is a public synonym for the USER_RECYCLEBIN data dictionary view, showing the recycle bin entries for the current user. DBAs can see all dropped objects via the DBA_RECYCLEBIN data dictionary view.

NOTE
As of Oracle Database 12c release 1 (12.1.0.2), the recycle bins are local to the root container and each pluggable database and do not have a CON_ID column. This makes sense, because the tablespaces that are shared across all containers, such as SYSTEM, UNDO, and optionally TEMP, do not support the recycle bin even in a non-CDB environment.

As shown in the preceding listing, a user has dropped the AUTHOR table and its associated primary key index. Although they have been dropped, they are still available for flashback. The index cannot be recovered by itself (its CAN_UNDROP column value is NO, while the AUTHOR table's CAN_UNDROP value is YES).

You can use the FLASHBACK TABLE TO BEFORE DROP command to recover the table from the recycle bin:

```
SQL> flashback table author to before drop;

Flashback complete.
```

The table has been restored, along with its rows, indexes, and statistics.

What happens if you drop the AUTHOR table, re-create it, and then drop it again? The recycle bin will contain both of the tables. Each entry in the recycle bin will be identified via its SCN and the timestamp for the drop.

NOTE
The FLASHBACK TABLE TO BEFORE DROP command does not recover referential constraints.

To purge old entries from the recycle bin, use the PURGE command. You can purge all your dropped objects, all dropped objects in the database (if you are a DBA), all objects in a specific tablespace, or all objects for a particular user in a specific tablespace. You can use the RENAME TO clause of the FLASHBACK TABLE command to rename the table as you flash it back.

By default, the recycle bin is enabled in Oracle Database 12*c*. You can use the initialization parameter RECYCLEBIN to turn the recycle bin on and off; you can also turn the recycle bin on and off at the session level, as in this example:

```
alter session set recyclebin = off;
```

Temporarily disabling the recycle bin functionality does not affect objects currently in the recycle bin; even when the recycle bin is disabled, you can still recover objects currently in the recycle bin. Only objects dropped while the recycle bin is disabled cannot be recovered.

The Flashback Database Command

The FLASHBACK DATABASE command returns the database to a past time or SCN, providing a fast alternative to performing incomplete database recovery. Following a FLASHBACK DATABASE operation, in order to have write access to the flashed-back database, you must reopen it with an ALTER DATABASE OPEN RESETLOGS command. You must have the SYSDBA system privilege in order to use the FLASHBACK DATABASE command.

NOTE
The database must have been put in FLASHBACK mode with an ALTER DATABASE FLASHBACK ON command. The database must be mounted in exclusive mode but not open when that command is executed.

The syntax for the FLASHBACK DATABASE command is as follows:

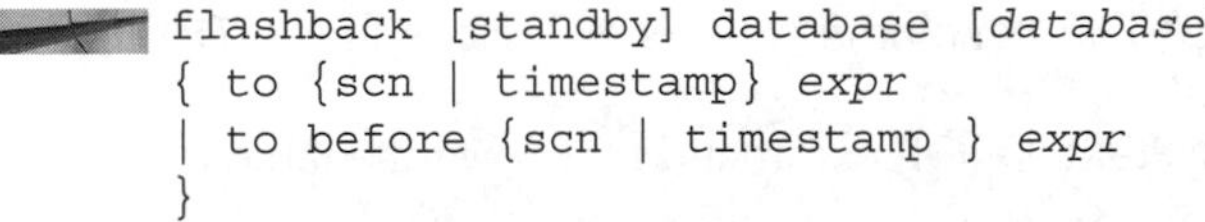

```
flashback [standby] database [database]
{ to {scn | timestamp} expr
| to before {scn | timestamp } expr
}
```

You can use either the TO SCN or TO TIMESTAMP clause to set the point to which the entire database should be flashed back. You can flash back TO BEFORE a critical point (such as a transaction that produced an unintended consequence for multiple tables). Use the ORA_ROWSCN pseudo-column to see the SCNs of the most recent row transactions.

If you have not already done so, you will need to shut down your database and enable flashback during the startup process using this sequence of commands:

```
startup mount;
alter database archivelog;
alter database flashback on;
alter database open;
```

NOTE
In a multitenant environment, you cannot flash back just a single PDB. The FLASHBACK DATABASE operation applies to the entire CDB (including the root container and all PDBs).

Two initialization parameter settings control how much flashback data is retained in the database. The DB_FLASHBACK_RETENTION_TARGET initialization parameter sets the upper limit (in minutes) for how far back in time the database can be flashed back. The DB_RECOVERY_FILE_DEST initialization parameter sets the size of the fast recovery area (see Chapter 13 for more information on setting up the fast recovery area). Note that the FLASHBACK TABLE command uses data already stored in the undo tablespace (it does not create additional entries), whereas the FLASHBACK DATABASE command relies on flashback logs stored in the fast recovery area.

You can determine how far back you can flash back the database by querying the V$FLASHBACK_DATABASE_LOG view. The amount of flashback data retained in the database is controlled by the initialization parameter and the size of the fast recovery area. The following listing shows the available columns in V$FLASHBACK_DATABASE_LOG and sample contents:

```
SQL> describe v$flashback_database_log

Name                                      Null?    Type
----------------------------------------- -------- -------
OLDEST_FLASHBACK_SCN                               NUMBER
OLDEST_FLASHBACK_TIME                              DATE
RETENTION_TARGET                                   NUMBER
FLASHBACK_SIZE                                     NUMBER
ESTIMATED_FLASHBACK_SIZE                           NUMBER
CON_ID                                             NUMBER

SQL> select * from v$flashback_database_log;

OLDEST_FLASHBACK_SCN OLDEST_FL RETENTION_TARGET FLASHBACK_SIZE
-------------------- --------- ---------------- --------------
ESTIMATED_FLASHBACK_SIZE     CON_ID
------------------------ ----------
             2977530 24-AUG-14             1440      104857600
                       0          0
```

You can verify the database's flashback status by querying V$DATABASE; the FLASHBACK_ON column will have a value of YES if the flashback has been enabled for the database:

```
SQL> select current_scn, flashback_on from v$database;

CURRENT_SCN FLASHBACK_ON
----------- ------------------
    2979255 YES
```

With the database open for over an hour, verify that the flashback data is available and then flash it back—you will lose all transactions that occurred during that time:

```
shutdown;
startup mount;
flashback database to timestamp sysdate-1/24;
```

Note that the FLASHBACK DATABASE command requires that the database be mounted in exclusive mode, which will affect its participation in any RAC clusters (see Chapter 12).

When you execute the FLASHBACK DATABASE command, Oracle checks to make sure all required archived and online redo log files are available. If the logs are available, the online datafiles are reverted to the time or SCN specified.

If there is not enough data online in the archive logs and the flashback area, you will need to use traditional database recovery methods to recover the data. For example, you may need to use a file system recovery method or a recent full RMAN backup followed by rolling the data forward.

Once the flashback has completed, you must open the database using the RESETLOGS option in order to have write access to the database:

```
alter database open resetlogs;
```

To turn off the Flashback Database option, execute the ALTER DATABASE FLASHBACK OFF command when the database is mounted but not open:

```
startup mount;
alter database flashback off;
alter database open;
```

You can use the Flashback options to perform an array of actions, including recovering old data, reverting a table to its earlier state, maintaining a history of changes on a row basis, and quickly restoring an entire database. All these actions are greatly simplified if the database has been configured to support Automatic Undo Management (AUM). Also, note that the FLASHBACK DATABASE command requires the modification of the database status. Although these requirements can present additional burdens to DBAs, the benefits involved in terms of the number of recoveries required and the speed with which those recoveries can be completed may be dramatic.

Using LogMiner

Oracle uses online redo log files to track every change that is made to user data and the data dictionary. The information stored in the redo log files is used to re-create the database, in part or in full, during recovery. To enable recovery of the database to a point in time after the database backup was made, you can maintain archived copies of the redo log files. The LogMiner utility provides a vital view into the modifications that have occurred within your database.

When you use LogMiner, you see both the changes that have been made (the SQL_*redo* column) and the SQL you can use to reverse those changes (the SQL_*undo* column). Thus, you can review the history of the database, without actually applying any redo logs, and obtain the code to reverse any problematic transactions. Using LogMiner, you can pinpoint the transaction under which corruption first occurred so that you can determine the correct point in time or System Change Number (SCN) to use as the endpoint for a database recovery.

If there were a small number of transactions that required rolling back, prior to LogMiner, you would have to restore the table to an earlier state (either using Flashback Table or recovering a single table using RMAN backups) and apply archived log files to bring the table forward to just before the corruption. When restoring the table and applying the archived log files, you would risk losing later transactions that you would like to retain. You can now use LogMiner to roll back only the transactions that are problematic without losing later, valid transactions.

LogMiner in its original form has had some limitations associated with its use. With the original approach, you could only review one log file at a time, and the interface to the tool was cumbersome to use. LogMiner includes a viewer for use with Oracle Cloud Control 12*c*. Both the manual approach to using LogMiner and the EM Cloud Control LogMiner Viewer are presented within this section.

How LogMiner Works

To run the LogMiner utility, you must have the EXECUTE privilege on the DMBS_LOGMNR package, the EXECUTE_CATALOG_ROLE role, the SELECT ANY DICTIONARY system privilege, and the SELECT ANY TRANSACTION system privilege. LogMiner requires a data dictionary to fully translate the redo log file contents and translate internal object identifiers and datatypes to object names and external data formats. If a data dictionary is not available, LogMiner will return the data in hex format and the object information as internal object IDs.

You have three choices for obtaining a data dictionary for LogMiner use:

- Extract the data dictionary information to a flat file.
- Extract the data dictionary to redo log files.
- Use the online data dictionary from the current database.

The LogMiner analysis usually requires that the data dictionary in use was generated from the same database that generated the redo log files. However, if you are using a flat file format or are using the data dictionary from redo log files, you can analyze the redo log files either from the database on which LogMiner is running or from another database. If, however, you are using the online catalog from the current database, you can only analyze redo log files from the current database.

Since you can run LogMiner from one database against the redo log files in another database, the character sets used on both databases must match. The hardware platform must also match the one used when the redo log files were generated.

Extracting the Data Dictionary

One potential problem with extracting the data dictionary to a flat file is that while you are extracting the data dictionary, someone else could be issuing DDL statements. Therefore, the extracted data dictionary could be out of sync with the database. When you use a flat file to store the data dictionary, fewer system resources are required than when you use redo log files.

When you extract the data dictionary to redo log files, no DDL statements can be processed during the time in which the data dictionary is extracted. Therefore, the dictionary will be in sync with the database; the extraction is more resource intensive, but the extraction process is faster.

To extract the data dictionary to either a flat file or to redo log files, you use the procedure DBMS_LOGMNR_D.BUILD. The data dictionary file is placed in a directory. Therefore, you must have write permission for the directory in which the file will be placed. To define the location of the directory, use the initialization parameter UTL_FILE_DIR. For example, to specify the location

/u01/app/ora_mine as the location for the LogMiner output, run the following command and restart the database:

```
alter system set UTL_FILE_DIR='/u01/app/ora_mine/dict' scope=spfile;
```

To execute the DBMS_LOGMNR_D.BUILD procedure, you must specify a filename for the dictionary, the directory pathname for the file, and whether you want the dictionary written to a flat file or redo log files. To extract the data dictionary to a flat file located in the directory **/u01/app/ora_mine/dict** with the filename **mydb_dictionary.ora**, you issue the following command:

```
begin
   dbms_logmnr_d.build
   (
    dictionary_filename => 'mydb_dictionary.ora',
    dictionary_location => '/u01/app/ora_mine/dict',
    options => dbms_logmnr_d.store_in_flat_file
   );
end;
/
```

Once you have the dictionary stored in a flat file, you can copy it to another platform to run LogMiner. You may need to run **dbmslmd.sql** on the other database to establish the correct environment. The **dbmslmd.sql** file can be found in the **$ORACLE_HOME/rdbms/admin** directory on a Linux system.

You can use DBMS_LOGMNR_D.STORE_IN_REDO_LOGS as the other option, which is more common if you're analyzing logs generated on the same database:

```
begin
   dbms_logmnr_d.build
   (
       options => dbms_logmnr_d.store_in_redo_logs
   );
end;
/
```

Analyzing One or More Redo Log Files

To analyze redo log files using LogMiner, follow these steps:

1. Start the LogMiner utility using the DBMS_LOGMNR.START_LOGMNR procedure. You can specify which redo log files to use when starting LogMiner by specifying the first log to use.
2. Query V$LOGMNR_CONTENTS to see the results.
3. Once you have finished viewing the redo logs, use DBMS_LOGMNR.END_LOGMNR to end the session:

   ```
   execute dbms_logmnr.end_logmnr;
   ```

The available subprograms for the DBMS_LOGMNR package are described in Table 16-1. Table 16-2 shows the parameters for the START_LOGMNR procedure.

Subprogram	Description
ADD_LOGFILE	Adds a file to the list of archive files to process.
START_LOGMNR	Initializes the LogMiner utility.
END_LOGMNR	Completes and ends a LogMiner session.
MINE_VALUE (*function*)	Returns the undo or redo column value of the column name specified by the COLUMN_NAME parameter for any row returned from V$LOGMNR_CONTENT.
COLUMN_PRESENT (*function*)	Determines if undo or redo column values exist for the column name specified by the COLUMN_NAME parameter for any row returned from V$LOGMNR_CONTENT.
REMOVE_LOGFILE	Removes a log file from the list of log files to be processed by LogMiner.

TABLE 16-1. *DBMS_LOGMNR Subprograms*

Options	Description
COMMITTED_DATA_ONLY	Only DMLs corresponding to committed transactions are returned if this option is set.
SKIP_CORRUPTION	Skips any corruption encountered in the redo log file during a select from V$LOGMNR_CONTENTS. This option works only if a block in the actual redo log file is corrupted and does not work if the corruption is in the header block.
DDL_DICT_TRACKING	Enables LogMiner to update the internal data dictionary if a DDL event occurs, to ensure that SQL_REDO and SQL_UNDO information is maintained and correct.
DICT_FROM_ONLINE_CATALOG	Instructs LogMiner to use the online data dictionary instead of a flat file or redo log file stored dictionary.
DICT_FROM_REDO_LOGS	Instructs LogMiner to use the data dictionary stored in one or more redo log files.
NO_SQL_DELIMITER	Instructs LogMiner not to place the SQL delimiter (;) at the end of reconstructed SQL statements.
NO_ROWID_IN_STMT	Instructs LogMiner not to include the ROWID clause in the reconstructed SQL statements.
PRINT_PRETTY_SQL	Instructs LogMiner to format the reconstructed SQL for ease of reading.
CONTINUOUS_MINE	Instructs LogMiner to automatically add redo log files to find the data of interest. Specify the starting SCN, date, or the first log to mine. LogMiner must be connected to the same database instance that is generating the redo log files.

TABLE 16-2. *Values for the START_LOGMNR Options*

To create a list of the redo log files that are available for analysis, you run the procedure DBMS_LOGMNR.ADD_LOGFILE with the NEW option as follows; this example uses a Linux file system:

```
begin
   dbms_logmnr.add_logfile
   (
    logfilename =>
      '+RECO/test12c/archivelog/2014_08_24/thread_1_seq_143.2005.856470967',
    options => dbms_logmnr.new
   );
   dbms_logmnr.start_logmnr
   (
    options =>
       dbms_logmnr.dict_from_online_catalog +
       dbms_logmnr.continuous_mine
   );
end;
/
```

After you've told LogMiner the location of the data dictionary and added the first redo log file, you can begin analyzing the redo log files using the DBMS_LOGMNR.START_LOGMNR package:

```
begin
   dbms_logmnr.start_logmnr
   (
    options =>
       dbms_logmnr.dict_from_online_catalog +
       dbms_logmnr.continuous_mine
   );
end;
/
```

If you do not enter start and end times or a range of SCN numbers, the entire file is read for every SELECT statement that you issue. To look at the redo and undo code, you select the SQL_REDO and SQL_UNDO columns as follows:

```
select sql_redo, sql_undo
from v$logmnr_contents;
```

Be sure to turn off LogMiner when you're done:

```
execute dbms_logmnr.end_logmnr;
```

Until Oracle Database 11*g*, a DBA had to use the Java-based LogMiner console, which was difficult to install and not completely integrated with Oracle Enterprise Manager Database Control (the predecessor to EM Cloud Control). This integration further enhances ease of use by integrating a task-based log mining operation with Flashback Transaction. Figure 16-1 shows the OEM interface for LogMiner.

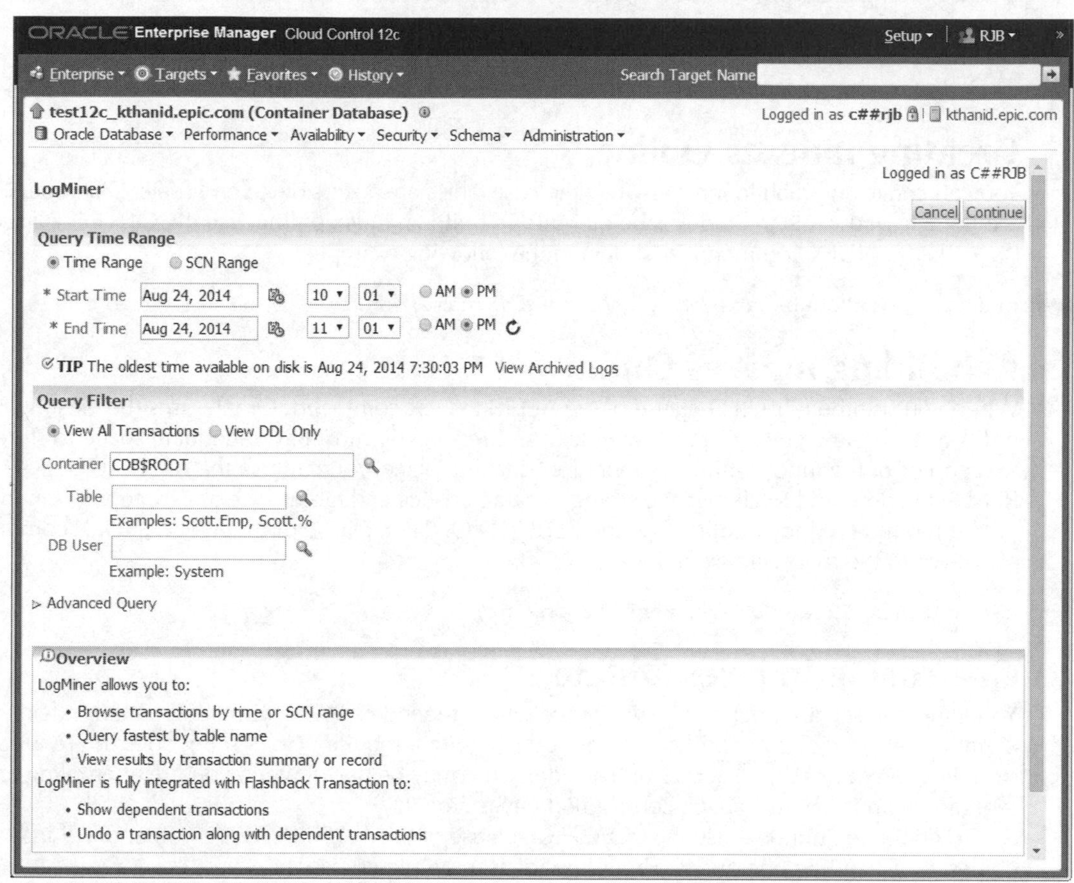

FIGURE 16-1. *OEM LogMiner and Flashback Transaction interface*

Online Object Reorganization

You can reorganize many database objects online. Options include the following:

- Creating indexes online
- Rebuilding indexes online
- Coalescing indexes online
- Rebuilding index-organized tables online

- Using the DBMS_REDEFINITION package to redefine a table online
- Moving a datafile online

In the following sections, you will see examples of each of these operations.

Creating Indexes Online

You can create and rebuild indexes while the base tables are accessible to end users. DDL operations are not allowed while the index is being built. To build an index online, use the ONLINE clause of the CREATE INDEX command, as shown in the following example:

```
create index auth$name on author (authorname) online;
```

Rebuilding Indexes Online

When you use the REBUILD clause of the ALTER INDEX command, Oracle uses the existing index as the data source for the new index. As a result, you must have adequate space to store two copies of the index while the operation is taking place. You can use the ALTER INDEX REBUILD command to change the storage characteristics and tablespace assignment for an index.

To rebuild the index online, use the REBUILD ONLINE clause of the ALTER INDEX command, as shown in the following example:

```
alter index ix_auth$name rebuild online;
```

Coalescing Indexes Online

You can coalesce an index to reclaim space within the index. When you coalesce an index, you cannot move it to another tablespace (as you can with a rebuild). Coalescing does not require storage space for multiple copies of the index, so it may be useful when you are attempting to reorganize an index in a space-constrained environment.

To coalesce an index, use the COALESCE clause of the ALTER INDEX command. All index coalesces are online operations. The following is a sample coalesce:

```
alter index auth$name coalesce;
```

Rebuilding Index-Organized Tables Online

You can use the ALTER TABLE . . . MOVE ONLINE command to rebuild an index-organized table (IOT) online. The overflow data segment, if present, is rebuilt if you specify the OVERFLOW keyword. For example, if the BOOKSHELF table is an index-organized table, you can rebuild it online via the following command:

```
alter table bookshelf move online;
```

When using this command, you cannot perform parallel DML. Also, the MOVE ONLINE option is only available for nonpartitioned index-organized tables.

Redefining Tables Online

You can change a table's definition while it is accessible by the application users. For example, you can partition a previously nonpartitioned table while it is being used—a significant capability for high-availability OLTP applications.

As of Oracle Database 11*g*, there are very few restrictions on what types of tables cannot be redefined online. Here are the key restrictions:

- After redefining a table with materialized view logs, the dependent materialized views must be refreshed with a complete refresh.
- The overflow table of an IOT must be redefined at the same time as the base IOT.
- Tables with fine-grained access control cannot be redefined online.
- Tables with BFILE columns cannot be redefined online.
- Tables with LONG and LONG RAW columns can be redefined, but the LONG and LONG RAW columns must be converted to CLOBs and BLOBs.
- Tables in the SYS and SYSTEM schemas cannot be redefined online.
- Temporary tables cannot be redefined online.

The following example shows the steps involved in redefining a table online. First, verify that the table can be redefined. For this example, the CUSTOMER table will be created in the SCOTT schema and then redefined:

```
create table customer
(name     varchar2(25) primary key,
 street   varchar2(50),
 city     varchar2(25),
 state    char(2),
 zip      number);
```

Next, verify that the table can be redefined by executing the CAN_REDEF_TABLE procedure of the DBMS_REDEFINITION package. Its input parameters are the username and the table name:

```
execute dbms_redefinition.can_redef_table('SCOTT','CUSTOMER');
```

The table is a candidate for online redefinition if the procedure returns the message

```
PL/SQL procedure successfully completed.
```

If it returns an error, the table cannot be redefined online, and the error message will give the reason.

Next, create an interim table, in the same schema, with the desired attributes of the redefined table. For example, we can partition the CUSTOMER table (to simplify this example, the TABLESPACE and STORAGE clauses for the partitions are not shown):

```
create table customer_interim
(name      varchar2(25) primary key,
 street    varchar2(50),
 city      varchar2(25),
 state     char(2),
 zip       number)
partition by range (name)
 (partition part1  values less than ('l'),
  partition part2  values less than (maxvalue))
;
```

You can now execute the START_REDEF_TABLE procedure of the DBMS_REDEFINITION package to start the redefinition process. Its input variables are the schema owner, the table to be redefined, the interim table name, and the column mapping (similar to the list of column names in a select query). If no column mapping is supplied, all the column names and definitions in the original table and the interim table must be the same.

```
execute dbms_redefinition.start_redef_table -
  ('SCOTT','CUSTOMER','CUSTOMER_INTERIM');
```

Next, create any triggers, indexes, grants, or constraints required on the interim table. In this example, the primary key has already been defined on CUSTOMER_INTERIM; you could add the foreign keys, secondary indexes, and grants at this point in the redefinition process. Create the foreign keys disabled until the redefinition process is complete.

NOTE

To avoid that manual step, you can use the COPY_TABLE_DEPENDENTS procedure to create all dependent objects on the interim table. Dependent objects supported via this method include triggers, indexes, grants, and constraints.

When the redefinition process completes, the indexes, triggers, constraints, and grants on the interim table will replace those on the original table. The disabled referential constraints on the interim table will be enabled at that point.

To finish the redefinition, execute the FINISH_REDEF_TABLE procedure of the DBMS_REDEFINITION package. Its input parameters are the schema name, original table name, and interim table name:

```
execute dbms_redefinition.finish_redef_table -
   ('SCOTT','CUSTOMER','CUSTOMER_INTERIM');
```

You can verify the redefinition by querying the table:

```
select table_name, high_value
from dba_tab_partitions
where table_owner = 'SCOTT';

TABLE_NAME                     HIGH_VALUE
------------------------------ ----------
CUSTOMER2                      '1'
CUSTOMER2                      MAXVALUE
```

To abort the process after executing the START_REDEF_TABLE procedure, execute the ABORT_REDEF_TABLE procedure (the input parameters are the schema, original table name, and interim table name).

Moving a Datafile Online

As of Oracle Database 12*c*, you can move a datafile while it's online. You might do this for a number of reasons:

- Migrating all datafiles to new storage

- Relocating infrequently used tablespaces to lower-cost or slower storage
- Moving read-only datafiles to optical media
- Moving datafiles into ASM storage from file system storage

Regardless of the reason, you want to keep your database as available as possible to users who have no idea that one or more datafiles in a tablespace are being moved. Here is an example of moving a datafile to an ASM diskgroup from a file system directory:

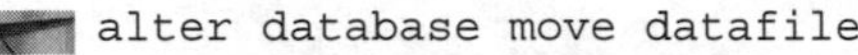

```
alter database move datafile
   '/u02/oradata/dw2010.dbf' to
   '+data12c/test12c/datafile/dw2010.imp';
```

When performing a move operation, ensure that there is enough space for a copy of the datafile at the destination location, because the source file must remain available until the operation is complete.

Summary

Many features of Oracle Database aid in maximizing ease of maintenance, availability, and recoverability. Some of the Flashback features of Oracle Database 12*c* fall into all three categories.

If you routinely have extra disk space available in each tablespace, then enable the recycle bin so that you can recover objects that were inadvertently dropped by a user, without having to resort to a more costly and time-consuming recovery effort.

Similarly, if you have set aside part of your fast recovery area for incremental changes to your database, then you can use Flashback Database to rewind the entire database to a point in time in the very recent past. This operation will typically be a fraction of the time required when using the only methods available in previous versions of the database, such as performing a full database restore operation and then recovering to a point in time right before the logical corruptions occurred.

Log Miner is a more precise tool—more like a scalpel than a hatchet—and if you have ARCHIVELOG mode enabled, you can query the archived redo log files to find out who made what changes and when. Having identified the changes, you can use Log Miner to extract the DML and DDL commands needed to reverse a very narrow set of changes while maintaining the logical consistency of the database.

Every version of Oracle Database brings new features that enable or enhance high availability. Oracle Database 12*c* is no exception. Creating or rebuilding tables and indexes, in addition to moving an entire datafile, can happen online with no downtime and minimal impact to online users.

PART IV

Networked Oracle

CHAPTER 17

Oracle Net

Distributing computing power across servers and sharing information across networks greatly enhances the value of the computing resources available. Instead of being a stand-alone server, the server becomes an entry point for intranets, the Internet, and associated websites.

Oracle's networking tool, Oracle Net Services (Oracle Net), can be used to connect to distributed databases. Oracle Net facilitates the sharing of data between databases, even if those databases are on different types of servers running different operating systems and communications protocols. It also allows for client/server applications to be created; the server can then function primarily for database I/O while the application can be fielded to a middle-tier application server. Also, the data presentation requirements of an application can be moved to front-end client machines. In this chapter, you will see how to configure, administer, and tune Oracle Net.

The installation and configuration instructions for Oracle Net depend on the particular hardware, operating system, and communications software you are using. The material provided here will help you get the most out of your database networking, regardless of your configuration.

Overview of Oracle Net

Using Oracle Net distributes the workload associated with database applications. Because many database queries are performed via applications, a server-based application forces the server to support both the CPU requirements of the application and the I/O requirements of the database (see Figure 17-1*a*). Using a client/server configuration (also referred to as a *two-tier architecture*) allows this load to be distributed between two machines. The first, called the *client,* supports the application that initiates the request from the database. The back-end machine on which the database resides is called the *server*. The client bears the burden of presenting the data, whereas the database server is dedicated to supporting queries, not applications. This distribution of resource requirements is shown in Figure 17-1*b*.

When the client sends a database request to the server, the server receives and executes the SQL statement that is passed to it. The results of the SQL statement, plus any error conditions that are returned, are then sent back to the client. Because of the client resources required, the client/server configuration sometimes is dubbed *fat-client architecture*. Although workstation costs have dropped appreciably over recent years, the cost impact to a company can still be substantial.

The more common, cost-effective architecture used with Oracle Net is a *thin-client* configuration (also referred to as a *three-tier architecture*). The application code is housed and executed using Java applets on a separate server from the database server. The client resource requirements become very low, and the cost is reduced dramatically. The application code becomes isolated from the database. Figure 17-2 shows the thin-client configuration.

The client connects to the application server. Once the client is validated, display management code is downloaded to the client in the form of Java applets. A database request is sent from the client through the application server to the database server; the database server then receives and executes the SQL statement that is passed to it. The results of the SQL statement, plus any error conditions that are returned, are then sent back to the client through the application server. In some versions of the three-tier architecture, some of the application processing is performed on the application server and the rest is performed on the database server. The advantage of a thin-client architecture is that you have low resource requirements and maintenance on the client side, medium resource requirements and central maintenance on the application server, and high resource but lower maintenance requirements on one or more back-end database servers.

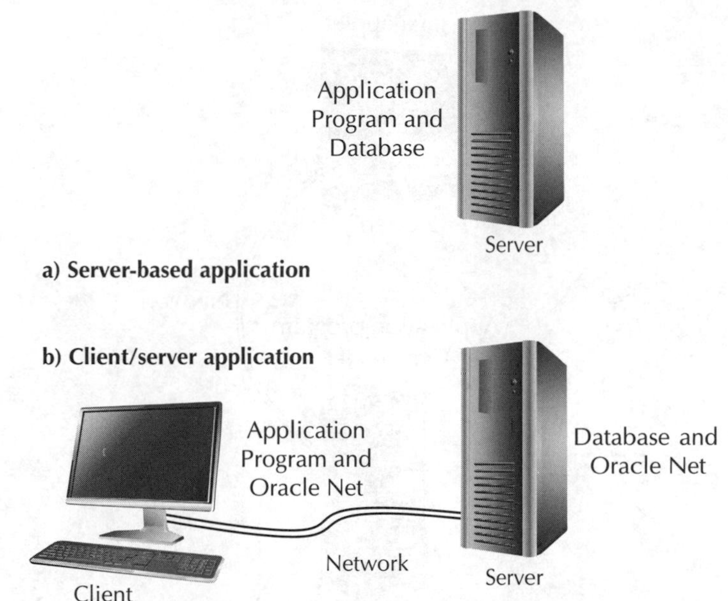

FIGURE 17-1. *Client/server architecture*

In addition to client/server and thin-client implementations, *server/server* configurations are often needed. In this type of environment, databases on separate servers share data with each other. You can then physically isolate each server from every other server without logically isolating the servers. A typical implementation of this type involves corporate headquarters' servers that communicate with departmental servers in various locations. Each server supports client applications, but it also has the ability to communicate with other servers in the network. This architecture is shown in Figure 17-3.

When one of the servers sends a database request to another server, the sending server acts like a client. The receiving server executes the SQL statement passed to it and returns the results plus error conditions to the sender.

When run on the clients and the servers, Oracle Net allows database requests made from one database (or application) to be passed to another database on a separate server. In most cases, machines can function both as clients and as servers; the only exceptions are operating systems with single-user architectures, such as network appliances. In such cases, those machines can only function as clients.

The end result of an Oracle Net implementation is the ability to communicate with all databases that are accessible via the network. You can then create synonyms that give applications true network transparency: The user who submits the query will not know the location of the data that is used to resolve it. In this chapter, you will see the main configuration methods and files used to manage inter-database communications, along with usage examples. You will see more detailed examples of distributed database management in Chapter 18.

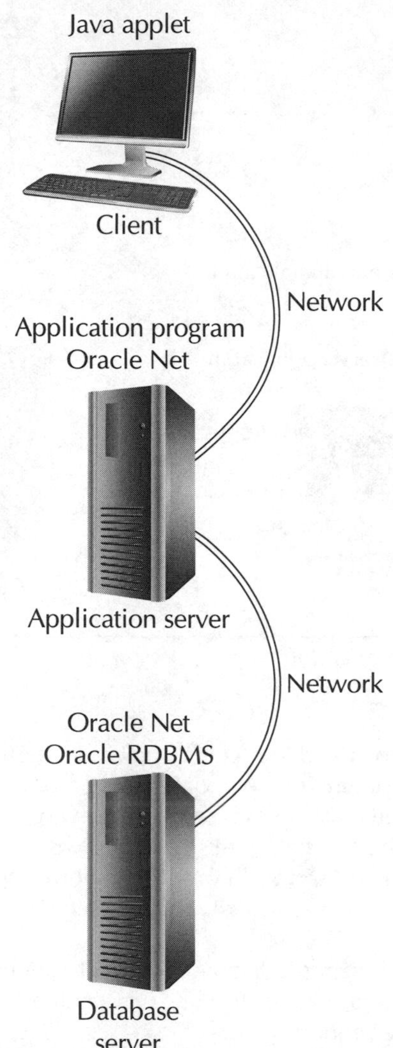

FIGURE 17-2. *Thin-client architecture*

Each object in a database is uniquely identified by its owner and name. For example, there will only be one table named EMPLOYEE owned by the user HR; there cannot be two tables of the same name and type within the same schema.

Within distributed databases, two additional layers of object identification must be added. First, the name of the instance that accesses the database must be identified. Next, the name of the server on which that instance resides must be identified. Putting together these four parts of the object's name—its server, its instance, its owner, and its name—results in a *global object name*.

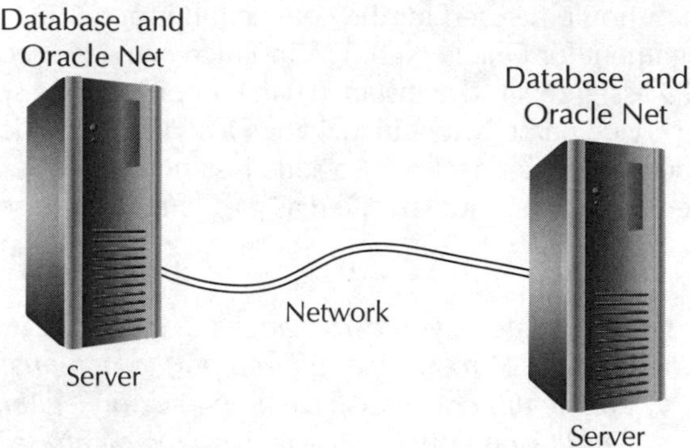

FIGURE 17-3. *Server/server architecture*

In order to access a remote table, you must know the table's global object name. DBAs and application administrators can set up access paths to automate the selection of all four parts of the global object name. In the following sections, you will see how to set up the access paths used by Oracle Net.

The foundation of Oracle Net is the Transparent Network Substrate (TNS), which resolves all server-level connectivity issues. Oracle Net relies on configuration files on the client and the server to manage the database connectivity. If the client and server use different communications protocols, the Oracle Connection Manager (described in a later section of this chapter) manages the connections. The combination of the Oracle Connection Manager and the TNS allows Oracle Net connections to be made independent of the operating system and communications protocol run by each server. Oracle Net also has the capability to send and receive data requests in an asynchronous manner; this allows it to support the shared server architecture.

Connect Descriptors

The server and instance portions of an object's global object name in Oracle Net are identified by means of a *connect descriptor.* A connect descriptor specifies the communications protocol, the server name, and the instance's service name to use when performing the query. Because of the protocol-independence of Oracle Net, the descriptor also includes hardware connectivity information. The generic format for an Oracle Net connect descriptor is shown in the following example, which uses the TCP/IP protocol and specifies a connection to an instance whose service name is LOC on a server named HQ (note that the keywords are protocol specific):

```
(DESCRIPTION=
   (ADDRESS=
      (PROTOCOL=TCP)
      (HOST=HQ)
      (PORT=1521))
   (CONNECT DATA=
      (SERVICE_NAME=LOC)))
```

In this connect descriptor, the protocol is set to TCP/IP, the server (HOST) is set to HQ, and the port on that host that should be used for the connection is port 1521 (which is the Oracle default registered port assignment for Oracle Net). The instance name is specified in a separate part of the descriptor as the SID assignment. The instance name or SID can be specified, but neither is required when the service name is specified. When a service name is specified, an instance name is only needed if you want to connect to a specific instance in a RAC database. The SID parameter is used when the service name is not specified as part of the database initialization parameters.

TIP
As part of your security strategy, you can change the default port for the Oracle listener from 1521 to another unused port to potentially thwart hackers. Changing this port may have no impact on legitimate database users, depending on how they connect to the database.

The structure for this descriptor is consistent across all protocols. Also, the descriptors can be automatically generated via the Net Configuration Assistant. As previously noted, the keywords used by the connect descriptors are protocol specific. The keywords to use and the values to give them are provided in the operating system–specific documentation for Oracle Net.

Net Service Names

Users are not expected to type in a connect descriptor each time they want to access remote data. Instead, the DBA can set up *net service names* (or *aliases*), which refer to these connect descriptors. Service names are stored in a file called **tnsnames.ora**. This file should be copied to all servers on the database network. Every client and application server should have a copy of this file as well.

On the server, the **tnsnames.ora** file should be located in the directory specified by the TNS_ADMIN environment variable. The file is usually stored in a common directory, such as the **$ORACLE_HOME/network/admin** directory on Unix or Linux systems. For a Windows server or client, this would be in the **\network\admin** subdirectory under your Oracle software home directory.

A sample entry in the **tnsnames.ora** file is shown in the following listing. This example assigns a net service name of LOC to the connect descriptor with the same name given earlier:

```
LOC=(DESCRIPTION=
    (ADDRESS=
       (PROTOCOL=TCP)
       (HOST=HQ)
       (PORT=1521))
    (CONNECT DATA=
       (SERVICE_NAME=LOC)))
```

A user wishing to connect to the LOC instance on the HQ server can now use the LOC net service name, as shown in this example:

```
sqlplus hr/hr@loc;
```

The "@" tells the database to use the net service name that follows it to determine which database to log into. If the username and password are correct for that database, a session is opened there and the user can begin using the database.

Net service names create aliases for connect descriptors, so you do not need to give the net service name the same name as the instance. For example, you could give the LOC instance the service name PROD or TEST, depending on its use within your environment. The use of synonyms to further enhance location transparency will be described in the section "Using Database Links" later in this chapter.

Replacing tnsnames.ora with Oracle Internet Directory

A *directory* is a specialized electronic database in which you store information about one or more objects. Your e-mail address book is an example of a directory. Within each of your e-mail address entries is information about the contact's name, e-mail address, home and business addresses, and so on. You can use the address book to locate a specific person with whom you want to correspond.

Oracle provides an electronic database tool called the Oracle Internet Directory (OID) for use in resolving user, server, and database locations as well as password and other important information storage. To support the deployment and maintenance of thousands of clients, the emphasis has moved from supporting many separate **tnsnames.ora** files on distributed machines to supporting one or more directories on centralized machines. See the section "Directory Naming with Oracle Internet Directory," later in this chapter, for more information about OID.

Listeners

Each database server on the network must contain a **listener.ora** file. The **listener.ora** file lists the names and addresses of all the listener processes on the machine and the instances they support. Listener processes receive connections from Oracle Net clients.

A **listener.ora** file has four parts:

- Header section
- Protocol address list
- Instance definitions
- Operational parameters

The **listener.ora** file is automatically generated by the Oracle Net Configuration Assistant tool (**netca** on Linux). You can edit the resultant file as long as you follow its syntax rules. The following listing shows sample sections of a **listener.ora** file—an address definition and an instance definition:

```
LISTENER =
 (ADDRESS_LIST =
    (ADDRESS=
     (PROTOCOL=IPC)
     (KEY=loc.world)
    )
    (ADDRESS=
     (PROTOCOL=TCP)
     (HOST=HR)
     (PORT=1521)
    )
 )
SID_LIST_LISTENER =
 (SID_DESC =
```

```
    (GLOBAL_DBNAME = loc.world)
    (ORACLE_HOME = /u00/app/oracle/product/12.1.0/grid)
    (SID_NAME = loc)
  )
 )
```

The first portion of this listing contains the protocol address list—one entry per instance. The protocol address list defines the protocol addresses on which a listener is accepting connections, including an interprocess calls (IPC) address-definition section. In this case, the listener is listening for connections to the service identified as **loc.world** as well as any requests coming from the HR machine on PORT 1521 using the TCP/IP protocol. The **.world** suffix is the default domain name for Oracle Net connections.

NOTE
Using SID_LIST_LISTENER is not required in Oracle Database 10g or later; it is required in previous versions of Oracle Net only if you monitor and manage the instance with Oracle Enterprise Manager.

The second portion of the listing, beginning with the SID_LIST_LISTENER clause, identifies the global database name as defined in the **init.ora** file for that database, the Oracle software home directory for each instance the listener is servicing, and the instance name or SID. The GLOBAL_DBNAME comprises the database name and database domain. The SID_LIST descriptor is retained for static database registration, for backward compatibility with earlier versions, and for use by Oracle Enterprise Manager. Databases dynamically register with the listener on database startup; a default installation of Oracle Database 12c on Linux only includes a **listener.ora** file with the LISTENER parameter, as in this sample **listener.ora** file from the RPT12C database used in examples throughout this book:

```
# listener.ora Network Configuration File:
/u00/app/oracle/product/12.1.0/grid/network/admin/listener.ora
# Generated by Oracle configuration tools.
LISTENER =
  (DESCRIPTION_LIST =
    (DESCRIPTION =
      (ADDRESS = (PROTOCOL = IPC)(KEY = EXTPROC1521))
      (ADDRESS = (PROTOCOL = TCP)(HOST = dw)(PORT = 1521))
    )
  )
# Cloud Control 12c agent settings
ENABLE_GLOBAL_DYNAMIC_ENDPOINT_LISTENER=ON        # line added by Agent
VALID_NODE_CHECKING_REGISTRATION_LISTENER=SUBNET # line added by Agent
```

For the listener on the server **dw** (for the database instance RPT12C), this **listener.ora** file does not even need to exist unless you want to add additional listeners or provide static registration entries: if there is no **listener.ora** file, the default listener name is LISTENER, the default value for PROTOCOL is TCP, the HOST parameter defaults to the server's host name, and the default value for PORT (the TCP/IP port number) is 1521. If you are using Oracle Cloud Control 12c to monitor this server and its databases, the agent software will add lines to this file as you can see in the previous example.

NOTE
*If you change the Oracle software home directory for an instance, you need to change the **listener.ora** file for the server.*

listener.ora Parameters

The **listener.ora** file supports a large number of parameters. The parameters should each be suffixed with the listener name. For example, the default listener name is LISTENER, so the LOG_FILE parameter is named LOG_FILE_LISTENER. The parameters in Table 17-1 apply whether you're using the Automatic Diagnostic Repository (ADR) or not.

Parameter	Description
DESCRIPTION	Serves as a container for listener protocol addresses.
ADDRESS	Specifies a single listener protocol address. Embedded within a DESCRIPTION.
IP	Specifies which IP address the listener listens on when a host name is specified and the HOST parameter specifies a host name. Values are FIRST, V4_ONLY, and V6_ONLY.
QUEUESIZE	Specifies the number of concurrent connection requests that the listener can accept on a TCP/IP or IPC listening endpoint.
RECV_BUF_SIZE	Specifies, in bytes, the buffer space for receive operations of sessions. Embedded within a DESCRIPTION.
SEND_BUF_SIZE	Specifies, in bytes, the buffer space for send operations of sessions. Embedded within a DESCRIPTION.
SID_LIST	Lists SID descriptions; configures service information for the listener; required for OEM, external procedure calls, and heterogeneous services.
SID_DESC	Specifies service information for a specific instance or service. Embedded within SID_LIST.
ENVS	Specifies environment variables for the listener to set prior to executing a dedicated server program or an executable specified via the PROGRAM parameter. Embedded within SID_DESC.
GLOBAL_DBNAME	Identifies the database service. Embedded within SID_DESC.
ORACLE_HOME	Specifies the Oracle software home directory for the service. Embedded within SID_DESC.
PROGRAM	Names the service executable program. Embedded within SID_DESC.

TABLE 17-1. *listener.ora Parameters, ADR or non-ADR*

Parameter	Description
SID_NAME	Specifies the Oracle instance name for the service. Embedded within SID_DESC.
CONNECTION_RATE_*listener_name*	Specifies the global rate for all listener endpoints that are rate limited, specified in number of connections per second.
RATE_LIMIT	Set to YES or NO and is embedded in the ADDRESS section.
SDU	Specifies the session data unit (SDU) size for data packet transfers. Values are 512 to 32768 bytes. Embedded within SID_DESC.
DIAG_ADR_ENABLED_*listener_name*	Set to ON or OFF to enable or disable ADR-related parameters.
ADMIN_RESTRICTIONS_*listener_name*	Disables run-time modification of listener parameters. Values are ON and OFF (the default).
CRS_NOTIFICATION_*listener_name*	Set to ON or OFF to notify Cluster Ready Services (CRS) when listener is started or stopped.
DEFAULT_SERVICE_*listener_name*	Specifies a default service name for the client when the service name is not specified.
INBOUND_CONNECT_TIMEOUT_*listener_name*	Specifies the time, in seconds, for the client to complete its connect request to the listener after the network connection has been established.
LOGGING_*listener_name*	Turns listener logging ON or OFF.
PASSWORDS_*listener_name*	Specifies an encrypted password for the listener process. The password can be generated via the Listener Control Utility (**lsnrctl**) or Oracle Net Manager.
SAVE_CONFIG_ON_STOP_*listener_name*	Set to TRUE or FALSE to specify whether runtime configuration changes are automatically saved to the **listener.ora** file.
SSL_CLIENT_AUTHENTICATION	Set to TRUE or FALSE to specify whether a client is authenticated with SSL.
WALLET_LOCATION	Specifies the location of certificates, keys, and trust points used by SSL for secure connections. For the WALLET_LOCATION parameter, you can specify the SOURCE, METHOD, METHOD_DATA, DIRECTORY, KEY, PROFILE, and INFILE subparameters.

TABLE 17-1. *listener.ora Parameters, ADR or non-ADR* (Continued)

You can modify the listener parameters after the listener has been started. If you use the SAVE_CONFIG_ON_STOP option, any changes you make to a running listener will be written to its **listener.ora** file. Examples of controlling the listener behavior are presented later in this chapter.

Parameter	Description
ADR_BASE_*listener_name*	Base directory to store trace and log files when ADR is enabled. Defaults to ORACLE_BASE, or ORACLE_HOME/log if ORACLE_BASE is undefined.
DIAG_ADR_ENABLED_*listener_name*	Set to ON (default) to use the ADR-related parameters; otherwise OFF.
LOGGING_*listener_name*	Defaults to ON for logging. This parameter is used for non-ADR tracing as well.
TRACE_LEVEL_*listener_name*	Turns tracing on with values other than OFF or 0. ■ 0/off: no trace ■ 4/user: user trace ■ 10/admin: administrative trace ■ 16/support: Oracle Support trace
TRACE_TIMESTAMP_*listener_name*	Adds a timestamp to every trace event in the format **dd-mon-yyyy hh:mi:ss:ms**

TABLE 17-2. *listener.ora Parameters, ADR*

If you are using ADR (by setting DIAG_ADR_ENABLED_*listener_name* to ON), then the parameters in Table 17-2 apply and non-ADR debugging parameters are ignored.

As you can see, using ADR means you have to specify fewer parameters in **listener.ora** in addition to letting Oracle manage your log and trace files for you. If you are not using ADR, then the **listener.ora** tracing-related parameters listed in Table 17-3 apply.

Parameter	Description
LOG_DIRECTORY_*listener_name*	Directory to store log files.
TRACE_DIRECTORY_*listener_name*	Directory to store trace files.
DIAG_ADR_ENABLED_*listener_name*	Set to ON (default) to use the ADR-related parameters; otherwise OFF.
LOG_FILE_*listener_name*	The name of the log file for the specified listener.
TRACE_FILE_*listener_name*	The name of the trace file for the specified listener.
TRACE_FILELEN_*listener_name*	Limits the size of each listener trace file in KB.
TRACE_FILENO_*listener_name*	Specifies the number of trace files to retain in conjunction with the TRACE_FILELEN parameter. Trace files are cycled much like online redo log files.

TABLE 17-3. *listener.ora Parameters, non-ADR*

Using the Oracle Net Configuration Assistant

The Oracle Net Configuration Assistant performs the initial network configuration steps after the Oracle software installation and automatically creates the default, basic configuration files. You can use the Oracle Net Manager tool to administer network services. The tools have graphical user interfaces for configuring the following elements:

- Listener
- Naming methods
- Local net service names
- Directory usage

Figure 17-4 shows the initial screen of the Oracle Net Configuration Assistant. As shown in Figure 17-4, Listener Configuration is the default option.

Configuring the Listener

Using the Oracle Net Configuration Assistant, you can configure a listener easily and quickly. When you select the Listener configuration option on the Welcome screen and click Next, you are given the choice to add, reconfigure, delete, or rename a listener. Select the Add option and click Next. The next step is to select a listener name. Figure 17-5 shows the Listener Name screen with the default listener name, LISTENER, displayed.

After selecting a listener name and clicking Next, you must select a protocol, as shown in Figure 17-6. The default protocol selected is TCP.

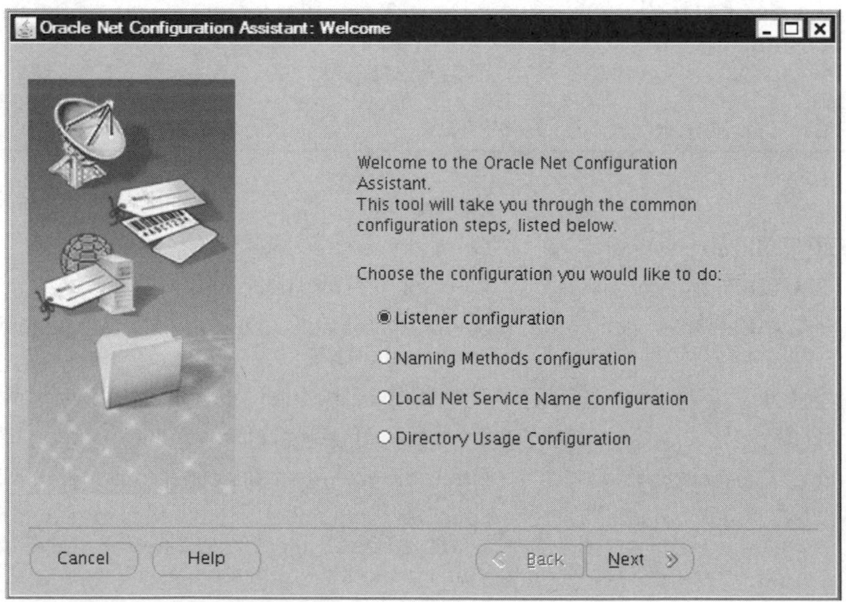

FIGURE 17-4. *Oracle Net Configuration Assistant: Welcome screen*

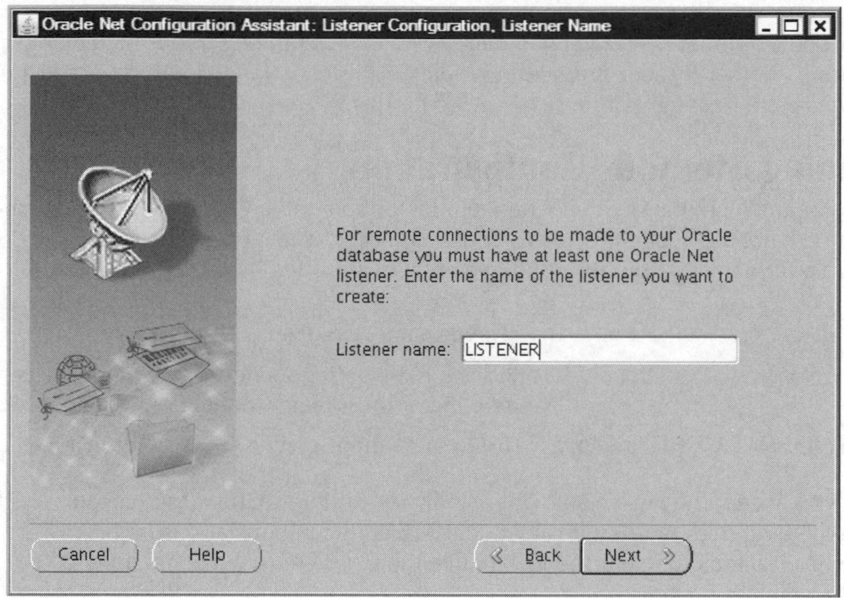

FIGURE 17-5. *Listener Configuration, Listener Name screen*

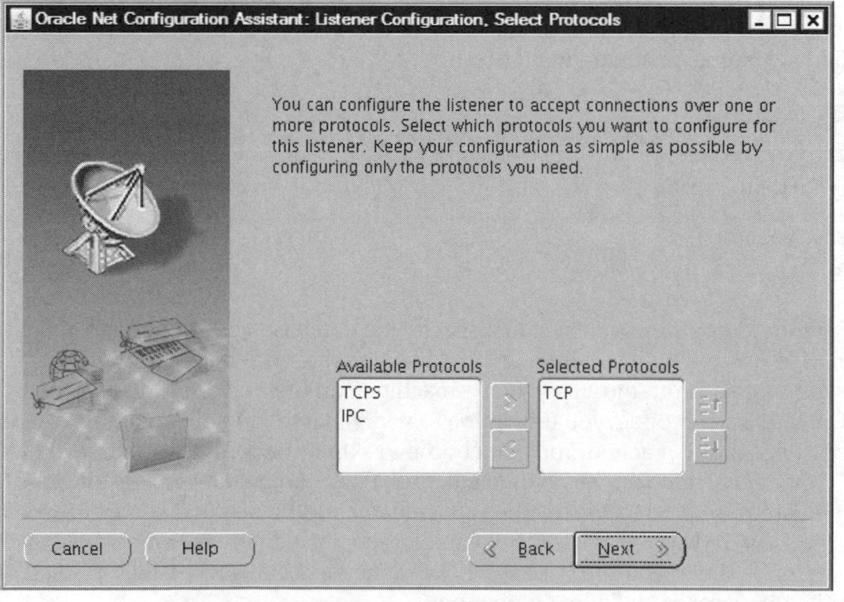

FIGURE 17-6. *Listener Configuration, Select Protocols screen*

After you select a protocol and click Next, you must designate a port number on which the new listener will listen. The default port number presented is 1521, but you are given the option to designate another port. After you click Next, the next three screens include a prompt to configure another listener, a request to indicate a listener you want to start, and a confirmation that the listener configuration is completed for this listener.

Naming Methods Configuration

Choosing the Naming Methods Configuration option of the Oracle Net Configuration Assistant (refer to Figure 17-4) enables you to configure net service names. There are many options available for naming methods. A couple of them are listed here:

Local	**The tnsnames.ora File**
Host Name	Uses a TCP naming service. You cannot use connection pooling or the Oracle Connection Manager with this option.
Sun NIS, DCE CDS, Directory	External naming services.

If you accept the Host Name option, you see an informational screen advising you that Host Name naming does not require any additional configuration "at this time." You are instructed that any time you add a database service in the future, you must make an entry in your TCP/IP host name resolution system.

Once you have selected the naming methods, the Oracle Net Configuration Assistant displays a confirmation screen.

Local Net Service Name Configuration

You can choose the Oracle Net Configuration Assistant's Local Net Service Name Configuration option (refer to Figure 17-4) to manage net service names. Five options are available for the Local Net Service Name Configuration tool:

- Add
- Reconfigure
- Delete
- Rename
- Test

For the Add option, you must first specify the database version you are going to access and the service name. Once you have entered the global service name or SID, you are prompted to enter the protocol. You must specify the machine name of the host and designate the listener port.

The next screen offers you the option to verify that the Oracle database you have specified can be successfully reached. You can choose to skip or perform the connection test. Once you have either chosen to test the connection, and it has completed successfully, or opted to skip the test, you are prompted to specify the service name for the new net service. By default, the service name you entered earlier is used, but you can specify a different name if you so choose. Finally, you are notified that your new local service name has been successfully created, and you are asked if you want to configure another one.

You can use the Reconfigure option to select and modify an existing net service name. You are prompted to select an existing net service name. The Database Version screen, the Service Name screen, and the Select Protocols screen are used as well as the TCP/IP Protocol screen. The option to test the database connection is offered, as well as a screen to enable you to rename the net service you are reconfiguring.

The Test option enables you to verify that your configuration information is correct, that the database specified can be reached, and that a successful connection can be made.

Directory Usage Configuration

A directory service provides a central repository of information for the network. The most common directory forms support the Lightweight Directory Access Protocol (LDAP). An LDAP server can provide the following features:

- Store net service names and their location resolution
- Provide global database links and aliases
- Act as a clearinghouse for configuration information for clients across the entire network
- Aid in configuring other clients
- Update client configuration files automatically
- House client information such as usernames and passwords

The Oracle Net Configuration Assistant's Directory Usage Configuration option supports both Oracle Internet Directory and Microsoft Active Directory. The Directory Type screen is shown in Figure 17-7 in a Linux environment; you would see an option for Microsoft Active Directory if you were running Oracle on Windows Server.

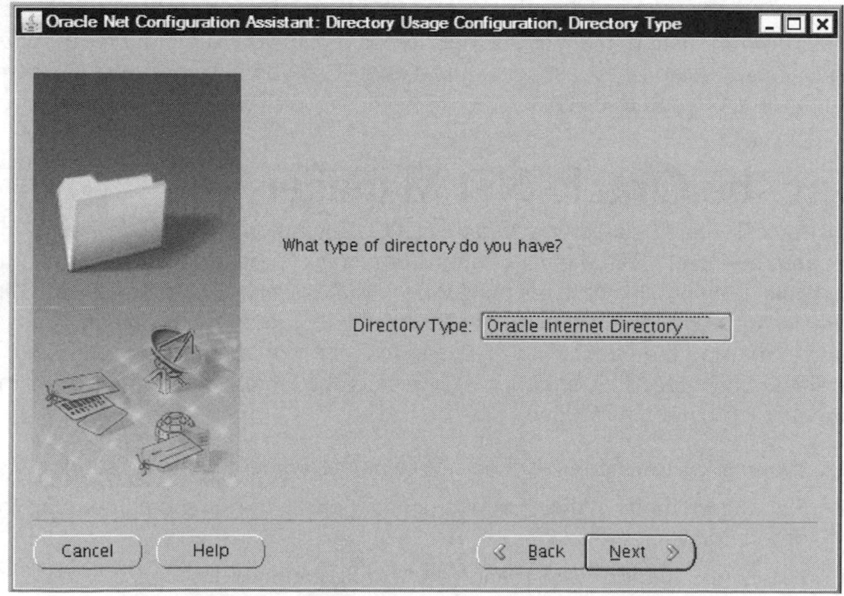

FIGURE 17-7. *Directory Usage Configuration, Directory Type screen*

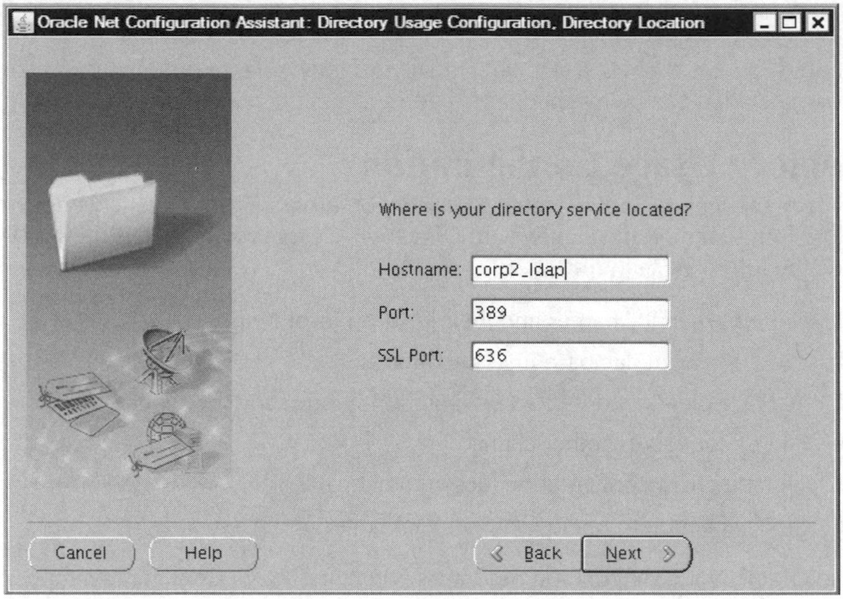

FIGURE 17-8. *Specifying an LDAP directory service*

Next, as shown in Figure 17-8, you are prompted to supply the directory service location host name, port, and SSL port. By default, the port is 389 and the SSL port is 636. Once you have specified this information, the tool attempts to connect to your directory repository and verify that you have already established a schema and a context. If you have not, you will receive an error message instructing you to do so.

Using the Oracle Net Manager

There is some overlap between the Oracle Net Configuration Assistant described in the preceding section and the Oracle Net Manager utility. Both tools can be used to configure a listener or a net service name. Both provide ease in configuring a Names service, local profile, and directory service. The Oracle Net Manager is not quite as user friendly but provides a more in-depth configuration alternative. You start the Oracle Net Manager on Linux with the **netmgr** command.

As shown in Figure 17-9, the opening screen of the Oracle Net Manager lists the basic functionality it provides, as follows:

- **Naming** Allows you to define simple names to identify the location of a service
- **Naming Methods** Allows you to define the way the simple names map to connect descriptors
- **Listeners** Supports the creation and configuration of listeners

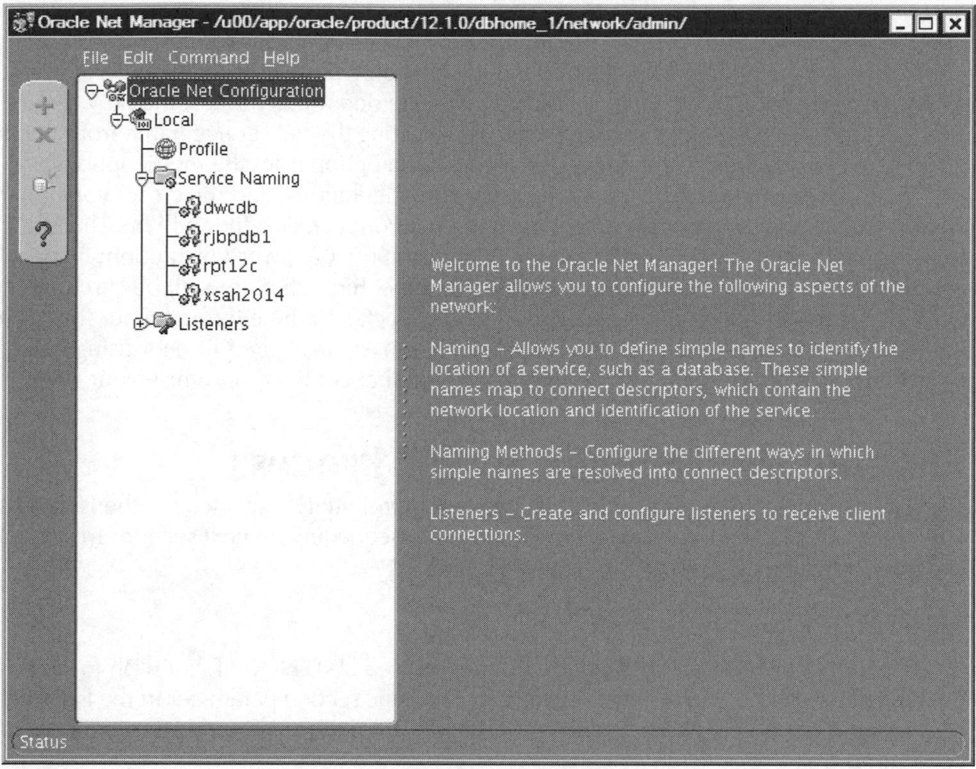

FIGURE 17-9. *Oracle Net Manager Console configuration window*

You can use Oracle Net Manager to manage your configuration files and test your connections. Options such as Oracle Advanced Security can be managed via the Oracle Net Manager. The Oracle Advanced Security option provides end-to-end encryption of data in a distributed environment. By default, your data will travel in clear text across the network unless you use Oracle's encryption or a hardware-based encryption.

You can create a new net service name for your **tnsnames.ora** file via the Oracle Net Service Names Wizard. Once you have specified a net service name, you are prompted to select the network protocol you want to use. The options are as follows:

- TCP/IP (Internet Protocol)
- TCP/IP with SSL (Secure Internet Protocol)
- Named Pipes (Microsoft Networking)
- IPC (Local Database)

The Oracle Net Manager will prompt you for each of the parameters required to establish a database connection and will modify your local **tnsnames.ora** file to reflect the information you provide. The information you will be prompted for is host, port number, service or SID name (depending on the Oracle version), and the connection type (either database default, shared server, or dedicated server). Finally, you are given the opportunity to test the new service name. You can also test existing net service names by selecting the net service name from the displayed list of services and then selecting the Test Connection option from the menu options.

The simpler you keep your client and server configurations, and the closer you adhere to the default values, the simpler the management of your configuration files will be. The Oracle Net Manager simplifies your configuration file administration. One word of caution: If you are using your listener to listen for connections from the Internet through a firewall, be sure that you do not leave a listener listening on the default port, 1521, because a hole through your firewall can leave you open to potential remote listener reconfiguration. An unsecured listener using default values can enable a hacker to obtain database information that could compromise your site.

Starting the Listener Server Process

The listener process is controlled by the Listener Control utility, executed via the **lsnrctl** command. The options available for the **lsnrctl** command are described in the next section. To start the listener, use this command:

```
lsnrctl start
```

This command will start the default listener (named LISTENER). If you wish to start a listener with a different name, include that listener's name as the second parameter in the **lsnrctl** command. For example, if you created a listener called ANPOP_LSNR, you could start it via the following command:

```
lsnrctl start anpop_lsnr
```

In the next section you will find descriptions of the other parameters available for the Listener Control utility.

After starting a listener, you can check that it is running by using the **status** option of the Listener Control utility. The following command can be used to perform this check:

```
[oracle@tettnang ~]$ lsnrctl status
LSNRCTL for Linux: Version 12.1.0.1.0 - Production on 10-JAN-2014 08:36:28
Copyright (c) 1991, 2013, Oracle.  All rights reserved.

Connecting to (ADDRESS=(PROTOCOL=tcp)(HOST=)(PORT=1521))
STATUS of the LISTENER
------------------------
Alias                     LISTENER
Version                   TNSLSNR for Linux: Version 12.1.0.1.0 - Production
Start Date                01-OCT-2013 10:22:55
Uptime                    100 days 23 hr. 13 min. 33 sec
Trace Level               off
Security                  ON: Local OS Authentication
SNMP                      OFF
Listener Parameter File
```

```
/u00/app/oracle/product/12.1.0/grid/network/admin/listener.ora
Listener Log File
/u00/app/oracle/diag/tnslsnr/tettnang/listener/alert/log.xml
Listening Endpoints Summary...
  (DESCRIPTION=(ADDRESS=(PROTOCOL=ipc)(KEY=EXTPROC1521)))
  (DESCRIPTION=(ADDRESS=(PROTOCOL=tcp)(HOST=tettnang.epic.com)(PORT=1521)))
  (DESCRIPTION=(ADDRESS=(PROTOCOL=tcps)(HOST=tettnang.epic.com)(PORT=5501))
    (Security=(my_wallet_directory=/u00/app/oracle/admin/XSAH2014/xdb_wallet))
    (Presentation=HTTP)(Session=RAW))
  (DESCRIPTION=(ADDRESS=(PROTOCOL=tcps)(HOST=tettnang.epic.com)(PORT=5500))
    (Security=(my_wallet_directory=/u00/app/oracle/admin/RPT12C/xdb_wallet))
    (Presentation=HTTP)(Session=RAW))
Services Summary...
Service "+ASM" has 1 instance(s).
  Instance "+ASM", status READY, has 1 handler(s) for this service...
Service "RPT12C" has 1 instance(s).
  Instance "RPT12C", status READY, has 1 handler(s) for this service...
Service "RPT12CXDB" has 1 instance(s).
  Instance "RPT12C", status READY, has 1 handler(s) for this service...
Service "XSAH2014.epic.com" has 1 instance(s).
  Instance "XSAH2014", status READY, has 1 handler(s) for this service...
Service "dwcdb" has 1 instance(s).
  Instance "dwcdb", status READY, has 1 handler(s) for this service...
Service "dwcdbXDB" has 1 instance(s).
  Instance "dwcdb", status READY, has 1 handler(s) for this service...
Service "rjbpdb1" has 1 instance(s).
  Instance "dwcdb", status READY, has 1 handler(s) for this service...
The command completed successfully
[oracle@tettnang ~]$
```

If the listener is named anything other than LISTENER in the **listener.ora** file, you must add the name of the listener to the **status** command. For example, if the listener is named ANPOP_LSNR, the command is

```
lsnrctl status anpop_lsnr
```

The **status** output will show if the listener has been started and the services it is currently supporting, as defined by its **listener.ora** file. The listener parameter file and its log file location will be displayed.

If you wish to see the operating system–level processes that are involved, use the following command. This example uses the Unix **ps -ef** command to list the system's active processes. The **grep tnslsnr** command then eliminates those rows that do not contain the term "tnslsnr."

```
[oracle@tettnang ~]$ ps -ef | grep tnslsnr
oracle    3756     1  0  2013 ?        00:06:52
   /u00/app/oracle/product/12.1.0/grid/bin/tnslsnr
   LISTENER -no_crs_notify -inherit
oracle   27106 21294  0 08:40 pts/0    00:00:00 grep tnslsnr
[oracle@tettnang ~]$
```

This output shows two processes: the listener process and the process that is checking for it. The first line of output is wrapped to the second line and may be truncated by the operating system.

Controlling the Listener Server Process

You can use the Listener Control utility, **lsnrctl**, to start, stop, and modify the listener process on the database server. Its command options are listed in Table 17-4. Each of these commands may be accompanied by a value; for all except the **set password** command, that value will be a listener name. If no listener name is specified, the default (LISTENER) will be used. Once within **lsnrctl**, you can change the listener being modified via the **set current_listener** command.

Command	Description
change_password	Sets a new password for the listener. You will be prompted for the old password for the listener.
exit	Exits **lsnrctl**.
help	Displays a list of the **lsnrctl** command options. You can also see additional options via the **help set** and **help show** commands.
quit	Exits **lsnrctl**.
reload	Allows you to modify the listener services after the listener has been started. It forces SQL*Net to read and use the most current **listener.ora** file.
save_config	Creates a backup of your existing **listener.ora** file and then updates your listener.ora file with parameters you have changed via **lsnrctl**.
services	Displays the services available, along with their connection history. It also lists whether each service is enabled for remote DBA or autologin access.
set	Sets parameter values. Options include the following: **current_listener** changes the listener process whose parameters are being set or shown. **displaymode** changes the format and level of detail for the **services** and **status** commands. **inbound_connect_timeout** sets the time, in seconds, for the client to complete its connection to the listener before being timed out. **log_directory** sets the directory for the listener log file. **log_file** sets the name of the listener log file. **log_status** sets whether logging is ON or OFF. **password** sets the listener password. **raw_mode** changes the **displaymode** format to show all data; only use **raw_mode** in conjunction with Oracle Support. **save_config_on_stop** saves your configuration changes to your **listener.ora** file when you exit **lsnrctl**. **startup_waittime** sets the number of seconds the listener sleeps before responding to a **lsnrctl start** command. **trc_directory** sets the directory for the listener trace file. **trc_file** sets the name for the listener trace file. **trc_level** sets the trace level (ADMIN, USER, SUPPORT, or OFF). See **lsnrctl trace**.

TABLE 17-4. *Listener Control (lsnrctl) Utility Commands*

Command	Description
show	Shows current parameter settings. Options are the same as the **set** options with the sole omission of the **password** command.
spawn	Spawns a program that runs with an alias in the **listener.ora** file.
start	Starts the listener.
status	Provides status information about the listener, including the time it was started, its parameter filename, its log file, and the services it supports. This can be used to query the status of a listener on a remote server.
stop	Stops the listener.
trace	Sets the trace level of the listener to one of four choices: OFF, USER (limited tracing), ADMIN (high level of tracing), or SUPPORT (for ORACLE Support).
version	Displays version information for the listener, TNS, and the protocol adapters.

TABLE 17-4. *Listener Control (lsnrctl) Utility Commands* (Continued)

TIP
Oracle best practices dictate not using a listener password in Oracle Database 12c. The default authentication mode for the listener is local OS authentication, which requires the listener administrator to be a member of the local ***dba*** *group.*

You can enter the **lsnrctl** command by itself to enter the **lsnrctl** utility shell, from which all other commands can then be executed.

The command options listed in Table 17-4 give you a great deal of control over the listener process, as shown in the following examples. In most of these examples, the **lsnrctl** command is first entered by itself. This places the user in the **lsnrctl** utility (as indicated by the LSNRCTL prompt). The rest of the commands are entered from within this utility. The following examples show the use of the **lsnrctl** utility to stop, start, and generate diagnostic information about the listener.

To stop the listener:

```
[oracle@tettnang ~]$ lsnrctl stop
LSNRCTL for Linux: Version 12.1.0.1.0 -
          Production on 10-JAN-2014 08:44:31
Copyright (c) 1991, 2013, Oracle.  All rights reserved.
Connecting to (ADDRESS=(PROTOCOL=tcp)(HOST=)(PORT=1521))
The command completed successfully
[oracle@tettnang ~]$
```

To show status information for the listener:

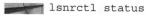

```
lsnrctl status
```

To list the status of a listener on another host, add a service name from that host as a parameter to the **status** command. The following example uses the HQ service name shown earlier in this chapter:

```
lsnrctl status hq
```

To list version information about the listener:

```
lsnrctl version
```

To list information about the services supported by the listener:

```
[oracle@tettnang ~]$ lsnrctl services
LSNRCTL for Linux: Version 12.1.0.1.0 -
   Production on 10-JAN-2014 08:46:57
Copyright (c) 1991, 2013, Oracle.  All rights reserved.
Connecting to (ADDRESS=(PROTOCOL=tcp)(HOST=)(PORT=1521))
Services Summary...
Service "+ASM" has 1 instance(s).
  Instance "+ASM", status READY, has 1 handler(s) for this service...
    Handler(s):
      "DEDICATED" established:0 refused:0 state:ready
         LOCAL SERVER
Service "RPT12C" has 1 instance(s).
  Instance "RPT12C", status READY, has 1 handler(s) for this service...
    Handler(s):
      "DEDICATED" established:0 refused:0 state:ready
         LOCAL SERVER
Service "RPT12CXDB" has 1 instance(s).
. . .
  Instance "dwcdb", status READY, has 1 handler(s) for this service...
    Handler(s):
      "DEDICATED" established:0 refused:0 state:ready
         LOCAL SERVER
The command completed successfully
[oracle@tettnang ~]$
```

The Oracle Connection Manager

The Oracle Connection Manager portion of Oracle Net acts as a router used to establish database communication links between otherwise incompatible network protocols as well as to take advantage of multiplexing and access control.

The advantage of the Oracle Connection Manager is that all servers do not have to use the same communications protocol. Each server can use the communications protocol that is best suited to its environment and will still be able to transfer data back and forth with other databases. This communication takes place regardless of the communications protocols used on the remote servers; the Oracle Connection Manager takes care of the differences between the protocols. The protocols supported by the Oracle Connection Manager are IPC, Named Pipes, SDP, TCP/IP, and TCP/IP with SSL.

You can use multiple access paths to handle different client requests. The Oracle Connection Manager will select the most appropriate path based on path availability and network load. The relative cost of each path is specified via the Network Manager utility when the Oracle Connection Manager is set up.

In an intranet environment, the Oracle Connection Manager can be used as a firewall for Oracle Net traffic. You can establish filtering rules to enable or disable specific client access using the Oracle Connection Manager. The filtering rules can be based on any of the following criteria:

- Destination host names or IP addresses for servers
- Destination database service name
- Source host names or IP addresses for clients
- Whether the client is using the Oracle Advanced Security option

The Oracle Connection Manager is used to enhance your firewall security by filtering out client access based on one or more aspects of the filtering rules you create. For example, you could specify that an IP address is to be refused access using the CMAN_RULES parameter within the **cman.ora** file.

The file **sqlnet.ora** may be used to specify additional diagnostics beyond the default diagnostics provided.

Using the Oracle Connection Manager

Oracle Net uses the Oracle Connection Manager to support connections within homogenous networks, reducing the number of physical connections maintained by the database. Two main processes and a control utility are associated with the Oracle Connection Manager, as follows:

CMGW	The gateway process that acts as a hub for the Connection Manager
CMADMIN	A multithreaded process responsible for all administrative tasks and issues
CMCTL	A utility that enables basic management functions for Oracle Connection Manager administration

The CMGW Process

The Connection Manager Gateway (CMGW) process registers itself with the CMADMIN process and listens for incoming connection requests. By default, this process listens on port 1630 using the TCP/IP protocol. The CMGW process initiates connection requests to listeners from clients and relays data between the client and server.

The CMADMIN Process

The multithreaded Connection Manager Administrative (CMADMIN) process performs many tasks and functions. The CMADMIN processes CMGW registrations and registers source route addressing information about the CMGW and listeners. The CMADMIN process is tasked with identifying all listener processes that support at least one database. Using Oracle Internet Directory, the CMADMIN performs the following tasks:

- Locates local servers
- Monitors registered listeners
- Maintains client address information
- Periodically updates the Connection Manager's cache of available services

The CMADMIN process handles source route information about the CMGW and listeners.

Configuring the Oracle Connection Manager

The **cman.ora** file, located by default in the **$ORACLE_HOME/network/admin** directory on a Unix system and in **%ORACLE_HOME%\network\admin** on a Windows system, contains the configuration parameters for the Oracle Connection Manager. The file contains protocol addresses of the listening gateway process, access control parameters, and profile or control parameters.

The complete set of **cman.ora** parameters is shown in Table 17-5.

Parameter	Description
ADDRESS	Specifies the protocol address (such as the protocol, the host, and the port) of the Connection Manager.
RULE	Specifies an access control rule list to filter incoming connections. Subparameters allow source and destination host names, IP addresses, and service names to be filtered.
PARAMETER_LIST	Specifies attribute values when overriding the default settings. The remainder of the parameters in this listing are subparameters within the PARAMETER_LIST setting.
ASO_AUTHENTICATION_FILTER	Specifies whether Oracle Advanced Security authentication settings must be used by the client. The default is OFF.
CONNECTION_STATISTICS	Specifies whether the SHOW_CONNECTIONS command displays connection statistics. The default is NO.
EVENT_GROUP	Specifies which event groups are logged. The default is NONE.
IDLE_TIMEOUT	Specifies the amount of time, in seconds, that an established connection can remain active without transmitting data. The default is 0.
INBOUND_CONNECT_TIMEOUT	Specifies, in seconds, how long the Oracle Connection Manager listener waits for a valid connection from a client or another instance of Oracle Connection Manager. The default is 0.
LOG_DIRECTORY	Specifies the destination directory for Oracle Connection Manager log files. The default is the **/network/log** subdirectory under the Oracle home directory.
LOG_LEVEL	Specifies the logging level (OFF, USER, ADMIN, or SUPPORT). The default is SUPPORT.
MAX_CMCTL_SESSIONS	Specifies the maximum number of concurrent local or remote sessions of the Oracle Connection Manager Control Utility allowable for a given instance. The default is 4.
MAX_CONNECTIONS	Specifies the maximum number of connections a gateway process can handle. The default is 256.
MAX_GATEWAY_PROCESSES	Specifies the maximum number of gateway processes that an instance of Oracle Connection Manager supports. The default is 16.

TABLE 17-5. *cman.ora Parameters*

Parameter	Description
MIN_GATEWAY_PROCESSES	Specifies the minimum number of gateway processes that an instance of Oracle Connection Manager must support. The default is 2.
OUTBOUND_CONNECT_TIMEOUT	Specifies, in seconds, the length of time that the Oracle Connection Manager instance waits for a valid connection to be established with the database server or with another Oracle Connection Manager instance. The default is 0.
PASSWORD_*instance_name*	The encrypted instance password, if set.
REMOTE_ADMIN	Specifies whether remote access to an Oracle Connection Manager is allowed. The default is NO.
SESSION_TIMEOUT	Specifies the maximum time, in seconds, allowed for a user session. The default is 0.
TRACE_DIRECTORY	Specifies the directory for the trace files. The default is the **/network/trace** subdirectory under the Oracle home directory.
TRACE_FILELEN	Specifies, in KB, the size of the trace file. The default is 0.
TRACE_FILENO	Specifies the number of trace files, used cyclically. The default is 0.
TRACE_LEVEL	Specifies the trace level (OFF, USER, ADMIN, or SUPPORT). The default is OFF.
TRACE_TIMESTAMP	Adds a timestamp to every trace event in the trace files. The default is OFF.

TABLE 17-5. *cman.ora Parameters* (Continued)

Using the Connection Manager Control Utility (CMCTL)

The Connection Manager Control Utility provides administrative access to CMADMIN and CMGW. The Connection Manager is started via the **cmctl** command. The command syntax is

```
cmctl command process_type
```

The default startup command from an operating system prompt is as follows:

```
cmctl start cman
```

The commands are broken into four basic types:

- Operational commands such as **start**
- Modifier commands such as **set**
- Informational commands such as **show**
- Command utility operations such as **exit**

Using the parameter REMOTE_ADMIN, you can control, but not start, remote managers. Unlike the Listener utility discussed earlier in this chapter, you cannot interactively set a password for the Oracle Connection Manager. To set a password for this tool, you put a plain-text password in the **cman.ora** file. The available command options for the **cmctl** command are shown in Table 17-6.

If the Connection Manager has been started, any client that has SOURCE_ROUTE set to YES in its **tnsnames.ora** file can use the Connection Manager. The Connection Manager reduces system resource requirements by maintaining logical connections while reusing physical connections.

Command	Description
ADMINISTER	Enables you to choose an instance of Oracle Connection Manager. The format is **administer -c** followed by the instance name, with an optional **using *password*** clause.
CLOSE CONNECTIONS	Terminates connections. You can specify the source, destination, service, state, and gateway process ID for the connections to terminate.
EXIT	Exits the Oracle Connection Manager Control utility.
HELP	Lists all CMCTL commands.
QUIT	Exits the Oracle Connection Manager Control utility.
RELOAD	Dynamically re-reads parameters and rules from the **cman.ora** file.
RESUME GATEWAYS	Resumes suspended gateway processes.
SAVE_PASSWORD	Saves the current password to the **cman.ora** configuration parameter file.
SET	Displays a list of parameters that can be modified within CMCTL. You can set values for ASO_AUTHENTICATION_FILTER, CONNECTION_STATISTICS, EVENT, IDLE_TIMEOUT, INBOUND_CONNECT_TIMEOUT, LOG_DIRECTORY, LOG_LEVEL, OUTBOUND_CONNECT_TIMEOUT, PASSWORD, SESSION_TIMEOUT, TRACE_DIRECTORY, and TRACE_LEVEL.
SHOW	Displays a list of parameters whose values can be displayed. You can show their values individually by specifically listing them after the **show** command (for example, **show trace_level**).
SHOW ALL	Displays the values of all parameters and rules.
SHOW DEFAULTS	Displays the default parameter settings.
SHOW EVENTS	Displays the events.
SHOW GATEWAYS	Displays the current status of specific gateway processes.
SHOW PARAMETERS	Displays current parameter settings.
SHOW RULES	Displays the current access control list.
SHOW SERVICES	Displays information on the Oracle Connection Manager services, including gateway handlers and the number of connections.
SHOW STATUS	Displays basic information about the instance and its current statistics.
SHOW VERSION	Displays the current version and name of the CMCTL utility.
SHUTDOWN	Shuts down specific gateway processes or the entire Oracle Connection Manager instance.
STARTUP	Starts the Oracle Connection Manager.
SUSPEND GATEWAY	Prevents gateway processes from accepting new client connections.

TABLE 17-6. *cmctl Command Options*

Directory Naming with Oracle Internet Directory

Oracle Internet Directory facilitates support for LDAP-compliant directory servers for centralized network names resolution management in a distributed Oracle network. For localized management, you can still use the **tnsnames.ora** file.

Oracle Internet Directory Architecture

The file **ldap.ora**, located in the **$ORACLE_HOME/network/admin** directory on a Unix system and in **%ORACLE_HOME%\network\admin** in a Windows environment, stores the configuration parameters to access a directory server. Oracle supports both the Oracle Internet Directory and Microsoft Active Directory LDAP protocols.

To resolve a connect descriptor using a centralized directory server, the steps are as follows:

1. Oracle Net, on behalf of the client, contacts the directory server to obtain the resolution for the connect identifier to a connect descriptor.
2. The directory server takes the connect identifier, locates the associated connect descriptor, and returns the descriptor to Oracle Net.
3. Oracle Net uses the resolved descriptor to make the connection request to the correct listener.

The directory server uses a tree structure in which to store its data. Each node in the tree is an *entry*. A hierarchical structure of entries is used, called a *directory information tree (DIT),* and each entry is identified by a unique *distinguished name (DN)* that tells the directory server exactly where the entry resides. DITs can be structured to use an existing Domain Name System (DNS), organizational or geographical lines, or Internet naming scheme.

Using a DIT that is organized along organizational lines, for example, the DN for the HR server could be this: **(dn: cn=HR, cn=OracleContext, dc=us, dc=ourcompany, dc=com)**. The lowest component of a DN is placed at the leftmost location of the DIT and moved progressively up the tree. The following illustration shows the DIT for this example.

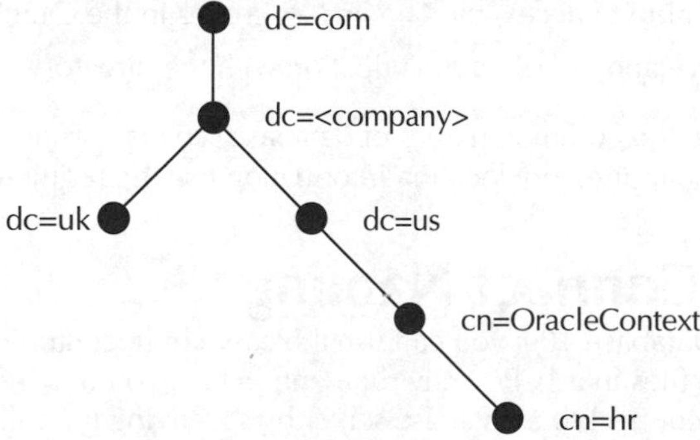

The commonly used LDAP attributes are as follows:

- **CommonName (cn)** Common name of an entry
- **Country (c)** Name of the country

- **Domain component (dc)** Domain component
- **Organization (o)** Name of organization
- **OrganizationalUnitName (ou)** Name of unit within the organization

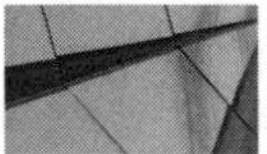

NOTE
*The value **cn=OracleContext** is a special entry in the directory server that supports directory-enabled features such as directory naming. The Oracle Context is created using the Oracle Net Configuration Assistant discussed earlier in this chapter.*

Setting Up an Oracle Internet Directory

As detailed earlier, you can use the Oracle Net Configuration Assistant or the Oracle Net Manager to perform the initial configuration tasks. Once the directory schema and Oracle Context have been established, you can begin to register service names with the directory service using the Oracle Net Manager. The Oracle Context area is the root of the directory subtree where all information relevant to Oracle software is stored.

When the Oracle Context is installed, two entities are created: OracleDBCreators and OracleNetAdmins. The OracleDBCreators entity with a DN of **(cn=OracleDBCreators, cn=OracleContext)** is created. Any user who is a member of OracleDBCreators can register a database server entry or directory client entry using the Oracle Database Configuration Assistant. A user assigned as a member of OracleNetAdmins can create, modify, and delete net service names and modify Oracle Net attributes of database servers using the Oracle Net Manager. If you are a directory administrator, you can add users to these groups.

Clients who want to look up information in the directory must meet the following minimum requirements:

- They must be configured to use the directory server.
- They must be able to access the Oracle Net entries in the Oracle Context.
- They must have anonymous authentication with the directory server.

The clients can use the common names of database servers and net service entries to perform the lookups, or additional directory location information may be required in the connection string.

Using Easy Connect Naming

Starting with Oracle Database 10*g*, you can use the easy connect naming method to eliminate the need for service name files in a TCP/IP environment; in fact, you may not need a **tnsnames.ora** file at all. Clients can connect to a database server by specifying the full connection information in their connect strings in this format as follows with the SQL*Plus CONNECT command:

```
connect username/password@[//]host[:port]
        [/service_name] [/server] [/instance_name]
```

The connection identifier elements are as follows:

Element	Description
//	Optional. Specify // for a URL.
Host	Required. Specify the host name or the IP address.
Port	Optional. Specify the port or use the default (1521).
service_name	Optional. Specify the service name. The default value is the host name of the database server.
server	Optional. Also known as connect_type in OCI, specifies the type of service handler: dedicated, shared, or pooled.
instance_name	Optional. Corresponds to the INSTANCE_NAME initialization parameter.

For example, you can connect to the LOC service with this syntax:

```
connect username/password@hq:1521/loc
```

In order to use easy connect naming, you must have Oracle Net Services 10*g* (or later) software installed on your client. You must be using the TCP/IP protocol, and no features requiring a more advanced connect descriptor are supported.

CAUTION
*Oracle Database 11*g *and 12*c *clients and database no longer support the use of Oracle Names; however, earlier versions of the client can still use Oracle Names to resolve naming for an Oracle Database 10*g *database.*

For URL or JDBC connections, prefix the connect identifier with a double slash (//):

```
connect username/password@[//][host][:port][/service_name]
```

Easy connect naming is automatically configured at installation. In your **sqlnet.ora** file, make sure EZCONNECT is added to the list of values in the NAME.DIRECTORY_PATH parameter listing; the default contents of **sqlnet.ora** for client installations of Oracle Database 11*g* and later have these two lines:

```
SQLNET.AUTHENTICATION_SERVICES= (NTS)
NAMES.DIRECTORY_PATH= (TNSNAMES, EZCONNECT)
```

In other words, when resolving service names, the Oracle client will first attempt a lookup using the **tnsnames.ora** file, then use Easy Connect.

Using Database Links

You should create *database links* to support frequently used connections to remote databases. Database links specify the connect descriptor to be used for a connection, and they may also specify the username to connect to in the remote database.

A database link is typically used to create local objects (such as views or synonyms) that access remote databases via server/server communications. The local synonyms for remote objects provide location transparency to the local users. When a database link is referenced by a SQL statement, it opens a session in the remote database and executes the SQL statement there. The data is then returned, and the remote session may stay open in case it is needed again. Database links can be created as public links (by DBAs, making the links available to all users in the local database) or as private links.

The following example creates a private database link called HR_LINK:

```
create database link hr_link
   connect to hr identified by hr
   using 'loc';
```

The CREATE DATABASE LINK command, as shown in this example, has three parameters:

- The name of the link (HR_LINK, in this example)
- The account to connect to
- The net service name

A public database link can be created by adding the keyword PUBLIC to the CREATE DATABASE LINK command, as shown in the following example:

```
create public database link hr_link
   connect to hr identified by hr
   using 'loc';
```

NOTE
Best practices for public database links would favor including the USING clause but not the CONNECT TO clause. You could then create a private database link with the same name that includes the CONNECT TO clause but not the USING clause. Subsequent changes to the service name for the data would require re-creating only the public link, while the private links and the user passwords would be unchanged.

If the LOC instance is moved to a different server, you can redirect the database links to LOC's new location simply by distributing a **tnsnames.ora** file that contains the modification or by revising the listing in the directory server. You can generate the revised entry for the **tnsnames.ora** file or directory server by using either the Oracle Net Configuration Assistant tool or the Oracle Net Manager, described previously in this chapter.

To use these links, simply add them as suffixes to the table names in commands. The following example creates a local view of a remote table, using the HR_LINK database link:

```
create view local_employee_view
as
select * from employee@hr_link
where office='Annapolis';
```

The FROM clause in this example refers to EMPLOYEE@HR_LINK. Because the HR_LINK database link specifies the server name, instance name, and owner name, the global object name for the table is known. If no account name had been specified, the user's account name would have been used instead. If HR_LINK was created without the CONNECT TO clause, the current username and password would be used to connect to the remote database.

In this example, a view was created in order to limit the records that users could retrieve. If no such restriction is necessary, a synonym can be used instead. This is shown in the following example:

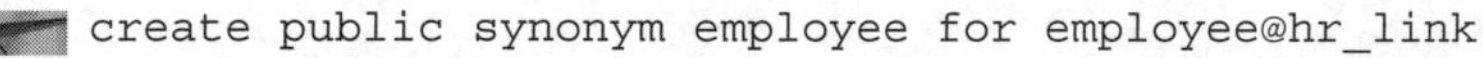

```
create public synonym employee for employee@hr_link;
```

Local users who query the local public synonym EMPLOYEE will automatically have their queries redirected to the EMPLOYEE table in the LOC instance on the HQ server. Location transparency has thus been achieved.

By default, a single SQL statement can use up to four database links. This limit can be increased via the OPEN_LINKS parameter in the database's SPFILE or **init.ora** file. If this value is set to 0, no distributed transactions are allowed.

Tuning Oracle Net

Tuning Oracle Net applications is fairly straightforward: Wherever possible, reduce the amount of data that is sent across the network, particularly for online transaction-processing applications. Also, reduce the number of times data is requested from the database. The basic procedures that should be applied include the following:

- The use of distributed objects, such as materialized views, to replicate static data to remote databases.
- The use of procedures to reduce the amount of data sent across the network. Rather than data being sent back and forth, only the procedure's error status is returned.
- The use of homogenous servers wherever possible to eliminate the need for connection managers.
- For OLTP applications only, the use of shared servers to support more clients with fewer processes.

The buffer size used by Oracle Net should take advantage of the packet sizes used by the network protocols (such as TCP/IP). If you send large packets of data across the network, the packets may be fragmented. Because each packet contains header information, reducing packet fragmentation reduces network traffic.

You can tune the size of the service layer buffer. The specification for the service layer data buffer is called SDU (Session Data Unit); if it is changed, this must be specified in your client and server configuration files. Oracle Net builds data into buffers the size of the SDU, so altering that size may improve your performance. The default size for the SDU is 8192 in Oracle Database 11*g*, and 2048 in earlier versions. For Oracle Database 12*c*, the default SDU size is 8192 for the client and a dedicated server; for a shared server it is 65535. If you will frequently be sending messages that are much larger than that, you can increase the SDU (up to a maximum of 2MB).

To configure the client to use a non-default SDU, add the new SDU setting to the client configuration files. For the change to apply to all connections, add the following parameter to the **sqlnet.ora** file:

```
DEFAULT_SDU_SIZE=32767
```

For the change to apply to only specific service names, modify their entries in the **tnsnames .ora** file:

```
LOC =(DESCRIPTION=
   (SDU=32767)
   (ADDRESS=
      (PROTOCOL=TCP)
      (HOST=HQ)
      (PORT=1521))
   (CONNECT DATA=
      (SERVICE_NAME=LOC)))
```

On the database server, configure the default SDU setting in the **sqlnet.ora** file:

```
DEFAULT_SDU_SIZE=32767
```

For shared server processes, add the SDU setting to the DISPATCHERS setting in the instance initialization parameter file:

```
DISPATCHERS="(DESCRIPTION=(ADDRESS=(PROTOCOL=tcp))(SDU=32767))"
```

For dedicated server processes, edit the entries in the **listener.ora** file:

```
SID_LIST_listener_name=
 (SID_LIST=
  (SID_DESC=
(SDU=32767)
(SID_NAME=loc)))
```

Oracle Net Services provides support for the Reliable Datagram Sockets (RDS) and Socket Direct Protocol (SDP) protocols on InfiniBand high-speed networks (such as those found in Oracle Exadata and Exalogic appliances). Applications using SDP place most of the messaging burden on the network interface card, thus reducing the CPU requirements of the application. If you are using an InfiniBand high-speed network (such as for communications among your application tiers), see the Oracle documentation for hardware and software configuration details.

Limiting Resource Usage

To limit the impact of unauthorized users on your system, you can reduce the duration for which resources can be held prior to authentication. The time-limiting parameters listed earlier in this chapter help to mitigate the performance problems caused by these unauthorized accesses. In the **listener.ora** file, set the INBOUND_CONNECT_TIMEOUT_*listener_name* parameter to terminate connections that are not authenticated by the listener within the specified time period. Failed connections will be logged to the listener log file. In the server-side **sqlnet.ora** file, set the SQLNET.INBOUND_CONNECT_TIMEOUT parameter to terminate connection attempts that cannot establish and authenticate connections within the specified interval. Set the server-side SQLNET.INBOUND_CONNECT_TIMEOUT parameter to a higher value than the INBOUND_CONNECT_TIMEOUT_*listener_name* parameter in the **listener.ora** file.

Using Compression

Once you've tuned the amount of data that needs to flow from client to server and vice versa, you can leverage a new feature of the Advanced Compression package in Oracle Database 12*c*: Advanced Network Compression. If you have additional CPU resources on both the client and server, then compressing the actual data stream will improve throughput and reduce elapsed time for Oracle Net messaging.

The settings you can use in **sqlnet.ora** to implement Advanced Network Compression are listed in Table 17-7.

Because the Advanced Network Compression feature is included as part of the Oracle Advanced Compression option, you must license the Advanced Compression option to leverage the Advanced Network Compression features.

Debugging Connection Problems

Oracle Net connections require that a number of communication mechanisms be properly configured. The connections involve host-to-host communication, proper identification of services and databases, and proper configuration of the listener server processes. In the event of connection problems when using Oracle Net, it is important to eliminate as many of these components as possible.

Start by making sure that the host the connection is trying to reach is accessible via the network. This can be checked via the **ssh** command:

```
ssh host_name
```

If this command is successful, you will be prompted for a username and password on the remote host. If the **ping** command is available to you, you may use it instead. The following command will check to see if the remote host is available and will return a status message:

```
ping host_name
```

If the host is available on the network, the next step is to check if the listener is running; you can use the **tnsping** utility provided by Oracle to verify Oracle Net connectivity to a remote database listener. The **tnsping** utility has two parameters: the net service name (from **tnsnames.ora**) to connect to, and the number of connections to attempt. The output from **tnsping** will include a listing showing the time required to connect to the remote database.

Parameter	Description
SQLNET.COMPRESSION	Enables or disables compression, values are ON or OFF. This must be set on both the client and server for compression to occur.
SQLNET.COMPRESSION_LEVELS	Specifies the compression level as either LOW or HIGH. Both the client and the server must have this set to HIGH for high compression levels to be used.
SQLNET.COMPRESSION_THRESHOLD	Specifies the minimum data size, in bytes, at which compression will occur. The default is 1024 bytes.

TABLE 17-7. *Advanced Network Compression Settings in sqlnet.ora*

For example, to determine if the Linux Oracle database server **tettnang** is accessible from a Windows client, use the **tnsping** command as follows:

```
C:\> tnsping tettnang
TNS Ping Utility for 64-bit Windows: Version 12.1.0.1.0 -
   Production on 10-JAN-2014 09:12:36
Copyright (c) 1997, 2013, Oracle.  All rights reserved.
Used parameter files:
c:\app\orabase3\product\12.1.0\dbhome_1\network\admin\sqlnet.ora
Used EZCONNECT adapter to resolve the alias
Attempting to contact
   (DESCRIPTION=(CONNECT_DATA=(SERVICE_NAME=))
   (ADDRESS=(PROTOCOL=TCP)(HOST=10.6.160.207)(PORT=1521)))
OK (40 msec)
C:\>
```

Note how **tnsping** under Windows used Easy Connect to obtain the TCP/IP address of the server **tettnang**, filled in default values, and located the listener on the Linux server successfully.

In addition to **tnsping**, you can use the **trcroute** utility to discover the path a connection takes to a remote database. The **trcroute** utility (similar to the Linux utility **traceroute**) reports on the TNS addresses of every node it travels through and reports any errors that occur. The command format is as follows:

```
trcroute net_service_name
```

In client/server communications, the same principles for debugging connection problems apply. First, verify that the remote host is accessible; most communications software for clients includes a **telnet** or **ping** command. If the remote host is not accessible, the problem may be on the client side. Verify that *other* clients are able to access the host on which the database resides. If they can, the problem is isolated to the client. If they cannot, the problem lies on the server side, and the server, its listener processes, and its database instances should be checked.

Summary

Using Oracle over a network is hard to avoid unless you're doing all your work on the database console. Therefore, it's imperative that you understand all components of the network infrastructure that connect Oracle Database to other Oracle Databases or clients.

Depending on the architecture of your network you may choose one of several different methods to connect to your database, whether by using a local **tnsnames.ora** file, the Easy Connect syntax, or an enterprise LDAP server. In any case you'll configure your **sqlnet.ora** file on the client to specify the allowed connect methods.

On the other side of the connection is the database whose listener hands off connection requests from the dispatcher(s) running on the server. In a clustered environment you will have a single address mapped in your DNS server to each node of the cluster. This ensures availability and reliability of your client connections.

With Oracle Database 12*c* you can dramatically improve throughput by specifying a compression level on both the client and server side. The Advanced Network Compression feature is similar in implementation to Advanced Compression in the database: less bandwidth used with minimal CPU overhead to perform the compress and decompress operations.

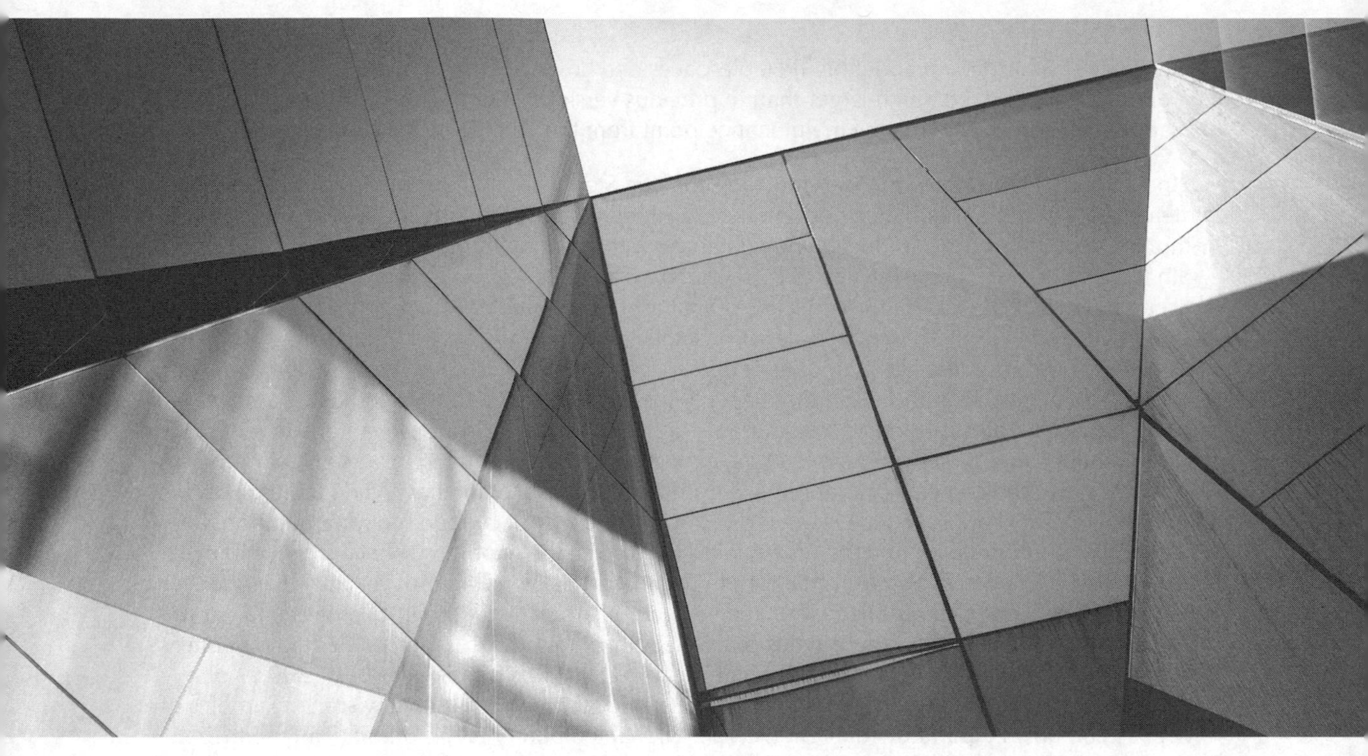

CHAPTER 18

Managing Large Databases

In Chapter 6, we talked about bigfile tablespaces and how they not only allow the total size of the database to be much larger than in previous versions of Oracle, but also ease administration by moving the maintenance point from the datafile to the tablespace.

In Chapter 4, I presented an overview of Automatic Storage Management (ASM) and how it can ease administration, enhance performance, and improve availability. The DBA can add one or more disk volumes to a rapidly growing database without bringing down the instance.

In this chapter, we'll revisit many of these database features, but with an emphasis on how they can be leveraged in a VLDB (Very Large Database) environment. Although these features surely provide benefits in all Oracle installations, they are especially useful in databases whose most heavily used resource is the amount of disk space allocated. First, we'll review the concepts behind bigfile tablespaces and delve more deeply into how they are constructed using a new ROWID format. I'll also show how transportable tablespaces are a distinct advantage in a VLDB environment because they bypass some of the export/import steps required in versions prior to Oracle9*i* to move the contents of a tablespace from one database to another. When tablespaces in a VLDB environment approach the exabyte size, both the extra space required for a traditional export and import operation and the time it takes to perform the export may become prohibitive. If you are using Oracle Database 11*g* or Oracle Database 12*c,* your tablespaces may even be transportable between different hardware and software platforms with minimal or no extra effort.

Next, we will review the various types of nontraditional (non-heap-based) tables that are often leveraged in a VLDB environment. Index-organized tables (IOTs) combine the best features of a traditional table with the fast access of an index into one segment; we'll review some examples of how IOTs can now be partitioned in Oracle 12*c*. Global temporary tables dramatically reduce space usage in the undo tablespace and redo logs for recovery purposes because the table contents only persist for the duration of a transaction or a session. External tables make it easy to access data in a non-Oracle format as if the data was in a table; as of Oracle 10*g,* external tables can be created using Oracle Data Pump (see Chapter 13 for an in-depth discussion of Data Pump). Finally, the amount of space occupied by a table can be dramatically reduced by using an internal compression algorithm when the rows are loaded using direct-path SQL*Loader and CREATE TABLE AS SELECT statements.

Table and index partitioning not only improves query performance but tremendously improves the manageability of tables in a VLDB environment by allowing you to perform maintenance operations on one partition while users may be accessing other partitions of the table. We will cover all the different types of partitioning schemes, including some of the partitioning features first introduced in Oracle 10*g*: hash-partitioned global indexes, list-partitioned IOTs, and LOB support in all types of partitioned IOTs. Oracle 11*g* brought even more partitioning options to the table: composite list-hash, list-list, list-range, and range-range. Other new partitioning schemes in Oracle Database 11*g* and Oracle Database 12*c* include automated interval partitioning, reference partitioning, application-controlled partitioning, and virtual column partitioning.

Bitmap indexes, available since Oracle 7.3, provide query benefits not only for tables with columns of low cardinality, but also for special indexes called *bitmap join indexes* that pre-join two or more tables on one or more columns. Oracle 10*g* removed one of the remaining obstacles for using bitmap indexes in a heavy, single-row insert, update, or delete environment: mitigating performance problems due to bitmap index fragmentation issues.

Creating Tablespaces in a VLDB Environment

The considerations for creating tablespaces in a small database (terabyte range or smaller) also apply to VLDBs: Spread out I/O across multiple devices, use a logical volume manager (LVM) with RAID capabilities, or use ASM. In this section, I will present more detail and examples for bigfile tablespaces. Because a bigfile tablespace contains only one datafile, the ROWID format for objects stored in a bigfile tablespace is different, allowing for a tablespace size as large as eight million terabytes, depending on the tablespace's block size.

Bigfile tablespaces are best suited for an environment that uses ASM, Oracle Managed Files (OMF), and Recovery Manager (RMAN) with a fast recovery area. See Chapter 6 for a detailed review of ASM; Chapter 14 presents RMAN from a command-line and Enterprise Manager Cloud Control perspective and leverages the fast recovery area for all backups. Finally, Chapter 6 describes OMF from a space-management perspective.

In the next few sections, I will present an in-depth look at creating a bigfile tablespace and specifying its characteristics; in addition, I will discuss the impact of bigfile tablespaces on both initialization parameters and data dictionary views. Finally, I will show you how the DBVERIFY utility has been revised as of Oracle 10*g* to allow you to analyze a single bigfile datafile using parallel processes.

Bigfile Tablespace Basics

Using bigfile tablespaces with a block size of 32KB, a datafile can be as large as 128 terabytes, with a maximum database size of 8 exabytes (EB). In contrast, a database using only smallfile tablespaces can have a maximum datafile size of 128 gigabytes (GB) and therefore a maximum database size of 8 petabytes (PB). Because a bigfile tablespace can only have one datafile, you never need to decide whether to add a datafile to the single datafile for the tablespace; once you turn on AUTOEXTEND, the single datafile will only increase in size at the increment you specify. If you are using ASM and OMF, you won't even need to know the name of the single datafile.

Given that the maximum number of datafiles in a database on most platforms is 65,533, and the number of blocks in a bigfile tablespace datafile is 2^{32}, you can calculate the maximum amount of space (M) in a single Oracle database as the maximum number of datafiles (D) multiplied by the maximum number of blocks per datafile (F) multiplied by the tablespace block size (B):

$$M = D * F * B$$

Therefore, the maximum database size, given the maximum block size and the maximum number of datafiles, is

65,533 datafiles * 4,294,967,296 blocks per datafile * 32,768 block size =
9,223,231,299,366,420,480 = 8EB

For a smallfile tablespace, the number of blocks in a smallfile tablespace datafile is only 2^{22}. Therefore, our calculation yields

65,535 datafiles * 4,194,304 blocks per datafile * 32,768 block size =
9,007,061,815,787,520 = 8PB

In Table 18-1, you can see a comparison of maximum datafile sizes for smallfile tablespaces and bigfile tablespaces given the tablespace block size. If for some reason your database size approaches 8EB, you may want to consider either some table archiving or splitting the database into multiple databases based on function. With even the largest commercial Oracle databases in the petabyte (PB) range in 2015, you may very well not bump up against the 8EB limit any time in the near future!

Tablespace Block Size	Maximum Smallfile Datafile Size	Maximum Bigfile Datafile Size
2KB	8GB	8TB
4KB	16GB	16TB
8KB	32GB	32TB
16KB	64GB	64TB
32KB	128GB	128TB

TABLE 18-1. *Maximum Tablespace Datafile Sizes*

Creating and Modifying Bigfile Tablespaces

Here is an example of creating a bigfile tablespace in a non-ASM environment:

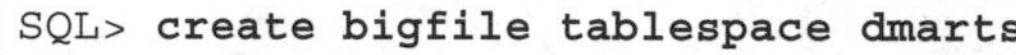

```
SQL> create bigfile tablespace dmarts
  2      datafile '+DATA' size 2500g
  3      autoextend on next 500g maxsize unlimited
  4      extent management local autoallocate
  5      segment space management auto;

Tablespace created.
```

In the example, you can see that EXTENT MANAGEMENT and SEGMENT SPACE MANAGEMENT are explicitly set, even though AUTO is the default for segment space management; bigfile tablespaces must be created as locally managed with automatic segment space management. Because the default allocation policy for both bigfile and smallfile tablespaces is AUTOALLOCATE, you don't need to specify it either. As a rule of thumb, AUTOALLOCATE is best for tablespaces whose table usage and growth patterns are indeterminate; as I've pointed out in Chapter 6, you use UNIFORM extent management only if you know the precise amount of space you need for each object in the tablespace as well as the number and size of extents.

Even though the datafile for this bigfile tablespace is set to autoextend indefinitely, the disk volume where the datafile resides may be limited in space; when this occurs, the tablespace may need to be relocated to a different disk volume. Therefore, you can see the advantages of using ASM: You can easily add another disk volume to the disk group where the datafile resides, and Oracle will automatically redistribute the contents of the datafile and allow the tablespace to grow—all of this occurring while the database (and the tablespace itself) is available to users.

By default, tablespaces are created as smallfile tablespaces; you can specify the default tablespace type when the database is created or at any time with the ALTER DATABASE command, as in this example:

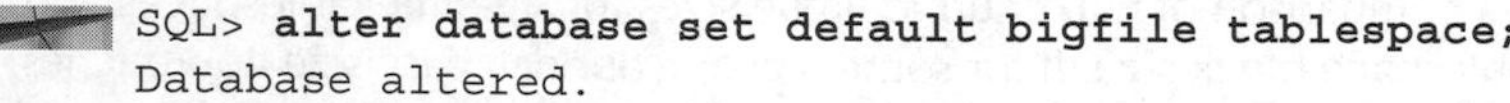

```
SQL> alter database set default bigfile tablespace;
Database altered.
```

Smallfile ROWID Component	Definition
OOOOOO	Data object number identifying the database segment (such as table, index, or materialized view)
FFF	Relative datafile number within the tablespace of the datafile that contains the row
BBBBBB	The data block containing the row, relative to the datafile
RRR	Slot number, or row number, of the row inside a block

TABLE 18-2. *Smallfile ROWID Format*

Bigfile Tablespace ROWID Format

To facilitate the larger address space for bigfile tablespaces, a new extended ROWID format is used for rows of tables in bigfile tablespaces. First, we will review the ROWID format for smallfile tablespaces in previous versions of Oracle and for Oracle 12*c*. The format for a smallfile ROWID consists of four parts:

```
OOOOOO FFF BBBBBB RRR
```

Table 18-2 defines each part of a smallfile ROWID.

In contrast, a bigfile tablespace only has one datafile, and its relative datafile number is always 1024. Because the relative datafile number is fixed, it is not needed as part of the ROWID; as a result, the part of the ROWID used for the relative datafile number can be used to expand the size of the block number field. The concatenation of the smallfile relative datafile number (FFF) and the smallfile data block number (BBBBBB) results in a new construct called an *encoded block number.* Therefore, the format for a bigfile ROWID consists of only three parts:

```
OOOOOO LLLLLLLLL RRR
```

Table 18-3 defines each part of a bigfile ROWID.

Bigfile ROWID Component	Definition
OOOOOO	Data object number identifying the database segment (such as table, index, or materialized view)
LLLLLLLLL	Encoded block number, relative to the tablespace and unique within the tablespace
RRR	Slot number, or row number, of the row inside a block

TABLE 18-3. *Bigfile ROWID Format*

DBMS_ROWID and Bigfile Tablespaces

Because two different types of tablespaces can now coexist in the database along with their corresponding ROWID formats, some changes have occurred to the DBMS_ROWID package.

The names of the procedures in the DBMS_ROWID package are the same and operate as before, except for a new parameter, TS_TYPE_IN, which identifies the type of tablespace to which a particular row belongs: TS_TYPE_IN can be either BIGFILE or SMALLFILE.

For an example of extracting ROWIDs from a table in a bigfile tablespace, we have a table called OE.ARCH_ORDERS in a bigfile tablespace named DMARTS:

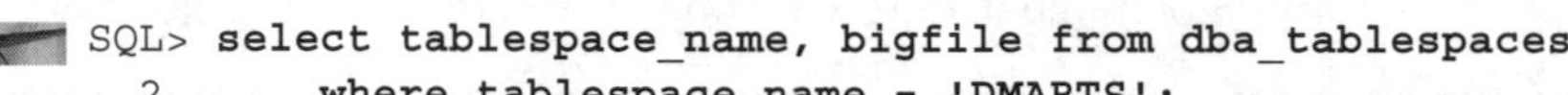

```
SQL> select tablespace_name, bigfile from dba_tablespaces
         where tablespace_name = 'DMARTS';

TABLESPACE_NAME                BIG
------------------------------ ---
DMARTS                         YES
```

As with tables in smallfile tablespaces in previous versions of Oracle and in Oracle 12*c*, we can use the pseudo-column ROWID to extract the entire ROWID, noting that the format of the ROWID is different for bigfile tables, even though the length of the ROWID stays the same. This query will also extract the block number in decimal format:

```
SQL> select rowid,
         dbms_rowid.rowid_block_number(rowid,'BIGFILE') blocknum,
         order_id, customer_id
     from oe.arch_orders
     where rownum < 11;

ROWID                BLOCKNUM   ORDER_ID CUSTOMER_ID
------------------ ---------- ---------- -----------
AAASAVAAAAAAAAUAAA         20       2458         101
AAASAVAAAAAAAAUAAB         20       2397         102
AAASAVAAAAAAAAUAAC         20       2454         103
AAASAVAAAAAAAAUAAD         20       2354         104
AAASAVAAAAAAAAUAAE         20       2358         105
AAASAVAAAAAAAAUAAF         20       2381         106
AAASAVAAAAAAAAUAAG         20       2440         107
AAASAVAAAAAAAAUAAH         20       2357         108
AAASAVAAAAAAAAUAAI         20       2394         109
AAASAVAAAAAAAAUAAJ         20       2435         144

10 rows selected.
```

For the row with the ORDER_ID of 2358, the data object number is AAASAV, the encoded block number is AAAAAAAAU, and the row number of the row, or slot, in the block is AAE; the translated decimal block number is 20.

NOTE
ROWIDs use base-64 encoding.

ROWID_INFO Parameter	Description
ROWID_IN	ROWID to be described
TS_TYPE_IN	Tablespace type (SMALLFILE or BIGFILE)
ROWID_TYPE	Returns ROWID type (restricted or extended)
OBJECT_NUMBER	Returns data object number
RELATIVE_FNO	Returns relative file number
BLOCK_NUMBER	Returns block number in this file
ROW_NUMBER	Returns row number in this block

TABLE 18-4. *ROWID_INFO Parameters*

The other procedures in the DBMS_ROWID package that use the variable TS_TYPE_IN to specify the tablespace type are ROWID_INFO and ROWID_RELATIVE_FNO.

The procedure ROWID_INFO returns five attributes for the specified ROWID via output parameters. In Table 18-4 you can see the parameters of the ROWID_INFO procedure.

In the following example, we'll use an anonymous PL/SQL block to extract the values for OBJECT_NUMBER, RELATIVE_FNO, BLOCK_NUMBER, and ROW_NUMBER for a row in the table OE.ARCH_ORDERS:

```
variable object_number number
variable relative_fno number
variable block_number number
variable row_number number

declare
   oe_rownum    rowid;
   rowid_type   number;
begin
   select rowid into oe_rownum from oe.arch_orders
      where order_id = 2358 and rownum = 1;
   dbms_rowid.rowid_info (rowid_in => oe_rownum,
       ts_type_in => 'BIGFILE',
       rowid_type => rowid_type,
       object_number => :object_number,
       relative_fno => :relative_fno,
       block_number => :block_number,
       row_number => :row_number);
end;

PL/SQL procedure successfully completed.

SQL> print
```

```
OBJECT_NUMBER
-------------
        73749

RELATIVE_FNO
------------
        1024

BLOCK_NUMBER
------------
          20

ROW_NUMBER
----------
         4

SQL>
```

Note that the return value for RELATIVE_FNO is always 1024 for a bigfile tablespace, and the BLOCK_NUMBER is 20, as you saw in the previous example that used the DBMS_ROWID .ROWID_BLOCK_NUMBER function.

Using DBVERIFY with Bigfile Tablespaces

The DBVERIFY utility, available since Oracle version 7.3, checks the logical integrity of an offline or online database. The files can only be datafiles; DBVERIFY cannot analyze online redo log files or archived redo log files. In previous versions of Oracle, DBVERIFY could analyze all of a tablespace's datafiles in parallel by spawning multiple DBVERIFY commands. However, because a bigfile tablespace has only one datafile, DBVERIFY has been enhanced to analyze parts of a bigfile tablespace's datafiles in parallel.

Using the **dbv** command at the Unix or Windows prompt, you can use two new parameters: START and END, representing the first and last block, respectively, of the file to analyze. As a result, you need to know how many blocks are in the bigfile tablespace's datafile; the dynamic performance view V$DATAFILE comes to the rescue, as you can see in the following example:

```
SQL> select file#, blocks, name from v$datafile;

     FILE#     BLOCKS NAME
---------- ---------- -------------------------------------------------
         1      96000 +DATA/dw/datafile/system.256.630244579
         2     109168 +DATA/dw/datafile/sysaux.257.630244581
         3       7680 +DATA/dw/datafile/undotbs1.258.630244583
         4        640 +DATA/dw/datafile/users.259.632441707
         5      12800 +DATA/dw/datafile/example.265.630244801
         6      64000 +DATA/dw/datafile/users_crypt.267.630456963
         7      12800 +DATA/dw/datafile/inet_star.268.632004213
         8       6400 +DATA/dw/datafile/inet_intl_star.269.632009933
         9       6400 /u02/oradata/xport_dw.dbf
        10       3200 +DATA/dw/datafile/dmarts.271.633226419

10 rows selected.
```

In the next example, you will see how to analyze datafile #9, the datafile for another bigfile tablespace in our database, XPORT_DW. At the operating system command prompt, you can analyze the file with five parallel processes, each processing 500 blocks, except for the last one:

```
$ dbv file=/u02/oradata/xport_dw.dbf start=1 end=1500 &
[1] 6444
$ dbv file=/u02/oradata/xport_dw.dbf start=1501 end=3000 &
[2] 6457
$ dbv file=/u02/oradata/xport_dw.dbf start=3001 end=4500 &
[2] 6466
$ dbv file=/u02/oradata/xport_dw.dbf start=4501 end=6000 &
[2] 6469
$ dbv file=/u02/oradata/xport_dw.dbf start=6001 &
[5] 6499
```

In the fifth command, we did not specify **end=**; if you do not specify **end=**, it is assumed that you will be analyzing the datafile from the starting point to the end of the file. All five of these commands run in parallel. You can also run DBVERIFY against datafiles in ASM disk groups, as in this example:

```
[oracle@kthanid ~]$ dbv file='+data12c/bob/datafile/users.259.863215269' \
                        start=1 end=1000

DBVERIFY: Release 12.1.0.2.0 - Production on Mon Nov 17 07:44:05 2014
Copyright (c) 1982, 2014, Oracle and/or its affiliates.  All rights reserved.
DBVERIFY - Verification starting : FILE =
     +data12c/bob/datafile/users.259.863215269

DBVERIFY - Verification complete

Total Pages Examined         : 640
Total Pages Processed (Data) : 68
Total Pages Failing   (Data) : 0
Total Pages Processed (Index): 33
Total Pages Failing   (Index): 0
Total Pages Processed (Lob)  : 2
Total Pages Failing   (Lob)  : 0
Total Pages Processed (Other): 520
Total Pages Processed (Seg)  : 0
Total Pages Failing   (Seg)  : 0
Total Pages Empty            : 17
Total Pages Marked Corrupt   : 0
Total Pages Influx           : 0
Total Pages Encrypted        : 0
Highest block SCN            : 0 (0.0)
[oracle@kthanid ~]$
```

Bigfile Tablespace Initialization Parameter Considerations

Although there are no new initialization parameters specific to bigfile tablespaces, the values of one initialization parameter and a CREATE DATABASE parameter can potentially be reduced because only one datafile is needed for each bigfile tablespace. The initialization parameter is DB_FILES, and the CREATE DATABASE parameter is MAXDATAFILES.

DB_FILES and Bigfile Tablespaces

As you already know, DB_FILES is the maximum number of datafiles that can be opened for this database. If you use bigfile tablespaces instead of smallfile tablespaces, the value of this parameter can be lower; as a result, because there are fewer datafiles to maintain, memory requirements are a bit lower in the System Global Area (SGA).

MAXDATAFILES and Bigfile Tablespaces

When creating a new database or a new control file, you can use the MAXDATAFILES parameter to control the size of the control file section allocated to maintain information about datafiles. Using bigfile tablespaces, you can make the size of the control file and the space needed in the SGA for datafile information smaller; more importantly, the same value for MAXDATAFILES using bigfile tablespaces means that the total database size can be larger.

Bigfile Tablespace Data Dictionary Changes

The changes to data dictionary views due to bigfile tablespaces include a new row in DATABASE_PROPERTIES and a new column in DBA_TABLESPACES and USER_TABLESPACES.

DATABASE_PROPERTIES and Bigfile Tablespaces

The data dictionary view DATABASE_PROPERTIES, as the name implies, contains a number of characteristics about the database, such as the names of the default and permanent tablespaces and various National Language Settings (NLS). Because of bigfile tablespaces, there is a new property in DATABASE_PROPERTIES called DEFAULT_TBS_TYPE that indicates the default tablespace type for the database if no type is specified in a CREATE TABLESPACE command. In the following example, you can find out the default new tablespace type:

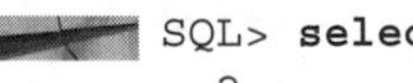

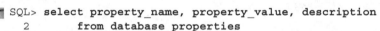

```
SQL> select property_name, property_value, description
  2        from database_properties
  3  where property_name = 'DEFAULT_TBS_TYPE';

PROPERTY_NAME      PROPERTY_VALUE   DESCRIPTION
------------------ ---------------- ------------------------
DEFAULT_TBS_TYPE   BIGFILE          Default tablespace type

1 row selected.
```

*_TABLESPACES, V$TABLESPACE, and Bigfile Tablespaces

The data dictionary views DBA_TABLESPACES and USER_TABLESPACES have a new column called BIGFILE. The value of this column is YES if the corresponding tablespace is a bigfile tablespace, as you saw in the query against DBA_TABLESPACES earlier in this chapter. The dynamic performance view V$TABLESPACE also contains this column.

Advanced Oracle Table Types

Many other table types provide benefits in a VLDB environment. Index-organized tables, for example, eliminate the need for both a table and its corresponding index, replacing them with a single structure that looks like an index but contains data like a table. Global temporary tables create a common table definition available to all database users; in a VLDB, a global temporary table shared by thousands of users is preferable to each user creating their own definition of the table, potentially putting further space pressure on the data dictionary. External tables allow you to use text-based files outside of the database without actually storing the data in an Oracle table. Partitioned tables, as the name implies, store tables and indexes in separate partitions to keep the availability of the tables high while keeping maintenance time low. Finally, materialized views preaggregate query results from a view and store the query results in a local table; queries that use the materialized view may run significantly faster because the results from executing the view do not need to be re-created. We will cover all these table types to varying levels of detail in the following sections.

Index-Organized Tables

You can store index and table data together in a table known as an *index-organized table (IOT)*. Significant reductions in disk space are achieved with IOTs because the indexed columns are not stored twice (once in the table and once in the index); instead, they are stored once in the IOT along with any non-indexed columns. IOTs are suitable for tables where the primary access method is through the primary key, although creating indexes on other columns of the IOT is allowed, to improve access by those columns.

In the following example, you will create an IOT with a two-part (composite) primary key:

```
create table oe.sales_summ_by_date
(     sales_date         date,
      dept_id            number,
      total_sales        number(18,2),
      constraint ssbd_pk primary key
          (sales_date, dept_id))
organization index tablespace xport_dw;
```

Each entry in the IOT contains a date, a department number, and a total sales amount for the day. All three of these columns are stored in each IOT row, but the IOT is built based on only the date and department number. Only one segment is used to store an IOT; if you build a secondary index on this IOT, a new segment is created.

Because the entire row in an IOT is stored as the index itself, there is no ROWID for each row; the primary key identifies the rows in an IOT. Instead, Oracle creates *logical ROWIDs* derived from the value of the primary key; the logical ROWID is used to support secondary indexes on the IOT.

If you still want to use an IOT for a frequently accessed set of columns but also include a number of infrequently accessed non-indexed columns, you can include these columns in an *overflow segment* by specifying the INCLUDING and OVERFLOW TABLESPACE clauses as in this example:

```
create table oe.sales_summ_by_date_full
(     sales_date         date,
      dept_id            number,
      total_sales        number(18,2),
      total_tax          number(18,2),
      country_code       number(8),
      constraint ssbd2_pk primary key
          (sales_date, dept_id))
organization index
including total_sales
tablespace xport_dw
overflow tablespace xport_ov;
```

The columns starting with TOTAL_TAX will be stored in an overflow segment in the XPORT_OV tablespace.

No special syntax is required to use an IOT; although it is built and maintained much like an index, it appears as a table to any SQL SELECT statement or other DML statements. Also, IOTs can be partitioned; information about partitioning IOTs is presented later in this chapter, in the section "Partitioned Index-Organized Tables."

Global Temporary Tables

Temporary tables have been available since Oracle8*i*. They are temporary in the sense of the data that is stored in the table, not in the definition of the table itself. The command CREATE GLOBAL TEMPORARY TABLE creates a temporary table; all users who have permissions on the table itself can perform DML on a temporary table. However, each user sees their own and only their own data in the table. When a user truncates a temporary table, only the data that they inserted is removed from the table. Global temporary tables are useful in situations where a large number of users need a table to hold temporary data for their session or transaction, while only needing one definition of the table in the data dictionary. Global temporary tables have the added advantage of reducing the need for redo or undo space for the entries in the table in a recovery scenario. The entries in a global temporary table, by their nature, are not permanent and therefore do not need to be recovered during instance or media recovery.

There are two different flavors of temporary data in a temporary table: temporary for the duration of the transaction, and temporary for the duration of the session. The longevity of the temporary data is controlled by the ON COMMIT clause; ON COMMIT DELETE ROWS removes all rows from the temporary table when a COMMIT or ROLLBACK is issued, and ON COMMIT PRESERVE ROWS keeps the rows in the table beyond the transaction boundary. However, when the user's session is terminated, all of the user's rows in the temporary table are removed.

In the following example, you create a global temporary table to hold some intermediate totals for the duration of the transaction. Here is the SQL command to create the table:

```
SQL> create global temporary table subtotal_hrs
  2      (emp_id              number,
  3       proj_hrs            number)
  4   on commit delete rows;

Table created.
```

For the purposes of this example, you will create a permanent table that holds the total hours by employee by project for a given day. Here is the SQL command for the permanent table:

```
SQL> create table total_hours (emp_id number, wk_dt date, tot_hrs number);
```

In the following scenario, you will use the global temporary table to keep the intermediate results, and at the end of the transaction, you will store the totals in the TOTAL_HOURS table. Here is the sequence of commands:

```
SQL> insert into subtotal_hrs values (101, 20);
1 row created.

SQL> insert into subtotal_hrs values (101, 10);
1 row created.
```

```
SQL> insert into subtotal_hrs values (120, 15);
1 row created.

SQL> select * from subtotal_hrs;

    EMP_ID   PROJ_HRS
---------- ----------
       101         20
       101         10
       120         15

SQL> insert into total_hours
  2      select emp_id, sysdate, sum(proj_hrs) from subtotal_hrs
  3          group by emp_id;
2 rows created.

SQL> commit;
Commit complete.

SQL> select * from subtotal_hrs;
no rows selected

SQL> select * from total_hours;

    EMP_ID WK_DT        TOT_HRS
---------- --------- ----------
       101 19-AUG-04         30
       120 19-AUG-04         15

SQL>
```

Notice that after the COMMIT, the rows are retained in TOTAL_HOURS but are not retained in SUBTOTAL_HRS because you specified ON COMMIT DELETE ROWS when you created the table.

NOTE

DDL can be performed on a global temporary table as long as there are no sessions currently inserting rows into the global temporary table.

There are a few other things to keep in mind when using temporary tables. Although you can create an index on a temporary table, the entries in the index are dropped along with the data rows, as with a regular table. Also, due to the temporary nature of the data in a temporary table, no recovery-related redo information is generated for DML on temporary tables; however, undo information is created in the undo tablespace and redo information to protect the undo. If all you do is insert and select from your global temporary tables, very little redo is generated. Because the table definition itself is not temporary, it persists between sessions until it is explicitly dropped.

As of Oracle Database 12*c*, statistics on a global temporary table can be specific to a session. This is important for global temporary tables whose contents and cardinality in one session vary widely from other sessions; in Oracle Database 11*g* there was only one set of statistics for a global temporary table, which made query optimization more difficult for queries containing global temporary tables.

External Tables

Sometimes you want to access data that resides outside of the database in a text format, but you want to use it as if it were a table in the database. Although you could use a utility such as SQL*Loader to load the table into the database, the data may be quite volatile or your user base's expertise might not include executing SQL*Loader at the Windows or Unix command line.

To address these needs, you can use *external tables,* which are read-only tables whose definition is stored within the database but whose data stays external to the database. There are a few drawbacks to using external tables: You cannot index external tables, and you cannot execute UPDATE, INSERT, and DELETE statements against an external table. However, in a data warehouse environment where an external table is read in its entirety for a merge operation with an existing table, these drawbacks do not apply.

You might use an external table to gather employee suggestions in a web-based front end that does not have access to the production database; in this example, you will create an external table that references a text-based file containing two fields: the employee ID and the comment.

First, you must create a *directory object* to point to the operating system directory where the text file is stored. In this example, you will create the directory EMPL_COMMENT_DIR to reference a directory on the Unix file system, as follows:

```
SQL> create directory empl_comment_dir as
         '/u10/Employee_Comments';
Directory created.
```

The text file in this directory is called **empl_sugg.txt**, and it looks like this:

```
$ cat empl_sugg.txt
101, The cafeteria serves lousy food.
138, We need a raise.
112, There are not enough bathrooms in Building 5.
138, I like the new benefits plan.
$
```

Because this text file has two fields, you will create the external table with two columns, the first being the employee number and the second being the text of the comments. Here is the CREATE TABLE command:

```
SQL> create table empl_sugg
       (employee_id       number,
        empl_comment      varchar2(250))
     organization external
       (type oracle_loader
        default directory empl_comment_dir
        access parameters
        (records delimited by newline
         fields terminated by ','
         (employee_id     char,
```

```
        empl_comment    char)
      )
      location('empl_sugg.txt')
     );
Table created.
SQL>
```

The first three lines of the command look like a standard CREATE TABLE command. The ORGANIZATION EXTERNAL clause specifies that this table's data is stored external to the database. Using the **oracle_loader** clause specifies the access driver to create and to load an external table as read-only. The file specified in the LOCATION clause, **empl_sugg.txt**, is located in the Oracle directory **empl_comment_dir**, which you created earlier. The access parameters specify that each row of the table is on its own line in the text file and that the fields in the text file are separated by a comma.

NOTE

*Using an access driver of **oracle_datapump** instead of **oracle_loader** allows you to unload your data to an external table; other than this initial unload, the external table is accessible for read access only through the **oracle_datapump** access driver and has the same restrictions as an external table created with the **oracle_loader** access driver.*

Once the table is created, the data is immediately accessible in a SELECT statement, as if it had been loaded into a real table, as you can see in this example:

```
SQL> select * from empl_sugg;

EMPLOYEE_ID EMPL_COMMENT
----------- ----------------------------------------------
        101  The cafeteria serves lousy food.
        138  We need a raise.
        112  There are not enough bathrooms in Building 5.
        138  I like the new benefits plan.

SQL>
```

Any changes made to the text file will automatically be available the next time you execute the SELECT statement.

Partitioned Tables

In a VLDB environment, partitioned tables help to make the database more available and maintainable. A partitioned table is split up into more manageable pieces, called *partitions,* and can be further subdivided into *subpartitions.* The corresponding indexes on partitioned tables can be nonpartitioned, partitioned the same way as the table, or partitioned differently from the table.

Partitioned tables can also improve the performance of the database: Each partition of a partitioned table can be accessed using parallel execution. Multiple parallel execution servers can be assigned to different partitions of the table or to different index partitions.

For performance reasons, each partition of a table can and should reside in its own tablespace. Other attributes of a partition, such as storage characteristics, can differ; however, the column datatypes and constraints for each partition must be identical. In other words, attributes such as datatype and check constraints are at the table level, not the partition level. Other advantages of storing partitions of a partitioned table in separate tablespaces include the following:

- It reduces the possibility of data corruption in more than one partition if one tablespace is damaged.
- Each partition can be backed up and recovered independently.
- You have more control of partition-to–physical device mapping to balance the I/O load. Even in an ASM environment, you *could* place each partition in a different disk group; in general, however, Oracle recommends two disk groups, one for user data and the other for flashback and recovery data. There are few reasons to limit a partition to a subset of the tens or hundreds of disks in a typical RAID-based disk group.

Partitioning is transparent to applications, and no changes to SQL statements are required to take advantage of partitioning. However, in situations where specifying a partition would be advantageous, you can specify both the table name and the partition name in a SQL statement; this improves both parse and SELECT performance. Examples of syntax using explicit partition names in a SELECT statement are found later in this chapter, in the section "Splitting, Adding, and Dropping Partitions."

Creating Partitioned Tables

Several methods of partitioning are available in the Oracle database, and many of them were introduced in Oracle Database 10*g*, such as list-partitioned IOTs; other methods are new to Oracle 11*g*, such as composite list-hash, list-list, list-range, and range-range partitioning. In the next few sections, we'll cover the basics of range partitioning, hash partitioning, list partitioning, six types of composite partitioning, as well as interval partitioning, reference partitioning, application-controlled partitioning, and virtual column partitioning. I'll also show you how to selectively compress partitions within the table to save on I/O and disk space. Oracle Database 12*c* adds another new type of partitioning: interval-reference partitioning.

Using Range Partitioning Range partitioning is used to map rows to partitions based on ranges of one or more columns in the table being partitioned. Also, the rows to be partitioned should be fairly evenly distributed among each partition, such as by months of the year or by quarter. If the column being partitioned is skewed (for example, by population within each state code), another partitioning method may be more appropriate.

To use range partitioning, you must specify the following three criteria:

- Partitioning method (range)
- Partitioning column or columns
- Bounds for each partition

In the following example, you want to partition the catalog request table CAT_REQ by season, resulting in a total of four partitions per year:

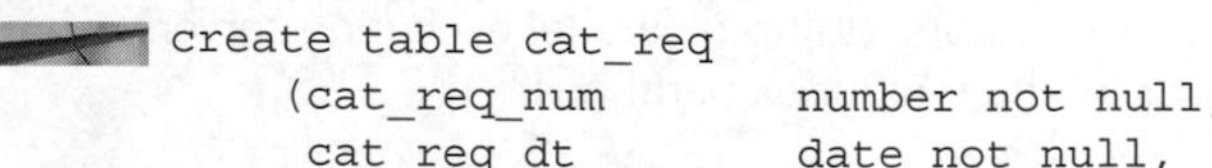

```
create table cat_req
   (cat_req_num        number not null,
    cat_req_dt         date not null,
```

```
     cat_cd               number not null,
     cust_num             number null,
     req_nm               varchar2(50),
     req_addr1            varchar2(75),
     req_addr2            varchar2(75),
     req_addr3            varchar2(75))
partition by range (cat_req_dt)
   (partition cat_req_spr_2014
         values less than (to_date('20140601','YYYYMMDD'))
         tablespace prd01,
     partition cat_req_sum_2014
         values less than (to_date('20140901','YYYYMMDD'))
         tablespace prd02,
     partition cat_req_fal_2014
         values less than (to_date('20141201','YYYYMMDD'))
         tablespace prd03,
     partition cat_req_win_2015
         values less than (maxvalue)
         tablespace prd04);
```

In the preceding example, the partitioning method is RANGE, the partitioning column is REQ_DATE, and the VALUES LESS THAN clause specifies the upper bound that corresponds to the dates for each season of the year: March through May (partition CAT_REQ_SPR_2014), June through August (partition CAT_REQ_SUM_2014), September through November (partition CAT_REQ_FAL_2014), and December through February (partition CAT_REQ_WIN_2015). Each partition is stored in its own tablespace—either PRD01, PRD02, PRD03, or PRD04.

You use MAXVALUE to catch *any* date values after 12/1/2014; if you had specified TO_DATE('20150301','YYYYMMDD') as the upper bound for the fourth partition, then any attempt to insert rows with date values after 2/28/2015 would fail. On the other hand, *any* rows inserted with dates before 6/1/2014 would end up in partition CAT_REQ_SPR_2014, even rows with a catalog request date of 10/1/1963! This is one case where the front-end application may provide some assistance in data verification, both at the low end and the high end of the date range.

The data dictionary view DBA_TAB_PARTITIONS shows you the partition components of the CAT_REQ table, as you can see in the following query:

```
SQL> select table_owner, table_name,
  2         partition_name, tablespace_name
  3  from dba_tab_partitions
  4  where table_name = 'CAT_REQ';

TABLE_OWNER     TABLE_NAME  PARTITION_NAME             TABLESPACE_NAME
--------------- ------------------------------------------ ---------------
OE              CAT_REQ     CAT_REQ_FAL_2014           PRD03
OE              CAT_REQ     CAT_REQ_SPR_2014           PRD01
OE              CAT_REQ     CAT_REQ_SUM_2014           PRD02
OE              CAT_REQ     CAT_REQ_WIN_2015           PRD04

4 rows selected.
```

Finding out the dates used in the VALUES LESS THAN clause when the partitioned table was created can be done in the same data dictionary view, as you can see in the following query:

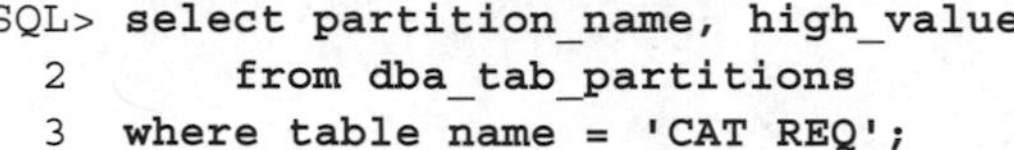

```
SQL> select partition_name, high_value
  2       from dba_tab_partitions
  3  where table_name = 'CAT_REQ';

PARTITION_NAME       HIGH_VALUE
-------------------- ----------------------------------------
CAT_REQ_FAL_2014     TO_DATE(' 2014-12-01 00:00:00', 'SYYYY-M
                     M-DD HH24:MI:SS', 'NLS_CALENDAR=GREGORIA
                     N')

CAT_REQ_SPR_2014     TO_DATE(' 2014-06-01 00:00:00', 'SYYYY-M
                     M-DD HH24:MI:SS', 'NLS_CALENDAR=GREGORIA
                     N')

CAT_REQ_SUM_2014     TO_DATE(' 2014-09-01 00:00:00', 'SYYYY-M
                     M-DD HH24:MI:SS', 'NLS_CALENDAR=GREGORIA
                     N')

CAT_REQ_WIN_2015     MAXVALUE

4 rows selected.
```

In a similar fashion, you can use the data dictionary view DBA_PART_KEY_COLUMNS to find out the columns used to partition the table, as in the following example:

```
SQL> select owner, name, object_type, column_name,
  2       column_position from dba_part_key_columns
  3  where owner = 'OE' and name = 'CAT_REQ';

OWNER     NAME          OBJECT_TYPE    COLUMN_NAME     COL
--------- ------------- -------------- --------------- ---
OE        CAT_REQ       TABLE          CAT_REQ_DT        1

1 row selected.
```

I will show you how to modify the partitions of a partitioned table later in this chapter, in the section "Managing Partitions."

Using Hash Partitioning Hash partitioning is a good option if the distribution of your data does not easily fit into a range partitioning scheme or the number of rows in the table is unknown, but you otherwise want to take advantage of the benefits inherent in partitioned tables. Rows are evenly spread out to two or more partitions based on an internal hashing algorithm using the partition key as input. The more distinct the values are in the partitioning column, the better the distribution of rows across the partitions.

To use hash partitioning, you must specify the following three criteria:

- Partitioning method (hash)
- Partitioning column or columns
- The number of partitions and a list of target tablespaces in which to store the partitions

For this example, you are creating a new customer table whose primary key is generated using a sequence. You want the new rows to be evenly distributed across four partitions; therefore, hash partitioning would be the best choice. Here is the SQL you use to create a hash-partitioned table:

```
create table oe.cust
     (cust_num          number not null primary key,
      ins_dt            date,
      first_nm          varchar2(25),
      last_nm           varchar2(35),
      mi                char(1),
      addr1             varchar2(40),
      addr2             varchar2(40),
      city              varchar2(40),
      state_cd          char(2),
      zip_cd            varchar2(10))
partition by hash (cust_num)
partitions 4
store in (prd01, prd02, prd03, prd04);
```

You do not necessarily have to specify the same number of partitions as tablespaces; if you specify more partitions than tablespaces, the tablespaces are reused for subsequent partitions in a round-robin fashion. If you specify fewer partitions than tablespaces, the extra tablespaces at the end of the tablespace list are ignored.

If you run the same queries that you ran for range partitioning, you may find some unexpected results, as you can see in this query:

```
SQL> select partition_name, tablespace_name, high_value
  2  from dba_tab_partitions
  3  where table_name = 'CUST';

PARTITION_NAME       TABLESPACE_NAME HIGH_VALUE
-------------------- --------------- --------------------
SYS_P1130            PRD01
SYS_P1131            PRD02
SYS_P1132            PRD03
SYS_P1133            PRD04

4 rows selected.
```

Because you are using hash partitioning, the HIGH_VALUE column is NULL.

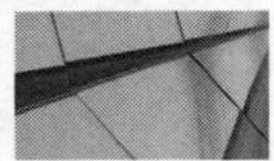

TIP
Oracle strongly recommends that the number of partitions in a hash-partitioned table be to a power of 2 to get an even distribution of rows in each table; Oracle uses the low-order bits of the partition key to determine the destination partition for the row.

Using List Partitioning List partitioning gives you explicit control of how each value in the partitioning column maps to a partition by specifying discrete values from the partitioning column. Range partitioning is usually not suitable for discrete values that do not have a natural and consecutive range of values, such as state codes. Hash partitioning is not suitable for assigning discrete values to a particular partition because, by its nature, a hash partition may map several related discrete values into different partitions.

To use list partitioning, you must specify the following three criteria:

- Partitioning method (list)
- Partitioning column
- Partition names, with each partition associated with a discrete list of literal values that place it in the partition

NOTE
As of Oracle 10g, list partitioning can be used for tables with LOB columns.

In the following example, you will use list partitioning to record sales information for the data warehouse into three partitions based on sales region: the Midwest, the western seaboard, and the rest of the country. Here is the CREATE TABLE command:

```
create table oe.sales_by_region_by_day
     (state_cd           char(2),
      sales_dt           date,
      sales_amt          number(16,2))
partition by list (state_cd)
    (partition midwest values ('WI','IL','IA','IN','MN')
          tablespace prd01,
     partition westcoast values ('CA','OR','WA')
          tablespace prd02,
     partition other_states values (default)
          tablespace prd03);
```

Sales information for Wisconsin, Illinois, and the other Midwestern states will be stored in the MIDWEST partition; California, Oregon, and Washington state will end up in the WESTCOAST partition. Any other value for state code, such as MI, will end up in the OTHER_STATES partition in tablespace PRD03.

Using Composite Range-Hash Partitioning As the name implies, range-hash partitioning uses range partitioning to divide rows first using the range method and then subpartitioning the rows within each range using a hash method. Composite range-hash partitioning is good for historical data with the added benefit of increased manageability and data placement within a larger number of total partitions.

To use composite range-hash partitioning, you must specify the following criteria:

- Primary partitioning method (range)
- Range partitioning column(s)
- Partition names identifying the bounds of the partition
- Subpartitioning method (hash)
- Subpartitioning column(s)
- Number of subpartitions for each partition or subpartition name

In the following example, you will track house and garden tool rentals. Each tool is identified by a unique tool number; at any given time, only about 400 tools are available for rental, although there may be slightly more than 400 on a temporary basis. For each partition, you want to use hash partitioning for each of eight subpartitions, using the tool name in the hashing algorithm. The subpartitions will be spread out over four tablespaces: PRD01, PRD02, PRD03, and PRD04. Here is the CREATE TABLE command to create the range-hash partitioned table:

```
create table oe.tool_rentals
  (tool_num       number,
   tool_desc      varchar2(50),
   rental_rate    number(6,2))
partition by range (tool_num)
   subpartition by hash (tool_desc)
   subpartition template (subpartition s1 tablespace prd01,
                          subpartition s2 tablespace prd02,
                          subpartition s3 tablespace prd03,
                          subpartition s4 tablespace prd04,
                          subpartition s5 tablespace prd01,
                          subpartition s6 tablespace prd02,
                          subpartition s7 tablespace prd03,
                          subpartition s8 tablespace prd04)
(partition tool_rentals_p1 values less than (101),
 partition tool_rentals_p2 values less than (201),
 partition tool_rentals_p3 values less than (301),
 partition tool_rentals_p4 values less than (maxvalue));
```

The range partitions are logical only; there are a total of 32 physical partitions, one for each combination of logical partition and subpartition in the template list. Note the SUBPARTITION TEMPLATE clause; the template is used for creating the subpartitions in every partition that doesn't have an explicit subpartition specification. It can be a real timesaver and reduce typing errors if the subpartitions are explicitly specified for each partition. Alternatively, you could specify the following clause, if you do not need the subpartitions explicitly named:

```
subpartitions 8 store in (prd01, prd02, prd03, prd04)
```

The physical partition information is available in DBA_TAB_SUBPARTITIONS, as for any partitioned table. Here is a query to find out the partition components of the TOOL_RENTALS table:

```
SQL> select table_name, partition_name, subpartition_name,
  2         tablespace_name
  3  from dba_tab_subpartitions
  4  where table_name = 'TOOL_RENTALS';

TABLE_NAME      PARTITION_NAME       SUBPARTITION_NAME      TABLESPACE
--------------- -------------------- ---------------------- ----------
TOOL_RENTALS    TOOL_RENTALS_P1      TOOL_RENTALS_P1_S1     PRD01
TOOL_RENTALS    TOOL_RENTALS_P1      TOOL_RENTALS_P1_S2     PRD02
TOOL_RENTALS    TOOL_RENTALS_P1      TOOL_RENTALS_P1_S3     PRD03
TOOL_RENTALS    TOOL_RENTALS_P1      TOOL_RENTALS_P1_S4     PRD04
TOOL_RENTALS    TOOL_RENTALS_P1      TOOL_RENTALS_P1_S5     PRD01
TOOL_RENTALS    TOOL_RENTALS_P1      TOOL_RENTALS_P1_S6     PRD02
TOOL_RENTALS    TOOL_RENTALS_P1      TOOL_RENTALS_P1_S7     PRD03
TOOL_RENTALS    TOOL_RENTALS_P1      TOOL_RENTALS_P1_S8     PRD04
TOOL_RENTALS    TOOL_RENTALS_P2      TOOL_RENTALS_P2_S1     PRD01
TOOL_RENTALS    TOOL_RENTALS_P2      TOOL_RENTALS_P2_S2     PRD02
. . .
TOOL_RENTALS    TOOL_RENTALS_P4      TOOL_RENTALS_P4_S8     PRD04

32 rows selected.
```

At the logical partition level, you still need to query DBA_TAB_PARTITIONS to obtain the range values, as you can see in the following query:

```
SQL> select table_name, partition_name,
  2          subpartition_count, high_value
  3   from dba_tab_partitions
  4  where table_name = 'TOOL_RENTALS';

TABLE_NAME       PARTITION_NAME      SUBPARTITION_COUNT HIGH_VALUE
---------------- ------------------- ------------------ -------------
TOOL_RENTALS     TOOL_RENTALS_P1                      8 101
TOOL_RENTALS     TOOL_RENTALS_P2                      8 201
TOOL_RENTALS     TOOL_RENTALS_P3                      8 301
TOOL_RENTALS     TOOL_RENTALS_P4                      8 MAXVALUE

4 rows selected.
```

Also note that either the partition name or subpartition name can be specified to perform manual partition pruning, as in these two examples:

```
select * from oe.tool_rentals partition (tool_rentals_p1);
select * from oe.tool_rentals subpartition (tool_rentals_p3_s2);
```

In the first query, a total of eight subpartitions are searched, TOOL_RENTALS_P1_S1 through TOOL_RENTALS_P1_S8; in the second query, only one out of the 32 total subpartitions is searched.

Using Composite Range-List Partitioning Similar to composite range-hash partitioning, composite range-list partitioning uses range partitioning to divide rows first using the range method and then subpartitioning the rows within each range using the list method. Composite range-list partitioning is good for historical data to place the data in each logical partition, further subdividing each logical partition using a discontinuous or discrete set of values.

NOTE
Range-list partitioning was introduced in Oracle 10g.

To use composite range-list partitioning, you must specify the following criteria:

- Primary partitioning method (range)
- Range partitioning column(s)
- Partition names identifying the bounds of the partition
- Subpartitioning method (list)
- Subpartitioning column
- Partition names, with each partition associated with a discrete list of literal values that place it in the partition

In the following example, we will expand on the previous "Sales by Region" list partitioning example and make the partitioned table more scalable by using the sales date for range partitioning, and we will use the state code for subpartitioning. Here is the CREATE TABLE command to accomplish this:

```
create table sales_by_region_by_quarter
     (state_cd           char(2),
      sales_dt           date,
      sales_amt          number(16,2))
partition by range (sales_dt)
     subpartition by list (state_cd)
       (partition q1_2014 values less than (to_date('20140401','YYYYMMDD'))
         (subpartition q1_2014_midwest values ('WI','IL','IA','IN','MN')
               tablespace prd01,
          subpartition q1_2014_westcoast values ('CA','OR','WA')
               tablespace prd02,
          subpartition q1_2014_other_states values (default)
               tablespace prd03
         ),
        partition q2_2014 values less than (to_date('20140701','YYYYMMDD'))
         (subpartition q2_2014_midwest values ('WI','IL','IA','IN','MN')
               tablespace prd01,
          subpartition q2_2014_westcoast values ('CA','OR','WA')
               tablespace prd02,
          subpartition q2_2014_other_states values (default)
               tablespace prd03
         ),
        partition q3_2014 values less than (to_date('20141001','YYYYMMDD'))
```

```
    (subpartition q3_2014_midwest values ('WI','IL','IA','IN','MN')
          tablespace prd01,
     subpartition q3_2014_westcoast values ('CA','OR','WA')
          tablespace prd02,
     subpartition q3_2014_other_states values (default)
          tablespace prd03
    ),
  partition q4_2014 values less than (maxvalue)
    (subpartition q4_2014_midwest values ('WI','IL','IA','IN','MN')
          tablespace prd01,
     subpartition q4_2014_westcoast values ('CA','OR','WA')
          tablespace prd02,
     subpartition q4_2014_other_states values (default)
          tablespace prd03
    )
  );
```

Each row stored in the table SALES_BY_REGION_BY_QUARTER is placed into one of 12 subpartitions, depending first on the sales date, which narrows the subpartition choice to three subpartitions. The value of the state code then determines which of the three subpartitions will be used to store the row. If a sales date falls beyond the end of 2014, it will still be placed in one of the subpartitions of Q4_2014 until you create a new partition and subpartitions for Q1_2015. Reorganizing partitioned tables is covered later in this chapter.

Using Composite List-Hash, List-List, and List-Range Partitioning Using list-hash, list-list, and list-range composite partitioning is similar to using range-hash, range-list, and range-range partitioning as discussed earlier in this section, except that you use the PARTITION BY LIST clause instead of the PARTITION BY RANGE clause as the primary partitioning strategy.

NOTE
*Composite list-hash partitioning and all subsequent partitioning methods in this chapter are new as of Oracle 11*g.

As an example, we'll re-create the SALES_BY_REGION_BY_QUARTER table (which uses a range-list scheme) using a list-range partitioning scheme instead, as follows:

```
create table sales_by_region_by_quarter_v2
     (state_cd            char(2),
      sales_dt            date,
      sales_amt           number(16,2))
partition by list (state_cd)
    subpartition by range(sales_dt)
        (partition midwest values ('WI','IL','IA','IN','MN')
          (
           subpartition midwest_q1_2014 values less than
                (to_date('20140401','YYYYMMDD')),
           subpartition midwest_q2_2014 values less than
                (to_date('20140701','YYYYMMDD')),
           subpartition midwest_q3_2014 values less than
                (to_date('20141001','YYYYMMDD')),
```

```
      subpartition midwest_q4_2014 values less than (maxvalue)
     ),
    partition westcoast values ('CA','OR','WA')
     (
      subpartition westcoast_q1_2014 values less than
           (to_date('20140401','YYYYMMDD')),
      subpartition westcoast_q2_2014 values less than
           (to_date('20140701','YYYYMMDD')),
      subpartition westcoast_q3_2014 values less than
           (to_date('20141001','YYYYMMDD')),
      subpartition westcoast_q4_2014 values less than (maxvalue)
     ),
    partition other_states values (default)
     (
      subpartition other_states_q1_2014 values less than
           (to_date('20140401','YYYYMMDD')),
      subpartition other_states_q2_2014 values less than
           (to_date('20140701','YYYYMMDD')),
      subpartition other_states_q3_2014 values less than
           (to_date('20141001','YYYYMMDD')),
      subpartition other_states_q4_2014 values less than (maxvalue)
     )
   );
```

This alternate partitioning scheme makes sense if the regional managers perform their analyses by date only within their regions.

Using Composite Range-Range Partitioning As the name implies, the range-range partitioning method uses a range of values in two table columns. Both columns would otherwise lend themselves to a range-partitioned table, but the columns do not need to have the same datatype. For example, a medical analysis table can use a primary range column of patient birth date, and a secondary range column of patient birth weight in ounces. Here is an example of a patient table using these two attributes:

```
create table patient_info
   (patient_id      number,
    birth_date      date,
    birth_weight_oz number)
partition by range (birth_date)
   subpartition by range (birth_weight_oz)
     (
      partition bd_1950 values less than (to_date('19501231','YYYYMMDD'))
       (
        subpartition bd_1950_4lb values less than (64),
        subpartition bd_1950_6lb values less than (96),
        subpartition bd_1950_8lb values less than (128),
        subpartition bd_1950_12lb values less than (192),
        subpartition bd_1950_o12lb values less than (maxvalue)
       ),
      partition bd_1960 values less than (to_date('19601231','YYYYMMDD'))
       (
```

```
   subpartition bd_1960_4lb values less than (64),
   subpartition bd_1960_6lb values less than (96),
   subpartition bd_1960_8lb values less than (128),
   subpartition bd_1960_12lb values less than (192),
   subpartition bd_1960_o12lb values less than (maxvalue)
  ),
partition bd_1970 values less than (to_date('19701231','YYYYMMDD'))
  (
   subpartition bd_1970_4lb values less than (64),
   subpartition bd_1970_6lb values less than (96),
   subpartition bd_1970_8lb values less than (128),
   subpartition bd_1970_12lb values less than (192),
   subpartition bd_1970_o12lb values less than (maxvalue)
  ),
partition bd_1980 values less than (to_date('19801231','YYYYMMDD'))
  (
   subpartition bd_1980_4lb values less than (64),
   subpartition bd_1980_6lb values less than (96),
   subpartition bd_1980_8lb values less than (128),
   subpartition bd_1980_12lb values less than (192),
   subpartition bd_1980_o12lb values less than (maxvalue)
  ),
partition bd_1990 values less than (to_date('19901231','YYYYMMDD'))
  (
   subpartition bd_1990_4lb values less than (64),
   subpartition bd_1990_6lb values less than (96),
   subpartition bd_1990_8lb values less than (128),
   subpartition bd_1990_12lb values less than (192),
   subpartition bd_1990_o12lb values less than (maxvalue)
  ),
partition bd_2000 values less than (to_date('20001231','YYYYMMDD'))
  (
   subpartition bd_2000_4lb values less than (64),
   subpartition bd_2000_6lb values less than (96),
   subpartition bd_2000_8lb values less than (128),
   subpartition bd_2000_12lb values less than (192),
   subpartition bd_2000_o12lb values less than (maxvalue)
  ),
partition bd_2010 values less than (to_date('20101231','YYYYMMDD'))
  (
   subpartition bd_2010_4lb values less than (64),
   subpartition bd_2010_6lb values less than (96),
   subpartition bd_2010_8lb values less than (128),
   subpartition bd_2010_12lb values less than (192),
   subpartition bd_2010_o12lb values less than (maxvalue)
  ),
partition bd_2020 values less than (maxvalue)
  (
   subpartition bd_2020_4lb values less than (64),
   subpartition bd_2020_6lb values less than (96),
```

```
        subpartition bd_2020_81b values less than (128),
        subpartition bd_2020_121b values less than (192),
        subpartition bd_2020_o121b values less than (maxvalue)
      )
    );
```

Using Interval Partitioning Interval partitioning automates the creation of new range partitions. For example, November, 2014 will almost certainly follow October, 2014, so using Oracle's interval partitioning saves you the effort and creates and maintains new partitions when needed. Here is an example of a range-partitioned table with four partitions and an interval definition of one month:

```
create table order_hist_interval
  (order_num      NUMBER(15),
   cust_id        NUMBER(12),
   order_dt       date,
   order_total    NUMBER(10,2)
  )
  partition by range (order_dt)
  interval(numtoyminterval(1,'month'))
    (partition p0 values less than (to_date('20060101','YYYYMMDD')),
     partition p1 values less than (to_date('20070101','YYYYMMDD')),
     partition p2 values less than (to_date('20090101','YYYYMMDD')),
     partition p3 values less than (to_date('20110101','YYYYMMDD'))
    );
```

Rows inserted with an ORDER_DT of July 1, 2014, or earlier will reside in one of the four initial partitions of ORDER_HIST_INTERVAL. Rows inserted with an ORDER_DT after July 1, 2014, will trigger the creation of a new partition with a range of one month each; the upper bound of each new partition will always be the first of the month, based on the value of the highest partition's upper limit. Looking in the data dictionary, this table looks somewhat like a pre-Oracle 11*g* range-partitioned table:

```
SQL> select table_name, partition_name, high_value
  2  from dba_tab_partitions
  3  where table_name = 'ORDER_HIST_INTERVAL';

TABLE_NAME                     PARTITION_NAME
------------------------------ ------------------------------
HIGH_VALUE
--------------------------------------------------------------------
ORDER_HIST_INTERVAL            P0
TO_DATE(' 2006-01-01 00:00:00', 'SYYYY-MM-DD HH24:MI:SS'
ORDER_HIST_INTERVAL            P1
TO_DATE(' 2007-01-01 00:00:00', 'SYYYY-MM-DD HH24:MI:SS'
ORDER_HIST_INTERVAL            P2
TO_DATE(' 2009-01-01 00:00:00', 'SYYYY-MM-DD HH24:MI:SS'
ORDER_HIST_INTERVAL            P3
TO_DATE(' 2012-01-01 00:00:00', 'SYYYY-MM-DD HH24:MI:SS'
```

However, suppose you add a row for November 11, 2014, as in this example:

```
SQL> insert into order_hist_interval
  2  values (19581968,1963411,to_date('20141111','YYYYMMDD'),420.11);

1 row created.

SQL>
```

There is now a new partition, as you can see when you query DBA_TAB_PARTITIONS again:

```
SQL> select table_name, partition_name, high_value
  2  from dba_tab_partitions
  3  where table_name = 'ORDER_HIST_INTERVAL';

TABLE_NAME                     PARTITION_NAME
------------------------------ ------------------------------
HIGH_VALUE
--------------------------------------------------------------------------------
ORDER_HIST_INTERVAL            P0
TO_DATE(' 2006-01-01 00:00:00', 'SYYYY-MM-DD HH24:MI:SS'
ORDER_HIST_INTERVAL            P1
TO_DATE(' 2007-01-01 00:00:00', 'SYYYY-MM-DD HH24:MI:SS'
ORDER_HIST_INTERVAL            P2
TO_DATE(' 2009-01-01 00:00:00', 'SYYYY-MM-DD HH24:MI:SS'
ORDER_HIST_INTERVAL            P3
TO_DATE(' 2011-01-01 00:00:00', 'SYYYY-MM-DD HH24:MI:SS'
ORDER_HIST_INTERVAL            SYS_P41
TO_DATE(' 2014-12-01 00:00:00', 'SYYYY-MM-DD HH24:MI:SS'
```

Note that partitions for July, August, September, and October of 2014 will not be created until order history rows are inserted containing dates within those months.

Using Reference Partitioning Reference partitioning leverages the parent-child relationships between tables to optimize partition characteristics and ease maintenance for tables that are frequently joined. In this example, the partitioning defined for the parent table ORDER_HIST is inherited by the ORDER_ITEM_HIST table:

```
create table order_hist
  (order_num      number(15) not null,
   cust_id        number(12),
   order_dt       date,
   order_total    number(10,2),
  constraint order_hist_pk primary key(order_num)
  )
  partition by range (order_dt)
    (partition q1_2014 values less than (to_date('20140401','YYYYMMDD')),
     partition q2_2014 values less than (to_date('20140701','YYYYMMDD')),
     partition q3_2014 values less than (to_date('20141001','YYYYMMDD')),
     partition q4_2014 values less than (to_date('20150101','YYYYMMDD'))
```

```
    )
;

create table order_item_hist
   (order_num       number(15),
    line_item_num   number(3),
    product_num     number(10),
    item_price      number(8,2),
    item_qty        number(8),
   constraint order_item_hist_fk
     foreign key (order_num) references order_hist(order_num)
   )
partition by reference(order_item_hist_fk)
;
```

Oracle automatically creates corresponding partitions with the same name for the ORDER_ITEM_HIST as in ORDER_HIST.

Using Interval-Reference Partitioning As you might expect, interval-reference partitioning (new to Oracle Database 12*c*) combines the features of both interval partitioning and reference partitioning discussed in previous sections. The key difference is that the parent table is interval-partitioned instead of range-partitioned. This gives you yet another option to manage parent-child tables with automated interval partitioning. Here is the example from the previous section rewritten to use interval-reference partitioning:

```
create table order_hist_interval_ref
   (order_num       NUMBER(15) not null,
    cust_id         NUMBER(12),
    order_dt        date,
    order_total     NUMBER(10,2)
   )
   partition by range (order_dt)
   interval(numtoyminterval(1,'month'))
     (partition p0 values less than (to_date('20060101','YYYYMMDD')),
      partition p1 values less than (to_date('20070101','YYYYMMDD')),
      partition p2 values less than (to_date('20090101','YYYYMMDD')),
      partition p3 values less than (to_date('20110101','YYYYMMDD'))
     );

create table order_item_hist
   (order_num       number(15),
    line_item_num   number(3),
    product_num     number(10),
    item_price      number(8,2),
    item_qty        number(8),
   constraint order_item_hist_fk
     foreign key (order_num) references order_hist_interval(order_num)
   )
partition by reference(order_item_hist_fk)
;
```

Any partition maintenance in the parent table (ORDER_HIST_INTERVAL) is automatically reflected in the child table (ORDER_ITEM_HIST). For example, converting a partition in the parent table from an interval partition to a conventional partition causes the same transformation in the child table.

Using Application-Controlled (System) Partitioning Application-controlled partitioning, also known as system partitioning, relies on the application logic to place rows into the appropriate partition. Only the partition names and the number of partitions are specified when the table is created, as in this example:

```
create table order_hist_sys_part
  (order_num      NUMBER(15) not null,
   cust_id        NUMBER(12),
   order_dt       date,
   order_total    NUMBER(10,2)
  )
  partition by system
    (partition p1 tablespace users1,
     partition p2 tablespace users2,
     partition p3 tablespace users3,
     partition p4 tablespace users4
    )
;
```

Any INSERT statements on this table must specify the partition number; otherwise, the INSERT will fail. Here is an example:

```
SQL> insert into order_hist_sys_part
  2  partition (p3)
  3  values (49809233,93934011,sysdate,122.12);

1 row created.

SQL>
```

Using Virtual Column Partitioning Virtual columns, available starting in Oracle Database 11*g*, can also be used as a partition key; any partition method that uses a regular column can use a virtual column. In this example, you create a partitioned table for order items based on the total cost of the line item—in other words, number of items multiplied by the item price:

```
create table line_item_value
  (order_num      number(15) not null,
   line_item_num  number(3) not null,
   product_num    number(10),
   item_price     number(8,2),
   item_qty       number(8),
   total_price    as (item_price * item_qty)
  )
partition by range (total_price)
(
   partition small  values less than (100),
   partition medium values less than (500),
```

```
    partition large  values less than (1000),
    partition xlarge values less than (maxvalue)
);
```

Using Compressed Partitioned Tables Partitioned tables can be compressed just as nonpartitioned tables can; in addition, the partitions of a partitioned table can be selectively compressed. For example, you may only want to compress the older, less often accessed partitions of a partitioned table and leave the most recent partition uncompressed to minimize the CPU overhead for retrieval of recent data. In this example, you will create a new version of the CAT_REQ table you created earlier in this chapter, compressing the first two partitions only. Here is the SQL command:

```
create table cat_req_2

    (cat_req_num        number not null,
     cat_req_dt         date not null,
     cat_cd             number not null,
     cust_num           number null,
     req_nm             varchar2(50),
     req_addr1          varchar2(75),
     req_addr2          varchar2(75),
     req_addr3          varchar2(75))
partition by range (cat_req_dt)
    (partition cat_req_spr_2014
          values less than (to_date('20140601','YYYYMMDD'))
          tablespace prd01 compress,
     partition cat_req_sum_2014
          values less than (to_date('20140901','YYYYMMDD'))
          tablespace prd02 compress,
     partition cat_req_fal_2014
          values less than (to_date('20141201','YYYYMMDD'))
          tablespace prd03 nocompress,
     partition cat_req_win_2015
          values less than (maxvalue)
          tablespace prd04 nocompress);
```

You do not have to specify NOCOMPRESS, because it is the default. To find out which partitions are compressed, you can use the column COMPRESSION in the data dictionary table DBA_TAB_PARTITIONS, as you can see in the following example:

```
SQL> select table_name, partition_name, compression
  2     from dba_tab_partitions
  3  where table_name = 'CAT_REQ_2';

TABLE_NAME        PARTITION_NAME       COMPRESS
----------------- -------------------- --------
CAT_REQ_2         CAT_REQ_FAL_2014     DISABLED
CAT_REQ_2         CAT_REQ_SPR_2014     ENABLED
CAT_REQ_2         CAT_REQ_SUM_2014     ENABLED
CAT_REQ_2         CAT_REQ_WIN_2015     DISABLED

4 rows selected.
```

Indexing Partitions

Local indexes on partitions reflect the structure of the underlying table and in general are easier to maintain than nonpartitioned or global partitioned indexes. Local indexes are *equipartitioned* with the underlying partitioned table; in other words, the local index is partitioned on the same columns as the underlying table and therefore has the same number of partitions and the same partition bounds as the underlying table.

Global partitioned indexes are created irrespective of the partitioning scheme of the underlying table and can be partitioned using range partitioning or hash partitioning. In this section, first I'll show you how to create a local partitioned index; next, I'll show you how to create both range-partitioned and hash-partitioned global indexes. In addition, I'll show you how to save space in a partitioned index by using key compression.

Creating Local Partitioned Indexes A local partitioned index is very easy to set up and maintain because the partitioning scheme is identical to the partitioning scheme of the base table. In other words, the number of partitions in the index is the same as the number of partitions and subpartitions in the table; in addition, for a row in a given partition or subpartition, the index entry is always stored in the corresponding index's partition or subpartition.

Figure 18-1 shows the relationship between a partitioned local index and a partitioned table. The number of partitions in the table is exactly the same as the number of partitions in the index.

In the following example, you will create a local index on the CUST table you created earlier in the chapter. Here is the SQL statement that retrieves the table partitions for the CUST table:

```
SQL> select partition_name, tablespace_name, high_value
  2  from dba_tab_partitions
  3  where table_name = 'CUST';

PARTITION_NAME       TABLESPACE_NAME HIGH_VALUE
-------------------- --------------- --------------------
SYS_P1130            PRD01
```

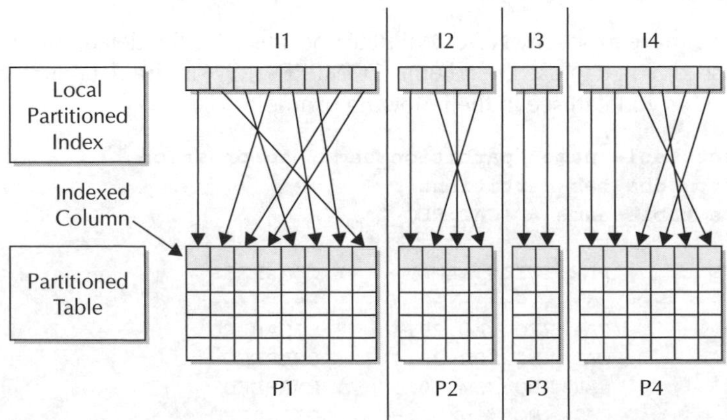

FIGURE 18-1. *Local partitioned index on a partitioned table*

```
SYS_P1131                PRD02
SYS_P1132                PRD03
SYS_P1133                PRD04

4 rows selected.
```

The command for creating the local index on this table is very straightforward, as you can see in this example:

```
SQL> create index oe.cust_ins_dt_ix on oe.cust (ins_dt)
  2        local store in (idx_1, idx_2, idx_3, idx_4);
Index created.
```

The index partitions are stored in four tablespaces stored outside of an ASM disk group—IDX_1 through IDX_4—to further improve the performance of the table, because each index partition is stored in a tablespace separate from any of the table partitions. You can find out about the partitions for this index by querying DBA_IND_PARTITIONS, as follows:

```
SQL> select partition_name, tablespace_name from dba_ind_partitions
  2       where index_name = 'CUST_INS_DT_IX';

PARTITION_NAME           TABLESPACE_NAME
------------------------ ---------------
SYS_P1130                IDX_1
SYS_P1131                IDX_2
SYS_P1132                IDX_3
SYS_P1133                IDX_4

4 rows selected.
```

Notice that the index partitions are automatically named the same as their corresponding table partitions. One of the benefits of local indexes is that when you create a new table partition, the corresponding index partition is built automatically; similarly, dropping a table partition automatically drops the index partition without invalidating any other index partitions, as would be the case for a global index.

Creating Range-Partitioned Global Indexes Creating a range-partitioned global index involves rules similar to those you use when creating range-partitioned tables. In a previous example, you created a range-partitioned table called CAT_REQ that contained four partitions based on the CAT_REQ_DT column. In this example, you will create a partitioned global index that will only contain two partitions (in other words, not partitioned the same way as the corresponding table):

```
create index cat_req_dt_ix on oe.cat_req(cat_req_dt)
  global partition by range(cat_req_dt)
  (partition spr_sum_2014
    values less than (to_date('20140901','YYYYMMDD'))
        tablespace idx_4,
   partition fal_win_2014
    values less than (maxvalue)
        tablespace idx_8);
```

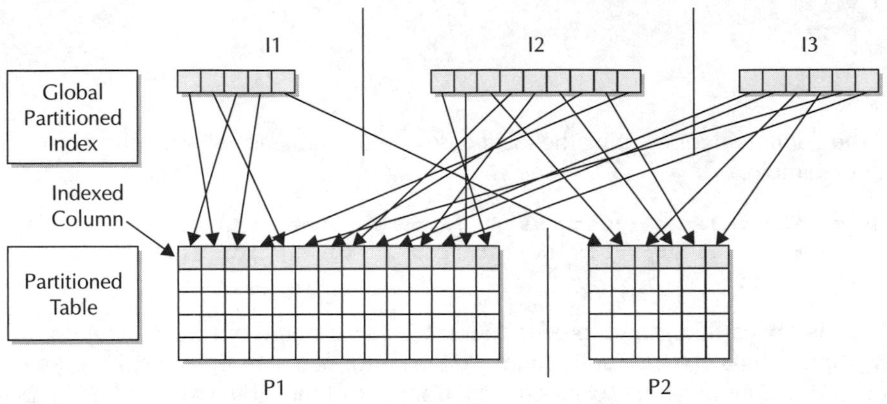

FIGURE 18-2. *Global partitioned index on a partitioned table*

Note that you specify two tablespaces to store the partitions for the index that are different from the tablespaces used to store the table partitions. If any DDL activity occurs on the underlying table, global indexes are marked as UNUSABLE and need to be rebuilt unless you include the UPDATE GLOBAL INDEXES clause (INVALIDATE GLOBAL INDEXES is the default). In the section "Managing Partitions" later in this chapter, we will review the UPDATE INDEX clause when you are performing partition maintenance operations on partitioned indexes.

Figure 18-2 shows the relationship between a partitioned global index and a partitioned table. The number of partitions in the table may or may not be the same as the number of partitions in the index.

Creating Hash-Partitioned Global Indexes As with range-partitioned global indexes, hash-partitioned global index CREATE statements share the syntax with hash-partitioned table CREATE statements. Hash-partitioned global indexes can improve performance in situations where a small number of a nonpartitioned index's leaf blocks are experiencing high contention in an OLTP environment. Queries that use either an equality or IN operator in the WHERE clause can benefit significantly from a hash-partitioned global index.

NOTE
*Hash-partitioned global indexes are new as of Oracle 10*g.

Building on our example using hash partitioning for the table CUST, you can create a hash-partitioned global index on the ZIP_CD column:

```
create index oe.cust_zip_cd_ix2 on oe.cust2(zip_cd)
  global partition by hash(zip_cd)
   (partition z1      tablespace idx_1,
    partition z2      tablespace idx_2,
    partition z3      tablespace idx_3,
    partition z4      tablespace idx_4,
    partition z5      tablespace idx_5,
```

```
partition z6        tablespace idx_6,
partition z7        tablespace idx_7,
partition z8        tablespace idx_8);
```

Note that the table CUST2 is partitioned using the CUST_NUM column, and it places its four partitions in PRD01 through PRD04; this index partition uses the ZIP_CD column for the hashing function and stores its eight partitions in IDX_1 through IDX_8.

Creating Nonpartitioned Global Indexes Creating a nonpartitioned global index is the same as creating a regular index on a nonpartitioned table; the syntax is identical. Figure 18-3 shows the relationship between a nonpartitioned global index and a partitioned table.

Using Key Compression on Partitioned Indexes If your index is nonunique and has a large number of repeating values for the index key or keys, you can use key compression on the index just as you can with a traditional nonpartitioned index. When only the first instance of the index key is stored, both disk space and I/O are reduced. In the following example, you can see how easy it is to create a compressed partitioned index:

```
create index oe.cust_ins_dt_ix on oe.cust (ins_dt)
   compress local
   store in (idx_1, idx_2, idx_3, idx_4);
```

You can specify that a more active index partition not be compressed by using NOCOMPRESS, which may save a noticeable amount of CPU for recent index entries that are more frequently accessed than the others in the index.

Partitioned Index-Organized Tables

Index-organized tables (IOTs) can be partitioned using either the range, list, or hash partitioning method; creating partitioned index-organized tables is syntactically similar to creating partitioned heap-organized tables. In this section, we'll cover some of the notable differences in how partitioned IOTs are created and used.

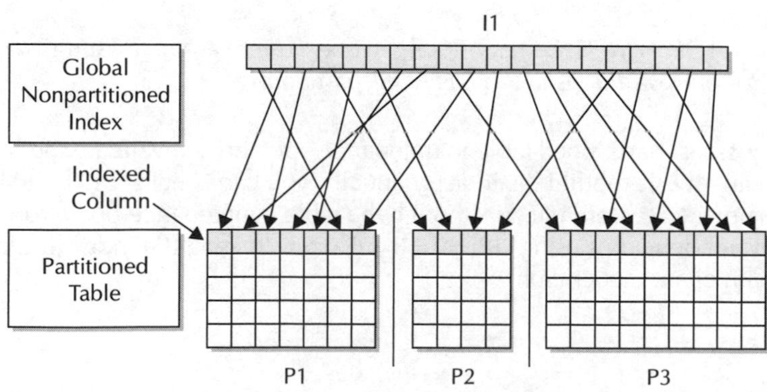

FIGURE 18-3. *Global nonpartitioned index on a partitioned table*

For a partitioned IOT, the ORGANIZATION INDEX, INCLUDING, and OVERFLOW clauses are used as they are for standard IOTs. In the PARTITION clause, you can specify the OVERFLOW clause as well as any other attributes of the overflow segment specific to a partition.

Since Oracle Database 10*g*, there is no longer the restriction that the set of partitioning columns must be a subset of the IOT's primary key columns; in addition, LIST partitioning is supported in addition to range and hash partitioning. In previous releases of Oracle, LOB columns were supported only in range-partitioned IOTs; as of Oracle 10*g*, they are supported in hash and list partitioning methods as well.

Managing Partitions

Fourteen maintenance operations can be performed on a partitioned table, including splitting a partition, merging partitions, and adding a new partition. These operations may or may not be available depending on the partitioning scheme used (range, hash, list, or one of the six composite methods). For composite partitions, these operations sometimes apply to both the partition and the subpartition, and sometimes to the subpartition only.

For partitioned indexes, there are seven different types of maintenance operations that vary depending on both the partitioning method (range, hash, list, or composite) as well as whether the index is a global index or a local index. In addition, each type of partitioned index may support automatic updates when the partitioning scheme is changed, thus reducing the occurrences of unusable indexes.

In the next couple sections, I'll present a convenient chart for both partitioned tables and partitioned indexes that shows you what kinds of operations are allowed on which partition types. For some of the more common maintenance operations, I'll give you some examples of how they are used, extending some of the examples I have presented earlier in this chapter.

Maintaining Table Partitions To maintain one or more table partitions or subpartitions, you use the ALTER TABLE command just as you would on a nonpartitioned table. In Table 18-5 are the types of partitioned table operations and the keywords you would use to perform them. The format of the ALTER TABLE command is as follows:

```
alter table <tablename> <partition_operation> <partition_operation_options>;
```

Table 18-6 contains the subpartition table operations.

CAUTION
Using the ADD PARTITION clause only works if there are no existing entries for new partitions in the DEFAULT partition.

In many cases, partitioned table maintenance operations invalidate the underlying index; while you can always rebuild the index manually, you can specify UPDATE INDEXES in the table partition maintenance command. Although the table maintenance operation will take longer, the most significant benefit of using UPDATE INDEXES is to keep the index available during the partition maintenance operation.

Partition Operation	Range & Composite Range-*	Interval & Composite Interval-*	Hash	List & Composite List-*	Reference
Add a partition	ADD PARTITION	ADD PARTITION	ADD PARTITION	N/A	
Coalesce a partition	N/A	N/A	COALESCE PARTITION	N/A	N/A
Drop a partition	DROP PARTITION	DROP PARTITION	DROP PARTITION	N/A	N/A
Exchange a partition	EXCHANGE PARTITION	EXCHANGE PARTITION	EXCHANGE PARTITION	EXCHANGE PARTITION	EXCHANGE PARTITION
Merge partitions	MERGE PARTITIONS	MERGE PARTITIONS	N/A	MERGE PARTITIONS	N/A
Modify default attributes	MODIFY DEFAULT ATTRIBUTES	MODIFY DEFAULT ATTRIBUTES	MODIFY DEFAULT ATTRIBUTES	MODIFY DEFAULT ATTRIBUTES	MODIFY DEFAULT ATTRIBUTES
Modify real attributes	MODIFY PARTITION	MODIFY PARTITION	MODIFY PARTITION	MODIFY PARTITION	MODIFY PARTITION
Modify list partitions: Add values	N/A	N/A	N/A	MODIFY PARTITION . . . ADD VALUES	N/A
Modify list partitions: Drop values	N/A	N/A	N/A	MODIFY PARTITION . . . DROP VALUES	N/A
Move a partition	MOVE PARTITION	MOVE PARTITION	MOVE PARTITION	MOVE PARTITION	MOVE PARTITION
Rename a partition	RENAME PARTITION	RENAME PARTITION	RENAME PARTITION	RENAME PARTITION	RENAME PARTITION
Split a partition	SPLIT PARTITION	SPLIT PARTITION	N/A	SPLIT PARTITION	N/A
Truncate a partition	TRUNCATE PARTITION	TRUNCATE PARTITION	TRUNCATE PARTITION	TRUNCATE PARTITION	TRUNCATE PARTITION

TABLE 18-5. *Maintenance Operations for Partitioned Tables*

Splitting, Adding, and Dropping Partitions In many environments, a "rolling window" partitioned table will contain the latest four quarters' worth of rows. When the new quarter starts, a new partition is created, and the oldest partition is archived and dropped. In the following example, you will split the last partition of the CAT_REQ table you created earlier in this chapter

Partition Operation	Composite *-Range	Composite *-Hash	Composite *-List
Add a subpartition	MODIFY PARTITION . . . ADD SUBPARTITION	MODIFY PARTITION . . . ADD SUBPARTITION	MODIFY PARTITION . . . ADD SUBPARTITION
Coalesce a subpartition	N/A	MODIFY PARTITION . . . COALESCE SUBPARTITION	N/A
Drop a subpartition	DROP SUBPARTITION	N/A	DROP SUBPARTITION
Exchange a subpartition	EXCHANGE SUBPARTITION	N/A	EXCHANGE SUBPARTITION
Merge subpartitions	MERGE SUBPARTITIONS	N/A	MERGE SUBPARTITIONS
Modify default attributes	MODIFY DEFAULT ATTRIBUTES FOR PARTITION	MODIFY DEFAULT ATTRIBUTES FOR PARTITION	MODIFY DEFAULT ATTRIBUTES FOR PARTITION
Modify real attributes	MODIFY SUBPARTITION	MODIFY SUBPARTITION	MODIFY SUBPARTITION
Modify list subpartitions: Add values	N/A	N/A	MODIFY SUBPARTITION . . . ADD VALUES
Modify list subpartitions: Drop values	N/A	N/A	MODIFY SUBPARTITION . . . DROP VALUES
Move a subpartition	MOVE SUBPARTITION	MOVE SUBPARTITION	MOVE SUBPARTITION
Rename a subpartition	RENAME SUBPARTITION	RENAME SUBPARTITION	RENAME SUBPARTITION
Split a subpartition	SPLIT SUBPARTITION	N/A	SPLIT SUBPARTITION
Truncate a subpartition	TRUNCATE SUBPARTITION	TRUNCATE SUBPARTITION	TRUNCATE SUBPARTITION

TABLE 18-6. *Maintenance Operations for Subpartitions of Partitioned Tables*

at a specific date and maintain the new partition with MAXVALUE, back up the oldest partition, and then drop the oldest partition. Here are the commands you can use:

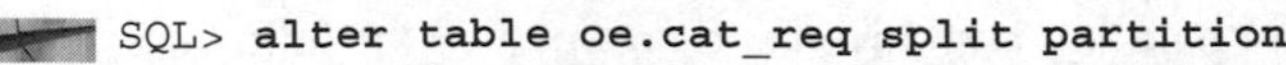

```
SQL> alter table oe.cat_req split partition
       cat_req_win_2015 at (to_date('20150101','YYYYMMDD')) into
       (partition cat_req_win_2015 tablespace prd04,
```

```
  4      partition cat_req_spr_2015 tablespace prd01);
Table altered.

SQL> create table oe.arch_cat_req_spr_2014 as
  2      select * from oe.cat_req partition(cat_req_spr_2014);
Table created.

SQL> alter table oe.cat_req
  2      drop partition cat_req_spr_2014;
Table altered.
```

The data dictionary view DBA_TAB_PARTITIONS reflects the new partitioning scheme, as you can see in this example:

```
SQL> select partition_name, high_value
  2      from dba_tab_partitions
  3  where table_name = 'CAT_REQ';

PARTITION_NAME        HIGH_VALUE
--------------------- ----------------------------------------
CAT_REQ_FAL_2014      TO_DATE(' 2014-12-01 00:00:00', 'SYYYY-M
                      M-DD HH24:MI:SS', 'NLS_CALENDAR=GREGORIA
                      N')

CAT_REQ_SUM_2014      TO_DATE(' 2014-09-01 00:00:00', 'SYYYY-M
                      M-DD HH24:MI:SS', 'NLS_CALENDAR=GREGORIA
                      N')

CAT_REQ_WIN_2015      TO_DATE(' 2015-01-01 00:00:00', 'SYYYY-M
                      M-DD HH24:MI:SS', 'NLS_CALENDAR=GREGORIA
                      N')
CAT_REQ_SPR_2015      MAXVALUE

4 rows selected.
```

Note that if you had dropped any partition other than the oldest partition, the next highest partition "takes up the slack" and contains any new rows that would have resided in the dropped partition; regardless of what partition is dropped, the rows in the partition are no longer in the partitioned table. To preserve the rows, you would use MERGE PARTITION instead of DROP PARTITION.

Coalescing a Table Partition You can coalesce a partition in a hash-partitioned table to redistribute the contents of the partition to the remaining partitions and reduce the number of partitions by one. For the new CUST table you created earlier in this chapter, you can do this in one easy step:

```
SQL> alter table oe.cust coalesce partition;
Table altered.
```

The number of partitions in CUST is now three instead of four:

```
SQL> select partition_name, tablespace_name
  2      from dba_tab_partitions
  3  where table_name = 'CUST';

PARTITION_NAME       TABLESPACE
-------------------- ----------
SYS_P1130            PRD01
SYS_P1131            PRD02
SYS_P1132            PRD03

3 rows selected.
```

Merging Two Table Partitions You may find out through various Oracle advisors that one partition of a partitioned table is infrequently used or not used at all; in this situation, you may want to combine two partitions into a single partition to reduce your maintenance effort. In this example, you will combine the partitions MIDWEST and WESTCOAST in the partitioned table SALES_BY_REGION_BY_DAY into a single partition, MIDWESTCOAST:

```
SQL> alter table oe.sales_by_region_by_day
  2      merge partitions midwest, westcoast
  3      into partition midwestcoast tablespace prd04;
Table altered.
```

Looking at the data dictionary view DBA_TAB_PARTITIONS, you can see that the table now has only two partitions:

```
SQL> select table_name, partition_name, tablespace_name, high_value
  2     from dba_tab_partitions
  3  where table_owner = 'OE' and
  4         table_name = 'SALES_BY_REGION_BY_DAY';

TABLE_NAME             PARTITION_NAME    TABLESPACE HIGH_VALUE
---------------------- ----------------- ---------- --------------------
SALES_BY_REGION_BY_DAY MIDWESTCOAST      PRD04      'WI', 'IL', 'IA', 'IN
                                                    ', 'MN', 'CA', 'OR',
                                                    'WA'

SALES_BY_REGION_BY_DAY OTHER_STATES      PRD03      default


2 rows selected.
```

Maintaining Index Partitions To maintain one or more index partitions or subpartitions, you use the ALTER INDEX command just as you would on a nonpartitioned index. Table 18-7 lists the types of partitioned index operations and the keywords you would use to perform them for the different types of partitioned indexes (range, hash, list, and composite). The format of the ALTER INDEX command is

```
alter index <indexname> <partition_operation> <partition_operation_options>;
```

Partition Operation	Index Type	Range	Hash/List	Composite
Add a partition	Global	N/A	ADD PARTITION (hash)	N/A
	Local	N/A	N/A	N/A
Drop a partition	Global	DROP PARTITION	N/A	N/A
	Local	N/A	N/A	N/A
Modify default attributes	Global	MODIFY DEFAULT ATTRIBUTES	N/A	N/A
	Local	MODIFY DEFAULT ATTRIBUTES	MODIFY DEFAULT ATTRIBUTES	MODIFY DEFAULT ATTRIBUTES [FOR PARTITION]
Modify real attributes	Global	MODIFY PARTITION	N/A	N/A
	Local	MODIFY PARTITION	MODIFY PARTITION	MODIFY [SUB] PARTITION
Rebuild a partition	Global	REBUILD PARTITION	N/A	N/A
	Local	REBUILD PARTITION	REBUILD PARTITION	REBUILD SUBPARTITION
Rename a partition	Global	RENAME PARTITION	N/A	N/A
	Local	RENAME PARTITION	RENAME PARTITION	RENAME [SUB] PARTITION
Split a partition	Global	SPLIT PARTITION	N/A	N/A
	Local	N/A	N/A	N/A

TABLE 18-7. *Maintenance Operations for Partitioned Indexes*

As with table partition maintenance commands, not all operations are available for every index partition type. You should note that many of the index partition maintenance options do not apply to local index partitions. By its nature, a local index partition matches the partitioning scheme of the table and will change when you modify the table's partitioning scheme.

Splitting a Global Index Partition Splitting a global index partition is much like splitting a table's partition. One particular global index partition may be a hotspot due to the index entries being stored in that particular partition; as with a table partition, you can split the index partition into two or more partitions. In the following example, you'll split one of the partitions of the global index OE.CAT_REQ_DT_IX into two partitions:

```
SQL> alter index oe.cat_req_dt_ix split partition
  2      fal_win_2014 at (to_date('20141201','YYYYMMDD')) into
  3        (partition fal_2014 tablespace idx_7,
  4         partition win_2015 tablespace idx_8);
Index altered.
```

The index entries for the FAL_WIN_2014 partition will now reside in two new partitions, FAL_2014 and WIN_2015.

Renaming a Local Index Partition Most characteristics of a local index are updated automatically when the corresponding table partition is modified. However, a few operations still may need to be performed on a local index partition, such as rebuilding the partition or renaming a partition that was originally named with a default system-assigned name. In this example, you will rename the local index partitions in the index OE.CUST_INS_DT_IX using more meaningful names:

```
SQL> alter index oe.cust_ins_dt_ix
  2      rename partition sys_P1130 to cust_ins_dt_ix_P1;
Index altered.

SQL> alter index oe.cust_ins_dt_ix
  2      rename partition sys_P1131 to cust_ins_dt_ix_P2;
Index altered.

SQL> alter index oe.cust_ins_dt_ix
  2      rename partition sys_P1132 to cust_ins_dt_ix_P3;
Index altered.
```

Materialized Views

Another type of table, called a *materialized view,* shares the characteristics of a table and a view. It is like a view in that it derives its results from a query against one or more tables; it is like a table in that it persists the result set of a view in a segment. Materialized views are useful in both OLTP and DSS systems. Frequent user queries against operational data may be able to use materialized views instead of the repeated joining of many highly normalized tables, and in a data warehouse environment the historical data can be aggregated ahead of time to make DSS queries run in a fraction of the time it would take to aggregate the data "on the fly."

The data in a materialized view can be refreshed on demand or incrementally, depending on the business need. Depending on the complexity of the view's underlying SQL statement, the materialized view can be quickly brought up to date with incremental changes via a *materialized view log.*

To create a materialized view, you use the CREATE MATERIALIZED VIEW command; the syntax for this command is similar to creating a standard view. Because a materialized view stores the result of a query, you can also specify storage parameters for the view as if you were creating a table. In the CREATE MATERIALIZED VIEW command, you also specify how the view will be refreshed. The materialized view can be refreshed either on demand or whenever one of the base tables changes. Also, you can force a materialized view to use materialized view logs for an incremental update, or you can force a complete rebuild of the materialized view when a refresh occurs.

Materialized views can automatically be used by the optimizer if the optimizer determines that a particular materialized view already has the results of a query that a user has submitted; the user does not even have to know that their query is using the materialized view directly instead of the base tables. However, to use query rewrite, the user must have the QUERY REWRITE system privilege and you have to set the value of the initialization parameter QUERY_REWRITE_ENABLED to TRUE.

Using Bitmap Indexes

An alternative to B-tree indexes, called *bitmap indexes,* provides query optimization benefits in environments that frequently perform joins on columns with low cardinality. In this section, we'll review the basics of bitmap indexes, create a bitmap index, and look at how bitmap indexes can be created ahead of time against columns in two or more tables.

Understanding Bitmap Indexes

A bitmap index is extremely useful in a VLDB environment when the column being indexed has a very low number of possible values, such as gender, where the possible values are usually M and F. A *bitmap index* uses a string of binary ones and zeros to represent the existence or nonexistence of a particular column value. Using bitmap indexes makes multiple AND and OR operations against several table columns very efficient in a query. Bitmap indexes are common in data warehouse and other VLDB environments where many low-cardinality columns exist, DML commands are done in bulk, and the query conditions frequently use columns with bitmap indexes.

The space requirements for a bitmap index are low as long as the cardinality is low; for example, a bitmap index on the GENDER column of the EMPLOYEES table would contain two bitmaps with a length equal to the number of rows in the table. If the EMPLOYEES table had 15 rows, the bitmaps for the GENDER column might look like the following:

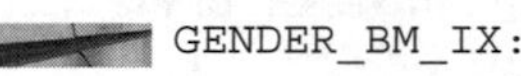

```
GENDER_BM_IX:
   F: 1 1 0 1 1 1 0 0 0 1 0 1 1 1 0
   M: 0 0 1 0 0 0 1 1 1 0 1 0 0 0 1
```

As you can see, the size of the bitmap index is directly proportional to the cardinality of the column being indexed; however, bitmap index blocks with all zeros are compressed to reduce storage space for bitmap indexes. A bitmap index on the LAST_NAME column of the EMPLOYEES table would be significantly larger, and many of the benefits of a bitmap index in this case might be outweighed by the space consumed by the index! Although there are exceptions to every rule, the cardinality can be up to ten percent of the rows and bitmap indexes will still perform well; in other words, a table with 1000 rows and 100 distinct values in a particular column will still most likely benefit from a bitmap index.

NOTE
The Oracle optimizer dynamically converts bitmap index entries to ROWIDs during query processing. This allows the optimizer to use bitmap indexes with B-tree indexes on columns that have many distinct values.

Previous to Oracle 10*g,* the performance of a bitmap would often deteriorate over time with frequent DML activity against the table containing the bitmap index. To take advantage of the improvements to the internal structure of bitmap indexes, you must set the COMPATIBLE initialization parameter to 10.0.0.0 or greater (to match your current release: if you're using Oracle Database 12*c,* you should have COMPATIBLE set to 12.1.0 or higher). Bitmap indexes that performed poorly before the COMPATIBLE parameter was adjusted should be rebuilt; bitmap indexes that performed adequately before the COMPATIBLE parameter was changed will perform better after the change. Any new bitmap indexes created after the COMPATIBLE parameter is adjusted will take advantage of all improvements.

Using Bitmap Indexes

Bitmap indexes are easy to create; the syntax is identical to that for creating any other index, with the addition of the BITMAP keyword. In the following example, you will add a GENDER column to the EMPLOYEES table and then create a bitmap index on it:

```
SQL> alter table hr.employees
  2      add (gender    char(1));
Table altered.

SQL> create bitmap index
  2      hr.gender_bm_ix on hr.employees(gender);
Index created.
```

Using Bitmap Join Indexes

As of Oracle9*i*, you can create an enhanced type of bitmap index called a *bitmap join index.* A bitmap join index is a bitmap index representing the join between two or more tables. For each value of a column in the first table of the join, the bitmap join index stores the ROWIDs of the corresponding rows in the other tables with the same value as the column in the first table. Bitmap join indexes are an alternative to materialized views that contain a join condition; the storage required for storing the related ROWIDs can be significantly lower than storing the result of the view itself.

In this example, you find out that the HR department is frequently joining the EMPLOYEES and DEPARTMENTS table on the DEPARTMENT_ID column. As an alternative to creating a materialized view, you decide to create a bitmap join index. Here is the SQL command to create the bitmap join index:

```
SQL> create bitmap index
  2       hr.emp_dept_bj_ix on hr.employees(hr.departments.department_id)
  3  from hr.employees, hr.departments
  4  where hr.employees.department_id = hr.departments.department_id;
Index created.
```

There are a few restrictions on bitmap join indexes:

- Only one of the tables in the bitmap join index can be updated concurrently by different transactions when the bitmap join index is being used.
- No table can appear more than once in the join.
- Bitmap join indexes cannot be created on an IOT or a temporary table.
- A bitmap join index cannot be created with the UNIQUE attribute.
- The join column(s) used for the index must be the primary key or have a unique constraint in the table being joined to the table with the bitmap index.

Summary

Chances are your database gets bigger rather than smaller every day. More customers are buying your merchandise online, for example, or more patients are being seen by doctors in your health system every day, and all of this information either should or must be retained over time for analytical or legal reasons. Therefore, Oracle Database 12*c* makes it easy to manage and access both current and historical data.

Bigfile tablespaces break past the limitations in datafile size for a tablespace (32GB for an 8KB block size, for example). Not only does this reduce the number of datafiles you need in your database but also enables maintenance of the tablespace at the tablespace level instead of the datafile level.

Table and index partitioning is the key feature of Oracle Database 12*c* (and the previous few versions!) that enables the timely access of rows from tables with millions or billions of rows. Even with an indexed table you may have to traverse billions of index entries to find the rows you need when all you need are the last three months' worth of rows in a patient visit table. Using an encounter date as the partitioning key means that even a full table scan on the last three months' worth of patient visits (the latest three partitions) will take seconds instead of hours.

Finally, bitmap indexes can speed up a class of queries where you typically have a low number of values in a column and you want to quickly filter a large percentage of those rows by using a very compact bitmap index whose format is literally a single bit for the existence of that column's value in the current row of the table. Bitmap join indexes take it a step further by pre-joining a column that's common to two tables, further speeding up any future joins between those two tables.

CHAPTER 19

Managing Distributed Databases

In a distributed environment, databases on separate servers (hosts) may be accessed during a single transaction or query. Each server can be physically isolated without being logically isolated from the other servers.

A typical distributed database implementation involves corporate headquarters servers that replicate data to departmental servers in various locations. Each database supports local client applications and also has the ability to communicate with other databases in the network. This architecture is shown in Figure 19-1.

Oracle Net allows this architecture to become reality. Run on all the servers involved, Oracle Net allows database requests made from one database (or application) to be passed to another database on a separate server. With this functionality, you can communicate with all the databases that are accessible via your network. You can then create synonyms that give applications true network transparency; the user who submits a query will not know the location of the data that is used to resolve it.

You can configure Oracle to support multimaster replication (in which all databases involved own the data and can serve as the source for data propagation) or single-master replication (in which only one database owns the data). When designing a replication configuration, you should try to restrict the ownership of data as much as possible. As the number of sources for propagation increases, the potential for errors to occur increases, as does the potential administration workload. In the following sections, you will see examples of the different replication capabilities available, followed by management techniques.

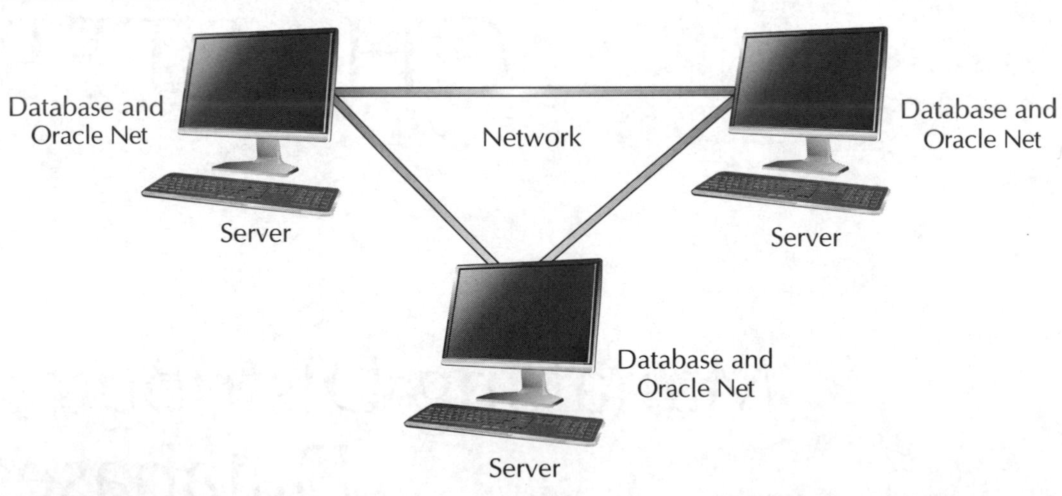

FIGURE 19-1. *Server/server architecture*

Remote Queries

To query a remote database, you must create a *database link* in the database in which the query will originate. The database link specifies the service name for the remote database and may also specify the username to connect to in the remote database. When a database link is referenced by a SQL statement, Oracle opens a session in the remote database, executes the SQL statement there, and returns the data. You can create database links as public links (created by DBAs, making the links available to all users in the local database) or as private links.

The following example creates a public database link called HR_LINK:

```
create public database link HR_LINK
connect to HR identified by employeeservices202
using 'hq';
```

NOTE
As of Oracle Database 11g, passwords are case-sensitive unless you set the initialization parameter SEC_CASE_SENSITIVE_LOGON to FALSE (the default is TRUE).

The CREATE DATABASE LINK command shown in this example has several parameters:

- The optional keyword PUBLIC, which allows DBAs to create links for all users in a database. An additional optional keyword, SHARED, is described later in this chapter.
- The name of the link (HR_LINK, in this example).
- The account to connect to. You can configure the database link to use the local username and password in the remote database. This link connects to a fixed username in the remote database.
- The service name (HQ, in this example).

To use the newly created link, simply add it as a suffix to table names in commands. The following example queries a remote table by using the HR_LINK database link:

```
select * from employees@hr_link
where office = 'ANNAPOLIS';
```

When you execute this query, Oracle will establish a session via the HR_LINK database link and query the EMPLOYEES table in that database. The WHERE clause will be applied to the EMPLOYEES rows, and the matching rows will be returned. The execution of the query is shown graphically in Figure 19-2.

The FROM clause in this example refers to EMPLOYEES@HR_LINK. Because the HR_LINK database link specifies the server name, instance name, and owner name, the full name of the table is known. If no account name had been specified in the database link, the user's account name and password in the local database would have been used during the attempt to log into the remote database.

The management of database links is described in the section "Managing Distributed Data," later in this chapter.

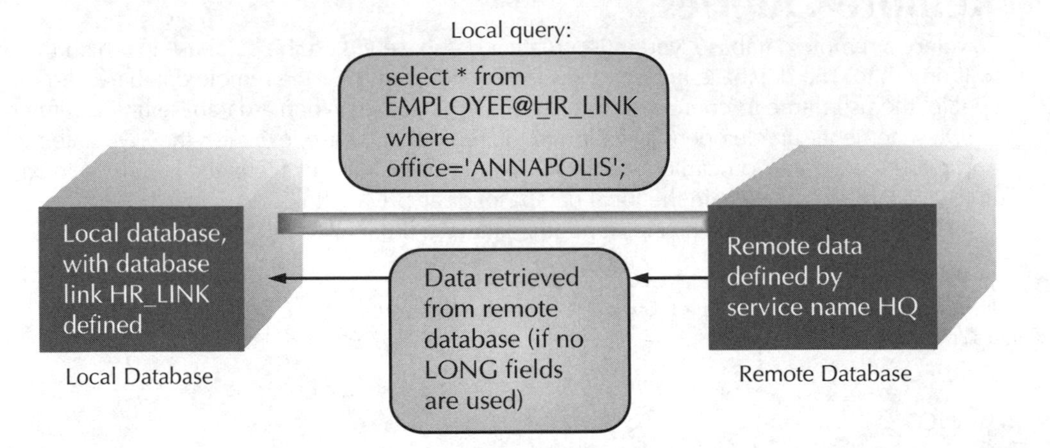

FIGURE 19-2. *Sample remote query*

Remote Data Manipulation: Two-Phase Commit

To support data manipulation across multiple databases, Oracle relies on *Two-Phase Commit (2PC)*. 2PC allows groups of transactions across several nodes to be treated as a unit; either the transactions all COMMIT or they all get rolled back. A set of distributed transactions is shown in Figure 19-3. In that figure, two UPDATE transactions are performed. The first UPDATE goes against a local table (EMPLOYEES); the second, against a remote table (EMPLOYEES@HR_LINK). After the two transactions are performed, a single COMMIT is then executed. If either transaction cannot COMMIT, both transactions will be rolled back.

Distributed transactions yield two important benefits: databases on other servers can be updated, and those transactions can be grouped together with others in a logical unit. The second benefit occurs because of the database's use of 2PC. Here are the two phases:

- **The prepare phase** An initiating node called the *global coordinator* notifies all sites involved in the transaction to be ready either to COMMIT or to roll back the transaction.
- **The commit phase** If there is no problem with the prepare phase, all sites COMMIT their transactions. If a network or node failure occurs, all sites roll back their transactions.

The use of 2PC is transparent to the users. If the node that initiates the transaction forgets about the transaction, a third phase, the *forget* phase, is performed. The detailed management of distributed transactions is discussed in the section "Managing Distributed Transactions," later in this chapter.

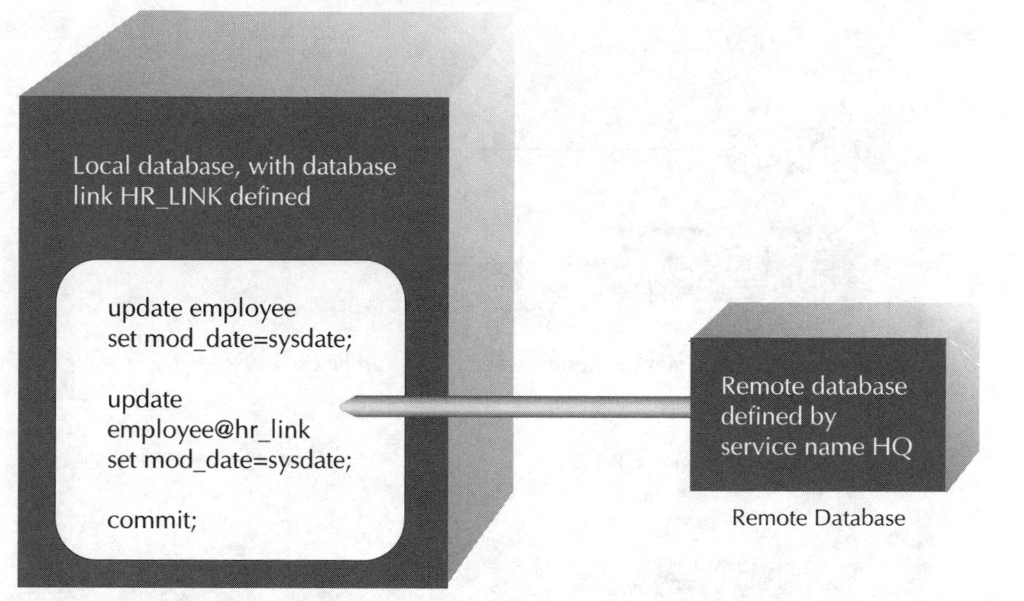

FIGURE 19-3. *Sample distributed transaction*

Dynamic Data Replication

To improve the performance of queries that use data from remote databases, you may wish to replicate that data on the local server. There are several options for accomplishing this, depending on which Oracle features you are using.

You can use *database triggers* to replicate data from one table into another. For example, after every INSERT into a table, a trigger may fire to insert that same record into another table—and that table may be in a remote database. Thus, you can use triggers to enforce data replication in simple configurations. If the types of transactions against the base table cannot be controlled, the trigger code needed to perform the replication will be unacceptably complicated.

When using Oracle's distributed features, you can use *materialized views* to replicate data between databases. You do not have to replicate an entire table or limit yourself to data from just one table. When replicating a single table, you may use a WHERE clause to restrict which records are replicated, and you may perform GROUP BY operations on the data. You can also join the table with other tables and replicate the result of the queries.

NOTE
You cannot use materialized views to replicate data using LONG, LONG RAW, or user-defined datatypes.

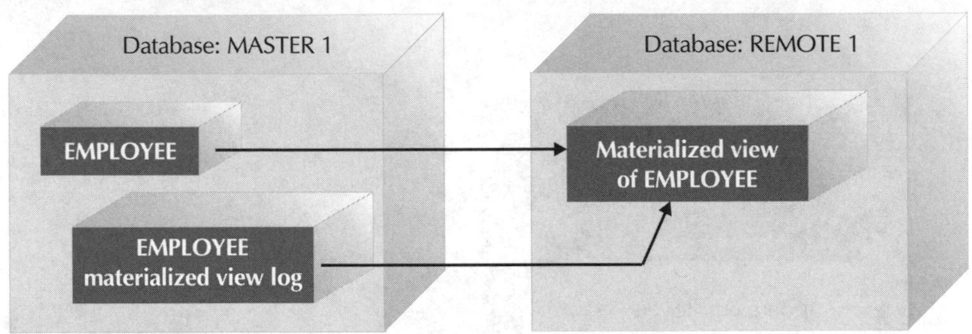

A simple materialized view; materialized view logs can be used.

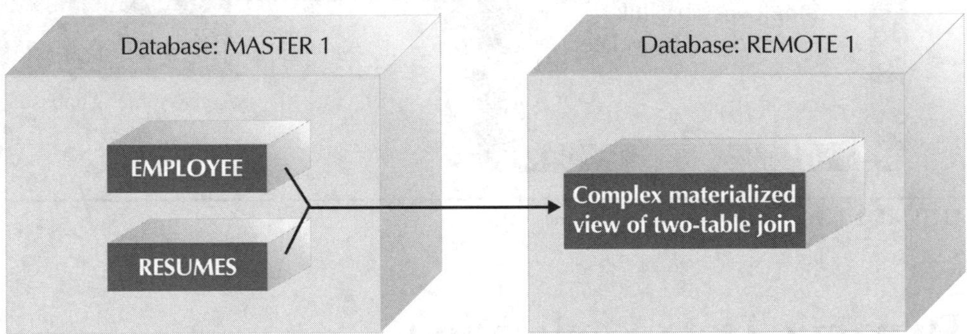

A complex materialized view; the result of the join is replicated.

FIGURE 19-4. *Replication with materialized views*

The data in the local materialized view of the remote table(s) will need to be refreshed. You can specify the refresh interval for the materialized view, and the database will automatically take care of the replication procedures. In many cases, the database can use a *materialized view log* to send over only transaction data (changes to the table); otherwise, the database will perform complete refreshes on the local materialized view. The dynamic replication of data via materialized views is shown in Figure 19-4.

You can use Data Guard to create and manage a standby database whose content is updated whenever the primary database's data changes. The standby database can be used as a read-only database to support reporting requirements and then returned to its status as a standby database. See Chapter 15 for details on the use and management of standby databases.

Managing Distributed Data

Before you can worry about managing transactions against remote databases, you have to get the data there and make it globally accessible to other databases. The following sections describe the requisite management tasks: enforcing location transparency and managing the database links, triggers, and materialized views.

NOTE
The examples in this chapter assume that you are using ***tnsnames.ora*** *files for your database service name resolution.*

The Infrastructure: Enforcing Location Transparency

To properly design your distributed databases for long-term use, you must start by making the physical location of the data transparent to the application. The name of a table within a database is unique within the schema that owns it. However, a remote database may have an account with the same name, which may own a table with the same name.

Within distributed databases, two additional layers of object identification must be added. First, the name of the instance that accesses the database must be identified. Next, the name of the host on which that instance resides must be identified. Putting together these four parts of the object's name—its host, its instance, its owner, and its name—results in a *global object name*. To access a remote table, you must know that table's global object name.

The goal of location transparency is to make the first three parts of the global object name—the host, the instance, and the schema—transparent to the user. The first three parts of the global object name are all specified via database links, so any effort at achieving location transparency should start there. First, consider a typical database link:

```
create public database link hr_link
connect to HR identified by employeeservices202
using 'hq';
```

NOTE
If the GLOBAL_NAMES initialization parameter is set to TRUE, the database link name must be the same as the global name of the remote database.

By using a service name (in this example, HQ), the host and instance name remain transparent to the user. These names are resolved via the local host's **tnsnames.ora** file. A partial entry in this file for the service name HQ is shown in the following listing:

```
HQ =(DESCRIPTION=
      (ADDRESS=
            (PROTOCOL=TCP)
            (HOST=HQ_MW)
            (PORT=1521))
      (CONNECT DATA=
            (SERVICE_NAME=LOC)))
```

The two lines in bold in this listing fill in the two missing pieces of the global object name. When a user references the HQ service name, the host name is HQ_MW and the service name is LOC. The SERVICE_NAME can be the instance name of the remote database. It is specified by the initialization parameter SERVICE_NAMES, and it can include several services. The default value for SERVICE_NAME is DB_UNIQUE_NAME.DB_DOMAIN. In a RAC database environment, each node can have additional service names in addition to the service name. A service specified by SERVICE_NAMES can run on several (or all, or just one) of the RAC instances. You would specify INSTANCE_NAME in **tnsnames.ora** instead of SERVICE_NAME if you want a specific database instance.

This **tnsnames.ora** file uses parameters for the TCP/IP protocol; other protocols may use different keywords, but their usage is the same. The **tnsnames.ora** entries provide transparency for the server and instance names.

The HR_LINK database link created via the code given earlier in this section will provide transparency for the first two parts of the global object name. But what if the data moves from the HR schema, or the HR account's password changes? The database link would have to be dropped and re-created. The same would be true if account-level security were required; you may need to create and maintain multiple database links.

To resolve the transparency of the schema portion of the global object name, you can modify the database link syntax. Consider the database link in the following listing:

```
create public database link HR_LINK
connect to current_user
using 'hq';
```

This database link uses the CONNECT TO CURRENT_USER clause. It will use what is known as a *connected user* database link: the remote database authenticates the connection request using the user's credentials on the server where the user executes the query. The previous examples were *fixed user* connections—the same credentials are used to authenticate the connection request regardless of the user making the request. Here is an example of using the connected user database link; not surprisingly, it looks identical to using a fixed user database link:

```
select * from employees@hr_link;
```

When the user references this link, the database will attempt to resolve the global object name in the following order:

1. It will search the local **tnsnames.ora** file to determine the proper host name, port, and instance name or service name.
2. It will check the database link for a CONNECT TO specification. If the CONNECT TO CURRENT_USER clause is found, it will attempt to connect to the specified database using the *connected user*'s username and password.
3. It will search the FROM clause of the query for the object name.

Connected user links are often used to access tables whose rows can be restricted according to the username that is accessing the tables. For example, if the remote database had a table named HR.EMPLOYEES, and every employee were allowed to see their own row in the table, then a database link with a specific connection, such as:

```
create public database link hr_link
connect to HR identified by employeeservices202
using 'hq';
```

would log in as the HR account (the owner of the table). If this specific connection is used, you cannot restrict the user's view of the records on the remote host. However, if a connected user link is used, and a view is created on the remote host using the USER pseudo-column, then only that user's data would be returned from the remote host. A sample database link and view of this type is shown in the following listing:

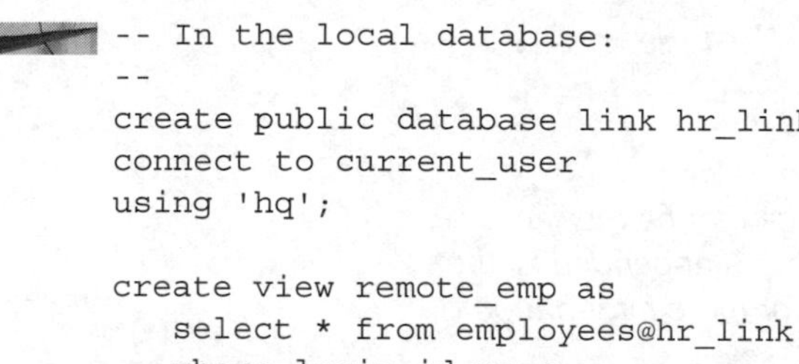

```
-- In the local database:
--
create public database link hr_link
connect to current_user
using 'hq';

create view remote_emp as
   select * from employees@hr_link
   where login_id=user;
```

Either way, the data being retrieved can be restricted. The difference is that when a connected user link is used, the data can be restricted based on the username in the remote database; if a fixed connection is used, the data can be restricted after it has been returned to the local database. The connected user link reduces the amount of network traffic needed to resolve the query and adds an additional level of location transparency to the data.

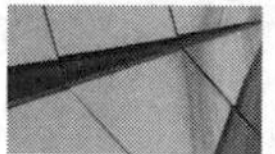

NOTE
If you are using the Virtual Private Database features of the Oracle Database, you can restrict access to rows and columns without maintaining views for this purpose. See Chapter 10 for details on Virtual Private Database options.

Connected user database links raise a different set of maintenance issues. The **tnsnames.ora** file must be synchronized across the servers (which in turn drive the adoption of an LDAP solution such as OID), and the username/password combinations in multiple databases must be synchronized. These issues are addressed in the next sections.

Database Domains

A *domain name service* allows hosts within a network to be hierarchically organized. Each node within the organization is called a *domain,* and each domain is labeled by its function. These functions may include COM for companies and EDU for schools. Each domain may have many subdomains. Therefore, each host will be given a unique name within the network; its name contains information about how it fits into the network hierarchy. Host names within a network typically have up to four parts; the leftmost portion of the name is the host's name, and the rest of the name shows the domain to which the host belongs.

For example, a host may be named HQ.MYCORP.COM. In this example, the host is named HQ and identified as being part of the MYCORP subdomain of the COM domain.

The domain structure is significant for two reasons. First, the host name is part of the global object name. Second, Oracle allows you to specify the DNS version of the host name in database link names, simplifying the management of distributed database connections.

To use DNS names in database links, you first need to add two parameters to your initialization file for the database. The first of these, DB_NAME, should be set to the instance name. The second parameter, DB_DOMAIN, is set to the DNS name of the database's host or is set to WORLD by default; the value cannot be NULL. DB_DOMAIN specifies the network domain in which the host resides. If a database named LOC is created on the HQ.MYCORP.COM server, its entries will be

```
DB_NAME = loc
DB_DOMAIN = hq.mycorp.com
```

NOTE
In a RAC environment, the INSTANCE_NAME cannot be the same as the DB_NAME. Typically, a sequential number is appended to the DB_NAME for each instance. See Chapter 12 for more information on configuring a RAC database.

To enable the usage of the database domain name, you must set the GLOBAL_NAMES parameter to TRUE in your SPFILE or initialization parameter file, as in this example:

```
GLOBAL_NAMES = true
```

NOTE
GLOBAL_NAMES is set to FALSE by default in Oracle Database 12c.

Once you have set these parameters, the database must be shut down and restarted for changes to DB_NAME or DB_DOMAIN.

NOTE
If you set GLOBAL_NAMES to TRUE, all your database link names must follow the rules described in this section; in other words, GLOBAL_NAMES ensures that database links have the same name as the database to which you connect using the link.

When you use this method of creating global database names, the names of the database links are the same as the databases to which they point. Therefore, a database link that points to the LOC database instance listed earlier would be named LOC.HQ.MYCORP.COM. Here is an example:

```
create public database link loc.hq.mycorp.com
using 'LOCSVC';
```

LOCSVC is the service name in **tnsnames.ora**. Oracle will append the local database's DB_DOMAIN value to the name of the database link. For example, if the database is in the HQ.MYCORP.COM domain, and the database link is named LOC, the database link will resolve to LOC.HQ.MYCORP.COM whenever it is referenced.

Using global database names establishes a link between the database name, database domain, and database link names. This, in turn, may make it easier to identify and manage database links. For example, you can create a public database link (with no connect string, as shown in the preceding example) in each database that points to every other database. Users within a database no longer need to guess at the proper database link to use; if they know the global database name, they know the database link name. If a table is moved from one database to another, or if a database is moved from one host to another, it is easy to determine which of the old database links must be dropped and re-created. Using global database names is part of migrating from standalone databases to true networks of databases.

Using Shared Database Links

If you use a shared server configuration for your database connections and your application will employ many concurrent database link connections, you may benefit from using *shared database links*. A shared database link uses shared server connections to support the database link connections. If you have multiple concurrent database link accesses into a remote database, you can use shared database links to reduce the number of server connections required.

To create a shared database link, use the SHARED keyword of the CREATE DATABASE LINK command. As shown in the following listing, you will also need to specify a schema and password for the remote database:

```
create shared database link hr_link_shared
connect to current_user
authenticated by hr identified by employeeservices202
using 'hq';
```

The HR_LINK_SHARED database link uses the connected user's username and password when accessing the HQ database, since this link specifies the CONNECT TO CURRENT_USER clause. In order to prevent unauthorized attempts to use shared links, the AUTHENTICATED BY clause is required for shared links. In this example, the account used for authentication is an application user's account, but you can also use an empty schema (that no user will ever log into) for authentication. The authentication account must have the CREATE SESSION system privilege. When users use the HR_LINK_SHARED link, connections will use the HR account on the remote database.

If you change the password on the authentication account, you will need to drop and re-create each database link that references the account. To simplify maintenance, create an account that is only used for authentication of shared database link connections. The account should only have the CREATE SESSION privilege; it should not have any privileges on any of the application tables.

If your application uses database links infrequently, you should use traditional database links without the SHARED clause. Without the SHARED clause, each database link connection requires a separate connection to the remote database. In general, use shared database links when the number of users accessing a database link is expected to be much larger than the number of server processes in the local database.

Managing Database Links

You can retrieve information about public database links via the DBA_DB_LINKS data dictionary view. You can view private database links via the USER_DB_LINKS data dictionary view. Whenever possible, separate your users among databases by application so that they may all share the same public database links. As a side benefit, these users will usually also be able to share public grants and synonyms.

The columns of the DBA_DB_LINKS data dictionary view are listed in the following table. The password for the link to use is not viewable via DBA_DB_LINKS; it is encrypted in the SYS.LINK$ table since Oracle Database 10*g* Release 2.

Column Name	Description
OWNER	The owner of the database link
DB_LINK	The name of the database link (such as HR_LINK in this chapter's examples)
USERNAME	The name of the account to use to open a session in the remote database if a specific connection is used
HOST	The connect string that will be used to connect to the remote database
CREATED	The creation date for the database link

NOTE
The number of database links that can be used by a single query is limited by the OPEN_LINKS parameter in the database's initialization file. Its default value is 4.

The managerial tasks involved for database links depend on the level to which you have implemented location transparency in your databases. In the best-case scenario, connected user links are used with service names or aliases; minimal link management in this scenario requires a consistent **tnsnames.ora** file among all hosts in the domain (or all hosts using the same LDAP server for name resolution) and that user account/password combinations are the same within the domain.

Synchronizing account/password combinations across databases may be difficult, but there are several alternatives. First, you may force all changes to user account passwords to go through a central authority. This central authority would have the responsibility for updating the password for the account in all databases in the network—a time-consuming but valuable task.

Second, you may audit user password changes made via the ALTER USER command by auditing the usage of that command (see Chapter 10). If a user's password changes in one database, it must be changed on all databases available in the network that are accessed via connected user links.

If any part of the global object name—such as a username—is embedded in the database link, a change affecting that part of the global object name requires that the database link be dropped and re-created. For example, if the HR user's password were changed, the HR_LINK database link with a specific connection defined earlier would be dropped with:

```
drop database link hr_link;
```

and the link would have to be re-created using the new account password:

```
create public database link hr_link
connect to HR identified by employeeservices404
using 'hq';
```

You cannot create a database link in another user's account. Suppose you attempt to create a database link in OE's account, as shown here:

```
create database link oe.hr_link
connect to hr identified by oe2hr
using 'hq';
```

In this case, Oracle will not create the HR_LINK database link in OE's account. Instead, Oracle will create a database link named OE.HR_LINK in the account that executed the CREATE DATABASE LINK command. To create private database links, you must be logged into the database in the account that will own the link.

NOTE
To see which links are currently in use in your session, query V$DBLINK.

Managing Database Triggers

If your data replication needs require synchronized changes in multiple databases, you can use database triggers to replicate data from one table into another. Database triggers are executed when specific actions happen. Triggers can be executed for each row of a transaction, for an entire transaction as a unit, or when system-wide events occur. When dealing with data replication, you will usually be concerned with triggers affecting each row of data.

Before creating a replication-related trigger, you must create a database link for the trigger to use. In this case, the link is created in the database that *owns* the data, accessible to the owner of the table being replicated:

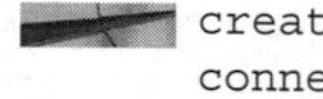

```
create public database link trigger_link
connect to current_user
using 'rmt_db_1';
```

This link, named TRIGGER_LINK, uses the service name RMT_DB_1 to specify the connection to a remote database. The link will attempt to connect to the database RMT_DB_1 using the same username and password as the account using the link.

The trigger shown in the following listing uses this link. The trigger is fired after every row is inserted into the EMPLOYEES table. Because the trigger executes after the row has been inserted, the row's data has already been validated in the local database. The trigger inserts the same row into a remote table with the same structure, using the TRIGGER_LINK database link just defined. The remote table must already exist.

```
create trigger copy_data
after insert on employees
for each row
begin
     insert into employees@trigger_link
     values
     (:new.Empno, :new.Ename, :new.Deptno,
     :new.Salary, :new.Birth_Date, :new.Soc_Sec_Num);
end;
/
```

This trigger uses the NEW keyword to reference the values from the row that was just inserted into the local EMPLOYEES table.

NOTE
If you use trigger-based replication, your trigger code must account for potential error conditions at the remote site, such as duplicate key values, space-management problems, or a shut down database.

```
select trigger_type,
       triggering_event,
       table_name
  from dba_triggers
 where trigger_name = 'COPY_DATA';
```

Sample output from this query is as follows:

```
TYPE             TRIGGERING_EVENT        TABLE_NAME
---------------- ----------------------- ------------
AFTER EACH ROW   INSERT                  EMPLOYEES
```

You can query the text of the trigger from DBA_TRIGGERS, as shown in this example:

```
set long 1000
select trigger_body
  from dba_triggers
 where trigger_name = 'COPY_DATA';

TRIGGER_BODY
-----------------------------------------------------
begin
     insert into employees@trigger_link
     values
     (:new.Empno, :new.Ename, :new.Deptno,
     :new.Salary, :new.Birth_Date, :new.Soc_Sec_Num);
end;
```

It is theoretically possible to create a trigger to replicate all possible permutations of data-manipulation actions on the local database, but this quickly becomes difficult to manage. For a complex environment, you should consider the use of materialized views. For the limited circumstances described earlier, triggers are a very easy solution to implement. The overhead of using triggers for replication purposes is significant, however, so if you use this method, be sure to perform enough tests on bigger tables to determine if the overhead is acceptable.

NOTE
If you use triggers for your data replication, the success of a transaction in the master database is dependent on the success of the remote transaction.

Managing Materialized Views

You can use materialized views to aggregate, pre-join, or replicate data. In an enterprise database environment, data generally flows from an online transaction-processing database into a data warehouse. Normally, the data is prestaged, cleansed, or otherwise processed and then moved into the data warehouse. From there, the data may be copied to other databases or data marts.

You can use materialized views to pre-compute and store aggregate information within a database, to dynamically replicate data between distributed databases, and synchronize data updates within replicated environments. In replication environments, materialized views enable local access to data that would normally have to be accessed remotely. A materialized view may be based on another materialized view.

In large databases, materialized views help to improve the performance of queries that involve aggregates (including sum, count, average, variance, standard deviation, minimum, and maximum) or table joins. Oracle's query optimizer will automatically recognize that the materialized view could be used to satisfy the query—a feature known as *query rewrite*.

NOTE
For best results, make sure the statistics on the materialized view are kept current. Since Oracle Database 10g, statistics on all database objects are collected on a regular basis during predefined maintenance windows as part of the automated maintenance tasks infrastructure (AutoTask windows).

You can use initialization parameters to configure the optimizer to automatically rewrite queries to use the materialized views whenever possible. Because materialized views are transparent to SQL applications, they can be dropped or created without any impact on the execution of the SQL code. You can also create partitioned materialized views, and you can base materialized views on partitioned tables.

Unlike regular views, materialized views store data and take up physical space in your database. Materialized views are populated with data generated from their base queries, and they are refreshed on demand or on a scheduled basis. Therefore, whenever the data accessed by the base query changes, the materialized views should be refreshed to reflect the data changes. The data refresh frequency depends on how much data latency your business can tolerate in the processes supported by the materialized views. You'll see how to establish your refresh rate later in this chapter.

The materialized view will create several objects in the database. The user creating the materialized view must have the CREATE MATERIALIZED VIEW, CREATE TABLE, and CREATE VIEW privileges as well as the SELECT privilege on any tables that are referenced but are owned by another schema. If the materialized view is going to be created in another schema, the user creating the materialized view must have the CREATE ANY MATERIALIZED VIEW privilege and the SELECT privilege to the tables that are referenced in the materialized view if the tables are owned by another schema. To enable query rewrite on a materialized view that references tables within another schema, the user enabling query rewrite must have the GLOBAL QUERY REWRITE privilege or be explicitly granted the QUERY REWRITE privilege on any referenced table within another schema. The user must also have the UNLIMITED TABLESPACE privilege. Materialized views can be created in the local database, and pull data from the remote master database, or materialized views can reside on the same database server on which the data is located.

If you plan to use the query rewrite feature, you must put the following entry in your initialization parameter file:

```
query_rewrite_enabled=true
```

NOTE
If the OPTIMIZER_FEATURES_ENABLE parameter is set to 10.0.0 or higher, then QUERY_REWRITE_ENABLED defaults to TRUE.

A second parameter, QUERY_REWRITE_INTEGRITY, sets the degree to which Oracle must enforce query rewriting. At the safest level, Oracle does not use query rewrite transformations that rely on unenforced relationships. The valid values for QUERY_REWRITE_INTEGRITY are ENFORCED (Oracle enforces and guarantees consistency and integrity), TRUSTED (query rewrite is supported for declared relationships), and STALE_TOLERATED (query rewrite is supported even if the materialized views are inconsistent with their underlying data). By default, QUERY_REWRITE_INTEGRITY is set to ENFORCED.

Materialized View Planning

Before you can create a materialized view, you must make several decisions, including:

- Whether the materialized view is to be populated with data during creation or after
- How often the materialized view is to be refreshed
- What type of refreshes to perform
- Whether to maintain a materialized view log or not
- Whether the refresh should be in-place or out-of-place

You can either have data loaded to the materialized view upon its creation using the BUILD IMMEDIATE option of the CREATE MATERIALIZED VIEW command, or add the BUILD DEFERRED clause to pre-create the materialized view but not populate it until the first time it is used. The advantage of populating the view on creation is that the data will be available immediately when you make the materialized view available. However, if the materialized view is not going to be used right away and the underlying data changes rapidly, the data in the materialized view will become stale rapidly. If you wait to have the materialized view populated, the view will not be populated with data until the package DBMS_MVIEW.REFRESH is automatically executed, and your users must wait for the view to populate before any data is returned, thus causing a one-time performance degradation. If a standard view already exists and you want to convert it to a materialized view, you can use the PREBUILT keyword option.

You must also decide how much stale data is tolerable in terms of your company's needs. You can base your decision on how frequently the data changes in the table on which the materialized view is based. If your management does not have to have up-to-the-minute information on which to base decisions, you might only need to refresh your materialized view once an hour or once a day. If it is critical for the data to be absolutely accurate at all times, you may need to perform fast refreshes every five minutes throughout the day and night.

There are four forms of refresh when specifying a refresh method during materialized view creation: REFRESH COMPLETE, REFRESH FAST, REFRESH FORCE, and NEVER REFRESH. In a fast (incremental) refresh, materialized view logs are used to track the data changes that have occurred within the table since the last refresh. Only changed information is populated back to the materialized view, on a periodic basis, based on the refresh criteria you have established. The materialized view log is maintained in the same database and schema as the master table for the materialized view. Because the fast refresh just applies changes made since the last refresh, the time taken to perform the refresh should generally be very short.

A new type of incremental refresh introduced in Oracle Database 12*c* is called partition change tracking (PCT), which is somewhat of a hybrid between log-based incremental refreshes and full refreshes. If a base table is partitioned, only the corresponding materialized view partition needs to be refreshed.

In a complete refresh, the data within the materialized view is completely replaced each time the refresh is run. The time required to perform a complete refresh of the materialized view can be substantial. You can either have the refresh performed each time transactions are committed on the master table (REFRESH ON COMMIT) or have it performed only when the DBMS_MVIEW .REFRESH procedure is run (REFRESH ON DEMAND).

When you specify REFRESH FORCE, the refresh process first evaluates whether or not a fast refresh can be run. If it can't, a complete refresh will be performed. If you specify NEVER REFRESH as the refresh option, the materialized view will not be refreshed. If you do not have a materialized view log created and populated, only complete refreshes can be executed. Oracle Database 12*c* introduces another type of refresh: *out-of-place materialized view refresh*. During any type of refresh (COMPLETE, FAST, FORCE, or PCT), the current copy of the materialized view is maintained while a new version is built. Once completed, the current version is dropped and the new copy is renamed. This dramatically improves the availability of the materialized view, with the cost being the additional storage required to build a new copy of the materialized view.

Creating a Materialized View

A sample command used to create the materialized view is shown in the following listing. In this example, the materialized view is given a name (STORE_DEPT_SAL_MV) and its storage parameters are specified as well as its refresh interval and the time at which it will be populated with data. In this case, the materialized view is told to use the complete refresh option and to not populate the data until the DBMS_MVIEW.REFRESH procedure is run. Query rewrite is enabled. This materialized view's base query is as follows:

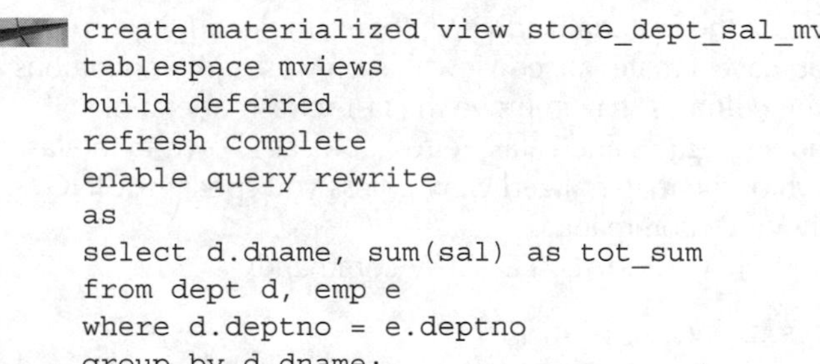

```
create materialized view store_dept_sal_mv
tablespace mviews
build deferred
refresh complete
enable query rewrite
as
select d.dname, sum(sal) as tot_sum
from dept d, emp e
where d.deptno = e.deptno
group by d.dname;
```

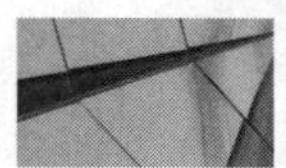

NOTE
A materialized view query cannot reference tables or views owned by the user SYS.

The following example shows another example of a materialized view creation, using the REFRESH FAST ON COMMIT clause. To support fast refreshes when commits occur, you will need to create a materialized view log on the base table. See "Managing Materialized View Logs" later in this chapter for details.

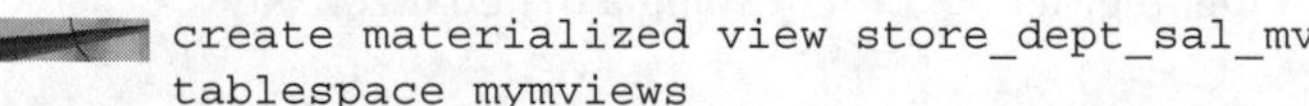

```
create materialized view store_dept_sal_mv
tablespace mymviews
```

```
parallel
build immediate
refresh fast on commit
enable query rewrite
as
select d.dname, sum(sal) as tot_sum
  from dept d, emp e
 where d.deptno = e.deptno
group by d.dname;
```

In this example, the same base query is used, but the materialized view is created with REFRESH FAST ON COMMIT so that a fast refresh occurs every time a transaction is committed in any of the materialized view's base queries. This materialized view will be populated with data on creation, and the inserted rows will be loaded in parallel. Query rewrite is enabled as well.

NOTE

The fast refresh option will not be used unless a materialized view log is created on the base table for the materialized view. Oracle can perform fast refreshes of joined tables in materialized views.

For both of these examples, the materialized view uses the default storage parameters for its tablespace. You can alter the materialized view's storage parameters via the ALTER MATERIALIZED VIEW command, as in this example:

```
alter materialized view store_dept_sal_mv pctfree 5;
```

The two most frequently used operations against a materialized view are query execution and fast refresh. Each of these actions requires different resources and has different performance requirements. You may index the base table of the materialized view; for example, adding an index to improve query performance. If you have a materialized view that only uses join conditions and fast refresh, indexes on the primary key columns may improve the fast refresh operations. If your materialized view uses both joins and aggregates and is fast refreshable, as shown in the last example, an index is automatically created for the materialized view unless you specify USING NO INDEX in the CREATE MATERIALIZED VIEW command.

To drop a materialized view, use the DROP MATERIALIZED VIEW command:

```
drop materialized view STORE_DEPT_SAL_MV;
```

Using the out-of-place option for a materialized view (new as of Oracle Database 12*c*), the creation of a materialized view created out-of-place is the same as for a materialized view that will be refreshed in-place, with the difference being the parameters you specify in the call to DBMS_MVIEW.REFRESH.

Using DBMS_MVIEW and DBMS_ADVISOR

There are multiple supplied packages you can use to manage and evaluate your materialized views, including DBMS_MVIEW, DBMS_ADVISOR, and DBMS_DIMENSION.

The DBMS_MVIEW package subprograms are shown in Table 19-1; this package is used to perform management tasks such as evaluating, registering, or refreshing a materialized view.

Subprogram	Description
BEGIN_TABLE_REORGANIZATION	A process to preserve the data needed for a materialized view refresh is performed, used prior to reorganizing the master table.
END_TABLE_REORGANIZATION	Ensures that the materialized view master table is in the proper state and that the master table is valid, at the end of a master table reorganization.
ESTIMATE_MVIEW_SIZE	Estimates the size of a materialized view, in bytes and rows.
EXPLAIN_MVIEW	Explains what is possible with an existing or proposed materialized view. (Is it fast refreshable? Is query rewrite available?)
EXPLAIN_REWRITE	Explains why a query failed to rewrite, or which materialized views will be used if it rewrites.
I_AM_A_REFRESH	The value of the I_AM_REFRESH package state is returned, called during replication.
PMARKER	Used for Partition Change Tracking. Returns a partition marker from a ROWID.
PURGE_DIRECT_LOAD_LOG	Used with data warehousing, this subprogram purges rows from the direct loader log after they are no longer needed by a materialized view.
PURGE_LOG	Purges rows from the materialized view log.
PURGE_MVIEW_FROM_LOG	Purges rows from the materialized view log.
REFRESH	Refreshes one or more materialized views that are not members of the same refresh group.
REFRESH_ALL_MVIEWS	Refreshes all materialized views that do not reflect changes to their master table or master materialized view.
REFRESH_DEPENDENT	Refreshes all table-based materialized views that depend on either a specified master table or master materialized view. The list can contain one or more master tables or master materialized views.
REGISTER_MVIEW	Enables an individual materialized view's administration.
UNREGISTER_MVIEW	Used to unregister a materialized view at a master site or master materialized view site.

TABLE 19-1. *DBMS_MVIEW Subprograms*

To refresh a single materialized view, use DBMS_MVIEW.REFRESH. Its two main parameters are the name of the materialized view to be refreshed and the method to use. For the method, you can specify 'c' for a complete refresh, 'f' for fast refresh, and '?' for force. Here's an example:

```
begin
   dbms_mview.refresh(
      'store_dept_sal_mv',
      method => 'c'
   );
end;
```

If you are refreshing multiple materialized views via a single call to DBMS_MVIEW.REFRESH, list the names of all the materialized views in the first parameter and their matching refresh methods in the second parameter, as in this example:

```
execute dbms_mview.refresh('mv1,mv2,mv3','cfc');
```

In this example, the materialized view MV2 will be refreshed via a fast refresh, whereas the other will use a complete refresh.

Refreshing a materialized view using out-of-place refresh is very similar to refreshing a materialized view using in-place refresh, the only difference being one parameter to the procedure DBMS_MVIEW.REFRESH, as in this example:

```
begin
   dbms_mview.refresh(
      'store_dept_sal_mv',
      method => 'c',
      out_of_place => true
   );
end;
```

Since the outside table (the future version of the materialized view to be refreshed) is loaded using direct path I/O, it can be significantly faster than an in-place complete refresh.

You can use a separate procedure in the DBMS_MVIEW package to refresh all the materialized views that are scheduled to be automatically refreshed. This procedure, named REFRESH_ALL, will refresh each materialized view separately. It does not accept any parameters. The following listing shows an example of its execution:

```
execute dbms_mview.refresh_all;
```

Because the materialized views will be refreshed via REFRESH_ALL consecutively, they are not all refreshed at the same time (in other words, not in parallel). Therefore, a database or server failure during this procedure may cause the local materialized views to be out of sync with each other. In this case, simply rerun this procedure after the database has been recovered. As an alternative, you can create refresh groups, as described in the next section.

Using the SQL Access Advisor

You can use the SQL Access Advisor to generate recommendations for the creation and indexing of materialized views. The SQL Access Advisor may recommend specific indexes (and types of indexes) to improve the performance of joins and other queries. The SQL Access Advisor may also generate recommendations for altering a materialized view so that it supports query rewrite or fast refreshes. You can execute the SQL Access Advisor from within Oracle Enterprise Manager or via executions of the DBMS_ADVISOR package.

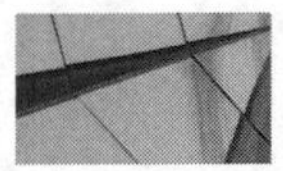

NOTE
For best results from the DBMS_ADVISOR package, you should gather statistics about all tables, indexes, and join columns prior to generating recommendations.

To use the SQL Access Advisor, either from Oracle Cloud Control 12*c* or via DBMS_ADVISOR, perform the following steps:

1. Create a task.
2. Define the workload.
3. Generate recommendations.
4. View and implement recommendations.

You can create a task in one of two ways: by executing the DBMS_ADVISOR.CREATE_TASK procedure or by using the DBMS_ADVISOR.QUICK_TUNE procedure (as shown in the next section).

The workload consists of one or more SQL statements plus the statistics and attributes that relate to the statement. The workload may include all SQL statements for an application. The SQL Access Advisor ranks the entries in the workload according to statistics and business importance. The workload is created using the DBMS_ADVISOR.CREATE_SQLWKLD procedure. To associate a workload with a parent Advisor task, use the DBMS_ADVISOR.ADD_SQLWKLD_REF procedure. If a workload is not provided, the SQL Access Advisor can generate and use a hypothetical workload based on the dimensions defined in your schema.

Once a task exists and a workload is associated with it, you can generate recommendations via the DBMS_ADVISOR.EXECUTE_TASK procedure. The SQL Access Advisor will consider the workload and the system statistics and will attempt to generate recommendations for tuning the application. You can see the recommendations by executing the DBMS_ADVISOR.GET_TASK_SCRIPT function or via data dictionary views. Each recommendation can be viewed via USER_ADVISOR_RECOMMENDATIONS (there are "ALL" and "DBA" versions of this view available as well). To relate recommendations to a SQL statement, you will need to use the USER_ADVISOR_SQLA_WK_STMTS view and USER_ADVISOR_ACTIONS.

NOTE
See Chapter 6 for more examples of using the DBMS_ADVISOR package.

When you execute the GET_TASK_SCRIPT procedure, Oracle generates an executable SQL file that will contain the commands needed to create, alter, or drop the recommended objects. You should review the generated script prior to executing it, particularly noting the tablespace specifications. Later in this chapter, you will see how to use the QUICK_TUNE procedure to simplify the tuning advisor process for a single command.

To tune a single SQL statement, use the QUICK_TUNE procedure of the DBMS_ADVISOR package. QUICK_TUNE has two input parameters, a task name and a SQL statement. Using QUICK_TUNE shields the user from the steps involved in creating workloads and tasks via DBMS_ADVISOR.

For example, the following procedure call evaluates a query:

```
execute dbms_advisor.quick_tune(dbms_advisor.sqlaccess_advisor, -
     'mv_tune','select publisher from bookshelf');
```

NOTE
The user executing this command needs the ADVISOR system privilege.

The recommendations generated by QUICK_TUNE can be viewed via the data dictionary view USER_ADVISOR_ACTIONS, but they are easier to read if you use the DBMS_ADVISOR procedures to generate a script file. The recommendation in this example is to create a materialized view to support the query. Because only one SQL statement was provided, this recommendation is given in isolation and does not consider any other aspects of the database or application.

You can use the CREATE_FILE procedure to automate the generation of a file containing the scripts needed to implement the recommendations. First, create a directory object to hold the file:

```
create directory scripts as 'e:\scripts';
grant read on directory scripts to public;
grant write on directory scripts to public;
```

Next, execute the CREATE_FILE procedure. It has three input variables: the script (generated by GET_TASK_SCRIPT, to which you pass the name of the task), the output directory, and the name of the file to be created.

```
execute dbms_advisor.create_file(dbms_advisor.get_task_script('mv_tune'),-
'scripts','mv_tune.sql');
```

The **mv_tune.sql** file created by the CREATE_FILE procedure will contain commands similar to those shown in the following listing. Depending on the specific version of Oracle, the recommendations may differ.

```
Rem  Username:         PRACTICE
Rem  Task:             MV_TUNE
Rem

set feedback 1
set linesize 80
set trimspool on
set tab off
set pagesize 60

whenever sqlerror CONTINUE
```

```
CREATE MATERIALIZED VIEW "PRACTICE"."MV$$_021F0001"
    REFRESH FORCE WITH ROWID
    ENABLE QUERY REWRITE
    AS SELECT PRACTICE.BOOKSHELF.ROWID C1,
"PRACTICE"."BOOKSHELF"."PUBLISHER" M1
FROM PRACTICE.BOOKSHELF;

begin
  dbms_stats.gather_table_stats('"PRACTICE"',
'"MV$$_021F0001"',NULL,dbms_stats.auto_sample_size);
end;
/

whenever sqlerror EXIT SQL.SQLCODE

begin
dbms_advisor.mark_recommendation('MV_TUNE',1,'IMPLEMENTED');
end;
/
```

The MARK_RECOMMENDATION procedure allows you to annotate the recommendation so that it can be skipped during subsequent script generations. Valid actions for MARK_RECOMMENDATION include ACCEPT, IGNORE, IMPLEMENTED, and REJECT.

You can use the TUNE_MVIEW procedure of the DBMS_ADVISOR package to generate recommendations for the reconfiguration of your materialized views. TUNE_MVIEW generates two sets of output results, one for the creation of new materialized views and the other for the removal of previously created materialized views. The end result should be a set of materialized views that can be fast refreshed, replacing materialized views that cannot be fast refreshed.

You can view the TUNE_MVIEW output via the USER_TUNE_MVIEW data dictionary view, or you can generate its scripts via the GET_TASK_SCRIPT and CREATE_FILE procedures shown in the previous listings.

The supplied programs for the DBMS_ADVISOR package are shown in Table 19-2.

An additional package, DBMS_DIMENSION, provides these two procedures:

DESCRIBE_DIMENSION	Shows the definition of the input dimension, including owner, name, levels, hierarchies, and attributes.
VALIDATE DIMENSION	Verifies that the relationships specified in a dimension are correct.

You can use the DBMS_DIMENSION package to validate and display the structure of your dimensions.

Enforcing Referential Integrity Among Materialized Views

The referential integrity between two related tables, both of which have simple materialized views based on them, may not be enforced in their materialized views. If the tables are refreshed at different times, or if transactions are occurring on the master tables during the refresh, it is possible for the materialized views of those tables to not reflect the referential integrity of the master tables.

Subprocedure	Description
ADD_SQLWKLD_REF	Adds a workload reference to an Advisor task.
ADD_SQLWKLD_STATEMENT	Adds a single statement to a workload.
CANCEL_TASK	Cancels a currently executing task operation.
CREATE_FILE	Creates an external file from a PL/SQL CLOB variable.
CREATE_OBJECT	Creates a new task object.
CREATE_SQLWKLD	Creates a new workload object.
CREATE_TASK	Creates a new Advisor task in the repository.
DELETE_SQLWKLD	Deletes an entire workload object.
DELETE_SQLWKLD_REF	Deletes a link between the current task and a workload data object. This procedure is deprecated as of Oracle Database 11*g*.
DELETE_SQLWKLD_STATEMENT	Deletes one or more statements from a workload.
DELETE_TASK	Deletes the specified task from the repository.
EXECUTE_TASK	Executes the specified task.
GET_REC_ATTRIBUTES	Retrieves specific recommendation attributes from a task.
GET_TASK_SCRIPT	Creates and returns an executable SQL script of the Advisor recommendations.
IMPORT_SQLWKLD_SCHEMA	Imports data into a workload based on the contents of one or more schemas. This procedure is deprecated as of Oracle Database 11*g*.
IMPORT_SQLWKLD_SQLCACHE	Imports data into a workload from the current SQL cache. This procedure is deprecated as of Oracle Database 11*g*.
IMPORT_SQLWKLD_STS	Imports data into a workload from a SQL Tuning Set.
IMPORT_SQLWKLD_SUMADV	Imports data into a workload from the current SQL cache.
IMPORT_SQLWKLD_USER	Imports data into a workload from the current SQL cache.
INTERRUPT_TASK	Stops a currently executing task, ending its operations as it would at a normal exit.
MARK_RECOMMENDATION	Sets the annotation status for a particular recommendation.
QUICK_TUNE	Performs an analysis on a single SQL statement.
RESET_TASK	Resets a task to its initial state.
SET_DEFAULT_SQLWKLD_PARAMETER	Imports data into a workload from schema evidence.
SET_DEFAULT_TASK_PARAMETER	Modifies a default task parameter.
SET_SQLWKLD_PARAMETER	Sets the value of a workload parameter.

TABLE 19-2. *DBMS_ADVISOR Subprograms*

Subprocedure	Description
SET_TASK_PARAMETER	Sets the specified task parameter value.
TUNE_MVIEW	Shows how to decompose a materialized view into two or more materialized views or to restate the materialized view in a way that is more advantageous for fast refresh and query rewrite.
UPDATE_OBJECT	Updates a task object.
UPDATE_REC_ATTRIBUTES	Updates an existing recommendation for the specified task.
UPDATE_SQLWKLD_ATTRIBUTES	Updates a workload object.
UPDATE_SQLWKLD_STATEMENT	Updates one or more SQL statements in a workload.
UPDATE_TASK_ATTRIBUTES	Updates a task's attributes.

TABLE 19-2. *DBMS_ADVISOR Subprograms* (Continued)

If, for example, the EMPLOYEES and DEPARTMENTS tables are related to each other via a primary key/foreign key relationship, then simple materialized views of these tables may contain violations of this relationship, including foreign keys without matching primary keys. In this example, that could mean employees in the EMPLOYEES materialized view with DEPTNO values that do not exist in the DEPARTMENTS materialized view.

This problem has a number of potential solutions. First, time the refreshes to occur when the master tables are not in use. Second, perform the refreshes manually (see the following section for information on this) immediately after locking the master tables or quiescing the database. Third, you may join the tables in the materialized view, creating a complex materialized view that will be based on the master tables (which will be properly related to each other). Fourth, you can force the materialized view updates to occur when transactions are committed in the primary database.

Using refresh groups provides another solution to the referential integrity problem. You can collect related materialized views into *refresh groups*. The purpose of a refresh group is to coordinate the refresh schedules of its members. Materialized views whose master tables have relationships with other master tables are good candidates for membership in refresh groups. Coordinating the refresh schedules of the materialized views will maintain the master tables' referential integrity in the materialized views as well. If refresh groups are not used, the data in the materialized views may be inconsistent with regard to the master tables' referential integrity.

Manipulation of refresh groups is performed via the DBMS_REFRESH package. The procedures within that package are MAKE, ADD, SUBTRACT, CHANGE, DESTROY, and REFRESH, as shown in the following examples. Information about existing refresh groups can be queried from the USER_REFRESH and USER_REFRESH_CHILDREN data dictionary views.

NOTE

Materialized views that belong to a refresh group do not have to belong to the same schema, but they do have to be all stored within the same database.

You can create a refresh group by executing the MAKE procedure in the DBMS_REFRESH package, whose calling parameters are shown here:

```
DBMS_REFRESH.MAKE
(name IN VARCHAR2,
 list IN VARCHAR2, |
  tab IN DBMS_UTILITY.UNCL_ARRAY,
 next_date IN DATE,
 interval IN VARCHAR2,
 implicit_destroy IN BOOLEAN := FALSE,
 lax IN BOOLEAN := FALSE,
 job IN BINARY INTEGER := 0,
 rollback_seg IN VARCHAR2 := NULL,
 push_deferred_rpc IN BOOLEAN := TRUE,
 refresh_after_errors IN BOOLEAN := FALSE,
 purge_option IN BINARY_INTEGER := NULL,
 parallelism IN BINARY_INTEGER := NULL,
 heap_size IN BINARY_INTEGER := NULL);
```

All but the first four of the parameters for this procedure have default values that are usually acceptable. The LIST and TAB parameters are mutually exclusive. You can use the following command to create a refresh group for materialized views names LOCAL_EMP and LOCAL_DEPT:

```
execute dbms_refresh.make
   (name => 'emp_group', -
    list => 'local_emp, local_dept', -
    next_date => sysdate, -
    interval => 'sysdate+7');
```

NOTE
The LIST parameter, which is the second parameter in the listing, has a single quote at its beginning and at its end, with none between. In this example, two materialized views—LOCAL_EMP and LOCAL_DEPT—are passed to the procedure via a single parameter.

The preceding command will create a refresh group named EMP_GROUP, with two materialized views as its members. The refresh group name is enclosed in single quotes, as is the list of members—but not each member.

If the refresh group is going to contain a materialized view that is already a member of another refresh group (for example, during a move of a materialized view from an old refresh group to a newly created refresh group), you must set the LAX parameter to TRUE. A materialized view can only belong to one refresh group at a time.

To add materialized views to an existing refresh group, use the ADD procedure of the DBMS_REFRESH package, whose parameters are as follows:

```
DBMS_REFRESH.ADD
(name IN VARCHAR2,
 list IN VARCHAR2, |
  tab IN DBMS_UTILITY.UNCL_ARRAY,
 lax IN BOOLEAN := FALSE);
```

As with the MAKE procedure, the ADD procedure's LAX parameter does not have to be specified unless a materialized view is being moved between two refresh groups. When this procedure is executed with the LAX parameter set to TRUE, the materialized view is moved to the new refresh group and is automatically deleted from the old refresh group.

To remove materialized views from an existing refresh group, use the SUBTRACT procedure of the DBMS_REFRESH package, as in the following example:

```
DBMS_REFRESH.SUBTRACT
(name IN VARCHAR2,
 list IN VARCHAR2, |
  tab IN DBMS_UTILITY.UNCL_ARRAY,
 lax IN BOOLEAN := FALSE);
```

As with the MAKE and ADD procedures, a single materialized view or a list of materialized views (separated by commas) may serve as input to the SUBTRACT procedure. You can alter the refresh schedule for a refresh group via the CHANGE procedure of the DBMS_REFRESH package; here are the parameters:

```
DBMS_REFRESH.CHANGE
(name IN VARCHAR2,
 next_date IN DATE := NULL,
 interval IN VARCHAR2 := NULL,
 implicit_destroy IN BOOLEAN := NULL,
 rollback_seg IN VARCHAR2 := NULL,
 push_deferred_rpc IN BOOLEAN := NULL,
 refresh_after_errors IN BOOLEAN := NULL,
 purge_option IN BINARY_INTEGER := NULL,
 parallelism IN BINARY_INTEGER := NULL,
 heap_size IN BINARY_INTEGER := NULL);
```

The NEXT_DATE parameter is analogous to the START WITH clause in the CREATE MATERIALIZED VIEW command. For example, to change the EMP_GROUP's schedule so that it will be replicated every three days, you can execute the following command (which specifies a NULL value for the NEXT_DATE parameter, leaving that value unchanged):

```
execute dbms_refresh.change
(name => 'emp_group',
 next_date => null,
 interval => 'sysdate+3');
```

After this command is executed, the refresh cycle for the EMP_GROUP refresh group will be changed to every three days.

NOTE
Refresh operations on refresh groups may take longer than comparable materialized view refreshes. Group refreshes may also require significant undo segment space to maintain data consistency during the refresh.

You can manually refresh a refresh group via the REFRESH procedure of the DBMS_REFRESH package. The REFRESH procedure accepts the name of the refresh group as its only parameter. The command shown here will refresh the refresh group named EMP_GROUP:

```
execute dbms_refresh.refresh('emp_group');
```

To delete a refresh group, use the DESTROY procedure of the DBMS_REFRESH package, as shown in the following example. Its only parameter is the name of the refresh group.

```
execute dbms_refresh.destroy(name => 'emp_group');
```

You may also implicitly destroy the refresh group. If you set the IMPLICIT_DESTROY parameter to TRUE when you create the group with the MAKE procedure, the refresh group will be deleted (destroyed) when its last member is removed from the group (usually via the SUBTRACT procedure).

NOTE
For performance statistics related to materialized view refreshes, query V$MVREFRESH.

Managing Materialized View Logs

A *materialized view log* is a table that maintains a record of modifications to the master table in a materialized view. It is stored in the same database as the master table and is only used by simple materialized views. The data in the materialized view log is used during fast refreshes. If you are going to use fast refreshes, create the materialized view log before creating the materialized view.

To create a materialized view log, you must be able to create an AFTER ROW trigger on the table, so you need CREATE TRIGGER and CREATE TABLE privileges. You cannot specify a name for the materialized view log.

Because the materialized view log is a table, it has the full set of table storage clauses available to it. The following example shows the creation of a materialized view log on a table named EMPLOYEES:

```
create materialized view log on employees tablespace data2;
```

The PCTFREE value for the materialized view log can be set very low (even 0), since there will not be any updates to this table! The size of the materialized view log depends on the number of changes that will be processed during each refresh. The more frequently all the materialized views that reference the master table are refreshed, the less space is needed for the log.

You can modify the storage parameters for the materialized view log via the ALTER MATERIALIZED VIEW LOG command. When using this command, specify the name of the master table. An example of altering the EMPLOYEES table's materialized view log is shown in the following listing:

```
alter materialized view log on employees pctfree 10;
```

To drop a materialized view log, use the DROP MATERIALIZED VIEW LOG command, as in this example:

```
drop materialized view log on employees;
```

Purging the Materialized View Log

The materialized view log contains transient data; records are inserted into the log, used during refreshes, and then deleted. If multiple materialized views use the same master table, they share the same materialized view log. If one of the materialized views is not refreshed for a long period, the materialized view log may never delete any of its records. As a result, the space requirements of the materialized view log will grow.

To reduce the space used by log entries, you can use the PURGE_LOG procedure of the DBMS_MVIEW package. PURGE_LOG takes three parameters: the name of the master table, a NUM variable, and a DELETE flag. The NUM variable specifies the number of least recently refreshed materialized views whose rows will be removed from the materialized view log. For example, if you have three materialized views that use the materialized view log and one of them has not been refreshed for a very long time, you would use a NUM value of 1.

The following listing shows an example of the PURGE_LOG procedure. In this example, the EMPLOYEES table's materialized view log will be purged of the entries required by the least recently used materialized view:

```
execute dbms_mview.purge_log
(master => 'employees',
    num => 1,
   flag => 'delete');
```

To further support maintenance efforts, Oracle provides two materialized view–specific options for the TRUNCATE command; if you want to truncate the master table without losing its materialized view log entries, you can use the TRUNCATE command with options like the following:

```
truncate table employees preserve materialized view log;
```

If the EMPLOYEES table's materialized views are based on primary key values (the default behavior), the materialized view log values will still be valid following an export/import of the EMPLOYEES table. However, if the EMPLOYEES table's materialized views are based on ROWID values, the materialized view log would be invalid following an export/import of the base table (since different ROWIDs will most likely be assigned during the import). In that case, you should truncate the materialized view log when you truncate the base table, as in this example:

```
truncate table employees purge materialized view log;
```

What Kind of Refreshes Can Be Performed?

To see what kind of refresh and rewrite capabilities are possible for your materialized views, you can query the MV_CAPABILITIES_TABLE table. The capabilities may change between versions, so you should reevaluate your refresh capabilities following Oracle software upgrades. To create this table, execute the **utlxmv.sql** script located in the directory **$ORACLE_HOME/rdbms/admin**.

The columns of MV_CAPABILITIES_TABLE are shown here:

```
desc MV_CAPABILITIES_TABLE

 Name                                      Null?    Type
 ----------------------------------------- -------- ----------------
 STATEMENT_ID                                       VARCHAR2(30)
 MVOWNER                                            VARCHAR2(30)
```

```
MVNAME                                      VARCHAR2(30)
CAPABILITY_NAME                             VARCHAR2(30)
POSSIBLE                                    CHAR(1)
RELATED_TEXT                                VARCHAR2(2000)
RELATED_NUM                                 NUMBER
MSGNO                                       NUMBER(38)
MSGTXT                                      VARCHAR2(2000)
SEQ                                         NUMBER
```

To populate MV_CAPABILITIES_TABLE, execute the procedure DBMS_MVIEW.EXPLAIN_MVIEW, using the name of the materialized view as the input value, as in this example:

```
exec dbms_mview.explain_mview('local_category_count');
```

The script **utlxmv.sql** provides guidance on the interpretation of the column values, as in this listing:

```
CREATE TABLE MV_CAPABILITIES_TABLE
 (STATEMENT_ID     VARCHAR(30),  -- Client-supplied unique statement
identifier
 MVOWNER          VARCHAR(30),  -- NULL for SELECT based EXPLAIN_MVIEW
 MVNAME           VARCHAR(30),  -- NULL for SELECT based EXPLAIN_MVIEW
 CAPABILITY_NAME  VARCHAR(30),  -- A descriptive name of the particular
                                -- capability:
                                -- REWRITE
                                --   Can do at least full text match
                                --   rewrite
                                -- REWRITE_PARTIAL_TEXT_MATCH
                                --   Can do at least full and partial
                                --   text match rewrite
                                -- REWRITE_GENERAL
                                --   Can do all forms of rewrite
                                -- REFRESH
                                --   Can do at least complete refresh
                                -- REFRESH_FROM_LOG_AFTER_INSERT
                                --   Can do fast refresh from an mv log
                                --   or change capture table at least
                                --   when update operations are
                                --   restricted to INSERT
                                -- REFRESH_FROM_LOG_AFTER_ANY
                                --   can do fast refresh from an mv log
                                --   or change capture table after any
                                --   combination of updates
                                -- PCT
                                --   Can do Enhanced Update Tracking on
                                --   the table named in the RELATED_NAME
                                --   column.  EUT is needed for fast
                                --   refresh after partitioned
                                --   maintenance operations on the table
                                --   named in the RELATED_NAME column
                                --   and to do non-stale tolerated
```

```
                                 --   rewrite when the mv is partially
                                 --   stale with respect to the table
                                 --   named in the RELATED_NAME column.
                                 --   EUT can also sometimes enable fast
                                 --   refresh of updates to the table
                                 --   named in the RELATED_NAME column
                                 --   when fast refresh from an mv log
                                 --   or change capture table is not
                                 --   possible.
  POSSIBLE         CHARACTER(1), -- T = capability is possible
                                 -- F = capability is not possible
  RELATED_TEXT     VARCHAR(2000),-- Owner.table.column, alias name, etc.
                                 -- related to this message.  The
                                 -- specific meaning of this column
                                 -- depends on the MSGNO column.  See
                                 -- the documentation for
                                 -- DBMS_MVIEW.EXPLAIN_MVIEW() for details
  RELATED_NUM      NUMBER,       -- When there is a numeric value
                                 -- associated with a row, it goes here.
                                 -- The specific meaning of this column
                                 -- depends on the MSGNO column.  See
                                 -- the documentation for
                                 -- DBMS_MVIEW.EXPLAIN_MVIEW() for details
  MSGNO            INTEGER,      -- When available, QSM message #
                                 -- explaining why not possible or more
                                 -- details when enabled.
  MSGTXT           VARCHAR(2000),-- Text associated with MSGNO.
  SEQ              NUMBER);      -- Useful in ORDER BY clause when
                                 -- selecting from this table.
```

Once the EXPLAIN_MVIEW procedure has been executed, you can query the MV_CAPABILITIES_TABLE to determine your options:

```
select capability_name, msgtxt
from mv_capabilities_table
where msgtxt is not null;
```

For the LOCAL_BOOKSHELF materialized view, the query returns the following:

```
CAPABILITY_NAME
------------------------------
MSGTXT
------------------------------------------------------------
PCT_TABLE
relation is not a partitioned table

REFRESH_FAST_AFTER_INSERT
the detail table does not have a materialized view log

REFRESH_FAST_AFTER_ONETAB_DML
see the reason why REFRESH_FAST_AFTER_INSERT is disabled
```

```
REFRESH_FAST_AFTER_ANY_DML
see the reason why REFRESH_FAST_AFTER_ONETAB_DML is disabled

REFRESH_FAST_PCT
PCT is not possible on any of the detail tables in the
materialized view

REWRITE_FULL_TEXT_MATCH
query rewrite is disabled on the materialized view

REWRITE_PARTIAL_TEXT_MATCH
query rewrite is disabled on the materialized view

REWRITE_GENERAL
query rewrite is disabled on the materialized view

REWRITE_PCT
general rewrite is not possible or PCT is not possible on
any of the detail tables

PCT_TABLE_REWRITE
relation is not a partitioned table

10 rows selected.
```

Because the QUERY REWRITE clause was not specified during the creation of this materialized view, the query rewrite capabilities are disabled for the LOCAL_BOOKSHELF table. Fast refresh capabilities are not supported, because the base table does not have a materialized view log. If you change your materialized view or its base table, you should regenerate the data in MV_CAPABILITIES_TABLE to see the new options.

As shown in the preceding listing, the LOCAL_BOOKSHELF materialized view cannot use a fast refresh because its base table does not have a materialized view log. Here are some other constraints that will limit your ability to use fast refreshes:

- The materialized view must not contain references to nonrepeating expressions such as SYSDATE and ROWNUM.
- The materialized view must not contain references to RAW or LONG RAW datatypes.
- For materialized views based on joins, ROWIDs from all tables in the FROM list must be part of the SELECT list.
- If there are outer joins, all the joins must be connected by ANDs, the WHERE clause must have no selections, and unique constraints must exist on the join columns of the inner join table.
- For materialized views based on aggregates, the materialized view logs must contain all columns from the referenced tables, must specify the ROWID and INCLUDING NEW VALUES clauses, and must specify the SEQUENCE clause.

See the *Oracle Database Data Warehousing Guide 12c Release 1 (12.1)* for additional restrictions related to fast refreshes of complex aggregates.

NOTE
You can specify an ORDER BY clause in the CREATE MATERIALIZED VIEW command. The ORDER BY clause will only affect the initial creation of the materialized view; it will not affect any refreshes.

Using Materialized Views to Alter Query Execution Paths

For a large database, a materialized view may offer several performance benefits. You can use materialized views to influence the optimizer to change the execution paths for queries. This feature, called *query rewrite,* enables the optimizer to use a materialized view in place of the table queried by the materialized view, even if the materialized view is not named in the query. For example, if you have a large SALES table, you may create a materialized view that sums the SALES data by region. If a user queries the SALES table for the sum of the SALES data for a region, Oracle can redirect that query to use your materialized view in place of the SALES table. As a result, you can reduce the number of accesses against your largest tables, thus improving the system performance. Further, because the data in the materialized view is already grouped by region, summarization does not have to be performed at the time the query is issued.

NOTE
You must specify ENABLE QUERY REWRITE in the materialized view definition for the view to be used as part of a query rewrite operation.

To use the query rewrite capability effectively, you should create a dimension that defines the hierarchies within the table's data. To execute the CREATE DIMENSION command, you must have the CREATE DIMENSION system privilege. In this example, countries are part of continents, so you can create tables and dimensions to support this hierarchy:

```
create dimension geography
   level country_id       is country.country
   level continent_id     is continent.continent
   hierarchy country_rollup (
      country_id            child of
      continent_id
   join key country.continent references continent_id);
```

To enable a materialized view for query rewrite, you must place all the master tables for the materialized view in the materialized view's schema, and you must have the QUERY REWRITE system privilege. In general, you should create materialized views in the same schema as the tables on which they are based; otherwise, you will need to manage the permissions and grants required to create and maintain the materialized views.

NOTE
You can enable or disable query rewrite at the SQL statement level via the REWRITE and NOREWRITE hints. When using the REWRITE hint, you can specify materialized views for the optimizer to consider.

For query rewrite to be enabled, you must set the following initialization parameters:

- OPTIMIZER_MODE = ALL_ROWS or FIRST_ROWS or FIRST_ROWS_*n*
- QUERY_REWRITE_ENABLED = TRUE
- QUERY_REWRITE_INTEGRITY = STALE_TOLERATED, TRUSTED, or ENFORCED

By default, QUERY_REWRITE_INTEGRITY is set to ENFORCED; in this mode, all constraints must be validated. The optimizer only uses fresh data from the materialized views and only uses those relationships that are based on ENABLED and VALIDATED primary, unique, or foreign key constraints. In TRUSTED mode, the optimizer trusts that the data in the materialized view is fresh and that the relationships declared in dimensions and constraints are correct. In STALE_TOLERATED mode, the optimizer uses materialized views that are valid but contain stale data as well as those that contain fresh data.

If you set QUERY_REWRITE_ENABLED to FORCE, the optimizer will rewrite queries to use materialized views even when the estimated query cost of the original query is lower.

If query rewrite occurs, the explain plan for the query will list the materialized view as one of the objects accessed, along with an operation listed as "MAT_VIEW REWRITE ACCESS." You can use the DBMS_MVIEW.EXPLAIN_REWRITE procedure to see if rewrite is possible for a query and which materialized views would be involved. If the query cannot be rewritten, the procedure will document the reasons.

NOTE
Query rewrite decisions are based on the costs of the different execution paths, so your statistics should be kept up to date.

EXPLAIN_REWRITE takes three input parameters—the query, a materialized view name, and a statement identifier—and can store its output in a table. Oracle provides the CREATE TABLE command for the output table in a script named **utlxrw.sql** in the **$ORACLE_HOME/rdbms/admin** directory. The **utlxrw.sql** script creates a table named REWRITE_TABLE.

You can query REWRITE_TABLE for the original cost, rewritten cost, and the optimizer's decision. The MESSAGE column will display the reasons for the optimizer's decision.

If you have used the BUILD DEFERRED option of the CREATE MATERIALIZED VIEW or ALTER MATERIALIZED VIEW command, the query rewrite feature will not be enabled until after the first time the materialized view is refreshed.

NOTE
If bind variables have been used within the query, the optimizer will not rewrite it even though query rewrite has been enabled.

Managing Distributed Transactions

A single logical unit of work may include transactions against multiple databases. For example, a COMMIT may be executed after two tables in separate databases have been updated. Oracle will transparently maintain the integrity between the two databases by ensuring that all the transactions involved either COMMIT or roll back (using the ROLLBACK command or a session failure) as a group. This is accomplished automatically via Oracle's Two-Phase Commit (2PC) mechanism.

The first phase of the 2PC is the *prepare* phase. In this phase, each database instance involved in a transaction prepares the data that it will need to either COMMIT or roll back the data. Once prepared, an instance is said to be "in doubt." The destination instances notify the initiating instance for the transaction (known as the *global coordinator*) of their status.

Once all instances are prepared, the transaction enters the commit phase, and all nodes are instructed to COMMIT their portion of the logical transaction. The databases all COMMIT the data at the same logical time, preserving the integrity of the distributed data.

NOTE
All databases that perform a COMMIT in a distributed transaction use the same System Change Number (SCN), which is the highest SCN of all databases involved in the transaction.

Resolving In-Doubt Transactions

Transactions against standalone databases may fail due to problems with the database server; for example, there may be a media failure. Working with distributed databases increases the number of potential failure causes during a set of related transactions.

When a distributed transaction is pending, an entry for that transaction will appear in the DBA_2PC_PENDING data dictionary view. When the transaction completes, its DBA_2PC_PENDING record is removed. If the transaction is pending but is not able to complete, its record stays in DBA_2PC_PENDING.

The RECO (Recoverer) background process periodically checks the DBA_2PC_PENDING view for distributed transactions that failed to complete. Using the information there, the RECO process on a node will automatically attempt to recover the local portion of an in-doubt transaction. It then attempts to establish connections to any other databases involved in the transaction and resolves the distributed portions of the transaction. The related rows in the DBA_2PC_PENDING view in each database are then removed.

NOTE
You can enable and disable the RECO process via the ENABLE DISTRIBUTED RECOVERY and DISABLE DISTRIBUTED RECOVERY clauses of the ALTER SYSTEM command.

The recovery of distributed transactions is performed automatically by the RECO process. You can manually recover the local portions of a distributed transaction, but this will usually result in inconsistent data between the distributed databases. If a local recovery is performed, the remote data will be out of sync.

To minimize the number of distributed recoveries necessary, you can influence the way that the distributed transaction is processed. The transaction processing is influenced via the use of *commit point strength* to tell the database how to structure the transaction.

Commit Point Strength

Each set of distributed transactions may reference multiple hosts and databases. Of those, one host and database can normally be singled out as being the most reliable, or as owning the most critical data. This database is known as the *commit point site*. If data is committed there, it should be committed for all databases. If the transaction against the commit point site fails, the transactions against the other nodes are rolled back. The commit point site also stores information about the status of the distributed transaction.

The commit point site will be selected by Oracle based on each database's *commit point strength*. This is set via the initialization file, as shown in the following example:

```
commit_point_strength=100
```

The values for the COMMIT_POINT_STRENGTH parameter are set on a scale relative to other nodes participating in distributed transactions. In the preceding example, the value is set to 100 (the default is 1). If another database has a value of 200 for this parameter, that database would be the commit point site for a distributed transaction involving those two databases. The COMMIT_POINT_STRENGTH cannot exceed 255.

Because the scale is relative, you should set up a site-specific scale. Set the commit point on your most reliable database to 200. Then, grade the other servers and databases relative to the most reliable database. If, for example, another database is only 80 percent as reliable as the most reliable database, assign it a commit point strength of 160 (80 percent of 200). Fixing a single database at a definite point (in this case, 200) allows the rest of the databases to be graded on an even scale. This scale should result in the proper commit point site being used for each transaction.

Monitoring Distributed Databases

Several key environmental performance measures must be taken into account for databases:

- The performance of the host
- The distribution of I/O across disks and controllers
- The usage of available memory

For distributed databases, you must also consider the following:

- The capacity of the network and its hardware
- The load on the network segments
- The usage of different physical access paths between hosts

None of these can be measured from within the database. The focus of monitoring efforts for distributed databases shifts from being database-centric to being network-centric. The database becomes one part of the monitored environment, rather than the only part that is monitored.

You still need to monitor those aspects of the database that are critical to its success, such as the free space in tablespaces. However, the *performance* of distributed databases cannot be measured except as part of the performance of the network that supports them. Therefore, all performance-related tests, such as stress tests, must be coordinated with the network management staff. That staff may also be able to verify the effectiveness of your attempts to reduce the database load on the network.

The performance of the individual hosts can usually be monitored via a network monitoring package. This monitoring is performed in a top-down fashion, from network to host to database. Use the monitoring system described in Chapter 6 as an extension to the network and host monitors.

Tuning Distributed Databases

When you're tuning a standalone database, the goal is to reduce the amount of time it takes to find data. As described in Chapter 8, you can use a number of database structures and options to increase the likelihood that the data will be found in the buffer cache or via an index.

When working with distributed databases, you have an additional consideration: Because data is now not only being retrieved but also being shipped across the network, the performance of a query is made up of the performance of these two steps. You must therefore consider the ways in which data is being transferred across the network, with a goal of reducing the network traffic.

A simple way to reduce network traffic is to replicate data from one node to another. You can do this manually (via the SQL*Plus COPY command), or it can be done automatically by the database (via materialized views). Replicating data improves the performance of queries against remote databases by bringing the data across the network once, usually during a slow period on the local host. Local queries can use the local copy of the data, eliminating the network traffic that would otherwise be required.

Let's consider a simple task: selecting a value from a sequence. A company has created a distributed application in which a new sequence value is generated for each row. However, the sequence is local, whereas the insert is being performed in a far distant database. Because the trigger that generates the sequence value is executed for each row, each insert generates a remote operation to generate the next sequence value.

The impact of this design is apparent when a session's trace file is examined:

```
SELECT NEWID_SEQ.NEXTVAL
FROM
 DUAL

call     count       cpu    elapsed       disk      query    current        rows
------- ------  -------- ---------- ---------- ---------- ----------  ----------
Parse        1      0.01       0.13          0          0          0           0
Execute     53      0.01       0.01          0          0          0           0
Fetch       53      0.06       6.34          0        159          0          53
------- ------  -------- ---------- ---------- ---------- ----------  ----------
total      107      0.09       6.50          0        159          0          53

Misses in library cache during parse: 0
Optimizer goal: CHOOSE

Rows     Execution Plan
-------  ---------------------------------------------------
      0  SELECT STATEMENT   GOAL: CHOOSE
      0   SEQUENCE (REMOTE)
      0    TABLE ACCESS (FULL) OF 'DUAL'

Elapsed times include waiting on following events:
  Event waited on                             Times   Max. Wait  Total Waited
  ----------------------------------------   Waited  ----------  ------------
  SQL*Net message to dblink                      53        0.00          0.00
  SQL*Net message from dblink                    53        0.13          6.29
```

In this case, the query is very simple—it selects the next value of the sequence from the DUAL table. But the sequence is remote (as seen in the execution plan), so the time required to fetch the values is 6.29 seconds for 53 rows, out of a total of 6.5 seconds. To tune the application, you either need to reduce the number of trips (such as by performing batch operations instead of row-by-row operations) or eliminate the remote architecture component of the INSERT. If the remote object (the sequence) and the local object (the DUAL table) can reside on the same database, the wait times associated with the remote operations can be eliminated.

NOTE
*Since Oracle Database 10g, the DUAL table is an internal table, not a physical table, and therefore does not generate consistent gets as long as you don't use * as the column list in a query referencing DUAL.*

Two problems commonly arise with replicated solutions: First, the local data may become out of sync with the remote data. This is a standard problem with derived data; it limits the usefulness of this option to tables whose data is fairly static. Even if a simple materialized view is used with a materialized view log, the data will not be refreshed continuously—only when scheduled.

The second problem with the replicated data solution is that the copy of the table may not be able to pass updates back to the master table. That is, if a read-only materialized view is used to make a local copy of a remote table, the snapshot cannot be updated. If you are using materialized views, you can use updatable materialized views to send changes back to the master site, or you can use writable materialized views to support local ownership of data.

Any updates that must be processed against replicas must also be performed against the master tables. If the table is frequently updated, then replicating the data will not improve your performance unless you are using Oracle's multimaster replication options. When there is multisite ownership of data, users can make changes in any database designated as an owner of the data. The management of Oracle's multimaster replication is very involved and requires creating a database environment (with database links and so on) specifically designed to support multidirectional replication of data. See the Oracle replication documentation for details on implementing a multimaster environment.

The performance of the refreshes generally won't concern your users. What may concern them is the validity and timeliness of the data. If the remote tables are frequently modified and are of considerable size, you are almost forced to use simple materialized views with materialized view logs to keep the data current. Performing complete refreshes in the middle of a workday is generally unacceptable. Therefore, it is the *frequency* of the refreshes rather than the size of them that determines which type of materialized view will better serve the users. After all, users are most concerned about the performance of the system while they are using it; refreshes performed late at night do not directly affect them. If the tables need to be frequently synchronized, use simple materialized views with materialized view logs.

As was noted previously in this chapter, you may index the underlying tables that are created by the materialized view in the local database. Indexing should also help to improve query performance, at the expense of slowing down the refreshes.

Another means of reducing network traffic, via remote procedure calls, is described in Chapter 8. That chapter also includes information on tuning SQL and the application design. If the database was properly structured, tuning the way the application processes data will yield the most significant performance improvements.

Summary

Distributed databases spread out the workload in a database environment to improve both performance and availability. However, merely spreading out the database or replicating a database across multiple locations is only valuable if you can ensure transactional integrity at each site. Therefore, Oracle uses Two-Phase Commit to ensure that a distributed transaction is treated atomically with a single COMMIT point.

To further enhance transparency and usability, you can use database links between databases to give you the flexibility to change the actual location of a database object without any changes to the application or any awareness of the actual location of the database objects to end users.

Use of materialized views is another key element in a distributed environment or even in a standalone environment. Creating a materialized view pre-aggregates the results of a query to improve performance for users who may run the query several times a day and not be aware that they are accessing the aggregate and not the actual tables in the query. The materialized view can be kept up to date on a continuous basis whether the source tables are all in a single database or are in several databases in a distributed environment.

Index

References to figures are in italics.

B

D

E

J

K

L

M

N

O

P

Q

R

S

U

V